Frommer's

South Pacific

10th Edition

by Bill Goodwin

Here's what the critics say about Frommer's:

"Amazingly easy to use. Very portable, very complete."

—*Booklist*

"Detailed, accurate, and easy-to-read information for all price ranges."
—*Glamour Magazine*

"Hotel information is close to encyclopedic."

—*Des Moines Sunday Register*

"Frommer's Guides have a way of giving you a real feel for a place."
—*Knight Ridder Newspapers*

WILEY

Wiley Publishing, Inc.

Wiley Publishing, Inc.

111 River St.
Hoboken, NJ 07030-5774

ISBN-13: 978-0-471-76980-4
ISBN-10: 0-471-76980-0

Editor: Risa Wyatt
Production Editor: Eric T. Schroeder
Cartographer: Elizabeth Puhl
Photo Editor: Richard Fox
Production by Wiley Indianapolis Composition Services

Front cover photo: Cook Islands, Aitutaki: Girl relaxing in hammock
Back cover photo: French Polynesia, Bora Bora: Aerial view of island and lagoon

For information on our other products and services or to obtain technical support, please contact our Customer Care Department within the U.S. at 800/762-2974, outside the U.S. at 317/572-3993 or fax 317/572-4002.

Wiley also publishes its books in a variety of electronic formats. Some content that appears in print may not be available in electronic formats.

Manufactured in the United States of America

5 4 3 2 1

Contents

List of Maps   vii

What's New in the South Pacific   1

1   The Best of the South Pacific   4

1 The Most Beautiful Islands 4
2 The Best Beaches 6
3 The Best Honeymoon Destinations ...7
4 The Best Family Vacations 9
5 The Best Cultural Experiences 10
6 The Best of the Old South Seas 11

7 The Best Dining Experiences 11
8 The Best Island Nights 13
9 The Best Buys 14
10 The Best Diving & Snorkeling 15
11 The Best Sailing 15
12 The Best Offbeat Travel Experiences ...16

2   Planning Your Trip to the South Pacific   17

1 The Islands in Brief 17
2 Visitor Information 22
3 Entry Requirements & Customs 23
4 Money 26
   Island Time vs. Island Service 28
5 When to Go 29
6 Travel Insurance 30
7 Health & Safety 31
   Insects & Other Critters 33
8 Specialized Travel Resources 33
   Frommers.com: The Complete
   Travel Resource 35

9 Planning Your Trip Online 36
10 The 21st-Century Traveler 38
   Configuring Your Laptop 39
11 Getting There & Getting Around 40
12 Packages for the Independent
   Traveler 46
   Flying with Film & Video 48
13 The Active Traveler 49
14 Tips on Accommodations 51
15 Recommended Reading 53

3   Suggested South Pacific Itineraries   57

1 Two Weeks in Fiji 57
2 Two Weeks in Tahiti & French
   Polynesia 59

3 A Week in The Cook Islands 61
4 A Week in the Samoas 62
5 A Week in Tonga 64

4   Introducing Fiji   66

1 Fiji Today: The Regions in Brief 66
   Diving in Fiji 70

2 Fiji Yesterday: History 101 71
3 The Islanders 74

A Holy Meal 75

"Grog" Etiquette 76

4 Languages 78

5 Visitor Information & Entry
Requirements 80

6 Money 81

The Fiji Dollar & the U.S. Dollar 82

7 When to Go 82

8 Getting There & Getting Around 83

Fast Facts: Fiji 89

5 Viti Levu   94

1 Nadi 94

Fast Facts: Nadi 95

A Side Trip to Lautoka 98

Don't Miss a Meke 111

2 The Mamanuca & Yasawa
Islands .114

*How to Choose Your Offshore
Resort* .122

3 The Coral Coast 126

Fast Facts: The Coral Coast 127

4 Pacific Harbour & Beqa Island 137

5 Suva 140

Fast Facts: Suva 142

Walking Tour: Suva 144

*A Side Trip Back in Time to
Levuka* .152

6 Rakiraki & Northern Viti Levu 156

6 Northern Fiji: Savusavu & Taveuni   159

1 Savusavu 159

Fast Facts: Savusavu 162

2 Taveuni .169

Fast Facts: Taveuni 170

3 Resorts on Qamea & Matagi
Islands .177

7 Introducing French Polynesia   179

1 French Polynesia Today: The Islands
in Brief .179

2 French Polynesia Yesterday:
History 101 183

Sexy Skin 184

3 The Islanders 187

Sex & the Single Polynesian 188

4 Languages 189

5 Visitor Information & Entry
Requirements 190

6 Money 192

7 When to Go—Climate, Holidays
& Events 193

*French Polynesia Calendar of
Events* .194

8 Getting There & Getting Around . . .195

9 Seeing the Islands by Cruise Ship
& Yacht .198

10 Dining Out in French Polynesia 201

Fast Facts: French Polynesia 203

8 Tahiti   207

1 Arriving & Getting Around 208

Fast Facts: Tahiti 212

2 Exploring Tahiti 214

Walking Tour: Papeete 217

The Moon & Six Million 225

3 Golf, Hiking & Watersports 229

4 Shopping 230

Buying Your Black Pearl 232

5 Where to Stay 232

6 Where to Dine 237

Don't Miss Les Roulottes 237

Dining with a Belle View 239

A Most Indecent Song & Dance . . .241

7 Island Nights 242

9   Moorea   244

1 Getting Around 245

Fast Facts: Moorea 246

2 Exploring Moorea 247

Tiki Theatre Village 252

3 Safari Expeditions, Lagoon
Excursions & Dolphin-Watching . . .252

4 Fishing, Hiking, Watersports &
Other Outdoor Activities 253

5 Shopping 255

6 Where to Stay 256

The Bali Hai Boys 258

7 Where to Dine 261

8 Island Nights 264

10   Bora Bora   266

1 Arriving & Getting Around 267

Fast Facts: Bora Bora 268

2 Exploring Bora Bora 270

A Side Trip to Maupiti 271

3 Safari Expeditions & Lagoon
Excursions 272

4 Diving, Fishing & Watersports 273

5 Shopping 274

6 Where to Stay 274

7 Where to Dine 280

8 Island Nights 282

11   Huahine & the Other Islands of French Polynesia   283

1 Huahine .283

Fast Facts: Huahine 284

2 Raiatea & Tahaa 292

Fast Facts: Raiatea & Tahaa 294

3 Rangiroa 300

Fast Facts: Rangiroa 301

4 Tikehau .304

5 Manihi 305

6 Fakarava 305

12   Rarotonga & the Cook Islands   307

1 The Cook Islands Today 307

2 The Cook Islands Yesterday:
History 101 308

All in the Family 310

3 The Cook Islanders 311

4 Language 312

5 Visitor Information & Entry
Requirements 312

6 Money 313

*The New Zealand Dollar & the
U.S. Dollar* 313

7 When to Go 313

*The Cook Islands Calendar of
Events* 315

8 Getting to Rarotonga & Getting
Around 316

Fast Facts: Rarotonga 319

9 Exploring Rarotonga 323

10 Fishing, Hiking, Diving & Other
Outdoor Activities 328

11 Shopping on Rarotonga 330

12 Where to Stay on Rarotonga 332

13 Where to Dine on Rarotonga 338
Cook Islands Chow 338

14 Island Nights on Rarotonga 342
Don't Miss an Island Night 343

15 Aitutaki 343
Fast Facts: Aitutaki 344

13 Samoa   351

1 Samoa Today 351

2 Samoa Yesterday: History 101 353
The Teller of Tales 354

3 The Samoan People 355

4 The Samoan Language 358

5 Visitor Information & Entry
Requirements 359

6 Money 360
The Samoan Tala & U.S. Dollar 361

7 When to Go 361

8 Getting There & Getting Around . . .362
Fast Facts: Samoa 366

9 Exploring Apia & the Rest of Upolu . . .369

10 Watersports, Golf & Other
Outdoor Activities 377

11 Shopping 378

12 Where to Stay on Upolu 378
Hot Dogs & Hamburgers 379
Beach Fales at Aleipata 383

13 Where to Dine in Apia 384
Don't Miss a Fiafia 385

14 Island Nights on Upolu 386

15 Savai'i 386
Manono & Apolima 388

14 American Samoa   391

1 American Samoa Today 391

2 History 101 392

3 Visitor Information & Entry
Requirements 393

4 Money 393

5 When to Go 394

6 Getting There & Getting Around . . .394

Fast Facts: American Samoa 396

7 Exploring American Samoa 398
*Seeing American Samoa as a Day
Trip from Apia* 400

8 National Park of American Samoa . . .402

9 Where to Stay 403

10 Where to Dine 405

15 The Kingdom of Tonga   406

1 Tonga Today 406

2 History 101 408

3 The Tongans 410
What Day Is It? 411

4 Language .412

5 Visitor Information & Entry
Requirements 413

6 Money 414
The Pa'anga & the U.S. Dollar 414

7 When to Go 415

8 Getting to Tonga &
Getting Around 416
Fast Facts: Tonga 419

9 Exploring Tongatapu 422

10 Island Excursions, Watersports &
Other Outdoor Activities 427

11 Shopping on Tongatapu 429

12 Where to Stay on Tongatapu 430

13 Where to Dine on Tongatapu 433

Dine Like a Tongan 434

14 Island Nights on Tongatapu 436

15 Vava'u 436

Fast Facts: Vava'u 438

16 Ha'apai .444

Appendix: The South Pacific in Depth   447

1 A Shared History 447

2 The Islanders 451

3 The Islands & the Sea 454

Index   458

List of Maps

The South Pacific   18

Two Weeks in Fiji   59

Two Weeks in Tahiti & French
Polynesia   61

A Week in the Cook Islands   62

A Week in the Samoas   63

A Week in Tonga   64

The Fiji Islands   69

Viti Levu & Ovalau   99

Nadi   105

Walking Tour: Suva   145

Northern Fiji   161

The Society Islands & the Northern
Tuamotus   181

Tahiti   209

Walking Tour: Papeete   219

Moorea   249

Bora Bora   269

Huahine   285

Rarotonga   317

The Samoa Islands   363

Apia   371

Pago Pago   399

Nuku'alofa   417

To my father, with love and with grateful thanks for supporting my being a writer rather than a lawyer

Acknowledgments

I owe a debt of gratitude to many individuals and organizations without whose help this book would have been impossible to research and write. You will become acquainted with many of them in these pages, and it will be your good fortune if you meet them in the islands.

I am particularly grateful to Dany Panero, Céline Teihotaata Al Keahi, Jonathan Reap, and Leila Laille of Tahiti Tourisme; Viliame Gavoka, Keti Wagavonovono, Jo Rayawa, and Julia Hazelman of the Fiji Visitors Bureau; Chris Wong of the Cook Islands Tourism Corporation; Matafeo Reupena Matafeo of the Samoa Tourism Authority; Virginia F. Samuelu of the American Samoa Office of Tourism; and Vainga Palu, Sione Finau Moala-Mafi, Sandradee Fonua, and Bruno Toke of the Tonga Visitors Bureau.

My deep personal thanks go to Anne Simon, Suzanne McIntosh, Nancy Monseaux, Max Parrish, Curtis and Judy Moore, and Bill and Donna Wilder, whose generosity over the years have made this book possible; to my sister, Jean Goodwin Santa-Maria, who has consistently given much-needed moral support; to Dick Beaulieu, always a font of information, advice, and ice-cold Fiji Bitters; and to David Hunt, with whom I have shared many Sundays on Tonga's islets.

I am truly blessed to have all of them in my life.

—Bill Goodwin

An Invitation to the Reader

In researching this book, we discovered many wonderful places—hotels, restaurants, shops, and more. We're sure you'll find others. Please tell us about them, so we can share the information with your fellow travelers in upcoming editions. If you were disappointed with a recommendation, we'd love to know that, too. Please write to:

Frommer's South Pacific, 10th Edition
Wiley Publishing, Inc. • 111 River St. • Hoboken, NJ 07030-5774

An Additional Note

Please be advised that travel information is subject to change at any time—and this is especially true of prices. We therefore suggest that you write or call ahead for confirmation when making your travel plans. The authors, editors, and publisher cannot be held responsible for the experiences of readers while traveling. Your safety is important to us, however, so we encourage you to stay alert and be aware of your surroundings. Keep a close eye on cameras, purses, and wallets, all favorite targets of thieves and pickpockets.

About the Author

Bill Goodwin is one of the world's experts on travel to the South Pacific. Before falling in love with the islands, he was an award-winning newspaper reporter and then legal counsel and speechwriter for two influential U.S. senators—Sam Nunn of Georgia and the late Sam Ervin of North Carolina. In 1977 he and a friend sailed a 41-foot yacht from Annapolis, Maryland, to Tahiti. He left the boat in Papeete and, with girlfriend and backpack, spent more than a year exploring French Polynesia, American Samoa, Samoa, Tonga, Fiji, New Zealand, and Australia. Altogether he has spent several years in the South Pacific, including one researching and writing the first edition of this book in 1986–87. He has revisited many times since then. At home, he also is the author of *Frommer's Virginia*.

Frommer's Star Ratings, Icons & Abbreviations

Every hotel, restaurant, and attraction listing in this guide has been ranked for quality, value, service, amenities, and special features using a **star-rating system.** In country, state, and regional guides, we also rate towns and regions to help you narrow down your choices and budget your time accordingly. Hotels and restaurants are rated on a scale of zero (recommended) to three stars (exceptional). Attractions, shopping, nightlife, towns, and regions are rated according to the following scale: zero stars (recommended), one star (highly recommended), two stars (very highly recommended), and three stars (must-see).

In addition to the star-rating system, we also use **seven feature icons** that point you to the great deals, in-the-know advice, and unique experiences that separate travelers from tourists. Throughout the book, look for:

Finds	Special finds—those places only insiders know about
Fun Fact	Fun facts—details that make travelers more informed and their trips more fun
Kids	Best bets for kids and advice for the whole family
Moments	Special moments—those experiences that memories are made of
Overrated	Places or experiences not worth your time or money
Tips	Insider tips—great ways to save time and money
Value	Great values—where to get the best deals

The following **abbreviations** are used for credit cards:

AE	American Express	DISC	Discover	V	Visa
DC	Diners Club	MC	MasterCard		

Frommers.com

Now that you have the guidebook to a great trip, visit our website at **www.frommers.com** for travel information on more than 3,000 destinations. With features updated regularly, we give you instant access to the most current trip-planning information available. At Frommers.com, you'll also find the best prices on airfares, accommodations, and car rentals—and you can even book travel online through our travel booking partners. At Frommers.com, you'll also find the following:

- Online updates to our most popular guidebooks
- Vacation sweepstakes and contest giveaways
- Newsletter highlighting the hottest travel trends
- Online travel message boards with featured travel discussions

What's New
in the South Pacific

Seen as safe destinations, many South Pacific island countries are in the midst of a tourism boom. This is particularly true in Fiji and the Cook Islands, where record numbers of visitors have spurred the construction of new hotels and resorts. Many are already open, while others were under construction during my recent tour of the islands. Others are on the drawing board. (I lost count of how many times I met someone in the islands who was planning to build the resort of his or her dreams!) Many properties have been upgraded, and in some cases their names changed. With values rising astronomically, some long-time owners have cashed in by selling their hotels.

Here's a recap of recent changes affecting travelers.

PLANNING YOUR TRIP For complete information about planning your trip to the South Pacific, see chapter 2.

Air Tahiti Nui (www.airtahitinui.com) now flies non-stop between New York and Papeete. The same plane goes on to Sydney, Australia, and back to Tahiti.

Australians and New Zealanders can now reach Fiji, the Cook Islands, and Tonga via **Pacific Blue** (www.flypacific blue.com), the lower-fare subsidiary of Sir Richard Branson's Virgin Blue. It also flies to Samoa as **Polynesian Blue**, which has taken over most international services of **Polynesian Airlines.**

FIJI For complete information on Fiji, see chapters 4 through 6.

The French-based Accor Hotels (www. accorhotels.com) now has a significant presence in Fiji. Built from scratch, its 296-unit **Sofitel Fiji Resort & Spa** (© 675 1111) has joined the ranks of large hotels on Denarau Island. After a thorough facelift, the former Fiji Dominion International Hotel is now the **Mercure Hotel Nadi** (© 672 0272). Accor also was in the process of refurbishing the Fiji Mocambo, near Nadi airport, and turning it into the **Novotel Hotel Nadi.** In the Mamanuca Islands, it has taken over the renovated **Sofitel Vomo Island Resort** (© 666 7955; www.vomofiji. com), which is now back to luxury status.

The Sheraton Royal Denarau Resort also has been upgraded and renamed **The Westin Denarau Island Resort & Spa** (© 675 0000; www.starwoodspa collection.com).

Also vastly improved are the Robert Trent Jones, Jr. links and the former Pacific Harbour International Hotel, now known collectively as **The Pearl South Pacific** (© 345 0022; www.thepearl southpacific.com). Across the Queens Road, the country's best Fijian cultural center has reopened as the **Pacific Harbour Arts Village** (© 345 0065; www. artsvillage.com).

On a small islet in the Beqa Lagoon off Pacific Harbour, the luxurious **Royal**

Davui Island Fiji (© **330 7090;** www. royaldavui.com) has added to the ranks of the country's small, top-end resorts. It joins **Lalati Resort & Spa** (© **347 2033;** www.latali-fiji.com) and the **Beqa Lagoon Resort** (© **330 4042;** www. beqalagoonresort.com), both on Beqa Island, in catering to both honeymooners and divers.

In Suva, the old YWCA building has been converted into **JJ's on the Park** (© **330 5055;** www.jjsfiji.com.fj), offering a boutique hotel alternative to the city's business-oriented properties.

Once among the region's top family destinations, northern Fiji's **Matangi Island Resort** no longer accepts children.

TAHITI & FRENCH POLYNESIA

For complete information on French Polynesia, see chapters 7 through 11.

The hotel building boom also continues in French Polynesia, especially on Bora Bora, where three super-luxurious properties are due to open in 2006: The **InterContinental Resort and Thalasso Spa Bora Bora** (www.boraboraspa. interconti.com), the **St. Regis Resort Bora Bora** (www.starwoodspacollection. com), and the **Four Seasons Bora Bora** (www.fourseasons.com).

On Tahiti itself, the **Radisson Plaza Resort Tahiti** (© **48 88 88;** www. radisson.com) is a bit inconvenient to downtown Papeete but provides a black-sand beach plus modern in-room amenities such as high-speed Internet access. The **Sofitel Maeva Beach Tahiti** has reopened after a thorough renovation. The InterContinental Tahiti Beachcomber Resort is now known simply as the **InterContinental Resort Tahiti,** although locals still refer to it as the Beachcomber.

The InterContinental Moorea Beachcomber Resort has changed its name to the **InterContinental Resort and Spa Moorea.** The **Sofitel Ia Ora** was recently closed for 6 months for a much needed overhaul. On the lower end of the scale, American-born Mark Walker offers inexpensive bungalows and campsites at **Mark's Place Paradise** (© **56 43 02;** www.marks-place-paradise.com).

On Huahine, the **Sofitel Heiva** has closed. **Relais Mahana** has temporarily shut its doors while undergoing a serious upgrade.

The Bora Bora Beach Resort is now the **Novotel Bora Bora Beach Resort** and is one of the island's best values. The InterContinental Bora Bora Beachcomber Resort has been renamed the **InterContinental Le Moana Resort.** New on Bora Bora is the inexpensive **Rohotu Fare Lodge** (© **70 77 99;** www. rohotulodge.com). Perched on a hillside, its three romantic bungalows have lagoon and mountain views.

In the Tuamotu Islands, the new **Novotel Rangiroa Beach Resort** (© **93 13 50;** www.novotel.com) offers 38 comfortable bungalows beside a rocky beach.

THE COOK ISLANDS

For complete information on these islands, see chapter 12.

A series of back-to-back hurricanes early in 2005 forced several Rarotonga establishments to repair, renovate, and improve. Among them, the **Crown Beach Resort** (© **23-953;** www.crown beach.com) has emerged as one of the island's best hotels.

Rarotonga's most luxurious new resort is **Rumours of Romance** (© **22-551;** www.rumours-rarotonga.com), although its units are close together.

The Little Polynesian has added six luxurious bungalows to its inventory, plus a swimming pool.

One of the region's top family hotels, **The Rarotongan Beach Resort & Spa,** now pitches its 48 upgraded "beachfront junior suites" primarily to couples.

Cookbook author Sue Carruthers has vastly improved Rarotonga's dining scene with her **Tamarind House Restaurant &**

Bar (© 26-487), in a colonial-era lagoonside house near Avarua.

On Aitutaki, the eight-unit **Etu Moana** (© 31-458; www.etumoana.com) has brought a new standard of luxury to the island's bungalow-only establishments. Nearby, Are Tamanu has expanded to 22 bungalows and become **Are Tamanu Beach Village.** It has added a restaurant and bar. **Samade on the Beach** now has 12 bungalows to go with its funky beach-side restaurant.

SAMOA For complete information on Samoa, see chapter 13.

The biggest and best addition to Samoa is the 140-unit **Aggie Grey's Lagoon, Beach Resort & Spa** (© 45-611; www.aggiegreys.com), near the airport on Upolu's western end. Many features at the historic Aggie Grey's Hotel in Apia have been replicated here, including a restaurant and bar under a huge Samoa *fale.* The in-town hotel is now known as **Aggie Grey's Hotel & Bungalows.**

Coconuts Beach Club has replaced some of its units with deluxe garden suites, all with outdoor showers. Nearby **Sinalei Reef Resort & Spa** now has a spa and three beachside suites, one of them fit for a president.

Pacific Quest Marine Adventures has gone out of business. Watersports and other aquatic activities are now centered at Samoa's beachside resorts.

AMERICAN SAMOA For complete information on American Samoa, see chapter 14.

With the demise of **Samoa Air,** domestic flights are now provided by **Inter Island Airways** (© 699 5700; www.interislandair.com), which also flies between the two Samoas.

The derelict **Rainmaker Hotel** has finally closed, but Tom and Ta'aloga Drabble, who did an excellent job earlier with their Sadie Thompson Inn, have converted 46 of its beachside rooms into **Sadie's By The Sea** (© 633 5714; www.sadiethompsoninn.com).

THE KINGDOM OF TONGA For complete information on the Kingdom of Tonga, see chapter 15.

Domestic air service has been in a state of flux since **Royal Tongan Airlines** folded in 2004. At present, **Peau Vava'u** (© 28-325; www.peauvavau.to) is flying from Tongatapu to Hapai'i and Vava'u. **Airlines Tonga** (© 24-506; www.airlines tonga.com) also is flying those routes as well as serving the other islands in Tonga. But beware: Tongans love monopolies, and one of them could wind up being the only one flying anywhere.

Although the kingdom still lacks a modern resort hotel, accommodations improved with the opening of **The Black Pearl Suites** (© 28-393; thepearl@ kalianet.to). In addition to 10 units, it has one of Nuku'alofa's better restaurants.

Tonga has replaced its 5 percent sales tax with a 15 percent "consumption tax" on every purchase made in the kingdom, including hotel rooms and airline tickets.

1

The Best of the South Pacific

My own love affair with the South Pacific doesn't go back quite that far, but Tahiti, Fiji, Samoa, Rarotonga, and Tonga have conjured up romantic images of an earthly paradise since European sailors brought home tales of their tropical splendor and uninhibited people in the 1760s. When I did wash ashore, I quickly understood why these remote outposts came to have such a reputation. These are some of the most beautiful islands in the world—if not *the* most beautiful. They are blessed with some of the most gorgeous beaches the planet has to offer, and their lagoons offer some of the globe's most fabulous diving and snorkeling.

Picking the best of the South Pacific is no easy task. I cannot, for example, choose the friendliest island, for the people of Tahiti and French Polynesia, the Cook Islands, Fiji, Samoa, American Samoa, and the Kingdom of Tonga are among the most welcoming folks on earth. Their fabled history has provided fodder for famous books and films, their culture inspires hedonistic dreams, and their big smiles and genuine hospitality are prime attractions everywhere in the South Pacific. Personally, I like all the islands and all the islanders, which further complicates my chore to no end.

In this chapter, I point out the best of the best—not necessarily to pass qualitative judgment, but to help you choose among many options. I list them here in the order in which they appear in the book.

Your choice of destination will depend on why you are going to the islands. You can scuba dive to exhaustion or just sit on the beach with a trashy novel. You can share a 300-room hotel with package tourists or get away from it all on a tiny islet. Even out there, you can be left alone with your lover or join your fellow guests at lively dinner parties. You can totally ignore the Pacific Islanders around you or enrich your own life by learning about theirs. You can listen to the day's events on CNN International or see what the South Seas were like a century ago. Those decisions are all yours.

For a preview of each South Pacific country, see "The Islands in Brief" in chapter 2.

1 The Most Beautiful Islands

"In the South Seas," Rupert Brooke wrote in 1914, "the Creator seems to have laid himself out to show what He can do." How right the poet was, for all across the South Pacific lie some of the world's most dramatically beautiful islands. In my opinion, the best of the lot have jagged mountain peaks plunging into aquamarine lagoons. Here are some that you see on the travel posters and in the brochures:

- **The Yasawa Islands** (Fiji): This ranks as the South Pacific's hottest destination of late, especially for backpackers. A chain of long, narrow islands off the northwest coast of Viti Levu, Fiji's main island, the Yasawas have some of the region's best beaches. Despite the inroads of tourism, however, the group remains mostly populated by Fijians who live in traditional villages. See chapter 5.

- **Ovalau** (Fiji): The sheer cliffs of Ovalau kept the town of Levuka from becoming Fiji's modern capital, but they create a dramatic backdrop to an old South Seas town little changed in the past century. Ovalau has no good beaches, which means it has no resorts to alter its landscape. See "A Side Trip Back in Time to Levuka" in chapter 5.

- **Qamea and Matagi Islands** (Fiji): These little jewels off the northern coast of Taveuni are lushly beautiful, with their shorelines either dropping precipitously into the calm surrounding waters or forming little bays with idyllic beaches. See "Resorts on Qamea & Matagi Islands" in chapter 6.

- **Moorea** (French Polynesia): I think Moorea is the most beautiful island in the world. Nothing to my mind compares with its sawtooth ridges and the great dark-green hulk of Mount Rotui separating glorious Cook's and Opunohu bays. The view from Tahiti of Moorea's dinosaur-like skyline is unforgettable. See chapter 9.

- **Bora Bora** (French Polynesia): The late James Michener thought that Bora Bora was the most beautiful island in the world. Although tourism has turned this gem into sort of an expensive South Seas Disneyland since Michener's day, development hasn't altered the incredible beauty of Bora Bora's basaltic tombstone towering over a lagoon ranging in color from yellow to deep blue. See chapter 10.

- **Rarotonga** (Cook Islands): Only 32km (20 miles) around, the capital

of the Cook Islands boasts the beauty of Tahiti—with hints of Moorea—but without the development and the high prices of French Polynesia. See chapter 12.

- **Aitutaki** (Cook Islands): A junior version of Bora Bora, Aitutaki sits at the apex of a shallow, colorful lagoon, which from the air looks like a turquoise carpet laid on the deep blue sea. See "Aitutaki" in chapter 12.

- **Upolu** (Samoa): Robert Louis Stevenson was so enraptured with Samoa that he spent the last 5 years of his life in the hills of Upolu. The well-weathered eastern part of the island is ruggedly beautiful, especially in Aliepata, where a cliff virtually drops down to one of the region's most spectacular beaches. See "Exploring Apia & the Rest of Upolu" in chapter 13.

- **Savai'i** (Samoa): One of the largest Polynesian islands, this great volcanic shield slopes gently on its eastern side to a chain of gorgeous beaches. There are no towns on Savai'i, only traditional Samoan villages interspersed among rain forests, which adds to its unspoiled beauty. See "Savai'i" in chapter 13.

- **Tutuila** (American Samoa): A primary reason to go to American Samoa these days is to see the physical beauty of Tutuila and its magnificent harbor at Pago Pago. If you can ignore the tuna canneries and huge stacks of shipping containers, this island is right up there with Moorea. See chapter 14.

- **Vava'u** (Tonga): One of the South Pacific's best yachting destinations, hilly Vava'u is shaped like a jellyfish, with small islands instead of tentacles trailing off into a quiet lagoon. Waterways cut into the center of the main island, creating the picturesque and perfectly protected Port of Refuge. See "Vava'u" in chapter 15.

2 The Best Beaches

Because all but a few South Pacific islands are surrounded by coral reefs, there are few surf beaches in the region. Tahiti has a few, but they all have heat-absorbing black volcanic sand. Otherwise, most islands (and all but a few resorts) have bathtublike lagoons that lap on coral sands draped by coconut palms. Fortunately for the environmentalists among us, some of the most spectacular beaches are on remote islands and are protected from development by the islanders' devotion to their cultures and villages' land rights. Here are a few that stand out from the many.

- **Yasawa Island** (Fiji): One of the most spectacular beaches I've ever seen is on Yasawa Island, northernmost of the gorgeous chain of the same name. This long expanse of deep sand is broken by a teapotlike rock outcrop, which also separates two Fijian villages, whose residents own this land. Blue Lagoon Cruises and oceangoing cruise ships stop here; otherwise, the Fijians keep it all to themselves. There are other good beaches on Yasawa, however, and two of them are at Yasawa Island Resort and Oarsman's Bay Lodge. See "The Yasawa Islands" in chapter 5.

- **Vatulele Island Resort Beach** (Vatulele Island, Fiji): Nearly a kilometer (½ mile) of deep white sand fronts the deluxe Vatulele Island Resort, off the south shore of Viti Levu, Fiji's main island. Guests can have dinner out on the beach or get a bird's-eye view from a private gazebo overlooking the sands. See "A Resort on Vatulele Island" in chapter 5.

- **Natadola Beach** (The Coral Coast, Fiji): Fiji's main island of Viti Levu doesn't have the high-quality beaches found on the country's small islands, but Natadola is an exception. Until recently this long stretch was spared development, but a big resort is coming. See "The Coral Coast" in chapter 5.

- **Horseshoe Bay** (Matagi Island, Fiji): Home of one of the region's best-value resorts, Matagi is an extinct volcano whose crater fell away on one side and formed picturesque Horseshoe Bay. The half-moon beach at its head is one of the finest in the islands, but you will have to be on a yacht or a guest at Matangi Island Resort to enjoy it. See "Resorts on Qamea & Matagi Islands" in chapter 6.

- **Temae Plage Publique** (Moorea, French Polynesia): The northeastern coast of Moorea is fringed by a nearly uninterrupted stretch of white-sand beach which commands a glorious view across a speckled lagoon to Tahiti sitting on the horizon across the Sea of the Moon. See "Exploring Moorea" in chapter 9.

- **Matira Beach** (Bora Bora, French Polynesia): Beginning at the Hotel Bora Bora, this fine ribbon of sand stretches around skinny Matira Point, which forms the island's southern extremity, all the way to the Club Med. The eastern side has views of the islands of Raiatea and Tahaa. See "Exploring Bora Bora" in chapter 10.

- **Avea Beach** (Huahine, French Polynesia): My favorite resort beach is at Relais Mahana, a small hotel on Auea Bay near Huahine's southern end. Trees grow along the white beach, which slopes into a lagoon deep enough for swimming at any tide. The resort's pier goes out to a giant coral head, a perfect and safe place to snorkel, and the lagoon here is protected from the trade winds, making it safe for sailing. See "Where to Stay on Huahine" in chapter 11.

- **Titikaveka Beach** (Rarotonga, Cook Islands): On Rarotonga's southern coast, Titikaveka is blessed with palm trees draped over a long beach of brilliant white sand, and the lagoon here is the island's best for swimming and snorkeling. See "Exploring Rarotonga" in chapter 12.

- **Beach on One Foot Island** (Aitutaki, Cook Islands): The sands on the islets surrounding Aitutaki gleam pure white, like talcum. Tiny One Foot Island has the best beach here, with part of it along a channel whose coral bottom is scoured clean by strong tidal currents. Another stretch runs out to a sandbar known as Nude Island—a reference not to clothes but to a lack of vegetation. See "Exploring Aitutaki" in chapter 12.

- **Lalomanu Beach** (Upolu, Samoa): In the Aleipata district on the eastern end of Upolu, a clifflike mountain forms a dramatic backdrop to the deep sands of Lolomanu Beach, which faces a group of small islets offshore. On a clear day you can see American Samoa from here. This is a great place to stay in an open-air "beach fale." See "Exploring Apia & the Rest of Upolu" in chapter 13.

- **Return to Paradise Beach** (Upolu, Samoa): This idyllic stretch of white sand and black rocks overhung by coconut palms gets its name from *Return to Paradise,* the 1953 Gary Cooper movie that was filmed here. Surf actually pounds on the rocks. See "Exploring Apia & the Rest of Upolu" in chapter 13.

- **Manase Beach** (Savai'i, Samoa): The long stretch of white sand fronting Manase village on the north shore of Savai'i is another great place to spend a night in an open-air beach fale. See "Savai'i" in chapter 13.

3 The Best Honeymoon Destinations

Whether you're on your honeymoon or not, the South Pacific is a marvelous place for romantic escapes. After all, romance and the islands have gone hand-in-hand since the bare-breasted young women of Tahiti gave rousing welcomes to the 18th-century European explorers.

I've never stayed anywhere as romantic as a thatch-roof bungalow built on stilts over a lagoon, with a glass panel in its floor for viewing fish swimming below you and steps leading from your front deck into the warm waters below. You'll find lots of these in French Polynesia—especially on Bora Bora, the South Pacific's most famous (and expensive) honeymoon destination—and a handful more in the Cook Islands and in Samoa.

One caveat is in order: Many overwater bungalows are relatively close together, meaning that your honeymooning next-door neighbors will be within earshot if not eyeshot. ("It can be like watching an X-rated video," a hotel manager once confessed, "but without the video.") Therefore, if you're seeking a high degree of privacy and seclusion they won't be your best choice.

On the other hand, many of the South Pacific's small, relatively remote offshore resorts offer as much privacy as you are likely to desire. These little establishments would also fall into another category: The Best Places to Get Away from It All. They are so romantic that a friend of mine says her ideal wedding would be to rent an entire small resort in Fiji, take her wedding party with her, get married in Fijian costume beside the beach, and make the rest of her honeymoon a diving vacation. Most resorts covered in this book are well aware of such desires, and they offer wedding packages complete with traditional ceremony and costumes. Choose your resort, and then contact the management for details about their wedding packages.

In the meantime, here's what the two best honeymoon destinations have to offer:

- **Fiji:** Fiji has one of the world's finest collections of small offshore resorts. These little establishments have two advantages over their French Polynesian competitors. First, they have less than 20 bungalows each, instead of the 40 or more found at the French Polynesian resorts, which means they are usually more widely spaced than their Tahitian cousins. Second, they are on islands all by themselves. Together, these two advantages multiply the privacy factor several fold.

  The atmosphere at **Turtle Island Resort** (p. 124) and the **Vatulele Island Resort** (p. 135), both in the luxurious, superexpensive category, is active. Guests have the choice of dining alone in their bungalows or at lively dinner parties hosted by the engaging owners. **Yasawa Island Resort** sits on one of the prettiest beaches and has a very low-key, friendly ambience. It has very large bungalows, the choice being the secluded honeymoon unit that sits by its own beach. If you can't get that, be sure to reserve one of the newer units because a communal pathway runs just outside the bedroom windows of the older bungalows. See p. 125. Much less luxurious but also much less expensive, **Matamanoa Island Resort** caters exclusively to couples, making it a good choice for honeymooners on a budget. See p. 121.

  In central Fiji off Suva, **The Wakaya Club** has the largest bungalows in Fiji, plus a palatial mansion with its own pool, perched high atop a ridge. The staff leaves the guests to their own devices. You might see a movie star or two relaxing at Wakaya. See p. 154.

Off Taveuni, **Matangi Island Resort** is one of the region's best values for honeymooners. One of its widely spaced bungalows is built 20 feet up in a Pacific almond tree, and two more are carved into the side of a cliff (they are reserved for honeymooners). See p. 178. Among my favorite places to stay are the charming, old South Seas–style bungalows and stunning central building at **Qamea Resort and Spa.** Kerosene lanterns romantically light the 52-foot-high thatch roof of Qamea's main building, and each bungalow has an outdoor shower and its own hammock strung across the front porch. See p. 178.

- **French Polynesia:** The resorts here have the region's best selection of overwater bungalows. Invariably these are the most expensive style of accommodation in French Polynesia.

  On Tahiti, which most visitors now consider a way station to the other islands, the **Inter-Continental Tahiti Beachcomber Resort** has overwater bungalows that face the dramatic outline of Moorea across the Sea of the Moon. See p. 233. Some of those at **Le Meridien Tahiti** also have this view. See p. 233.

  On Moorea, the units at the **Club Bali Hai** are the among the oldest— and the least expensive—overwater bungalows in the islands, but they enjoy an unparalleled view of the jagged mountains surrounding Cook's Bay. See p. 257. Some overwater units at the **Sofitel Ia Ora** face Tahiti across the Sea of the Moon, and they're built over Moorea's most colorful lagoon. See p. 257. The **Moorea Pearl Resort** has a few perched on the edge of the clifflike reef, making for superb snorkeling right off your front deck. See p. 256.

Bora Bora has several hundred over-water bungalows, and many more will be there by the time you plan your trip. Meantime, the largest and most luxurious are at the **Bora Bora Nui Resort** (p. 275), although they don't look out to pillarlike Mount Ote-manu, which rises across the famous lagoon. Along with Cook's Bay on Moorea, this is one of the most pho-tographed scenes in the entire South Pacific. For that signature vista, you have to stay at the **Sofitel Motu** (p. 278) or at the **Hotel Bora Bora** (p. 276). Other bungalows at the Hotel Bora Bora sit right on the reef's edge. Ashore, the Hotel Bora Bora has large, luxurious bungalows that boast their own courtyards with swimming pools. Equally private though less luxe are the garden units at the **Bora Bora Pearl Beach Resort;** you can cavort to your heart's content in their wall-enclosed patios, which have sun decks and splash pools. See p. 276. The smaller but well-appointed overwater units at the friendly **Hotel Maitai Polynesia** are the least expensive on Bora Bora. See p. 279.

On Huahine, units at the **Te Tiare Beach Resort** have some of the largest decks of any overwater bunga-lows (one side is completely shaded by a thatch roof). See p. 290. The most charming of all overwater units are at the **Le Taha'a Private Island & Spa,** a luxurious resort on a small islet off Tahaa. Some of these espy Bora Bora on the horizon. See p. 298.

Out at the huge atoll known as Rangiroa, in the Tuamotu archipel-ago, **Hotel Kia Ora** has bungalows over the world's second-largest lagoon. See p. 302. On the adjacent atoll, overwater bungalows at the new **Tikehau Pearl Beach Resort** actually sit over the rip tides in a pass that lets the sea into the lagoon. See p. 304. On Manihi atoll, units at the **Manihi Pearl Beach Resort** are cooled by the almost constantly blowing trade winds. Isolated on their own islets, the Pearl Beach resorts on Tikihau and Manihi more closely approximate Fiji's offshore resorts than any others in French Polynesia. See p. 305.

4 The Best Family Vacations

There are no Disney Worlds or other such attractions in the islands. That's not to say that children won't have a fine time here, for more and more resorts are mak-ing provisions for families as well as hon-eymooners. Kids will enjoy themselves most if they like being around the water.

A family can vacation in style and comfort at large resorts like the big resorts on Denarau Island in Fiji, or Shangri-la's Fijian Resort on the Coral Coast, but here are some of the best smaller estab-lishments that welcome families with children.

- **Castaway Island Resort** (Mamanuca Islands, Fiji): One of Fiji's oldest resorts but thoroughly refurbished,

Castaway has plenty to keep both adults and children occupied, from a wide array of watersports to a kids' playroom and a nursery. There's even a nurse on duty. See p. 119.
- **Jean-Michel Cousteau Fiji Islands Resort** (Savusavu, Fiji): The South Pacific's finest family resort encour-ages parents to enroll their kids in an exceptional environmental education program. It keeps the youngsters both educated and entertained from sunup to bedtime. See p. 164.
- **InterContinental Resort and Spa Moorea** (Moorea, French Polynesia): Most resorts in French Polynesia are designed for romance, not children.

The one notable exception is the Moorea Beachcomber, which has an attractive pool, a calm lagoon, the widest selection of watersports in French Polynesia, and a kids' program. See p. 259.

- **The Rarotongan Beach Resort & Spa** (Rarotonga, Cook Islands): Rising like a phoenix after years of government-owned neglect, this is now the best international-standard resort on Rarotonga. Although it caters to everyone from honeymooners to families, the Rarotongan's children's program is tops in the Cook Islands. See p. 336.

5 The Best Cultural Experiences

The South Pacific Islanders are justly proud of their ancient Polynesian and Fijian cultures, and they eagerly inform anyone who asks about both their ancient and modern ways. Here are some of the best ways to learn about the islanders and their lifestyles.

- **Fijian Village Visits** (Fiji): Many tours from Nadi and from most offshore resorts include visits to traditional Fijian villages, whose residents stage welcoming ceremonies (featuring the slightly narcotic drink kava) and then show visitors around and explain how the old and the new combine in today's villages. See "Sightseeing Tours" in chapter 5.
- **Tiki Theatre Village** (Moorea, French Polynesia): Built to resemble a pre-European Tahitian village, this cultural center on Moorea has demonstrations of handicraft making and puts on a nightly dance show and feast. It's a bit commercial, and the staff isn't always fluent in English, but this is the only place in French Polynesia where one can sample the old ways. See "Exploring Moorea" in chapter 9.
- **Rarotonga** (Cook Islands): In addition to offering some of the region's most laid-back beach vacations, the people of Rarotonga go out of their way to let visitors know about their unique Cook Islands way of life. A morning spent at the **Cook Islands Cultural Village** and on a **cultural tour** of the island is an excellent educational experience. For a look at flora and fauna of the island, and their traditional uses, **Pa's Cross-Island Mountain Trek** cannot be topped. See "Exploring Rarotonga" in chapter 12.

- **Samoa:** The entire country serves as a cultural storehouse of *fa'a Samoa,* the traditional Samoan way of life. Most Samoans still live in villages featuring *fales* (oval houses), some of which have stood for centuries—although tin roofs have replaced thatch. The island of Savai'i is especially well preserved. A highlight of any visit to Savai'i should be a **tour** with Warren Jopling, a retired Australian geologist who has lived on Samoa's largest island for many years. Not only does he know the forbidding lava fields like the back of his hand, but everyone on Savai'i knows him, which helps make his cultural commentaries extremely informative. See "Savai'i" in chapter 13.
- **Tongan National Centre** (Nuku'alofa, Tonga): Artisans turn out classic Tongan handicrafts, and a museum exhibits Tongan history, including the robe worn by Queen Salote at the coronation of Queen Elizabeth II in 1953; and the carcass of Tui Malila, a Galápagos turtle that Captain James Cook reputedly gave to the king of Tonga in 1777, and which lived until 1968. The center also has island-night dance shows and feasts of traditional Tongan food. See "Exploring Tongatapu" in chapter 15.

6 The Best of the Old South Seas

Many South Pacific islands are developing rapidly, with modern, fast-paced cities replacing what were sleepy backwater ports, such as those at Papeete in French Polynesia and Suva in Fiji. However, there are still many remnants of the old South Sea days of coconut planters, beach bums, and missionaries.

- **Levuka** (Ovalau Island, Fiji): No other town has remained the same after a century as has Levuka, Fiji's first European-style town and its original colonial capital in the 1870s. The dramatic cliffs of Ovalau Island hemmed in the town and prevented growth, so the government moved to Suva in 1882. Levuka looks very much as it did then, with a row of clapboard general stores along picturesque Beach Street. See "A Side Trip Back in Time to Levuka" in chapter 5.

- **Taveuni Island** (Northern Fiji): Like Savai'i, Fiji's third-largest and most lush island has changed little since Europeans started coconut plantations there in the 1860s. With the largest remaining population of indigenous plants and animals of any South Pacific island, Taveuni is a nature lover's delight. See "Taveuni" in chapter 6.

- **Huahine** (French Polynesia): Of the French Polynesian islands frequented by visitors, Huahine has been the least affected by tourism, and its residents are still likely to give you an unprompted Tahitian greeting, *"Ia orana!"* As on Aitutaki, agriculture is still king on Huahine, which makes it the "Island of Fruits." There are ancient *marae* (temples) to visit, and the only town, tiny Fare, is little more

than a collection of Chinese shops fronting the island's wharf, which comes to life when ships pull in. See "Huahine" in chapter 11.

- **Aitutaki** (Cook Islands): Although it is now one of the hottest destinations in the South Pacific, the little island of Aitutaki is still very much old Polynesia, with most of its residents still farming and fishing for a living. The crystal-clear lagoon is something to behold. See "Aitutaki" in chapter 12.

- **Apia** (Samoa): Despite a sea wall along what used to be a beach and two large high-rise buildings sitting on reclaimed land, a number of clapboard buildings and 19th-century churches make Apia look much as it did when German, American, and British warships washed ashore during a hurricane here in 1889. See "Exploring Apia & the Rest of Upolu" in chapter 13.

- **Savai'i** (Samoa): One of the largest of all Polynesian islands, this great volcanic shield also is one of the least populated, with the oval-shaped houses of traditional villages sitting beside freshwater bathing pools fed by underground springs. See "Savai'i" in chapter 13.

- **Neiafu** (Vava'u, Tonga): Although Nuku'alofa, the capital on the main island of Tongatapu, gets most of the ink about Tonga, the little village of Neiafu on the sailor's paradise of Vava'u has remained untouched by development. Built by convicted adulteresses, the Road of the Doves still winds above the dramatic Port of Refuge, just as it did in 1875. See "Vava'u" in chapter 15.

7 The Best Dining Experiences

You won't be stuck eating island-style food cooked in an earth oven (see "Feasts

from Underground Ovens" in the appendix), nor will you be limited to the rather bland tastes of New Zealanders and Australians, which predominate at many restaurants. Wherever the French go, fine food and wine are sure to follow, and French Polynesia is no exception. The East Indians brought curries to Fiji, and chefs trained there have spread those spicy offerings to the other islands. Many chefs in Tonga are from Germany and Italy and specialize in their own "native" food. Chinese cuisine of varying quality can be found everywhere.

Wine connoisseurs will have ample opportunity to sample the vintages from nearby Australia, where abundant sunshine produces renowned full-bodied, fruit-driven varieties, such as chardonnay, semillon, Riesling, shiraz, Hermitage, cabernet sauvignon, and merlot. New Zealand wines are also widely available, including distinctive whites, such as chenin blanc, sauvignon blanc, and soft merlot. Freight and import duties drive up the cost of wine, so expect higher prices than at home.

- **Chefs The Restaurant** (Nadi, Fiji): Chef Eugeme Gomes's establishment has gourmet cuisine, excellent service, and lots of little touches that make for Fiji's finest dining experience. There's a branch in Suva, too. See p. 112.
- **Vilisite's Seafood Restaurant** (The Coral Coast, Fiji): This seaside restaurant, owned and operated by a friendly Fijian woman named Vilisite, doesn't look like much from the outside, but it offers a handful of excellent seafood meals to augment a terrific view along Fiji's Coral Coast from the veranda. See p. 136.
- **Old Mill Cottage** (Suva, Fiji): Diplomats and government workers pack this old colonial cottage at breakfast and lunch for some of the region's best and least expensive local fare. Offerings range from English-style roast chicken with mashed potatoes and peas to Fijian-style *palusami* (fresh fish wrapped in taro leaves and steamed in coconut milk). See p. 155.
- **Auberge du Pacifique** (Papeete, Tahiti): Award-winning chef Jean Galopin has been blending French and Polynesian cuisines at his lagoonside restaurant—with a removable roof to let in starlight—since 1974. He's even written a cookbook about Tahitian cooking. See p. 238.
- **Le Lotus** (Papeete, Tahiti): The most romantic setting of any South Pacific restaurant is in this overwater dining room at the Tahiti Beachcomber Inter-Continental Resort. Even if the food weren't gourmet French and the service highly efficient and unobtrusive, the view of Moorea on a moonlit night makes an evening here special. See p. 238.
- **Linareva Floating Restaurant and Bar** (Moorea, French Polynesia): With luck you won't get queasy while dining at chef Eric Lussiez's charming restaurant, which occupies the original ferry that plied between Tahiti and Moorea. His menu highlights fresh seafood excellently prepared in the classic French fashion. See p. 263.
- **Bloody Mary's Restaurant & Bar** (Bora Bora, French Polynesia): A fun evening at the South Pacific's most famous restaurant is a must-do experience when on Bora Bora. That's because Bloody's offers the most unique and charming dining experience in the islands. Come early for a drink at the friendly bar, then pick your fresh seafood from atop a huge tray of ice. After eating heavy French fare elsewhere for a few days, the sauceless fish from the grill will seem downright refreshing. See p. 280.
- **La Villa Mahana** (Bora Bora, French Polynesia): Corsican chef Damien Rinaldi Devio also offers relief from traditional French sauces at his little

restaurant, where he uses "exotic" spices to enliven fresh fish and beef dishes. See p. 280.

- **Tamarind House Restaurant & Bar** (Rarotonga, Cook Islands): Noted restaurateur and cookbook author Sue Carruthers brings the seasonings of her native Kenya to this charmer in a seaside colonial house. See p. 341.
- **Sails Restaurant and Bar** (Apia, Samoa): Ian and Lyvia Black have turned Robert Louis Stevenson's first Samoan home into one of the South Pacific's best casual restaurants,

complete with tables on an upstairs veranda overlooking historic Beach Road and Apia Harbour. You'll never forget the Commodore Sashimi. See p. 385.

- **Seaview Restaurant** (Nuku'alofa, Tonga): In a country where restaurants come and go, this German-owned establishment in an old waterfront home has provided Nuku'alofa's best cuisine for years. Tonga is the last island nation with a reliable supply of spiny tropical lobsters, so go for one here. See p. 435.

8 The Best Island Nights

Don't come to the South Pacific islands expecting opera and ballet, or Las Vegas–style floor shows, either. Other than pub-crawling to bars and nightclubs with music for dancing, evening entertainment here consists primarily of island nights, which invariably feature feasts of island foods followed by traditional dancing.

In the cases of French Polynesia and the Cook Islands, of course, the hip-swinging traditional dances are world famous. They are not as lewd and lascivious today as they were in the days before the missionaries arrived, but they still have plenty of suggestive movements to the primordial beat of drums. By contrast, dancing in Fiji, Tonga, and the Samoas is much more reserved, with graceful movements, terrific harmony, and occasional action in a war or fire dance.

- **French Polynesia:** Hotels are the places in which to see Tahitian

dancing. The resorts rely on village groups to perform a few times a week. The very best shows are during the annual *Heiva i Tahiti* festival in July; the winners then tour the other islands in August for minifestivals at the resorts. See "Island Nights" in chapters 8 through 10.

- **The Cook Islands:** Although the Tahitians are more famous for their dancing than the Cook Islanders, many of their original movements were quashed by the missionaries in the early 19th century. By the time the French took over in 1841 and allowed dancing again, the Tahitians had forgotten much of the old movements. They turned to the Cook Islands, where dancing was—and still is—the thing to do when the sun goes down. In the Cooks the costumes tend to be more natural and less colorful than in

Weekend Pub Crawling

Fundamentalist Christians may own Sundays in the islands, but Friday and Saturday nights definitely belong to the sinners. That's because bar-hopping—or pub-crawling as it's known out here—is *the* thing to do after dark on weekends. Every island has its favorite bars, which are packed until the wee hours on Friday night, until midnight on Saturday. There's a dark side, however, for fights can break out, and drunken driving is a problem on those nights.

the Tahitian floor shows, but the movements tend to be more active, suggestive, and genuine. There's an island night show every evening except Sunday on Rarotonga. The best troupes usually perform at the Edgewater Resort and the Rarotongan Beach Resort, but ask around. The best public performances are during the annual Dancer of the Year contest in April and the Constitution Week celebrations in August. See "Island Nights on Rarotonga" in chapter 12.

- **Samoa:** Among the great shows in the South Pacific are *fiafia* nights in the magnificent main building at Aggie Grey's Hotel in Apia. This tradition

was started in the 1940s by the late Aggie Grey, who at the show's culmination personally danced the graceful *siva*. Nowadays the show includes a rousing fire dance around the adjacent pool. See "Island Nights on Upolu" in chapter 13.

- **Tonga:** The weekly shows at the Tongan National Centre are unique, for this museum provides expert commentary before each dance, explaining its movements and their meanings. That's a big help, since all songs throughout the South Pacific are in the native languages. See "Island Nights on Tongatapu" in chapter 15.

9 The Best Buys

Take some extra money along, for you'll spend it on handicrafts, black pearls, and tropical clothing.

For the locations of the best shops, see the shopping sections in chapters 5 through 15.

- **Black Pearls:** Few people will escape French Polynesia or the Cook Islands without buying at least one black pearl. That's because the shallow, clear-water lagoons of French Polynesia's Tuamotu archipelago and the Manihiki and Penrhyn atolls in the Cook Islands are the world's largest producers of the beautiful dark orbs. The seemingly inexhaustible supply has resulted in fierce competition by vendors ranging from market stalls to high-end jewelry shops. See chapters 8 through 12.
- **Handicrafts:** Although many of the items you will see in island souvenir shops are actually made in Asia, locally produced handicrafts are the South Pacific's best buys. The most widespread are hats, mats, and baskets woven of *pandanus* or other fibers, usually by women who have maintained this ancient art to a high

degree. Tonga has the widest selection of woven items, although Samoa and Fiji are making comebacks. The finely woven mats made in Tonga and the Samoas are still highly valued as ceremonial possessions and are seldom for sale to tourists. See chapters 5, 13, and 15.

Before the coming of European traders and printed cotton, the South Pacific islanders wore garments made from the beaten bark of the paper mulberry tree. The making of this bark cloth, widely known as *tapa,* is another preserved art in Tonga, Samoa (where it is called *siapo*), and Fiji (where it is known as *masi*). The cloth is painted with dyes made from natural substances, usually in geometric designs that have ancestries dating back thousands of years. Tapa is an excellent souvenir because it can be folded and brought back in a suitcase. See chapters 5, 13, and 15.

Woodcarvings are also popular. Spears, war clubs, knives made from sharks' teeth, canoe prows, and cannibal forks are some examples. Many carvings, however, tend to be produced for the tourist trade and often lack the imagery of bygone days, and some may be machine-produced today. Carved tikis are found in most South Pacific countries, but many of them resemble the figures of the New Zealand Maoris rather than figures indigenous to those countries. The carvings from Fiji and the Marquesas Islands of French Polynesia are the best of the lot today. See chapters 5 and 8 through 12.

- **Tropical Clothing:** Colorful hand-screened, hand-blocked, and hand-dyed fabrics are very popular in the islands for making dresses or the wraparound skirt known as *pareu* in Tahiti and Rarotonga, *lava-lava* in the Samoas and Tonga, and *sulu* in Fiji. Heat-sensitive dyes are applied by hand to gauzelike cotton, which is then laid in the sun for several hours. Flowers, leaves, and other designs are placed on the fabric, and as the heat of the sun darkens and sets the dyes, the shadows from these objects leave their images behind on the finished product. See chapters 5 through 15.

10 The Best Diving & Snorkeling

All the islands have excellent scuba diving and snorkeling, and all but a few of the resorts either have their own dive operations or can easily make arrangements with a local company. Here are the best:

- **Fiji:** With nutrient-rich waters welling up from the Tonga Trench offshore and being carried by strong currents funneling through narrow passages, Fiji is famous for some of the world's most colorful soft corals. This is especially true of the Somosomo Strait between Vanua Levu and Taveuni in northern Fiji, home of the Rainbow Reef and its Great White Wall. The Beqa Lagoon is also famous for having plentiful soft corals. See chapters 5 and 6.

- **Rangiroa, Manihi, and Fakarava** (French Polynesia): Like those surrounding most populated islands, some lagoons in French Polynesia have been relatively "fished out" over the years. That's not to say that diving in such places as Moorea and Bora Bora can't be world class, but the best is at Rangiroa, Manihi, and Fakarava in the Tuamotu Archipelago. All are more famous for their abundant sea life, including sharks, than colorful soft corals. Go to Rangiroa to see sharks; go to the others to see more fish than you imagined ever existed. See chapter 11.

- **Tonga:** The north shore of the main island of Tongatapu fronts a huge lagoon, where the government has made national parks of the Hakaumama'o and Malinoa reefs. The best diving in Tonga, however, is around unspoiled Ha'apai and Vava'u. See "Ha'apai" and "Vava'u" in chapter 15.

11 The Best Sailing

One would think that the South Pacific is a yachting paradise, and it certainly gets more than its share of cruising boats on holiday from Australia and New Zealand or heading around the world (the region is on the safest circumnavigation route). However, the reefs in most places make sailing a precarious undertaking, so yachting is not that widespread. It has only recently gained a toehold in Fiji. There are only two places where you can charter a yacht and sail it yourself:

- **Raiatea** (French Polynesia): Firms have charter fleets based in Raiatea in the Leeward Islands of French Polynesia. Raiatea shares a lagoon with

Tahaa, a hilly island indented with long bays that shelter numerous anchorages. Boats can be sailed completely around Tahaa without leaving the lagoon, and both Bora Bora and Huahine are just 32km (20 miles) away over blue water. See "Raiatea & Tahaa" in chapter 11.

- **Vava'u** (Tonga): The second most popular yachting spot, Vava'u is virtually serrated by well-protected bays like the nearby Port of Refuge. Chains of small islands trail off the south side of Vava'u like the tentacles of a jellyfish, creating large and very quiet cruising grounds. Many anchorages are off deserted islands with their own beaches. See "Vava'u" in chapter 15.

12 The Best Offbeat Travel Experiences

Some cynics might say that a visit to the South Pacific itself is an offbeat experience, but there are a few things to do that are even more unusual.

- **Getting Asked to Dance** (everywhere): I've seen so many traditional South Pacific dance shows that I now stand by the rear door, ready to beat a quick escape before those lovely young women in grass skirts can grab my hand and force me to make a fool of myself trying to gyrate my hips up on the stage. It's part of the tourist experience at all resorts, and it's all in good fun.
- **Swimming with the Sharks** (Bora Bora, French Polynesia): A key attraction in Bora Bora's magnificent lagoon is to snorkel with a guide, who actually feeds a school of sharks as they thrash around in a frenzy. I prefer to leave this one to the Discovery Channel. See "Exploring Bora Bora" in chapter 10.
- **Riding the Rip** (Rangiroa and Manihi, French Polynesia): Snorkelers will never forget the flying sensation as they ride the strong currents ripping through a pass into the lagoons at Rangiroa and Manihi. See "Rangiroa" and "Manihi" in chapter 11.
- **Sleeping in a Beach Fale** (Samoa): Even if you don't like to camp, you'll enjoy every minute spent in one of Samoa's beach fales—little thatch-roof buildings perched beside one of that country's lovely beaches. Forget privacy, since most are open-sided in traditional Samoan fashion. But why block the view with unnecessary walls? And the neighbors you meet could become lifetime friends. See "Where to Stay on Upolu" and "Where to Stay & Dine on Savai'i" in chapter 13.
- **Worshipping with the King** (Nuku'alofa, Tonga): It's not every day you get to see a real-life king, but you can in Tonga. In fact, you can even go to church with him on Sunday, or perhaps watch him ride by in his big, black SUV other days of the week. See "How To Survive Sunday in Tonga" in chapter 15.
- **Cave Swimming** (Samoa and Tonga): Boats can go right into Swallows Cave on one of the small islands that make up beautiful Vava'u, but you have to don masks and snorkels and follow a guide underwater into Mariner's Cave, whose only light comes from the passage you just swam through. See "Exploring Vava'u" in chapter 15. You also have to swim underwater into the Piula Cave Pool in Samoa. See "Exploring Apia & the Rest of Upolu" in chapter 13.

2

Planning Your Trip to the South Pacific

Drawn by the islands' beauty and charm—as well as their reputation as a safe haven in this time of international terrorism—record numbers of visitors are discovering this vast and varied paradise. This is especially true of Australians and New Zealanders, for whom the islands are as convenient as the Caribbean is to Americans and Canadians, or the Greek Isles are to Europeans. The tourism boom is bringing new airlines, resorts, tours, and other facilities. In other words, change is in the air out here. Now more than ever, wise planning is essential to get the most out of your time and money in this vast and varied modern paradise.

Fiji, Tahiti and French Polynesia, the Cook Islands, Samoa, American Samoa, and the Kingdom of Tonga have their own sources of information, entry requirements, currency, government, customs, laws, internal transportation, styles of accommodation, and food. In this chapter I give a brief description of the islands and tell you how to plan your trip in general. This information augments, but is not a substitute for, the chapters devoted to each destination.

1 The Islands in Brief

Most of the islands covered in this book are part of the Polynesian Triangle, which stretches across the vast Pacific Ocean from Hawaii to New Zealand to Easter Island. With the exception of Fiji, they are variations on an overall cultural theme. Each has carved its own identity, yet each is fundamentally Polynesian. Sitting on the border between Polynesia and the Melanesian islands to the west, Fiji has its own distinctive culture blending elements from both areas. The Fijians also share their islands with East Indians, who add a starkly contrasting culture to the mix.

Every country offers a great variety of activities, so be sure to read "The Active Traveler," later in this chapter.

Let's take a quick tour to see what each island country or territory contributes to this smorgasbord.

FIJI

Because its international airport at **Nadi** is the region's major transportation hub, Fiji is a prime place with which to begin or end a trip to the South Pacific. In fact, more than twice as many people of every income bracket visit Fiji each year as come to any other South Pacific island destination.

This lush country of 300-plus islands has something for everyone—from lying on some of the region's best beaches to diving on some of the world's most colorful reefs, from cruising to intriguing outer islands to hiking into the mountainous interior.

Although its beaches aren't the best in Fiji, the Nadi area is home to **Denarau Island,** the country's largest resort area. Still developing, Denarau has an 18-hole

The South Pacific

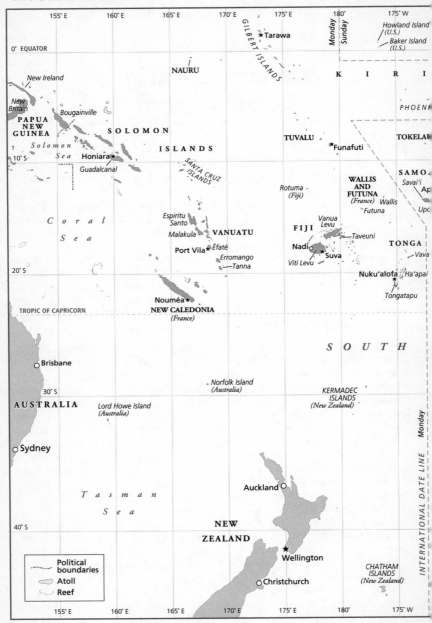

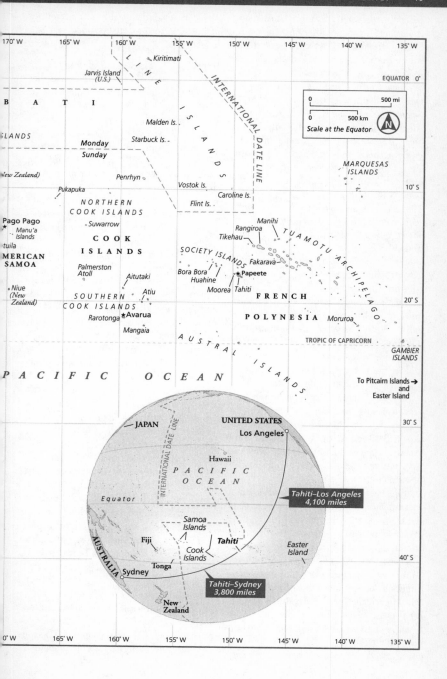

golf course, a tennis center, a marina, and three large hotels (with more to come). From Denarau you can cruise out to the **Mamanuca** and **Yasawa** islands, all little specks of land which are home to fine beaches, a host of watersports, and a wide range of offshore resorts.

From Nadi, the Queen's Road goes south to the **Coral Coast,** Fiji's first resort area and still host to several family-oriented resorts, and to **Pacific Harbour,** site of the country's top cultural center and golf course. Pacific Harbour is the departure point for rafting trips on the Navua River and to the island of **Beqa** (pronounced *Beng*-ga), whose surrounding lagoon proffers some of its best diving and snorkeling.

The Queen's Road ends in **Suva,** Fiji's cosmopolitan capital city. Suva gives a glimpse through its rainy climate of the era when Great Britain ruled here. A 10-minute flight from nearby Nausori Airport will whisk you to the island of **Ovalau,** where the country's first European-style town, **Levuka,** still looks like it did in the late 1800s, before the government moved the capital to Suva.

Up in Northern Fiji, **Savusavu** and **Taveuni** will transport you back in time to the Fiji of colonial coconut plantations. Between them lies the **Somosomo Strait,** home to the Great White Wall and its Rainbow Reef, as well as other world-class dive sites.

Fiji has the South Pacific's most fascinating mix of peoples. A bit more than half are extremely friendly, easygoing Fijians, most of whom still live in traditional villages surrounded by vegetable gardens. About 44% or so are industrious—and sometimes abrasive—East Indians whose ancestors came to work the sugar-cane plantations that make Fiji the most self-sufficient of the South Pacific countries. Although the contrasting Fijian-Indian cultures has resulted in political unrest and three coups since 1987, it also makes this an interesting place to get into a conversation.

FRENCH POLYNESIA

If there is a "major league" of dramatically beautiful islands, then Tahiti and her French Polynesian sisters dominate it. This is especially true of **Moorea** and **Bora Bora,** which provide Hollywood with many of its choice "stock shots" of glorious tropical settings. Moorea's jagged, shark's-teeth ridges serrate the horizon like the back of some primordial dinosaur resting on the sea just 20km (12 miles) west of Tahiti. One of the world's most romantic honeymoon destinations, Bora Bora is famous for its world-class lagoon, out of which rises the main island topped by the dramatic, tombstonelike Mt. Otemanu.

High and well watered, **Tahiti** is the largest of the French Polynesian islands and was the first to be discovered by European explorers in the late 18th century. A great majority of the territory's population lives on Tahiti, especially in and around **Papeete,** the capital. Today this busy little city has so many cars, trucks, and motor scooters that it can take up to 2 hours to commute to work from the outlying regions. Although Papeete has lost much of its old South Seas charm, Tahiti's rural areas still display aspects of traditional Polynesia.

Even more of Old Polynesia exists on the territory's third most beautiful island, **Huahine,** which locals call "wild" because of its undeveloped status. Here you can explore some of the region's most important archaeological sites. Nearby, the adjacent islands of **Raiatea** and **Tahaa** are even more natural. The two islands are enclosed by one large lagoon, making them French Polynesia's prime sailing grounds.

Off to the northeast, the line of atolls known as the **Tuamotu Archipelago** boasts French Polynesia's top scuba diving destinations. **Rangiroa,** which encloses the world's second largest lagoon, is known for its clear waters, which are home to thousands of sharks. Sitting next to Rangiroa, **Tikehau** is considerably smaller, and its one international-standard resort sits on an islet all to itself. Also much smaller and shallower than the lagoon at Rangiroa, the fish-filled lagoon at **Manihi** makes it the world's largest producer of black pearls. Farther afield, **Fakarava** possesses the world's third largest lagoon.

Even farther afield are the wildly beautiful **Marquesas Islands,** recently made famous by TV's "Survivor" reality show, which filmed one season here.

Thanks to many tons of francs poured in by the French government, the territory is the most developed, and has the highest standard of living, of any South Pacific island country. The flip side of that coin is that everyone pays high prices for almost everything, local residents and visitors alike. Indeed, French Polynesia is the most expensive South Pacific destination. As one local resident of these gorgeous islands says, "Here, you must pay for the view."

THE COOK ISLANDS

Only 800km (500 miles) west of Tahiti (virtually next door in this part of the world), the tiny Cook Islands have much in common with French Polynesia, both in physical beauty and people.

Barely 32km (20 miles) around, **Rarotonga** is a miniature Tahiti in terms of its mountains, beaches, and reefs—but in terms of development, it's like Tahiti was some 50 years ago. Unlike Papeete, however, the capital of the Cook Islands, **Avarua,** remains a quiet little backwater, a picturesque village without a stoplight. Yet no other South Pacific destination has as many hotels, restaurants, daytime activities, and nightclubs packed into so small a space as does Rarotonga.

Among the outer islands, **Aitutaki** bears the same relationship to Rarotonga

as Bora Bora does to Tahiti. A small central island sits at the apex of a shallow but spectacular aquamarine lagoon fringed by some of the region's whitest, talcumlike sand beaches. Long a backwater, Aitutaki is now a thriving destination, thanks to new hotels and beach-bungalow establishments. Even if you don't stay there, it's worth a side trip to Aitutaki just to take a lagoon excursion out to the little islands fringing the reef.

The Cook Islanders share with the Tahitians a fun-loving lifestyle, many old Polynesian legends and gods, and about 60% of their native language. The Cooks were governed by New Zealand from 1901 until 1965 and still are associated with New Zealand. Consequently, Cook Islanders speak English fluently, which makes it easy for English-speaking travelers to take advantage of the South Pacific's most informative cultural tours and exhibits. They also pay less for almost everything and use the New Zealand dollar as their local currency, which means the Cooks are more affordable than French Polynesia.

THE SAMOAS

Independent **Samoa** (formerly known as Western Samoa) is like a cultural museum, especially when compared with its much smaller cousin, **American Samoa.** The peoples of both are related by family and tradition, if not by politics. Samoan culture still exists in the American islands, and it is preserved to a remarkable degree in Samoa, relatively unchanged by modern materialism. Traditional Samoan villages, with their turtle-shaped houses, rest peacefully along the coasts of the two main western Samoan islands, **Upolu** and **Savai'i.** Although Samoa has been experiencing a good economy, time seems to have forgotten some of the weather-beaten, clapboard buildings that distinguish **Apia,** the country's picturesque capital. Although tourism is not a major industry, the country has three luxury beach resorts from which you can fan out and meet the friendly Samoans. Experiencing their unique culture and visiting their truly remarkable and undeveloped beaches (one of which was the setting for the Gary Cooper movie *Return to Paradise*) are highlights of any visit. You can even sleep right on the sands in one of the country's numerous beach *fales* (small, open-air huts).

Tutuila, the main island in American Samoa, rivals the dramatic beauty of Moorea and Bora Bora in French Polynesia. The mountains drop straight down into fabled **Pago Pago,** the finest harbor in the South Pacific and the main reason that the United States has had a presence there since 1890. This American influence has resulted in a blend of cultures: the Samoan emphasis on extended families and communal ownership of property, especially land, and the Western desire for business and progress. The result of the latter is that Pago Pago harbor is dominated—and polluted—by two large tuna canneries, and large stacks of shipping containers often block the splendid views. The road around the harbor is often clogged with vehicles as American Samoans rush past their traditional villages on their way to American-style shopping centers.

TONGA

From his Victorian palace in **Nuku'alofa,** King Taufa'ahau Tupou IV of Tonga rules over a nobility that carries European titles but is in reality a pure Polynesian system of high chiefs. Despite grumbling among his commoner subjects in recent years, the king, his family, and the nobles control the government and all the land, of which they are obligated to provide 3.4 hectares (8½ acres) to every Tongan adult male.

While the relatively flat main island of **Tongatapu** offers little in the way of dramatic scenic beauty, and accommodations here are below international standard, the adjacent lagoon provides excellent boating, snorkeling, fishing, and diving. The crown jewel of this little kingdom is hilly **Vava'u,** which presents long and narrow fjords and a plethora of deserted islands; these features make it one of the South Pacific's leading yachting and whale-watching centers. **Neiafu,** the only town on Vava'u, is a reminder of the old days of traders and beach bums.

Indeed, Tonga is the heart of the South Pacific "Bible Belt." Things are slow on Sunday in most island countries, but they almost stop completely in Tonga—except for church, picnics at the beautiful beaches, and escapes to resorts on tiny islets offshore.

2 Visitor Information

The best sources for data about the specific island countries are their tourist information offices (see the individual country chapters).

A good source for general information is the **South Pacific Tourism Organization (SPTO),** P.O. Box 13119, Suva, Fiji Islands (© **679/330-4177;** fax 679/330-1995; www.spto.org).

Another general source is the **Pacific Asia Travel Association (PATA),** an industry trade association based in Bangkok, Thailand. It has a North American office in the Latham Square Building, 1611 Telegraph Ave., Suite 1515, Oakland, CA 94612 (© **510/625-2055;** fax 510/625-2044; www.pata.org).

The U.S. Department of State maintains a **Travel Advisory** (© **202/647-5225;** http://travel.state.gov) to keep you abreast of political or other problems throughout the world and posts travel warnings and other timely information on its website, www.travel.state.gov.

The East-West Center at the University of Hawaii gathers news from throughout the islands on its **Pacific Islands Report** website, http://pidp.east westcenter.org/pireport. It's the best single source for breaking news stories, and it has links to newspapers, news services, universities, and other useful sites.

Another useful site for regional news is posted by the Fiji-based *Pacific Magazine* (www.pacificmagazine.net).

3 Entry Requirements & Customs

ENTRY REQUIREMENTS

All South Pacific countries require each new arrival to have a **passport** that will be valid for the duration of the visit, as well as an onward or return airline ticket. Your passport should be valid for 6 months beyond the date you expect to return home. See chapters 4, 7, 12, 13, 14, and 15 for details about each country's entry requirements.

Safeguard your passport in an inconspicuous, inaccessible place and keep a copy of the critical pages, with your passport number, in a separate place. If you lose your passport, you can go to a U.S. embassy in Fiji or Samoa, or the governor of American Samoa can issue a temporary replacement passport. Australia, New Zealand, and the United Kingdom have high commissioners in Fiji, Samoa, and Tonga.

Note that the International Civil Aviation Organization (ICAO) recommends that *every* individual who travels by air have his or her own passport. In response, many countries are now requiring that children be issued their own passport to travel internationally, where before those under 16 or so may have been able to travel on a parent or guardian's passport.

The only vaccination required anywhere in the South Pacific is for yellow fever, and then only if you're coming from an infected area of South America or Africa.

GETTING A PASSPORT
RESIDENTS OF THE UNITED STATES   American citizens and residents can obtain passport applications at most post offices and at regional passport offices. The fee for a new passport is US$97; for a renewal, US$67.

Whether you're applying in person or by mail, you can download passport applications from the **U.S. State Department** website at **http://travel.state.gov**. For general information, call the **National Passport Agency** (© 202/647-0518). To find your regional passport office, either check the U.S. State Department website or call the **National Passport Information Center** (© 900/225-5674); the fee is US55¢ per minute for automated information and US$1.50 per minute for operator-assisted calls.

Firms in many large cities will expedite passport applications—at additional fees, of course. Look under "Passport" or "Passport & Visa Services" in the Yellow Pages in your local phone book. Nationally, **American Passport Express** (© 800/841-6778; www.americanpassport.com) will process your passport in a week for a fee plus the cost of the passport itself.

RESIDENTS OF CANADA   Canadian citizens can pick up passport applications at one of 28 regional passport offices, from Canada Post offices, from most travel agencies, or downloaded from **Passport Canada,** Department of Foreign Affairs and International Trade, Ottawa, ON K1A 0G3 (© 800/567-6868; www.ppt.gc.ca).

Applications may be submitted at any Passport Canada office, at post office, or sent to Passport Canada, 70 Crémazie St., Gatineau, QC J8Y 3P2. They must be accompanied by two identical passport-size photographs and proof of Canadian

Tips Getting Hitched in the Islands

The South Pacific islands are marvelous places to get married, and most resorts have romantic wedding packages including traditional ceremonies, often right on the beach. Getting officially married in the islands, however, is easy only in Fiji and the Cook Islands. It is impractical in French Polynesia, where a 30-day residency is required. Legal or not, many couples still opt for island wedding ceremonies during their honeymoons. The resorts will tell you what documents you need to bring and what local formalities you need to execute before your wedding.

citizenship. Processing takes 5 to 10 days if you apply in person, or about 3 weeks by mail. Canadian children who travel must have their own passport. However, if you hold a valid Canadian passport issued before December 11, 2001, that bears the name of your child, the passport remains valid for you and your child until it expires.

RESIDENTS OF THE UNITED KINGDOM   To pick up an application for a standard 10-year passport (5-year. passport for children under 16), visit the nearest Passport Office, major post office, or travel agency. You can also contact the **United Kingdom Passport Service** at ⓒ **0870/571-0410** or visit its website at www.passport.gov.uk. Processing takes about 2 weeks (1 week if you apply at the Passport Office).

RESIDENTS OF IRELAND   You can apply for a 10-year passport at the **Passport Office,** Setanta Centre, Molesworth Street, Dublin 2 (ⓒ **01/671-1633;** www.irlgov.ie/iveagh). The fee is €75. Those under age 18 and over 65 must apply for a 3-year passport, which costs €15. You can also apply at 1A South Mall, Cork (ⓒ **021/272-525**) or at most main post offices.

RESIDENTS OF AUSTRALIA   You can pick up an application from your local post office or any branch of Passports Australia, but you must schedule an interview at the passport office to present your application materials. Call the **Australian Passport Information Service** at ⓒ **131-232,** or visit the government website at www.passports.gov.au.

RESIDENTS OF NEW ZEALAND You can pick up a passport application at any New Zealand Passports Office or download it from their website. Contact the **Passports Office** at ⓒ **0800/225-050** in New Zealand or 04/474-8100, or log on to www.passports.govt.nz.

CUSTOMS
WHAT YOU CAN BRING INTO THE SOUTH PACIFIC
Each South Pacific country or territory has its own customs laws. See chapters 4, 7, 12, 13, 14, and 15 for information about what you can take into them.

WHAT YOU CAN TAKE HOME FROM THE SOUTH PACIFIC
Returning **U.S. citizens** who have been in the South Pacific for at least 48 hours are allowed to bring back, once every 30 days, US$800 worth of merchandise duty-free (US$1,200 from American Samoa). You'll be charged a flat rate of 4% duty on the next US$1,000 worth of purchases. Be sure to have your receipts handy, since you must list every item if you're over the duty-free limits. On mailed gifts, the duty-free limit is US$100 (US$200 for American Samoa). In addition, adults can bring back 200 cigarettes (age 18 and older) and one liter of alcoholic beverages (age 21 and older).

You cannot bring fresh foodstuffs into the United States; tinned foods, however, are allowed. For more information, contact the **U.S. Bureau of Customs & Border Protection,** 1300 Pennsylvania Ave. NW, Washington, DC 20229 (© 877/287-8867; www.customs.gov), and request the free pamphlet *Know Before You Go.* (Click on "Traveler Information," then "Know Before You Go Brochure.")

For a summary of **Canadian** rules, get the booklet *I Declare,* from the **Canada Customs and Revenue Agency** (© 800/461-9999 in Canada, or 204/983-3500; www.ccra-adrc.gc.ca). Canada allows its citizens a C$750 exemption; adults are allowed to bring back duty-free one carton of cigarettes, one can of tobacco, 40 imperial ounces of liquor, and 50 cigars; check age requirements with your home province's tobacco and drinking laws. In addition, you're allowed to mail gifts to Canada valued at less than C$60 a day, provided they're unsolicited and don't contain alcohol or tobacco (write on the package "Unsolicited gift, under C$60 value"). All valuables should be declared on the Y-38 form before departure from Canada, including serial numbers of valuables you already own, such as expensive foreign cameras. *Note:* The C$750 exemption can be used once a year and only after an absence of 7 days.

U.K. citizens age 17 or over have a customs allowance of 200 cigarettes; 50 cigars; 250g of smoking tobacco; 2 liters of still table wine; 1 liter of spirits or strong liqueurs (over 22% by volume); 2 liters of fortified wine, sparkling wine or other liqueurs; 60ml perfume; 250ml of toilet water; and £145 worth of all other goods, including gifts and souvenirs. People under 17 are not entitled to the tobacco and alcohol allowances. For more information, contact **HM Customs & Excise** at © 0845/010-9000 (from outside the U.K., 020/8929-0152), or consult their website at www.hmce.gov.uk.

The duty-free allowance in **Australia** is A$400 for adults and A$200 for those under 18. Personal property mailed back from the islands should be marked "Australian goods returned" to avoid payment of duty. Upon returning to Australia, citizens age 18 or over can bring in 250 cigarettes or 250g of loose tobacco, and 2.25 liters of alcohol. If you're returning with valuable goods you owned before your trip to the South Pacific, such as foreign-made cameras, you should file form B263. A helpful brochure, available from Australian consulates or Customs offices, is *Know Before You Go.* For more information, call the **Australian Customs Service** at © 1300/363-263, or log on to www.customs.gov.au.

The duty-free allowance for **New Zealand** is NZ$700. Citizens over 17 can bring in 200 cigarettes, or 50 cigars, or 250g of tobacco (or a mixture of all three if their combined weight doesn't exceed 250g); plus 4.5 liters of wine and beer, or 1.125 liters of liquor. New Zealand currency does not carry import or export restrictions. You should fill out a certificate of export, listing the valuables you are taking out of the country; that way, you can bring them back without paying

---

Tips **Be Careful What You Buy**

Some South Pacific governments restrict the export of antique carvings and other artifacts of historic value. If a piece looks old, check before you buy. Jewelry made of shells and of pink or black coral is available in many countries, as is scrimshaw, but items made of black coral and whalebone cannot legally be brought back to the United States and most other Western countries.

duty. Most questions are answered in a free pamphlet available at New Zealand consulates and Customs offices: *New Zealand Customs Guide for Travellers, Notice no. 4.* For more information, contact **New Zealand Customs,** The Customhouse, 17–21 Whitmore St., Box 2218, Wellington (© **04/473-6099** or 0800/428-786; www.customs.govt.nz).

4 Money

CURRENCIES

The Cook Islands use New Zealand dollars, and American Samoa spends U.S. greenbacks. Otherwise, each South Pacific country has its own currency— Fiji dollars (F$), French Pacific francs (CFP), Samoan tala (S$), and Tongan pa'anga (T$). See the individual country chapters for details. U.S., Australian, and New Zealand dollars are accepted widely in the islands (Euros, too, in French Polynesia), and the local banks will change other major currencies.

The major banks have ATMs (see below) and exchange booths at the international airports with the same rates as in the cities and towns.

Before you leave home, if you can find a bank which has the local currencies–not a likely prospect–you can avoid lines at the airport banks and ATMs by changing enough money to cover airport incidentals and transportation to your hotel. Otherwise, bring a few U.S., Australian, or New Zealand dollars or Euros to tide you over.

You'll get a better rate by exchanging currency or traveler's checks at a bank or currency exchange shop, not a hotel or store.

To find exchange rates, go to **www.xe.com/ucc**, which gives the present exchange rates for French Pacific francs, Fiji dollars, Samoan tala, Tongan pa'anga, and the New Zealand dollar.

ATMs

Banks in all the main towns have **automated teller machines (ATMs),** at which you can use your Visa or MasterCard (but not necessarily those without such an international affiliation) to withdraw local currency against your credit card or check (debit) card account. I tell you in the "Fast Facts" in each section whether an island has ATM machines. Be sure to read the information—or check with the banks or tourist offices in the main towns—before heading off cash-less to an outer island.

When I use credit or debit cards, I get a better exchange rate than if I had changed traveler's checks, and I avoid the local banks' fees for changing traveler's checks (see below).

Visa and MasterCard tack on a 1% currency conversion fee, and many American banks add up to 5% as their own "foreign transaction fee." Visa and MasterCard have already converted the other currency into dollars by the time it hits

---

Tips **Small Change**

When you change money (or after you've withdrawn local currency from an ATM), ask for some small bills or loose change. Petty cash will come in handy for public transportation (South Pacific taxi drivers never seem to have change for large bills). Consider keeping the small money separate from your larger bills, so that it's readily accessible and you'll be less of a target for theft.

<Tips **Getting Rid of Your Left-over Currency**

Use your left-over currency to pay part of your hotel bill when leaving the South Pacific. Put the rest on your credit card. It will save you the trouble of having to change it at the airport.

---

your bank, so this additional fee is nothing but a gouge. To my mind, it's also grounds for finding another bank.

I have a Capital One credit card which charges no foreign transaction fee, and it has no annual fee. Read your own card member agreement—or better yet, call your bank's customer service department—for charges.

Also ask if they levy a fee even if you pay in dollars, or when you charge a U.S. dollar purchase to an overseas company or Website and the vendor sends the transaction through a foreign bank.

You may be charged lower fees by using your debit or ATM card, as opposed to a credit card, but even then your bank may charge you for using another bank's ATM. For example, my commercial bank tacks on $1.75 per transaction for using its Visa check card in someone else's ATM plus the 1% Visa foreign transaction fee. On the other hand, my credit union charges no fees for my using its Visa check/debit card to withdraw cash overseas, and it even rebates the 1% charged by Visa. Obviously I use my credit union card to withdraw cash from ATMs overseas.

I carry the two debit cards so that if my credit union card doesn't work in a bank's ATM, I have a back-up.

One way to avoid the charges is to pay for your airfare and hotel in U.S. dollars before leaving home, such as through a travel agent.

Be sure you know your **personal identification number (PIN)** for each card before you leave home and be sure to find out your daily withdrawal limit before you depart.

TRAVELER'S CHECKS

Traveler's checks are something of an anachronism from the days before the ATM. I carry a few hundred dollars' worth in case the ATMs are broken, have run out of cash, or for some reason won't accept my credit or debit card (more likely in French Polynesia than elsewhere), but I did not cash a single check during my recent three-month trip. Banks in all the main towns will cash, and most major hotels, resorts, restaurants, and car-rental firms will accept, traveler's checks issued by American Express, Thomas Cook, Visa, Bank of America, Citicorp, and MasterCard.

You won't necessarily be able to cash traveler's checks on many outer islands, which often have limited, if any, banking facilities, so read the applicable "Fast Facts" section in each of the following chapters before heading to an outer island. Also note that banks in French Polynesia and some other countries charge fees of up to US$5 per transaction.

You can get traveler's checks at almost any bank or from an **American Express** office. You'll pay a service charge ranging from 1% to 4%. You can also get American Express traveler's checks over the phone by calling ℂ **800/221-7282** (www.americanexpress.com); Amex gold and platinum cardholders who use this number are exempt from the 1% fee.

Visa offers traveler's checks at Citibank locations nationwide, as well as at several other banks. The service charge ranges between 1.5% and 2%. Call ℂ **800/ 732-1322** (www.visa.com) for information. **MasterCard** also offers traveler's checks. Call ℂ **800/223-9920** (www. mastercard.com) for a location near you.

AAA members can obtain checks without a fee at most AAA offices.

CREDIT CARDS

Most hotels, car-rental companies, restaurants, and large shops accept Visa and MasterCard, and some accept American Express. Only the major hotels and car-rental firms accept Diners Club. Leave your Discover card at home; it isn't accepted anywhere in the islands. Always ask first, and when you're away from the main towns, don't count on putting anything on plastic.

TIPPING & TAXES

Although the custom is changing, tipping is considered contrary to the Polynesian and Melanesian traditions of hospitality and generosity. You may get that "Where's-my-tip?" look from a porter as he delays leaving your room, and there's a sign in a Tahiti restaurant proclaiming that "Tipping Is Not Illegal." Nevertheless, you don't have to tip out here. That's not to say that a gratuity isn't in order for truly outstanding service. I usually give a small tip to porters who wrestle with my heavy international bags.

You will not be socked with a service charge on your hotel and restaurant bills. So for the most part, you can forget that hidden 15% or more your vacation could cost in the United States or Europe.

Hotel rooms are subject to an additional levy everywhere, and most countries impose a hidden "value-added tax." Except in Tonga, direct sales taxes aren't added to your restaurant, bar, shopping, and other bills as they are in the United States.

Fun Fact   Island Time vs. Island Service

There's an old story about a 19th-century planter who promised a South Pacific islander a weekly wage and a pension if he would come to work on his copra plantation. *Copra* is dried coconut meat, from which oil is pressed for use in soaps, cosmetics, and other products. Hours of backbreaking labor are required to chop open the coconuts and extract the meat by hand.

The islander was sitting by the lagoon, eating fruit he had picked from nearby trees while hauling in one fish after another. "Let me make sure I understand you," said the islander. "You want me to break my back working for you for 30 years. Then you'll pay me a pension so I can come back here and spend the rest of my life sitting by the lagoon, eating fruit from my trees and the fish I catch? I may not be sophisticated, but I am not stupid."

The islander's response reflects an attitude still prevalent in the South Pacific, where many people don't have to work in the Western sense. Here life moves at a slow pace. The locals call it "island time."

Consequently, do not expect the same level of service rendered in most hotels and restaurants back home. The slowness is not slothful inattention; it's just the way things are done here. Your drink will come in due course. If you must have it immediately, order it at the bar. Otherwise, relax with your friendly hosts and enjoy their charming company.

5 When to Go

THE CLIMATE

The South Pacific islands covered in this book lie within the tropics. Compared to the pronounced winters and summers of the temperate zones, there is little variation from one island group to the next: They are warm and humid all year. The only question is: Will it rain, or will it shine?

Although local weather patterns have changed in the past 20 years, making conditions less predictable, local residents recognize two distinct seasons, which may bear on when you choose to visit.

A cooler and more comfortable **dry season** occurs during the austral winter, from May to October. The winter trade wind blows fairly steadily during these months, bringing generally fine tropical weather throughout the area. Daytime high temperatures reach the delightful upper 70s (24°C–27°C) to low 80s (28°C–30°C) in French Polynesia, Samoa, and Fiji, with early morning lows in the high 60s (18°C–20°C). Rarotonga in the Cook Islands and Tongatapu in Tonga are farther from the equator and see cooler temperatures, with the highs in the 60s or low 70s (15°C–23°C). Breezy wintertime nights can feel chilly in those islands.

The austral summer from November through April is the warmer and more humid **wet season.** Daytime highs climb into the upper 80s (30°C–33°C) throughout the islands, with nighttime lows around 70°F (21°C). Low-pressure troughs and tropical depressions can bring several days of rain at a time, but usually heavy rain showers are followed by periods of very intense sunshine. An air-conditioned hotel room or bungalow will feel like heaven during this humid time of year. This is also the season for tropical cyclones (hurricanes), which can be devastating and should never be taken lightly. Fortunately, they usually move fast enough that their major effect on visitors is a day or two of heavy rain and wind. If you're caught in one, the hotel employees are experts on what to do to ensure your safety.

Another factor to consider is the part of an island that you'll visit. Because moist trade winds often blow from the east, the eastern sides of the high, mountainous islands tend to be wetter all year than the western sides.

Also bear in mind that the higher the altitude, the lower the temperature. If you're going up in the mountains, be prepared for much cooler weather than you'd have on the coast.

THE BUSY SEASON

July and August are the busiest tourist season in the South Pacific. That's when Australians and New Zealanders visit the islands to escape the cold back home. It's also when residents of Tahiti head to their own outer islands, in keeping with the traditional July-August holiday break in France. Many Europeans also visit the islands during this time.

Moments When the Moon Is Full

The islands are extraordinarily beautiful anytime, but the play of moonlight on the lagoons and ocean, and the black silhouettes the mountains cast against the sky, make them magical when the moon is full. Keep that in mind when planning your trip—and especially if it's your honeymoon.

There also are busy miniseasons at school holiday time in Australia and New Zealand. These periods vary, but in general they are from the end of March through the middle of April, 2 weeks in late May, 2 weeks at the beginning of July, 2 weeks in the middle of September, and from mid-December until mid-January. You can get a list of Australian holidays at **www.oztourism.com.au** (click on the "Holiday dates" link); for New Zealand go to **www.tourism.org.nz** (the "Utilities and Holidays" link).

Some South Pacific hoteliers raise their rates during the busy periods.

From Christmas through the middle of January is a good time to get a hotel reservation in the South Pacific, but airline seats can be hard to come by, since thousands of islanders fly home from overseas.

HOLIDAYS & SPECIAL EVENTS

The chapters of this book list each country's festivals and special events, which can change the nature of a visit to the South Pacific. The annual *Heiva Nui* in French Polynesia, the King's Birthday in Tonga, and the week of Constitution Day in Rarotonga are just three examples, and every country has at least one such major celebration. These are the best times to see traditional dancing, arts, and sporting events. Be sure to make your reservations well in advance if you want to visit at celebration time, for hotel rooms and airline seats can be in short supply.

6 Travel Insurance

Check your existing insurance policies and credit-card coverage before you buy travel insurance. You may already be covered for lost luggage, cancelled tickets or medical expenses. The cost of travel insurance varies widely, depending on the cost and length of your trip, your age, health, and the type of trip you're taking.

TRIP-CANCELLATION INSURANCE (TCI)

Trip-cancellation insurance helps you get your money back if you have to back out of a trip, if you have to go home early, or if your travel supplier goes bankrupt. Allowed reasons for cancellation can range from sickness to natural disasters (the islands occasionally get whacked by a hurricane). Trip-cancellation insurance is a good buy if you're getting tickets well in advance—who knows what the state of the world, or of your airline, will be in 9 months? Insurance policy details vary, so read the fine print—and especially make sure that your airline or cruise line is on the list of carriers covered in case of bankruptcy.

For more information, contact one of the following recommended insurers: **Access America** (© 866/807-3982; www.access america.com); **Travel Guard International** (© 800/826-4919; www.travel guard.com); **Travel Insured International** (© 800/243-3174; www.travel insured.com); and **Travelex Insurance Services** (© 888/457-4602; www.travelex-insurance.com).

MEDICAL INSURANCE

Hospitals and clinics are widespread in the South Pacific, but the quality varies a great deal from place to place. You can get a broken bone set and a coral scrape tended, but treating more serious ailments likely will be beyond the capability of the local hospital everywhere except in Tahiti. For this reason, I always buy a travel insurance policy that includes medical evacuation in case of life-threatening injury or illness. Otherwise, the cost of a flying ambulance would wipe out my life's savings.

Check with your insurer, particularly if you're insured by an HMO, about the extent of its coverage while you're overseas. With the exception of certain HMOs and Medicare/Medicaid, your medical insurance should cover medical treatment—even hospital care—overseas (don't forget to bring your insurance ID card!). However, most out-of-country hospitals make you pay your bills up front, and they send you a refund after you've returned home and filed the necessary paperwork. If you do get medical treatment in the islands, save all of your receipts!

If you require additional medical insurance, try **MEDEX International** (© 800/527-0218 or 410/453-6300; www.medexassist.com) or **Travel Assistance International** (© 800/821-2828 or 202/331-1596 www.travelassistance. com; for general information on services, call the company's Worldwide Assistance Services, Inc., at © **800/777-8710**).

LOST-LUGGAGE INSURANCE
On U.S. domestic flights, checked baggage is covered up to US$2,500 per ticketed passenger. On international flights (including US portions of international trips), baggage is limited to approximately US$9.07 per pound, up to approximately US$635 per checked bag. If you plan to check items more valuable than the standard liability, see if your valuables are covered by your homeowner's policy, get baggage insurance as part of your comprehensive travel-insurance package, or buy Travel Guard's Bag-Trak product. Don't buy insurance at the airport, as it's usually overpriced. Be sure to take any valuables or irreplaceable items with you in your carry-on luggage, as many valuables (including books, money, and electronics) aren't covered by airline policies.

If your luggage is lost, immediately file a lost-luggage claim at the airport, detailing the luggage contents. For most airlines, you must report delayed, damaged, or lost baggage within 4 hours of arrival. The airlines are required to deliver luggage, once found, directly to your house or destination free of charge.

CAR-RENTAL INSURANCE
If you hold a private auto insurance policy, you probably are covered in the United States, but not necessarily abroad, for loss or damage to the car and liability in case a passenger is injured. The credit card you used to rent the car also may provide some coverage. Check your own auto insurance policy, the rental company policy, and your credit card coverage for the extent of coverage.

Even if you have such coverage, rental car companies in the islands are likely to require that you pay for any damages on the scene and sort it out with your insurer or credit card company when you get home. Given the hassles this can cause, I always buy the collision damage waiver and liability policies offered by the local companies. It adds to the cost, but it's a relatively small price to pay for peace of mind.

7 Health & Safety

STAYING HEALTHY
The South Pacific islands covered in this book pose no major health problems for most travelers, although it's a good idea to have your tetanus, hepatitis-A, and hepatitis-B vaccinations up to date.

There are plenty of mosquitoes (see the "Insects & Other Critters" box below), but they do not carry deadly endemic diseases such as malaria. From time to time the islands will experience an outbreak of **dengue fever,** a viral disease borne by the *Adës aegypti* mosquito, which lives indoors and bites only during daylight hours. Dengue seldom is fatal in adults, but you should take extra precautions to keep children from being bitten by mosquitoes if the disease is present. (Other precautions should be taken if you are traveling with **children;** see "Tips for Travelers with Specialized Travel Resources," below.)

Among minor illnesses, the islands have the common cold and occasional outbreaks of influenza and conjunctivitis (pink eye).

Cuts, scratches, and all open sores should be treated promptly in the tropics. I always carry a tube of antibacterial ointment and a small package of adhesive bandages such as Band-Aids.

Throughout the islands, sexual relations before marriage—heterosexual, homosexual, and bisexual—are more or less accepted (abstinence campaigns fall on deaf ears). Both male and female prostitution is common in the larger towns. HIV is present in the islands, so if you intend to engage in sex with strangers, you should exercise *at least* the same caution in choosing them, and in practicing safe sex, as you would at home.

Tap water is safe to drink in the city of Papeete on Tahiti, on parts of the island of Bora Bora, on Rarotonga in the Cook Islands, and in the main towns in Fiji. You can buy bottled spring water in most grocery stores. See "Fast Facts" in the following chapters for particulars.

If you have a chronic condition, check with your doctor before visiting the islands. For conditions like epilepsy, diabetes, or heart problems, wear a **MedicAlert Identification Tag** (© **800/825-3785;** www. medicalert.org), which will alert doctors to your condition and give them access to your records through MedicAlert's 24-hour hot line.

Pack **prescription medications** in your carry-on luggage, and carry prescription medications in their original containers. Bring along copies of your prescriptions in case you lose your pills or run out. Carry the generic name of medicines, since local pharmacies primarily carry medications manufactured in France, Australia, and New Zealand, and the brand names might be different than in the United States.

And don't forget **sunglasses** and an extra pair of **contact lenses** or **prescription glasses.** You can easily replace your contacts and prescription lenses only in French Polynesia, the Cook Islands, and Fiji.

SMOKING LOWDOWN

Although antismoking campaigns and hefty taxes have reduced the practice to a large extent, cigarette smoking is still more common in the islands, and especially in French Polynesia, than in Western countries. Most office buildings and the airlines are smoke-free, but nonsmoking sections in restaurants are rare. Not all hotels have nonsmoking rooms, so don't assume you'll get a non-smoking room without asking for one.

STAYING SAFE

While international terrorism is a threat throughout the world, the South Pacific islands are among the planet's safest destinations. Tight security procedures are in effect at the major airports, but once you're on the outer islands, you are unlikely to see a metal detector, nor is anyone likely to inspect your carry-on.

The region has seen increasing property theft in recent years, however, including occasional break-ins at hotel rooms and resort bungalows. Although street crimes against tourists are still relatively rare, friends of mine who live here don't stroll off Papeete's busy boulevard Pomare after dark, and they keep a sharp eye peeled everywhere in Fiji. For that matter, you should stay alert wherever you are after dusk.

Don't leave valuable items in your hotel room, in your rental car, or unattended anywhere. See the "Fast Facts" in the following chapters for specific precautions.

Women should not wander alone on deserted beaches any time, since some Polynesian men may consider such behavior to be an invitation for instant amorous activity.

Tips Insects & Other Critters

"You will find that we Cook Islanders are among the friendliest people in the South Pacific," a sign in a Cook Island resort advises its guests. "Amongst all the friendly people we also have the friendliest ants, roaches, geckos, crabs, and insects, who are all dying to make your acquaintance."

Indeed, the South Pacific islands have multitudes of mosquitoes, roaches, ants, houseflies, and other insects. **Ants** are omnipresent here so don't leave crumbs or dirty dishes lying around your room. Many beaches and swampy areas also have invisible **sand flies**—the dreaded "no-see-ums" or "no-nos"—which bite the ankles around daybreak and dusk.

Insect repellent is widely available in island shops. The most effective contain a high percentage of "deet" (N,N-diethyl-m-toluamide).

I light a mosquito coil in my non-air-conditioned rooms at dusk in order to keep the pests from flying in, and I start another one at bedtime. Grocery stores throughout the islands carry these inexpensive coils. I have found the Fish brand coils, made by the appropriately named Blood Protection Company, to work best.

Don't be frightened by those little **geckos** (lizards) crawling around the rafters of even the most expensive bungalows. They're harmless to us humans but lethal to insects.

Also, don't be surprised to see a multitude of dogs, chickens, pigs, and squawking myna birds, even in the finest restaurants.

When heading outdoors, keep in mind that injuries often occur when people fail to follow instructions. Believe the experts who tell you to stay on the established trails. Hike only in designated areas, follow the marine charts if piloting your own boat, carry rain gear, and wear a life jacket when canoeing or rafting. Mountain weather can be fickle at any time. Watch out for sudden storms that can leave you drenched and send bolts of lightning your way.

8 Specialized Travel Resources

TRAVELERS WITH DISABILITIES

Most disabilities shouldn't stop anyone from traveling, even in the South Pacific islands, where ramps, handles, accessible toilets, automatic opening doors, telephones at convenient heights, and other helpful aids in Western countries are just beginning to appear.

Some hotels provide rooms specially equipped for people with disabilities. Such improvements are ongoing; I have pointed out some of them in this book, but inquire when making a reservation whether such rooms are available.

The major international airlines make special arrangements for disabled persons. Be sure to tell them of your needs when you reserve. Although most local airlines use small planes that are not equipped for disabled passengers, their staffs go out of their way to help everyone get in and out of the craft.

GAY & LESBIAN TRAVELERS

Although homosexuality is officially frowned upon by local laws and by some religious leaders, especially in Fiji, an old Polynesian custom makes the South Pacific a relatively friendly destination for gay men.

In the islands, many families with a shortage of female offspring rear young boys as girls, or at least relegate them to female chores around the home and village. These males-raised-as-girls are known as *mahus* in Tahiti, *magus* in Samoa, and *fakaleitis* in Tonga. Some of them grow up to be heterosexual; others become homosexual or bisexual and, often appearing publicly in women's attire, actively seek the company of tourists. Some dance the female parts in traditional island night shows. You'll see them throughout the islands; many hold jobs in hotels and restaurants.

On the other hand, women were not considered equal in this respect in ancient times, and lesbianism was discouraged.

The International Gay & Lesbian Travel Association (IGLTA) (© **800/448-8550** or 954/776-2626; fax 954/776-3303; www.iglta.org) is the trade association for the gay and lesbian travel industry, and offers an online directory of gay and lesbian-friendly travel businesses; go to their website and click on "Members."

SENIOR TRAVEL

Children are cared for communally in the South Pacific's extended family systems, and so are senior citizens. Most islanders live with their families from birth to death. Consequently, the local governments don't provide programs and other benefits for persons of retirement age. You won't find many senior citizen discounts. Children get them; seniors don't.

Nevertheless, mention the fact that you're a senior citizen when you first make your travel reservations. All major airlines and many chain hotels offer discounts for seniors.

Elderhostel, 75 Federal St., Boston, MA 02110-1941 (© **877/426-8056;** www.elderhostel.org), arranges study programs for those 55 and over (and a spouse or companion of any age) in the United States and in more than 80 countries. Most include airfare, accommodations in university dorms or modest inns, meals, and tuition. One recent trip included a 2-week cruise to the Marquesas Islands in French Polynesia.

Members of **AARP,** 601 E St. NW, Washington, DC 20049 (© **888/687-2277** or 202/434-2277; www.aarp.org), get discounts on hotels, airfares, and car rentals. AARP offers members a wide range of benefits, including *AARP: The Magazine* and a monthly newsletter. Anyone over 50 can join.

FAMILY TRAVEL

The islanders adore infants and young children, but childhood does not last as long in the South Pacific as it does in Western societies. As soon as they are capable, children are put to work, first caring for their younger siblings and cousins and helping out with household chores, later tending the village gardens. It's only as teenagers, and then only if they leave their villages for town, that they know unemployment in the Western sense. Accordingly, few towns and villages have children's facilities, such as playgrounds, outside school property.

On the other hand, the islanders invariably love children and are very good at babysitting. Just make sure you get one who speaks English. The hotels can take care of this for you.

The larger hotels in Fiji and the Cook Islands cater to Australian and New Zealander families with ample activities to keep everyone occupied. Even some smaller resorts, such as **Jean-Michel Cousteau Fiji Islands Resort** in northern Fiji, welcome families (see chapter 6). Although most are oriented for couples, many French Polynesian resorts now also welcome children. Best is the

Inter-Continental Moorea Resort and Spa (see chapter 9).

Some resorts do not accept children at all; I point those out in the establishment listings, but you should ask to make sure. Even if they do, check whether the hotel can provide cribs and other needs, and if they have children's menus.

Disposable diapers, cotton swabs (known as Buds, not Q-Tips), and baby food are sold in many main-town stores, but you should take along a supply of such items as children's aspirin, a thermometer, adhesive bandages, and special medications. Make sure your children's vaccinations are up to date before you leave home. If your children are very small, perhaps you should discuss your travel plans with your family doctor.

Remember to protect youngsters with ample sunscreen.

Other tips: Some tropical plants and animals may resemble rocks or vegetation, so teach your youngsters to avoid touching or brushing up against rocks, seaweed, and other objects. If your children are prone to swimmer's ear, use vinegar or preventive drops before they go swimming in freshwater streams or lakes. Have them shower soon after swimming or suffering cuts or abrasions.

Rascals in Paradise, One Daniel Burnham Court, Suite 105-C, San Francisco, CA 94107 (© **415/921-7000;** fax 415/921-7050; www.rascalsinparadise. com), specializes in organizing South Pacific tours for families with kids, including visits with local families and children.

WOMEN TRAVELERS

The South Pacific islands are relatively safe for women traveling alone, but don't let the charm of warm nights and smiling faces lull you into any less caution than you would exercise at home. *Do not* wander alone on deserted beaches. In the old days this was an invitation for sex. If that's what you want today, then that's what you're likely to get. Otherwise, it could result in your being raped.

And don't hitchhike alone, either.

STUDENT TRAVEL

The South Pacific islands have one of the most developed backpacker industries in the world, but you won't find any student discounts.

Frommers.com: The Complete Travel Resource

For an excellent travel-planning resource, we highly recommend **Frommers. com** (www.frommers.com), voted Best Travel Site by *PC Magazine*. We're a little biased, of course, but we guarantee that you'll find the travel tips, reviews, monthly vacation giveaways, bookstore, and online-booking capabilities thoroughly indispensable. Among the special features are our popular **Destinations** section, where you'll get expert travel tips, hotel and dining recommendations, and advice on the sights to see for more than 3,500 destinations around the globe; the **Frommers.com Newsletter,** with the latest deals, travel trends, and money-saving secrets; our **Community** area featuring **Message Boards,** where Frommer's readers post queries and share advice (sometimes even our authors show up to answer questions); and our **Photo Center,** where you can post and share vacation tips. When your research is done, the **Online Reservations System** (www.frommers. com/book_a_trip) takes you to Frommer's preferred online partners for booking your vacation at affordable prices.

If you're going on to New Zealand and Australia, you'd be wise to get an **international student I.D. card,** which offers savings on plane tickets. It also provides basic health and life insurance and a 24-hour help line. The card is available from **STA Travel** (© **800/781-4040;** www.statravel.com), the world's biggest student travel agency. If you're not in North America, there's probably a local number in your country.

If you're no longer a student but are still under 26, you can get an **International Youth Travel Card (IYTC)** for the same price from the same people. The card offers some discounts (but not on museum admissions).

Travel CUTS (© **800/667-2887** or 416/614-2887; www.travelcuts.com) offers similar services for both Canadians and U.S. residents. Irish students may prefer to turn to **USIT** (© **01/602-1904;** www.usitnow.ie), an Ireland-based specialist in student, youth, and independent travel.

SINGLE TRAVELERS

Having traveled alone through the South Pacific for more years than I care to admit, I can tell you it's a great place to be unattached. After all, this is the land of smiles and genuine warmth toward strangers. The attitude soon infects visitors: All I've ever had to do to meet my fellow travelers is wander into a hotel bar, order a beer, and ask the persons next to me where they are from and what they have done in Fiji, Tahiti, and so on.

The two hottest destinations for singles—especially backpackers—are Fiji and the Cook Islands. Fiji has dozens of resorts aimed at this low-budget market, including the rocking **Beachcomber Island Resort** (see chapter 5).

Even couples-oriented French Polynesia has a playground especially suited to singles: The **Club Med** on Bora Bora (see chapter 10).

Unfortunately, the solo traveler is often forced to pay a "single supplement" charged by many resorts, cruise lines, and tours for the privilege of sleeping alone.

TravelChums (© **212/799-6464;** www.travelchums.com) is an Internet-only travel-companion matching service hosted by respected New York–based Shaw Guides travel service.

Based in Canada, **Travel Buddies Singles Travel Club** (© **800/998-9099;** www.travelbuddiesworldwide.com) runs small, intimate, single-friendly group trips and will match you with a roommate free of charge and save you the cost of single supplements.

TRAVELING WITH PETS

Don't even think about bringing your pet. Every country will quarantine Fido until you are ready to fly home.

9 Planning Your Trip Online

SURFING FOR AIRFARES

The "big three" online travel agencies, **Expedia.com, Travelocity.com,** and **Orbitz.com,** sell most of the air tickets bought on the Internet. (Canadian travelers should try expedia.ca and Travelocity. ca; U.K. residents can go for expedia.co.uk and opodo.co.uk.) Each has different deals with the airlines and may offer different fares on the same flights, so it's wise to shop around. Expedia and Travelocity will also send you **e-mail notification** when a cheap fare becomes available to your favorite destination.

Of the smaller travel agency websites, **SideStep** (www.sidestep.com) has gotten the best reviews from Frommer's authors. It's a browser add-on that purports to "search 140 sites at once," but in reality only beats competitors' fares as often as other sites do.

By all means check **airline websites,** especially those which fly to the islands, and the sites of the package tour companies specializing in the South Pacific, some of whom sell air tickets separately from hotel rooms (see "Getting There & Getting Around," below). You can often shave a few bucks from a fare by booking directly through the airline and avoiding a travel agency's transaction fee. But you'll get these discounts only by **booking online:** Most airlines now offer online-only fares that even their phone agents know nothing about.

I don't like such uncertainty, but if you're willing to give up some control over your flight details, use an opaque fare service like **Priceline** (www.priceline.com; www.priceline.co.uk for Europeans) or **Hotwire** (www.hotwire.com). Both offer rock-bottom prices in exchange for travel on a "mystery airline" at a mysterious time of day, often with a mysterious change of planes en route. It's sort of like buying a car, a horse-trading process I personally detest. If you're new at this, the helpful folks at **BiddingForTravel** (www.bidding fortravel.com) do a good job of demystifying Priceline's prices. Priceline and Hotwire are great for flights within North America and between the U.S. and Europe.

For much more about airfares and savvy air-travel tips and advice, pick up a copy of *Frommer's Fly Safe, Fly Smart* (Wiley Publishing, Inc.).

SURFING FOR HOTELS

Shopping online for hotels is generally done one of two ways: by booking through the hotel's own website or through an independent booking agency. These Internet hotel agencies have multiplied in mind-boggling numbers of late, competing for the business of millions of consumers surfing for accommodations around the world. This competitiveness

can be a boon to consumers who have the patience and time to shop and compare the online sites for good deals—but shop they must, for prices can vary considerably from site to site. And keep in mind that hotels at the top of a site's listing may be there for no other reason than that they paid money to get the placement.

The best independent site for South Pacific hotel discount shopping is Fiji-based **www.Travelmaxia.com**, where scores of properties throughout the region post their specials. You can search by country for resorts, hotels, bed-and-breakfasts, dive operators, and cruises.

Another tactic is to check with the South Pacific **inbound tour operators.** In addition to selling tours and day trips to visitors already in the islands (that is, at hotel activities desks), these companies put together the local elements of tour packages—such as hotel rooms and airport transfers—for overseas wholesalers. They have the advantage of being on the scene and thus familiar with the properties. Some sell directly to inbound visitors as well as other tour companies. In Fiji, two small companies specialize in discount travel arrangements, including hotel rooms: **Impulse Fiji** (www.impulsefiji. com) and **Sun Vacations** (www.sun vacationsfiji.com). In French Polynesia, **Tahiti Nui Travel** (www.tahitinuitravel. com) has a variety of local packages in French Polynesia. Based on Rarotonga, **Island Hopper Vacations** (www.island hoppervacations.com) books hotels and puts together local packages in both the Cook Islands and the Samoas.

Of the "big three" sites, **Expedia** offers a long list of deals and "virtual tours" or photos of available rooms so you can see what you're paying for (a feature that helps counter the claims that the best rooms are often held back from bargain booking websites).

Travelocity posts unvarnished customer reviews and ranks its properties according to the AAA rating system. Also reliable are **Hotels.com** and **Quikbook.com.** An excellent free program, **TravelAxe** (www.travelaxe.net), can help you search multiple hotel sites at once, even ones you may never have heard of—and conveniently lists the total price of the room, including the taxes and service charges.

Another booking site, **Travelweb** (www.travelweb.com), is partly owned by the hotels it represents (including the Starwood chain, which has properties in Fiji and French Polynesia). Therefore, it plugs directly into the hotels' reservations systems—unlike independent online agencies, which have to fax or e-mail reservation requests to the hotel, a portion of which get misplaced in the shuffle. More than once, travelers have arrived at the hotel, only to be told that they have no reservation.

It's a good idea to **get a confirmation number** and **make a printout** of any online booking transaction.

SURFING FOR RENTAL CARS

All of the South Pacific's major car rental firms are franchises; they're owned by local interests and not by the big companies such as Avis and Budget. They also are relatively small operations. Consequently, you're unlikely to find them featured in big discounts and special deals on the major firms' websites. The best deals will appear on their own sites, which I give in the following chapters.

All the major online travel agencies offer rental-car reservations services, so it never hurts to look there. Priceline and Hotwire work well for rental cars, too. The only mystery is which major rental company you get, and for most travelers the difference between Hertz, Avis, and Budget is negligible.

---

10 The 21st-Century Traveler

INTERNET ACCESS IN THE SOUTH PACIFIC

E-mail is as much a part of life in the South Pacific islands as it is anywhere else these days, but most Internet connections here are glacially slow compared to even dial-up connections in Western countries. High-speed access is a mere infant out here.

Access is also relatively expensive. Every local Internet service provider (ISP) charges by the minute rather than by the month, and many hotels slap a whopping fee on top of that. (My Internet and phone bills for checking my e-mail and bank sites from Tahiti hotel rooms have topped US$50!) Consequently, don't expect people in the South Pacific to reply to your e-mail immediately. Patience definitely is a virtue when dealing with folks out here.

The easiest way to get your e-mail on the Web is at your hotel, resort, or hostel. Most have computers for guest use. Or you can go to one of the numerous cybercafes in the islands.

To retrieve your e-mail, ask your ISP if it has a Web-based interface tied to your existing e-mail account. If not, you can use the free **mail2web** service (www.mail2web.com) to view and reply to your home e-mail. For more flexibility, you may want to open a free, Web-based e-mail account with **Yahoo! Mail** (mail.yahoo.com). Microsoft's Hotmail is another popular option. Your home ISP may be able to forward your e-mail to the Web-based account automatically.

Since no major international ISP has a local access number in the islands, you can't just plug in your laptop, program in the local access number, and go online as

Configuring Your Laptop

If you brought a laptop, you can sign up for a temporary dial-up Internet account from the local service providers and go online from your hotel room (see the "Fast Facts" in chapters 4, 7, 12, 13, and 15 for details). In addition to the service providers' fees and the cost of local calls to gain access, most hotels add an additional charge, so it's anything but free. If you elect to go this route, here's how to set up your computer in Windows XP, 2000, and 98:

- Double-click on **Control Panel** in Windows XP (My Computer in Windows 98).
- Double-click **Network Connections** in XP (Dial-Up Networking in 98).
- Double-click **Create a New Connection** in XP (Make New Connection in 98).
- Name the new connection anything you want.
- Click **Configure** and set the maximum speed of your modem to not more 57,600kbps. Click **OK**.
- Leave the Area Code box blank and in Telephone Number box type (with no spaces) **the number you must dial to reach an outside line (0 or 9), a comma, and the local access number.** Don't change the Country box. Click **OK**.
- After you have created your new connection, double-click **Network Connections** in XP (My Computer, Dial-Up Networking in 98), and the icon for your new connection. Click **Connect**. When the connection is made, enter *both* your name and your password.
- From then on, you can double-click **My Computer, Dial-Up Networking,** your local connection icon, and **Connect**. After the connection is made, load your browser, and you're online.

you would at home. On the other hand, you can use your own computer from any hotel room with a phone, provided you sign up for a **temporary local Internet access account.** For details see "Fast Facts" in the destination chapters and the "Configuring Your Laptop" box this chapter.

If you bring your laptop, be sure to include a **connection kit** of the right power, plus phone adapters (French in French Polynesia, American in American Samoa, Australian elsewhere) and a spare phone cord.

There are a growing number of Wi-Fi (wireless fidelity) "hotspots" in the islands. Many are in coffee shops or hotel bars, so you can sip a cuppa or a cold one while answering your e-mail. The hotspots are not free, and some require that you purchase a prepaid usage card.

The easiest way to take advantage of Wi-Fi is to buy a laptop with built- in wireless (most new models have it). If your old machine doesn't have it, you will need to buy a 802.11b or 802.11g wireless card to plug into your computer's PCMICA slot.

USING A CELLPHONE

Known as "mobiles" over here, cellphones are prevalent throughout the islands. No North American wireless company operates in the South Pacific, and many

American phones won't work since all the islands use the Global System for Mobiles (GSM) technology. Although the technology is gaining in popularity worldwide, only T-Mobile and Cingular/AT&T Wireless use this quasi-universal system in the U.S. In Canada, Microcell and some Rogers customers are GSM. All Europeans and most Australians use GSM. Call your wireless company to see if your phone is GSM.

If you do have a GSM phone, you may be able to use it in the islands if your home provider has a roaming agreement with the local phone companies. If it doesn't, you may still use your phone (1) if it transmits and receives on the 900 mHz band; (2) it has been "unlocked" from its SIM card, the removable computer chip which stores your and your provider's information; and (3) you rent or buy a local SIM card.

The Travel Insider (www.thetravel insider.info) has an excellent explanation of all this as well as a phone unlocking service. Click on "Road Warrior Resources" and "International Cellphone Service."

In a worst-case scenario, you can always rent a phone. One of the first things you'll see after clearing Customs at Nadi airport in Fiji is a mobile phone rental booth. Most hotels will make the arrangements for you elsewhere.

Should you want to rent a phone or SIM card before leaving the U.S., good wireless rental companies offering phones for use in Fiji and French Polynesia are **InTouch USA** (✆ **800/872-7626;** www.intouch global.com) and **RoadPost** (✆ **888/290-1606** or 905/272-5665; www.roadpost. com). Be sure to compare their rental and air time prices to those offered in the islands (see the "Fast Facts" in chapters 4 and 7).

11 Getting There & Getting Around

BY PLANE
A few cruise ships stop in the islands, but today all but a handful of visitors fly to the islands. Because populations are small, flights are not nearly as frequent to and among the islands as Westerners are used to at home. There may be only one flight weekly between some countries, and flights that are scheduled today may be eliminated tomorrow. The airlines have relatively few planes, so mechanical problems can cause delays.

Many of the outer-island airstrips are unlit, so there are few connecting flights after dark. It's wise to consult a travel agent or contact the airlines to find out what's happening at present. See the "Getting Around" sections in the following chapters for details.

Also, you are likely be limited to 10 kilograms (22 lb.) of baggage on small interisland planes, as opposed to 20 kilograms (44 lb.) or more on international flights (see "Baggage Allowances," below).

The distances out here are enormous, so be prepared for long flights: 10½ hours or more from Los Angeles to Fiji, 7½ hours or more to Tahiti.

THE AIRPORTS
Most flights to the islands from North America depart from Los Angeles International Airport (LAX, in airline parlance). A few flights go from other West Coast cities and from Vancouver, B.C. Australians and New Zealanders can get there from Auckland, Wellington, Christchurch, Sydney, Melbourne, or Brisbane, depending on the carrier.

If you don't live in a city where flights to the South Pacific originate, then you will have to pay to get there in order to make a connection. Some carriers offer "feeder" or "add-on" fares to cover the connecting flights. Be sure to ask about them.

Each island country has just one main international airport: **Nadi (NAN)** and in a few cases **Suva (SUV)** in Fiji; **Papeete**

(PPT) on Tahiti in French Polynesia; **Rarotonga (RAR)** in the Cook Islands; **Apia (APW)** in Samoa; **Pago Pago (PPG)** in American Samoa; and **Tongatapu (TBU),** the main island in Tonga. Only Nadi (pronounced *Nahn*-dee) has enough international traffic to be considered a regional hub.

THE AIRLINES

Here in alphabetical order are the airlines with service to the islands:

- **Air New Zealand** (© **800/262-1234** or 310/615-1111; www.airnew zealand.com) has the most extensive network to and from the islands, including several flights a week linking Los Angeles and San Francisco to Fiji, Tahiti, the Cook Islands, Samoa, and Tonga. Within the islands, its weekly "Coral Route" service links Fiji to Rarotonga in the Cook Islands, from where you can connect to and from Tahiti, Los Angeles, and Auckland. Air New Zealand flies to several Australian cities, so Aussies can reach most of the South Pacific islands through Auckland. It links Japan, Hong Kong, Singapore, Seoul, Taipei, and Beijing to Auckland, with connections on to the islands. Air New Zealand is a member of the Star Alliance, which includes United Airlines and several other carriers. This means you can get to the islands from many cities in the United States, Canada, and Europe on an Air New Zealand even if your ticket is issued by one of these other airlines.

- **Air France** (© **800/321-4538**; www. airfrance.com) flies to Tahiti from Paris, Los Angeles, and Tokyo.

- **Air Pacific** (© **800/227-4446**; www.airpacific.com), Fiji's fine international airline, has several weekly nonstop flights between Los Angeles and Fiji, and one from Vancouver, B.C. via Honolulu. From the south, it links Fiji to Sydney, Brisbane, and Melbourne in Australia, and Auckland, Wellington, and Christchurch in New Zealand (some of those flights go directly to Suva). It provides nonstop service between Fiji and Tokyo in Japan. Within the region, it offers two flights per week linking Nadi to Samoa and Tonga, and it goes west to Vanuatu and Solomon Islands. It code-shares with both American Airlines (which provides feeder service from many U.S. and Canadian cities to Los Angeles) and Qantas Airways. In fact, all

---

Tips **Reserve Early & Always Reconfirm**

Planes do not always fly between all the island countries every day in this sparsely populated, far-flung region. When planning your trip, therefore, first find out the airlines' schedules, which will determine the dates you can travel.

By all means book your domestic inter-island flights well in advance. You may not get on a plane at all if you wait until you arrive in the islands to take care of this important chore.

Once here, *always* reconfirm your return flight as soon as you arrive on an outer island, primarily so that the local airline will know where to reach you in case of a schedule change. Avoid booking a return flight from an outer island on the same day your international flight is due to leave for home; give yourself plenty of leeway in case the weather or mechanical or scheduling problems prevent the plane from getting to and from the outer island on time.

American Airlines and Qantas passengers bound for Fiji actually travel on Air Pacific.

- **Air Tahiti Nui** (© **877/824-4846;** www.airtahitinui.com), French Polynesia's national airline, has more flights—all on relatively new Airbus planes—between Tahiti and Los Angeles than any other airline. Some of those depart early afternoon California time and arrive in Papeete before dark, thus enabling you to connect to Moorea that evening. Most of its return flights are overnight, but you arrive in Los Angeles early enough in the morning to make convenient connections. It also has non-stop flights between New York's John F. Kennedy International Airport and Papeete. As we went to press it was planning to expand that service from New York on to Paris. On the other end, the New York–Tahiti plane keeps going to Sydney in Australia. New York–Papeete is a 12-hour flight, but you don't have to change airlines in Los Angeles. Air Tahiti Nui also links Paris, Tokyo, and Auckland to Papeete, and it has a code-share arrangement with Virgin Atlantic permitting direct ticketing from London to Sydney (via Hong Kong) on Virgin Atlantic, thence to Papeete via Air Tahiti Nui.
- **Freedom Air** (www.freedom.co.nz), the low-fare subsidiary of Air New Zealand, has service between several New Zealand cities and Fiji.
- **Hawaiian Airlines** (© **800/367-5320** in the continental U.S., Alaska, and Canada, or 808/838-1555 in Honolulu; www.hawaiianair.com) flies from Los Angeles, San Francisco, Portland, and Seattle to Tahiti and to American Samoa. You must change planes in Honolulu, which can result in delays and even an unexpected Hawaiian layover.
- **Pacific Blue** (www.flypacificblue. com), the international subsidiary of the Australian cut-rate domestic airline Virgin Blue (itself an offshoot of Sir Richard Branson's Virgin Atlantic), has low-fare service from Sydney via Auckland to and from Fiji, the Cook Islands, and Tonga. It also flies to Samoa disguised as Polynesian Blue (see below).
- **Polynesian Airlines** (© **800/264-0823;** www.polynesianairlines.com), the national carrier of Samoa, connects its home base at Apia to American Samoa and Tonga.
- **Polynesian Blue** (www.polynesian blue.com), a joint venture between Polynesian Airlines and Pacific Blue, has low-fare service to Samoa from Sydney and Auckland.
- **Qantas Airways** (© **800/227-4500;** www.qantas.com), the Australian carrier, has flights between Los Angeles and Fiji and Los Angeles and Tahiti. Its Fiji-bound passengers fly on Air Pacific planes.
- In addition, **LanChile Airlines** (© **800/735-5526;** www.lanchile. com) flies at least weekly between Santiago, Chile, and Tahiti by way of Easter Island. **Japan Airlines** (www. jal.co.jp) flies between Tokyo and Tahiti. **Korean Air** (www.korean air.com) has service between Seoul and Fiji.

BAGGAGE ALLOWANCES

How many bags you can carry on board and check (and how much they can weigh) varies somewhat by airline, so always check with your chosen carrier before packing.

Only one rule is set in stone: Passengers on flights to or from the continental United States may check two bags each weighing up to 30kg (66 lb.), with total dimensions (height, width, and length) of both not exceeding 158cm (62 in.). The allowance on flights to and from Hawaii and the South Pacific may be limited to 30kgs (66 lb.) per economy class passengers, 32kgs (70 lb.) for first and business class.

Although domestic U.S. allowances may be less, you can check this much baggage if you're connecting to an international flight.

In general, first-class passengers on other international flights are entitled to 40kg (88 lb.) of checked luggage, business-class passengers to 30 kilograms (66 lb.), and economy-class passengers to 20 kilograms (44 lb.). Some airlines, including Air New Zealand and Air Pacific, strictly enforce these limits and make you pay extra for each kilogram over the maximum.

In addition to a small handbag or purse, all international passengers are permitted one carry-on bag with total measurements not exceeding 115 centimeters (45 in.). Carry-on hoarders can stuff all sorts of things into a laptop bag; as long as it has a laptop in it, it's still considered a personal item (remember, however, you must remove your laptop and pass it through security separately).

Note: Many domestic air carriers in the islands limit their baggage allowance to 10kg (22 lb.). Check with the individual airlines to avoid showing up at the check-in counter with too much luggage. Most hotels in the main towns have storage facilities where you can leave your extra bags during side trips.

FLYING FOR LESS: TIPS FOR GETTING THE BEST AIRFARE

The Pacific Ocean hasn't shrunk since it took 10 days and more than 83 hours in the air for Australian aviator Charles Kingsford Smith to become the first person to fly across it in 1928. Even though you can now board a jetliner in Los Angeles in the evening and be strolling under the palm trees of Tahiti or Fiji by the crack of dawn, the distances still run into

the thousands of miles. Consequently, transportation costs may be the largest single expense of your trip to the South Pacific.

Be sure to shop all the airlines mentioned above to see who has the best deals. Keep calling and checking the websites if no attractive fare is available at first because wholesalers and groups often reserve blocks of low-cost seats in advance but release some of them near the date of departure. Occasionally a carrier will hold a last-minute sale to get rid of unused seats, so always ask for the *lowest* fare.

Australians and New Zealanders can save with Air New Zealand's **South Pacific Airpass,** which provides between 2 and 10 flight coupons. Travel must begin in a South Pacific country, including Australia and New Zealand, and must conclude within 30 days.

SEASONAL & PROMOTIONAL FARES Depending on the carrier, the South Pacific has four airfare seasons: High, or peak season, is from December through February. One shoulder season includes March and April; a second runs from September through November. Least expensive, the basic season runs from May through August (when the weather is at its finest in the islands). Fares can vary by as much as 25%, depending on the season.

The major airlines serving the South Pacific usually have special fares, especially during the slower seasons. Check the airline websites or ask their reservations agents what special deals are offered when you want to fly.

Also check the travel section of your Sunday newspaper for discounts. Look especially for ads run by discounters and consolidators (see below).

Note: The lowest-priced fares are often nonrefundable, require advance purchase of 1 to 3 weeks and a certain length of stay, and carry penalties for changing dates of travel.

GETTING THROUGH THE AIRPORT

Security procedures at U.S. airports are more stable and consistent than ever. Generally, you'll be fine if you arrive at the airport **2 hours** before a domestic flight and **3 hours** before an international flight; if you show up late, tell an airline employee and he or she will probably whisk you to the front of the line.

These same times apply for your return flight, but check with the airlines in the islands to make sure.

Whatever the airport, you must have a **current, government-issued photo ID** such as a passport, and if you've got an e-ticket, print out the **official confirmation page.** You'll need to show your confirmation and your ID at the security checkpoint and at the ticket counter.

The federal government has phased out **gate check-in** at all U.S. airports. And **e-tickets** have made paper tickets nearly obsolete. Passengers with e-tickets can beat the ticket-counter lines by using airport **electronic kiosks** or even **online check-in** from your home computer. Online check-in involves logging on to your airlines' website, accessing your reservation, and printing out your boarding pass—and the airline may even offer you bonus miles to do so! If you're using a kiosk at the airport, bring the credit card you used to book the ticket or your frequent-flier card. Print out your boarding pass from the kiosk and simply proceed to the security checkpoint with your pass and photo ID. If you're checking bags or looking to snag an exit-row seat, you will be able to do so using most airline kiosks. Even the smaller airlines are employing the kiosk system, but always call your airline to make sure these alternatives are available.

Curbside check-in is also a good way to avoid lines, although a few airlines still ban curbside check-in; call before you go.

If you have trouble standing for long periods of time, tell an airline employee; the airline will provide a wheelchair. Speed up security by **not wearing metal objects** such as big belt buckles or clanky earrings. If you've got metallic body parts, a note from your doctor can prevent a long chat with the security screeners. Keep in mind that only **ticketed passengers** are allowed past security, except for folks escorting disabled passengers or children.

Tips Coping with Jet Lag

Except for Air Tahiti Nui's afternoon departures from Los Angeles bound for the islands (see "The Airlines"), flights from North America leave after dark, which means you will fly overnight and cross at least two time zones. This invariably translates into jet lag. Here are some tips for combating this malady:

- Reset your watch to your destination time before you board the plane.
- Drink lots of water before, during, and after your flight. Avoid alcohol.
- Exercise and sleep well for a few days before your trip.
- Daylight is the key to resetting your body clock. At the website for Outside In (www.bodyclock.com), you can get a customized plan of when to seek and avoid light.
- If you need help getting to sleep and staying asleep, some doctors recommend taking either the hormone melatonin or the sleeping pill Ambien—but not together. Take 2 to 5 milligrams of melatonin about 2 hours before your planned bedtime.

Federalization has stabilized **what you can carry on** and **what you can't.** The general rule is that sharp things are out, nail clippers are okay; cigarette lighters are out but matches are okay. Food and beverages must be passed through the X-ray machine—but security screeners can't make you drink from your coffee cup. Bring food in your carry-on rather than checking it. Explosive-detection machines used on checked luggage occasionally mistake food (especially chocolate, for some reason) for bombs.

The **Transportation Security Administration** (TSA) has issued a list of restricted items; check details on its website (www.tsa.gov/public).

Expect tight security at the main South Pacific airports but not at small strips on the outer islands.

DISCOUNTERS & CONSOLIDATORS

Discounters are travel agents who buy airline seats and hotel rooms at wholesale prices and pass on some of their savings to you. Until recently they were the only way to get the big discounts, but today some wholesalers who specialize in the South Pacific engage in the same practice and are more likely to offer the best deals (see "Packages for the Independent Traveler," below).

There are still numerous discounters, many of them in the United States and abroad. Start by looking in Sunday newspaper travel sections; U.S. travelers should focus on the *New York Times, Los Angeles Times, Miami Herald,* and *The Washington Post.* For less-developed destinations, small travel agents who cater to immigrant communities in large cities often have the best deals.

Many discounters—as well as some full-service travel agents—sell tickets provided by **consolidators,** which are sometimes called bucket shops. Consolidators buy and resell seats on the major international carriers that otherwise would go

unfilled, especially during the slow seasons. Consolidator deals can be riskier than direct buys from a carrier, but they can result in substantial savings on tickets that have fewer restrictions than you would get with an advance-purchase ticket bought directly from an airline.

Beware, however, that bucket shop tickets are usually nonrefundable or rigged with stiff cancellation penalties, often as high as 50% to 75% of the ticket price, and some put you on charter airlines with questionable safety records.

Generally it's best to ask a travel agent to comparison shop for you. Always compare the deals he or she comes up with to those offered directly by the airlines and wholesalers, inquire about any and all restrictions there may be, and pay by credit card.

Several reliable consolidators are worldwide and available on the Internet. **STA Travel** (© **800/781-4040;** www.statravel.com) is now the world's leader in student travel, thanks to their purchase of Council Travel (see "Student Travel," earlier in this chapter). It also offers good fares for travelers of all ages. **Flights.com** (© **800/TRAV-800;** www.flights.com) started in Europe and has excellent fares worldwide, but particularly to that continent. It also has local websites in 12 countries. **Air Tickets Direct** (© **800/778-3447;** www.airticketsdirect.com) is based in Montreal and leverages the currently weak Canadian dollar for low fares.

BY CRUISE SHIP

Although the days of great liners plying the Pacific are long gone, occasionally it may be possible to reach the islands on a cruise ship making an around-the-world voyage or being repositioned, say, from Alaska to Australia. In addition to Princess Cruises (see below), other companies likely to have ships in the South Pacific include **Cunard Line** (© **800/528-6273;** www.cunardline.com), whose vessels include the *Queen Elizabeth II,* and **Orient Lines** (© 800/333-7300; www.orientlines.com).

Most sell tickets through travel agents, although some offer them directly to the public on their websites.

The only company whose ships regularly visit more than one country covered in this book is **Princess Cruises** (© 800/774-6237; www.princesscruises.com). Some of its *Tahitian Princess* itineraries are extended from French Polynesia to the Cook Islands and Samoa (see chapter 7).

Lindblad Expeditions (© 800/EXPEDITION; www.expeditions.com) occasionally has exploratory voyages from Easter Island to Tahiti, from there to Fiji, and from Fiji to Papua New Guinea.

You can also click on **www.cruise critic.com**, where you can check out cruises throughout the world; **www.cruise411.com**, which has itineraries, deck plans, and other information; and **www.cruisepage.com**, with reviews of more than 300 ships.

Your best bet for steaming through the islands, however, is to fly to Fiji or Tahiti and take one of the ships based there (see chapters 5 and 7).

12 Packages for the Independent Traveler

In addition to searching for the lowest airfare, you may want to consider booking your flight as part of a travel package. Buying a package tour is simply a way to get the airfare, accommodations, and other elements of your trip (such as car rentals, airport transfers, and sometimes even meals and activities) at the same time and often at discounted prices—kind of like one-stop shopping. In fact, package tours usually provide the best bargains available, especially to expensive French Polynesia.

Package tours are not the same thing as escorted tours, which are structured tours with a group leader. Scant few escorted tours go to the South Pacific islands except as add-ons to tours primarily of Australia and New Zealand.

The costs are kept down because wholesale tour operators (known as wholesalers in the travel industry) can make volume bookings on the airlines and at the hotels. Packages traditionally were then sold through retail travel agents, but many wholesalers now deal directly with the public, thus passing savings along to you, rather than part of their commissions to retail agents.

Travel packages are listed in the travel section of many Sunday newspapers. Or check ads in magazines such as *Arthur Frommer's Budget Travel Magazine, Travel & Leisure, National Geographic Traveler,* and *Condé Nast Traveler.*

Airlines offer air-and-hotel packages, so be sure to check the Web sites of **Air New Zealand, Air Pacific, Air Tahiti Nui,** and the other South Pacific carriers (see "The Airlines," earlier).

Following in alphabetical order are some reputable American-based companies that sell package tours. Some will discount air tickets and hotel rooms separately; that is, not as part of a package. Be sure to shop for the best deal among them.

- **Blue Pacific Vacations** (© 800/798-0590; www.bluepacificvacations.com), a division of France Vacations, is headed by John Biggerstaff and Ken Jordan, two veterans of Tahiti tourism. They will customize tours to most French Polynesian islands.
- **Brendan Worldwide Vacations** (© 800/421-8446 or 818/785-9696; www.brendanvacations.com) provides packages to Fiji and French Polynesia.
- **Go-Today** (© 800/227-3235; www.go-today.com), based in Washington State, offers discount-priced packages to Fiji and French Polynesia.

- **Islands in the Sun** (© 800/828-6877 or 310/536-0051; www.islands inthesun.com), the largest and oldest South Pacific specialist, offers packages to all the islands.
- **Jetabout Island Vacations** (© 800/348-8145; www.jetabouttahiti vacations.com) of El Segundo, CA, offers a wide variety of packages to Fiji and Tahiti.
- **Journey Pacific** (© 800/704-7094; www.journeypacific.com) is a Las Vegas–based agency offering packages to Fiji and Tahiti.
- **Newmans South Pacific Vacations** (© 800/421-3326; www.newmans vacations.com) offers packages to the islands, including Samoa and Tonga. It's a branch of a long-established New Zealand company.
- **Pacific Destination Center** (© 800/227-5317; www.pacific-destinations. com) is owned and operated by Australian-born Janette Ryan, who offers some good deals to the islands.
- **Pleasant Holidays** (© 800/742-9244; www.pleasantholidays.com), a huge company best known for its Pleasant Hawaiian and Pleasant Mexico operations, offers packages to Fiji and French Polynesia.
- **Solace** (© 800/548-5331; www. solace1.com) specializes in trips to French Polynesia, the Cook Islands, and Fiji. It offers fares and rates below those published by the airlines and hotels.
- **South Pacific Holidays** (© 800/940-1712; www.spac.com), based in Vancouver, Washington, offers packages to high-end resorts and less expensive diving destinations in Fiji.
- **Sunspots International** (© 800/334-5623 or 503/666-3893; www. sunspotsintl.com), based in Portland, Oregon, has trips to all the islands. It has particular expertise in the Cook Islands, Samoa, and Tonga.
- **Tahiti Discount Travel** (© 877/426-7262; www.tahiti-discount travel.com) is owned by former employees of the defunct Discover Wholesale Travel, once the leader in budget packages. Today they arrange some of the lowest-priced packages to French Polynesia.
- **Tahiti Legends** (© 800/200-1213; www.tahiti-legends.com) is run by former officials of Islands in the Sun. It sells tours to French Polynesia, the Cook Islands, and Fiji under the names **Pacific Legends** (www.pacific legends.com).
- **Tahiti Vacations** (© 800/553-3477; www.tahitivacation.com), a subsidiary of Air Tahiti, French Polynesia's domestic airline, specializes in French Polynesia but also has packages to Fiji, the Cook Islands, and Tonga. It frequently offers the least expensive packages available to Tahiti and Moorea.

A FEW CAUTIONS There are some drawbacks to package tours: The least expensive tours may put you up at a bottom-end hotel. And because the lower costs depend on volume, some more expensive tours could send you to a large, impersonal property. You might find that once you're in the islands, you want to shift to that cozy bungalow down the road; if you do, you might lose the accommodation portion of the money you've paid. Some hoteliers will endorse your vouchers to another property if you're unhappy with theirs; others will not. And because the tour prices are based on double occupancy, the single traveler is almost invariably penalized. You could end up traveling with strangers who become friends for life; they could also be loudmouthed bores.

In other words, ask about the **accommodation choices** and prices for each. Then look up the hotels' reviews in this

Tips   Flying with Film & Video

Never pack film—developed or undeveloped—in checked bags, as the new, more powerful scanners in many airports can fog film. Scanners can damage film carried onboard as well. X-ray damage is cumulative; the slower the film, and the more times you put it through a scanner, the more likely the damage. Film under 800 ASA is usually safe for up to five scans. If you're taking your film through additional scans, U.S. regulations permit you to demand hand inspections. In international airports, you're at the mercy of officials. Store your film in baggies, so you can remove it easily before you go through scanners.

Most photo supply stores sell pouches designed to block X-rays. The pouches fit both film and loaded cameras. They should protect your film in checked baggage, but they also may raise alarms and result in a hand inspection.

Carry-on scanners will not damage memory cards in digital cameras, videotape in video cameras, CD-ROMs, or hard drives in laptops, but the magnetic fields emitted by the walk-through security gateways and hand-held inspection wands will. If you plan to travel extensively, you may want to play it safe and hand-carry your digital equipment or ask that it be inspected by hand. Be sure your batteries are charged, as you may be required to turn your electronic devices on to ensure that they're what they appear to be.

Film Safety for Traveling on Planes, FSTOP (© 888/301-2665; www. f-stop.org), provides additional tips for traveling with film and equipment.

guide and check their rates for your specific dates of travel online. If I don't recommend the hotel in this book (there usually is a good reason or two), then check it out thoroughly online, particularly in chat rooms and message boards such as you'll find at www.frommers. com.

You'll also want to find out what **type of room** you get. If you need a certain type of room, ask for it; don't take whatever is thrown your way. Request a non-smoking room, a quiet room, a room with a view, or whatever you fancy.

Most tour companies require payment in advance of travel. If possible, pay by credit card, which will give you some protection in case the company doesn't come

through with the tour. Also consider buying both trip cancellation and trip interruption insurance (see "Travel Insurance" and "Health & Safety," earlier in this chapter).

Finally, look for **hidden expenses.** Ask whether airport departure fees and taxes are included in the total cost.

If you decide to go for a package, read the fine print carefully. You might not want all the "extras" that are included, such as all meals (why pay in advance for all meals in places like French Polynesia, where dining out can be a major extracurricular activity?). And don't think the free manager's welcoming party is any big deal; you might be invited anyway, even if you're not on the tour.

13 The Active Traveler

The South Pacific islands are a dream if you're an active traveler, and especially if you're into diving, snorkeling, swimming, boating, and other watersports. You can also play golf and tennis, or hike into the jungle-clad mountainous interiors of the islands. Kayaking is popular everywhere, and Fiji has river rafting. There's good biking along the many roads skirting colorful lagoons. You can engage in these activities everywhere, although some islands are better than others. I point out the best in the following chapters, but here's a brief rundown of my favorites.

BIKING

Relatively flat roads circle most of the islands I cover in this book, making for easy and scenic bike riding. In fact, bicycles are one of my favorite means of getting around. It's simple and inexpensive to rent bikes on all the islands in French Polynesia, the Cook Islands, Samoa, and Tonga. In fact, many hotels and resorts provide bikes for their guests to use.

DIVING & SNORKELING

Most of the islands have very good to great diving and snorkeling. Virtually every lagoon-side resort has a dive operator, and many will let snorkelers go along. Liveaboard dive boats also operate in Fiji and French Polynesia. See chapters 4 and 7. respectively.

Fiji is on every diver's list of world-class destinations for colorful soft corals. This is especially true in northern Fiji, where nutrient-rich waters bathe the reefs in the Somosomo Strait, between Vanua Levu and Taveuni islands. Here you'll find famous Rainbow Reef and its Great White Wall. See chapter6.

French Polynesia is famous for its bountiful sealife, from harmless tropical fish to hammerhead sharks. You'll see plenty of creatures at Moorea, Bora Bora, Huahine, and Raiatea-Tahaa, but the best

diving and snorkeling is in the huge lagoons of Rangiroa, Tikehau, Manihi, and Fakarava in the Tuamotu Islands. See chapters 9, 10, and 11.

The shallow lagoons in the Cook Islands and the Samoas are fine for snorkeling, but most diving is in open water outside the reef, where you'll see ample sealife swimming in caves and canyons. Tonga offers a mix, with lagoon diving off Tongatapu and Vava'u and open-water dives off the island of Eu'a. See chapters 12, 13, and 15.

Most resorts offer dive packages to their guests, and the American-based **PADI Travel Network** (© 800/729-7234; www.padi.com) puts together packages for divers of all experience levels.

DEEP-SEA FISHING

Charter boats in every country will take you in search of marlin, swordfish, tuna, mahi-mahi, and other game fish. For example, a lucky Australian angler recently snagged a record-breaking 328.8kg (723 lbs.) black marlin off Vava'u in Tonga (see chapter 15).

French Polynesia has two ways to cast your line while living aboard in luxury. Based in Bora Bora, the *Tara Vana* (www.taravana.com) is a 50-foot sail-powered game-fishing boat. In the Tuamotus, **Haumana Cruises** (www.tahiti-fly-fishing-cruises.com) uses a 17-cabin yacht. See chapters 10 and 11, respectively.

GOLF & TENNIS

Most islands have at least one golf course, and some hotels and resorts have tennis courts, but generally this is not the place for a vacation consisting primarily of golf and tennis.

The one exception is Fiji, where **Denarau Golf & Racquet Club** is a modern complex with an 18-hole resort course and 10 tennis courts near Nadi. Fiji also is home to the region's most picturesque course, **The Pearl Championship Golf Course & Country** at Pacific Harbour. As we went to press, Fiji native Veejay Singh was designing a course at a new resort at Natadola Beach. See chapter 5.

French Polynesia's lone course on the south coast of Tahiti was about to be joined by a new set of links on Moorea. See chapter 8.

The Cook Islands have two 9-hole courses, one on Rarotonga and one on Aitutaki. Both are famous for their antenna guy-wire obstacles, which are in play. See chapter 12. Samoa has two courses and Tonga one. See chapters 13 and 15, respectively.

HIKING

These aren't the Rocky Mountains, nor are there blazed trails out here, but hiking in the islands is a lot of fun.

In Fiji you can trek into the mountains and stop at—or stay in—native Fijian villages. **Adventures Fiji,** an arm of Fiji's Rosie the Travel Service (www.rosie fiji.com), has guided hikes ranging from 1 to 10 days into the mountains of Viti Levu, with meals and accommodations provided by Fijian villagers. See chapter 5. On Taveuni island, you can hike a spectacular coastal trail to a waterfall or up to **Lake Tagimaucia,** in a crater at an altitude of more than 800m (2,700 ft.). It's home of the rare *tagimaucia* flower. See chapter 6.

Tahiti and Moorea have several trails into the highlands, some of which run along spectacular ridges. You'll need a guide for the best hikes, but you can easily hire them on both islands. See chapters 8 and 9.

Rarotonga in the Cook Islands is famous for its Cross-Island Trek, which runs across the mountains from coast-to-coast, as well as other trails. You can do the Cross-Island hike on your own, as part of a group, or with a guide. See chapter 12.

HORSEBACK RIDING

Although I prefer sipping a cold drink, a great way to experience a South Pacific sunset is from the back of a horse while riding along a beach. You can do just that in Fiji (see chapter 5), on Moorea and Huahine in French Polynesia (see chapters 9 and 11), and on Rarotonga in the Cook Islands (see chapter 12).

The ranches on Moorea and Huahine also have daytime rides into the mountains.

RIVER RAFTING

Only Fiji has rivers long enough and swift enough for white-water rafting. The best is the Navua River on Viti Levu, which starts in the mountainous interior and flows swiftly down to a flat delta on the island's south coast. Local companies offer trips using traditional *bilibilis* (bamboo rafts) on the lower, slow-flowing section of the river. The American-based **Rivers Fiji** (© **800/346-6277;** www. riversfiji.com) uses inflatable rafts for white-water trips up in the highlands. See chapter 5.

SAILING & KAYAKING

All but a few beachfront resorts have canoes, kayaks, small sailboats, sailboards, and other toys for their guests' amusement. Since most of these properties sit beside lagoons, using these craft is not only fun, it's relatively safe. They are most fun where you can paddle or sail across the lagoon to uninhabited islets out on the reef, such as on Moorea's northwest coast and off Muri Beach on Rarotonga in the Cook Islands. See chapters 9 and 12, respectively.

Sea kayaking is popular throughout the islands, especially among Fiji's many small islands. See chapters 5 and 6. In Samoa, you can take kayak tours of the small islands of Manono and Apolima with **Ecotour Samoa** (www.ecotour samoa.com). See chapter 13. In Tonga,

Friendly Islands Kayak Company (www.fikco.com) leads trips through Vava'u's islets. See chapter 15.

The region's reef-strewn waters make charter-boat sailing a precarious undertaking. The exceptions are the Leeward Islands in French Polynesia and Vava'u in Tonga, where you can rent sailboats with or without skippers. Two leading companies, **The Moorings** (© **800/535-7289;** www.moorings.com) and **Sunsail Yacht Charters** (© **800/327-2276;** www.sunsail.com), have operations at both locations. See chapters 11 and 15. You can charter boats with captains in Fiji. See chapter 5.

14 Tips on Accommodations

The South Pacific has a wide range of accommodations, from deluxe resort hotels on their own islands to mom-and-pop guesthouses and dormitories with bunk beds.

TYPES OF ROOMS

My favorite type of hotel accommodates its guests in individual bungalows set in a coconut grove beside a sandy beach and quiet lagoon. If that's not the quintessential definition of the South Seas, then I don't know what is! Some of these in French Polynesia, the Cook Islands, and Samoa are super-romantic bungalows that actually stand on stilts out over the reef (although I should point out that some of these overwater units tend to be close together and thus less private than bungalows ashore elsewhere). Others are as basic as tents. In between they vary in size, furnishings, and comfort. In all, you enjoy your own place. The bungalows are usually built or accented with thatch and other native materials but they contain most of the modern conveniences. An increasing number of these accommodations are air-conditioned, which is a definite plus during the humid summer months from November through March. All but a few bungalows have ceiling fans, which usually will keep you comfortable during the rest of the year. Hotels of this style are widespread in the South Pacific.

With the exception of French Polynesia, the major tourist markets for the island countries are Australia and New Zealand. Accordingly, the vast majority of hotels are tailored to Aussie and Kiwi tastes, expectations, and uses of the English language.

Unlike the usual U.S. hotel room, which likely has two huge beds, the standard Down Under room has a double or queen-size bed and a single bed that also serves as a settee. The room may or may not have a bathtub but always has a shower. There will be tea, instant coffee, sugar, creamer, and an electric jug to heat water (that's usually what I mean by "coffeemaker" in my hotel descriptions). Televisions are numerous but are not yet universal, but most hotels have radios whose selections are limited to the one, two, or three stations on the island.

Rooms are known to South Pacific reservation desks as "singles" if one person books them, regardless of the number and size of beds they have. Singles are slightly less expensive than other rooms. A unit is a "double" if it has a double bed and is reserved for two persons who intend to sleep together in that bed. On the other hand, a "twin" has two twin beds; it is known as a "shared twin" if two unmarried people book them and don't intend to sleep together. Third and fourth occupants of any room are usually charged a few dollars on top of the double or shared twin rates.

Some hotel rooms, especially in Rarotonga and the Cook Islands, have kitchenettes equipped with a small refrigerator (the "fridge"), hot plates (the "cooker"), pots, pans, crockery, silverware, and utensils. Establishments with cooking facilities

> ### ⟨Tips⟩ It Could Pay to Ask
>
> All South Pacific hotels pay travel agents and wholesalers 30% or more of their rates for sending clients their way, and they may even sell blocks of rooms at even more of a discount during slow periods. Some hotels may give you the benefit of at least part of this commission if you book directly instead of going through an airline or travel agent.
>
> Many also have "local" rates for islanders, which they may extend to visitors if business is slow. It never hurts to ask politely for a discounted or local rate.

but no restaurants often call themselves motels rather than hotels, especially in the Cook Islands. Having a kitchenette can result in quite a saving on breakfasts and light meals.

SAVING ON YOUR HOTEL ROOM

The rate ranges quoted in this book are known as **rack rates,** or published rates; that is, the maximum a property charges for a room. These prices are becoming less meaningful as more and more hotels engage in "yield management," under which they change their rates almost daily depending on how many people are booked in for a particular night. In other words, you may not know what the price of a room is until you call the hotel or book online for a particular date. Nevertheless, rack rates remain the best way of comparing prices.

You may be able to save on hotel rooms by booking them through the airlines, discounters, or wholesalers. One example is **Air New Zealand's "Go As You Please"** program, which offers reduced rates at a number of establishments everywhere that the airline flies. You book and pay for the rooms ahead through Air New Zealand's offices and agents (see "The Airlines," earlier in this chapter). You won't find this program online, so ask the airline for a brochure that lists the hotels and rates.

Just as consolidators pare the price of airline tickets by selling unused seats,

so do hotel brokers get rid of rooms hoteliers don't think they can sell at full price. The brokers may not offer the best deals you can find, but they're worth calling. You're probably better off dealing directly with a hotel, but if you don't like bargaining, this is certainly a viable option. Most of them offer online reservation services as well. One reputable provider offering South Pacific rooms is **Hotel Reservations Network** (© **800/715-7666;** www.hoteldiscounts.com).

See "Planning Your Trip Online," earlier in this chapter for tips on finding discounts on the Web.

LANDING THE BEST ROOM

Somebody has to get the best room in the house. It might as well be you.

You can start by joining the hotel's frequent-guest program, which may make you eligible for upgrades. A hotel-branded credit card usually gives its owner "silver" or "gold" status in frequent-guest programs for free.

Always ask about a corner room. They're often larger and quieter, with more windows and light, and they often cost the same as standard rooms.

When you make your reservation, ask if the hotel is renovating; if it is, request a room away from the construction. Ask about nonsmoking rooms, rooms with views, rooms with twin, queen-, or king-size beds. If you're a light sleeper, request a room away from vending machines, elevators, bars, and discos. Ask for a room that has been recently renovated or redecorated. If you aren't happy with your room, talk to the front desk. If they have another room, they may be willing to accommodate you.

Here are some other questions to ask before you book a room:

- What's the view like? If you're a cost-conscious traveler, you might be willing to pay less for a bungalow in the garden, especially if you don't plan to spend much time in the room.
- Does the room have air-conditioning or just ceiling fans? An important consideration between November and March.
- Is there good ventilation in the room? Some older hotels don't have windows on both sides of the building, which prevents the cooling trade winds from circulating.
- What is the noise level outside the room? If nighttime entertainment takes place alfresco, you might want to find out when show time is over.
- What's included in the price? Your room may be moderately priced, but if you're charged for beach chairs, towels, sports equipment, and other amenities, you could end up spending more than you bargained for.
- Is there a hotel pool, and is it fresh- or saltwater?
- Are airport transfers included?
- If it's off-season, will any facilities be shut down while you're there?
- If you're single, ask if there's a singles program. If it's off-season, inquire about the occupancy rate. If you're with a partner and looking for quiet, an empty resort might be fine; but if you're single and looking for fun, you might want to find a place that's a little more bustling.
- Are there children's programs?
- How far is the room from the beach?
- What is the dining plan? European Plan (EP; no meals), American Plan (AP; three meals), or Modified American Plan (MAP; breakfast and dinner)? You don't want to pay for three meals if eat out a lot.
- What is the cancellation policy?

15 Recommended Reading

Rather than list the hundreds of books about the South Pacific, I have picked some of my favorites that are likely to be available in the United States and Canada, either in bookstores or at your local library. A few out-of-print island classics have been reissued in paperback by **Mutual Publishing Company,** 125 Center St, Suite 210, Honolulu, HI 96816 (© **808/732-1709;** fax 808/ 734-4094; www.mutualpublishing.com).

GENERAL

If you have time for only one South Pacific book, read *The Lure of Tahiti* (1986). Editor A. Grove Day, himself an islands expert, includes 18 short stories, excerpts of other books, and essays. There is a little here from many writers mentioned below, plus selections from captains Cook, Bougainville, and Bligh.

The National Geographic Society's book *The Isles of the South Pacific* (1971), by Maurice Shadbolt and Olaf Ruhen, and Ian Todd's *Island Realm* (1974), are somewhat out-of-date coffee-table books but have lovely color photographs. *Living Corals* (1979), by Douglas Faulkner and Richard Chesher, shows what you will see underwater.

HISTORY & POLITICS

Several early English and French explorers published accounts of their exploits, but *The Journals of Captain James Cook* stand out as the most exhaustive and evenhanded. Edited by J. C. Beaglehole, they were published in three volumes (one for each voyage) in 1955, 1961, and 1967. A. Grenfell Price edited many of Cook's key passages and provides short transitional explanations in *The Explorations of Captain James Cook in the Pacific* (1971).

The explorers' visits and their consequences in Tahiti, Australia, and Antarctica are the subject of Alan Moorehead's excellent study *The Fatal Impact: The Invasion of the South Pacific, 1767–1840* (1966), a colorful tome loaded with sketches and paintings of the time.

Three other good books trace Tahiti's postdiscovery history. Robert Langdon's *Tahiti: Island of Love* (1979) takes the island's story up to 1977. David Howarth's *Tahiti: A Paradise Lost* (1985) covers the same early ground covered by Langdon but stops with France's taking possession in 1842. *The Rape of Tahiti* (1983), by Edward Dodd, covers the island from prehistory to 1900.

Mad About Islands (1987), by A. Grove Day, follows the island exploits of literary figures Herman Melville, Robert Louis Stevenson, Jack London, and W. Somerset Maugham. Also included are Charles Nordhoff and James Norman Hall, coauthors of the so-called "Bounty Trilogy" and other works about the islands (see "Fiction," below). *A Dream of Islands* (1980), by Gavan Dawes, tells of the missionary John Williams as well as of Melville, Stevenson, and the painter Paul Gauguin, who spent the final years of his life in French Polynesia.

Former *New York Times* reporter Robert Turnbull traveled the islands in the 1970s and reported his findings in *Tin Roofs and Palm Trees* (1977).

PEOPLES & CULTURES

Some of the most interesting accounts of island life were written by persons who lived among the islanders. Perhaps the most famous is *Coming of Age in Samoa*

(1928), in which Margaret Mead tells of her year studying promiscuous adolescent girls in the Manu'a islands of American Samoa. The book created quite a stir when it was published in a more modest time than the present. Her interpretation of Samoan sex customs was taken to task by New Zealander Derek Freeman in *Margaret Mead and Samoa: The Making and Unmaking of an Anthropological Myth* (1983).

Bengt Danielsson, a Swedish anthropologist who arrived in Tahiti on Thor Heyerdahl's *Kon Tiki* raft in 1947 and spent the rest of his life there, painted a broader picture of Polynesian sexuality in *Love in the South Seas* (1986). Heyerdahl tells his tale and explains his theory of Polynesian migration (since debunked) in *Kon Tiki* (1950). In 1936, Heyerdahl and his wife lived for a year in the Marquesas. His book, *Fatu-Hiva: Back to Nature* (1975), provides an in-depth look at Marquesan life at the time.

Two Americans gave unscholarly but entertaining accounts of Polynesian island life during the 1920s. Robert Dean Frisbie spent several years as a trader in the Cook Islands and told about it charmingly in *The Book of Puka-Puka* (1928; reprinted by Mutual in 1986). Robert Lee Eskridge spent a year on Mangareva in French Polynesia; his equally charming book is titled, appropriately, *Manga Reva* (1931; reprinted by Mutual in 1986).

TRAVELOGUES

Although the novelist Robert Louis Stevenson composed little fiction about the South Pacific during his years in Samoa (see chapter 13), he wrote articles and letters about his travels and about events leading to Germany's acquisition of the islands in 1890. Many of them are available in two collections: *In the South Seas* (1901) and *Island Landfalls* (1987). The latter includes three Stevenson short stories with South Seas settings: "The

> **Fun Fact** **Mutiny on the *Bounty***
>
> The most famous movies about the South Pacific are two *Mutiny on the Bounty* films based on the novel by Charles Nordhoff and James Norman Hall. The 1935 version starred Clark Gable as Fletcher Christian and Charles Laughton as a tyrannical Captain Bligh. (It actually was the second film based on the *Bounty* story; the first was an Australian production, starring Errol Flynn in his first movie role.) Although the 1935 version contained background shots of 40 Tahitian villages, most of the movie was filmed on Santa Catalina, off the California coast; neither Gable nor Laughton visited Tahiti. The 1962 remake with Marlon Brando and Trevor Howard, was actually filmed on Tahiti. It was the beginning of Brando's tragic real-life relationship with Tahiti. A 1984 version, *The Bounty,* not based on Nordhoff and Hall, was filmed in Opunohu Bay on Moorea and featured Mel Gibson as Christian and Anthony Hopkins as a more sympathetic (and historically accurate) Bligh.

Bottle Imp," "The Isle of Voices," and "The Beach at Falesá."

Sir David Attenborough, the British documentary film producer, traveled to Papua New Guinea, Vanuatu, Fiji, and Tonga in the late 1950s to film, among other things, Tongan Queen Salote's royal kava ceremony. Sir David entertainingly tells of his trips in *Journeys to the Past* (1983).

The travel writer and novelist Paul Theroux took his kayak along for a tour of the South Pacific and reported on what he found in *The Happy Isles of Oceania: Paddling the Pacific* (1992). The book is a fascinatingly frank yarn, full of island characters and out-of-the-way places. Tonga's royal family reportedly was so upset with Theroux's comments that he is banned from returning to the kingdom.

FICTION

Starting with Herman Melville's *Typee* (1846) and *Omoo* (1847)—semifictional accounts of his adventures in the Marquesas and Tahiti, respectively—the South Pacific has spawned a wealth of fiction. (Though set in the South Pacific Ocean, Melville's 1851 classic, *Moby Dick,* does not tell of the islands.)

After Melville came Julien Viaud, a French naval officer who fell in love with a Tahitian woman during a sojourn in Tahiti. As Pierre Loti, he wrote *The Marriage of Loti* (1880; reprinted by KPI in 1986), a classic tale of lost love.

W. Somerset Maugham's *The Moon and Sixpence* (1919) is a fictional account of the life of Paul Gauguin. Maugham changed the name to Charles Strickland and made the painter English instead of French. (Gauguin's own novel, *Noa Noa,* was published in English in 1928, long after his death.) Maugham also produced a volume of South Pacific short stories, *The Trembling of a Leaf* (1921; reprinted by Mutual in 1985). The most famous is "Rain," the tragic story of prostitute Sadie Thompson and the missionary she led astray in American Samoa. It was made into several movies. My favorite Maugham story is "The Fall of Edward Bernard," about a Chicagoan who forsakes love and fortune at home for "beauty, truth, and goodness" in Tahiti.

Next on the scene were Charles Nordhoff and James Norman Hall (more about them in chapters 7 and 8). Together they wrote the most famous of all South Pacific novels, *Mutiny on the Bounty* (1932). They followed that enormous success with two other novels: *Men Against the Sea* (1934), based on Captain

Bligh's epic longboat voyage after the mutiny; and *Pitcairn's Island* (1935), about Lt. Fletcher Christian's demise on the mutineers' remote hideaway.

(For a non-fiction retelling of the great tale, see Caroline Alexander's *The Bounty: The True Story of the Mutiny on the Bounty* [2003].)

Nordhoff and Hall later wrote *The Hurricane* (1936), a novel set in American Samoa that has been made into two movies filmed in French Polynesia. Hall also wrote short stories and essays, collected in *The Forgotten One* (1986).

The second most famous South Pacific novel appeared just after World War II— *Tales of the South Pacific* (1947), by James A. Michener. A U.S. Navy historian, Michener spent much of the war on Espiritu Santo in the New Hebrides (now Vanuatu). Richard Rodgers and Oscar Hammerstein turned the novel into the musical *South Pacific,* a huge Broadway hit; it was later made into the blockbuster movie.

Michener toured the islands a few years later and wrote *Return to Paradise* (1951), a collection of essays and short stories. The essays describe the islands as they were after World War II but before tourists began to arrive— near the end of the region's backwater, beachcomber days. His piece on Fiji predicts that country's Fijian–Indian problems.

3

Suggested South Pacific Itineraries

People often ask me where they should go in the South Pacific. Lacking the ability to read minds, I do not have an easy answer. In other words, it depends on what you want to see and do on your own vacation. What I can do is give you the benefit of my expertise so that you don't waste your valuable vacation time.

If you live in the United States, Canada, or Europe, the long flights here and back mean you will burn a day getting here and a day returning home. Consequently, you should spend more than 1 week out here. If you have only 1 week, spend it in one island country, or even on one island. (Also pick only one if your primary goal is to spend as much time as possible in the water.) I suggest itineraries in this chapter which will do some degree of justice to the Cook Islands, the Samoas, and Tonga, which are smaller than Fiji and French Polynesia. I recommend 2 weeks for either of the latter.

The vast distances and the infrequent—or in some cases nonexistent—air services between the islands make it impractical to see more than one South Pacific island country in less than 3 weeks. If you do island-hop between countries, you will devote several days to

packing, getting to the airports, standing in line at security checkpoints, waiting for flights, flying (usually in the middle of the night), clearing Customs and Immigration, getting to your new hotel, and recovering from your nocturnal ordeal. That will leave you just enough time to see the sites—and I don't mean *dive* sites.

That's not to say it is impossible to jump around from country to country. If you have 3 weeks or more, you can fly with Air New Zealand over its Coral Route from Fiji to Rarotonga to Tahiti, or vice versa. Air New Zealand pioneered this route in the days of flying boats, and one of its jets now flies from Auckland to Fiji and Rarotonga once a week. It turns around in Rarotonga and returns over the same route the next day.

However you construct your own itinerary, first find out the airlines' schedules and book all domestic inter-island flights well in advance. Do not wait until you arrive in the islands to take care of this important chore.

And remember the old travel agent's rule: Never stay at the most luxurious property first. In other words, anything after that will seem inferior, and you may come home disappointed.

1 Two Weeks in Fiji

This trip takes you to the highlights of Fiji. The Queens Road, a two-lane highway, links Nadi, the Coral Coast, and Suva, so you'll make this part of the trip overland.

Bus connections are available, but I always rent a car in order to have the maximum flexibility. Ferries run from Suva to Taveuni and Savusavu, but don't even think about taking them. Fly instead.

Days ❶–❷: Relaxing in Nadi

Take the first day to recover from your international flight lounging around the pool, shopping in Nadi Town, or sightseeing. Spend day 2 on land-based excursions, such as to the late Raymond Burr's **Garden of the Sleeping Giant** (p. 97); **Lautoka,** Fiji's second largest city (p. 98); and **Viseisei Village,** the country's oldest native Fijian village (p. 97). Finish off with some more shopping and dinner in Nadi.

Days ❸–❹: Exploring the Coral Coast ⟆

Get up early and drive south to the Coral Coast, on the southern coast of Viti Levu, Fiji's "mainland." Stop on the way at the **Sigatoka Sand Dunes National Park** (p. 129) and **Kula Eco Park** (p. 130), which I like because they give an interesting glimpse of Fiji's geology and wildlife. You can swim or snorkel in the afternoon, or hike to a waterfall with **Adventures in Paradise Fiji** (p. 130). Catch an evening show featuring the "fire walkers" from Beqa Island (p. 136).

Day ❺: Rafting on the Navua River ⟆⟆⟆

One of my favorite Fiji excursions is up the **Navua River,** which carves a dramatic gorge through Viti Levu's mountainous interior before spilling into a flood plain west of Suva. The usual trip takes you upriver on a fast speed boat but brings you back on a *bilibili* (bamboo raft). Or you can ride an inflatable boat over white waters with **Rivers Fiji** (p. 138).

Day ❻: Suva ⟆

On the way to Suva, Fiji's humid capital city, stop and see a presentation of native arts, crafts, and dancing at the **Pacific Harbour Arts Village,** the country's best cultural center (p. 137). Once in Suva, take a walking tour of downtown, ending at the **Fiji Museum** (p. 144). The city is the best place to do after-dark bar hopping (p. 156).

Day ❼: A Trip Back in Time to Levuka

A short trip from Suva to **Levuka** always highlights my visits to Fiji. The country's original capital, the old town has retained its 19th-century appearance, and its backdrop of sheer cliffs makes it one of the South Pacific's most beautiful towns. Get **Ovalau Watersports** (p. 152) to organize a morning walking tour and an afternoon excursion on Ovalau. Either catch the late afternoon flight back to Suva or overnight at the charming **Levuka Homestay** (p. 153).

Days ❽–❾: Exploring Taveuni ⟆⟆⟆

Take the early morning Air Fiji flight back to Nausori Airport near Suva and connect from there to **Taveuni,** Fiji's third largest island. Famous for world-class diving on the nearby **Great White Wall** and its **Rainbow Reef,** Taveuni also is a hiker's paradise. Stay near the airport, from where it's an easy trip to the waterfalls in **Bouma National Heritage Park** and the scenic **Lavena Coastal Walk** (p. 172). The next day hike to the mountaintop **Lake Tagimaucia,** where you might see the rare flower of the same name.

Days ❿–⓫: Savusavu: "Little America"

Spend your first day exploring **Savusavu,** on Fiji's second largest island, Vanua Levu. Although it is rapidly developing, the

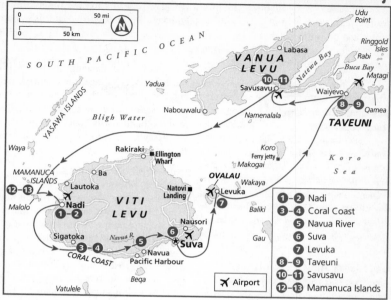

0 ─── **50 mi**
0 ─── **50 km**

SOUTH PACIFIC OCEAN

Udu Point

Ringgold Isles

Rabi
Buca Bay
Matagi

Labasa

VANUA LEVU

Yadua

Savusavu **⑩─⑪**

Natewa Bay

Waiyevo

⑧─⑨ Qamea

Nabouwalu

Namenalala

TAVEUNI

Bligh Water

YASAWA ISLANDS

Waya

Rakiraki

Ellington Wharf

Koro
Ferry jetty
Makogai

Koro Sea

Wakaya

Malolo

MAMANUCA ISLANDS **⑫─⑬**

Ba

Lautoka

OVALAU

Levuka **⑦**

Baliki

VITI LEVU

Natovi Landing

Nadi **①─②**

Nausori

Gau

Sigatoka **③─④**

Navua R.

⑤

Pacific Harbour

⑥ Suva

Navua

CORAL COAST

Beqa

Vatulele

①─② Nadi
③─④ Coral Coast
⑤ Navua River
⑥ Suva
⑦ Levuka
⑧─⑨ Taveuni
⑩─⑪ Savusavu
⑫─⑬ Mamanuca Islands

✈ Airport

town still recalls its days as a 19th-century copra (coconut oil) port. Stroll along the harbor, have lunch at the **Bula-Re Cafe** (p. 168), and visit the famous **Savusavu Hot springs,** where Fijians still cook their evening meals (p. 163). Stop by **Curly's Cruising/Bosun's Locker** (p. 163) to rent a kayak or arrange an excursion to a Fijian village. If you have brought your children, stay at **Jean-Michel Cousteau Fiji Islands Resort** (p. 164), one of the South Pacific's top family resorts.

Days ⑫–⑬: A Mamanuca Island Retreat

Spending at least 1 night on a small island in the Mamanucas is almost an essential ingredient of any trip to Fiji, whether it's at the raucous **Beachcomber Island Resort** (p. 123), the family-oriented **Plantation Island Resort** (p. 123), or a quiet couples-only hideaway like **Matamanoa Island Resort** (p. 121). They all have much better beaches than you'll find on the "mainland" of Viti Levu, and it'll give you a chance to rest up for your trip home.

Day ⑭: Last Minute Shopping in Nadi

If your homeward flight departs late at night, you can stay in the islands for an extra day. Otherwise spend your last day catching up on shopping or any excursions you might have missed in and around Nadi.

2 Two Weeks in Tahiti & French Polynesia

This itinerary takes you over the well-worn path through French Polynesia's Society Islands—Tahiti, Moorea, Huahine, and Bora Bora—plus a few days in Rangiroa, the largest atoll in the Tuamotu Archipelago. I suggest going to Rangiroa first because after the awesome mountainous beauty of the Society Islands, it may seem anticli-mactic to end your trip at a flat atoll. Tikihau, Manihi, or Fakarava, its Tuamotuan sisters, are almost as good and are worthy alternatives to Rangiroa. If you have only 1 week, omit Rangiroa and head to Moorea first, then to Huahine and Bora Bora. If you're on an expensive honeymoon, you won't regret ending it at **Le Taha'a Private Island & Spa** (p. 298).

Day ❶: Circling Tahiti ☆

Spend your first morning on a guided half-day **circle island** tour of Tahiti (p. 220). You won't have to drive or find your way around, so it's a good method of recover-ing while seeing the island. After a long French lunch, take a **walking tour** of downtown Papeete (p. 217). I like to stay in a hotel on Tahiti's west coast, where I can watch the sunset over Moorea, one of the region's most awe-inspiring sights.

Days ❷–❹: Riding the Rip on Rangiroa ☆☆

The world's second largest lagoon demands a full day excursion by boat to one of its two key sites: the **Pink Sands** or the **Blue Lagoon** (p. 301). Devote a full day to one of these trips. My choice would be the Blue Lagoon, actually a small lagoon within the large lagoon. On another day don your snorkel or diving gear and **ride the rip tide** through the main pass into the lagoon. Be sure to watch the dolphins playing in Ohotu Pass at sunset.

Days ❺–❼: Feeding the Sharks on Bora Bora ☆☆☆

A non-stop flight from Rangiroa will bring you to beautiful **Bora Bora,** which many consider the world's most beautiful island. Spend part of your first day here exploring the interior by four-wheel-drive "safari expedition" (p. 272). Devote a full day to a lagoon tour by boat, the top thing to do on Bora Bora. You'll get a fish-eye view of the island's dramatic peak, snorkel while watching your guide feed a school of reef sharks, and enjoy a fresh-fish lunch on a small islet on the fringing reef (p. 372).

Days ❽–❿: Old Polynesia on Huahine ☆☆

After the mile-a-minute activities on Bora Bora, **Huahine** will seem like a reserved Polynesian paradise. Spend your first day touring the historic *maraes* (ancient tem-ples) at Maeva village with Paul Atallah of **Island Eco Tours** (p. 287). The next day tour the lagoon, swim, snorkel, or go horseback riding. I always have a sunset drink while watching the boats coming and going at **Fare,** the island's charming main town.

Days ⓫–⓮: Seeing the Sights on Moorea ☆☆☆

While the lagoons are the highlights at Rangiroa and Bora Bora, the ruggedly gorgeous interior draws my eyes on **Moorea.** Whether it's on a regular guided tour, a four-wheel-drive safari excursion, or on your own, go up to the **Belvédère,** overlooking **Cook's** and **Opunohu** bays. Moorea's lagoon does have its good fea-tures, especially dolphin-watching excur-sions led by **Dr. Michael Poole** (p. 253). And don't miss a nighttime show at **Tiki Theatre Village,** one of the region's best cultural centers (p. 251). Moorea is only 7 minutes by plane from Tahiti, which makes it a snap to connect to Papeete and your flight home.

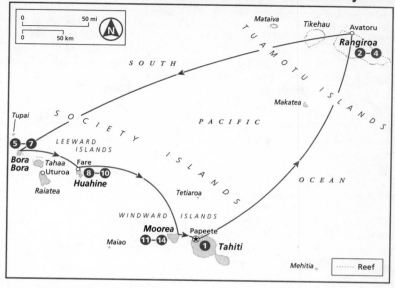

3 A Week in The Cook Islands

In many ways the Cook Islands are a microcosm of the South Pacific. Here in a small space are people as friendly as the Fijians, beautiful islands similar to those in French Polynesia, exposure to Polynesian culture rivaling that in Samoa and Tonga, and lots of outdoor activities. In other words, here you can easily see most of what the islands have to offer in 1 week. Since Rarotonga is less than a 2-hour flight from Tahiti, 3 from Fiji, this week can easily be added to your Fiji or French Polynesia visits.

Day ❶: Arrival & Recovery on Rarotonga ☆☆☆

My favorite thing to do after an all-night plane ride getting here is to head into **Avarua** for a cup of strong coffee at **The Cafe** (p. 341), then a stroll around the Cooks' little capital. Be sure to visit the **Cook Islands Library and Museum** (p. 323). Spend the afternoon recovering with a swim or a sail at **Muri Beach** (p. 325).

Day ❷: Sampling Cook Islands Culture ☆☆☆

The demonstrations at the **Cook Islands Cultural Village** and its guided tour

around Rarotonga (p. 327) will take most of this day. Later on don't miss one of the region's best **island nights** (p. 343), featuring a feast and a lively dance show. If it's Friday or Saturday, make the obligatory "crawl" through Avarua's pubs (p. 342).

Day ❸: A Walk Across Rarotonga ☆☆☆

Plan to spend this morning hiking the **Cross-Island Track,** which literally traverses Rarotonga from north to south, passing the base of the famous **Needle** on the way. You will learn much as well as enjoy the views on a guided trek with **Pa's**

A Week in the Cook Islands

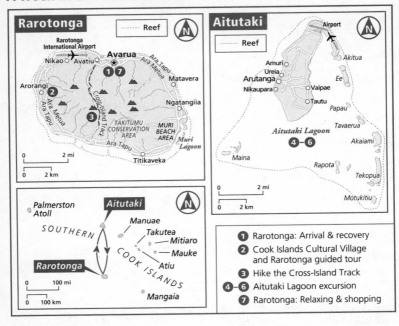

- ① Rarotonga: Arrival & recovery
- ② Cook Islands Cultural Village and Rarotonga guided tour
- ③ Hike the Cross-Island Track
- ④–⑥ Aitutaki Lagoon excursion
- ⑦ Rarotonga: Relaxing & shopping

Nature Walks (p. 328). If you're not up to walking and climbing, **Raro Safari Tours** will take you into the interior mountains via four-wheel-drive vehicle (p. 327).

Days ④–⑥: An Aitutaki Lagoon Excursion ✦✦✦

On day 4 take an early morning flight from Rarotonga to **Aitutaki.** Spend that afternoon exploring Aitutaki's main island, either on a guided tour or on your own via scooter or rental car. After sunset attend an island night buffet and dance show, preferably at **Samade on the Beach** (p. 349). Spend all of day 5 on an excursion out on the lagoon, one of the

South Pacific's most beautiful. You'll get to snorkel around tiny **One Foot Island,** one of my favorite things to do here. Have dinner at **Cafe Tupuna** (p. 350). Enjoy the morning of day 6 on the beach before flying back to Rarotonga.

Day ⑦: Relaxing & Shopping on Rarotonga

Spend the morning of your last day doing some shopping for black pearls, Tangaroa statues, and tropical clothing in Avarua (p. 330). In the afternoon head over to **Titikaveka** for Rarotonga's best snorkeling.

4 A Week in the Samoas

By being both Christian and conservative, Samoa and nearby American Samoa have maintained their traditional Polynesian cultures to a remarkable degree. I like this trip because it lets me examine the old way of life while still enjoying great beaches, reefs, and tropical scenery.

A Week in the Samoas

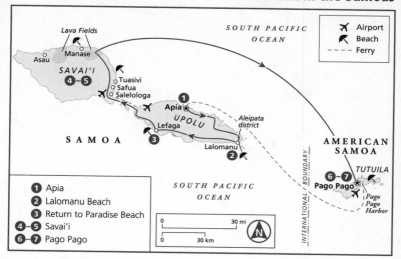

Day ❶: Arrival & Recovery on Upolu

Whether you stay in town or at a beachside resort, devote your first day to seeing **Apia,** the picturesque waterfront capital of independent Samoa. Stroll the promenade along the harbor and visit the nearby **Robert Louis Stevenson Museum & Grave,** where the great writer is buried on Mount Vaea overlooking Apia (p. 369). Don't miss a *fiafia* feast and show, especially at one of **Aggie Grey's** resorts (p. 378).

Day ❷: An Excursion to Lalomanu Beach ★★★

Few South Pacific beaches combine great sand, a colorful lagoon, and a dramatic backdrop as does the one at **Lalomanu** village (p. 374), on the eastern end of Upolu, Samoa's main island. The drive there takes 2 hours, so leave early to enjoy a full day at the beach. You can also overnight beside the lagoon in a **beach fale** (p. 383).

Day ❸: Return to Paradise Beach ★★★

In case you didn't get an eyeful at Lalomanu Beach, spend this day between the black rocks protruding at **Return to Paradise Beach,** on Upolu's southwestern coast, where Gary Cooper starred in the 1950s movie *Return to Paradise.*

Days ❹–❺: Savai'i ★★★

Spend 1 of your 2 days on Samoa's undeveloped and fascinating "Big Island" exploring the **Virgin's Grave** and other sites on the Savai'i **lava fields** with Warren Jopling of **Safua Tours** (p. 387). Plan to stay in or near the north shore village of **Manase,** perhaps in an open-air beach fale beside Manase's magnificent white sands (p. 390).

Days ❻–❼: A Slice of America in Pago Pago

Three good hotels now make this beautiful if somewhat commercialized American outpost worth a visit. Spend 1 day touring Tutuila's south shore, especially from the fabled harbor at **Pago Pago** to the island's eastern end. The winding road passes one gorgeous bay after another. If you're into hiking in this humid tropical climate, devote your second day to the **National Park of American Samoa** (p. 402).

A Week in Tonga

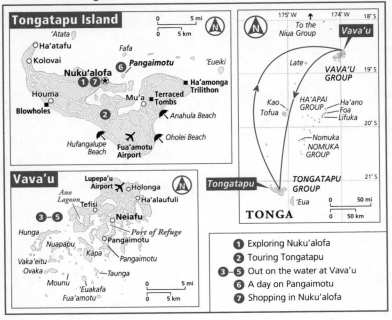

Tongatapu Island

'Atata
Ha'atafu
Kolovai
Fafa
Pangaimotu ⑥
Nuku'alofa ①⑦★
'Eueiki
Ha'amonga Trilithon
Houma
Mu'a Terraced Tombs
Blowholes
Anahula Beach
Hufangalupe Beach
Fua'amotu Airport
Oholei Beach
②

0 — 5 mi
0 — 5 km

Vava'u

Lupepa'u Airport
Holonga
Ano Lagoon
Tefisi
Ha'alaufuli
Neiafu
③–⑤
Hunga
Port of Refuge
Nuapapu
Pangaimotu
Vaka'eitu
Kapa
Pangaimotu
Ovaka
Taunga
Mounu
'Euakafa
Fua'amotu

0 — 5 mi
0 — 5 km

175° W   174° W   18° S
To the Niua Group   Vava'u
Late
VAVA'U GROUP   19° S
Kao   HA'APAI GROUP   Ha'ano
Tofua   Foa
Lifuka
Nomuka   20° S
NOMUKA GROUP
Tongatapu
TONGATAPU   21° S
GROUP
'Eua   0 — 50 mi
TONGA   0 — 50 km

① Exploring Nuku'alofa
② Touring Tongatapu
③–⑤ Out on the water at Vava'u
⑥ A day on Pangaimotu
⑦ Shopping in Nuku'alofa

5 A Week in Tonga

I approach the Kingdom of Tonga as two distinct destinations. On the one hand is the flat main island of Tongatapu, with its scruffy capital of Nuku'alofa, several historic sites worth observing out in the countryside, and little islets out in its harbor. On the other is hilly Vava'u, one of the South Pacific's sailing capitals. However you devise your own itinerary, give them equal time.

Day ①: Exploring Nuku'alofa

Most hotels on Tongatapu are in Nuku'alofa, so use the capital as your base. Spend your first day seeing sights such as the **Royal Palace** and the **Royal Tombs** (p. 425), and visiting the **Tongan National Cultural Centre** (p. 422). Don't miss dinner and a dance show at the center, either. Stop for coffee or lunch at **Friends Cafe** on the main street (p. 434).

Day ②: Touring Tongatapu

Spend your second day touring Tongatapu from end to end, with stops at the ancient **Ha'amonga Trilithon**, the **Blow Holes, Captain Cook's Landing Place**, and the exotic birds residing at the **Tongan Wildlife Centre** (p. 426). End up on the western shore, where you can sun and swim at **Ha'atafu** (p. 427).

Days ③–⑤: Out on the Water at Vava'u ★★★

One of the region's most picturesque destinations, **Vava'u** merits at least 3 days. If you're an avid sailor, this is the safest place in the South Pacific to charter a yacht and explore the many small islets dotting the lagoon. Even if you aren't into boating, spend 1 day on a lagoon tour to **Swallows Cave** and **Mariner's Cave** (p. 439). Vava'u also is the region's best place to go **whale watching** from June through October (p. 428).

Day ⑥: A Day on Pangaimotu ☆☆

Especially if it's a Sunday when nearly everything closes, spend this day at **Pangaimotu Island Resort,** a few minutes off Nuku'alofa (p. 428). Hanging over a beach beside the country's best swimming lagoon, this ramshackle but charming establishment is my favorite South Pacific bar. You'll have lots of local company out here on the Christian Sabbath.

Day ⑦: Shopping for Handicrafts ☆☆☆

Tongans produce the South Pacific's best handicrafts, so spend most of your last day exploring the shops in Nuku'alofa, especially the **Langafonua Women's Association Handicraft Centre** (p. 430).

4

Introducing Fiji

The thing I love most about these 300-plus islands isn't their palm-draped beaches, their blue lagoons, or their rugged mountains. It is the enormous friendliness of the Fijian people.

You'll see why as soon as you get off the plane, clear Customs and Immigration, and are greeted by a procession of smiling faces, all of them exclaiming an enthusiastic *"Bula!"* That one word—"health" in Fijian—expresses the warmest and most heartfelt welcome I have ever received anywhere.

This diverse country's great variety will also be immediately evident, for the taxi drivers who whisk us to our hotels and hostels are not Fijians of Melanesian heritage, but Indians whose ancestors migrated to Fiji from places like Calcutta and Madras. Now about 44% of the population, these Indo-Fijians have played major roles in making their nation economically as well as politically independent.

But their presence has also resulted in racial animosity and three political coups, most recently in 2000. Except for an occasional work stoppage or protest, however, visitors have not directly been affected by the political tensions, which exist primarily in Suva (the capital) and other towns. Fiji has remained calm since the coup of 2000, and with the country once again perceived as safe and affordable, tourism is booming as never before. In addition many new hotels and resorts have opened their doors since my recent visit.

In the tourist areas—and especially on Fiji's marvelous offshore islets—you'll find gorgeous white-sand beaches bordered by curving coconut palms, azure lagoons and colorful reefs offering world-class scuba diving and snorkeling, green mountains sweeping to the sea, and a tropical climate in which to enjoy it all.

Fiji has something for every pocketbook. Its wide variety of accommodation ranges from deluxe resorts nestled in tropical gardens beside the beach to down-to-basics hostels that cater to the young and the young-at-heart. Out on its 300-plus islands is the largest and finest collection of small, Robinson Crusoe–like offshore resorts in the entire South Pacific—if not the world.

Regardless of where you stay and what you do, you are in for a memorable time. The friendly Fijians will see to that.

1 Fiji Today: The Regions in Brief

From a strategic position in the southwestern Pacific some 5,152km (3,200 miles) southwest of Honolulu and 3,156km (1,960 miles) northeast of Sydney, Fiji is the transportation and economic hub of the South Pacific islands. **Nadi International Airport** is the main connection point for flights going to the other island countries, and Fiji's capital city, **Suva,** is one of the region's prime shipping ports and headquarters of most regional organizations.

Given the size and diversity of the country, any trip to Fiji requires careful planning to avoid disappointment. You could spend your entire vacation in Nadi, and although the tourism industry provides a host of activities to keep you busy there, you would miss the best parts of Fiji. This is a country of more than 300 gorgeous islands, and I think you should try to experience more than one.

By and large, the main island of Viti Levu does not have the best beaches in Fiji. Where it does have good sands, the reef offshore is more walkable than swimmable, especially at low tide. In other words, look beyond Nadi for good beaches and the best diving.

From a tourist's standpoint, Fiji is divided into several regions, each with its own special characteristics and appeal. Here's what each has to offer.

FIJI'S REGIONS IN BRIEF

The archipelago forms a horseshoe around the shallow, reef-strewn **Koro Sea,** much of which was dry land some 18,000 years ago during the last Ice Age. More than 300 islands and islets range in size from *Viti Levu* (Big Fiji), which is 10 times the size of Tahiti, to tiny atolls that barely break the surface of the sea. With a total land area of 18,187 sq. km (7,022 sq. miles), Fiji is slightly smaller than the state of New Jersey. Viti Levu has 10,803 sq. km (4,171 sq. miles), giving it more dry land than all the islands of French Polynesia put together.

ON VITI LEVU ISLAND

NADI   Most visitors arrive at Nadi International Airport, located among sugar-cane fields on Viti Levu's dry western side. Known as **Nadi,** this area is the focal point of much of Fiji's tourism industry, and it's where many tourists on package deals spend their time. There are a variety of hotels between the airport and predominately Indian **Nadi Town,** whose main industries are tourism and farming. Numerous handicraft, electronics, and clothing merchants wait to part you from your cash.

None of the airport hotels are on the beach, and even at **Denarau Island,** the country's major resort development, coastal mangrove forests make the beaches gray and the water offshore murky. There are many things to do in Nadi, but make it a stopover on the way to someplace if you have more than 1 or 2 days to spend in Fiji.

THE CORAL COAST   The **Queen's Road** runs around the south coast of Viti Levu through the resort area called the **Coral Coast.** Here you'll find comfortable hotels, luxury resorts, and fire-walking Fijians, but the beaches lead into very shallow lagoons. Most visitors staying on the Coast these days are tourists on packages. It's still a good choice for anyone who wants on-the-beach resort living while being able to conveniently see some of the country. Offshore, Vatulele Island Resort ranks as one of the world's finest small resorts.

PACIFIC HARBOUR & BEQA ISLAND   About 48km (30 miles) west of Suva, Pacific Harbour was developed in the early 1970s as a resort complete with golf course, private residences, shopping center, cultural center, and a seaside hotel. Because this area is in Viti Levu's rain belt, the project never reached its full potential. Nevertheless, its prime hotel has been renovated, as have the country's best cultural center and most scenic golf course. Pacific Harbour also is known for excellent deep-sea fishing, and it's the most convenient location for river rafting trips on the **Navua River.** It's also the jumping-off point for the **Beqa Lagoon,** which attracts divers from around the planet. Beqa has three comfortable hotels, including one of Fiji's newest luxury resorts.

NORTHERN VITI LEVU   An alternative driving route to Suva, the **King's Road** runs from Lautoka through the Sugar Belt of northern Viti Levu, passing through the predominately Indian towns of Ba and Tavua to **Rakiraki,** a Fijian village near the island's northernmost point and site of one of the country's few remaining colonial-era hotels. Jagged green mountains lend a gorgeous backdrop to the shoreline along the Rakiraki coast. Offshore, **Nananu-I-Ra Island** beckons backpackers.

Most of the King's Road is paved. East of Rakiraki, it follows deep, mountain-bounded **Viti Levu Bay,** one of the most beautiful parts of Fiji. From the head of the bay, the road then twists through the mountains, following the Wainbuka River until it emerges near the east coast at Korovou. A left turn there takes you to Natovi Wharf; and a right, to Suva. In other words, it's possible to drive or take buses all the way around Viti Levu via the Queen's and King's roads.

SUVA   The Queen's Road goes on to **Suva** (pop. 95,000), Fiji's busy capital and one of the South Pacific's most cosmopolitan cities. Remnants of Fiji's century as a British possession and the presence of so many Indians give the town a certain air of the colonial "Raj"—as if this were Agra or Bombay, not the boundary between Polynesia and Melanesia. On the other hand, Suva has modern high-rise buildings and lives at as fast a pace as can be found in the South Pacific west of Tahiti; this is no surprise because in many respects it's the bustling economic center of the region. The streets are filled with a melting-pot blend of Indians, Chinese, Fijians, other South Pacific islanders, "Europeans" (a term used in Fiji to mean persons of white skin, regardless of geographic origin), and individuals of mixed race.

ISLANDS OFF VITI LEVU

THE MAMANUCA ISLANDS   Beckoning off Nadi, the **Mamanuca Islands** offer day cruises and several offshore resorts of various sizes that appeal to a broad spectrum of travelers, from swinging singles to quieter couples and families. Generally speaking, they are in the driest part of Fiji, which means sunshine most of the time. Some are flat atolls so small you can walk around them in 5 minutes. Others are hilly, grassy islands reminiscent of the Virgin Islands in the Caribbean. Since the islands lie relatively close together, most offer excursions to the others. They also are close to Nadi, so you don't have to spend much extra money or time to get there.

THE YASAWA ISLANDS   A chain of gorgeous and relatively unspoiled islands stretching off north of the Mamanucas, the hilly **Yasawas** are often used as movie sets. Two versions of *The Blue Lagoon* were filmed here, the latest starring Brooke Shields as the castaway schoolgirl. Blessed with the best beaches in Fiji, the Yasawas are now one of the country's hottest destinations, especially among young backpackers. The islets have a host of inexpensive accommodations—a few of them attractive to anyone on a low budget, not just young backpackers.

BEQA ISLAND   A 30-minute boat ride off Pacific Harbour, rugged **Beqa** (pronounced Beng-*ga*) is best known for the surrounding **Beqa Lagoon,** one of Fiji's top diving destinations. Here you'll also find **Frigate Passage,** one of the world's best surfing spots (but

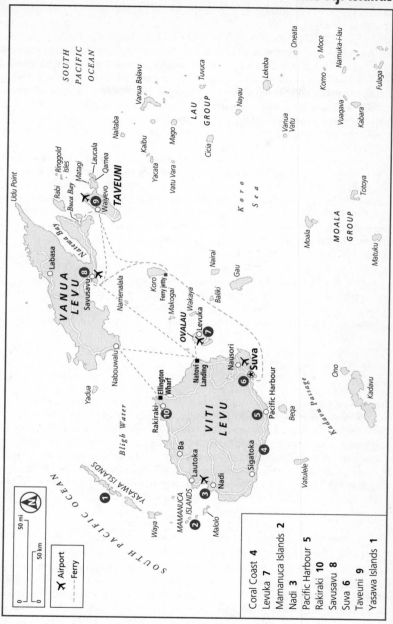

Coral Coast **4**
Levuka **7**
Mamanuca Islands **2**
Nadi **3**
Pacific Harbour **5**
Rakiraki **10**
Savusavu **8**
Suva **6**
Taveuni **9**
Yasawa Islands **1**

Diving in Fiji

Fiji is famous among divers as being the "Soft Coral Capital of the World" because of its enormous number and variety of colorful corals. These species grow well where moderate to heavy currents keep them fed, such as in the **Beqa Lagoon** and the **Astrolabe Reef,** both south of Viti Levu, and the **Great White Wall** and its **Rainbow Reef** in the **Somosomo Strait** between Vanua Levu and Taveuni in northern Fiji. In turn, the corals attract a host of fish. As one example, more than 35 species of angelfish and butterfly fish swim in these waters.

The Great White Wall is covered from between 23m and 60m (75–200 ft.) deep with pale lavender corals, which appear almost snow-white underwater. Near Qamea and Matagi, off Taveuni, are the appropriately named **Purple Wall,** a straight drop from 9m to 24m (30–80 ft.), and Mariah's Cove, a small wall as colorful as the Rainbow Reef. Also in the north, **Magic Mountain** on the Namena barrier reef around Moody's Namena has hard corals on top and soft ones on the sides, which attract an enormous number of small fish and their predators.

In Beqa Lagoon, the soft corals **Frigate Passage** seem to fall over one another, and **Side Streets** has unusual orange coral.

Even the heavily visited **Mamanuca Islands** off Nadi have their share of good sites, including **The Pinnacle,** a coral head rising 18m (60 ft.) from the lagoon floor, and a W-shaped protrusion from the outer reef. A drawback for some divers is that they don't have the Mamanuca sites all to themselves.

All but a few resorts in Fiji have dive operations on site, as will be pointed out in the following chapters.

One of the best ways to dive a lot of reefs in Fiji, and especially the out-of-the-way sites, is on a live-aboard dive boat. The best is the 101-foot-long, 10-passenger *Fiji Aggressor,* which makes weekly voyages from Suva through the reefs off eastern Viti Levu. It is equipped with a photo lab, video, and a high-speed canopied dive boat. You'll dive for 5½ days out of the week, making at least 2 dives per day. Rates begin at US$2,000 per person, including accommodations, meals, snacks, and unlimited diving, but not equipment. For information and reservations, contact **Aggressor Fleet** (© **800/348-2628** or 985/385-2628; fax 985/384-0817; www.aggressor.com).

not for novices, since the curling breakers slam onto the reef). Beqa has three comfortable hotels, including a small American-owned retreat and one of Fiji's top-end luxury resorts.

LEVUKA & OVALAU   Off Suva, the picturesque island of **Ovalau** is home to the historic town of **Levuka,** which has changed little in appearance since its days as a boisterous whaling port and the first capital of a united Fiji in the 1800s. Few places in the South Pacific have retained their frontier facade as has this living museum.

NORTHERN FIJI

Vanua Levu, Taveuni, and their nearby islands are known locally as "The North" because they comprise Fiji's Northern Province. Over on Vanua Levu, Fiji's second largest island, a little town with the exotic name **Savusavu** lies nestled in one of the region's most protected deep-water bays. Unlike Viti Levu, Savusavu and the Garden Isle of **Taveuni** are throwbacks to the old South Pacific, a land of copra plantations and small Fijian villages tucked away in the bush. Both have excellent places to stay, including fine resorts off Vanua Levu and near Taveuni's north coast on **Matagi** and **Qamea** islands. Both also have considerable amounts of freehold land; in fact, so many of my countrymen and women have bought parcels here that Fijians now facetiously refer to Savusavu as "Little America."

GOVERNMENT

Fiji is a republic governed by the 1998 constitution. The Westminster-style government has a 71-member parliament of 23 Fijians, 19 Indians, 1 Rotuman, 3 general electors (anyone who's a Fijian, Indian, Rotuman), and 25 open seats which any citizen can hold. The Great Council of Chiefs picks the country's largely figurehead president, who presides over an appointed senate with relatively little power.

ECONOMY

Tourism is far and away Fiji's largest and most profitable industry, and it keeps getting larger every year. High demand for the country's supply of rooms has spurred a hotel construction boom, which in turn has driven up the cost of real estate, particularly in the tourist areas. On the other hand, sugar and garment manufacturing—two more of Fiji's economic mainstays—have not kept pace. Grown primarily by Indian farmers, the sugar cane is harvested between June and November and crushed in five aging sugar mills operated by the government-owned Fiji Sugar Corporation; all the mills need repair and upgrading. The number of farmers has decreased since Fijian landowners have not renewed many of their land leases (some displaced farmers have moved into shanties around Suva). In addition, favorable import duties on both sugar and garments produced in Fiji have been, or are soon to be, withdrawn by the European Union, the United States, and Australia.

While Nadi and the Coral Coast have seen gains, unemployment is a persistent problem elsewhere. More than half the population is under 25, and there just aren't enough jobs being created for youngsters coming into the workforce. About 50% of all households live below the official poverty line or just above it. As a consequence, the country has seen a marked increase in burglaries, robberies, and other crimes.

Gold mining on northern Viti Levu also contributes to the economy, as do fishing, copra, timber, garments, furniture, coffee (you'll get a rich, strong brew throughout the country), and other consumer goods produced by small manufacturers (the Colgate toothpaste you buy in Fiji is made here). Fiji is also a major trans-shipment point for goods destined for other South Pacific islands.

2 Fiji Yesterday: History 101

The Dutch navigator Abel Tasman sighted some of the Fiji Islands in the 1640s, and Capt. James Cook visited one of the southernmost islands in 1774. After the mutiny on HMS *Bounty* off Tonga in April 1789, Capt. William Bligh and his loyal crewmen sailed their longboat between Viti Levu and Vanua Levu, where they barely escaped capture by Fijians in speedy *druas* (speedy war canoes). The passage between Viti Levu and Vanua Levu still is named Bligh Water.

European sandalwood, copra, and *bêche-de-mer* (sea cucumber) traders settled on Ovalau in the early 1820s and established the first urban-type town in Fiji at Levuka, but for many years the real power lay on Bau, a tiny island just off the eastern coast of Viti Levu. With the help of a Swedish mercenary named Charlie Savage, who supplied the guns, High Chief Tanoa of Bau extended his control over most of western Fiji. Bau's influence grew even more under his son and successor, Cakobau, who rose to the height of power in the 1840s. Cakobau never ruled over all the islands, however, for Enele Ma'afu, a member of Tonga's royal family, invaded the Lau Group in 1848 and exerted control over eastern Fiji. Ma'afu made the conquered Fijian chiefs marry Tongan women, which helps explain why many of Fiji's high chiefs today appear as much Polynesian as Melanesian.

> **Impressions**
>
> *Many of the missionaries were eaten, leading an irreverent planter to suggest that they triumphed by infiltration.*
>
> —James A. Michener, *Return to Paradise,* 1951

Ma'afu also brought along Wesleyan missionaries from Tonga, thus giving the Methodist church a foothold in Fiji (it still is the predominate denomination here). Although Cakobau converted to Christianity, many lesser chiefs, especially those in the mountains, saw the Wesleyan missionaries as a threat to their power and refused to convert or even to allow the missionaries to establish outposts in their villages. Some mountaineers made a meal of the Rev. Thomas Baker when he tried to convert them in 1867 (see "A Holy Meal" box, below).

FIJI BECOMES A COLONY   Cakobau's slide from power began July 4, 1849, when John Brown Williams, the American consul, celebrated the birth of his own nation. A cannon went off and started a fire that burned Williams's house. The Fijians promptly looted the burning building. Williams blamed Cakobau and demanded $5,000 in damages. Within a few years the U.S. claims against the chief totaled more than $40,000, an enormous sum in those days. In the late 1850s, with Ma'afu gaining power in the east, and disorder growing elsewhere in Fiji, Cakobau offered to cede the islands to Great Britain if Queen Victoria would pay the Americans. The British pondered his offer for 4 years before turning him down.

The early European settlers bought about 10 percent of the islands from the Fijians, sometimes fraudulently and often for whiskey and guns (this freehold property is a sore point with some modern Fijians, who would like to have it back). Claims and counterclaims to land ownership swept Fiji to the brink of race war. To avoid anarchy, the Europeans established a national government at Levuka and named Cakobau king of Fiji. Three years later they forced Cakobau to cede the islands to Great Britain. With no price tag attached, the British accepted. The Deed of Cession making Fiji a British colony was signed on October 10, 1874, at Nasovi village near Levuka.

Britain sent Sir Arthur Gordon as the colony's first governor. He allowed the Fijian chiefs to govern their villages and districts as they had done before and to advise him through a Great Council of Chiefs. He declared that native Fijian lands could not be sold, only leased. That decision has to this day helped to protect the Fijians, their land, and their customs, but it has helped fuel bitter animosity on the part of the land-deprived Indians.

Gordon prohibited the planters from using Fijians as laborers (not that many of them had the slightest inclination to work for someone else). When the planters switched to sugarcane in the 1870s, Sir Arthur convinced them to import indentured servants from India. The first 463 East Indians arrived on May 14, 1879 (see "The Islanders," below).

FIJI BECOMES INDEPENDENT   One of the highest-ranking Fijian chiefs, Ratu Sir Lala Sukuna, rose to prominence after World War I. (*Ratu* means "chief" in Fijian.) Born of high chiefly lineage, Ratu Sukuna was educated at Oxford, served in World War I, and worked his way up through the colonial bureaucracy to the post of chairman of the Native Land Trust Board, which governs all communally-owned Fijian land. He used the position as a platform to educate his people and to lay the foundation for the independent state of Fiji. As much as anyone, he was the father of modern, independent Fiji.

The road to independence was anything but smooth. The Indo-Fijians were highly organized, in political parties and trade unions, and they objected to a constitution that would institution-alize Fijian control of the government and Fijian ownership of most of the new nation's land. Key compromises were made in 1969, however, and on October 10, 1970—exactly 96 years after Cakobau signed the Deed of Cession—the Dominion of Fiji became an independent member of the British Commonwealth of Nations.

> **Impressions**
>
> *A hundred years of prodding by the British have failed to make the Fijians see why they should work for money.*
>
> —James A. Michener, *Return to Paradise*, 1951

RAMBO'S COUP   Under the 1970 constitution, Fiji had a Westminster-style Parliament consisting of an elected House of Representatives and a Senate composed of Fijian chiefs. For the first 17 years of independence, the Fijians maintained a majority—albeit a tenuous one—in the House of Representatives and control of the government under the leadership of the late Ratu Sir Kamisese Mara, the country's first prime minister.

Then, in a general election held in April 1987, a coalition of Indians and liberal Fijians voted Ratu Mara and his Alliance party out of power. Although a Fijian became prime minister, he named more Indians than Fijians to his cabinet. Shortly after the election, members of the predominantly Fijian army stormed into Parliament and overthrew the new government. It was the South Pacific's first military coup, and although peaceful, it took nearly everyone by surprise.

The coup leader was Col. Sitiveni Rabuka (pronounced "Ram-*bu-ka*"), whom local wags quickly nicknamed Rambo. A Fijian of nonchiefly lineage, Rabuka immediately became a hero to his "commoner" fellow Fijians. He abrogated the 1970 constitution, declared Fiji to be an independent republic, and set up an interim government with himself as minister of home affairs and army commander. In 1990 he promulgated a new constitution guaranteeing Fijians a parliamentary majority—thereby rankling the Indians. Rabuka's pro-Fijian party won the initial election, but he barely hung onto power in 1994 by forming a coalition with the European, Chinese, and mixed-race general-elector parliamentarians.

Fun Fact **The Count Confounded**

In 1917 Count Felix von Luckner arrived at Wakaya Island off eastern Viti Levu in search of a replacement for his infamous World War I German raider, the *Seeadler,* which had gone aground in the Cook Islands after shelling Papeete on Tahiti. A local constable became suspicious of the armed foreigners and notified the district police inspector. Only Europeans—not Fijians or Indians—could use firearms, so the inspector took a band of unarmed Fijians to Wakaya. Thinking he was up against a much larger armed force, von Luckner unwittingly surrendered.

THE 2000 INSURRECTION   Rabuka also appointed a three-person Constitutional Review Commission, which proposed the present constitution. Ratified in 1998, it led to general elections in 1999. Supported by many Fijians, Labor Party leader Mahendra Chaudhry won an outright majority of parliament and became Fiji's first Indian prime minister.

His tenure was short-lived, however. In May 2000 a disgruntled Fijian businessman named George Speight led a gang of armed henchmen into parliament. Demanding the appointment of an all-Fijian government, they held Chaudhry and several members of parliament hostage for 56 days. While negotiating with Speight with one hand, the army with the other disbanded the constitution and appointed an interim government headed by Fijian economist Laisenia Qarase. Speight released his hostages after being promised amnesty, but the army arrested him 2 weeks later and charged him with treason. Convicted by a civilian court, his death sentence was later commuted to life in prison. A number of other participants were convicted and sent to jail.

Fiji's supreme court then ruled that the 1998 constitution was still in effect and ordered fresh parliamentary elections in 2001, when caretaker leader Qarase became the legal prime minister of a Fijian-dominated government. Chaudhry was returned to parliament as leader of the opposition.

Qarase proposed a "Reconciliation, Tolerance, and Unity" bill, which opponents—including the army—claimed would grant amnesty to Speight and other participants in the 2000 insurrection. The proposed legislation was the most contentious issue in the general elections of May 2006, which returned Qarase's Fijian party to power.

3 The Islanders

Fiji's population was officially 834,494 in 2000, the most recent census. Indigenous Fijians made up 51%, Indo-Fijians 44%, and other Pacific islanders, Chinese, Europeans, and persons of mixed race the other 5%. Thanks to a high Fijian birth rate, the overall population has been rising slightly despite the country's losing thousands of Indo-Fijians since the 1987 military coups.

It's difficult to imagine peoples of two more contrasting cultures living side by side. "Fijians generally perceive Indians as mean and stingy, crafty and demanding to the extent of being considered greedy, inconsiderate and grasping, uncooperative, egotistic, and calculating," wrote Professor Asesela Ravuvu of the University of the South Pacific. On the other hand, he said, Indians see Fijians as *"jungalis"*—poor, backward, naive, foolish, and living on land they will not sell.

Given that these attitudes are not likely to change anytime soon, it is remarkable that Fijians and Indo-Fijians actually manage to coexist. Politically correct Americans may take offense at some things they can hear said in Fiji because racial distinctions are a fact of life here.

From a visitor's standpoint, the famously friendly Fijians give the country its laid-back South Seas charm while providing relatively good service at the hotels. For their part, the Indo-Fijians make this an easy country to visit by providing excellent maintenance of facilities and efficient and inexpensive services, such as transportation.

The 1998 constitution makes everyone, regardless of his or her race, a Fiji Islander.

THE FIJIANS

Today's indigenous Fijians are descended from a Melanesian people who came from the west and began settling here around 500 B.C. Over time they replaced the Polynesians, whose ancestors had arrived some 1,000 years beforehand, but not before adopting much of Polynesian culture and intermarrying enough to give many Fijians lighter skin than that of most other Melanesians, especially in the islands of eastern Fiji near the Polynesian Kingdom of Tonga. (This is less the case in the west and among the hill dwellers, whose ancestors had less contact with Polynesians in ancient times.) Similar differences occur in terms of culture. For example, whereas Melanesians traditionally

---

Fun Fact **A Holy Meal**

When meeting and talking to the smiling Fijians, it's difficult to imagine that hardly more than a century ago their ancestors were among the world's most ferocious cannibals. Today the only vestiges of this past are the four-pronged wooden cannibal forks sold in handicraft shops (they make interesting conversation pieces when used at home to serve hors d'oeuvres).

Yet in the early 1800s, the Fijians were so fierce that Europeans were slow to settle in the islands for fear of literally being turned into a meal. Back then, Fijian society was organized by tribes, which constantly warred with each other, usually with brutal vengeance. The winners hung captured enemy children by their feet from the rigging of their canoes, and they sometimes consecrated new buildings by burying live adult prisoners in holes dug for the support posts.

The ultimate insult, however, was to eat the enemy's flesh. Victorious chiefs were even said to cook and nibble on the fingers or tongues of the vanquished, relishing each bite while the victims watched in agony. "One man actually stood by my side and ate the very eyes out of a roasted skull he had, saying, '*Venaca, venaca,*' that is, very good," wrote William Speiden, the purser on the U.S. exploring expedition that charted Fiji in 1840.

More than 100 white-skinned individuals ended up with their skulls smashed and their bodies baked in an earth oven, including the Rev. Thomas Baker, who attempted to convert the Viti Levu highlanders in 1867. Instead of converting, they killed the reverend, tossed his body into an oven, and made a meal of him.

"Grog" Etiquette

Known as *kava* elsewhere in the South Pacific, the slightly narcotic drink Fijians call *yaqona* (yong-gona) or "grog" rivals Fiji Bitter beer as the national drink. You will likely have half a coconut shell of grog offered—if not shoved in your face—beginning at your hotel's reception desk. Fiji has more "grog shops" than bars.

And thanks to the promotion of *kavalactone,* the active ingredient, as a health-food answer to stress and insomnia in the United States and elsewhere, growing the root is an important part of the economy in the South Pacific. When fears surfaced a few years ago that kava could be linked to liver disease, locals commented that if that was true, then there would be few healthy livers in Fiji!

Yaqona has always played an important ceremonial role in Fijian life. No significant occasion takes place without it, and a *sevusevu* (welcoming) ceremony is usually held for tour groups visiting Fijian villages. Mats are placed on the floor, the participants gather around in a circle, and the yaqona roots are mixed with water and strained through coconut husks into a large carved wooden bowl, called a *tanoa.*

The ranking chief sits next to the tanoa during the welcoming ceremony. He extends in the direction of the guest of honor a cowrie shell attached to one leg of the bowl by a cord of woven coconut fiber. It's extremely impolite to cross the plane of the cord once it has been extended.

The guest of honor (in this case your tour guide) then offers a gift to the village (a kilogram or two of dried grog roots will do these days) and makes a speech explaining the purpose of his visit. The chief then passes the first cup of yaqona to the guest of honor, who claps once, takes the cup in both hands, and gulps down the entire cup of sawdust-tasting liquid in one swallow. Everyone else then claps three times.

Next, each chief drinks a cup, clapping once before bolting it down. Again, everyone else claps three times after each cup is drained. Except for the clapping and formal speeches, everyone remains silent throughout the ceremony, a tradition easily understood considering kava's numbing effect on the lips and tongue.

pick their chiefs by popular consensus, Fijian chiefs hold titles by heredity, in the Polynesian (or more precisely, Tongan) fashion.

Most Fijians still live in small villages along the coast and riverbanks or in the hills, and you will see many traditional thatch *bures,* or houses, scattered in the countryside away from the main roads. Members of each tribe cultivate and grow food crops in small "bush gardens" on plots of communally owned native land assigned to their families. More than 80% of the land in Fiji is owned by Fijians.

A majority of Fijians are Methodists, their forebears having been converted by Wesleyan missionaries who came to the islands in the 19th century. Along with the Great Council of Chiefs, the Methodist Church is a powerful political force.

THE TABUA   The highest symbol of respect among Fijians is the tooth of the sperm whale, known as a *tabua* (pronounced "tam-*bu*-a"). Like large mother-of-pearl shells used in other parts of Melanesia, tabuas in ancient times played a role similar to that of money in modern society and still have various ceremonial uses. They are presented to chiefs as a sign of respect, given as gifts to arrange marriages, offered to friends to show sympathy after the death of a family member, and used as a means to seal a contract or another agreement. It is illegal to export a tabua out of Fiji, and even if you did, the international conventions on endangered species prohibit your bringing them into the United States and most other Western countries.

> **Impressions**
>
> *It is doubtful if anyone but an Indian can dislike Fijians . . . They are one of the happiest peoples on earth and laugh constantly. Their joy in things is infectious; they love practical jokes, and in warfare they are without fear.*
>
> —James A. Michener, *Return to Paradise*, 1951

FIRE WALKING   Legend says that a Fijian god once repaid a favor to a warrior on Beqa island by giving him the ability to walk unharmed on fire. His descendants, all members of the Sawau tribe on Beqa, still walk across stones heated to white-hot by a bonfire—but usually for the entertainment of tourists at the hotels rather than for a particular religious purpose.

Traditionally, the participants—all male—had to abstain from women and coconuts for 2 weeks before the ceremony. If they partook of either, they would suffer burns to their feet. Naturally a priest (some would call him a witch doctor) would recite certain incantations to make sure the coals were hot and the gods were at bay and not angry enough to scorch the soles.

Today's fire walking is a bit touristy but still worth seeing. If you don't believe the stones are hot, go ahead and touch one of them—but do it gingerly.

Some Indians in Fiji engage in fire walking, but it's strictly for religious purposes.

FIJIAN ETIQUETTE   Fijian villages are easy to visit, but keep in mind that to the people who live in them, the entire village—not just an individual's house—is home. In your native land, you wouldn't walk into a stranger's living room without being invited, so find someone and ask permission before traipsing into a Fijian village. The Fijians are accommodating people, and it's unlikely they will say no; in fact, they may ask you to stay for a meal or stage a small yaqona ceremony in your honor (see "Grog" Etiquette box above). They are very tied to tradition, however, so ask first.

If you are invited to stay or eat in the village, a small gift to the chief is appropriate; F$10 (US$6) per person or a handful of dried kava root from the local market will do. The gift should be given to the chief or highest-ranking person present to

---

Moments   **Meeting the Friendly Fijians**

The indigenous Fijians are justly renowned for their friendliness to strangers, and many Indo-Fijians are as well educated and informed as anyone in the South Pacific. Together, these two peoples are fun to meet, whether it be over a hotel desk or while riding with them in one of their fume-belching buses.

accept it. Sometimes it helps to explain that it is a gift to the village and not payment for services rendered, especially if it's money you're giving.

Only chiefs are allowed to wear hats and sunglasses in Fijian villages, so it's good manners for visitors to take theirs off. Shoulders must be covered at all times. Fijians go barefoot and walk slightly stooped in their bures. Men sit cross-legged on the floor; women sit with their legs to the side. They don't point at one another with hands, fingers, or feet, nor do they touch each other's heads or hair. They greet each other and strangers with a big smile and a sincere *"Bula."*

THE INDO-FIJIANS

The *Leonidas,* a labor transport ship, arrived at Levuka from Calcutta on May 14, 1879, and landed 463 indentured servants destined to work Fiji's sugar-cane fields. As more than 60,000 Indians would do over the next 37 years, these first immigrants signed agreements (*girmits,* they called them) requiring that they work in Fiji for 5 years; they would be free to return to India after 5 more years. Most of them labored in the cane fields for the initial term of their girmits, living in "coolie lines" of squalid shacks hardly better than the poverty-stricken conditions most left behind in India.

After the initial 5 years, however, they were free to seek work on their own. Many leased plots of land from the Fijians and began planting sugarcane or raising cattle. To this day most of Fiji's sugar crop, the country's most important agricultural export, is produced on small leased plots. Other Indo-Fijians went into business in the growing cities and towns and, joined in the early 1900s by an influx of business-oriented Indians, thereby founded Fiji's modern merchant and professional classes.

> **Impressions**
>
> *The question of what to do with these clever Indians of Fiji is the most acute problem in the Pacific today. Within 10 years it will become a world concern.*
>
> —James A. Michener, *Return to Paradise,* 1951

Of the immigrants who came from India between 1879 and 1916, when the indenturing system ended, some 85% were Hindus, 14% were Muslims, and the remaining 1% were Sikhs and Christians. Fiji offered these adventurers far more opportunities than caste-controlled India. In fact, the caste system was scrapped very quickly by the Hindus in Fiji, and, for the most part, the violent relations between Hindus and Muslims that racked India were put aside on the islands.

Only a small minority of the Indo-Fijians went home after their girmits expired. They tended then—as now—to live in the towns and villages, and in the "Sugar Belt" along the drier north and west coasts of Viti Levu and Vanua Levu. Hindu and Sikh temples and Muslim mosques abound in these areas, and places such as Ba and Tavua look like small towns on the Indian subcontinent. On the southern coasts and in the mountains, the population is overwhelmingly Fijian. Indo-Fijians constituted more than half of Fiji's population prior to the 1987 and 2000 coups, but emigration (mostly to Australia, New Zealand, Canada, and the U.S.) has reduced their share to around 44%.

4 Languages

Fiji has three official languages. To greatly oversimplify the situation, the Fijians speak Fijian, the Indians speak Hindi, and they speak English to each other. Schoolchildren are taught in their native language until they are proficient (but not necessarily fluent) in English, which thereafter is the medium of instruction. Although you may not get into serious conversations in English with everyone here, you will have little trouble getting around and enjoying the country.

FIJIAN

Fijian is similar to the Polynesian languages spoken in Tahiti, the Cook Islands, Samoa, and Tonga in that it uses vowel sounds similar to those in Latin, French, Italian, and Spanish: *a* as in b*a*d, *e* as in s*a*y, *i* as in b*ee*, *o* as in g*o*, and *u* as in kangar*oo*.

Some Fijian consonants, however, sound very different from their counterparts in English, Latin, or any other language. In devising a written form of Fijian, the early Wesleyan missionaries decided to use some familiar Roman consonants in unfamiliar ways. It would have been easier for English speakers to read Fijian had the missionaries used a combination of consonants—*th*, for example—for the Fijian sounds. Their main purpose, however, was to teach Fijians to read and write their own language. Because the Fijians separate all consonant sounds with vowels, writing two consonants together confused them.

The missionaries came up with the following usage: *b* sounds like *mb* (as in reme*mb*er), *c* sounds like *th* (as in *th*at), *d* sounds like *nd* (as in Su*nd*ay), *g* sounds like *ng* (as in si*ng*er), and *q* sounds like *ng + g* (as in fi*ng*er).

The unusual pronunciation is most evident in Fijian names such as Nadi, which is pronounced *Nahn-di*. There are many other names of people and places that are equally or even more confusing.

Here are some Fijian names with their unusual pronunciations:

Ba	mBah	**Labasa**	Lam-*ba*-sa
Bau	mBau	**Mamanuca**	Ma-ma-*nu*-tha
Beqa	*mBeng*-ga	**Nadi**	*Nahn*-di
Buca	*mBu*-tha	**Tabua**	*Tam*-bua
Cakobau	Thack-*om*-bau	**Toberua**	Tom-*bay*-rua
Korotogo	Ko-ro-*ton*-go	**Tubakula**	Toom-ba-*ku*-la

You are likely to hear these Fijian words and phrases used during your stay:

English	Fijian	Pronunciation
hello	**bula**	*boo*-lah
hello (formal)	**ni sa bula**	nee sahm *boo*-lah
good morning	**ni sa yadra**	nee sah *yand*-rah
good night	**ni sa moce**	nee sah *mo*-thay
thank you	**vinaka**	vee-*nah*-kah
thank you very much	**vinaka vaka levu**	vee-*nah*-kah *vah*-ka *lay*-voo
house/bungalow	**bure**	*boo*-ray
tapa cloth	**masi**	*mah*-see
sarong	**sulu**	*sue*-loo

FIJI HINDI

The common everyday language spoken among the Indo-Fijians is a tongue peculiar to Fiji. Although it is based on Hindustani, it is different from that language as spoken in India. It grew out of the need for a common language among the immigrants who came from various parts of the subcontinent and spoke some of the many languages and dialects found in India and Pakistan. Thus it includes words from Hindi, Urdu, Tamil Nadu, a variety of Indian dialects, and even English and Fijian. You'll see what I mean by tuning into a Hindi radio station. If you want to impress the Indo-Fijians, try these phrases in Fiji Hindi:

English	Fiji Hindi	Pronunciation
hello and good-bye	**namaste**	na-*mas*-tay
how are you?	**kaise?**	ka-*ee*-say
good	**accha**	*ach*-cha
I'm okay	**Thik hai**	teak high
right or okay	**rait**	right

5 Visitor Information & Entry Requirements

VISITOR INFORMATION

The **Fiji Visitors Bureau,** P.O. Box 9217, Nadi Airport, Fiji Islands (② **672 2433;** fax 672 0141; www.bulafiji.com), provides maps, brochures, and other materials from the bureau's head office in the Colonial Plaza shopping center, on the Queens Road in Namaka, about halfway between Nadi Airport and Nadi Town. It also has an information desk in a historic colonial house at the corner of Thomson and Scott streets in the heart of Suva (② **330 2433**).

The bureau's award-winning website is a trove of up-to-date information (weather and currency exchange rates, for example) and is linked to the home pages of the country's airlines, tour operators, attractions, and hotels. It also has a directory of e-mail addresses.

Other Fiji Visitors Bureau offices are:

- **United States and Canada:** 5777 West Century Blvd., Suite 220, Los Angeles, CA 90045 (② **800/932-3454** or 310/568-1616; fax 310/670-2318; www. bulafijinow.com)
- **Australia:** Level 12, St. Martins Tower, 31 Market St., Sydney, NSW 2000 (② **02/9264-3399;** fax 02/9264-3060; www.bulafiji-au.com)
- **New Zealand:** 33 Scanlon St., Grey Lynn (P.O. Box 1179), Auckland (② **09/ 373-2533;** fax 09/376-4720; info@bulafiji.co.nz)
- **Germany:** Petersburger Strasse 94, 10247 Berlin (② **30/4225-6026;** fax 30/ 4225-6287; www.bulafiji.de).
- **Japan:** Noa Building, 14th Floor, 3–5, 2 Chome, Azabuudai, Minato-Ku, Tokyo 106 (② **03/3587-2038;** fax 03/3587-2563; www.bulafiji-jp.com)
- **United Kingdom:** Northcut House, 36 Southwark, Bridge Rd., London SE1 9EU (② **207/202-6369;** fax 207/928-0722; fiji@hillsbalfour.com).
- **Korea:** Suite 4008, Korea World Trade Center, Kangnam-gu, Samsung-dong, 159 Seoul (② **822/3452-5093;** fax 822/561-6921; www.bulafiji.or.kr).

If you have a TV in your room, you can tune in to the advertiser-supported **Visitor Information Network (VIN),** usually on channel 10, for tips about what to do and where to dine.

ENTRY REQUIREMENTS

Visitor permits good for stays of up to 4 months are issued upon arrival to citizens of the United States; all Commonwealth countries; most European, South American, and South Pacific island nations; and Mexico, Japan, Israel, Pakistan, South Korea, Thailand, Tunisia, and Turkey. You must have a passport valid for 6 months beyond your visit and an onward or return airline ticket.

Citizens of all other countries must apply for visas in advance from the Fiji embassies or consulates. In the United States, contact the **Embassy of Fiji,** 2233 Wisconsin Ave., Suite 240, NW, Washington, DC 20007 (© 202/337-8320; fax 202/337-1996; www.fijiembassy.org). Other Fiji embassies or high commissions are in Canberra, Australia; Wellington, New Zealand; London, England; Brussels, Belgium; Tokyo, Japan; Kuala Lumpur, Malaysia; Port Moresby, Papua New Guinea; and Beijing, China. Check your local phone book.

Persons wishing to remain longer than 4 months must apply for extensions from the **Immigration Department,** whose primary offices are at the Nadi International Airport terminal (© 672 2454; www.fiji.gov.fj) and in the Labour Department building on Victoria Parade in downtown Suva (© 321 1775).

Vaccinations are not required unless you have been in a yellow fever or cholera area shortly before arriving in Fiji.

Customs allowances are 200 cigarettes; 2 liters of liquor, beer, or wine; and F$400 (US$240) worth of other goods in addition to personal belongings. Pornography is prohibited. Firearms and nonprescription narcotic drugs are strictly prohibited and subject to heavy fines and jail terms. Pets will be quarantined. Any fresh fruits and vegetables must be declared and are subject to inspection and fumigation.

Note: Customs will x-ray *all* of your luggage upon arrival.

6 Money

The national currency is the Fiji dollar, which is divided into 100 cents and trades independently on the foreign exchange markets. The Fiji dollar is abbreviated "FID" by the banks and airlines, but I use **F$** in this book. Some hotels and resorts quote their rates in U.S. dollars, indicated here by **US$.**

As we went to press, one Fiji dollar was worth slightly less than US60¢. You find the rate at **www.xe.com**, a currency conversion site.

HOW TO GET LOCAL CURRENCY   An **ANZ Bank** branch in the international arrivals concourse at Nadi International Airport is open 24 hours a day, 7 days a week. There's an ATM on the wall outside the branch, where you can draw Fijian currency by using MasterCard or Visa credit or debit cards.

ANZ Bank, Westpac Bank, and **Colonial National Bank** have offices throughout the country where currency and traveler's checks can be exchanged. They all have

The Fiji Dollar & the U.S. Dollar

At this writing, F$1 = approximately US60¢ (or US$1 = approximately F$1.66), the rate of exchange used to calculate the U.S. dollar prices given in chapters 9 through 11. This rate may change by the time you visit, so use the following table only as a guide:

F$	US$	F$	US$
.25	.15	15	9.00
.50	.30	20	12.00
.75	.45	25	15.00
1	.60	30	18.00
2	1.20	35	21.00
3	1.80	40	24.00
4	2.40	45	27.00
5	3.00	50	30.00
6	3.60	75	45.00
7	4.20	100	60.00
8	4.80	125	75.00
9	5.40	150	90.00
10	6.00	200	120.00

ATMs at their Nadi and Suva offices and at their branches in Savusavu. Elsewhere bring credit cards, cash, and travelers checks. Banking hours nationwide are Monday to Thursday from 9:30am to 3pm and Friday from 9:30am to 4pm.

You can get a better rate for traveler's checks at **GlobalEX** offices in Nadi Town and Suva. See the "Fast Facts" sections in chapters 5 and 6 for specific currency exchange locations.

CREDIT CARDS   American Express, MasterCard, and Visa are widely accepted by the hotels, car-rental firms, travel and tour companies, large stores, and most restaurants. Don't count on using a Diners Club card outside the hotels. Leave your Discover card at home.

7 When to Go

THE CLIMATE

Although global warming has made the climate more unpredictable than in the past, the prevailing southeast trade winds temper Fiji's warm, humid, tropical climate during most of the year. Average high temperatures range from 83°F (28°C) during the austral winter (June–Sept) to 88°F (31°C) during the summer months (Dec–Mar). Evenings are in the warm and comfortable 70s (21°C–28°C) throughout the year.

The islands receive the most rain during the austral summer, but the amount depends on which side of each island the measurement is taken on. The north and west coasts tend to be drier (and warmer), and the east and south coasts wetter (and somewhat cooler but more humid). Nadi, on the west side of Viti Levu, gets considerably less rain than does Suva, on the southeast side (some 200 in. a year). Consequently, most of Fiji's resorts are on the western side of Viti Levu. Even during the wetter months, however, periods of intense tropical sunshine usually follow the rain showers.

Fiji is in the heart of the South Pacific cyclone belt and receives its share of hurricanes between November and April. Fiji's Meteorological Service is excellent at tracking hurricanes and issuing timely warnings, and the local travel industry is very adept at preparing for them. I've been through a few Fiji cyclones, and I've never let the thought of one keep me from returning every chance I get.

HOLIDAYS & EVENTS

Unlike other South Pacific island countries, Fiji has no grand national festivals around which to plan a visit. One exception is the annual **South Pacific World Music Festival,** which brings noted regional artists to Savusavu in late November or early December. Contact the Fiji Visitors Bureau or the Savusavu Tourism Association (www. fiji-savusavu.com) for details.

More likely to impact your visit is a seemingly interminable list of national holidays—so many of them, in fact, that the government pared the list a few years ago in a effort to improve the national economy.

At press time, all banks, government offices, and most private businesses are closed for New Year's Day, Good Friday, Easter Saturday, Easter Monday, Ratu Sukuna Day (May 30 or the Mon closest thereto), The Prophet Mohammed's Birthday (a Mon in mid-July), Fiji Day (the Mon closest to Oct 10), Deepawali (an Indian festival in late Oct or early Nov), Christmas Day, and December 26 (Boxing Day).

Banks take an additional holiday on the first Monday in August, and some businesses also close for various Hindu and Muslim holy days. And if Fiji wins the annual Hong Kong Sevens rugby tournament, don't expect anyone to be at work the next day!

8 Getting There & Getting Around

GETTING THERE

Air New Zealand, Air Pacific, and **Qantas Airways** fly to Fiji from North America, Australia, and New Zealand. **Pacific Blue** and **Freedom Airways** come here from Australia and New Zealand. See "Getting There & Getting Around" in chapter 2 for details.

ARRIVING & DEPARTING

ARRIVING AT NADI   Most international flights arrive at and depart from **Nadi International Airport,** about 11km (7 miles) north of Nadi Town. A few flights arrive from Auckland, Samoa, and Tonga at Nausori Airport, some 19km (12 miles) from Suva on the opposite side of the island. Both airports are used for domestic flights. They are the only lighted airstrips in the country, which means you don't fly domestically after dark. Because many international flights arrive during the night, at least a 1-night stay-over in Nadi will likely be necessary before you leave for another island.

Arriving passengers can purchase duty-free items at two shops in the baggage claim area before clearing Customs (they are in fierce competition, so it will pay to shop between them and ask for discounts). Imported liquor is expensive in Fiji, so if you drink, don't hesitate to buy two bottles here.

After clearing Customs, you emerge onto an air-conditioned concourse lined on both sides by airline offices, travel and tour companies, car-rental firms, and a 24-hour-a-day branch of the **ANZ Bank** (see "Money," above).

Touts for the inexpensive hotels will be milling about, offering free transportation to their establishments. The larger hotels will also have transportation available for their guests.

Taxis will be lined up to the right outside the concourse (see the table in "Getting Around," below, for fares to the hotels).

Local buses to Nadi and Lautoka pass the airport on the Queen's Road every day. To get to one, walk straight out of the concourse, across the parking lot, and through the gate to the road. Driving in Fiji is on the left, so buses heading for Nadi and its hotels stop on the opposite side, next to Raffles' Gateway Hotel; those going to Lautoka stop on the airport side of the road. You will see the covered bus stands. See "Getting Around Nadi" in chapter 5for details.

The Nadi domestic terminal and the international check-in counters are to the right of the arrival concourse as you exit Customs (or to the left, if you are arriving from the main road). There are several **snack bars** near the domestic counters, including the excellent **Republic of Cappuccino,** the local version of Starbucks.

The Left Luggage counter at the far end of the departures concourse provides **baggage storage** for about F$3 to F$6 (US$1.80–US$3.60) a day, depending on the size of the baggage. The counter is open 24 hours daily. The hotels all have baggage-storage rooms and will keep your extra stuff for free. The Left Luggage also has showers and rents towels.

A **post office,** in a separate building across the entry road from the main terminal, is open Monday to Friday from 8am to 4pm.

ARRIVING AT SUVA   Suva is served by **Nausori Airport,** on the flat plains of the Rewa River delta about 19km (12 miles) from downtown. The small terminal has a snack bar but few other amenities. Taxis between Nausori and downtown Suva cost about F$25 (US$15) each way.

DEPARTING   Fiji has no **departure tax** for either international or domestic flights.

Nadi Airport has a modern, air-conditioned international departure lounge with a currency exchange counter, snack bar, showers, and the largest duty-free shops in the South Pacific. Duty-free prices, however, are higher here than you'll pay elsewhere in the country, and there is no haggling.

Nausori Airport near Suva has a small duty-free shop in its departure lounge. Some of Air Pacific's flights bound from Samoa and Tonga to Nadi stop first at Nausori, where you will deplane and clear immigration.

GETTING AROUND
Fiji has an extensive and reliable transportation network of airlines, rental cars, taxis, ferries, and both long-distance and local buses. This section deals primarily with getting

---

Tips **Avoid Backtracking**

Most flights from Nadi to Taveuni stop in Savusavu going or coming, so don't let an uninformed travel agent book you back to Nadi or Suva in order to get from Taveuni to Savusavu.

> ## *Tips* Weigh Your Bag & Reconfirm Your Flight
>
> Baggage allowances on domestic flights may be 10 kilograms (22 lb.) instead of the 20 kilograms (44 lb.) allowed on international flights. Check with the airlines to avoid showing up with too much luggage. And always reconfirm your domestic return flights as soon as possible after arriving at your destination. Also, check in when the airlines tell you to; planes sometimes arrive and depart a few minutes early.

from one island or major area to another; see the "Getting Around" sections in chapters 5 and 6 for details on transportation within the local areas.

BY PLANE & HELICOPTER

The easiest way to get around the country is to fly with **Fiji Airlines** (© 800/ 294-4864 or 672 3016 in Nadi, 331 5755 in Suva; www.airpacific.com). or **Air Fiji** (© 877/247-3454 or 672 2521 in Nadi, 331 3666 in Suva; www.airfiji.net) Fiji Airlines is a subsidiary of Air Pacific, Fiji's international airline (see "Getting There & Getting Around," in chapter 2), which recently bought out Sun Air, a long-time domestic carrier. Both fly small planes from Nadi to the tourist destinations and have offices in the international concourse at Nadi International Airport and on Victoria Parade in Suva.

One-way fares as I write are about F$70 (US$42) to Malololailai Island (Plantation Island and Musket Cove resorts); F$85 (US$51) to Mana Island; F$156 (US$94) to Suva; F$220 (US$132) to Savusavu; and F$270 (US$162) to Taveuni. Suva to Taveuni costs about F$196 (US$118). You can save a bundle by booking roundtrip fares; ask the airlines for specifics.

If you're going to Suva, Taveuni, and Savusavu, you also can save with an **Air Pass** from Air Fiji. Any four flights cost US$270 if purchased in North America (the passes are not available in Fiji), with additional flights at US$90 each. Call or go to Air Fiji's website for details.

Pacific Islands Seaplanes (© 672 5643; www.fijiseaplanes.com) provides service throughout Fiji in its small, Canadian-built floatplanes, which use wheels to take off from Nadi airport and floats to land on water at the Mamanuca resorts. In other words, you can connect directly at the airport. **Turtle Airways** (© 877/SEE-FIJI or 672 2988 in Nadi; www.turtleairways.com) flies small seaplanes from Wailolaloa Beach on Nadi Bay to the Mamanuca and Yasawa resorts. Turtle has a special F$200 (US$120) one-way fare for backpackers staying at some hostels in the Yasawa Islands. **Island Hoppers** (© 672 0140; www.helicopters.com.fj) also will whisk you to the Mamanucas in one of its helicopters. If you have to ask how much these rides cost, you can't afford it.

BY RENTAL CAR

Rental cars are widely available in Fiji. Each company has its own pricing policy, and you can frequently find discounts, special deals, and some give-and-take bargaining over long-term and long-distance use. All major companies, and a few not so major, have offices in the commercial concourse at Nadi International Airport, so it's easy to shop around. Most are open 7 days a week, some for 24 hours a day. Give careful consideration to how far you will drive; it's 197km (118 miles) from Nadi Airport to

Suva, so an unlimited kilometer rate could work to your advantage if you plan to drive to Suva.

Avis (© **800/331-1212,** or 672 2233 in Nadi; www.avis.com.fj) has more than 50% of the business here, and for good reason: The Toyota dealer is the local agent, so it has the newest and best-maintained fleet. In addition to the office at Nadi Airport, Avis can be found in Suva (© **331 3833**), in Korolevu on the Coral Coast (© **653 0176**), and at several hotels.

The local Mazda and Suzuki dealer operates **Budget Rent-A-Car** (© **800/ 527-0700** or 672 2735; www.budget.com), so it also has good vehicles. Budget also is on Denarau Island (© **675 0888**), Suva (© **331 5899**), Sigatoka (© **650 9886**), Savusavu (© **881 1999**), and Taveuni (© **888 0291**).

Thrifty Car Rental (© **800/367-2277,** or 672 2935 in Nadi; www.thrifty.com), which is handled in Fiji by Rosie the Travel Service, also is good, with rates and cars comparable to Avis's.

Other international agencies here are **Hertz** (© **800/654-3131** or 672 3466; www. hertz.com), and **Europcar** (© **800/227-7368** or 672 5957; www.europcar.com).

The most reliable local companies are **Khan's Rental Cars** (© **679 0617** or 338 5033 in Suva; www.khansrental.com.fj) and **Carpenters Rentals** (© **672 2772,** or 332 8628 in Suva; rentals@carpenters.com.fj). I do not rent from other "kick-the-tires" local companies.

Rates at all range from about F$125 (US$75) upwards per day with unlimited kilometers. Add about F$20 (US$12) a day to reduce your collision damage liability. Your home **insurance** policy might cover any damages that occur in Fiji, but I strongly recommend getting local coverage when you rent a car. Even if you do, most policies require you to pay the first F$1,000 (US$600) or more of damages in any event.

All renters must be at least 21 years old, and a few companies require them to be at least 25 or have at least 2 years driving experience.

DRIVING RULES   Your valid home driver's license will be honored in Fiji. **Driving is on the left-hand side of the road. Seat belts** are mandatory. **Speed limits** are 80kmph (48 mph) on the open road and 50kmph (30 mph) in the towns and other built-up areas. Driving while talking on a **cellphone** is illegal. You must **stop for pedestrians** in all marked crosswalks.

Tips **Watch Out for Cows, Horses & Road Humps!**

Most roads in Fiji are narrow, poorly maintained, and crooked. Not all local drivers are well trained, experienced, or skilled, and some of them (including bus drivers) go much too fast for the conditions. Consequently, you should **drive defensively** at all times. Constantly be alert for potholes, landslides, hairpin curves, and various stray animals—cows and horses are a very real danger, especially at night.

Also keep an eye out for speed bumps known in Fiji as road humps. Most Fijian villages have them. Although big signs made to resemble traditional Fijian war clubs announce when you're entering and leaving villages on the Queen's Road, there are usually road humps between the clubs, so slow down! The humps are large enough to do serious damage to the bottom of a car, and no local rental insurance covers that.

Driving under the influence of alcohol or other drugs is a criminal offense in Fiji, and the police frequently throw up roadblocks and administer Breathalyzer tests to all drivers. Even if I have a rental, I take a taxi home after a session with friends at a local bar.

Gasoline (petrol) is readily available at service stations in all the main towns. Expect to pay about twice what you would pay in the United States and Canada, about the same as elsewhere.

BY BUS

Buses are plentiful and inexpensive in Fiji, and it's possible to go all the way around Viti Levu on them. I did it once by taking the Fiji Express from Nadi to Suva one morning, a local express to Rakiraki the next morning, and then another express to Lautoka and a local back to Nadi.

Best is the air-conditioned **Fiji Express** (© **672 3105** in Nadi, 331 2287 in Suva), which operates daily between Nadi airport and Suva. One bus leaves Nadi airport daily at 7:30am and stops at the major hotels along the Queen's Road before arriving at Suva about 11:30am. It departs Suva at 4:30pm and returns to Nadi at 8pm. Another bus begins its daily runs at 7:30am from the Holiday Inn Suva and arrives in Nadi about 11:30am. It begins its return to Suva at 1pm, arriving in the capital about 5pm. One-way fares run up to F$25 (US$15), depending on how far you go. You can book at any hotel tour desk.

Sunbeam Transport Ltd. (© **666 2822** in Lautoka, or 338 2704 in Suva) and **Pacific Transport Ltd.** (© **670 0044** in Nadi, or 330 4366 in Suva) operate express and regular buses going all the way around Viti Levu. They all stop at the domestic terminal at Nadi Airport and the markets at Nadi Town, Sigatoka, and Navua. The express buses take about 4 hours between Nadi and Suva, compared to 5 hours on the local "stages." All these buses cater to local residents, do not take reservations, and have no air-conditioning. The Nadi–Suva fare is about F$10 (US$6), express or local.

In addition to Sunbeam Transport Ltd., **Reliance Transport Bus Service** (© **666 3059** in Lautoka, or 338 2296 in Suva) and **Akbar Buses Ltd.** (© **669 4760** in Rakiraki) have express and local service between Lautoka and Suva via the King's Road. The Lautoka–Suva fare is about F$13 (US$8).

Fume-belching **local buses** use the produce markets as their terminals. The older buses have side windows made of canvas panels that are rolled down during inclement weather (they usually fly out the sides and flap in the wind like great skirts). They run every few minutes along the Queen's Road between Lautoka and Nadi Town, passing the airport and most of the hotels and restaurants along the way (see "Getting Around Nadi," in chapter 5).

Minivans scoot along between the Nadi market and Rodwell Road, just around the corner from the Suva Municipal Market. Those with yellow license tags with the prefix "LM" (licensed minivan) are regulated by the government. Others should be considered unsafe.

BY TAXI

Taxis are as abundant in Fiji as taxi meters are scarce. Some of the Nadi Airport taxi drivers have allegedly taken advantage of naive tourists, so make sure to settle on a fare to your destination before setting out (see the distance chart below). Some drivers will complain about short fares and will badger you for more business later on during your stay; politely ignore these entreaties.

> ⌒Tips **It Never Hurts to Bargain**
>
> In Nadi and on the Coral Coast, you will see the same taxi drivers stationed out-side your hotel every day. Usually they are paid on a salaried rather than a fare basis, so they may be willing to spend more time than usual showing you around. Also, they might charge you less than the government-regulated fares for long-distance trips, such as from Nadi to the Coral Coast or Suva, because many would rather earn one big fare a day than several small ones. It never hurts to bargain politely.

Not to be confused with minibuses, **"share taxis"** or "rolling taxis"—those not oth-erwise occupied—pick up passengers at bus stops and charge the bus fare. They are particularly good value on long-distance trips. A taxi returning to Suva, for example, will stop by the Nadi Town market and pick up a load of passengers at the bus fare rather than drive back to the capital empty. Ask around the local market bus stops if share taxis are available. You'll meet some wonderful Fijians that way.

Although the government sets all taxi fares, it has not raised them despite skyrock-eting fuel prices. Accordingly, many drivers will ask for a few dollars more than the official fare. Even if they don't, I usually give them a small tip anyway—provided they haven't pestered me or blared Indian music from their radios. The following are dis-tances from Nadi International Airport via the Queen's Road and the official govern-ment-regulated taxi fares:

From Nadi Airport to:	km	Miles	Approx. Taxi Fare
Tanoa/Mocambo Hotels	1.3	0.8	F$3.00 (US$1.80)
Skylodge Hotel	3.3	2.0	F$4.00 (US$2.40)
Dominion/Sandalwood Inn/ West Motor Inn	5.2	3.1	F$5.00 (US$3.00)
Sheraton/Denarau Island	15.0	9.3	F$20.00 (US$12.00)
Nadi Town	9.0	5.4	F$7.00 (US$4.20)
Fijian Resort	60.0	36.0	F$55.00 (US$33.00)
Sigatoka	70.0	42.0	F$60.00 (US$36.00)
Outrigger Reef Resort	78.0	46.8	F$65.00 (US$39.00)
Hideaway Resort	92.0	55.2	F$68.00 (US$40.80)
The Warwick Fiji	104.0	62.4	F$80.00 (US$48.00)
Pacific Harbour	148.0	88.8	F$145.00 (US$87.00)
Suva	197.0	118.2	F$165 (US$99.00)

BY FERRY

As an alternative to flying, you can take one of the ferries that run between the main islands. The schedules can change abruptly depending on the weather and the condi-tion of the ships, however, so I don't recommend them unless you have unlimited time. Call the operators for the latest information.

During my recent visit, **Suilven Shipping Ltd.** (© **331 8247** in Suva; www. suilvenshipping.com) was operating the cleanest and most reliable ferry between Suva, Savusavu, and Taveuni. It was fully air-conditioned and had economy and first-class lounges in addition to a deluxe "Prime Minister's Cabin." It departed Suva thrice weekly, usually on Monday, Wednesday, and Friday. Fares for the 11-hour run to Savusavu started at F$52 (US$31).

Venu Shipping Ltd. (© **339 5000** in Suva) was running the *Sinu-a-Wasa Tolu* between Suva and Savusavu three times a week, with extensions to Taveuni twice a week. Both first- and economy-class cabins are air-conditioned and have airline-style seats. Fares from Suva to Savusavu began at F$39 (US$24) for economy. You can book at Tairoa's Travel in Suite 8, Epworth House, Nina Street in Suva (© **330 5889**).

Patterson Shipping Services (© **331 5644** in Suva; patterson@connect.com.fj) has bus–ferry connections from Natovi Wharf (north of Suva on eastern Viti Levu) to Buresala Landing on Ovalau and to Nabouwalu on Vanua Levu. You connect by bus from Suva to Natovi, from Buresala to Levuka, and from Nabouwalu to Labasa (local buses connect Labasa to Savusavu). The Suva–Levuka fare costs about F$25 (US$15), while the Suva–Labasa fare is about F$45 (US$27). Patterson's office is in Suite 1–2, Epworth House, Nina Street in Suva.

Based at Taveuni, the small ferry *Amazing Grace* (© **888 0320** on Taveuni, 927 1372 in Savusavu,) crosses the Somosomo Strait between Buca Bay on Vanua Levu and Waiyevo on Taveuni. One-way fare is F$20 (US$12), including a bus ride from Savusavu to Buca Bay.

FAST FACTS: Fiji

The following facts apply to Fiji in general. For more specific information, see the "Fast Facts" sections in chapters 5 and 6.

American Express Fiji does not have a full-service American Express representative.

Business Hours Stores are generally open Monday to Friday from 8am to 4:30pm, although many close for lunch from 1 to 2pm, and many stay open until 5:30pm. Saturday hours are from 8:30am to noon in town, but many sub-urban stores stay open until 6pm and even 8pm. Shops in most hotels stay open until 9pm every day. Government office hours are Monday to Thursday from 8am to 1pm and 2 to 4:30pm, Friday from 8am to 1pm and 2 to 4pm.

Camera/Film **Caines Photofast,** the largest processor of Kodak films, has shops in the main towns.

Climate See "When to Go," earlier in this chapter.

Clothing Modest dress is the order of the day, particularly in the villages. As a rule, don't leave the hotel swimming pool or the beach in bathing suits or other skimpy attire. That includes low-slung pants and shorts which show everything from your navel down to your you-know-what. If you want to run around half naked, go to Tahiti, where the French think it's all right. The Fijians do not. Do not enter a Fijian village wearing a hat or sunglasses, or with your shoulders uncovered.

Fijian men and women wear *sulus,* the wraparound skirts known as *pareus* in Tahiti and the Cook Islands and *lava-lavas* in the Samoas. Fijian women wear *chambas,* or hip-length blouses, over their sulus. Many Indian women wear saris, lengths of cloth wrapped and pleated around the body.

Drug Laws Marijuana is grown illegally up in the hills, but one drive past the Suva Gaol will convince you not to get caught buying it—or smuggling narcotics or dangerous drugs into Fiji.

Drugstores The main towns have reasonably well-stocked drugstores. Their medicines are likely to be from Australia or New Zealand. The large Morris Hedstrom department stores throughout Fiji carry a wide range of toiletries, including Coppertone, Colgate, and many other brands that are familiar to Americans.

Electricity Electric current in Fiji is 240 volts, 50 cycles. Many hotels have converters for 110-volt shavers, but these are not suitable for hair dryers. The plugs are the angled two-prong types used in Australia and New Zealand. Outlets have separate on/off switches mounted next to them.

E-mail Most hotels and resorts will send and receive e-mail for their guests. Cybercafes in Nadi, Suva, and Savusavu have computer terminals, as does **Connect Internet Services** (or simply "Connect" to the locals), Fiji's major Internet service provider (✆ **670 7359** in Nadi, 330 0100 in Suva; www.connect.com.fj). No U.S. Internet service provider has a local access number in Fiji. If you take your laptop, you can sign up for temporary dial-up access through Connect. See the "Fast Facts" section in chapter 5 for Connect's locations in Nadi Town and Suva. There's a F$33 (US$20) fee for 1 month's access, plus a F8¢ (US5¢) a minute access fee, which will be billed to your hotel room. (Be careful, for some hotels add a whopping service fee on top of Connect's charges.) See the "Configuring Your Laptop" box in chapter 2 for how to set up your computer.

Embassies/Consulates The **U.S. Embassy** is at 31 Loftus St., Suva (✆ **331 4466**; www.amembassy-fiji.gov). Other major diplomatic missions in Suva are **Australia**, 37 Princes Rd., Tamavua (✆ **338 2211**); **New Zealand,** 10th Floor, Reserve Bank of Fiji Bldg., Pratt St. (✆ **331 1422**); **United Kingdom,** Victoria House, 47 Gladstone Rd. (✆ **331 1033**); **Japan,** 2nd Floor, Dominion House, Thomson St. (✆ **330 2122**); **France,** 7th Floor, Dominion House, Thomson St. (✆ **331 2233**); **People's Republic of China,** 147 Queen Elizabeth Dr. (✆ **330 0215**); and **South Korea,** 8th Floor, Vanua House, Victoria Parade (✆ **330 0977**).

Emergencies The emergency telephone number for **fire** and **ambulance** is ✆ **911** throughout Fiji. The **police** emergency number is **917.**

Firearms Guns are illegal in Fiji, and persons found with them could be fined severely and sentenced to jail.

Gambling There are no casinos in Fiji but you can play the local lottery.

Healthcare Medical and dental care in Fiji are not up to the standards common in the industrialized world. Most hotels have private physicians on call or can refer one. Doctors are listed at the beginning of the White Pages section of the Fiji telephone directory, under the heading "Medical Practitioners." See the "Fast Facts" sections in chapters 5 and 6 for specific doctors.

Hitchhiking Local residents seldom hitchhike, so the custom is not widespread, nor do I recommend it. Women traveling alone should never hitchhike in Fiji.

Insects Fiji has no dangerous insects, and its plentiful mosquitoes do not carry malaria. The only dangerous animal is the bolo, a venomous snake that is docile and rarely seen.

Liquor Laws The legal drinking age is 21. Both beer and spirits are produced locally and are considerably less expensive than imported brands, which are taxed heavily. If you drink quality brands of liquor, bring some with you. Fiji Bitter and Fiji Gold are the local beers. Fiji Bitter served in a bottle is known as a "Stubbie." Fiji Gold is a much lighter lager than Fiji Bitter. Most bars also sell Budweiser from the United States and most Australian and New Zealand beers.

Maps Most bookstores and hotel gift shops sell maps of Fiji.

Newspapers/Magazines Three national newspapers are published in English: the *Fiji Times* (www.fijivillage.com), the *Daily Post* (www.fijipost.com), and the *Fiji Sun* (www.sun.com.fj). All are tabloids and appear daily. They carry a few major stories from overseas. The international editions of *Time* and the leading Australian and New Zealand daily newspapers are available at some bookstores and hotel shops. The latter usually are several days old before they reach Fiji. Published monthly in Suva, the excellent *Pacific Magazine* (www.pacific islands.net) covers South Pacific regional news.

Pets You will need advance permission to bring any animal into Fiji; if not, your pet will be quarantined.

Post Office All the main towns have post offices operated by Fiji Post, and there is a branch at Nadi International Airport, across the entry road from the terminal. Allow at least a week for delivery of airmail letters between Fiji and North America. Surface mail can take 2 months or more. Post offices usually are open Monday to Friday from 8am to 4pm. Mail moves faster if you use "Fiji Islands" on envelopes and packages sent here.

Radio/TV The Fijian government operates three nationwide radio networks whose frequencies depend on the location of the relay transmitters. Radio Fiji 1 carries programming in Fijian. Radio Fiji 2 is Hindi. Radio Fiji Gold broadcast in English and sounds very much like a popular-music station in Western countries. Radio Fiji 1 and Radio Fiji Gold both carry news bulletins on the hour and full world, regional, and local news reports and weather bulletins daily at 7am and 6pm. Several privately owned English-language FM stations can be heard in Suva and Nadi.

Fiji has one broadcast channel which could be received around Suva, Nadi, and Lautoka. The local news and weather comes on at 6pm daily. The published schedules are carried in the local newspapers. Many hotels have Sky TV, a pay system with the BBC, sports, and a few other channels.

Safety Fiji has experienced a serious increase in crime in recent years. Property theft is commonplace, and armed robberies—once virtually nonexistent—have become more frequent. A tourist's chances of being robbed or assaulted in Fiji are lower than in the centers of most large American cities, but caution is advised at all times. Stick to the main streets after dark, and take a taxi back to your hotel if you're out late at night. Do not leave valuables in your hotel room or unattended elsewhere, including in rental cars and tour buses.

Women should not wander alone on deserted beaches and should be extremely cautious about accepting an offer to have a few beers outside a bar or to be given a late-night lift back to their hotel or hostel.

Taxes Fiji imposes a 12.5% value added tax (VAT) on most goods and services, which is included in most prices. These are known as "VAT-inclusive prices," or VIP for short. Hotels are not required to include it in the rates they quote outside Fiji, so be sure to ask whether a hotel room rate or other price includes the VAT. You will not be entitled to a VAT refund when you leave the country.

In addition, Fiji imposes a 3% tax on all hotel expenditures: rooms, restaurants, bars, and activities. The hotel tax may or may not be included in the rates advertised overseas.

Fiji does not have airport departure taxes.

Telephone/Fax International calls can be dialed directly into Fiji from most areas of the world. The international country code is **679**. There are no area codes within Fiji.

Several international long-distance carriers have access numbers their customers can call from within Fiji to reach their international networks: **AT&T** (✆ **00-48-901008**); **AT&T Canada** (✆ **00-48-901009**); **MCI** (✆ **00-48-901002**); **Sprint** (✆ **00-48-901003**); **Hawaii Telecom** (✆ **00-48-901004**); **Verizon** (✆ **00-48-901007**); **Bell South** (✆ **00-48-901010**); and **Teleglobe Canada** (✆ **00-48-901005**). These numbers can be dialed toll free from any Phonecard public phone (see below). Check the front of the Fiji phone book white pages for Australian, New Zealand, and other phone companies.

The numbers for **directory assistance** in Fiji are ✆ **011** for domestic information, ✆ **022** for international numbers. On the Web you can look up numbers at **www.whitepages.com.fj**.

Pay phones are located at all post offices and in many other locations. You can make local, domestic long-distance ("trunk"), or international calls without operator assistance from any of them. They accept only prepaid Fiji Telecom **Phonecards,** not coins. Post offices and many shops (including the gift shops in the Nadi Airport terminal) sell Phonecards in denominations up to F$50 (US$30). Peel the tape off the back of the card to reveal your user identification. Calls to the United States cost about F$3 (US$1.80) a minute when dialed directly. You *cannot* use your AT&T or other phone company credit cards from a Phonecard phone.

To call outside Fiji, dial **00** first, then the country code (**1** for the U.S. and Canada), and the area code and phone number. No prefix is required for domestic long distance calls.

Vodaphone Fiji (✆ **672 6226**; www.vodafone.com.fj) rents cellphones and GSM-compatible SIM cards at its desk in the arrivals concourse at Nadi airport. Phones cost F$6 (US$3.60) a day, SIM cards F$2 (US$1.20), plus F95¢ (US57¢) per minute for outgoing calls to land lines, F52¢ (US31¢) to other mobile phones. All incoming calls are free. Vodaphone will pre-authorize a credit of F$200 (US$120) on your credit card, to which it will bill your rental and usage fees. The desk is staffed daily from 5am to 11pm and for every major international flight.

Time Local time in Fiji is 12 hours ahead of Greenwich Mean Time from March 1 to October 31. Daylight saving time is in effect from November 1 to February 28, when local time is 13 hours ahead of GMT. Although the 180° meridian passes through Taveuni, all of Fiji is west of the international date line, so it's one day ahead of the United States and shares the same day with Australia and New Zealand. Translated: When it's 5am on Tuesday in Fiji, it's noon on Monday in New York and 9am on Monday in Los Angeles.

Tipping Tipping is discouraged throughout Fiji unless truly exceptional service has been rendered. That's not to say that the porter won't give you that where's-my-money look once he figures out you're an American.

Water Except during periods of continuous heavy rain, the tap water in the main towns and at the resorts is safe to drink. The famous "Fiji" and other bottled waters are widely available at shops and hotels.

Weights/Measures Fiji uses the metric system.

5

Viti Levu

You will begin your visit at Nadi International Airport, a modern facility located among sugar cane fields on the dry western side of Viti Levu (Big Land), Fiji's largest island. Known locally as the "mainland," Viti Levu is 10 times the size of Tahiti. Fiji's capital city of **Suva** lies 197km (118 miles) from the airport; that's less than halfway around the island. By comparison, the road all the way around the main part of Tahiti is 116km (72 miles). In fact, at 10,803 sq. km (4,171 sq. miles), Viti Levu has more dry land than all the islands of French Polynesia put together.

The booming **Nadi** area is the focal point of much of Fiji's tourism industry, and it's where many tourists on package deals spend their time, especially on **Denarau Island,** the country's largest resort development. There are many things to do in Nadi, but if you have more than 1 or 2 days to spend in Fiji, you will make it a stopover on the way to someplace else.

From Nadi, it's an easy hop over to the pleasant resorts out in the little **Mamanuca Islands,** which have the beaches and clear lagoons the mainland lacks. Farther out, the even more beautiful, less developed, and increasingly popular **Yasawa Islands** have the best beaches in Fiji. The small, low-key cruise ships of **Blue Lagoon Cruises** ply the Yasawas, which have two of Fiji's most luxurious offshore resorts and some of its best backpacker retreats.

The usual route heads south from Nadi along the Queen's Road to the **Coral Coast,** which has widely spaced resorts with gorgeous scenery and Fijian villages in between. Although its beaches are not as good as those on the offshore islands, the Coral Coast was Fiji's first major resort area and still attracts visitors in search of a beachside vacation on the mainland.

On the Queen's Road between the Coral Coast and Suva, **Pacific Harbour** has Fiji's best cultural center and one of its two top golf courses. It also is the jumping-off point for **Beqa Island** and great diving in its surrounding lagoon.

With a population of about 100,000, often rainy **Suva** is one of the South Pacific's largest and most cosmopolitan cities. Remnants of Fiji's century as a British possession and the presence of so many Indians give it a certain air of the colonial "Raj."

From Suva, you can go the other way around back to Nadi, along the King's Road from Lautoka, through the sugar cane fields of **northern Viti Levu,** where Rakiraki beckons, with its charming colonial-era hotel.

1 Nadi

Although you won't see much of the real Fiji if you spend your entire vacation in Nadi, this area has more activities to keep you busy than any other part of the country. That's because the international airport and a dry climate combine to make it the country's main tourist center. The lagoon off Nadi is usually murky from runoff coming from the area's sugar cane fields, however, so this is not the most ideal place in Fiji for a beach vacation.

Despite the murk, many visitors spend their entire Fiji vacation on pancake-flat **Denarau Island,** about 7km (4⅓ miles) to the west of Nadi Town. It's only technically an island, for merely a narrow creek through a mangrove forest separates it from the mainland. Denarau is home to a huge real estate project known in its entirety as **Denarau Island Resort Fiji** (www.denarau.com). To my mind—and many local folks'—it's a generic tropical resort development that could be in Hawaii, Florida, or Australia's Gold Coast. It includes large Sheraton, Westin, and Sofitel resorts, a 150-unit time-share complex, innumerable homes and condos, an 18-hole golf course, and **Port Denarau,** a marina where most of the area's cruises are based. In addition, big new Hilton and Radisson resorts are expected to open by 2007.

The tourism boom has made **Nadi**—as the area around the international airport is known—the fastest-growing part of Fiji. New homes, stores, shopping centers, and office buildings are popping up along the 9km (5½ miles) of traffic-heavy Queen's Road between the airport and **Nadi Town,** a 7-block strip lined with handicraft, souvenir, and other shops. The only reason I go into Nadi Town these days is to dine at some of the country's better restaurants.

From Nadi, it's an easy 33km (20-mile) side trip to **Lautoka,** Fiji's second-largest city. Lautoka offers a genteel contrast to tourist-oriented Nadi Town.

GETTING AROUND NADI

All of Fiji's major international and local **car-rental** firms have offices in the international arrival concourse of Nadi International Airport. See "Getting There & Getting Around," in chapter 4.

Taxis gather outside the arrival concourse at the airport and are stationed at the larger hotels. Ask the reception desk to call one, or contact **Taxi 2000** (© **672 1350**), one of the more reliable companies whose cabs are radio dispatched. The aggressive drivers will find you in Nadi Town. A taxi fare chart is available under "Getting There & Getting Around" in chapter 4.

I often take the **local buses** which ply the Queen's Road between the markets in Nadi Town and Lautoka frequently during daylight, every 30 minutes after dark. Tell the driver where you're going; he'll tell you how much to pay when you board. Fares vary according to the length of the trip. No more than F65¢ (US39¢) will take you anywhere between the airport and Nadi Town.

FAST FACTS: Nadi

The following facts apply specifically to Nadi and Lautoka. For more information, see "Fast Facts: Fiji" in chapter 4.

Bookstores Bookshops here are actually stationery stores. Hotel boutiques are the best places to buy magazines and books.

Camera/Film **Caines Photofast** has a film and 1-hour processing shop on Queen's Road in Nadi Town (© **670 1608**). Most of the hotel gift shops also sell film. You can transfer your digital images from memory card to CD at **Coconut**

Internet Cafe, on the second floor of Jack's Handicrafts on the Queen's Road in Nadi Town (© **679 0744;** see "E-mail," below).

Currency Exchange **ANZ Bank, Westpac Bank,** and **Colonial National Bank** have offices with ATM machines in Namaka and on the Queen's Road in Nadi Town. ANZ Bank has an ATM at the Port Denarau marina on Denarau Island, and its airport office is open 24 hours a day. You'll get a better rate for currency and travelers checks at the **GlobalEX** offices at the airport and on the Queen's Road in Nadi Town.

Drugstores There are three drugstores on the Queen's Road in Nadi Town. **Budget Pharmacy** (© **670 0064**) is the best stocked.

E-mail All hotels and hostels have computers for their guests to access the Internet, and there are numerous Internet kiosks in the Nadi Airport terminal. In Nadi Town, the most comfortable place to check your e-mail is **Coconut Internet Cafe,** on the second floor of Jack's Handicrafts on the Queen's Road in Nadi Town (© **679 0744**). Open Monday to Friday 8am to 6pm, Saturday 8am to 5pm. Fiji's major Internet service provider operates **Connect Cafe,** at the bridge in Nadi Town (© **670 7359**), where you can sit on the riverside terrace and sip an espresso or latte. It's open Monday to Friday 8am to 5pm, Saturday 8am to 4pm. You'll pay about F$1 (US60¢) for 10 minutes at either. If you have your laptop, you can sign up for temporary access at Connect Cafe. On Denarau Island, the **Republic of Cappuccino** (© **675 0989**), in front of the Sheraton Villas, has high speed access for F25¢ (US15¢) per minute. (High speed here is 512kbs; that's not lightening, but it's much better than 56kbs dial-up.)

Emergencies/Police The emergency phone number for **police** is © **917.** Dial © **911** for **fire** and **ambulance.** The Fiji **police** have stations at Nadi Town (© **670 0222**) and at the airport terminal (© **672 2222**).

Eyeglasses For optical needs, try **Eyesite,** on the Queen's Road in Nadi Town (© **670 7178**).

Hairdressers/Barbers The **Tanoa International Hotel** (© **672 0277**) has a unisex hair salon (see "Where to Stay in Nadi," later).

Healthcare The government-operated **Lautoka Hospital** (© **666 3337**) is the region's main facility. There is a **government medical clinic** in Nadi Town (© **670 0362**). **Dr. Ram Raju,** 2 Lodhia St., Nadi Town (© **670 0240** or 976333 mobile), has treated many visitors, including me. Ask your hotel staff to recommend a **dentist** in private practice.

Information You can get brochures and other information from the tour companies in the arrivals concourse at Nadi Airport. The main office of **Fiji Visitors Bureau** (© **672 2433;** www.bulafiji.com) is in the Colonial Plaza shopping center, on the Queen's Road in Namaka. Other so-called Tourist Information Centres are in reality travel agents or tour operators.

Laundry/Dry Cleaning **Flagstaff Laundry & Dry Cleaning** (© **672 2161**), on Northern Press Road in Martintar, has 1-day laundry and dry-cleaning service.

Post Office The Nadi Town post office, on Hospital Road near the south end of the market, is open Monday to Friday 8am to 4pm, Saturday 8am to noon. It has a well-stocked stationery store in the lobby. A small airport branch is across the main entry road from the terminal (go through the gates and turn left). It is open Monday to Friday 8am to 4pm, Saturday 8am to noon.

Water The tap water is safe to drink.

EXPLORING THE NADI AREA

Most hotel and hostel activity desks, or the reception-desk staffs, will make reservations or arrangements for all activities.

Round-trip bus transportation from the Nadi area hotels is included in the price of the tours and outings; that is, a bus will pick you up within 30 minutes or so of the scheduled departure time for Nadi area trips, 1 hour or more for those on the Coral Coast. Children under 12 years of age pay half fare on most activities.

SIGHTSEEING TOURS

You can easily waste a lot of time driving around this area without seeing much of anything, so I recommend at least a half-day guided sightseeing tour with a reputable company.

My favorite half-day tour goes north of Nadi Airport to the **Garden of the Sleeping Giant** ✸✸✸. The late Raymond Burr, star of TVs *Perry Mason* and *Ironside,* started this lovely, 50-acre orchid range, north of the airport, in 1977 to house his private collection of tropical orchids (he once also owned Naitoba, a small island in the Lau Group). It sits at the base of "Sleeping Giant Mountain," whose profile forms the outline of a man fast asleep. There's much more here than orchids, however, and the guides will describe a variety of local plants and their uses.

You can get here on your own by rental car or taxi. Look for the sign at Wailoko Road off the Queen's Road between Nadi and Lautoka. It's open Monday to Saturday from 9am to 5pm. Entrance fees are F$12 (US$7.20) for adults, F$6 (US$3.60) for children, including guided tour and a fruit drink.

From there the tour stops at historic **Viseisei Village,** on the Queen's Road about halfway between Nadi and Lautoka. One legend says that the first Fijians settled here. Today it's a typical, fairly prosperous Fijian village, with some modern houses and some shacks of concrete block and tin, a small handicraft shop, and the usual road humps that bring traffic to a crawl.

Coral Sun Fiji (✆ **672 3105;** www.coralsunfiji.com.fj) charges about F$60 (US$36) for its orchids and village tour.

Fun Fact The First Village

Viseisei village between Nadi and Lautoka reputedly is where the great canoe *Kaunitoni* came out of the west and deposited the first Fijians some 3,000 years ago. From there, as the legend goes, they dispersed all over the islands. The yarn is helped by the local district name Vuda, which means "our origin" in Fijian, and Viseisei, which means "to scatter."

FLIGHTSEEING & SKYDIVING

Island Hoppers Fiji (© 672 0410; www.helicopters.com.fj), **Turtle Airways** (© 672 2389; www.turtleairways.com), and **Pacific Islands Seaplanes** (© 672 5643; www.fijiseaplanes.com) all offer sightseeing flights over Denarau Island, Nadi Bay, the Mamanucas, and Vuda Point north of Nadi between Viseisei village and Lautoka. Call them or inquire at any hotel activities desk for prices and reservations.

I've never had the courage to put my life in someone's hands while falling to Denarau Island from 10,000 feet up in the air, but you can with **Skydive Fiji** (© 672 8166; www.skydivefiji.com.fj). Prices start at F$348 (US$209).

A Side Trip to Lautoka

Fiji's second-largest town (pop. 30,000), **Lautoka** is a pleasant seaport of broad avenues, green parks, and a row of towering royal palms marching along the middle of **Vitogo Parade,** the main drag running from the harbor to the heart of town.

Tourism may rule Nadi, but sugar is king in Lautoka. The **Fiji Sugar Corporation**'s huge mill was built in 1903 and is one of the largest crushing operations in the southern hemisphere. If you pass the industrial port, you'll also see a mountain of wood chips ready for export; the chips are a prime product of the country's timber plantations.

The stores along Vitogo Parade mark the boundary of Lautoka's business district; behind them are several blocks of shops and the lively **Lautoka Market,** which doubles as the bus station and is second in size only to Suva's Municipal Market. Handicraft stalls at the front of the market offer a variety of goods, especially when cruise ships are in port. Shady residential streets trail off beyond the playing fields of **Churchill Park** on the other side of Vitogo Parade. The Hare Krishnas have their most important temple in the South Pacific on Tavewa Avenue. (There have been robberies here, so stick to the busy main streets.)

The southern end of downtown gives way to a large park and picturesque promenade along the harbor. Beside it are the **Waterfront Hotel** (© 666 4777; www.tanoahotels.com), offering Lautoka's best digs, and the **West Wards Bar n' Grill** (© 666 1247), its best pub.

Local buses leave the market in Nadi Town every half hour for the Lautoka Market from Monday to Saturday between 6am and 8pm. The fare is no more than F$3 (US$1.80), depending on where you get on. The one-way taxi fare to Lautoka is about F$25 (US$15) from Nadi. Rosie the Travel Service has a half-day Lautoka excursion from Nadi for F$45 (US$27) per person; book at any hotel activity desk.

If you're driving yourself from Nadi, you will come to two traffic circles on the outskirts of Lautoka. Take the second exit off the first one and the first exit off the second. That will take you directly to the post office and the southern end of Vitogo Parade.

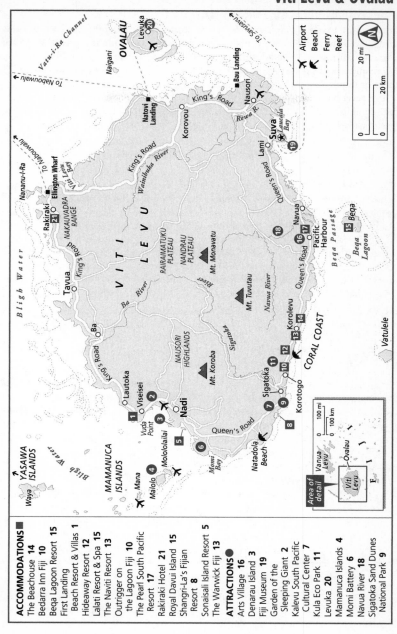

Viti Levu & Ovalau

Legend:
- Airport
- Beach
- Ferry
- Reef

20 mi
20 km

OVALAU
Levuka 20

Naigani

To Nabouwalu →

Vatu-i-Ra Channel

Natovi Landing

Bau Landing
Nausori
King's Road
Korovou
Rewa R.
Suva 19
Lami
Levuka Bay
Queen's Road

Nananu-i-Ra

To Nabouwalu →

To Savusavu →

Ellington Wharf
Rakiraki
Viti Levu Bay

NAKAUVADRA RANGE

King's Road

Waimbuka River

Bligh Water

Tavua

King's Road

Ba River

Ba

King's Road

Lautoka
Viseisei 2
Nadi 3
Vuda Point 1
Mololoilailai 5
6
Queen's Road
Momi Bay
Natadola Beach

Mololo
Mana 4

YASAWA ISLANDS
Waya

MAMANUCA ISLANDS

Bligh Water

V I T I   L E V U

RAIRAIMATUKU PLATEAU
NANDRAU PLATEAU
Mt. Monavatu

Mt. Tuvutau

Navua River

Sigatoka River

NAUSORI HIGHLANDS
Mt. Koroba

Sigatoka 11
Korotogo
7 9 10 12
8
13 14
Korolevu
CORAL COAST
16 17 18
Navua
Pacific Harbour 15
Beqa
Beqa Lagoon
Beqa Passage

Vatulele

Area of detail
100 mi
100 km
Vanua Levu
Ovalau
Viti Levu
F I

ACCOMMODATIONS
The Beachouse **14**
Bedarra Inn Fiji **10**
Beqa Lagoon Resort **15**
First Landing
  Beach Resort & Villas **1**
Hideaway Resort **12**
Lalati Resort & Spa **15**
The Naviti Resort **13**
Outrigger on
  the Lagoon Fiji **10**
The Pearl South Pacific
  Resort **17**
Rakiraki Hotel **21**
Royal Davui Island **15**
Shangri-La's Fijian
  Resort **8**
Sonaisali Island Resort **5**
The Warwick Fiji **13**

ATTRACTIONS
Arts Village **16**
Denarau Island **3**
Fiji Museum **19**
Garden of the
  Sleeping Giant **2**
Kalevu South Pacific
  Cultural Center **7**
Kula Eco Park **11**
Levuka **20**
Mamanuca Islands **4**
Momi Battery **6**
Navua River **18**
Sigatoka Sand Dunes
  National Park **9**

99

EXPLORING VITI LEVU FROM NADI

If you don't have time to stay elsewhere, you can make day trips from Nadi to other parts of Viti Levu. Some key Coral Coast and Pacific Harbour area activities provide transportation from the Nadi area hotels.

RAFTING ON THE NAVUA RIVER   Best of these—in fact, it's one of Fiji's top experiences—is a full-day rafting trip on the **Navua River,** between Pacific Harbour and Suva on Viti Levu's south coast. The tour visits a Fijian village that puts on a *yaqona* ceremony, a lunch of local-style foods, and a traditional dance show. Price is about F$135 (US$81) from the Nadi hotels, less from those on the Coral Coast. Be sure to opt for the variation of this tour which includes a ride down the river on a *bili-bili* (bamboo raft). See "River Rafting" under "Pacific Harbour & Beqa Island," later in this chapter.

THE CORAL COAST   Other fine outdoor excursions are the waterfall and cave tours offered by Rusi Brown's **Adventures in Paradise Fiji** (© **652 0833;** wfall@ connect.com.fj), on the Coral Coast. You can also go for a ride on the **Coral Coast Railway Co.** (© **652 0434**), based outside Shangri-La's Fijian Resort. I'm most fond of the trip to lovely Natadola Beach, where you swim (bring your own towel) and have a barbecue lunch. Another Coral Coast tour visits the town of Sigatoka and the meandering river and fertile valley of the same name. The best part of this trip for animal lovers is **Kula Eco Park.** These full-day trips cost about F$125 (US$75) from Nadi. See "What to See & Do on the Coral Coast," later in this chapter.

SUVA DAY TRIPS   Full-day guided tours go from Nadi to Suva, picking up guests at the Coral Coast hotels in between. From Nadi you'll spend a total of 8 hours riding in the bus for a 4-hour stay in Suva, so think about staying overnight and riding the Fiji Express back to Nadi tomorrow. You'll pay about F$84 (US$51) per person from Nadi, less from the Coral Coast hotels.

GREEN TURTLE TOURS   Aimed primarily at backpackers but suitable for all of us with young hearts, **Green Turtle Fiji** (© **0800 672 8889** toll free in Fiji or 672 8889 in Nadi; www.greenturtleholidays.com) has two long-distance day tours from Nadi. One goes via the Kings Road to **Nananu-I-Ra island,** off northern Viti Levu, for a bit of swimming and snorkeling (see "Northern Viti Levu," later in this chapter). Another takes in the Momi Battery, Sigatoka Sand Dunes, and other historic sites on the Coral Coast. Either costs F$145 (US$87) per person.

The company also has overland trips on Viti Levu ranging from 2 days and 1 night to 7 days and 6 nights. The 2-day trip includes a night in a Fijian village and costs F$315 (US$189).

Green Turtle sends its vans all the way around Viti Levu every day. You can sightsee all the way around in 1 day for F$300 (US$180), or buy a travel pass for F$345

Tips Take a Day Trip to a Small Island

No visit to Fiji is complete without exploring a small offshore island. So when in Nadi, put at least a day trip to one of the Mamanuca or Yasawa islands high on your list of things to do. You'll find more details in the "The Mamanuca & Yasawa Islands" section, later in this chapter.

(US$207) and get off and on at will. It will arrange accommodation in hostels or Fijian villages for F$110 (US$66) a night, including meals.

Green Turtle Tours is a branch of Dr. Steve Brown's successful Samoa operation (see chapter 13).

BOATING, GOLF, HIKING & OTHER OUTDOOR ACTIVITIES

The Nadi area offers a host of sporting and outdoor activities to suit almost every interest. Most of these are near Nadi, but some require a boat trip to the Mamanuca Islands or a bus ride to other locations on Viti Levu, such as white-water rafting on the Navua River (see "River Rafting" under "Pacific Harbour & Beqa Island," later in this chapter).

The resorts on Denarau Island have watersports equipment and activities.

FISHING ⭐⭐ The Denarau Island hotels and all the resorts in the Mamanucas offer sportfishing as a pay-extra activity for their guests. On the mainland, **South Sea Cruises** (© 675 0500; www.ssc.com.fj) has a fleet of fishing boats and guides based at Port Denarau. Offshore, that same company operates under the name **Pleasure Marine** (© 675 0500), with boats at Musket Cove Resort and Mana Island Resort.

GOLF & TENNIS The 18-hole, 7,150-yard, par-72 links at the **Denarau Golf & Racquet Club** ⭐⭐ (© 675 0477; www.denaraugolf.com.fj) occupy most of Denarau Island, with the club house opposite the Sheraton Fiji Resort. Its barbecue-style restaurant and bar serve breakfast, lunch, and dinner at moderate prices. It also has locker rooms with showers. Greens fees are F$100 (US$60) for guests of the two big resorts and F$110 (US$66) for those of us who can't afford to stay there. The course is open daily from 7am to dark.

The club's six Wimbledon-standard grass tennis courts are open daily from 7am to dark, and its four all-weather courts stay open until 10pm. Fees are F$25 (US$15) per person per hour on grass, F$20 (US$12) per hour on the hard courts. Lessons are available, and proper tennis attire is required.

The **Novotel Nadi Hotel** (© 672 2000) has a 9-hole executive course, and the hotel tour desks can arrange for you to play at the 18-hole **Nadi Airport Golf Club** (© 672 2148) near Newtown Beach, behind the airport. The latter is a 5,882-yard, par-70 course which isn't particularly challenging or well kept, but the setting, on the shores of Nadi Bay, is attractive.

HIKING In addition to Adventures in Paradise's waterfall hikes on the Coral Coast (see later in this chapter), **Adventure Fiji** (© 672 2935 or 672 2755; www.rosiefiji. com), an arm of Rosie Holidays, takes trekkers (as hikers are known in these parts) on 1-day walks some 600m (2,000 ft.) up into the Nausori Highlands above Nadi. I found this hike to be fascinating but strenuous; in fact, you have to be between 10 and 45 years old to sign up. Wear walking shoes with excellent traction that you don't mind getting wet, for the sandy trail goes into and out of steep valleys and crosses streams. Most of this walk is through grasslands with no shade, so wear sunscreen. We had a long midday break in a Fijian village, where we shared a local-style lunch sitting cross-legged in a simple Fijian home. The cost is about F$80 (US$48) per person. The company also has 4-, 6-, and 10-day hikes across central Viti Levu, ranging from about F$600 to F$1,450 (US$360–US$870), including transfers, guide, accommodation, and meals provided by Fijian villagers along the way.

Fun Fact Where "V. Singh" Started Swinging

The Nadi Airport Golf Club plays second fiddle to the manicured links at the Denarau Golf & Racquet Club these days, but it was here that one V. Singh won the Grade A Open Championship in 1981. That would be Vijay Singh, one of the world's top professional golfers. Before he started playing, the Fiji native served as caddy for his father, who was club president. Vijay Singh lives in Florida and is seldom seen hereabouts.

HORSEBACK RIDING   You can ride along Wailoaloa Beach in Nadi with a local man known as **Babba** (*©* **679 3652**), who charges F$25 (US$15) an hour.

A 20-minute drive south of Nadi Town, **Sonaisali Island Resort** (*©* **670 6011;** www.sonaisali.com) has guided horseback rides through the tropical vegetation on its 105-acre private island. A 1-hour ride costs F$19 (US$11) per hour. Riders must be at least 8 years and not weigh over 138 kilograms (275 lb.). Reservations are required.

JET BOATS   For a thrill-a-minute carnival ride afloat, **Jet Fiji** (*©* **675 0400;** www.jetfiji.com) will take you twisting and turning through the mangrove-lined creeks behind Denarau Island. Heart-stopping 360° turns are guaranteed to get the adrenaline flowing and the clothes wet. The half-hour rides depart every 30 minutes daily from Port Denarau. A shuttle connects the nearby Sheratons; there are scheduled pickups from other Nadi area hotels, so call for reservations. Price is about F$80 (US$48) for adults and F$40 (US$24) for children. Note that Jet Fiji was planning to operate on the Sigatoka River, which should be a much more scenic ride.

SCUBA DIVING & SNORKELING   Serious divers head elsewhere in Fiji (see the "Diving in Fiji" box in chapter 4), but you can go underwater with **Aqua Blue** (*©* **672 6111;** www.aquabluefiji.com), on Wailoaloa Beach, which provides dive guides and teaches courses. Expect to pay about F$135 (US$81) for a single-tank dive. You can also go snorkeling with Aqua Blue for F$50 ($30). The Denarau Island resorts have dive operators on premises.

SHOPPING IN NADI

Haggling is not considered to be polite when dealing with Fijians, and the better stores now have fixed prices. Bargaining is still acceptable, however, when dealing with Indo-Fijian merchants in many small shops. They will start high, you will start low, and somewhere in between you will find a mutually agreeable price. I usually knock 40% off the asking price as an initial counteroffer and then suffer the merchants' indignant snickers, secure in the knowledge that they aren't about to kick me out of the store. After all, the fun has just begun.

To avoid the hassles of bargaining, visit **Jack's Handicrafts** (Fiji's largest merchant), **Prouds,** and **Tappoo,** all of which have branches in Nadi Town, Sigatoka, Suva, and in the shopping arcades of the larger hotels. The upstairs rooms in Jack's Handicrafts in Nadi Town are filled with clothing and leather goods. Tappoo carries a broad range of merchandise, including electronics, cameras, and sporting goods. Prouds concentrates on jewelry, perfumes, and watches.

You'll have innumerable choices of tropical clothing here, but for the most unusual items in the entire South Pacific, head out to **Michoutouchkine Creations** ✸✸✸ at the Sheraton Fiji (© **675 0518**). This little shop carries the colorful creations of Nicolai Michoutouchkine and Aloi Pilioki, two noted Vanuatu artists whose unique squiggly swirls and swooshes distinguish each of their shirts, blouses, pant suits, and beach towels.

"DUTY-FREE" SHOPPING

Fiji has the most developed shopping industry in the South Pacific, as will be very obvious when you walk along the main thoroughfare in Nadi Town. The Fiji government charges a flat 10% import tax on merchandise brought into the country, however, so despite their claims to the contrary, the stores aren't "duty free." I have found much better prices and selections on the Internet and at large-volume dealers such as Best Buy and Circuit City in the United States, so shop around at home first so that you can compare the price in Fiji. Also the models offered in the duty-free shops here are seldom the latest editions.

You should have no problems buying watches, cameras, and electronic gear from large merchants such as Prouds and Tappoo, but if you decide to make a purchase from a small store, get receipts that accurately describe your purchases. Make sure all guarantee and warranty cards are properly completed and stamped by the merchant. Examine all items before making payment. If you later find that the item is not what you expected, return to the shop immediately with the item and your receipt. As a general rule, purchases are not returnable and deposits are not refundable. Always pay for your duty-free purchases by credit card. That way, if something goes wrong after you're back home, you can call for help from the large financial institution that issued the card.

If you missed anything, you'll get one last chance at the huge shops in the departure lounge at Nadi Airport.

HANDICRAFTS

Fijians produce a wide variety of handicrafts, such as carved *tanoa* (kava) bowls, war clubs, and cannibal forks; woven baskets and mats; pottery (which has seen a renaissance of late); and *masi (*tapa*)* cloth. Although generally not of the quality of those produced in Tonga, they are made in prolific quantities. Be careful when buying souvenirs and some woodcarvings, however, for many of today's items are machine-made, and many smaller items are imported from Asia. Only with masi can you be sure of getting a genuine Fijian handicraft.

Tips Beware of Sword Sellers

Fijians are extremely friendly people, but beware of so-called **sword sellers.** These are Fijian men who carry bags under their arms and approach you on the street. "Where you from, States?" will be their opening line, followed by, "What's your name?" If you respond, they will quickly inscribe your name on a sloppily carved wooden sword. They expect you to buy the sword, whether you want it or not. They are especially numerous in Suva, but they will likely come up to you in Nadi, too. The Fiji government discourages this practice but has had only limited success in stopping it. The easiest way to avoid this scam is to not tell any stranger your name and walk away as soon as you see the bag.

The larger shops sell some very fine face masks and *nguzunguzus* (noozoo-noozoos), the inlaid canoe prows carved in the Solomon Islands, and some primitive art from Papua New Guinea. (Although you will see plenty hanging in the shops, the Fijians never carved masks in the old days.)

The largest and best-stocked shop on Queen's Road is **Jack's Handicrafts** $\mathcal{R}\mathcal{R}$ (① **670 0744**). It has a wide selection of handicrafts, jewelry, T-shirts, clothing, and paintings by local artists. The prices are reasonable and the staff is helpful rather than pushy. The Chefs The Restaurant complex is on premises (see "Where to Dine in Nadi," later in this chapter), and you can check your e-mail at **Coconet Internet Cafe** on the second floor. Jack's Handicrafts has other outlets including the shopping arcade of the Sheraton Fiji Resort (① **670 1777**), at the Tokatoka Resort Hotel (① **672 0400**), and in Sigatoka (① **650 0810**).

Other places to look are **Nadi Handicraft Center** (① **670 2357**), opposite the Bank of Hawaii on the other side of Queen's Road, and **Nad's Handicrafts** (① **670 3588**), near the north end of town. Nadi Handicraft Center has an upstairs room that carries clothing, leather goods, jewelry, and black pearls. Nad's usually has a good selection of Fijian pottery.

WHERE TO STAY IN NADI

Most Nadi-area hotels are on or near the Queen's Road, either near the airport or in **Martintar,** a suburban area halfway between the airport and Nadi Town. An advantage of Martintar is that you can walk from your hotel to several restaurants and bars. Only the resorts on **Denarau Island** and beside **Wailoaloa Beach** actually sit beside a beach. Even if they do, runoff from the mountains, hills, cane fields, and coastal mangrove swamps perpetually leaves Nadi Bay less than clear.

Touts bombard young travelers arriving at Nadi Airport with offers of cheap accommodation, for this area has a host of backpacker hostels, all of them in fierce competition with each other. My choices are Aquarius Fiji, Nadi Bay Resort Hotel, Horizon Beach Resort, and Nomads Skylodge (see below). For more information check the website of the **Fiji Backpackers Association** (www.fiji-backpacking.com), an organization of reputable hostel owners.

ON DENARAU ISLAND

You can get around Denarau on a free "Bula Bus." One shuttles between the big resorts and the Denarau Golf & Racquet Club, while another runs once an hour between the resorts and the Port Denarau marina. There's a deli and a Republic of Cappuccino coffee shop (with high-speed Internet access) in front of the Sheraton Denarau Villas. The beachfront resorts all have scuba diving and snorkeling gear, kayaks, sailboats, and other toys for their guests' entertainment.

Tips **Last-Minute Plans**

If you're making last-minute plans, contact **Impulse Trips Fiji,** P.O. Box 10000, Nadi Airport (① **672 3952;** fax 672 5064; www.impulsefiji.com), which sells "unused" hotel rooms at reduced rates. It saves you the trouble of asking the front desk for a discount on rooms that would otherwise go unused. You can also get discounts on airline tickets and hotel rooms if you book in advance on the company's website.

Nadi

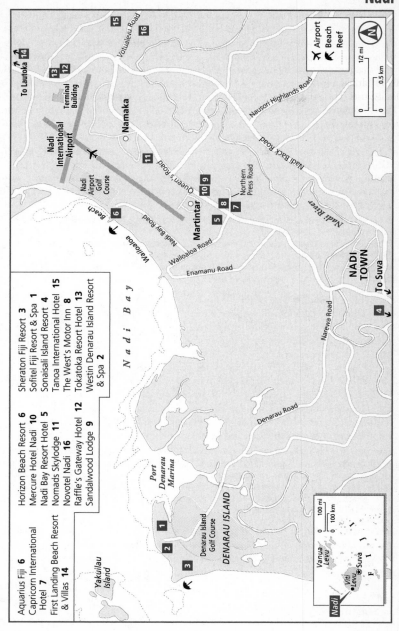

Aquarius Fiji 6
Capricorn International Hotel 7
First Landing Beach Resort & Villas 14

Horizon Beach Resort 6
Mercure Hotel Nadi 10
Nadi Bay Resort Hotel 5
Nomads Skylodge 11
Novotel Nadi 16
Raffle's Gateway Hotel 12
Sandalwood Lodge 9

Sheraton Fiji Resort 3
Sofitel Fiji Resort & Spa 1
Sonaisali Island Resort 4
Tanoa International Hotel 15
The West's Motor Inn 8
Tokatoka Resort Hotel 13
Westin Denarau Island Resort & Spa 2

Sheraton Fiji Resort 🏝🏝 Contrasting sharply with the dark-wood, handicraft-accented public areas of its sister property, The Westin Denarau Island Resort & Spa, the white marble lobby of this 1987-vintage hotel is strongly reminiscent of a U.S. shopping mall (it does indeed have some very fine shops). In other words, this Sheraton could be put down in any tropical resort location, not necessarily in the South Seas. Its large, bright, spacious, and tropically decorated rooms have ocean views from their private terraces or balconies. The four food choices here (none of them inexpensive) include fine dining in the swanky Ports O' Call. Planters Bar is a dimly lit pub with disco dancing after 9pm. There's a private island across the lagoon where guests can swim, snorkel, and sunbathe.

The resort also manages the 184 adjacent condos known as the **Sheraton Denarau Villas.** Built around a courtyard, one end of which opens to a beachside swimming pool and bar, these are among Nadi's fanciest digs. They come in various sizes, ranging from a single room to a three-bedroom apartment, and are appointed with all the comforts, including full kitchens and washers and dryers.

P.O. Box 9761, Nadi (Denarau Island). ✆ 800/325-3535 or 675 0777. Fax 675 0818. www.sheraton.com. 292 hotel units, 184 condos. US$330–US$535 double; US$435–US$1,065 condo. AE, DC, MC, V. **Amenities:** 4 restaurants; 3 bars; outdoor pool; golf course; tennis courts; exercise room; watersports equipment rentals; bike rentals; children's programs; concierge; activities desk; car-rental desk; business center; shopping arcade; salon; 24-hr. room service; massage; babysitting; laundry service. *In room:* A/C, TV, dataport, minibar, kitchen (in condos), coffeemaker, hair dryer, iron, safe.

Sofitel Fiji Resort & Spa 🏝🏝🏝 Fiji's largest outdoor swimming pool and its best big-hotel dining highlight this luxury resort, which opened at the end of 2005. The central building sports a gleaming open-air lobby overlooking the pool and beach. The spacious guest quarters are in three-story buildings lined up along the beach. Furnished and equipped in European style, they range from ocean-view rooms to presidential suites. I prefer the "junior suites" with romantic Jacuzzis hidden behind louvered windows on their balconies. Under the direction of European chefs, the central kitchen provides excellent fare for three food outlets, including a fine-dining seafood restaurant. Meeting space in the central building is high-tech, including wireless Internet access. Although it lacks the Fijian charm of The Westin Denarau Island Resort & Spa, I admire the food and modern amenities here.

Private Mail Bag 396, Nadi Airport (Denarau Island). ✆ 800/763-4835 or 675 1111. Fax 675 1122. www.sofitel.com.fj. 296 units. F$430–F$2,000 (US$258–US$1,200). AE, DC, MC, V. **Amenities:** 3 restaurants; 5 bars; outdoor pool; fitness center; spa; Jacuzzi; watersports equipment rentals; children's programs; game room; concierge; activities desk; car-rental desk; business center; wireless Internet access (central building); shopping arcade; 24-hr. room service; babysitting; laundry service; free coin-op washers and dryers; concierge-level rooms. *In room:* A/C, TV, dataport, minibar, fridge, coffeemaker, hairdryer, iron, safe.

The Westin Denarau Island Resort & Spa 🏝🏝🏝 Once known as The Regent of Fiji and more recently as the Sheraton Royal Denarau Resort, this venerable property first opened its doors in 1972. Starwood Hotels, which now owns it as well as the nearby Sheraton Fiji, recently upgraded it to luxury status. Fortunately, it still maintains more Fijian charm than any other large hotel here. Covered by a peaked wooden roof and laden with artifacts, the dark, breezy foyer opens to an irregularly shaped pool and the gray-sand beach. The rooms are in a series of two-story, motel-style blocks grouped in "villages" surrounded by thick, lush tropical gardens and linked by covered walkways to the central building. With lots of varnished wood trim, exposed timbers, and masi cloth accents, the spacious units also ooze tropical charm. Guests here can use the private island shared with the Sheraton Fiji, while guests there can use the fitness center and full-service spa here.

P.O. Box 9761, Nadi Airport (Denarau Island, 7km/4.5 miles west of Nadi Town). ℭ 800/325-3535 or 675 0000. Fax 675 0259. www.sheraton.com. 274 units. US$475–US$600 double, US$1,130 suite. AE, DC, MC, V. **Amenities:** 5 restaurants; 4 bars; outdoor pool; golf course; tennis courts; exercise room; watersports equipment rentals; children's programs; game room; concierge; activities desk; car-rental desk; shopping arcade; 24-hr. room service; massage; babysitting; laundry service. *In room:* A/C, TV, high-speed dataport, minibar, coffeemaker, hair dryer, iron, safe.

AT WAILOALOA BEACH

Wailoaloa Beach, about 3km (2 miles) off the Queens' Road, is a long strip of grayish brown sand fringing Nadi Bay. Although it was built as a tract housing project, the area known as Newtown Beach is the home of both suburbanites and several back-packer-oriented establishments.

Aquarius Fiji 𝒜   Canadian Terrence Buckley merged these two beachside condos into Fiji's most luxurious budget-priced resort. Although backpackers usually occupy the five downstairs rooms with 2, 6, or 10 bunk beds (each unit is air-conditioned and has its own bathroom), the eight spacious rooms upstairs are suitable for anyone searching for an inexpensive beachside stay. The four upstairs rooms facing the bay are particularly attractive since they have large balconies overlooking the beach and a small outdoor swimming pool. The other four upstairs units have smaller balconies facing the mountains. Downstairs, a restaurant, bar, and TV lounge open to the pool.

P.O. Box 7, Nadi (17 Wasawasa Rd., Newtown Beach). ℭ 672 6000. Fax 672 6001. www.aquarius.com.fj. 8 units (all w/bathroom), 18 dorm beds. F$79–F$89 (US$48–US$54) double; F$25–F$28 (US$15–US$17) dorm bed. AE, MC, V. **Amenities:** Restaurant; bar; outdoor pool; activities desk; laundry service. *In room:* A/C, no phone.

Horizon Beach Resort   This two-story clapboard house across an open lot from Wailoaloa Beach is a good choice if you don't want to spend the money to stay at the nearby Aquarius Fiji. The rooms are spacious if not luxurious and have their own bathrooms with hot-water showers. Superior units are air-conditioned; the others have fans. The dorm beds are in two rooms; one with eight bunks is air-conditioned. There's a pool and an open-air restaurant serving inexpensive meals. Fijian musicians perform at night at the bar. At press time owners were building a more luxurious **Smugglers Cove Beach Resort** next door (www.smugglersbeachfiji.com).

P.O. Box 1401, Nadi (Wasawasa Rd., Newtown Beach). ℭ 672 2832. Fax 672 4578. www.horizonbeachfiji.com. 14 units (all w/bathroom), 16 dorm beds. F$40–F$70 (US$24–US$42) double, F$10–F$18 (US$6–US$11) dorm bed. Rates include continental breakfast. AE, MC, V. **Amenities:** Restaurant; bar; outdoor pool; activities desk; laundry service. *In room:* A/C (all rooms and 8 dorm beds), no phone.

IN THE MARTINTAR AREA

Capricorn International Hotel   Cleanliness and very firm mattresses are trade-marks at this budget property, along with its Suva sister, the Capricorn Apartment Hotel (see "Where to Stay in Suva," later in this chapter). Least expensive are the standard rooms, which are entered from the rear and have window walls instead of bal-conies overlooking a lush tropical courtyard with a pool and a hot tub (they are the highlight here). I would opt for a unit with a balcony or patio. These more spacious units have glass shower stalls with doors instead of French-style showers, which can result in wet tile floors. Six family units have kitchens and two bedrooms. This is often the least expensive hotel on package tours.

P.O. Box 9043, Nadi Airport (Queen's Rd., at Wailoaloa Rd.). ℭ 672 0088. Fax 672 0522. www.capricornfiji.com. 68 units. F$85–F$160 (US$51–US$96) double. Rates include continental breakfast. AE, DC, MC, V. **Amenities:** Restaurant;

bar; outdoor pool; spa; Jacuzzi; activities desk; limited room service; babysitting; laundry service. *In room:* A/C, TV, kitchen (family units), fridge, coffeemaker, iron (family units).

Mercure Hotel Nadi   Accor Hotels also has given this motel, formerly the Dominion International, a major reworking. Now sporting modern European decor and furniture, the spacious rooms are in two white, three-story buildings flanking a tropical garden surrounding a swimming pool and wooden deck. The rooms have desks, shower-only bathrooms with French-style "bowl" hand basins, and glass doors sliding open to patios or balconies. Some have king beds, others both double and single beds. A few units are equipped for guests with disabilities.

P.O. Box 9178, Nadi Airport (Queen's Rd.). ✆ **800/637-2873** or 672 0272. Fax 672 0187. www.accorhotels.com.fj. 85 units. F$190–F$225 (US$115–US$135) double. AE, DC, MC, V. **Amenities:** Restaurant; bar; outdoor pool; tennis court; game room; activities desk; salon; limited room service; massage; babysitting; laundry service. *In room:* A/C, TV, fridge, coffeemaker, hair dryer.

Nadi Bay Resort Hotel   Although suitable for any cost-conscious traveler, 110 dormitory beds make this Nadi's largest backpacker establishment. Behind its walls you'll find three bars, two sophisticated restaurants serving reasonably priced meals, an air-conditioned TV lounge, and courtyards with two swimming pools (usually surrounded by a multitude of nubile young bodies!). There's even a hair salon, a massage parlor, and a 70-seat theater for watching movies and sporting events on TV. In addition to the dormitories, its five buildings hold standard motel rooms and apartments. The property is directly under Nadi Airport's flight path, however, so jets occasionally roar overhead in the middle of the night. Lower priced units and dorms are not air-conditioned.

NAP 0359, Nadi Airport (Wailoaloa Rd.). ✆ **672 3599.** Fax 672 0092. www.fijinadibayhotel.com. 42 units (19 w/bathroom), 110 dorm beds. F$66–F$125 (US$40–US$75) double; F$21–F$25 (US$13–US$15) dorm bed. AE, MC, V. Room rates include continental breakfast; dormitory rates do not. **Amenities:** 2 restaurants; 3 bars; 2 outdoor pools; activities desk; salon; massage; laundry service. *In room:* A/C (most units), fridge, coffeemaker, no phone.

Nomads Skylodge   Nomads World, an Australian company specializing in accommodations and tours for backpackers and other budget-minded travelers, runs this sprawling, 11-acre property and has converted 13 of its units into air-conditioned dormitories, each with four or six bunk beds, private lockers (bring a lock), and its own bathroom. The Spartan "economy" motel rooms have no TVs, phones, or other such amenities, but the "superior" units in the main building and cottages still do. One cottage has cooking facilities. Imported sand forms a small faux beach by the swimming pool.

P.O. Box 9222, Nadi Airport (Queen's Road). ✆ **672 2200.** Fax 671 4330. www.nomadsskylodge.com.fj. 53 units. F$69–F$140 (US$42–US$84) double; F$21–F$25 (US$13–US$15) dorm bed. AE, DC, MC, V. **Amenities:** Restaurant; bar; outdoor pool; activities desk; game room; laundry service; coin-op washers and dryers. *In room:* A/C, fridge (superior units and cottages), coffeemaker (superior units and cottages).

Sandalwood Lodge 🏆 *Value*   "Clean and comfortable at a sensible price" is the appropriate motto at John and Ana Birch's family-operated establishment, which I have long found to be Nadi's best value, provided you don't need a restaurant on the premises. Quietly situated about 300 yards off the Queen's Road behind the Mercure Hotel Nadi, the Birch's spacious New Zealand–style motel consists of three two-story buildings flanking a nicely landscaped lawn with a rock-bordered pool. Units in the Orchid Wing are somewhat larger than the others and have queen-size beds instead of a double. Every unit has a kitchen and sofa bed.

P.O. Box 9454, Nadi Airport (near Queen's Rd.) ✆ **672 2044.** Fax 672 0103. sandalwood@connect.com.fj. 34 units. F$76–F$92 (US$46–US$55) double. AE, DC, MC, V. **Amenities:** Outdoor pool; babysitting; laundry service; coin-op washer and dryer. *In room:* A/C, TV, kitchen, coffeemaker, iron (in Orchid Wing).

The West's Motor Inn   The main part of this gay-friendly but not exclusively gay establishment is more like a Key West inn than a motel. Lending charm, a courtyard swimming pool partially wraps around—and is shaded by—an ancient mango tree. The best units have wooden louvered windows and doors opening to this pleasant vista. Although they lack such a view, the least expensive rooms in the rear of the main building and in an annex appeal to cost-conscious travelers. There's a piano bar here at night (see "Island Nights in Nadi," later).

P.O. Box 10097, Nadi Airport (Queen's Rd., near Northern Press Rd.). © 672 0044. Fax 672 0071. www.hexagonfiji.com. 82 units. F$67–F$131 (US$40–US$79) double. AE, DC, MC, V. **Amenities:** Restaurant; bar; outdoor pool; activities desk; laundry service. *In room:* A/C, TV (in deluxe units), fridge, coffeemaker, hair dryer (in deluxe units).

NEAR THE AIRPORT

Novotel Nadi   Formerly the Fiji Mocambo, this sprawling hotel atop a hill was getting a much-needed facelift after being taken over and renamed in 2006 by Accor Hotels. All rooms have excellent views across the cane fields to the mountains. Best are units on the top floor, which have peaked ceilings that give them the feel of bungalows. The open-air coffee shop down by the swimming pool is open 24 hours, and you can practice your swing at the hotel's 9-hole executive golf course. Note that the hotel was open but being upgraded at press time, so the information below—especially the room rates—may change.

P.O. Box 9195, Nadi Airport (Votualevu Rd). © **800/942-5050** or 672 2000. Fax 672 0324. www.novotel.com.fj. 128 units. F$202–F$337 (US$121–US$202) double. AE, DC, MC, V. **Amenities:** 2 restaurants; 2 bars; outdoor pool; 9-hole golf course; 2 tennis courts; game room; activities desk; business center; shopping arcade; 24-hr. room service; babysitting; laundry service. *In room:* A/C, TV, fridge, coffeemaker, hair dryer, iron.

Raffle's Gateway Hotel   Along with the more entertaining Tokatoka Resort Hotel next door, this older property (no connection whatsoever to Singapore's famous Raffles Hotel) is Nadi's most convenient place to wait for a flight at the airport just across Queen's Road. And as at the Tokatoka, you can slip down a water slide into a swimming pool, this one shaped like a figure eight. The tiny, least expensive "standard" rooms can barely hold their double beds and are devoid of TVs and most other amenities. The best units have sitting areas and patios or balconies. The roadside main building houses a 24-hour coffee shop.

P.O. Box 9891, Nadi Airport (Queen's Rd., directly opposite airport). © 672 2444. Fax 672 0620. www.rafflesgateway. com. 93 units. F$75–F$188 (US$45–US$113) double. AE, DC, MC, V. **Amenities:** 2 restaurants; bar; 2 outdoor pools; tennis court; game room; activities desk; 24-hr. room service; babysitting; laundry service. *In room:* A/C, TV, fridge, coffeemaker, hair dryer, safe.

Tanoa International Hotel 🐦🐦   Until renovations at the nearby Novotel Nadi are finished, this motel will remain the top place to stay near the airport. The bright public areas open onto a lush garden with a waterfall splashing into a modest swimming pool. Shingle-covered walkways lead to medium-size, motel-style rooms in two-story blocks. Most units have a double and a single bed, combination tub-and-shower bathrooms, and balconies or patios. Refurbished superior rooms have king-size beds, large desks, sofas, and walk-in showers. Dignitaries often take the two luxurious one-bedroom suites. The open-air restaurant by the pool is open 24 hours.

P.O. Box 9203, Nadi Airport (Votualevu Rd). © **800/835-7742** or 672 0277. Fax 672 0191. www.tanoahotels.com. 135 units. F$220–F$280 (US$132–US$168) double; F$350–F$500 (US$210–US$300) suite. AE, DC, MC, V. **Amenities:** Restaurant; bar; outdoor pool; 2 tennis courts; exercise room; activities desk; salon; 24-hr. room service; Jacuzzi; sauna, massage; babysitting; laundry service; coin-op washers and dryers. *In room:* A/C, TV, dataport, fridge (stocked in suites), coffeemaker, hair dryer, iron.

Tokatoka Resort Hotel *(Kids)*   The highlight at this modern complex, at the edge of sugar cane fields across the Queen's Road from the airport, is an unusual combination swimming pool–restaurant-bar at the rear of the property, which makes it a favorite of families with children. You'll find Nadi's most varied mix of accommodations here, from hotel rooms to apartments to two-bedroom bungalows, many of them equipped with cooking facilities. The poolside restaurant is open 24 hours a day for snacks and a blackboard meal menu. Some units are equipped for guests with disabilities.

P.O. Box 9305, Nadi Airport (Queen's Rd., opposite airport). **(©) 672 0222.** Fax 672 0400. www.hexagonfiji.com. 112 units. F$158–F$350 (US$95–US$210) double. AE, DC, MC, V. **Amenities:** Restaurant; bar; outdoor pool; spa; playground; game room; tour desk; 24-hr. room service; babysitting; laundry service; coin-op washers and dryers. *In room:* A/C (except villa living rooms), TV, kitchen (in some units), fridge, coffeemaker.

SOUTH OF NADI

Sonaisali Island Resort   You drive through cane fields and ride a boat across a narrow muddy channel to this modern resort set on a flat, 105-acre island. The lagoon is very shallow here at low tide, so imported sand held in place by a seawall serves as the main beach. You can also frolic in an attractive rock-lined pool with a swim-up bar (a rarity in Fiji). A large shingled roof covers all other common facilities, including an air-conditioned fine-dining restaurant. The tropically-attired guest quarters include spacious hotel rooms, but the top choice are the airy duplex bungalows out in the lush gardens—some of the largest *bures* on Viti Levu. Beachside bungalows have small Jacuzzi tubs on their front porches (these are *duplex* units, however, so don't expect the ultimate in privacy). Three of the units have two bedrooms each and are attractive to families. I wouldn't spend my entire vacation here (as many Australians and New Zealanders do), but this is a viable alternative to the Denarau Island resorts for a bay-side stopover.

P.O. Box 2544, Nadi (Sonaisali Island, 20 min. south of Nadi Town). **(©) 670 6011.** Fax 670 6092. www.sonaisali.com. 123 units. F$473 (US$284) double. F$557–F$782 (US$334–US$469) bungalow. Rates include full breakfast. AE, DC, MC, V. **Amenities:** 2 restaurants; 4 bars; outdoor pool; tennis court; spa; Jacuzzi; watersports equipment rentals; game room; activities desk; business center; salon; 24-hr. room service; massage; babysitting; laundry service. *In room:* A/C, TV, minibar, coffeemaker, hair dryer, iron, safe.

NORTH OF NADI

First Landing Beach Resort & Villas   The creation of American Jim Dunn and Australian George Stock, this little resort sits beachside at Vuda Point, near where the first Fijians came ashore 3 millennia ago. Vuda Point Marina and the country's major oil storage tanks are nearby, but the grounds here are festooned with coconut palms and other tropical plants. The foliage and picturesque waterside setting make the resort's restaurant a favorite weekend lunch retreat for local residents. There's an attractive outdoor swimming pool, and Jim and George have dredged the shallow reef to create a swimming hole and small islet offshore. There's a dive operator at the adjacent marina. The duplex guest bungalows are comfortably furnished with both king-size and single beds, and their bathrooms have whirlpool tubs. The beachfront units also sport charming screened porches. The resort also has four two-bedroom, two-bath villas. Although not as spacious as Sonaisali Island Resort, this is another good choice for a layover.

P.O. Box 348, Lautoka (at Vuda Point, 15km/9 miles north of Nadi Airport). **(©) 666 6171.** Fax 666 8882. www.first landingfiji.com. 40 units. F$305–F$860 (US$183–US$516) double. Rates include full breakfast. AE, DC, MC, V. **Amenities:** Restaurant; bar; outdoor pool; spa; activities desk; car-rental desk; 24-hr. room service; babysitting; laundry service. *In room:* A/C, dataport, fridge (stocked on request), coffeemaker, hair dryer, safe.

> ## *Tips* Don't Miss a *Meke*
>
> Like most South Pacific islanders, the Fijians in pre-European days steamed their food in an earth oven, known here as a *lovo*. They would use their fingers to eat the huge feasts (mekes) that emerged, then would settle down to watch traditional dancing and perhaps polish off a few cups of yaqona.
>
> The ingredients of a lovo meal are *buaka* (pig), *doa* (chicken), *ika* (fish), *mana* (lobster), *moci* (river shrimp), *kai* (freshwater mussels), and various vegetables, such as dense *dalo* (taro root), spinachlike *rourou* (taro leaves), and *lumi* (seaweed). Most dishes are cooked in sweet *lolo* (coconut milk). The most plentiful fish is the *walu,* or Spanish mackerel.
>
> Fijians also make delicious *kokoda* (ko-*kon*-da), their version of fresh fish marinated in lime juice and mixed with fresh vegetables and coconut milk. Another Fijian specialty is *palusami,* a rich combination of meat or fish baked in banana leaves or foil with onions, taro leaves, and coconut milk.
>
> Most resort hotels have mekes on their schedule of weekly events. Traditional Fijian dance shows follow the meals. Unlike the fast, hip-swinging, suggestive dancing of Tahiti and the Cook Islands, Fijians follow the custom of the Samoas and Tonga, with gentle movements taking second place to the harmony of their voices. Only in the spear-waving war dances do you see much action.

WHERE TO DINE IN NADI

Someone quipped to me recently that "the only thing Fiji has in common with good food is that they are both four letter words and both start with F." Which is to say, Fiji is not French Polynesia when it comes to fine dining. Don't expect exceptional cuisine outside the exclusive resorts.

You will find Fijian-style dishes on many menus (see the "Don't Miss a *Meke*" box, below), as well as Indian curries, which bodes well for vegetarians, since most Hindus eat nothing but vegetables.

Most curries here are on the mild side, but you can ask for it extra spicy and get it so hot you can't eat it. Curries are easy to figure out from the menu: lamb, goat, beef, chicken, vegetarian. If in doubt, ask the waiter or waitress. *Roti* is the round, lightly fried bread normally used to pick up your food (it is a hybrid of the round breads of India and Pakistan). *Puri* is a soft, puffy bread, and *papadam* is round, crispy, and chiplike. The entire meal may come on a round steel plate, with the curries, condiments, and rice in their own dishes arranged on the larger plate. The authentic method of dining is to dump the rice in the middle of the plate, add the smaller portions around it, and then mix them all together.

The local **McDonald's** is on the Queen's Road about 1km (½ mile) north of Nadi Town. Most interesting are the vegetable McNuggets and the McVegetable burger, a tasty fried vegetable curry patty.

ON DENARAU ISLAND

Cardo's Steakhouse & Bar ⊛ STEAKS/SEAFOOD/PIZZA   Although it may relocate into a shopping complex being developed at the marina, this restaurant in a colonial-style building beside the narrow, muddy waterway at Port Denarau is the best place outside the resorts to dine with a view. Choice tables on the wraparound porch offer a view across the water and cane fields to the green mountains rising beyond. This vista is especially gorgeous on a moonlit night, but bring insect repellent. Owner Cardo is known throughout Fiji for providing quality chargrilled steaks and fish, and they're his best offerings here. This is a pleasant spot to breakfast before a cruise or a hair-raising ride on a Jet Fiji, or to chill afterwards.

Port Denarau Marina. *©* **992 6460.** Reservations recommended for dinner. Breakfast F$4.50–F$7.50 (US$2.50–US$4.50); pizza F$11–F$25 (US$6.50–US$15); main courses F$20–F$42 (US$12–US$25). AE, MC, V. Daily 7am–10:30pm.

IN NADI TOWN

Chefs The Restaurant *RRR* *Value* INTERNATIONAL   Executive Chef Eugene Gomes, who left the Sheraton Fiji to open the dining complexes at Jack's Handicrafts here, shows off his culinary skill here at Fiji's top restaurant. Given the favorable exchange rate of the U.S. dollar against its Fijian counterpart, dining here is a good bargain—and you get another 10% discount if you purchase F$100 (US$60) worth of merchandise from Jack's (bring your receipt). The service is extraordinarily attentive, and the cuisine is very well presented. Menus vary with the season. The stars are wonderful pan-fried *pakapaka* (snapper) under a sweet brown apple sauce or king prawns perfectly chargrilled and served with a salad of Boston lettuce and a slightly Roqueforty dressing. There's also grilled beef tenderloin and rack of lamb to satisfy Australian and New Zealand patrons.

Sangayam Rd. (behind Jack's Handicrafts). *©* **670 3131.** Reservations recommended. Main courses F$24–F$38 (US$15–US$23). AE, DC, MC, V. Mon–Sat 6–10pm.

Continental Cakes & Pizza BAKERY/PIZZA   This store-front bakery isn't much to look at, but it supplies the major hotels with bread, cakes, and pastries. It's my favorite place in town for a morning coffee and one of the crispiest croissants in the South Pacific (and that includes Tahiti). Later on you can order thin-crust pizzas and made-to-order submarine sandwiches on fresh bread. For an afternoon sugar high, try a slice of German black forest cake.

Queen's Rd. (opposite Mobil station). *©* **670 3595.** Breakfast F$8–F$9 (US$5–US$5.50), cakes and pastries F$1.50–F$4 (US$90¢–US$2.50); sandwiches and pizzas F$4–F$24 (US$2.50–US$15). MC, V. Mon–Sat 8am–7pm.

Corner Cafe *R* *Value* CAFETERIA   One of chef Eugene Gomes's operations, this pleasant cafeteria is my favorite place to stop for a snack, an ice cream, or a quick lunch in Nadi Town. The cafeteria menu is varied: pastries and coffee (you can get a latte here), hot dogs and hamburgers, sandwiches and salads, roast chicken, and fish and chips. I love the luscious creamy Thai curry chicken. You can also order from the adjacent Saffron's menu (see below).

Queen's Rd. (in Jack's Handicrafts building). *©* **670 3131.** Sandwiches, burgers, and hot dogs F$4.50–F$6.50 (US$2.50–US$4); meals F$8.50–F$12 (US$5–US$7). AE, DC, MC, V. Mon–Sat 8am–6pm.

The Edge *RR* INTERNATIONAL   Chef Eugene Gomes's third dining establishment, this air-conditioned cafe offers a variety of hamburgers, and many of the same Asian stir-fries and Thai curries offered at The Corner, but here they are served at your table. The menu also features a few simple but tasty selections, such as seafood lasagna, chicken enchiladas, and stir-fried beef. Cool and casual, The Edge is a fine place to take a shopping break over a cup of cappuccino, espresso, or herbal tea.

Sagayam Rd. (behind Jack's Handicrafts). ☎ **670 3131**. Salads, sandwiches, burgers F$13–F$14 (US$7.50–US$8.50); main courses F$13–F$30 (US$8–US$18). AE, DC, MC, V. Mon–Sat 9am–10pm.

Mama's Pizza Inn ITALIAN   If you need a tomato sauce fix, follow the aroma of garlic to Robin O'Donnell's establishment. Her wood-fired pizzas range from a small plain model to a large deluxe version with all the toppings. Just remember that this is Nadi, not New York or Naples, so adjust your expectations accordingly. She also has spaghetti with tomato-and-meat sauce, lasagna, and fresh salads. There's a suburban Mama's in the Colonial Plaza shopping mall on the Queen's Road north of Martintar (☎ **672 0922**).

Queen's Rd., Nadi Town, opposite Mobil Station. ☎ **670 0221**. Pizzas F$6–F$24 (US$3.50–US$15); pastas F$8.50–F$9.50 (US$5–US$5.70). MC, V. Daily 10am–11pm.

Saffron ✦ NORTHERN INDIAN/VEGETARIAN   Sharing quarters in Jack's Handicrafts with the Corner Cafe (see above), this is executive chef Eugene Gomes's ode to the tandoori cooking of northern India and Pakistan, although his menu also features a number of vegetarian and other dishes from around the subcontinent. Punjabi chicken *tikka* is always popular, although I'm addicted to the butter chicken curry. You'll be greeted with a complimentary basket of crispy *papadam* chips with dipping sauce (an Indian version of Mexican tortilla chips and salsa). To me, this is Fiji's best curry restaurant.

Queen's Rd., Nadi Town (in Jack's Handicrafts building). ☎ **670 1233**. Reservations accepted. Main courses F$8–F$42 (US$5–US$25). AE, DC, MC, V. Mon–Sat 11am–2:30pm and 5:30–9:30pm, Sun 5:30–9:30pm.

IN THE MARTINTAR AREA

Joelle Richard's **Aroma's Cafe,** next to the Mercure Hotel Nadi (☎ **672 6779**), is tops on Martintar's restaurant row for rich Fijian coffee, fresh morning muffins, and made-to-order sandwiches and salads. Her menu switches to pizzas after 4pm. Open daily 8am to 10:30pm.

I seldom recommend Mexican restaurants in the islands, since the chow usually looks more like the real thing than it tastes. That said, you can order tacos and burritos at the **Lazy Cactus Restaurant,** across from The West's Motor Inn (☎ **762 6890**). Another option is the simple but inexpensive steaks and seafood served at **Ed's Bar** (☎ **672 4650**), across from the Bounty Restaurant & Bar.

A suburban version of the **Mama's Pizza Inn** resides in the Colonial Plaza shopping center on the Queen's Road north of Martintar (☎ **672 0922**). It has the same menu, prices, and hours as its Nadi Town mama (see above).

The Bounty Bar & Restaurant ✦ ⓥalue INTERNATIONAL/FIJIAN   This has long been one of my favorite South Pacific pubs. A TV and two New Zealand–style standup drinking tables back in a corner draws a mixed clientele of tourists, resident expatriates, and parliamentarians. The menu stars grilled steaks, and you will get the best hamburger in town here, too. The "Bounty *ika* roast" is a variation of that sweet palusami, a South Pacific dish of fish or pork steamed with coconut milk inside taro leaves. You can order breakfast anytime. If you don't like karaoke, grab one of the outdoor tables after 9pm to escape the "music."

Queen's Rd., Martintar. ☎ **672 0840**. Reservations accepted. Breakfast F$3.50–F$11 (US$2–US$6.50); lunch F$5–F$17 (US$3–US$10); main courses F$12–F$48 (US$7–US$29). AE, MC, V. Daily 9am–11pm (bar later Fri–Sat).

Piranha's Restaurant & Bar INTERNATIONAL/VEGETARIAN   You can dine in cool comfort inside Pradeep and Lenoma Singh's urbane restaurant, but their best

---

⟨Tips⟩ Keep an Eye on Your Beer Mug

Bartenders in Fiji are taught to keep your beer mug full and your pockets empty—that is, they don't ask if you want another beer, they keep pouring until you tell them emphatically to stop.

---

tables are outside in the gardens or on the covered patio. The menu ranges widely from New Zealand rack of lamb to local snapper baked with coconut milk and chili in banana leaves. Locals love the barbecued baby back ribs, although I found them to taste a bit "porky." Vegetarians have four main course choices here. The attentive service is among the best in Fiji.

Queens' Rd., Martintar (at Northern Press Rd.). ℂ **672 8051**. Reservations recommended. Main courses F$27–F$40 (US$16–US$24). MC, V. Tues–Sun 5–11pm.

ISLAND NIGHTS IN NADI

The large hotels usually have something going on every night. As noted in the "Don't Miss a *Meke*" box, above, this might be a special meal followed by a Fijian dance show. The large hotels also frequently have live entertainment in their bars during the cocktail hour. Check with any hotel activities desk to see what's happening.

The Martintar area has some of Nadi's most comfortable bars. Always popular is my favorite, **The Bounty Bar & Restaurant** (ℂ **672 0840**), which draws many expatriate residents to its sports TV and friendly bar. It resorts to karaoke after 9pm. Across the Queen's Road, the outdoor tables at **Ed's Bar** (ℂ **672 4650**) are popular with expats, surfers, and backpackers during the early evening, with locals later. Next door to the Mercure Hotel Nadi, you can dance the night away at **Frequency Lounge** (ℂ **672 6779**), which shares a pizza kitchen with Aroma's Cafe. See "Where to Dine in Nadi," above, for more information.

The cafe at **The West's Motor Inn,** on the Queen's Road in Martintar (ℂ **672 0044**), usually becomes a pleasant, gay-friendly piano bar from Monday to Saturday. See "Where to Stay in Nadi," earlier in this chapter.

2 The Mamanuca & Yasawa Islands ⟨★⟨★

The Great Sea Reef off northwest Viti Levu encloses a huge lagoon. Here, usually calm waters surround the nearby Mamanuca and Yasawa island groups with speckled shades of yellow, green, and blue as the sea changes from shallow to deep. With ample sunshine and some of Fiji's best beaches, they are great places to escape for a day or longer.

The **Mamanuca Group,** as it's officially known, consists of small flat atolls and hilly islands ranging from 8km to 32km (4–20 miles) west of Nadi. Day cruises have been going to the Mamanucas since the dawn of Fiji's modern tourism in the early 1960s. The Mamanucas have some of the country's oldest offshore resorts, which are still very popular with Australians and New Zealanders on 1- or 2-week holidays.

North of the Mamanucas, the **Yasawa Islands** stretch as much as 100km (60 miles) from Nadi. Lt. Charles Wilkes, commander of the U.S. exploring expedition that charted Fiji in 1840, said the Yasawa Islands reminded him of "a string of blue beads lying along the horizon." For the most part, Fijians still live in small villages huddled among the curving coconut palms beside some of the South Pacific's most awesomely beautiful beaches. But the Yasawas are changing rapidly, with more than 2 dozen small, low-budget "resorts" aimed at backpackers (we called them hostels in my youth), who now see a bit of beach time in the Yasawas as an essential part of their Fiji experience. Rather than tour around Fiji, many backpackers today simply head for the Yasawas.

GETTING TO THE ISLANDS

The Mamanuca and Yasawa resorts arrange transfers for their guests (all of them require reservations), either by boat from the Port Denarau marina, or by seaplane or helicopter from Nadi. See "Getting There & Getting Around" in chapter 4.

The quickest, easiest, and most expensive way to the islands is via seaplane or helicopter. **Turtle Airways** (© 672 2988; www.turtleairways.com) and **Pacific Island Seaplanes** (© 672 5643; www.fijiseaplanes.com) both provide seaplane service to the islands; the flights are on a charter basis arranged by the resorts. Turtle has a special one-way fare for backpackers headed to the Yasawas (call or check the website). It's even more expensive, but **Island Hoppers** (© 672 0140; www.helicopters.com.fj) flies its helicopters to most of the moderate and expensive resorts. **Sun Air** (© 672 3016) flies nine-seat planes several times a day from Nadi Airport to Malololailai, home of Plantation and Musket Cove resorts, and to Mana Island.

Most folk, however, take one of the fast, air-conditioned catamarans providing daily ferry service from Port Denarau to and from the islands.

If you're going to Musket Cove or Plantation Island resorts on Malololailai Island, you can take the *Malolo Cat* (© 672 0774) from Port Denarau. One-way fares are about F$70 (US$42).

South Sea Cruises (© 675 0500; www.ssc.com.fj) operates two fast catamarans from Port Denarau. The *Tiger V* goes to most of the Mamanuca resorts three times daily. It goes as far as Mana Island, from where you will have to transfer to Matamanoa and Tokoriki resorts by speedboat. The bright yellow *Yasawa Flyer* makes daily voyages to and from the Yasawas. It goes as far north as Nacula Island, a 4-hour voyage from Port Denarau. From there, the inexpensive resorts send long boats to pick up their guests (some charge extra). Round-trip fares range up to F$100 (US$60) per person to the Mamanucas, F$120 (US$72) to the Yasawas.

A subsidiary of South Sea Cruises, **Awesome Adventures Fiji** (© 670 5006; www.awesomefiji.com) has a "Bula Pass" allowing unlimited island-hopping via the *Yasawa Flyer* for 7, 14, and 21 days. These cost F$250 (US$150), F$369 (US$221), and F$399 (US$239) per person, respectively. The company also has packages including accommodation and meals at the Yasawa hostels. These are easily arranged at any Nadi area hostel, but since the choices are many and complicated, I would check the website or visit Awesome Adventures' main office, on the Queen's Road at the bridge in Nadi Town.

Tips Take a Big Boat

Some inexpensive properties will offer to take you to the islands in their own small craft for less money than you would pay on the *Tiger V* or the *Yasawa Flyer.* These rides take at least an hour to the Mamanucas, several hours to the Yasawas, and the boats can be small, poorly equipped, and perhaps lacking covers to protect you from the elements. One of them sank a few years ago, fortunately without the loss of life. Take my advice and take one of the bigger boats.

If you arrived at Nadi in the middle of the night and just can't wait to get to your offshore paradise, **SeaFiji** (© **672 5961;** www.seafiji.net) provides 24-hour water taxi service to the islands from Port Denarau.

SEEING THE ISLANDS ON DAY TRIPS FROM NADI

Even if you're laying over in Fiji for just a short time, you should get out to the islands for a day from Nadi or the Coral Coast. Most of the trips mentioned below depart from the Port Denarau marina on Denarau Island. Bus transportation from the Nadi or Coral Coast hotels to the marina is included in their prices (you'll pay more from the Coral Coast). Children pay half fare on all the day trips.

My favorite is **Beachcomber Day Cruises** *֍֍֍* (© **666 1500;** www.beachcomber fiji.com), which goes to youth-oriented Beachcomber Island Resort (see "Resorts in the Mamanucas Islands," below). Despite the advent of so many inexpensive properties elsewhere, Beachcomber still is the most popular stop for young people seeking sand, sun, and suds—but beware if you have fundamentalist eyes: young European women have been known to drop their tops at Beachcomber. You'll pay F$77 (US$46) for bus transportation, the cruise, and an all-you-can-eat buffet lunch on Beachcomber Island. Swimming is free, but snorkeling gear, scuba diving, and other activities cost extra.

You can sightsee through the Mamanucas on the *Tiger V* (© **675 0500;** www. ssc.com.fj; see "Getting to the Islands," above). The sightseeing-only voyage costs about F$60 (US$36). I prefer taking the morning voyage, getting off at **South Sea Island, Malolo Island Resort, Castaway Island Resort, Mana Island Resort,** or **Bounty Island** (see "Resorts in the Mamanuca Islands," below, before making your decision). These include a buffet lunch, swimming and sunbathing, and cost between F$85 and F$120 (US$51–US$72).

It's a long day (9am to 6pm), but you can ride the *Yasawa Flyer* (© **675 0500;** www.ssc.com.fj) on its daily voyages through the Yasawas and back for F$120 (US$72) roundtrip. You won't be able to luxuriate on any beaches, as the boat stops at each property only long enough to put off and pick up passengers and their luggage. It's the only way to take in the Yasawas in 1 day. Or you can get off at **Waya Island** for lunch and a guided tour of a Fijian village, which will give you more of a glimpse into Fijian life than the Mamanuca day trips.

Captain Cook Cruises (© **670 1823;** www.captaincook.com.au) uses the *Ra Marama,* a 33m (110-ft.) square-rigged brigantine built in Singapore during the 1950s and once the official yacht of Fiji's colonial governors-general, for the 1-hour sail out to Tivua Island, an uninhabited 4-acre islet in the Mamanucas. A traditional Fijian welcoming ceremony greets you at the island, where you can swim, snorkel, and canoe over 500 acres of surrounding coral gardens (or see the colors from a glass-bottom boat). Lunch and drinks are included in the F$97 (US$58) charge. I've never

---

Moments Sand Between My Toes

Nothing relaxes me more than running sand between my toes at one of Fiji's small get-away-from-it-all resorts. If I have a day to spare in Nadi, I head out to Beachcomber Island Resort, where the floor of the bar and dining room is nothing but sand. And with all those young folks running around out on the beach, I feel like I'm 25 again.

done it, but you can stay overnight on Tivua for F$287 (US$172) per person, double occupancy, including meals. Accommodation is in two bures with cool freshwater showers.

Malamala Island (© 670 2444) is a 6-acre islet studded with palm trees and circled with white-sand beaches. The only inhabitants will be you and your fellow passengers, who will use Malamala's only building, a thatch bure, for a barbecue lunch. Guests are taken to the island on the glass-bottom boat *Tropic Sea.* The F$89 (US$54) price includes lunch, a beer or drink from the bar, snorkel gear, and coral viewing.

You will have more options on **Malololailai Island,** home of Plantation Island and Musket Cove resorts. You can visit them on a day cruise via the *Malololo Cat* (© 672 0744) for F$55 (US$33) roundtrip, or fly over on **Sun Air** (© 672 3016; www.fiji.to) for F$140 (US$84) roundtrip. You can hang out at the two resorts, shop at Louis and Georgie Czukelter's **Art Gallery** on the hill above Musket Cove (no phone), and dine at **Anandas Restaurant and Bar** (© 672 2333) by the airstrip. You can book at the restaurant to play the island's short 9-hole golf course; fees are F$20 (US$12).

Seafari Cruise is what South Sea Cruises (© 675 0500) calls its rent-a-boat service at Port Denarau. You design your own cruise to the Mamanuca Islands, such as picnicking at a deserted beach or picking your own snorkeling spots. Prices depend on the size of the boat. The largest can hold up to 20 passengers.

SAILING THROUGH THE ISLANDS

Because of Fiji's reef-strewn waters, the government will not permit strictly "bare boat" yacht charters, but you can rent both boat and skipper or local guide for extended cruises through the islands. The marina at **Musket Cove Resort** (see "Resorts in the Mamanuca Islands," below) is a mecca for cruising yachts, some of whose skippers take charters for a living. Contact the resort for details.

The *Whale's Tale* ⚓⚓ (© 672 2455; funcruises@connect.com.fj), a luxury, 30m (100-ft.) auxiliary sailboat owned by American Paul Myers, takes no more than 12 guests on day cruises from Port Denarau through the Mamanucas. The F$170 (US$102) per person cost includes a continental breakfast with champagne on departure; a buffet lunch prepared on board; and all beverages, including beer, wine, liquor, and sunset cocktails. The *Whale's Tale* is also available for charters ranging from 1 day in the Mamanucas to 3 days and 2 nights in the Yasawas. Rates depend on the length of trip.

Based at Mana Island, the **MV** *Seaspray* (© 675 0500; www.ssc.com.fj), a 25m (83-ft.) schooner that starred in the 1960s TV series *Adventures in Paradise,* based on James A. Michener's short stories, sails through the outer Mamanucas. These trips stop for swimming and snorkeling at the same beach on rocky Modriki Island upon which Tom Hanks filmed the movie *Castaway*—Hanks did *not* live on the islet all by himself during production. The cruises range from F$135 to F$165 (US$81–US$99) for adults, depending on where you board, including morning tea, lunch, beer, wine, and soft drinks. You pay more to come out from Port Denarau to Mana on the *Tiger V,* less from the Mamanuca resorts.

For longer trips, the 17m (50-ft.) *Pelorous Jack* (© 651 0100; www.robinson crusoeislandfiji.com) sails on 5-day, 4-night cruises from Port Denarau to the Yasawa Islands and to Robinson Crusoe Island off Natadola Beach. These cost F$495 (US$297) per person including all meals. It spends 3 nights at anchor in the Yasawas, 2 days at Robinson Crusoe Island, a basic and inexpensive resort which passengers on

---

Fun Fact **Drop-Dead Good Looks**

The late actor Gardner McKay, who sailed around on the MV *Seaspray* while starring as Capt. Adam Troy, walked away from the boob tube after the popular TV series *Adventures in Paradise* bit the dust in the 1960s. At first he opted for real dust—as in riding across the Sahara Desert with the Egyptian Camel Corps. He went on to crew on yachts in the Caribbean and hike the Amazonian jungles before settling down as a novelist, poet, playwright, and newspaper drama critic. Despite his drop-dead good looks, he never acted again.

---

the Coral Coast Railway may visit (see "What to See & Do on the Coral Coast," later in this chapter).

CRUISING THROUGH THE ISLANDS

Started with a converted American crash vessel in the 1950s by Capt. Trevor Withers, who had worked on the original *Blue Lagoon* movie starring Jean Simmons, **Blue Lagoon Cruises** ✸✸✸ (© **818/554-5000** or 666 1622; fax 666 4098; www.blue lagooncruises.com) are one of the South Pacific's best. They're so popular, in fact, that they're often booked solid more than 2 months in advance of each daily departure.

Two of Blue Lagoon's vessels are 38m (126-ft.) -long ships capable of carrying 54 passengers in 26 air-conditioned cabins. Two others, the 54m (181-ft.) *Yasawa Princess* and the 47m (155-ft.) *Nanuya Princess,* carry up to 66 passengers each, in 33 staterooms. The newest vessel, the sleek 56m (185-ft.) *Mystique Princess,* looks as if she should belong to a Greek shipping magnate, and her 35 staterooms do indeed approach tycoon standards.

Most cruises range from 3 to 7 nights through the Yasawas, with one of the 7-night voyages designed especially for scuba divers. They depart Lautoka and arrive in the Yasawas in time for a welcoming cocktail party and dinner on board. They then proceed to explore the islands, stopping in little bays for snorkeling, picnics or lovo feasts on sandy beaches, and visits with the Yasawans in their villages. The ships anchor in peaceful coves at night, and even when they cruise from island to island, the water is usually so calm that only incurable landlubbers get seasick. In the one major variation from this theme, the *Mystique Princess* makes week-long "historical and cultural" cruises to Northern Fiji, with stops at Levuka, Savusavu, Taveuni, and several remote islands.

Rates range from about F$3,000 to F$8,000 (US$1,800–US$4,800) per cabin double occupancy, depending on the length of the voyage, the season, and the cabin's location. All meals, activities, and taxes are included. Singles and children staying in their parents' cabins pay supplements.

A less expensive alternative is **Captain Cook Cruises** (© **670 1823;** www.captain cook.com.fj). This Australian-based firm uses the 120-passenger MV *Reef Escape* for most of its 3- to 7-night cruises from Port Denarau to the Mamanucas and Yasawas. The *Reef Escape* has a swimming pool, spa, and sauna. Prices begin at F$1,067 (US$640) per person double occupancy. More appealing to adventurous souls are its 3- and 4-day "sailing safaris" on its tall-ship *Spirit of the Pacific,* which sails through the islands during daylight but deposits you ashore at its Barefoot Lodge at night. These start at F$510 (US$306) per person.

My, what an inefficient way to fish.

Ring toss, good. Horseshoes, bad.

Faster! Faster! Faster!

We take care of the fiddly bits, from providing over 43,000 customer reviews of hotels, to helping you find our best fares, to giving you 24/7 customer service. So you can focus on the only thing that matters. Goofing off.

travelocity
You'll never roam alone.™

travelocity.com   1-888-TRAVELOCITY   AOL Keyword: Travel

So many places, so little time?

Frommers.com

TOKYO — 7766 miles
LONDON — 3818 miles
TORONTO — 4682 miles
SYDNEY — 5087 miles
NEW YORK — 4947 miles
LOS ANGELES — 2556 miles
HONG KONG — 5638 miles

Frommers.com makes the going fast and easy.

Find a destination. ✓ Buy a guidebook. ✓ Book a trip. ✓ Get hot travel deal
Enter to win vacations. ✓ Check out the latest travel news.
Share trip photos and memories. ✓ And much more.

Frommers.com
Rated #1 Travel Web Site by *PC Magazine*

RESORTS IN THE MAMANUCA ISLANDS

The Mamanucas have several resorts in addition to those I recommend below, and more were under construction during my recent visit. One to look for will be **Likuliku Lagoon Resort** (© 672 4275; www.likulikulagoon.com), on Malolo Island, which was slated to have Fiji's first overwater bungalows.

The **Mamanuca Hotel Association,** Private Mail Bag, Nadi Airport (© 670 0144; fax 670 2336; www.fijiresorts.com), has information about all the resorts.

They all have scuba dive operators on premises. The excellent U.S. firm **Aqua-Trek** (© 800/541-4334 or 670 2413; www.aquatrek.com) is at Mana Island Resort, while **Subsurface Fiji Diving and Watersports** (© 666 6738; www.subsurfacefiji.com) staffs 14 of the resorts. See the "Diving in Fiji" box in chapter 4 for more information.

EXPENSIVE

Another top-end resort (i.e., more than US$2,000 double, all-inclusive) is the superprivate **Wadigi Island Resort** (© 672 0901; www.wadigi.com), which attracts celebrities to its three spacious bungalows on a tiny islet within sight of Malolo Island Fiji. **Lomani Island Resort** (© 666 8212; www.lomaniisland.com) is a boutique hotel sharing the picturesque beach on Malololailai with Plantation Island Resort.

Castaway Island Resort 🐾🐾 (Kids)   Built in the mid-1960s of logs and thatch, Castaway maintains its rustic, Fijian-style charm despite many improvements over the years. The central activities building, perched on a point with white beaches on either side, has a thatch-covered roof, and the ceilings of the bures are lined with genuine masi cloth. Although the guest bures sit relatively close together in a coconut grove, their roofs sweep low enough to provide some privacy. Located upstairs at the beachside watersports shack, the Sundowner Bar appropriately faces west toward the Great Sea Reef. Guests have wood-fired pizzas there or dine in the central building, usually at umbrella tables on a stone beachside patio. This is a very good family resort, with a nurse on duty and the staff providing a wide range of activities, from learning Fijian to sack races. Consequently, couples seeking a quiet romantic retreat should look elsewhere during school holiday periods. Australian restaurateur Geoff Shaw owns both this resort and the Outrigger on the Lagoon Fiji on the Coral Coast (see "The Coral Coast," below), and the two often have attractive joint packages including helicopter transfers between them.

Private Mail Bag, Nadi Airport (Qalito Island, 21km/13 miles off Nadi). © 800/888-0120 or 666 1233. Fax 666 5753. www.castawayfiji.com. 66 units. US$405–US$1,060 bungalow. AE, DC, MC, V. **Amenities:** 2 restaurants; 3 bars; outdoor pool; tennis court; watersports equipment rentals; children's programs; game room; activities desk; massage; babysitting; laundry service. *In room:* Minibar, coffeemaker, hair dryer, iron, no phone.

Sofitel Vomo Island Resort 🐾🐾🐾   One of the most interesting aspects of this luxury resort is Vomo Island itself. An unusual clump of land, it features a steep, 550-foot-high hill on one end and a perfectly flat, 200-acre shelf surrounded by a reef edged by brilliantly colorful corals on the other. Plans were to install a signature fine-dining restaurant on a black-rock outcrop at the end of the plateau, where it will have a view of the steep cliffs on Vomolailai (Little Vomo), an islet offshore. Vomolailai has a small beach, where you can go for private picnics. The main restaurant sits adjacent to the beach, a deck-surrounded pool, and a stylish bar. It serves excellent Asian-influenced cuisine, with dinners often taken poolside. Some of the luxurious guest bungalows climb the hill to provide views of the reef and sea, although I prefer those along a fine stretch of beach. Some of the beach bures are in duplex buildings, so ask for a self-standing one if you don't want next-door neighbors. On the other hand, about half of the duplex units interconnect, making them good choices for well-heeled families. All of the well-equipped units have sitting areas with sofas, and their large bathrooms have both showers and two-person Jacuzzis. Vomo sits on the border between the Mamanuca and Yasawa islands. Most guests get here by seaplane or helicopter.

P.O. Box 5650, Lautoka (Vomo Island, 32km/20 miles northwest of Nadi). © 666 7955. Fax 666 7997. www. vomofiji.com. 29 units. F$825–F$1,100 (US$495–US$660) bungalow. Rates include meals, soft drinks, and activities except scuba diving and deep-sea fishing. AE, DC, MC, V. **Amenities:** Restaurant; bar; outdoor pool; pitch-and-put golf course; tennis court; spa; watersports equipment; children's program (during Australian school holidays); limited room service; massage; babysitting; laundry service. *In room:* A/C, minibar, coffeemaker, hair dryer, safe.

Tokoriki Island Resort ⨕   Almost as far away from Nadi as its nearest neighbor, Matamanoa Island Resort, this adults-only property sits beside a wide beach stretching 1.5km (1 mile) on hilly Tokoriki Island. Although it doesn't have Matamanoa's deep sand, once you get past rock shelves along the shoreline, the bottom slopes gradually into a safe lagoon with colorful coral gardens protected by a barrier reef. The resort itself sits on a flat shelf of land backed by a steep hill (a 4km/2½-mile hiking trail leads up to the ridgeline). Lined up along the beach, most of the spacious units have separate sleeping and living areas equipped with wet-bars, and both indoor and outdoor showers. Five luxurious honeymoon units have daybeds under thatched-roofs next to their own plunge pools. A central thatch-topped bar divides the one-room central building into lounge and dining areas. The latter opens to a swimming pool, and guests can take their excellent meals alfresco during fair weather, either by the pool or on private decks by the beach. Other than scuba diving, there are no motorized watersports here.

P.O. Box 10547, Nadi Airport (Tokoriki Island, 32km/20 miles off Nadi). © 666 1999. Fax 666 5295. www. tokoriki.com. 34 units. F$1,000–F$1,500 (US$600–US$900) bungalow. AE, MC, V. No children under 12 accepted. **Amenities:** Restaurant; bar; 2 outdoor pools; tennis court; spa; watersports equipment rentals; game room; massage; laundry service. *In room:* A/C, minibar, coffeemaker, hair dryer, iron.

MODERATE

The 10-unit **Navini Island Resort** (© 666 2188; www.navinifiji.com.fj) and 66-unit **Treasure Island Resort** (© 666 6999; www.fiji-treasure.com) occupy tiny atoll-like islets. Within sight of Beachcomber Island, Treasure is one of the oldest Mamanuca resorts, but it underwent a facelift in 2005.

Malolo Island Fiji 🄺ⁱᵈˢ   Although it draws mostly couples, this resort is a good choice for families with children. Among adults it's notable for having an outdoor spa, a grownups-only lounge, and one of the best beachside bars in Fiji—a thatched-roof building with a lagoonside deck and a lunchtime dining area under a sprawling shade tree. Two other restaurants and bars occupy a two-story building at the base of a hill at the rear of the property. They open to two swimming pools, one especially suited for children since it has a walk-in sand bottom under a tarp to provide shade, the other good for grownups since it sports a swim-up bar. Most of the guest bungalows are duplexes. Of these, 18 have separate bedrooms; the others are studios. In addition, an upstairs family unit can sleep eight persons.

P.O. Box 10044, Nadi Airport (Malolo Island, 25km/15 miles off Nadi). © 666 9192. Fax 666 9197. www.malolo island.com. 49 units. F$521–F$608 (US$313–US$365) double; F$1,013 (US$608) family unit. AE, DC, MC, V. **Amenities:** 3 restaurants; 3 bars; 2 outdoor pools; spa; watersports equipment rentals; children's programs; game room; activities desk; massage; babysitting; laundry service. *In room:* A/C, fridge, coffeemaker, hair dryer, iron, no phone.

Mana Island Resort   One of the largest off Nadi, this lively resort attracts Japanese singles and honeymooners, plus Australian and New Zealand couples and families. It's a popular day-trip destination from Nadi (see "Seeing the Islands on Day Trips From Nadi," earlier in this chapter). Seaplanes, planes, and helicopters also land here. Since this also is the major transfer point for the outer Mamanuca Islands, you'll have a *lot* of company on Mana. Accommodations include varied bungalows, town houses, and hotel rooms. Least expensive are the few original Garden units that remain; they have ceiling fans but not air-conditioners and can be quite warm at midday. Seven honeymoon models are the most luxurious units in the Mamanucas. Situated by themselves on the beach north of the airstrip, they feature Jacuzzis and butler service. Six executive beachfront bures have their own hot tubs. The newest units are two-story, town house–style oceanfront suites with upstairs bedrooms and two bathrooms.

P.O. Box 610, Lautoka (Mana Island, 32km/20 miles off Nadi). © **665 0423.** Fax 665 0788. www.manafiji.com. 160 units. F$360–F$950 (US$216–US$570) double. Rates include full buffet breakfast. AE, DC, MC, V. **Amenities:** 3 restaurants; 3 bars; outdoor pool; 2 tennis courts; Jacuzzi; watersports equipment rentals; children's programs; game room; activities desk; massage; babysitting; laundry service; coin-op washers and dryers. *In room:* A/C (except in Garden units), minibar (in executive and honeymoon units), fridge, coffeemaker, hair dryer, iron, safe.

Matamanoa Island Resort 🌴🌴   The farthest of all Mamanuca resorts off Nadi, this intimate, adults-oriented complex (no kids under 12 can stay here) sits on a small island consisting of two steep hills. The bungalows, a motel-like block of rooms, a horizon-edge pool, and a central building with bar and open-air dining room occupy a small flat point on one end of the island overlooking a beach of deep, white sand. The reef shelf falls away steeply here, resulting in great snorkeling even at low tide. For scuba divers, this is the closest of all Mamanuca resorts to the outer reef. They aren't the most luxurious in Fiji, but each of the spacious, rectangular bungalows is spacious and comfortable. The 13 motel rooms are much smaller than the bungalows and do not face the beach, but they are air-conditioned (the bures have two ceiling fans).

P.O. Box 9729, Nadi Airport (Matamanoa Island, 33km/21 miles off Nadi). © **666 0511.** Fax 666 0069. www.matamanoa.com. 33 units. F$330 (US$198) double room; F$510 (US$306) bungalow. Rates include breakfast. AE, DC, MC, V. Children under 12 not accepted. **Amenities:** Restaurant; bar; outdoor pool; tennis court; watersports equipment rentals; activities desk; massage; laundry service. *In room:* A/C (in rooms), fridge, coffeemaker, hair dryer.

Musket Cove Resort   One of three Australians who own Malololailai Island, Dick Smith founded this retreat in 1977. It has grown considerably since then, and it now has a marina where cruising yachties call from June to September. They congregate at an open-air bar under a thatch roof out on a tiny man-made island reached by the marina's pontoons. "Dick's Place" has been retained as the name of the pleasant bar and restaurant next to two swimming pools, one with a real yacht protruding from its side, as if it has run aground. Although a broad mud bank appears here at low tide,

---

Tips **Keeping You Entertained**

Don't worry about staying busy at the offshore resorts. You can do as much or as little as you like. All the resorts have canoes, kayaks, sailboards, snorkeling gear, and other equipment for your use, and each has a scuba diving operation. In addition, Fijians make music most evenings and stage meke feasts at least 1 night a week at all the resorts.

Dick has dredged out a swimming beach area. Accommodations range from air-conditioned hotel rooms to luxury villas with living rooms, full kitchens, and master bedrooms downstairs and two bedrooms upstairs, each with its own private bathroom. Musket Cove also manages Armstrong Villas at Musket Cove, a group of two-bedroom condo bungalows on a man-made island. These have kitchens and phones. You should check the website and consult with the reservationist when booking your unit to make sure you'll have the in-room amenities you desire.

Private Mail Bag, Nadi Airport (Malololailai Island, 14km/9 miles off Nadi). 877/313-1464 or 672 2371. Fax 672 0378. www.musketcovefiji.com. 55 units. F$250 (US$150) double; F$446–F$512 (US$268–US$307) bungalow; F$638 (US$383) villa. AE, DC, MC, V. **Amenities:** 2 restaurants; 2 bars; 3 outdoor pools; 9-hole golf course; spa; watersports equipment rentals; bike rentals; activities desk; massage; babysitting; laundry service; coin-op washers and dryers. *In room:* A/C (in villas only), kitchen (villas and some rooms), fridge, coffeemaker, hair dryer, iron, safe, no phone (in bungalows).

How to Choose Your Offshore Resort

Fiji has one of the world's finest collections of offshore resorts—small establishments with islands all to themselves. They all have lovely beach settings and modern facilities, and without exception they are excellent places to get away from it all. The major drawback of any offshore resort, however, is that you've done just that. You won't see much of Fiji while you're basking in the sun on a tiny rock some 40km (25 miles) at sea. Consider them for what they have to offer but not as bases from which to explore the country.

You can check your e-mail, but you're unlikely to have a television in your bungalow at Fiji's offshore resorts, and you may not get a telephone, either. If you must be in touch with the world every minute of every day, stay on the "mainland" of Viti Levu. Come out here with one goal in mind: relaxation.

Although the Mamanuca and Yasawas have more offshore resorts than anywhere else in Fiji, others are on Vatulele Island off the Coral Coast, Beqa Island off Pacific Harbour, on Wakaya Island off Suva, on Namenalala Island off Savusavu, and on Qamea and Matagi islands off Taveuni. If you decide to stay at one of them, I suggest you read all my descriptions of them before making your choice.

Pay attention to what I say about the resorts' styles. For example, if you don't enjoy getting to know fellow guests at sometimes raucous parties, you might not like Vatulele Island or Turtle Island resorts, but you might love The Wakaya Club or Yasawa Island Resort. If you like a large establishment with lively, Club Med–like ambience, you might prefer Mana Island and Plantation Island resorts. Many other resorts offer peace, quiet, and few fellow guests—and no children. In other words, choosing carefully could mean the difference between a miserable week or a slice of heaven.

In most cases, you'll have no place to dine other than your resort's food outlets. Be sure to inquire about meal plans if food is not already included in the rates. All but a few of the island resorts provide free snorkeling gear, kayaks, and other watersports equipment. They charge extra for scuba diving and other motorized sports. In other words, you'll pay extra if you get in a boat with a motor.

Plantation Island Resort *Kids*   One of the oldest, largest, and most diverse of the Mamanuca resorts, Plantation primarily attracts Australian couples and families, plus day-trippers from Nadi. Like Mana Island, it has a Club Med–style atmosphere of nonstop activity. It shares Malololailai Island with Musket Cove Resort, but this end boasts one of the South Pacific's most picturesque palm-draped beaches, shallow though the lagoon may be at low tide. The resort has four types of accommodations: duplex bures suitable for singles or couples, two-bedroom bungalows for families, and motel-style rooms, some in a two-story building next to the beach, others surrounding a swimming pool and removed from the resort action (the latter are known as Plantation Village). All units have phones, but only the hotel rooms are air-conditioned. A large central building beside the beach has a bar, dance floor, lounge area, coffee shop, and restaurant. For a meal guests can also wander over to Musket Cove or Ananda's, a barbecue-oriented restaurant near the airport. There's a children's playroom with a full-time baby-sitter, making this a good choice for families.

P.O. Box 9176, Nadi Airport (Malololailai Island, 14km/9 miles off Nadi). © 666 9333. Fax 666 9200. www.plantationisland.com. 170 units. F$247–F$371 (US$148–US$223) double; F$371–F$545 (US$223–US$327) bungalow. AE, DC, MC, V. **Amenities:** 2 restaurants; 2 bars; 3 outdoor pools; 9-hole golf course; tennis courts; watersports equipment rentals; children's programs; game room; activities desk; salon; massage; babysitting; laundry service; coin-op washers and dryers. *In room:* A/C (in hotel rooms), fridge, coffeemaker.

INEXPENSIVE

While Beachcomber Island continues to be the most popular Mamanuca resort with low-budget travelers, you can get away from the crowds at nearby **Bounty Island** (© 666 7461; www.fiji-bounty.com), which has 22 bures and 50 dorm beds. Its flat, 48-acre island is much larger than Beachcomber's. The bungalows range from F$140 to F$234 (US$84–US$140), while a dorm bed costs F$46 (US$28), including meals.

Also occupying a tiny islet, **South Sea Island** (© 675 0500; www.ssc.com.fj) has accommodations, but it is more of a day-trip destination.

Near the main pass through the Great Sea Reef, the American-operated **Tavarua Island Resort** (© 805/687-4551 in the U.S.; www.tavarua.com) began as a surfer camp but now caters to everyone.

On Mana Island, **Mereani's Backpacker Inn** (© 670 3466; mereanis backpack@connect.com.fj) is on the beach about 200 yards south of the luxurious Mana Island Resort. Simple rooms cost F$80 to F$130 (US$48–US$78), dorm beds F$45 (US$28), and camp sites F$25 (US$15) per person, including meals in the beachside dining room. Also on Mana is **Ratu Kini Backpackers** (© 672 1959; fax 672 0552; www.ratukini.com), offering dormitories or simple houses for F$45 (US$27) per person a day for a dorm bed, F$75 to F$110 (US$45–US$66) for bungalows, including all meals. At this writing, guests at either could use Mana Island Resort's watersports facilities, which are operated by Awesome Adventures Fiji.

Beachcomber Island Resort *Value*   Back in 1963, Fiji-born Dan Costello bought an old Colonial Sugar Refining Company tugboat, converted it into a day cruiser, and started carrying tourists on day trips out to a tiny atoll known then as Tai Island. The visitors liked it so much that some of them didn't want to leave. Today it still packs in the young, young-at-heart, and other like-minded souls in search of fun, members of the opposite sex, and a relatively inexpensive vacation (considering that all-you-can-eat meals are included in the rates). The youngest-at-heart cram into the coed dormitories. If you want more room, you can have or share a semiprivate lodge. And if you want your own bure, you can have that, too—just don't expect luxury.

Rates also include a wide range of activities; you pay extra for sailboats, canoes, wind-surfing, scuba diving, water-skiing, and fishing trips.

P.O. Box 364, Lautoka (Tai Island, 19km/12 miles off Lautoka). © 800/521-7242 or 666 1500. Fax 666 4496. www.beachcomberfiji.com. 36 units, 102 dorm beds. F$315–F$345 (US$189–US$207) double bure; F$265 (US$159) double lodge; F$79 (US$48) dorm bed. Rates include all meals. AE, DC, MC, V. **Amenities:** Restaurant; bar; outdoor pool; miniature golf; watersports equipment rentals; massage; laundry service. *In room:* Fridge, coffeemaker, no phone.

RESORTS IN THE YASAWA ISLANDS

Once quiet, sleepy, and devoid of most tourists except a few backpackers and well-heeled guests at Turtle Island and Yasawa Island Resort, this gorgeous chain has seen an explosion of accommodations in recent years, most of them owned by villagers and aimed at budget-conscious travelers. In fact, the Yasawas are one of the hottest back-packer destinations in Fiji, if not the entire South Pacific.

EXPENSIVE

Turtle Island ✿✿✿ Enjoying the most picturesque setting of any resort in Fiji, this venerable little getaway nestles beside an idyllic, half-moon-shaped beach and looks out on a nearly landlocked body of water, which American owner Richard Evanson has dubbed "the Blue Lagoon" (see the box "Turtle Time for *The Blue Lagoon*," below). Ceiling fans whirl from the sprawling branches of a *baka* tree, which shades a dining and entertainment area beside the beach and central building. Supplied by the resort's own garden, the kitchen serves excellent meals dinner-party fashion at a long, polished table in the beachside dining room. If you don't want company, you can dine alone on the beach or on a pontoon floating on the lagoon. The beach turns into a sand bar at low tide, but you can swim and snorkel then off a long pier over the Blue Lagoon. Everything is included in the rates except Hawaiian-style therapeutic mas-sage. A dozen of the superluxe, widely spaced bungalows have two-person spa tubs embedded in the floors of their enormous bedrooms or bathrooms. Much of the fur-niture is constructed of tree limbs, including four-poster king-size beds equipped with mosquito netting. In a few bungalows, the front porch has a lily pond on one side and a queen-size bed under a roof on the other. A few bungalows are more modest (no spa tubs), but one of these, on a headland with a 360° view of the lagoon and surround-ing islands, is the most private of all. Every unit has its own kayaks and a hammock

---

Fun Fact **Turtle Time for *The Blue Lagoon***

San Franciscan Richard Evanson graduated from Harvard Business School, made a bundle in cable television, got divorced, ran away to Fiji, and in 1972 bought Nanuya Levu, an island in the Yasawas. Growing lonely and bored, he decided to build Turtle Island, a small resort, on his hilly, 500-acre retreat. By 1980 he had completed three bures. Then a Hollywood producer leased the entire island as a set for a second version of *The Blue Lagoon,* starring the then-teenage Brooke Shields. Clocks were set ahead 1 hour to maximize daylight, and the resort still operates on "Turtle Time," an hour ahead of the rest of Fiji. The movie's most familiar scenes were shot on Devil's Beach, one of Nanuya Levu's dozen gor-geous little stretches of sand wedged between rocky headlands.

strung between shade trees by the beach. Only couples and singles are accepted here, except during certain family weeks in July and at Christmas. Instead of a phone in your bungalow, you will have a two-way radio to call for room service.

P.O. Box 9317, Nadi Airport (Nanuya Levu Island, 80km/50 miles north of Nadi, a 30-min. seaplane ride). (C) 877/288-7853 or 672 2921 for reservations, 666 3889 on the island. Fax 672 0007. www.turtlefiji.com. 14 units. US$1,975–US$2,390 per couple. Rates include meals, drinks, all activities including game fishing and 1 scuba dive per day. Round-trip seaplane transfers US$790 per couple. 6-night stay required. AE, DE, MC, V. Children under 12 not accepted except during family weeks in July and at Christmas. **Amenities:** Restaurant; bar; limited room service; massage; laundry service. *In room:* Minibar, coffeemaker, hair dryer, iron, safe, no phone.

Yasawa Island Resort 🐢🐢🐢   This luxurious resort sits in a small indention among steep cliffs that line the west coast of skinny, relatively dry Yasawa Island, northernmost of the chain. The Great Sea Reef is far enough offshore here that surf can slap against shelves of black rock just off a beach of deep white sand. Or you can dip in a saltwater swimming pool, a feature which Turtle and Vatulele resorts don't have. Most of the large, air-conditioned guest bures are long, 93 sq. m (1,000 sq. ft.) rectangular models with thatch roofs over white stucco walls. A door leads from the bathroom, which has an indoor shower, to an outdoor shower and a private sunbathing patio. A few other one- and two-bedroom models are less appealing but are better arranged for families (although children under 12 are allowed here only during Jan) and have fine views from the side of the hill backing the property. Best of all is the remote, extremely private Lomolagi honeymoon bure, which has its own beach. Guests all dine together for once-weekly Fijian-style lovos, but otherwise they can choose their own spacious seating arrangements or dine in their bungalows on the beach.

P.O. Box 10128, Nadi Airport (Yasawa Island, 100km/60 miles north of Nadi, 35 min. by charter flight). (C) 672 2266. Fax 672 4456. www.yasawa.com. 18 units. US$820–US$1,500 double. Rates include room, all meals, and nonmotorized watersports, but no drinks. Round-trip transfers US$350 per person. AE, DC, MC, V. Children under 12 not accepted except in Jan. **Amenities:** Restaurant; bar; outdoor pool; tennis court; spa; limited room service; massage; laundry service. *In room:* A/C, kitchen (2 units), minibar, coffeemaker, hair dryer, iron, safe.

INEXPENSIVE

The Yasawas have more than 2 dozen resorts designed to appeal to cost-conscious travelers. Some of the best in the central Yasawas near Turtle Island have banded together as **Nacula Tikina,** or Fijibudget.com ((C) 877/733-3454 or 672 2921; www.fijibudget. com), which promotes them and handles bookings.

In addition to Oarsman's Bay Lodge on Nacula Island (see below), they include **Safe Landing Resort,** a similar property but with not as good a beach, also on Nacula. Rates range from F$75 (US$45) for a Fijian-style bure sharing a bathroom to F$200 (US$120) for a family-size bungalow with its own bathroom. Dorm beds cost F$17–F$23 (US$10–US$14), or you can camp for F$11 (US$7) per person.

Nearby Tavewa Island has four basic properties. **David's Place** ((C) 672 1820), **Coral View Resort** ((C) 666 6644), and **Otto & Fanny's** ((C) 666 6481) are three of the oldest backpacker retreats in the Yasawas, but they reside beside a long, gorgeous beach. Each charges about F$80 to F$90 (US$48–US$33) for a bure, F$45 (US$27) for a dorm bed, including meals. More luxurious, so-to-speak, is **Kingfisher Lodge** ((C) 666 1462), with one modern bungalow.

West Side Waters Sports ((C) 666 1462; westside@connect.com.fj) provides daily dive trips for all of the central Yasawa retreats and teaches introductory and PADI certification courses.

Oarsman's Bay Lodge ⟨⟨⟨ (Value)   Sitting on Nacula Island beside one of Fiji's finest beaches, this is the best inexpensive retreat in the Yasawas. Although owned by Fijians, it was designed and built by Richard Evanson of Turtle Island (see above), so in some respects this is an inexpensive version of his super-luxury resort. A live tree helps support the central building with a sand-floor dining room and bar (there is no communal kitchen here). Steep stairs lead upstairs to a one-room coed dorm, whose residents share toilets and warm-water showers with guest camping on the grounds. Although the tin-roof guest bungalows are a bit cramped, they are nicely appointed with wooden cabinets, full-length mirrors, reading lights over their double beds, porches with hammocks and chairs, screened louvered windows, and bathrooms with solar-heated showers. Paddle boats and canoes are available, plus gear for fabulous snorkeling. Backpacking or not, you'll find this no-frills resort to be an extraordinary bargain.

P.O. Box 9317, Nadi Airport (Nacula Island, 85km/52 miles north of Nadi, a 30-min. seaplane ride). © **877/288-7853** or 672 2921. Fax 672 0007. www.fijibudget.com. 6 units, 13 dorm beds. F$125 (US$77) double; F$42 (US$25) dorm bed; F$25 (US$15) per person campsite w/tent rental; F$20 (US$12) per person campsite without tent. MC, V. **Amenities:** Restaurant; bar; watersports equipment rentals. *In room:* No phone.

Octopus Resort   If you decide to stop in the southern Yasawas, your best bet is this resort beside a fine beach on Waya, the most rugged island in the Yasawas. Accommodation is in traditional Fijian-style bures, about half of them facing the beach, and in Poppy's Lodge, a modern building with two interconnecting rooms. Although devoid of amenities found at more expensive resorts, every unit has its own bathroom and outdoor shower with solar-heated water. The clean dorm can accommodate 13 guests. The sand-floor restaurant specializes in freshly caught seafood and locally-grown vegetables. There's good snorkeling right off the beach here (gear is free).

P.O. Box 1861, Lautoka (Waya Island). © **666 6442** or 666 6337. Fax 666 6210. www.octopusresort.com. 14 units (all w/bathroom), 13 dorm beds, 2 tents. F$90–F$199 (US$54–US$119) bungalow, F$30 (US$18) dorm bed. 2-night minimum stay required. MC, V. **Amenities:** Restaurant; bar; watersports equipment rentals, massage, laundry service. *In room:* No phone.

3 The Coral Coast ⟨⟨

Long before big jets began bringing loads of visitors to Fiji, many affluent local residents built cottages on the dry southwestern shore of Viti Levu as sunny retreats from the rain and high humidity of Suva. When visitors started arriving in big numbers during the early 1960s, resorts sprang up among the cottages, and promoters gave a new, more appealing name to the 50km (30-mile) stretch of beaches and reef on either side of the town of Sigatoka: the Coral Coast.

The appellation was apt, for coral reefs jut out like wide shelves from the white beaches that run between mountain ridges all along this picturesque coastline. In most spots the lagoon just reaches snorkeling depth at high tide, and when the water retreats, you can put on your reef sandals or a pair of old sneakers and walk out nearly to the surf pounding on the outer edge of the shelf.

Frankly, the Coral Coast is now overshadowed by other parts of Fiji. Its large hotels cater primarily to meetings, groups, and families from Australia and New Zealand on 1-week holidays. Nevertheless, it does have some dramatic scenery, it has some of the country's better historical sites, and it's a central location from which to see both the Suva and Nadi sides of Viti Levu.

GETTING TO THE CORAL COAST: THE QUEEN'S ROAD

Visitors can reach the Coral Coast from Nadi International Airport by taxi, bus, or rental car along the Queen's Road (see "Getting There & Getting Around" in chapter 4).

The drive from Nadi to Shangri-La's Fijian Resort takes about 45 minutes. After a sharp right turn at the south end of Nadi Town, the highway runs well inland, first through sugar cane fields undulating in the wind and then past acre after acre of pine trees planted in orderly rows, part of Fiji's national forestry program. The blue-green mountains lie off to the left; the deep-blue sea occasionally comes into view off to the right.

GETTING AROUND THE CORAL COAST

The large hotels have car-rental desks as well as taxis hanging around their main entrances. Express buses between Nadi and Suva stop at Shangri-La's Fijian Resort, the Outrigger on the Lagoon Fiji, the Hideaway Resort, and the Warwick Fiji. Local buses ply the Queen's Road and will stop for anyone who flags them down. See "Getting There & Getting Around" in chapter 4 for more information.

FAST FACTS: The Coral Coast

The following information applies to the Coral Coast. If you don't see an item here, see "Fast Facts: Nadi," earlier in this chapter, and "Fast Facts: Fiji" in chapter 4.

Camera/Film **Caines Photofast** has a shop on Market Road in Sigatoka (© 650 0877). Most hotel boutiques sell color print film and provide 1-day processing.

Currency Exchange **ANZ Bank** and **Westpac Bank** have branches with ATMs on the riverfront in Sigatoka. The Outrigger on the Lagoon Fiji and The Naviti resorts have ATMs, and others likely will by the time you arrive (see "Where to Stay on the Coral Coast," below).

Drugstores **Patel Pharmacy** (© 650 0213) is on Market Road in Sigatoka.

E-mail **Le Cafe Pizza Town,** in Sigatoka Town (© 652 0668), and **Le Cafe,** on Korotogo Drive (© 652 0877), next to the Outrigger on the Lagoon Fiji resort, both have computer terminals for e-mail and web surfing (see "Where to Dine on the Coral Coast," later in this chapter).

Emergencies The emergency phone number for **police** is © 917; for **fire** and **ambulance** dial © 911. The Fiji **police** has posts at Sigatoka (© 650 0222) and at Korolevu (653 0322).

Healthcare The government-run **Sigatoka Hospital** (© 650 0455) can handle minor problems.

Post Office Post offices are in Sigatoka and Korolevu.

WHAT TO SEE & DO ON THE CORAL COAST

Hotel reception or tour desks can make reservations for most of the activities and day cruises mentioned under "Nadi" and "The Mamanuca & Yasawas Islands," earlier in this chapter. From the Coral Coast, you will likely pay more for Nadi-based activities than if you were staying on the west coast. On the other hand, you are closer to such activities as the rafting trips on the Navua River (see "Pacific Harbour & Beqa Island," later in this chapter).

From here you can easily take advantage of the golf, fishing, and diving at Pacific Harbour and see the sights in Suva.

I have organized the attractions below in the order in which you will come to them from Nadi; that is, from west to east.

MOMI BATTERY

The Queen's Road branches off toward the coast and **Momi Bay,** 16km (10 miles) south of Nadi Town. The first 5km (3 miles) of this road is improved, since it leads to a large Marriott hotel project being developed on Momi Bay. Turn right at the signpost beside a school and follow a rough dirt track another 4km (2½ miles) to **Momi Battery.** Built by American forces during World War II to protect the main pass through the Great Sea Reef, the concrete bunkers and naval guns are now a National Trust of Fiji historical park. The drive is worth it just for the splendid view over the lagoon and western coast of Viti Levu. The park does not have toilets or drinking water. It's open daily from 9am to 5pm. Admission is F$3 (US$2) adults, F$1 (US60¢) for students.

NATADOLA BEACH

Off the Queen's Road 35km (21 miles) south of Nadi, the mostly paved Maro Road runs down to **Natadola Beach** 🌴🌴🌴, the only exceptionally beautiful beach on Viti Levu. A big resort is going up here, including a golf course designed by Vijay Singh. Meantime, Natadola has a grassy, parklike area all along it. A break in the reef allows some surf to break here, especially on the south end. Already here is **Natadola Beach Resort** (© 672 1001; www.natadola.com), a small, Spanish-style hotel with a dining room and bar in a shady courtyard. Rather than drive here, I would wait and take the Coral Coast Railway train from Shangri-La's Fijian Resort (see below).

CORAL COAST RAILWAY 🌴

Based outside Shangri-La's Fijian Resort, the **Coral Coast Railway Co.** (© 652 0434) uses two restored sugar cane locomotives for a variety of tours on narrow-gauge railroads through the cane fields, across bridges, and along the coast. The best pulls you to lovely Natadola Beach, where you swim (bring your own towel) and have a barbecue lunch at the beach. These outings cost about F$105 (US$63) from the Nadi hotels and F$98 (US$59) from those on the Coral Coast, including lunch. These "Natadola BBQ Bash" trips run daily, departing Shangri-La's Fijian resort at 10am and returning at 4pm.

A variation of the Natadola Beach trip includes a boat ride out to **Robinson Crusoe Island** (© 651 0200; www.robinsoncrusoeislandfiji.com), a basic offshore resort, for swimming, snorkeling, and a picnic lunch. These excursions cost about F$145 (US$87) from Nadi, F$130 (US$78) from the Coral Coast. Water-skiing is extra. The boat doesn't run every day, so call ahead.

The other locomotive makes trips east to Sigatoka on the Coral Coast. A half-day version takes you to Sigatoka town for shopping and sightseeing. It costs F$60 (US$36) from the Nadi area, F$55 (US$33) from the Coral Coast. It also makes all-day "Ratu's Scenic Inland" tours into the Sigatoka Valley. These cost F$123 (US$74) from Nadi, F$120 (US$72) from the Coral Coast.

The company also has sundown tours, which include a kava welcoming ceremony and dinner. These cost F$75 (US$45) from Nadi, F$69 (US$42) from the Coral Coast hotels.

Children pay half, and all fares are somewhat less expensive if you provide your own transportation to the station.

KALEVU SOUTH PACIFIC CULTURAL CENTRE &

Well worth a visit if you're interested in island life and history, the **Kalevu South Pacific Cultural Centre,** opposite Shangri-La's Fijian Resort (*C* **652 0200**), presents demonstrations of traditional kava processing, handicraft making, lovo cooking, and fishing. The cultural exhibits include not just Fiji but Samoa, Kiribati (in the central Pacific), and New Zealand. The center offers half- and full-day tours of the complex for F$69 (US$42) and F$99 (US$60), respectively, including transportation and a traditional island lunch cooked in an earth oven. The other days it offers 1-hour tours of the grounds and Fiji historical museum for F$25 (US$15). Call for schedules and reservations. The center is open daily from 9am to 4pm. You can also get refreshment here, or attend a Fijian meke nightly, at Gecko's Restaurant (see "Where to Dine on the Coral Coast," later).

SIGATOKA SAND DUNES NATIONAL PARK

The pine forests on either side of the Queen's Road soon give way to rolling fields of mission grass before the sea suddenly emerges at a viewpoint above Shangri-La's Fijian Resort on Yanuca Island. After you pass the resort, watch on the right for the visitor center for **Sigatoka Sand Dunes National Park** (*C* **652 0243**). Fiji's first national park protects high sand hills, which extend for several miles along the coast. About two-thirds of them are stabilized with grass, but some along the shore are still shifting sand (the surf crashing on them is dangerous). Ancient burial grounds and pieces of pottery dating from 5 B.C. to A.D. 240 have been found among the dunes, but be warned: Removing them is against the law. Exhibits in the visitor center explain the dunes and their history. Rangers are on duty daily from 8am to 6pm. Admission to the visitors center is free, but adults pay F$8 (US$5), students F$3 (US$1.80) to visit the actual dunes. Call ahead for a free guided tour. (*Note:* You must go to the visitors center before visiting the dunes, which are not accessible from Club Masa, about 1km/½ mile toward Sigatoka.)

SIGATOKA TOWN

About 3km (2 miles) from the sand dunes visitor center, the Queen's Road enters **Sigatoka** (pop. 2,000), the commercial center of the Coral Coast. This quiet, predominantly Indo-Fijian town is perched along the west bank of the **Sigatoka River,** Fiji's longest waterway. The broad, muddy river lies on one side of the main street; on the other is a row of stores. The river is crossed by the Melrose Bridge, built in 1997 and named in honor of Fiji's winning the Melrose Cup at the Hong Kong Sevens rugby matches. The old bridge it replaced is now for pedestrians only.

SIGATOKA VALLEY

From Sigatoka, you can go inland along the west bank of the meandering river, flanked on both sides by a patchwork of flat green fields of vegetables that give the **Sigatoka Valley** its nickname: "Fiji's Salad Bowl." The pavement ends about 1km (½ mile) from the town; after that, the road surface is poorly graded and covered with loose stones.

The residents of **Lawai** village at 1.5km (1 mile) from town offer Fijian handicrafts for sale. Two kilometers (1¼ miles) farther on, a small dirt track branches off to the left and runs down a hill to **Nakabuta,** the "Pottery Village," where the residents make and sell authentic Fijian pottery. This art has seen a renaissance of late, and you will find bowls, plates, and other items in handicraft shops elsewhere. Tour buses from Nadi and the Coral Coast stop there most days.

If you're not subject to vertigo, you can look forward to driving past Nakabuta: the road climbs steeply along a narrow ridge, commanding panoramic views across the large Sigatoka Valley with its quiltlike fields to the right and much smaller, more rugged ravine to the left. It then winds its way down to the valley floor and the **Sigatoka Agricultural Research Station,** on whose shady grounds some tour groups stop for picnic lunches. The road climbs into the interior and eventually to Ba on the northwest coast; it intersects the **Nausori Highlands** Road leading back to Nadi, but it can be rough or even washed out during periods of heavy rain. Unless they have a four-wheel-drive vehicle or are on an organized tour with a guide, most visitors turn around at the research station and head back to Sigatoka.

TAVUNI HILL FORTIFICATION
A sign at the eastern end of the Sigatoka River bridge points inland to the **Tavuni Hill Fortification,** built by an exiled Tongan chief as a safe haven from the ferocious Fijian hill tribes living up the valley. Those highlanders constantly fought wars with the coastal Fijians, and they were the last to give up cannibalism and convert to Christianity. When they rebelled against the Deed of Cession to Great Britain in 1875, the colonial administration sent a force of 1,000 men up the Sigatoka River. They destroyed all the hill forts lining the river, including Tavuni. Today the fort is a Fiji Heritage Project that's open to the public Monday to Friday 8am to 4pm, Saturday 8:30am to 1:30pm. Admission is F$6 (US$3.50) for adults and F$3 (US$1.80) for children.

KULA ECO PARK ★★
Opposite the Outrigger on the Lagoon Fiji, **Kula Eco Park** (© 650 0505; www.fijiwild.com) is Fiji's only wildlife park. Along the banks of a stream in a tropical forest, it has a fine collection of rainbow-feathered tropical birds and an aquarium stocked with examples of local sea life. Allow 2 hours here, since this is one of the South Pacific's best places to view local flora and fauna in a natural setting. Children will love it. It's open daily 10am to 4pm. Admission is F$15 (US$9) for adults, F$7.50 (US$4.50) for children under 12.

WATERFALL & CAVE TOURS ★★
You won't soon forget the waterfall and cave tours offered by Rusi Brown's **Adventures in Paradise Fiji** (© 652 0833; wfall@connect.com.fj), near the Outrigger on the Lagoon Fiji. The waterfall tour goes to Biausevu village in the Korolevu Valley. A tour bus takes you to the village, where you'll be welcomed at a traditional yaqona ceremony. Then comes a 30-minute hike along a rocky stream to the falls, which plunge straight over a cliff into a swimming hole. The sometimes slippery trail fords the stream seven times, so wear canvas or reef shoes or a pair of strap-on sandals. Wear a bathing suit and bring a towel if you want to take a very cool and refreshing dip after the sweaty hike. You'll be treated to a barbecue lunch.

On Rusi's other excursion, you'll spend 45 minutes inside the Naihehe Cave, which was used as a fortress by Fiji's last cannibal tribe, and then return via a bilibili raft on the Sigatoka River (the cave is a 35-minute drive up the Sigatoka Valley). You'll have a picnic lunch before the raft ride.

Rusi charges F$99 (US$60) per person for either tour, which run on alternate days. Add F$20 (US$13) from Nadi. Book at any hotel activities desk.

> **Tips Fijian Art: Don't Steal It, Come Here**
>
> Tessa Miller's **Namana Gallery** ☆☆, on Korotogo Drive west of the Outrigger on the Lagoon Fiji (② 650 0218), is one of the best places to buy local art, especially works by Fred Whippy, Fiji's most prolific painter. "If you like the art hanging in your hotel room," says Tessa, "don't steal it. Come here." While browsing, you can partake of fresh Fijian coffee, muffins, and rolls, and you can check your e-mail for F$3 (US$1.80) for 15 minutes. Namana Gallery is open Monday to Friday from 8am to 6pm, Saturday from 10am to 6pm. Follow the old beach road off the traffic circle at Korotogo; the gallery is the first building on the left.

WATERSPORTS & OTHER OUTDOOR ACTIVITIES

Most hotels have abundant sports facilities, including diving, for their guests (see "Where to Stay on the Coral Coast," below).

A joint project between an American couple and Votua villagers, **Mike's Divers,** on the Queen's Road between The Naviti and the Warwick Fiji (② 650/879-0421 in the U.S., or 653 0222; www.dive-fiji.com), provides scuba diving at F$150 (US$90) for two tanks, and teaches PADI certification courses. The base is a short boat ride to the outer reef and Morgan's Wall, one of the Coral Coast's most famous sites.

SHOPPING ON THE CORAL COAST

In Sigatoka Town, you can do some serious hunting at **Sigatoka Handicraft Centre** (no phone), in a tin-roof shack on the main street beside the river. Operated by local women, it has carvings, shell jewelry, masi cloth, and other items made in Fiji. **Jack's Handicrafts, Prouds,** and **Tappoo** have large stores across the street.

Prices at relaxed, "browse-in-peace" **Baravi Handicrafts** ☆☆ (② 652 0364), in Vatukarasa village 13km (8 miles) east of Sigatoka, are somewhat lower than you'll find at the larger stores, and it has a snack bar that sells excellent coffee made from Fijian-grown beans. The shop buys woodcarvings and pottery directly from village artisans. It's open Monday to Saturday 7:30am to 6pm, Sunday 8:30am to 5pm. Vatukarasa also has a roadside stall where you might find unusual seashells.

WHERE TO STAY ON THE CORAL COAST
EXPENSIVE

Outrigger on the Lagoon Fiji ☆☆ *Kids*   This fine lagoonside resort compensates for Mother Nature's having robbed its beach of most sand with one of the most attractive swimming pools in Fiji. You can still go kayaking, spy-boarding and snorkeling at high tide, but the gorgeous pool is the center of attention here. In a way, the Outrigger is two hotels in one. Most of the accommodations are hotel rooms in modern five-story hillside buildings at the rear of the property. The resort also offers thatched-roof guest bungalows and restaurants that resemble a traditional Fijian village in a coconut grove down by the lagoon. These rooms all have balconies, with spectacular views from the upper floor units. Hotel rooms in the Reef Wing, a three-story lagoonside building (and the last remnant of The Reef Resort which once stood here), are smaller than their hillside counterparts and better suited to couples than families. You'll have butler service down in the comfortable guest bures, which have masi-lined peaked ceilings. The beachfront bungalows are the pick of the litter. A few others are joined to make family units. Australian restaurateur Geoff Shaw, who owns both this resort and Castaway Island Resort (see "Resorts in the Mamanuca Islands," earlier in this chapter), sees to it that everyone is well fed in an intimate fine-dining restaurant, a large open-air, buffet-style dining room, and a midday restaurant by the pool.

P.O. Box 173, Sigatoka (Queen's Rd., 78km/49 miles from Nadi Airport, 8km/5 miles east of Sigatoka). (C) 800/ 688-7444 or 650 0044. Fax 652 0074. www.outrigger.com. 254 units. F$500–F$600 (US$300–US$360) double; F$600–F$1,080 (US$360–US$648) bungalow. AE, DC, MC, V. **Amenities:** 3 restaurants; 4 bars; outdoor pool; 2 tennis courts; exercise room; Jacuzzi; watersports equipment rentals; children's programs; game room; activities desk; car-rental desk; business center; shopping arcade; salon; massage; babysitting; laundry service; coin-op washers and dryers. *In room:* A/C, TV, dataport, fridge, coffeemaker, hair dryer, iron, safe.

Shangri-La's Fijian Resort ★★★   Fiji's largest hotel, "The Fijian" occupies all 105 acres of flat Yanuca Island, which is joined to the mainland by a short, one-lane causeway. Yanuca is bordered by a crystal clear lagoon and a coral-colored sand beach, both superior to those at Denarau Island near Nadi. Needless to say, there are a host of watersports activities here, including diving, or you can play tennis or knock around the 9-hole golf course. Covered walkways wander through thick tropical foliage to link the hotel blocks to three main restaurant-and-bar buildings, both adjacent to swimming pools. The spacious rooms and suites occupy two- and three-story buildings, all on the shore of the island. Each room has a view of the lagoon and sea from its own private balcony or patio. The suites have separate bedrooms and two bathroom sinks. While The Fijian draws many families, its Ocean Premier units on one end of the sprawling property are reserved for couples. The Fijian's restaurants have something for everyone's taste, if not necessarily for everyone's pocketbook, and four bars are ready to quench any thirst. A full-service spa was due to open in late 2006, as were half a dozen honeymoon bungalows.

Private Mail Bag (NAPO 353), Nadi Airport (Yanuca Island, 60km/36 miles from Nadi Airport, 10km/6 miles west of Sigatoka). (C) **800/942-5050** or 652 0155. Fax 652 0402. www.shangri-la.com. 436 units. F$396–F$523 (US$237–US$314) double, F$666–F$731 (US$400–US$438) suite, F$950 (US$570) bungalow. AE, DC, MC, V. **Amenities:** 4 restaurants; 4 bars; 3 outdoor pools; 9-hole golf course; 4 tennis courts; fitness center; watersports equipment rentals; bike rentals; children's programs; game room; concierge; activities desk; car-rental desk; business center; shopping arcade; salon; 24-hr. room service; massage; babysitting; laundry service. *In room:* A/C, TV, dataport, fridge, coffeemaker, hair dryer, iron, safe.

The Warwick Fiji   Sitting on a palm-fringed beach with a bit more sand than you'll find at the Outrigger or the Hideaway, this complex reflects distinctive architecture from its origins as the Hyatt Regency Fiji. A sweeping roof supported by wood beams covers a wide reception and lobby area bordered on either end by huge carved murals depicting Capt. James Cook's discovery of Fiji in 1779. A curving staircase descends from the center of the lobby into a large square well, giving access to the dining and recreation areas on the lagoon level. The medium-size guest rooms are in two- and three-story blocks that flank the central building. Each room has its own balcony or patio with a view of the sea or the tropical gardens surrounding the complex. The most expensive units are suites, which directly face the lagoon from the ends of the buildings. The sand-floored Wicked Walu, under a thatch roof on a tiny island offshore, is the choice dining spot here. A free shuttle runs between The Warwick and its more family-oriented sister, The Naviti Resort. Construction was due to begin in 2006 on a complex of 40 deluxe bungalows, which is to have its own swimming pool.

P.O. Box 100, Korolevu (104km/62 miles from Nadi Airport, 32km/20 miles east of Sigatoka). (C) **800/448-8355** or 653 0555. Fax 653 0010. www.warwickfiji.com. 250 units. F$350–F$550 (US$210–US$330) double; F$732 (US$439) suite. AE, DC, MC, V. **Amenities:** 4 restaurants; 5 bars; 2 outdoor pools; 4 tennis courts; exercise room; spa; Jacuzzi;

watersports equipment rentals; children's programs; activities desk; car-rental desk; business center; shopping arcade; salon; 24-hr. room service; massage; babysitting; laundry service; coin-op washers and dryers; concierge-level rooms. *In room:* A/C, TV, dataport, minibar, coffeemaker, hair dryer, iron, safe.

MODERATE

Near the Hideaway Resort, the American-owned **Tambua Sands** (© 650 0399; www.tambuasandsfiji.com) offers a restaurant, bar, swimming pool, and 25 bungalows in a lagoonside coconut grove. Rates range from F$193 to F$240 (US$116–US$144) per bungalow.

Hideaway Resort 🌴🌴 *Value*   This is the best all-bungalow resort on the Coral Coast. It occupies a narrow strip of land between the Queen's Road and the lagoon that's long enough so that families, singles, and couples don't get in each other's way or disturb each other's sleep (or lack thereof). For the most peace and quiet, opt for a duplex "deluxe villa" on the far end of the property. With pastel stucco walls and both his-and-her indoor showers as well as outdoor showers, these are like smaller and less expensive versions of the bungalows at Vatulele Island Resort (see "A Resort on Vatulele Island," below). The 16 original, A-frame bungalows here are much closer to the action. Other units are in modern, duplex bungalows with tropical furnishings and shower-only bathrooms. A few larger family units here can sleep up to five persons. The main building opens to a beachside pool with a waterfall and a water slide; this vista is especially appealing at night, when a flame shoots from the top of a mid-pool post. Lively evening entertainment features a Fijian meke feast once a week, Beqa island fire-walking, and Club Med–style cabaret shows. As has happened at the Outrigger on the Lagoon Fiji (see above), most of the beach has eroded, but you can follow a trail out on the reef and observe a coral restoration project being undertaken in cooperation with local villagers.

P.O. Box 233, Sigatoka (Queen's Rd., 92km/55 miles from Nadi Airport, 21km/13 miles east of Sigatoka). © 650 0177. Fax 652 0025. www.hideawayfiji.com. 112 units. F$320–F$510 (US$192–US$306) bungalow. AE, DC, MC, V. **Amenities:** Restaurant; bar; outdoor pool; miniature golf; tennis court; exercise room; watersports equipment rentals; children's programs; game room; concierge; activities desk; car-rental desk; salon; massage; babysitting; laundry service; coin-op washers and dryers. *In room:* A/C, dataport, fridge, coffeemaker, hair dryer, iron, safe.

The Naviti Resort *Value*   A sister of The Warwick Fiji (see above), this recently expanded resort attracts mainly Australians and New Zealanders lured by its extensive activities and optional all-inclusive rates. The resort sits on 40 acres of coconut palms waving in the trade wind beside a lovely beach and dredged lagoon (you can wade to two islets). Or you can lounge beside two swimming pools, one with a shaded swim-up bar. Double-deck covered walkways lead from the central complex to two- and three-story concrete block buildings, two of them constructed in 2005. The older wings hold some of Fiji's largest hotel rooms (baths have both tubs and walk-in showers). The two-room suites on the ends of the older buildings are especially spacious. The best units here, however, are 16 beachside bungalows, ranging from studios to two-bedrooms. Fijian-shaped shingle roofs cover a coffee shop, a candlelit restaurant for fine dining, and a large lounge where a band plays for dancing most evenings. A fine Chinese restaurant looks out on an unchallenging 9-hole golf course.

P.O. Box 29, Korolevu (Queen's Road, 97km/58 miles from Nadi Airport, 26km/16 miles east of Sigatoka). © 800/448-8355 or 653 0444. Fax 653 0099. www.navitiresort.com.fj. 224 units. F$315–F$340 (US$189–US$204) double; F$565 (US$339) suite or bungalow. Rates include breakfast. All-inclusive rates available. AE, DC, MC, V. **Amenities:** 3 restaurants; 3 bars; outdoor pool; 9-hole golf course; 5 tennis courts; exercise room; spa; Jacuzzi; watersports equipment rentals; bike rentals; children's programs; game room; activities desk; car-rental desk; salon; limited room service; babysitting; laundry service. *In room:* A/C, TV, dataport, fridge, coffeemaker, hair dryer, iron, safe.

INEXPENSIVE

Although not nearly as charming as The Beachhouse, the simple **Tubakula Beach Bungalows** (© **650 0097;** www.fiji4less.com) sits in a lagoonside coconut grove almost next door to the Outrigger on the Lagoon Fiji, thus putting the restaurants on Korotogo Drive within walking distance. The downstairs of each A-frame bungalow has a lounge, kitchen, bathroom, and bedroom; upstairs is a sleeping loft. Each can sleep six persons, so sharing one represents good value. The 24 dorm beds are in European-style houses. Rates range from F$80 to F$100 (US$48–US$60) for a bungalow, F$18 (US$11) for a dorm bed.

The Beachouse ⟨ₑ Andrew Waldken-Brown, a European who was born in Fiji, and his Australian wife, Jessica, have turned his family's old vacation cottage—beside one of the finest beaches on the Coral Coast—into this excellent backpacker resort. Built in the old South Seas style of tin roof, clapboard sides, and big windows with push-out, prop-up shutters, the charming cottage serves as lounge, bar, and dining room providing inexpensive meals. Andrew and Jessica gave their airy, two-story dorms the ultimate in luxuries—well, at least as far as backpackers are concerned. Each dorm is screened and has its own ceiling fan, and all beds have reading lights. Upstairs is aimed at couples, with partitions separating roomettes, but the walls don't reach the ceiling; the accommodations also have ceiling fans and mosquito-netted double beds. Better for couples are garden rooms in a separate building; each has a double bed and two settees for lounging. All guests, including campers who can pitch their tents on the spacious lawn, share clean toilets and a modern communal kitchen.

P.O. Box 68, Korolevu (105km/65 miles from Nadi Airport, 37km/23 miles east of Sigatoka). © **0800/653 0530** toll-free in Fiji, or 653 0500. www.fijibeachouse.com. 12 units (none w/bathroom), 64 dorm beds. F$77 (US$46) double; F$25 (US$15) dorm bed; F$16 (US$10) per person camping. MC, V. **Amenities:** Restaurant; bar; bike and watersports equipment rentals; massage. *In room:* No phone.

Bedarra Inn–Fiji ⟨*Value* This comfortable inn began life as a private home with bedrooms on either end of a great, two-story central hall, which opened to a veranda overlooking a swimming pool and the lagoon. The beach is across a dead-end road known as Sunset Strip, which was the main drag before the Queen's Road was diverted around the new Outrigger on the Lagoon Fiji, a short walk from here. Today a square bar, lounge furniture, and potted palms occupy the great hall, and a romantic restaurant has taken over the veranda (see "Where to Dine on the Coral Coast," below). Upstairs, another veranda wraps around the house. Inside, guests can opt for two-bedroom budget suites capable of sleeping up to four persons, or standard hotel-style rooms, each equipped with a king-size bed but not air-conditioners (ceiling fans kick up a breeze). Out back, a two-room bure can accommodate four persons. To the side of the house, a two-story motel block holds 16 air-conditioned rooms, all with traditional oak furniture and large bathrooms with walk-in showers. Four of these also have cooking facilities.

P.O. Box 1213, Sigatoka (Sunset Strip, 78km/47 miles from Nadi Airport, 8km/5 miles east of Sigatoka). © **650 0476.** Fax 652 0166. www.bedarrafiji.com. 20 units. F$129–F$175 (US$77–US$105) double. AE, MC, V. **Amenities:** Restaurant; bar; outdoor pool; game room; activities desk; laundry service. *In room:* A/C (in motel rooms), dataport, kitchen (in 4 units), fridge, coffeemaker, hair dryer, no phone.

A RESORT ON VATULELE ISLAND

A flat, raised coral atoll 48km (30 miles) south of Viti Levu, **Vatulele Island** is known for its unusual red shrimp—that is, they're red while alive, not just after being cooked. The only way to see them, however, is to stay at Vatulele Island Resort, which is accessible only from Nadi Airport,

Vatulele Island Resort ⭐⭐⭐   A favorite haunt of Hollywood stars (it was built by Australian movie producer Henry Crawford, who has since sold it), this super-luxe resort resides beside a gorgeous, 1km (½ mile)–long beach of brilliantly white sand. In a blend of Santa Fe and Fijian native architectural styles, the bures and main building have thick adobe walls supporting Fijian thatch roofs. Most meals here are dinner parties inside the main building or on the adjacent patio. You can dine anytime and anyplace you want, however, including in your bure, down in the cool wine cellar, out on the beach, or in The Folly, a cabana that sits all by itself on a headland at one end of the beach. During the day you can take a picnic lunch out on a tiny nearby islet known for good reason as "Nookie Island." Although staff members play guitars and sing island songs, the nightly dinner parties *are* the entertainment at Vatulele, and they can go into the wee hours. Seemingly vast distances and thick native forest separate the spacious bures, which a previous manager described as being "orgasm distance" apart. Most of these are L-shaped and have a lounge and raised sleeping areas under one roof; another roof covers an enormous bathroom that can be entered both from the bed/dressing area and from a private, hammock-swung patio. At the far end of the property, the private, exquisitely designed Pink House delights honeymooners with its own private beach, plunge pool, and a unique two-person, face-to-face tub in the middle of its large bathroom. The Hollywood types often opt for the terrific views from The Point, a 2-story villa with a private pool sitting on a headland. You'll have free use of an array of non-motorized watersports equipment and pay extra only for scuba diving, deep-sea fishing, and massage.

P.O. Box 9936, Nadi Airport (Vatulele Island, 50km/30 miles south of Viti Levu, a 30-min. flight from Nadi). ℂ 800/828-9146 or 672 0300. Fax 672 0062. www.vatulele.com. 19 units. US$888–US$1,880 bungalow. Rates include room, food, bar, all activities except sport fishing and scuba diving. 4-night minimum stay required. Round-trip transfers US$450 per person. AE, DC, MC, V. Children under 12 not accepted. **Amenities:** Restaurant; bar; tennis court; 24-hr. room service; massage; laundry service. *In room:* Minibar, coffeemaker, hair dryer, safe, no phone.

WHERE TO DINE ON THE CORAL COAST

In Sigatoka Town next to Jack's Handicrafts, Roshni and Jean-Pierre Gerber's clean **Le Cafe Pizza Town** (ℂ **652 0668**) offers a mixed menu of sandwiches, salads, curries, spaghetti, pizzas, fish and chips, and other snacks. You can check your e-mail here, too. Prices range from F$6.50 to $F16 (US$4–US$9.50). Credit cards are not accepted. Le Cafe is open Monday to Saturday from 9am to 5pm. The Gerbers—she's from Fiji, he's a Swiss chef—also serve dinners at Le Cafe in Korotogo (see below).

Although her original restaurant is better (see below), **Vilisite's Seafood Restaurant No. 2** is on the Queen's Road in Sigatoka west of the river (ℂ **650 1030**). It's open daily from 10am to 9:30pm.

Many Coral Coast hotels have special nights, such as meke feasts of Fijian foods cooked in a lovo, served buffet style, and followed by traditional dancing.

Bedarra Inn Restaurant INTERNATIONAL   Overlooking a lush tropical garden surrounding a swimming pool, the veranda of the Bedarra Inn Fiji (see "Where to Stay on the Coral Coast," above) is the most romantic place to dine here. The menu offers an uninspired but varied selection, including tender steaks under peppercorn or red wine sauce, fresh local fish panfried with lemon caper sauce, crumbed veal slices topped with asparagus, a vegetarian pasta, and a spicy version of spaghetti carbonara. You can also try Fijian dishes such as palusami and *ika vakalolo* (fish steamed in coconut milk).

Korotogo Drive, Korotogo, west of the Outrigger on the Lagoon Fiji. ℭ **650 0476**. Reservations recommended. Main courses F$18–F$26 (US$11–US$16). AE, MC, V. Daily 7am–10pm.

Gecko's Restaurant REGIONAL   Occupying the veranda of one of the Western-style buildings at The Kalevu Cultural Museum, this pleasant restaurant offers a more affordable if not-as-good alternative to the dining rooms at Shangri-La's Fijian Resort across the Queen's Road. You can have a breakfast of omelets and other egg dishes all day here. Lunch features a choice of sandwiches, burgers, fish and chips, curry, stir-fries, and other local favorites. Dinner sees a wide-ranging menu, which includes the house specialty, mud crabs with coconut cream, chili, or Chinese-style black bean. There are Fijian meke shows here every night (call to see what's on).

Queen's Rd., in Kalevu Cultural Museum opposite Shangri-La's Fijian Resort. ℭ **652 0200**. Reservations accepted. Breakfast F$5–F$8 (US$3–US$5); lunch F$5–F$11 (US$3–US$6.50); main courses F$12–F$26 (US$7–US$16). MC, V. Daily 10am–10pm.

Le Cafe ☆☆ INTERNATIONAL   In addition to running Le Cafe Town in Siga-toka, Roshni and Jean-Pierre Gerber turn their attention to this little establishment, where they oversee the production of fish and chips, Indian curries, Italian pastas, and some reasonably good pizzas. The nightly specials board features the likes of fresh fish filet with lemon butter sauce, pepper or garlic steak, garlic prawns, and local lobster with Mornay sauce. A special lunch and dinner menu offers substantial servings of fish and chips, spaghetti, or burgers for F$7.50 (US$4.50). Even if you don't dine here, the thatch-topped bar out front is a great place for a sunset cocktail during happy hour from 5 to 7pm daily.

Sunset Strip, Korotogo, west of the Outrigger on the Lagoon Fiji. ℭ **652 0877**. Reservations accepted. Breakfast F$6.50–F$9.50 (US$4–US$5.50); lunch F$7.50 (US$4.50); pizzas and main courses F$7–F$20 (US$4–US$12). No credit cards. Daily 8am–10pm (bar later).

Vilisite's Seafood Restaurant ☆☆ *Value* SEAFOOD/INDIAN/CHINESE   Vil-isite (sounds like "Felicity"), a friendly Fijian who lived in Australia, operates one of the few places in Fiji where you can dine right by the lagoon's edge. Come in time for a sunset drink and bring a camera, for the westward view from Vilisite's veranda belongs on a postcard. Her well-prepared cuisine is predominately fresh local seafood—fish, shrimp, lobster, octopus—in curry, garlic, and butter, or coconut milk (the Fijian way). She offers only five full seafood meals at dinner, or you can choose from chop suey, curry, shrimp, or fish and chips. Vilisite will arrange rides for dinner parties of four or more from as far away as the Outrigger on the Lagoon Fiji, but be sure to ask about the cost. You won't soon forget the view or this extraordinarily friendly Fijian, who certainly knows how to cook.

Queen's Road, Korolevu, between the Warwick and the Naviti. ℭ **653 0054**. Reservations recommended. Lunch F$4.50–F$19 (US$2.50–US$12); full dinners F$7–F$45 (US$4–US$27). MC, V. Daily 8am–10pm.

ISLAND NIGHTS ON THE CORAL COAST

Coral Coast nightlife centers around the hotels and whatever Fiji meke shows they are sponsoring.

The **Fijian fire walkers** from Beqa, an island off the south coast (remember, it's pronounced M-*bengga*, not *Beck*-a), parade across the steaming stones to the incanta-tions of "witch doctors" at least once a week at the **Hideaway Resort** (ℭ **650 0177**), **Outrigger on the Lagoon Fiji** (ℭ **650 0044**), and the **Warwick Fiji** (ℭ **653 0010**). Call them or ask at your hotel for the schedule.

Gecko's Restaurant (© 652 0200) in the Kalevu South Pacific Cultural Center has a 1-hour Fijian dance show Monday to Friday nights and a 3-hour version on Sunday evening. Call for reservations. The **Hideaway Resort** (© 650 0177) has a South Pacific show on Sunday and its excellent cabaret shows during the week.

4 Pacific Harbour & Beqa Island

Pacific Harbour was begun in the early 1970s as a recreation-oriented, luxury residential community and resort (translated: a real estate development). A number of expatriates have built homes here and have their own tourist information website at **www.pacificharbour-fiji.com.** Given the heat, humidity, and amount of rain it gets, Pacific Harbour is not the place to come for a typical beach vacation. On the other hand, it does have an excellent golf course, fine deep-sea fishing, fabulous scuba diving out in the **Beqa Lagoon,** and rafting trips on the nearby **Navua River.** In fact, local promoters aren't far wrong when they describe Pacific Harbour as "The Adventure Capital of Fiji."

It's also my favorite place to experience Fijian culture without visiting a village. Formerly known as the Pacific Harbour Cultural Centre & Market Place but now the **Arts Village,** a shopping center on the Queen's Road serves both tourists and residents of the real estate development. It consists of colonial-style clapboard buildings joined by covered walkways. In addition to restaurants, a grocery store, ice cream and massage parlors, boutiques, handicraft shops, and a swimming pool, it is home to Fiji's best cultural center (see below).

Offshore, rugged **Beqa Island** is nearly cut in two by a long bay, making it one of Fiji's more scenic spots. Most of Fiji's famous fire walkers come from Dakuibeqa, Naceva, and Ruka villages on Beqa. The island is surrounded by Beqa Lagoon, where more than a dozen dive sites feature both soft and hard corals. Among them is **Frigate Passage,** which has both a 48-meter (158-foot) wall for divers and huge waves for surfers.

GETTING TO PACIFIC HARBOUR & GETTING AROUND

Pacific Harbour is on the Queen's Road, 30km (50 miles) west of Suva. The express buses between Nadi and Suva stop at The Pearl South Pacific Resort, where you'll also find taxis waiting in the parking lot. See "Getting There & Getting Around" in chapter 4 for more information.

WHAT TO SEE & DO IN PACIFIC HARBOUR
VISITING THE ARTS VILLAGE 🏯🏯

Fiji's best cultural center is the **Arts Village** (© 345 0065; www.artsvillage.com), on the Queen's Road. Formerly known as the Pacific Harbour Culture Centre, it has been greatly spiffed up in recent years. Its centerpiece is a lakeside Fijian village, complete with thatched-roofs over the grand chief's bure and the tallest traditional temple in Fiji. Two tours depart every hour Monday to Saturday. The "island boat tour" wanders around the edges of the village, while the "island temple tour" takes you into the village for visits with Fijians working at carving, weaving, boat building, and other crafts. These cost F$15 (US$9) each for adults. I suggest getting here for a 9am tour, then watching the 11am show of traditional dancing and singing (and fire walking on Tues and Thurs). Admission is F$15 (US$9), or F$20 (US$12) when the fire walkers perform. Children 6 to 16 are charged half.

FISHING, GOLF & SCUBA DIVING

FISHING   The waters off southern Viti Levu are renowned for their big game fish, especially when the tuna and mahimahi are running from January to May and when big wahoos pass by in June and July. The women's world records for wahoo and trevally were set here. **Xtasea Charters** (© 345 0280; www.xtaseacharters.com) and **Tropical Fishing & Water Sports** (© 992 3233; www.sportfishingfiji.com) can tailor excursions—from going for big ones offshore to trolling for smaller but exciting catch inshore. A full day of fishing costs about F$500 (US$300) for half a day, F$800 (US$480) for a full day.

GOLF   Robert Trent Jones, Jr. designed the scenic 18-hole, par-72 **The Pearl South Pacific Championship Golf Course** (© 345 0905), on the north side of the Queen's Road. Some of its fairways cross lakes; others cut their way through narrow valleys surrounded by jungle-clad hills. Greens fees are F$40 (US$24), and the pro shop has equipment for rent.

SCUBA DIVING & SNORKELING 🐠🐠   San Francisco–based **Aqua-Trek** (© 800/ 541-4334 or 345 0324; fax 345 0324; www.aquatrek.com) has expeditions to Beqa Lagoon. Aqua-Trek also teaches resort diving and a full range of PADI courses. A two-tank dive costs F$170 (US$102).

RIVER RAFTING & KAYAKING 🐠🐠🐠

Videos and brochures often feature tourists lazily floating down a Fijian river on a raft made of bamboo poles lashed together. In the old days, mountain-dwelling Fijians really did use **bilibilis**—flimsy bamboo rafts—to float their crops down river to market. They would discard the rafts and walk home. Today you can ride your own bilibili down the Navua River, between Pacific Harbour and Suva. The award-winning **Discover Fiji Tours** (© 345 0180; www.discoverfijitours.com) takes you upriver by motorized canoe and usually brings you back on a bilibili (ask if the bilibili ride is included before you sign up).

The river itself is a scenic delight as it cuts its way through the foothills. Depending on how much it has rained recently, you'll have a few gentle rapids to negotiate, and you'll stop for dips in waterfalls that tumble right into the river. Wear swimsuits and sandals, but bring a sarong to wear in a typical Fijian village, where you'll be welcomed at a yaqona ceremony.

These full-day trips cost about F$85 (US$51) from Pacific Harbour, more from the Nadi and Coral Coast hotels. Children pay about half fare. Reservations and a minimum of two passengers are required.

Discover Fiji Tours also has 1½-hour hikes through a rainforest to a waterfall, plus rafting-hiking trips. Call or check the website for details.

If you're into serious white-water rafting, the South Pacific's best is with **Rivers Fiji** 🐠🐠🐠 (© 800/446-2411 in the U.S., or 345 0147; fax 345 0148; www.riversfiji. com). This American-owned outfit uses modern inflatable rafts and kayaks for trips through the Upper Navua River Gorge, the "Grand Canyon of Fiji" and an official conservation area. I have met experienced rafters who say the Navua Gorge was one of their top experiences. The adventures cost about US$150 per person. It also has 1- and 2-day inflatable kayaking trips—"funyacking," it calls them—on the 'Luva River, another picturesque waterway up in the Namosi Highlands, for US$110 and US$365 per person, respectively. And it has 6-day trips combining the Upper Navua River Gorge, the 'Luva, and sea kayaking in the Beqa Lagoon. Reservations are essential.

WHERE TO STAY IN PACIFIC HARBOUR

If you're on a low budget, check out **Tsulu Beach House & Apartments.** Part of the Arts Village (see above), it was under construction during my recent visit.

The Pearl South Pacific   Formerly the Pacific Harbour International Hotel, and before that the Centra Resort Pacific Harbour, this three-story lagoonside resort is now Fiji's "coolest, sexiest, most stylish" hotel, to quote its general manager. In fact, it's so cool, sexy, and stylish that it would be more at home in New York or Sydney—or even Suva—than here beside a beach of deep, gray sand. Jazz music permeates the public areas, from the lobby bar before a waterfall wall to the huge day-bed loungers, where you can literally stretch out while enjoying a drink or reading a book. Each of the original hotel rooms also has a day bed on its balcony or patio. Some of them have been turned into luxurious, one-bedroom "Penthouse Suites," each with hardwood floors and its own decor. Dining choices include an informal restaurant, a fine-dining outlet, and a bar out by the beach and swimming pool, where Sunday jazz brunches draw crowds of well-heeled locals.

P.O. Box 144, Deuba. ☎ **345 0022.** Fax 345 0262. www.thepearlsouthpacific.com. 78 units. F$300–F$360 (US$180–US$216) double; F$640 (US$384) suite. AE, DC, MC, V. **Amenities:** 4 restaurants; 4 bars; outdoor pool; golf course; 3 tennis courts; spa; watersports equipment rentals; game room; activities desk; 24-hr. room service; laundry service. *In room:* A/C, TV, high-speed dataport, minibar, fridge, coffeemaker, hairdryer.

WHERE TO STAY ON BEQA ISLAND

Cost-conscious travelers can stay at **Lawaki Beach House** (☎ **992 1621** or 926 9229; www.lawakibeachhouse.com), on Beqa's southwestern coast. It has two simple but comfortable bures with bathrooms and porches, a six-person dormitory, and space for campers. Rates range from F$52 (US$31) to F$95 (US$57) per person, including meals.

Guests arrive at the Beqa Island resorts by 30- to 45-minute boat ride from Pacific Harbour or by seaplane or helicopter from Nadi.

Beqa Lagoon Resort   On the island's north shore and once known as Marlin Bay Resort, this is the oldest hotel on Beqa, and it was showing its age during my recent visit, especially the main lagoonside building with the bar and restaurant. One advantage is that you can go scuba diving off the beach. Accommodations are in a variety of bungalows, from beachfront units with their own plunge pools to half a dozen beside a manmade pond with lily pads. Many feature Indian and Asian furniture. Least expensive are four rooms in a two-story building.

P.O. Box 112, Deuba. ☎ **330 4042.** Fax 330 4028. www.beqalagoonresort.com. 25 units. F$438–F$585 (US$263–US$351) bungalow. AE, MC, V. **Amenities:** Restaurant; bar; outdoor pool; watersports equipment rentals; limited room service; massage; babysitting; laundry service. *In room:* A/C, fridge, coffeemaker, hairdryer, safe, no phone.

Lalati Resort & Spa ★★ *Value*   Minnesotans Clint and Jayne Carlson operate this pleasant little resort at the mouth of the narrow bay that nearly slices Beqa in two. As a result, it enjoys one of the most picturesque views of any Fiji resort. A jagged peak gives way to the azure Beqa Lagoon, while Viti Levu's southern coast lines the horizon. All buildings have tin roofs and ship-plank siding, lending a South Seas plantation ambience to the property. Bathrooms in the spacious guest bures open to both living rooms and bedrooms. The bures lack airconditioning, but ceiling fans whip up a breeze. All but two of them face the beach and shallow lagoon. Dining here is family-style in the central building. A swimming pool fronts the full-service spa, which has an air-conditioned lounge with TV and DVD player. Meals and non-motorized watersports are included in the rates. Smoking is not allowed in any of the buildings here.

P.O. Box 166, Deuba. © **347 2033.** Fax 347 2034. www.lalati-fiji.com. 7 units. US$290 per person. Rates include all meals. AE, MC, V. Children under 14 not accepted. **Amenities:** Restaurant; bar; outdoor pool; exercise room; spa; Jacuzzi; watersports equipment rentals; limited room service; massage; laundry service. *In room:* Minibar, coffeemaker, hairdryer, no phone.

Royal Davui Island Fiji 🐠🐠🐠   On a rocky, 8-acre islet off Beqa's southwestern coast, Royal Davui provides competition for Fiji's other top-end, luxury resorts. The island has no flat land, however, so all but one of the bungalows sit up on the hillside. The trade-off for not being able to step from your bure onto the beach is that you will have a wonderful view. (Westward-facing units espy the sunset but can become warm in the afternoon sun, so I prefer one looking east toward Beqa.) Individually designed to fit among the rocks and old-growth forest, these spacious units have living rooms and bedrooms in separate buildings joined by a hallway. Each has a private plunge pool off the living room balcony, while their bedroom balconies hold two lounge chairs. There are whirlpool tubs as well as showers in the bathrooms, plus two unusual flat sinks with water pouring from mirrors above. Part of each bathroom roof retracts to let in fresh air or sunshine. A walkway leads from the four-level reception building up to the open-air restaurant and bar. Guests can dine under the shade of a huge banyan tree (a remote, private space for honeymooners is facetiously dubbed the "fertilizer table").

P.O. Box 3171, Lami. © **330 7090.** Fax 331 1500. www.royaldavui.com. 16 units. US$1,013–US$1,350 double. Rates include meals, non-alcoholic beverages, all activities except scuba diving, game fishing, spa treatments. **Amenities:** Restaurant; bar; outdoor pool; spa; watersports equipment; limited room service; massage; laundry service. *In room:* A/C, dataport, minibar, coffeemaker, hairdryer, iron, safe.

WHERE TO DINE IN PACIFIC HARBOUR

Oasis Restaurant REGIONAL   Owned by English expatriates Monica Vine and Colin Head, this airy dining room with widely spaced tables makes an excellent pit stop if you're driving between Nadi and Suva. The house specialty is vinegary London-style fish and chips. You can get tasty burgers, sandwiches, salads, curries, omelets, and English-style breakfasts all day. Evening sees the likes of pan-fried mahimahi, perhaps caught by one of the charter boat skippers having a cold one at Colin's friendly corner bar. Monica and Colin will let you use their computer with Internet access for F20¢ (US12¢) per minute.

Queen's Rd., in Pacific Harbour Arts Village. © **345 0617.** Reservations accepted. Breakfast F$6–F$16 (US$3.50–US$9.50); snacks, sandwiches, and lunch F$5.50–F$16 (US$3.50–US$9.50); main courses F$15–F$40 (US$9–US$24). MC, V. Mon–Sat 9:30am–2:30pm and 6–10pm, Sun 10am–2:30pm and 6–10pm.

5 Suva ⭐

Neither the likelihood of frequent showers nor an occasional deluge should discourage you from visiting Suva, Fiji's vibrant, sophisticated capital city. Grab your umbrella and wander along its broad avenues lined with grand colonial buildings and orderly parks left over from the British Empire. Its streets will be crowded with Fijians, Indians, Chinese, Europeans, Polynesians, and people of various other ancestries.

Suva sprawls over a hilly, 26 sq. km (10 sq. mile) peninsula jutting like a thumb from southeastern Viti Levu. To the east lies windswept **Laucala Bay** and to the west, Suva's busy harbor and the suburbs of **Lami Town** and **Walu Bay.** Jungle-draped

Impressions
The English, with a mania for wrong decisions in Fiji, built their capital at
Suva, smack in the middle of the heaviest rainfall . . . Yet Suva is a superb
tropical city.
—James A. Michener, *Return to Paradise,* 1951

mountains rise to heights of more than 1,200m (4,000 ft.) on the mainland to the
north, high enough to condense moisture from the prevailing southeast trade winds
and create the damp climate that cloaks the city in lush green foliage all year round.

Suva was a typical Fijian village in 1870, when the Polynesia Company sent a group
of Australians to settle land it acquired in exchange for paying Chief Cakobau's foreign debts. The Aussies established a camp on the flat, swampy, mosquito-infested
banks of **Nubukalou Creek,** on the western shore of the peninsula. When they failed
to grow first cotton and then sugar, speculators convinced the new British colonial
administration to move the capital from Levuka in 1882.

The business heart of the city still sits near Nubukalou Creek, and you can see most
of the city's sights and find most of its shops, interesting restaurants, and lively
nightspots along historic **Victoria Parade,** the main drag.

On the beautiful island of Ovalau, some 32km (20 miles) east of Viti Levu, the old
town of Levuka still looks much as it did during its heydays before the government
moved to Suva. In contrast to Suva, never-changing Levuka remains a charming example of what South Pacific towns were like in the 1870s. Levuka makes a good day trip
from Suva—if you don't mind risking not getting back the same day—or longer if you
don't need accommodations with modern amenities.

GETTING TO SUVA & GETTING AROUND
GETTING TO SUVA
Suva is served by **Nausori Airport,** 19km (12 miles) northeast of downtown near the
Rewa River town of Nausori. Buses ostensibly meet incoming flights, but they are so
unreliable that you should plan to take a taxi. Fares between the airport and Suva are
F$25 (US$15) each way. Allow at least 30 minutes for the ride during midday, an
hour during morning and evening rush hours. See "Getting There & Getting
Around" in chapter 4 for more information.

If you're driving from the Nadi side of Viti Levu, don't leave without a good map
of Suva, which has a confusing maze of streets, especially at night (I seldom drive in
Suva after dark).

GETTING AROUND SUVA
Hundreds of **taxis** prowl the streets of Suva. Some have meters, but don't count on it.
As a rule of thumb, F$2 to F$3.50 (US$1.20–US$2.10) will get you to the sites of
interest, F$7 (US$4.20) to the Raintree Lodge. If the taxi has a meter, make sure the
driver drops the flag. The main **taxi stand** is on Central Street, behind the Air Pacific
office in the CML Building on Victoria Parade (② 331 2266), and on Victoria Parade
at Sukuna Park (no phone). I have been very satisfied with **Black Arrow Taxis** (② 330
0541 or 330 0139 in Suva, or 347 7071 in Nausori) and **Nausori Taxi & Bus Service** (② 347 7583 in Nausori, or 330 4178 in Suva), which is based at the Holiday
Inn Suva parking lot. Other taxis gather at the Suva Municipal Market.

Usually crowded, local **buses** fan out from the municipal market from before day-break to midnight Monday to Saturday (they have limited schedules on Sunday). The fares vary but should be no more than F$1 (US60¢) to most destinations in and around Suva. If you're going to ride the bus for the fun of it, do it in Nadi, where you won't get lost and aren't as likely to be robbed.

See "Getting There & Getting Around" in chapter 4 for the phone numbers of the major **car rental** firms.

FAST FACTS: Suva

The following facts apply to Suva. If you don't see an item here, see "Fast Facts: Fiji" in chapter 4.

Bookstores The region's largest store is **University Book Centre** (✆ 331 2500; www.uspbookcentre.com), on the University of the South Pacific campus on Laucala Bay Road (you can order online). Downtown, **Dominion Book Centre,** in Dominion Arcade on Thomson Street behind the Fiji Visitors Bureau (✆ 330 4334), has the latest news magazines and books on the South Pacific. Another good downtown choice is the book section of **Proud's** department store (✆ 331 8686), in the Suva Central building on Renwick Road at Pratt Street.

Camera/Film **Caines Photofast,** corner of Victoria Parade and Pratt Street (✆ 331 3211), sells a wide range of film and provides 1-hour processing of color-print film.

Currency Exchange **ANZ Bank, Westpac Bank,** and **Colonial National Bank** have offices with ATMs on Victoria Parade, south of the Fiji Visitors Bureau. ANZ has a walk-up currency exchange window which is open Monday to Friday from 9am to 6pm, Saturday from 9am to 1pm. **GlobelEX,** on Victoria Parade at Gordon Street, cashes travelers checks.

Drugstores **Suva City Pharmacy,** on Victoria Parade in the General Post Office building (✆ 331 7400), is the city's best drug store. It's open Monday to Friday from 8:30am to 5:30pm, Saturday from 8:30am to 2pm.

E-mail Suva has dozens of Internet cafes, many of them on Victoria Parade, and wireless "hotspots" were being set up as I write. Operated by Fiji's major Internet service provider, **Connect Internet Cafe,** in the General Post Office building (✆ 330 0777), has high-speed broadband access for F$5 (US$3) an hour. It's open Monday to Friday 8:30am to 8pm, Saturday 9am to 8pm, Sunday 10am to 6pm. You can print your e-mails, scan documents, and burn CDs here. The country's overseas phone company, **Fiji International Telecommunications Ltd. (FINTEL),** has dial-up and broadband access at its headquarters (✆ 330 1655). It's open Monday to Saturday from 8am to 8pm and charges F$1.50 (US90¢) for 15 minutes of dial-up access, F$5 (US$3) an hour for broadband. If you brought your wireless-capable laptop, there's a hotspot at the **Republic of Cappuccino** branch on Renwick Road at Pratt Street (✆ 330 0082). It's open Monday to Friday 7am to 10pm, Saturday 8am to 10pm, Sunday 9am to 7pm. The cost is F$5 ($3) per hour.

Emergencies/Police The emergency phone number for **police** is ☏ **917**. For **fire** and **ambulance** dial ☏ **911**. Fiji Police's **central station** is on Joske Street, between Pratt and Gordon streets (☏ **331 1222**).

Eyeglasses Dr. Guy Hawley, an American eye specialist, practices at **Asgar & Co. Ltd.**, Queensland Insurance Centre, Victoria Parade (☏ **330 0433**).

Hairdressers/Barbers **Edge Hair Design,** Queensland Insurance Centre, Victoria Parade (☏ **330 3404**).

Healthcare Most expatriate residents go to the private **Suva Private Hospital,** 120 Amy St. (☏ **331 3355**). It's open 24 hours a day. **Colonial War Memorial Hospital,** at the end of Ratu Mara Road at Brown Street (☏ **331 3444**), is the public hospital, but go to Suva Private Hospital if at all possible.

Information The **Fiji Visitors Bureau** (☏ **330 2433**) has an information center in a restored colonial house at the corner of Thomson and Scott streets, in the heart of Suva. Open Monday to Thursday 8am to 4:30pm, Friday 8am to 4pm, Saturday 8am to noon.

Laundry/Dry Cleaning **Flagstaff Laundry & Drycleaners,** 62 Bau St. (☏ **330 1214**), has full 1-day service.

Libraries **Suva City Library** on Victoria Parade (☏ **331 3433**) has a small collection of books on the South Pacific. It's open Monday, Tuesday, Thursday, and Friday 9:30am to 6pm; Wednesday noon to 6pm; Saturday 9am to 1pm. The library at the **University of the South Pacific** (☏ **331 3900**) has one of the largest collections in the South Pacific. The university is on Laucala Bay Road.

Maps The Fiji Visitors Bureau has maps (see "Information," above). The excellent *Suva and Lami Town* from the Department of Lands & Surveys is often available at Dominion Book Centre (see "Bookstores," above).

Post Office Fiji Post's General Post Office is on Thomson Street, opposite the Fiji Visitor's Bureau. Open Monday to Friday 8am to 4:30pm, Saturday 9am to noon.

Restrooms **Sukuna Park,** on Victoria Parade, has attended (and therefore reasonably clean) public restrooms, on the side next to McDonald's. You must pay F67¢ (US40¢) to use the toilets, or F$1.20 (US72¢) for a shower. Open Monday to Saturday 8am to 3:45pm.

Safety Street crime is a serious problem in Suva, so be alert at all times. Do not wander off Victoria Parade after dark; take a taxi. The busy blocks along Victoria Parade between the Fiji Visitors Bureau and the Holiday Inn Suva are relatively safe during the evenings (a local wag says the many prostitutes on the main drag keep the robbers away!), but protect valuables from pickpockets. See "Safety" under "Fast Facts: Fiji" in chapter 4.

Telephone/Fax You can make international calls, send faxes, and surf the 'net at **Fiji International Telecommunications Ltd. (FINTEL),** in its colonial-style building on Victoria Parade. Open Monday to Saturday 8am to 8pm.

Water The tap water is safe to drink.

EXPLORING SUVA

Although you could easily spend several days poking around the capital, most visitors come here for only a day, usually on one of the guided tours from Nadi or the Coral Coast. That's enough time to see the city's highlights, particularly if you make the walking tour described below.

Sitting on a ridge about 1km (½ mile) southeast of downtown, the **Parliament of Fiji,** on Battery Road off Vuya Road (© **330 5811**), resides under a modern shingle-covered version of a traditional Fijian roof. There are no organized tours, and access has been restricted since the 2000 coup, so call the main number or check with the Fiji Visitors bureau before coming up here. If you can get in (and another coup isn't in progress, God forbid!), you can watch the debates from the visitors' gallery.

THE TOP ATTRACTIONS

Fiji Museum ✿✿✿   You'll see a marvelous collection of war clubs, cannibal forks, tanoa bowls, shell jewelry, and other relics here, in one of the South Pacific's finest museums. Although some artifacts were damaged by Suva's humidity while they were hidden away during World War II, much remains. Later additions include the rudder and other relics of HMS *Bounty,* burned and sunk at Pitcairn Island by Fletcher Christian and the other mutineers in 1789 but recovered in the 1950s by the famed *National Geographic* photographer Luis Marden. Don't miss the masi cloth and Indian art exhibits in the air-conditioned upstairs galleries. The gift shop is worth a browse.

In Thurston Gardens, Ratu Cakobau Rd. off Victoria Parade. © **331 5944.** www.fijimuseum.org.fj. Admission F$7 (US$4.20) adults, F$5 (US$3) students w/IDs. Guided tours F$3 (US$1.80). Mon–Thurs and Sat 9am–4:30pm, Fri 9:30am–4pm, Sun 1–4:30pm.

Suva Municipal Market ✿✿✿   A vast array of tropical produce is offered for sale at Suva's main supply of food, the largest and most lively market in the South Pacific. If they aren't too busy, the merchants will appreciate your interest and answer your questions about the names and uses of the various fruits and vegetables. The market teems on Saturday morning, when it seems as if the entire population of Suva shows up to shop and select television programs for the weekend's viewing. Few sights say as much about urban life in the modern South Pacific as does that of a Fijian carrying home in one hand a bunch of taro roots tied together with pandanus, and in the other a collection of rented videocassettes stuffed into a plastic bag. The bus station is behind the market on Rodwell Road.

Usher St. at Rodwell Road. No phone. Free admission. Mon–Fri 5am–6pm, Sat 5am–1pm.

WALKING TOUR	SUVA

Start:	**The Triangle**
Finish:	**Government House**
Time:	**2½ hours**
Best Time:	**Early morning or late afternoon**
Worst Time:	**Midday, or Saturday afternoon and Sunday, when the market and shops are closed and downtown is deserted**

Begin at the four-way intersection of Victoria Parade, Renwick Road, and Thomson and Central streets. This little island in the middle of heavy traffic is called The Triangle.

Walking Tour: Suva

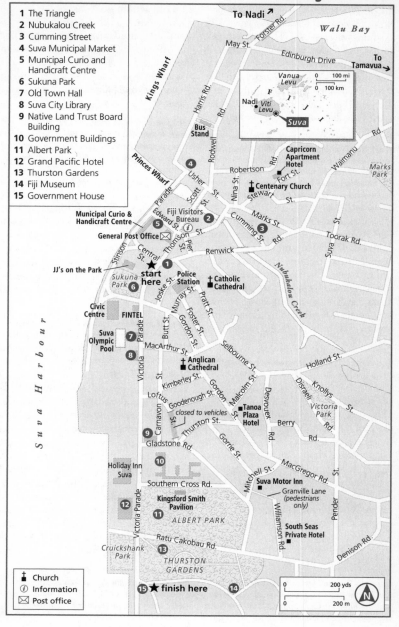

1 The Triangle
2 Nubukalou Creek
3 Cumming Street
4 Suva Municipal Market
5 Municipal Curio and
  Handicraft Centre
6 Sukuna Park
7 Old Town Hall
8 Suva City Library
9 Native Land Trust Board
  Building
10 Government Buildings
11 Albert Park
12 Grand Pacific Hotel
13 Thurston Gardens
14 Fiji Museum
15 Government House

✝ Church
ⓘ Information
✉ Post office

To Nadi ↗

Walu Bay

To Tamavua ↗

May St.
Forster Rd.
Edinburgh Drive

Vanua Levu   0   100 mi
                    0   100 km
Nadi • Viti Levu
F I J I
Suva

Kings Wharf
Harris Rd.
Rodwell Rd.

Bus Stand

Waimanu Rd.
Marks Park

Princes Wharf
Usher St.
Scott St.
Nina St.

Robertson
Fort St.
Capricorn Apartment Hotel

Parade
Edward St.
Pier St.
Stewart St.
✝ Centenary Church

Municipal Curio & Handicraft Centre
Fiji Visitors Bureau ⓘ
Marks St.
Toorak Rd.

General Post Office ✉
Thomson St.
Cumming St.

Central St.
Renwick Rd.

JJ's on the Park
Stinson Parade
★ start here
Police Station
✝ Catholic Cathedral
Suva Rd.

Sukuna Park
Joske St.
Nubukalou Creek

Civic Centre   FINTEL
Butt St.
Murray St.
Pratt St.
Foster St.

Suva Olympic Pool
Victoria Parade
MacArthur St.
Gordon St.
Selbourne St.
Holland St.

✝ Anglican Cathedral
Kimberley St.
Malcolm St.
Disraeli St.
Knollys St.
Victoria Park

Loftus St.
Carnavon St.
Goodenough St.
closed to vehicles
Gordon St.
Devoux Rd.
Victoria St.

Tanoa Plaza Hotel
Thurston St.
Berry Rd.

Gladstone Rd.
Gorrie St.
MacGregor Rd.

Holiday Inn Suva
Southern Cross Rd.
Mitchell St.
Suva Motor Inn
Pender St.
Granville Lane (pedestrians only)

Kingsford Smith Pavilion
Williamson Rd.
South Seas Private Hotel
Denison Rd.

ALBERT PARK

Victoria Parade
Ratu Cakobau Rd.

Cruickshank Park
THURSTON GARDENS

★ finish here

0   200 yds
0   200 m

Suva Harbour

145

❶ The Triangle

Now the center of Suva, in the late 1800s this spot was a lagoon fed by a stream that flowed along what is now Pratt Street. A marker in the park commemorates Suva's becoming the capital, the arrival of Fiji's first missionaries, the first public land sales, and Fiji's becoming a colony. Three of the four dates are slightly wrong.

From The Triangle, head north on Thomson Street, bearing right between the Fiji Visitors Bureau and the old Garrick Hotel (now the Sichuan Pavilion Restaurant), whose wrought-iron balconies recall a more genteel but non-air-conditioned era. Continue on Thomson Street to Nubukalou Creek.

❷ Nubukalou Creek

The Polynesia Company's settlers made camp beside this stream and presumably drank from it. A sign on the bridge warns against eating fish from it today—with good reason, as you will see and smell. Across the bridge, smiling Fijian women wait under a flame tree in a shady little park to offer grass skirts and other handicraft items for sale.

Pass to the left of the Fijian women across the bridge for now, and head down narrow Cumming Street.

❸ Cumming Street

This area, also on reclaimed land, was home of the Suva market until the 1940s. Cumming Street was lined with saloons, yaqona grog shops, and curry houses known as lodges. It became a tourist-oriented shopping mecca when World War II Allied servicemen created a market for curios. When import taxes were lifted from electronic equipment and cameras in the 1960s, Cumming Street merchants quickly added the plethora of duty-free items you'll find there today. Browse for a while.

Return to Thomson Street, turn right, and then turn left on Usher Street. Follow Usher Street past the intersection at Rodwell Road and Scott Street to the Suva Municipal Market.

❹ Suva Municipal Market

This market is a beehive of activity, especially on Saturday mornings (see "The Top Attractions," above). Big ships from overseas and small boats from the other islands dock at Princes Wharf and Kings Wharf beyond the market on Usher Street.

Head south along wide Stinson Parade, back across Nubukalou Creek and along the edge of Suva's waterfront to Edward Street and the gray tin roofs of the Municipal Curio and Handicraft Centre.

❺ Municipal Curio and Handicraft Centre

In yet another bit of cultural diversity, you can haggle over the price of handicrafts at stalls run by Indians. (Don't try to haggle at those operated by Fijians.) It's best to wait until you have visited the Government Handicraft Centre before making a purchase (see "Shopping in Suva," below).

Continue on Stinson Parade past Central Street. The gray concrete building on the corner is the YWCA. When you get there, cut diagonally under the palms and flame trees across Sukuna Park.

❻ Sukuna Park

This park is named for Ratu Sir Lala Sukuna, founding father of independent Fiji. This shady waterfront park is a favorite brown-bag lunch spot for Suva's office workers. On the west side is the harbor and on the east, Victoria Parade. For many years only a row of flame trees separated this broad avenue from the harbor, but the shallows have been filled and the land has been extended into the harbor by the width of a city block. The large auditorium that stands south of the park is the Suva Civic Centre.

Head south on the seaward side of Victoria Parade and pass the cream-colored colonial-style headquarters of FINTEL, the country's electronic link to the world. You'll come to the old Town Hall.

❼ Old Town Hall

A picturesque Victorian-era building, it features an intricate, ornamental wrought-iron portico. Built as an auditorium in the early 1900s and named Queen Victoria Memorial Hall, this lovely structure was later used as the Suva Town Hall (city offices are now in the modern Suva City Hall adjacent to the Civic Centre on the waterfront). The stage still stands at the rear of the Chinese restaurant.

Continue south on Victoria Parade until you come to the Suva City Library.

❽ Suva City Library

The U.S. industrialist and philanthropist Andrew Carnegie gave Fiji £1,500 sterling to build this structure. The central portion of the colonnaded building opened in 1909, with an initial collection of 4,200 books. The wings were added in 1929. Books on Fiji and the South Pacific are shelved to the left of the main entrance. (See "Fast Facts: Suva," above, for the library's hours.)

Keep going along Victoria Parade, past Loftus Street, to the corner of Gladstone Road, locale for the Native Land Trust Board Building.

❾ Native Land Trust Board Building

This site is known locally as Naiqaqi (The Crusher) because a sugar-crushing mill sat here during Suva's brief and unsuccessful career as a cane-growing area in the 1870s. Ratu Sir Lala Sukuna, who prepared his people for independence (see "Fiji Yesterday: History 101," in chapter 4), served as chairman of the Native Land Trust Board, which collects and distributes rents on the 80% of the country that is owned by the Fijians.

Across Gladstone Road you can't miss the imposing gray edifice and clock tower of the Government Buildings.

❿ Government Buildings

Erected between 1937 and 1939 (although they look older), these British-style gray stone buildings house the High Court, the prime minister's office, and several government ministries. Parliament met here until 1987, when Colonel Rabuka and gang marched in and arrested its leaders; Parliament now meets in a new complex on Ratu Sukuna Road in the Muanikau suburb. The clock tower is known as "Fiji's Big Ben." When it works, it chimes every 15 minutes from 6am to midnight.

Walk past the large open field on the south side of the building; this is Albert Park.

⓫ Albert Park

This park is named for Queen Victoria's consort, Prince Albert. The pavilion opposite the Government Buildings, however, is named for Charles Kingsford Smith, the Australian aviator and first person to fly across the Pacific. Smith was unaware that a row of palm trees stretched across the middle of Albert Park, his intended landing place. A local radio operator figured out Smith's predicament, and the colonial governor ordered the trees cut down immediately. The resulting "runway" across Albert Park was barely long enough, but Smith managed to stop his plane within a few feet of its end on June 6, 1928.

Opposite the park on Victoria Parade stands the Grand Pacific Hotel.

⓬ Grand Pacific Hotel

Vacant for years, this historic hotel was scheduled for restoration at press time. The Union Steamship Company built the "GPH" in 1914 to house its transpacific passengers during their stopovers in Fiji. The idea was to make them think they had never gone ashore, for rooms in the GPH were like first-class staterooms, complete with saltwater bathrooms and plumbing fixtures identical to those on an ocean liner. All rooms were on the second floor, and guests could step outside on a 15-foot-wide veranda overlooking the harbor and walk completely around the building—as if walking on the deck. When members of the British royal family visited Fiji, they stood atop the wrought-iron portico, the "bow" of the

---

Fun Fact **My Word!**

Before the government buildings on Victoria Parade were erected between 1937 and 1939, the land under them was a swampy area called Naiqaqi, or Crusher, for the sugar mill that operated from 1873 to 1875 where the Native Lands Trust Board Building now stands. Naiqaqi was populated by shacks, some of them houses of ill-repute.

Local residents tell of a sailor who often visited the shacks while his ship was in port. He left Suva in 1931 for a long voyage, carrying with him fond memories of Naiqaqi—and, in particular, of one of its residents, a beautiful young woman named Annie.

The sailor's next visit to Suva was in 1940. Instead of a swamp, he found an imposing gray stone building standing where the old, familiar shacks had been.

"My word!" he exclaimed upon seeing the great new structures, "Annie has done well!"

Grand Pacific, and addressed their subjects massed across Victoria Parade in Albert Park.

Continue south on Victoria Parade to the corner of Ratu Cakobau Road, and enter Thurston Gardens.

⑬ Thurston Gardens

Originally known as the Botanical Gardens, this cool, English-like park is named for its founder, the amateur botanist Sir John Bates Thurston, who started the gardens in 1881. Henry Marks, scion of a family who owned a local trading company, presented the drinking fountain in 1914. After G. J. Marks, a relative and lord mayor of Suva, was drowned that same year in the sinking of the SS *Empress* in the St. Lawrence River in Canada, the Marks family erected the bandstand in his memory. Children can climb aboard the stationary *Thurston Express,* a narrow-gauge locomotive once used to pull harvested cane to the crushing mill.

Walk to the southeast corner of the gardens, where you will find the Fiji Museum.

⑭ Fiji Museum

At this fascinating museum, you can see relics and artifacts of Fiji's history (see "The Top Attractions," above). After touring the complex, take a break at the museum's cafe, under a lean-to roof on one side of the main building; it serves soft drinks, snacks, and curries.

Backtrack through the gardens to Victoria Parade and head south again until, just past the manicured greens of the Suva Bowling Club on the harbor, you arrive at the big iron gates of Government House.

⑮ Government House

This is the home of Fiji's president, guarded like Buckingham Palace by spit-and-polish, *sulu*-clad Fijian soldiers. The original house, built in 1882 as the residence of the colonial governor, was struck by lightning and burned in 1921. The present rambling mansion was completed in 1928 and opened with great fanfare. It is closed to the public, but a colorful military ceremony marks the changing of the guard the first week of each month. Ask the Fiji Visitors Bureau whether a ceremony will take place while you're there.

From this point, Victoria Parade becomes Queen Elizabeth Drive, which skirts the peninsula to Laucala Bay. With homes and gardens on one side and the lagoon on the other, it's a lovely walk or drive. The manicured residential area in the rolling hills behind Government House is known as The Domain. An enclave of British civil servants in colonial times, it is now home to the Fiji parliament, government officials, diplomats, and affluent private citizens.

COLO-I-SUVA FOREST PARK

At an altitude of 121 to 182m (400 to 600 feet), **Colo—I-Suva Forest Park,** on the Prince's Road 11km (6½ miles) from downtown Suva (© **332 0211**), provides a cool, refreshing respite from the heat—if not the humidity—of the city below. You can hike the system of trails through the heavy indigenous forests and stands of mahogany to one of several lovely waterfalls that cascade into swimming holes. Bring walking shoes with good traction because the trails are covered with gravel or slippery soapstone. The park is open daily 8am to 4pm. Admission is F$5 (US$3). Take a taxi or the Sawani bus, which leave Suva Municipal Market every 30 minutes. If you drive, do not leave valuables in your vehicle.

SHOPPING IN SUVA

If you took the walking tour of Suva, you already have a good idea of where to shop for handicrafts, cameras, electronic gear, and clothing. The largest and most reliable merchants are **Jack's Handicrafts,** at Thomson and Pier streets, opposite the Fiji Visitors Bureau; **Prouds,** in the Suva Central building on Renwick Road at Pratt Street; and **Tappoo,** which has a large store at the corner of Thomson and Usher streets. Note that Jack's has a very small handicraft section here; it's mostly a clothing and accessories outlet. The prices are fixed in these stores.

Suva has some fine tropical clothing outlets, several of them on Victoria Parade near the Regal Theatre. The upmarket resort- and beachwear specialist **Sogo Fiji** is on Victoria Parade, opposite the theater.

HANDICRAFTS

Before buying handicrafts, be sure to visit the Fiji Museum and its excellent shop (see "The Top Attractions," above).

Government Handicraft Centre ℛ *(Value)*   Founded in 1974 to continue and promote Fiji's handicrafts, this shop has a limited selection of authentic merchandise here (no war clubs carved in Asia are sold in this shop). Special attention is given to rural artisans who cannot easily market their works. You will see fine woodcarvings, woven goods, pottery, and masi cloth, and you will learn from the fixed prices just how much the really good items are worth. The Fijian staff is friendly and helpful.

Corner of Victoria Parade and MacArthur St., in rear of Ratu Sukuna House. © **331 5869.** Mon–Thurs 8am–4:30pm, Fri 8am–4pm, Sat 8am–12:30pm.

Municipal Curio and Handicraft Centre   Having checked out the government center, you can visit these stalls and bargain with the Indian merchants (but not with the Fijians) from a position of knowledge, if not strength. Be careful, however, for some of the work here is mass produced and aimed at cruise-ship passengers who have only a few hours to do their shopping in Fiji.

Tips **Sword Sellers Are in Suva, Too**

Suva is crawling with the **sword sellers** I warned you about under "Shopping in Nadi," earlier in this chapter. The government requires these scam artists to stay in Thurston Park near the Fiji Museum, but you could be approached anywhere. Avoid them!

Municipal Car Park, Stinson Parade, on the waterfront. © **331 3433.** Mon–Thurs 8am–4:30pm, Fri 8am–4pm, Sat 8am–noon.

WHERE TO STAY IN SUVA
MODERATE
Holiday Inn Suva ✦   Formerly the Centra Suva and before that the Suva Travelodge, this is the unofficial gathering place for the city's movers and shakers. The waterfront location couldn't be better, for Suva Harbour laps one side, the stately government buildings sit across Victoria Parade on the other, and the business district is a 3-block walk away. All units have been upgraded in recent years, which makes the mustiness caused by Suva's humid climate less apparent. Upstairs over the lobby, rooms 263 to 281 face the harborside lawn and swimming pool, but they are less humid. The *Fiji Times* is delivered to your room daily on request. One room is equipped for guests with disabilities.

P.O. Box 1357, Suva (Victoria Parade, opposite government buildings). © **800/465-4329** or 330 1600. Fax 330 0251. www.holiday-inn.com. 130 units. F$230–F$380 (US$138–US$228) double. AE, DC, MC, V. **Amenities:** Restaurant; bar; outdoor pool; access to nearby health club; activities desk; business center; 24-hr. room service; babysitting; laundry service; coin-op washers and dryers. *In room:* A/C, TV, high-speed dataport, minibar, coffeemaker, hair dryer, iron, safe.

JJ's on the Park   Suva's only luxury boutique hotel, JJ's on the Park isn't much to look at from the outside, since it occupies the former YWCA Building, a stained concrete structure five stories high on the north side of Sukuna Park. But go inside and you'll find its comfortable rooms and suites Suva's best equipped—including wireless Internet access and a fax-copier-printer machine on each unit's desk. In addition, butlers stationed on each floor will cater to your every whim (they'll even take you shopping during the day or bar hopping at night). Obviously JJ's attracts business travelers seeking more luxuries and services than elsewhere. Accommodations range from smaller rooms without balconies to suites with two balconies and separate bedrooms. Balcony or not, every unit has a harbor view.

P.O. Box 12499, Suva (Stinson Parade, north side of Sukuna Park). © **330 5055.** Fax 330 5002. www.jjsfiji.com.fj. 22 units. F$250 (US$150) double; F$450–F$650 (US$271–US$390) suite. AE, DC, MC, V. No children accepted. **Amenities:** Restaurant; bar; access to nearby health club; activities desk; wireless Internet access; 24-hr. room service; laundry service. *In room:* A/C, TV, fax machine, high-speed dataport, minibar, coffeemaker, hairdryer, iron, safe.

Tanoa Plaza Hotel   Even *sans* balcony, you will have a commanding view over Suva, the harbor, and the south coast of Viti Levu from the top floors of this curving, nine-story building. Best of all are the executive suites on the top floor, which are larger and better appointed than the smallish regular rooms. The neighborhood is quiet and residential, yet the hotel is a 3-block walk from the shops on Victoria Parade (during the day, anyway; take a taxi at night). A first-floor restaurant serves breakfast, lunch, and dinner. There's a swimming pool on the shady side of the building.

P.O. Box 112, Suva (corner Malcolm and Gordon sts.). © **331 2300.** Fax 331 1300. www.tanoahotels.com. 60 units. F$195–F$215 (US$117–US$129) double; F$410 (US$246) suite. AE, DC, MC, V. **Amenities:** Restaurant; bar; outdoor pool; 24-hr. room service; babysitting; laundry service. *In room:* A/C, TV, dataport, minibar, coffeemaker, iron, safe.

INEXPENSIVE
Capricorn Apartment Hotel *Value*   Although it's a steep, 2-block walk uphill from Cumming Street, Mulchand Patel's super-clean establishment is popular with Australians and New Zealanders who like to do their own cooking. The three-story, L-shaped building looks out on Suva Harbour and down the mountainous coast.

Private balconies off each apartment share the view, as does a pear-shaped swimming pool on the Capricorn's grounds. Tropical furniture adorns all units, and the mattresses here are new and among the firmest in Fiji. Mulchand and his friendly staff make sure these roomy efficiencies are kept spotless. Each unit has an air-conditioner, although (unscreened) windows on both sides of the building let the cooling trade winds blow through. The reception staff will sell you canned goods from its small on-premises store or have "Dial-A-Meal" delivered to your room.

P.O. Box 1261, Suva (top end of Saint Fort St.). © 330 3732. Fax 330 3069. www.capricorn-hotels-fiji.com. 34 units. F$95–F$125 (US$57–US$75) double. AE, DC, MC, V. **Amenities:** Outdoor pool; babysitting; laundry service. *In room:* A/C, TV, data port; kitchen, coffeemaker, safe.

Homestay Suva ✦✦✦ *Value*   One of the top bed-and-breakfasts in the South Pacific islands, this gorgeous 1920s-vintage colonial home sits atop a ridge in the expensive Tamavua suburb. You will enjoy a stunning view while having breakfast or lounging on the covered veranda, which overlooks a ridge-top swimming pool and the south coast of Viti Levu. The choice room is appropriately named Harbor View. Another upstairs room, the Nukulau, looks eastward across Laucala Bay to little Nukulau Island on the far-off reef. Three other rooms in the main house lack a view. Four more private and spacious lodge units in a building a few steps from the main house have kitchens and private balconies overlooking Walu Bay. Many guests here are business types, including women traveling alone. Call for directions if you're driving, or take a taxi from downtown for F$3.50 (US$2.10).

265 Prince's Rd. (P.O. Box 16172, Suva). © 337 0395. Fax 337 0947. homestaysuva@connect.com.fj. 9 units (all w/bathroom). F$185–F$225 (US$111–US$135) double. Rates include full breakfast. AE, MC, V. **Amenities:** Outdoor pool; laundry service. *In room:* A/C, TV, kitchen (in lodge units), no phone.

Nanette's Homestay Suva *Finds*   Almost hidden away on a side street behind Colonial War Memorial Hospital, Nanette MacAdam's two-story, white concrete house looks smaller from the road than it is. Upstairs she has a lounge, kitchen, and four breezy rooms, all with private bathrooms. One has its own balcony. Downstairs are three apartments. Two of these have two bedrooms, and one of these has two bathrooms. All three have fully modern kitchens. The apartments are popular with overseas workers on assignment to the hospital. Guests are treated to continental breakfast, and they can barbecue on the big veranda off the guest lounge.

56 Extension St. (behind Colonial War Memorial Hospital). © 331 6316. Fax 331 6902. nanettes@connect.com.fj. 7 units (all w/bathroom). F$110 (US$66) double, F$120–F$190 (US$72–US$114) apartment. Rates include continental breakfast. MC, V. **Amenities:** Laundry service. *In room:* A/C, TV (apartments only), kitchen (apartments only), no phone.

Raintree Lodge   Backpackers flock to this rustic lodge beside a nearly round, quarry-turned-lake high in the hills near Colo-I-Suva Forest Park (see above). The climes are cool up here, and although "Raintree" refers to an acacia tree, it can rain a lot in this forest. Except for the vehicles passing on Prince's Road, you'll hear very little except the songs of tropical birds. Built of pine and overlooking the lake, the bungalows are spacious, and their beds have mosquito nets (the windows are screened, too). All have ceiling fans and bathrooms with showers. Dormitories range in size from seven private rooms with double beds to a hall with 21 bunk beds. Their occupants and those camping out on the lawn share toilets, hot-water showers, and a kitchen. Locals love to drive up here for lunch and dinner at the rustic and inexpensive **Raintree Restaurant,** where they vie for tables on the lakeside veranda. The lodge is F$7 (US$4) by taxi or F90¢ (US54¢) by public bus from downtown Suva.

A Side Trip Back in Time to Levuka

You might think you've slipped into *The Twilight Zone* as you stroll down historic Beach Street in Levuka, Fiji's first capital, on the ruggedly beautiful island of Ovalau. Everything in Levuka seems to be frozen at 1882, when the colonial administration moved to Suva: ramshackle dry-goods stores with false fronts, clapboard houses with tin roofs to keep dry, and shaded verandas to keep cool, and round clocks in the baroque tower of Sacred Heart Catholic Church.

The 360m (1,200-ft.) walls of basalt create a soaring backdrop to the town and put Ovalau in the big leagues of dramatic tropical beauty. The island has very little flat land and no decent beach, however, so it has not attracted resort or hotel development and is off the well-beaten tourist track.

Air Fiji (© 877/247-3454 in the U.S., 331 3666 in Suva, or 672 2251 in Nadi; www.airfiji.net) has an early morning flight from Nausori airport to Ovalau and a late afternoon flight back to Nausori. The round-trip fare is about F$155 (US$93). Rainy weather or delays can cause the late afternoon flight to be canceled, so bring your toothbrush just in case.

Begin your tour at the **Levuka Community Centre** (© 344 0356), where you can get information. It and the local library occupy the quaint old **Morris Hedstrom** store built by Levukans Percy Morris and Maynard Hedstrom in 1878. More importantly, check in next door with the German-operated **Ovalau Watersports** (© 344 0611; www.owlfiji.com), which in addition to offering snorkeling tours and scuba diving (there are some terrific sites nearby, including a wreck in the harbor), arranges hiking excursions and island tours. I highly recommend a walking tour of town.

P.O. Box 11245, LBE, Suva (Prince's Rd., Colo-I-Suva, opposite post office). © 332 0562. Fax 332 0113. www.raintree lodge.com. 4 units, 45 dorm beds. F$140 (US$84) bungalow; F$60 (US$36) double dorm room; F$20–F$22 (US$12–US$13) dorm bed; F$13 (US$7.50) per person camping. AE, MC, V. **Amenities:** Restaurant; bar; laundry service; coin-operated washers and dryers. *In room:* TV, fridge, coffeemaker, no phone.

South Seas Private Hotel   Most backpackers stay at the Raintree Lodge (see above), but those who opt for the city often end up at this large barrackslike wooden structure with a long sunroom across the front (it can get hot in the afternoons). It's a friendly establishment with dormitories, basic rooms, a rudimentary communal kitchen, a TV lounge, and hand-wash laundry facilities. Bed linen is provided, but bring your own towel or pay a small deposit to use one of theirs. There's a refundable key deposit, too. Showers have both hot and cold water. The rooms have fans which operate from 3pm to 8am.

P.O. Box 2086, Government Bldgs., Suva (Williamson Rd. off Ratu Cakobau Rd., behind Albert Park). © 331 2296. Fax 330 8646. www.fiji4less.com. 34 units (one w/bathroom), 42 dorm beds. F$45 (US$27) double room w/bathroom; F$35 (US$21) double room no bathroom; F$14 (US$8) dorm bed. AE, MC, V. *In room:* No phone.

Suva Motor Inn ☆ ⟨Value⟩   This three-story hotel is popular with business travelers who can't afford the rates elsewhere. It's a good bet for budget-minded couples and families. Just uphill from Albert Park near the Government Buildings, the L-shaped

A waterside park at **Nasova** village, south of town past a smelly tuna cannery, commemorates Chief Cakobau's ceding Fiji to Great Britain in 1874. To the north, a British warship showed the Fijians how much firepower it packed in 1849 by shelling a headland known as **Gun Rock**. In between are many historic buildings, including **Levuka Public School,** founded in 1879 and still one of Fiji's best educational institutions, and the **Ovalau Club,** scene of after-work libation.

Don't miss the **Royal Hotel** (© **344 0024;** www.royallevuka.com), built in 1852 and "modernized" in the 1890s. Rooms in the old building are extremely basic, but the Royal has modern cottages out front. Rooms cost F$35–F$60 (US$21–US$36) double, while cottages go for F$80–F$115 (US$48–US$69).

The town's best digs are the four rooms in John and Marilyn Milesi's **Levuka Homestay** (© **344 0777;** www.levukahomestay.com), which enjoys a marvelous view over the town. Rates are F$140 (US$84) double, including full breakfast. If you don't stay at the Royal Hotel, backpackers head for **Mary's Holiday Lodge** (© **344 0013**), on Beach Street, where 13 simple rooms cost F$35 (US$21) double; 20 dorm beds, F$15 (US$9) each, including breakfast.

You get a decent meal at the inexpensive **Whale's Tale Restaurant** (© **344 0235**), in one of Beach Street's old stores. Ovalau Watersports shares space with **Cafe Levuka,** where you can get a cup of coffee and check your e-mail. **Westpac Bank** has an ATM. For advance information, go to **www.levukafiji. com.**

structure bends around a tropical courtyard with a two-level swimming pool with a Jacuzzi and a water slide. Opening to this vista is a small restaurant and a lively bar, which attract business types after work. Accommodation is in spacious studios and two-bedroom apartments, all with tropical cane-and-wicker furniture. The studios are fully air-conditioned, but only the master bedrooms of the apartments are cooled. Apartments have full kitchens; studios have refrigerators, toasters, coffeemakers, and microwave ovens. The staff will assist in arranging activities and excursions.

P.O. Box 2500, Government Bldgs., Suva (corner of Mitchell and Gorrie sts.). © **331 3973.** Fax 330 0381. www. hexagonfiji.com. 47 units. F$150 (US$90) double; F$195 (US$117) apt. AE, DC, MC, V. **Amenities:** Restaurant; bar; outdoor pool; laundry service; coin-op washers and dryers. *In room:* A/C, TV, kitchen (apartments only), fridge, coffeemaker.

A SUPER-LUXURY RESORT ON WAKAYA ISLAND

The Wakaya Club, Fiji's most luxurious and exclusive resort, is on Wakaya Island, an uplifted, tilted coral atoll in the Koro Sea. Beaches fringe Wakaya's north and east coasts, and cliffs fall into the sea on its western side. There are still relics of a Fijian fort on the cliffs. Legend says a chief and all his men leapt off the cliff to their deaths from there rather than be roasted by a rival tribe. The spot is known as Chieftain's Leap.

The Wakaya Club 🏖🏖🏖 A 20-minute flight by private plane from Nausori Airport, 50 minutes from Nadi, this superdeluxe beachside facility is the brainchild of Canadian entrepreneur David Gilmour, who also introduced us to "Fiji" bottled water. Gilmour has sold off pieces of Wakaya for deluxe getaway homes. For a small fortune you can rent one of these villas, including Gilmore's own Japanese-influenced mansion high on a ridge overlooking the resort. Nicole Kidman (a regular guest) and other Hollywood types who don't own a private villa—or can't borrow a friend's—feel right at home in the club's large, super-luxurious bungalows. The food here is of gourmet quality and outstandingly presented. Guests dine in a huge thatched-roof beachside building or outside, either on a patio or under two gazebo-like shelters on a deck surrounding a pool with its own waterfall. Compared to Turtle Island and Vatulele Island resorts, where a party atmosphere often prevails, here the excellent, unobtrusive Fijian staff leaves the guests alone. Your wish is their command. When all is said and done, this is Fiji's most luxurious resort.

P.O. Box 15424, Suva (Wakaya Island, Lomaviti Group). 📞 **344 0128.** Fax 970/920-1225 or 344 0406. www. wakaya.com. 9 units. US$1,980–US$2,800 double. Rates include meals, bar, all activities except deep-sea fishing, scuba diving courses, and massages. Round-trip transfers US$960 per couple from Nadi, US$480 from Suva. AE, DC, MC, V. **Amenities:** Restaurant; bar; outdoor pool; 9-hole golf course; tennis courts; 24-hr. room service; massage; babysitting; laundry service. *In room:* Minibar, coffeemaker, hair dryer.

WHERE TO DINE IN SUVA
MODERATE

JJ's on the Park INTERNATIONAL On the harbor side of JJ's hotel, this lively bistro sports a Southwestern adobe theme, although a quesadilla here is less likely to be Tex-Mex than of the chicken curry variety. Better bets are substantial servings of fish and chips, burgers, salads, steaks, and rack of lamb. At dinner check the specials board for the fresh fish of the day. The bar here is a good place to slake a thirst during your walking tour of Suva.

In JJ's on the Park, Stinson Parade, north side of Sukuna Park. 📞 **330 5005.** Reservations recommended at dinner. Breakfast F$6.50–F$13 (US$4–US$8); burgers, sandwiches, and salads F$12–F$21 (US$7–US$13); main courses F$23–F$33 (US$14–US$20). AE, DC, MC, V. Mon–Wed 7am–10pm, Thurs–Sat 7am–11pm (bar later).

L'Opera Ristorante Italiano 🏖🏖 ITALIAN Don't be turned off by the location next to a karaoke bar, for a long paneled corridor hung with historic photographs will lead you to this elegant restaurant and Suva's most refined dining. The chef frequently changes his menu, which ranges up and down the Italian "boot" but always reflects his Tuscan birthplace. Dinners are served in true Italian fashion, beginning with an *apertivo* drink, followed in order by antipasto, pasta, and a fish or meat *secondi* (main course). The weekday fixed price lunch is good value at F$22 (US$13). There's an extensive Sunday brunch here.

59 Gordon St. at Kimberly St. 📞 **331 8602.** Reservations highly recommended. Pasta F$19–F$25 (US$12–US$15); main courses F$29–F$40 (US$18–US$24). AE, MC, V. Daily 11:30am–2:30pm and 6–10:30pm.

Malt House Brewery & Restaurant 🏖🏖 *Finds* INTERNATIONAL Paul and Noeleene Roadley's microbrewery is a South Seas version of a German beer hall, but if you don't mind the noise, you're in for some of Suva's best fare. Stop first at the bar, where the tender will offer small tastes to help you decide among the lager, ale, and dark beers. You'll have lots of company because the Malt House is popular among the capital's movers and shakers. Romantic dining is out of the question here, but the noise shouldn't distract from sautéed pakapaka (snapper), beef schnitzel, and fish and chips with either tempura or herb-crumbed breading. The excellent wood-fired pizzas are large enough to feed two persons, and the salads are dinner-size, too.

88 Jerusalem Rd., Vatuwaqa (4km/2½ miles from downtown; take a taxi). ℂ 337 1515. Reservations accepted. Pizza F$17–F$19 (US$10–US$11); main courses F$18–F$28 (US$11–US$17). AE, MC, V. Daily 11am–10pm.

Tiko's Floating Restaurant SEAFOOD/STEAKS   Locals like to take out-of-town guests to this floating restaurant, which served years ago with Blue Lagoon Cruises. One hopes they don't lean to seasickness, for the old craft does tend to roll a bit when freighters kick up a wake going in and out of the harbor. Your best bets are the nightly seafood specials, such as *walu* (Spanish mackerel) and pakapaka (snapper). It's not the best in town, but the fish is fresh, the service is attentive, and a terrific musician-singer usually provides dinner music—all of which makes for a pleasant night out.

Stinson Parade at Sukuna Park. ℂ **331 3626.** Reservations recommended. Main courses F$16–F$36 (US$9.50–US$22). AE, DC, MC, V. Mon–Fri noon–2pm; Mon–Sat 6–10pm.

INEXPENSIVE

Bad Dog Cafe ⊛ 🄥alue PIZZA/STEAKS/SEAFOOD   Expatriate residents and professional Suvans—from their mid-20s on up—congregate in this sophisticated pub for after-work drinks and then hang around for good food, including some of the South Pacific's best pizzas. One pie will feed two adults of moderate appetite. Nor will you go wrong with marinated and seared sushi-grade yellow fin tuna, or a char-grilled steak. An attractive, energetic, and good-natured wait staff help make this Suva's top pub.

Victoria Parade, at MacArthur St. ℂ 331 2884. Burgers, sandwiches, and salads F$8.50–F$12 (US$5–US$7); pizza F$14 (US$8.50); main courses F$10–F$18 (US$6–US$11). AE, MC, V. Mon–Wed 11am–11pm, Thurs–Sat 11am–1am, Sun 5–11pm.

Hare Krishna Restaurant ⊛ 🄥alue VEGETARIAN INDIAN   This clean, casual restaurant specializes in a wide range of very good vegetarian curries—eggplant, cabbage, potatoes and peas, okra, and papaya to name a few—each seasoned delicately and differently from the others. Interesting pastries, breads, side dishes, and salads (such as cucumbers and carrots in yogurt) cool off the fire set by some of the curries. The items are displayed cafeteria-style near the entrance to the second-floor dining room, or get the all-you-can-eat *thali* sampler and try a little of everything. Downstairs has an excellent yogurt and ice cream bar; climb the spiral stairs to reach the dining room. The Hare Krishnas allow no alcoholic beverages or smoking.

16 Pratt St. ℂ 331 4154. Curries F$1.50–F$8.50 (US$1–US$5). No credit cards. Dining room Mon–Sat 11am–2:30pm; downstairs snack bar Mon–Thurs 8am–7pm, Fri 8am–8pm, Sat 8am–3pm.

Old Mill Cottage ⊛⊛⊛ 🄥alue FIJIAN/INDIAN/EUROPEAN   One of the few remaining late-19th-century homes left in Suva's diplomatic-government section, these adjoining two-room clapboard cottages offer some of the most extraordinary home cooking in the South Pacific. You'll order at the cafeteria-like counters, one for breakfast, one for lunch. You'll have a choice of daily specials such as Fijian palusami, mild Indian curries, or European-style mustard-baked chicken with real mashed potatoes and peas. The vegetable plate is good value, since you can pick and choose from more than a dozen European, Fijian, and Indian selections. Diplomats (the U.S. Embassy is out the back door) and government executives pack the place at midday.

47–49 Carnavon St., near corner of Loftus St. ℂ 331 2134. Breakfasts F$3–F$8 (US$2–US$5); meals F$5–F$8.50 (US$3–US$5). No credit cards. Mon–Fri 7am–6pm, Sat 7am–5pm.

FOOD COURTS & COFFEE SHOPS

The city has two shopping mall–style food courts serving inexpensive European, Chinese, and Indian dishes. **Dolphins Food Court** is in the high-rise FNPF Place building on Victoria Parade at Loftus Street. The other is on the second floor of **Suva Central,** a modern building on Renwick Road at Pratt Street.

If you're hankering for a Big Mac, head for the **McDonald's** on Victoria Parade at the northern edge of Sukuna Park. If it's bird you want, there's a **Kentucky Fried Chicken** on Victoria Parade next to the General Post Office.

Republic of Cappuccino ☞ COFFEE BAR   "The Rock" to trendy locals, this Starbucks-style coffee shop (the U.S. chain hasn't arrived yet) occupies the triangular corner of FNPF Place, on the Victoria Parade side of Dolphins Food Court. You can listen to recorded jazz while drinking your latte or cappuccino (made with strong, Fiji-grown beans) and eating your brownie, cake, or quiche at the tall tables by the big storefront windows. A second Suva location, on Renwick Road at Pratt Street (✆ **330 0082**), near the Fiji Visitors Bureau, has wireless Internet access for your laptop (see "Fast Facts: Suva" earlier).

Victoria Parade at Loftus St., in FNPF Place bldg. ✆ **330 0333.** Coffee F$2.50–F$4 (US$1.50–US$2.50); pastries and sandwiches F$2–F$5 (US$1.20–US$3). No credit cards. Mon–Fri 7am–11pm, Sat 8am–11pm, Sun 9am–7pm.

ISLAND NIGHTS IN SUVA

Nocturnal activities in Suva revolve around going to the movies and then hitting the bars—until the wee hours on Friday, the biggest night out.

Movies are a big deal, especially the first-run Hollywood and "Bollywood" Indian flicks at **Village 6 Cinemas,** on Scott Street at Nubukalou Creek, a modern, American-style emporium with six screens and a games arcade upstairs. Check the newspapers for what's playing and show times. You can pig out on popcorn, candy, and soft drinks. Locals flock here on Sunday afternoon, when these plush, air-conditioned theaters offer a comfortable escape from Suva's daytime heat and humidity.

Blues and jazz fans gravitate to **Birdland,** a basement pub at 6 Carnavon St., east of Loftus Street (✆ **330 3833**), which has live music Thursday night. A more mature crowd gathers a few doors away in **The Barn** (✆ **330 7845**), where the waiters and bouncers wear cowboy hats and other Western garb. **Trap's Bar,** 305 Victoria Parade, 2 blocks south of the Pizza Hut (✆ **331 2922**), is a popular watering hole where you're not likely to witness a fight. A band usually plays in the back room on weekends. **O'Reilly's,** on MacArthur Street off Victoria Parade (✆ **331 2968**), is an Irish-style pub that serves Guinness stout and sports on TVs (and it can get a bit rough, depending on who's winning the rugby matches).

Victoria Parade has a number of loud discotheques frequented by the young, noisy crowd. Just walk along; you'll hear them.

Remember: Suva has a serious crime problem, so be careful when bar hopping. Guard your valuables, and always take a taxi to and from your hotel after dark.

6 Rakiraki & Northern Viti Levu

Few travelers will be disappointed by the scenic wonders on the northern side of Viti Levu. Cane fields climb valleys to green mountain ridges. Cowpokes round up cattle on vast ranches. Dramatic cliffs and spires bound a stunning bay. A narrow mountain road winds along the Wainibuka River, once called the "Banana Highway" because in preroad days Fijians used it to float their crops down to Suva on disposable bilibili rafts made of bamboo. A relatively dry climate beckons anyone who wants to catch a few rays, and there's great diving on the reefs off Viti Levu's northernmost point.

THE KING'S ROAD IN NORTHERN VITI LEVU

The only way to get to northern Viti Levu is via the **King's Road,** which runs for 290km (180 miles) from Nadi Airport around the island's northern side to Suva—93km (58 miles) longer than the Queen's Road to the south. The King's Road is paved all the way to Viti Levu Bay on the island's north side, but the unpaved portion through the central mountains can be treacherous. I would not drive through the mountains during the rainy season from November through April, when bridges can wash out.

Scheduled local and express buses run the entire length of the King's Road, as do unscheduled share taxis (see "Getting There & Getting Around" in chapter 4). From the Nadi side, the buses depart from the Lautoka Market. The hotels and backpackers' resorts provide their guests with transportation from Nadi (see "Where to Stay in Northern Viti Levu," below).

The King's Road officially begins at Lautoka. To reach it by car from Nadi, follow the Queen's Road north and take the second exits off of both traffic circles in Lautoka.

From Lautoka, the King's Road first crosses a fertile plain and then ascends into hills dotted with cattle ranches before dropping to the coast and entering the gorgeous **Ba Valley,** Fiji's most productive sugar-growing area. Populated mostly by Indo-Fijians, this valley of steep hills is second only to Suva in both population and economic importance. Many of the country's most successful businesses are headquartered in the town of **Ba,** a prosperous farming community on the banks of the muddy Ba River. Indeed, the commercial center of Ba is a mirror image of many towns in India. From Ba, the King's Road continues to **Tavua,** another predominately Indo-Fijian sugar town backed by its own much smaller valley that reaches up to the mountains.

RAKIRAKI

The enchanting peaks of the **Nakauvadra Range** keep getting closer to the sea as you proceed eastward toward Rakiraki. Legend says the mountains are home to Degei, the prolific spiritual leader who arrived with the first Fijians and later populated the country. As the flat land is squeezed between foothills and sea, cane fields give way to the grasslands and mesas of the 17,000-acre Yaqara Estate, Fiji's largest cattle ranch. Offshore, conelike islands begin to dot the aquamarine lagoon.

Although everyone calls this area Rakiraki, the chief commercial town is actually **Vaileka,** about 1km (½ mile) off the King's Road.

Vaileka itself is home to the **Penang Mill,** the only one of Fiji's five sugar mills that produces solely for domestic consumption (the others export all their sugar). There also is a 9-hole **Penang Golf Course** near the mill, which visitors may play (arrange at the Rakiraki Hotel; see "Where to Stay in Northern Viti Levu," below).

⌐ Fun Fact 900 Men for Dinner

Just before you reach the well-marked junction of the King's Road and the Vaileka cut-off, look on the right for the **Grave of Udre Udre.** Legend says the stones at the base of the tombstone represent every one of the 900 men this renowned cannibal chief had for dinner.

Rakiraki itself is a Fijian village (with the usual car-destroying road humps) on the King's Road, about 1km (½ mile) past the Vaileka junction. It's home of the *Tui Ra,* the high Fijian chief of Ra district, which encompasses all of northern Viti Levu. He likes to stroll over to the Rakiraki Hotel, on the village's eastern boundary.

After the village, a paved road leads to **Ellington Wharf,** the jumping-off point for **Nananu-I-Ra,** a semiarid island about 15 minutes offshore, which has low-budget retreats (see "Where to Stay in Northern Viti Levu," below).

WHERE TO STAY IN NORTHERN VITI LEVU

The area's most luxurious accommodation is at **Wananavu Beach Resort** (© **669 4433;** fax 669 4499; www.wananavu.com), on Viti Levu's northernmost point. The resort's marina is the launching pad for diving trips to the colorful reefs offshore. The dining room, bar, and guest bungalows have great ocean views from their hillside perches. All units here are air-conditioned but none has a phone or TV. Rates range from F$235 to F$600 (US$141–US$360).

Rakiraki Hotel ☝ This establishment is one of the few remaining colonial-era hotels in Fiji, and that means lots of charm unhurried by the pace of modern tourism. The two clapboard roadside buildings were built as guesthouses when U.S. soldiers were stationed nearby during World War II. One houses a tongue-and-groove-paneled bar and dining room, where guests enjoy home-cooked meals. The other has an old-fashioned hall down the middle with five rooms to either side. They have private bathrooms but not phones. Two rooms have four beds each, and are rented on a dormitory basis. Out in the back, three modern two-story motel blocks have 36 rooms outfitted to international standards, with air-conditioning units, phones, and tiled shower-only bathrooms. Behind all is a garden full of tropical fruits and vegetables, which the chef raids daily. The friendly staff will arrange excursions to Vaileka and to Fijian villages, horseback riding, golfing, scuba diving, and treks into the highlands.

P.O. Box 31, Rakiraki (Rakiraki village, on King's Rd., 2.5km/1½ miles east of Vaileka, 132km/82 miles from Nadi Airport). © **800/448-8355** or 669 4101. Fax 669 4545. www.tanoahotels.com. 41 units. F$85–F$120 (US$51–US$72) double, F$30 (US$18) dorm bed. AE, DC, MC, V. **Amenities:** Restaurant; bar; outdoor pool; tennis court; babysitting; laundry service. *In room:* A/C (in most units), TV, fridge, coffeemaker, hair dryer.

NANANU-I-RA ISLAND

Hilly, anvil-shaped Nananu-I-Ra island, a 15-minute boat ride from Ellington Wharf, has long been popular as a sunny retreat for local Europeans who own beach cottages there (the island is all freehold land). Although young backpackers today are more likely to head for the Yasawas, some still stop off here for a few days on their way by bus and ferry from Nadi to Savusavu and Taveuni.

Of the backpackers' resorts, **Betham's Beach Cottages** (©/fax **669 4132;** www. bethams.com.fj) and **MacDonald's Nananu Beach Cottages** (© **669 4633;** www. macsnananu.com) are like a relaxing but polite visit to grandma's (translated: no loud parties or topless sunbathing). All have dorm beds for about F$20 (US$12) per person and cottages from about F$50 to F$125 (US$30–US$75) single or double. **Dive Nananu** (www.divenananu.com) teaches PADI courses from its base at the backpacker-friendly **Nananu Island Lodge** (© **0800 669 4290** toll free in Fiji, or 669 4290; www.nananuislandlodge.com), which has cottages, a dorm, and campsites.

These properties promote heavily at Nadi's inexpensive hotels and hostels, so you will have no trouble getting the full details.

Northern Fiji:
Savusavu & Taveuni

To me, the pristine islands of northern Fiji are what the old South Seas are all about. Compared to busy Viti Levu, "The North" takes us back to the old days of *copra* (dried coconut meat) planters, of Fijians living in small villages in the hills or beside crystal-clear lagoons. You will feel the slow, peaceful pace of life up here as soon as you get off the plane.

The rolling plains of northern **Vanua Levu,** the country's second-largest island, are devoted to sugarcane farming and are of little interest to anyone who has visited Nadi. In fact, **Labasa,** a predominately Indo-Fijian town and Vanua Levu's commercial center, reminds me of Dorothy Parker's quip about Philadelphia: "There is no there there."

But Vanua Levu's southern side is quite another story. Over here, rugged mountains drop to coconut plantations, to an old trading town with the singsong name of **Savusavu,** and to villages where smiling people go about life at the ageless pace of tropical islands everywhere.

Across the Somosomo Strait lies **Taveuni,** Fiji's lush "Garden Isle," where the country's largest population of indigenous plants and animals makes things even more like they used to be. One of my favorite little beachside inns resides on Taveuni, and I am a great fan of two offshore resorts almost within hailing distance: on **Qamea** and **Matagi** islands.

The north is where I come to experience the natural wonders of Fiji—to "ecotour" in today's vogue terminology. It's also where you'll find some of the world's best scuba diving, for the strong currents in and around the Somosomo Strait feed a vast collection of colorful soft corals. Other South Pacific locations have more abundant sea life, but northern Fiji is unsurpassed for coral viewing.

1 Savusavu ★★

Savusavu is Vanua Levu's major sightseeing attraction, primarily because of its volcanic hot springs and magnificent scenic harbor—a bay so large and well protected by surrounding mountains that the U.S. Navy chose it as a possible "hurricane hole" for the Pacific Fleet during World War II. Today it is one of Fiji's major sailing centers and a popular stop for cruising yachties, who can clear Customs and Immigration here. The blue waters of the bay also are home to Fiji's first black pearl farm.

The paved Cross-Island Road from Labasa runs along the eastern shore, through Savusavu town, and out to **Lesiaceva Point** at the end of a peninsula that forms the southern side of the bay and protects it from the Koro Sea.

The **Hibiscus Highway** starts at Savusavu and cuts south across the hilly peninsula to the airstrip before continuing along the south shore to Buca Bay. Although 19km (11½ miles) of it is paved, this road is neither a highway nor lined with hibiscus (cows grazing beneath the palms ate them all), but it does run along a picturesque, island-dotted lagoon through the heart of Vanua Levu's copra region. This area has Fiji's largest concentration of freehold land, which Americans have been buying in recent years. So many Yanks have bought here, in fact, that residents elsewhere in Fiji facetiously refer to Savusavu as "Little America." Although you'll drive past thousands of coconut palms, there are now as many housing developments as copra plantations along the Hibiscus Highway.

The coastal plain here is primarily a raised limestone shelf, meaning that the reef is shallow and the beaches cannot hold a candle to the sands on Taveuni (see "Taveuni," later in this chapter). Keep that in mind as you plan your vacation.

GETTING TO SAVUSAVU

Air Pacific may start flying here from Nadi by the time you make your travels. In the meantime, **Air Fiji** and **Sun Air** both fly from Nadi to Savusavu, and Air Fiji comes here from Suva. Their flights between Nadi and Taveuni usually stop here briefly, so don't let your travel agent send you all the way back to Nadi in order to get to Taveuni. The tiny Savusavu airstrip is on Vanua Levu's south coast. The hotels send buses to meet guests who have reservations.

Suilven Shipping Ltd. (© 331 8247 in Suva; www.suilvenshipping.com) and **Venu Shipping Ltd.** (© 339 5000 in Suva) operate ferries to Savusavu from Suva. **Patterson Shipping Services** (© 331 5644 in Suva; patterson@connect.com.fj) has bus-ferry connections from Natovi Wharf (north of Suva on eastern Viti Levu) to Nabouwalu on Vanua Levu. You connect by bus from Suva to Natovi and from Nabouwalu to Labasa. Local buses connect Labasa to Savusavu.

See "Getting There & Getting Around" in chapter 4 for more information.

Buses fan out from the market in Savusavu town to various points on Vanua Levu, including Buca (*Boo*-tha) Bay, from whence the small ferry *Amazing Grace* crosses the Somosomo Strait to and from Taveuni daily (© 927 1372 in Savusavu, 888 0320 on Taveuni). One-way fare is F$20 (US$12), including the bus ride from Savusavu to Buca Bay. Call for schedules and reservations.

GETTING AROUND SAVUSAVU

Budget Rent-A-Car (© 800/527-0700 or 885 0377 in Savusavu, 672 2735 in Nadi; www.budget.com) and **Carpenters Rentals** (© 885 0122 in Savusavu, 672 2772 in Nadi; rentals@carpenters.com.fj) both have offices in Savusavu.

An incredible number of **taxis** gather by the market in Savusavu when they're not hauling passengers. The cars of **Paradise Cab** (© 885 0018 or 956026) and **Michael's Taxi** (© 995 5727) are air-conditioned. Fares from Savusavu are F$4.50 (US$2.70) to the airstrip, F$7 (US$4.20) to Namale Resort, F$12 (US$7) to Koro Sun Resort, and F$6 (US$3.60) to the Jean-Michel Cousteau Fiji Islands Resort on Lesiaceva Point.

Moments **The Way It Used to Be**

The old South Pacific of copra plantation and trading boat days still lives in Savusavu and Taveuni. It rains more in Fiji's north, but that makes the steep hills lushly green. The diving and snorkeling here are world class.

Northern Fiji

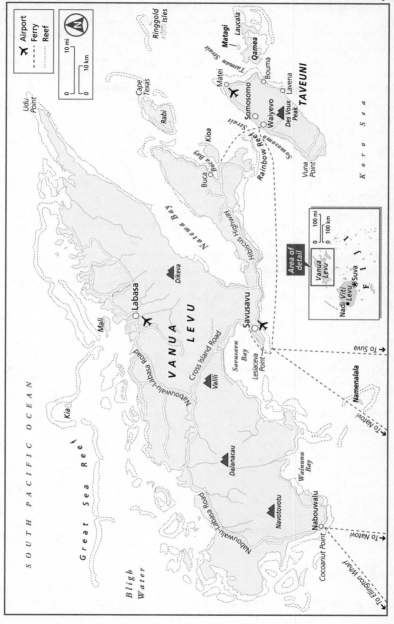

Airport
Ferry
Reef

10 mi
10 km

Ringgold Isles

Laucala
Matagi
Qamea

Tasman Strait

Matei
Bouma
Lavena
Somosomo
Waiyevo TAVEUNI
Des Voux Peak

Somosomo Strait

Cape Texas

Rabi

Kioa

Buca Bay

Buca

Rainbow Reef

Vuna Point

Koro Sea

Natewa Bay

Udu Point

Dikeva

Hibiscus Highway

Labasa

VANUA LEVU

Savusavu

Cross Island Road

Savusavu Bay

Lesiaceva Point

To Suva

Area of detail

100 mi
100 km

Vanua Levu

Nadi Viti Levu ✹Suva

F I J I

Mali

Nabouwalu-Labasa Road

Vaili

To Natovi

Namenalala

Kia

Dalanacau

Wainunu Bay

SOUTH PACIFIC OCEAN

Great Sea Reef

Navotovotu

Nabouwalu-Labasa Road

Nabouwalu

To Natovi

Bligh Water

Cocoanut Point

To Ellington Wharf

Local buses fan out from the Savusavu market to various points on the island. Most of them make three or four runs a day to outlying destinations, but ask the drivers when they will return to town. The longest runs should cost about F$6 (US$3.60), with local routes in the F55¢ to F$1 (US33¢–US60¢) range.

You can rent **mountain bikes** from **Curly's Cruising/Bosun's Locker,** on the main street opposite Waitui Marina (© **885 0122**). They cost F$15 (US$9) for a half day, F$25 (US$15) for a full day.

FAST FACTS: Savusavu

The following facts apply to Savusavu. If you don't see an item here, check "Fast Facts: Fiji" in chapter 4.

Currency Exchange **ANZ Bank, Westpac Bank,** and **Colonial National Bank** have offices with ATMs on the main street.

Drugstores **Shiloah Clinic/Drugs,** in the Palm Court shops on the main street (© **932 2544**), opposite Waitui Marina. Open Monday to Friday 9am to 1pm and 2 to 5pm, Sunday 9am to noon.

E-mail **Curly's Cruising/Bosun's Locker** (© **885 0122**), opposite Waitui Marina, charges F18¢ (US11¢) a minute online. **Savusavu Real Estate & Internet Centre,** in the Copra Shed (© **885 0929**), charges F20¢ (US12¢) per minute, but it's air-conditioned. **Bula-Re Cafe** (© **885 0377;** see "Where to Dine in Savusavu," later) charges F25¢ (US15¢) a minute.

Emergencies In an emergency phone © **917** for police, © **911** for **fire** or **ambulance.** The **police station** (© **885 0222**) is east of town.

Healthcare **Dr. Joeli Taoi** has an office in the Palm Court shops (© **885 0721**), on the main street. The **government hospital** (© **885 0800**) is east of town, in the government compound.

Information Best bet for local information is **Curly's Cruising/Bosun's Locker** (© **885 0122**), opposite Waitui Marina (see "Organized Tours," below). You can find information on the Web at the Savusavu Tourism Association's site (**www.fiji-savusavu.com**).

Post Office The post office is on the main street near the east of the downtown commercial district. It's open Monday to Friday 8am to 5pm, Saturday 8am to noon.

Safety Savusavu generally is a safe place to visit, but don't tempt the mortals. Keep an eye on your personal property.

Water The tap water in town and at the resorts is safe to drink.

EXPLORING SAVUSAVU

For practical purposes, Savusavu has only one street, and that runs along the shore for about 1.5km (1 mile). The modern **Copra Shed,** an old warehouse that has been turned into modern shops and a cafe, stands about midway along the shore. The airlines have their offices in the Copra Shed, along with tour operators, the Savusavu

Yacht Club, and restaurants. A bit farther along is **Waitui Marina,** where cruising yachties come ashore.

Highlights of a stroll along the bay-hugging avenue are the gorgeous scenery and the volcanic **hot springs.** Steam from underground rises from the beach on the west end of town, and you can see more white clouds floating up from the ground between the sports field and the school, both behind the Shell station. A concrete pot has been built to make a natural stove in which local residents place meals to cook slowly all day. Overlooking the springs and bay, the **Savusavu Hot Springs Hotel** has great views (see "Where to Stay in Savusavu," below).

ORGANIZED TOURS

More than likely your hotel will have a choice of guided excursions in and around Savusavu. If not, **Curly's Cruising/Bosun's Locker,** on the main street opposite Waitui Marina (© **885 0122**), has a series of tours and excursions. One goes to Naidi village, on the Hibiscus Highway, for a look at traditional Fijian lifestyles, and another takes you to a copra and beef plantation, where you can see the modern-day version of the old South Seas coconut plantation. Either of these costs F$25 (US$15) per person. Another trip goes to Waisali Rainforest Reserve, a 116-hectare (290-acre) national forest up in the central mountains, which includes a visit to a waterfall. It costs F$40 (US$24). They have a full-day tour to Labasa for F$90 (US$54) per person.

SHOPPING FOR BLACK PEARLS

Marine biologist Justin Hunter spent more than 10 years working in the U.S. before coming home to Savusavu and founding Fiji's first black-pearl farm out in the bay. You can shop for the results at **J. Hunter Pearls,** on the western end of town (© **885 0821;** www.pearlsfiji.com). Prices range from F$20 ($12) up to F$2,000 (US$1,200) for loose pearls. Hunter has them set in jewelry, too, as well as some interesting items made from the mother-of-pearl shells (I love my salad forks made from gleaming shells with tree branch handles). Open Monday to Friday 8am to 5pm, Saturday 8am to 1pm. You can take a free 30-minute boat tour of the farm at 9:30am and 1:30pm weekdays.

DIVING, KAYAKING & OTHER WATERSPORTS

Most of the resorts have complete diving facilities, as noted in "Where to Stay in Savusavu," below. A very long boat ride is required to dive on the Rainbow Reef and Great White Wall, which are more easily reached from Taveuni than from Savusavu. But that's not to say that there aren't plenty of colorful reefs near here, including the Namena Reef, a wonderful barrier formation that nearly encircles Moody's Namena (see "A Resort on Namenalala Island," below).

In addition to its land-based excursions (see "Exploring Savusavu," above), **Curly's Cruising/Bosun's Locker,** on the main street opposite Waitui Marina (© **885 0122;** fax 885 0344; www.ecodivers-tours.com), has snorkeling trips to colorful reefs offshore starting at F$25 (US$15) per person. It also rents single and double ocean kayaks, starting at F$15 (US$9) and F$20 (US$12), respectively, per hour, and sailing catamarans for F$15 (US$9) per hour. Curly's offers a full-day guided paddling trip to a Fijian village and will tailor 3- to 14-day paddling excursions along the northern and western coasts of Savusavu Bay. You'll stay in the villages and dine with the villagers, so consider these to be "soft adventure" excursions. Contact Curly's for schedules and prices.

⌐Tips   When to Go Diving in Northern Fiji

Diving in northern Fiji is best from late May through October, when visibility reaches 120 feet and more. Because of the strong currents, however, dives to such outer reef sites as the Great White Wall and Rainbow Reef can be strenuous any time of year.

There are usually several sailboats doing day cruises and longer charters here. Check with Curly's for information and reservations. You can also contact the Savusavu Hot Springs Hotel (see "Where to Stay in Savusavu," below) for deep-sea fishing.

The gray-sand beaches around Savusavu aren't the main reason to come here. The nearest beach to town is a shady stretch on Lesiaceva Point just outside the Jean-Michel Cousteau Fiji Islands Resort, about 5km (3 miles) west of town, which is the end of the line for westbound buses leaving Savusavu market. There also is a half-moon beach at Naidi Bay, an extinct volcanic crater, just west of Namale Resort on the Hibiscus Highway. The road skirts the bay, but the beach is not easy to see. Take a taxi or ask the bus driver to let you off at Naidi Bay—not Naidi village or nearby Namale Resort. The bar and restaurant at Namale Resort are not open to walk-in customers, so bring something to drink and eat.

TUI TAI ADVENTURE CRUISES ✿✿

Ecotourism takes to sea with **Tui Tai Adventure Cruises** (© 877/682-5433 or 885 3032; www.tuitai.com), which uses the 140-foot sailing schooner *Tui Tai* to make 3-, 4-, and 5-day voyages from Savusavu. The boat goes to Koro, where guests visit a private plantation; Taveuni, where they visit Bouma Falls; Kioa, where they spend time in that island's one village; and to the Ringgold Isles, inside an extensive reef system east of Vanua Levu. It carries mountain bikes for land excursions and kayaks and snorkel gear for exploring the shoreline and reefs. The *Tui Tai* can accommodate 24 guests in air-conditioned cabins. Rates range from F$2,630 (US$1,578) double for a 3-night cruise to F$3,580 (US$2,148) double for a 5-nighter, including all meals and activities. If space is available, you can go along on just its first day, around Savusavu Bay, for F$150 (US$90).

WHERE TO STAY IN SAVUSAVU
EXPENSIVE

Jean-Michel Cousteau Fiji Islands Resort ✿✿✿ *Kids*   This joint venture between the deluxe Post Ranch Inn of Big Sur, California, and Jean-Michel Cousteau, son of the late Jacques Cousteau, looks like an old-time Fijian village set in a flat palm grove beside the bay on Lesiaceva Point. This "environmentally correct" resort is great for adults and especially for families, since its educational Bula Camp is the South Pacific's best program for children.

Reception and the resort's bar are under a large thatched roof built like a chief's *bure* (bungalow), and the dining room is covered by a taller roof, constructed to resemble a priest's bure. These impressive buildings sit next to an infinity pool just steps from one of the better beaches in the area. The large, luxurious thatched-roof guest bures have ceiling fans to augment the natural breezes flowing through floor-to-ceiling wooden jalousie windows that make up the front and rear walls. Most have porches strung with hammocks. Sitting by themselves at the point, split-level "villas" are more spacious and private; they are for adults only except during school holiday periods. A new luxurious honeymoon unit has a spa tub in its large outdoor bathroom; needless to say, it's reserved for adults all the time. Some but not all units here have phones.

A host of watersports includes snorkeling, kayaking, sailing, and scuba diving. The resort also offers environmentally oriented activities such as visits to rain and mangrove forests. An on-site marine biologist gives lectures and leads bird-watching expeditions and visits to Fijian villages. You can scuba dive with guides skilled in marine biology. The resort has a custom-built dive boat that's capable of reaching the famous Namena Reef, which surrounds Moody's Namena (see "A Resort on Namenalala Island," below), in about 1 hour.

Post Office, Savusavu (Lesiaceva Point, 5km/3 miles west of town). © **800/246-3454** or 885 0188. Fax 885 0430. www.fijiresort.com. 25 units. US$535–US$1,950 double. Rates include meals, soft drinks, airport transfers, and all activities except scuba diving. AE, MC, V. **Amenities:** Restaurant; bar; 3 outdoor pools; tennis court; spa; watersports; scuba diving; children's program; activities desk; wireless Internet access (in main bldg.); limited room service; massage; babysitting; laundry service. *In room:* Minibar, coffeemaker, hair dryer, iron, safe, phone (in villas only).

Koro Sun Resort ⊛ *Value*   A fine value for dollar, this property on Vanua Levu's southern coast has been considerably upgraded in recent years by its American owners, who will gladly sell you a piece of paradise and build a custom-designed home on it (the resort rents villas already built by its landowners). The Hibiscus Highway runs along the shoreline, separating the property from the lagoon. There is a bit of beach here, and a swimming hole has been dredged into the shallow reef. A lagoonside restaurant and bar sit on a landfill by a marina, also blasted into the reef. Koro Sun sports two outdoor pools (the more attractive reserved for adults only), and a 9-hole, par-3 golf course beneath the coconut palms of an old plantation. A dirt track leads around the golf course and through a rain forest to the resort's own refreshing cascades, where there's a spa in two screen bungalows (you can easily work up a sweat just getting a treatment in this humid climate). The land turns quickly from flat coastal shelf to hills, where most of the guest bungalows are perched, thus commanding views through the palms to the sea. All these hillside units have screened porches. One has a separate bedroom, another has two bedrooms. The octagonal honeymoon bure is the most deluxe and private. Down at sea level, the "garden" units lack views but have small front yards behind picket fences, plus four-poster beds with mosquito nets. All bungalows have outdoor showers behind high rock walls.

Private Bag, Savusavu (Hibiscus Hwy., 16km/10 miles east of town). © **877/567-6786** or 885 0262. Fax 885 0355. www.korosunresort.com. 18 units. US$360–US$550 double. Rates include meals, nonmotorized watersports. AE, MC, V. **Amenities:** 2 restaurants; 2 bars; 2 outdoor pools; 9-hole golf course; 2 tennis courts; spa; free use of mountain bikes, snorkeling gear, and sea kayaks; scuba diving; children's programs; high-speed Internet kiosk; massage; babysitting; laundry service. *In room:* A/C, minibar, coffeemaker, hair dryer, no phone.

Namale Fiji Islands Resort & Spa ⊛⊛⊛   This luxurious resort is owned by toothy American motivational author and speaker Anthony Robbins, who visits several times a year and conducts get-a-grip seminars here from January to April. Robbins obviously finds any dull moment distasteful, for he has built an air-conditioned gym with a wall-size TV for watching sports via satellite, a basketball court, an electronic golf simulator, and a full-size bowling alley (I kid you not). These indoor toys will come in handy since the climate here is borderline rain forest, and the pebbly beaches are not reason alone to spend your entire vacation here. Nevertheless, Namale has excellent scuba diving and deep-sea fishing (the only two activities demanding an

---

Fun Fact **Do I Have a Deal for You**

Namale Resort has been a working copra plantation since the 1860s, when an Englishman bought it from the local chief for 10 rifles.

---

extra fee), plus windsurfing, horseback riding, and hiking. After all that, you can be pampered in the full-service spa, the most beautiful in Fiji. As my travel writing friend John (Johnny Jet) DiScala once wisecracked, this is "the kind of place Americans come when they really don't want to leave home."

This area has been geologically uplifted, so all buildings are on a shelf 10 to 20 feet above sea level. The guest quarters are widely scattered in the blooming tropical gardens, thus affording honeymoon-like privacy if not a setting directly beside the lagoon. Crown jewels here are two houses. The "Dream House" is a two-bedroom, two-bathroom minimansion with a kitchen, its own small pool, a whirlpool bathtub, and indoor and outdoor showers. Similarly equipped, the "Bula House" has only one bedroom, but there are two guest bungalows outside, and it has a Jacuzzi on its deck. Both the Dream and Bula houses have drop-down movie screens with wraparound sound systems (again, I kid you not). Your children can stay with you in the houses, but only if they're at least 12 years old (they are not allowed in the other bungalows unless you rent one just for them).

A deluxe honeymoon bure has its own swimming pool plus a sunken bathtub and two-person shower. Four more honeymoon bures have bathrooms with Jacuzzi tubs, separate showers with indoor and outdoor entrances, and their own ceiling fans. Six older bures are much less spectacular, but they are attractively appointed nonetheless. If you're traveling by yourself, you can stay in one of these, but not in the larger units. You'll have a walkie-talkie instead of a phone.

P.O. Box 244, Savusavu (Hibiscus Hwy., 11km/7 miles east of town). (C) **800/727-3454** or 885 0435. Fax 885 0400 or 619/535-6385 in the U.S. www.namalefiji.com. 13 bungalows, 2 houses. US$850–US$1,250 double, US$1,950–US$2,100 house. Rates include meals, drinks, all activities except spa services, scuba diving, and fishing. No children under 12 accepted. Villas require 4-night minimum stay. AE, MC, V. **Amenities:** Restaurant; 2 bars; 2 outdoor pools; tennis court; exercise room; Jacuzzi; watersports; free bikes; game room; high-speed Internet kiosk; massage; free laundry service; basketball court. *In room:* Kitchen (in houses), minibar, coffeemaker, hair dryer, iron, safe no phone.

INEXPENSIVE

Operated by an Indo-Fijian family of the Christian persuasion, **David's Budget Holiday House** ((C) **885 0149**) offers rooms and a dorm in a simple wood frame house in a quiet setting on Nakama Road near the hot springs. It charges F$30 (US$18) for a room, F$15 (US$9) for a dorm bed. Credit cards are not accepted.

Savusavu Hot Springs Hotel *Value*   Once a Travelodge motel, this three-story structure sits on a hill in town, and its motel-style rooms take advantage of the view by having sliding glass doors that open to balconies. The air-conditioned units on the third and fourth floors have the best vantage. The less expensive rooms on the lower levels are equipped with ceiling fans but lack air-conditioners. Ground floor rooms are devoted to dormitory-style accommodation, which makes this the local backpacker's choice. Most of these have double beds while two are equipped with four bunk beds each. There no longer is a restaurant here, although guests are treated to continental breakfast in the former dining room overlooking an outdoor pool. This isn't a fancy establishment, but it's clean, comfortable, friendly, and a very good value.

P.O. Box 208, Savusavu (in town). (✆ 714/840-1250 or 885 0195. Fax 885 0430. hotspringshotel@connect.com.fj. 48 units. F$95–F$155 (US$57–US$93) double; F$25 (US$15) dorm bed. Rates include continental breakfast. AE, MC, V. **Amenities:** Bar; outdoor pool; massage; babysitting; laundry service; coin-op washers and dryers. *In room:* A/C (some units), fridge, coffeemaker.

COTTAGE RENTALS

As on Taveuni (see "Where to Stay on Taveuni," later in this chapter), a number of American and other expatriates have purchased land and built homes in or near Savusavu. Some live here permanently and have constructed rental cottages on their properties. Others rent out their homes when they're not here, either through rental programs such as at Koro Sun Resort (see above) or on the Internet. Not all are licensed by the Fiji government, which has cracked down on owners who do not have licenses and thus do not pay value-added and hotel bed taxes on their rentals. You don't want someone from the Fiji Hotel Licensing Board knocking on your door in the middle of your siesta, so if you rent a cottage, make sure it is fully licensed.

You won't have this problem at **Tropic Splendor** (✆ **851 0152** or 991 7931; www.tropic-splendor-fiji.com), on the north shore of Savusavu Bay, a 20-minute drive from town. Deserting the deserts of New Mexico, owners Susan Stone and Jeffery Mather relocated to this lush setting in 2001, and they make sure you have all the comforts of home in their guest bungalow beside a beach of powdery, cocoa-color sand. It has ceiling fans, a TV with DVD player, a king-size bed, a big wrap-around porch, outdoor shower, and other amenities. They charge F$360 (US$216) per day, with discounts for longer stays.

CAMPING

You can pitch your own tent, rent one of theirs, or stay in a four-bed dormitory at **Yau Kolo Cafe and Camp Ground** (✆ **885 3089;** yaukolo@yahoo.com), in a jungle like setting 13km (8 miles) east of Savusavu on the Hibiscus Highway. Virtually next door to Koro Sun Resort, it has a cafe (consequently, there is no communal kitchen here) offering very good, inexpensive meals, or you can sip cold Fiji Bitters in the "beer garden" (I recently spent an entire Sunday afternoon doing just that). A campsite costs F$12 (US$7) per person a night, or you can rent a tent with bed and bedding for F$30 (US$18) double. Dorm beds cost F$20 (US$12) per night. All rates include breakfast. The communal bathrooms have cold-water showers.

A RESORT ON NAMENALALA ISLAND

Covered with dense native forest and bush, dragon-shaped Namenalala is a 110-acre rocky ridge protruding from the Koro Sea about 32km (20 miles) south of Vanua Levu. The huge Namena barrier reef sweeps down from Vanua Levu and surrounds it with a gorgeous lagoon, which is an officially protected marine reserve. A large colony of boobies nest on the island, and **sea turtles** climb onto some of the South Pacific's most gorgeous beaches to lay their eggs from November through February.

Moody's Namena 🌟🌟 *Value*   Originally from Pennsylvania, Tom and Joan Moody (she pronounces her name "Joanne") opened this peaceful, remote resort in 1986. The Moodys have perched all but one of their comfortable bungalows up on the ridge so that they have commanding views of the ocean but not of one another. The walls of the hexagonal structures slide back to render both views and cooling breezes, so you will sleep under a mosquito net. Solar power runs the reading lights and fans, but you won't be able to plug in your hairdryer or shaver. Instead of treading sandy paths among palm trees, you climb crushed-rock pathways along the wooded ridge to the central building, where the Moodys provide excellent meals. They serve wine with dinner and sell beer, but they do not have a license, so bring some duty-free booze if you drink spirits. OCCUPIED/UNOCCUPIED signs warn guests that someone else is already cavorting on four of the island's five private beaches. Other activities include hiking, kayaking, swimming, snorkeling, deep-sea fishing, and scuba diving among the colorful reefs and sea turtles. Tom does not teach scuba diving, so you must be certified in advance. The Moodys will have you brought out from Savusavu on a fast sportfishing boat, a voyage of 1½ hours, or arrange to charter a seaplane for the 1-hour flight from Nadi.

Private Mail Bag, Savusavu. (C) **881 3764.** Fax 881 2366. www.moodysnamenafiji.com. 6 units. US$285 per person (5-night minimum stay required). Rates include meals, nonalcoholic beverages, boat transfers from Savusavu, all activities except scuba diving. MC, V. Closed Mar–Apr. No children under 16 accepted. **Amenities:** Restaurant; bar; game room; massage; laundry service. *In room:* Coffeemaker, no phone.

WHERE TO DINE IN SAVUSAVU

You can grab an inexpensive breakfast, lunch, or cold beer at **Decked Out Cafe,** on the main street opposite the Copra Shed (C **885 2929**). Order at the counter and enjoy your cake, sandwich, burger, hot dog, fruit salad, or pizza at a picnic table on a covered deck with a view of the harbor across the main street. No item costs over F$7 (US$4). Open Monday to Saturday 7am to 2:30pm. No credit cards.

Bula-Re Cafe ✻ INTERNATIONAL   For the money, this German-operated restaurant facing the harbor serves the best food in town. That's especially true of its awesome toasted sesame-seed salad dressing. The house special is chicken schnitzel-style, but the menu ranges all over the world, from British fish and chips to Fijian *palusami.* Spicy Indian-style curry prawns with almond rice will excite your taste buds. Vegetarians will have several choices here, including veggie pasta with a spicy cheese and curry sauce. Wednesday is *lovo* night here, featuring a buffet of earth-oven Fijian foods for F$17 (US$10) per person. You can get an espresso or latte to accompany breakfast or to recharge later on. You can also check your e-mail here.

Main street, east end of town opposite the post office. (C) **885 0377.** Reservations recommended for dinner. Breakfast F$5–F$7 (US$3–US$4); main courses F$6.50–F$17 (US$4–US$10). No credit cards. Mon–Sat 9am–9:30pm, Sun 5–10pm.

Captain's Cafe INTERNATIONAL   With seating inside or outside on a deck over the bay, this cafe is a pleasant place for a morning coffee, an outdoor lunch, and good steaks at dinner. Fresh fish is surprisingly good, too, especially the mahimahi in lemon butter. Other offerings are sandwiches, burgers, side salads, garlic bread, and reasonably good pastas and pizzas.

Main street, in the Copra Shed. (C) **885 0511.** Burgers and sandwiches F$7–F$9 (US$4–US$5.50); pizza F$7–F$20 (US$4–US$12); main courses F$16–F$17 (US$9.50–US$10). No credit cards. Daily 7:30am–8:30pm.

Surf 'n' Turf *(finds* INTERNATIONAL   Formerly a chef at Jean-Michel Cousteau Fiji Islands Resort, Atesh Prasad now puts his skills to good use at this upstairs restaurant, the most refined in town. The dining room is air-conditioned, or you can sit at one of three tables on a narrow balcony overlooking the main street (it's noisy and often hot out here during the day but acceptable for dinner). As the name implies, a combination of steak and tropical lobster tail leads the list here, but Atesh also cooks very good Indian curries.

Main street, opposite the municipal market. © **881 0966**. Reservations accepted. Main courses F$12–F$50 (US$7–US$30). No credit cards. Daily 10am–2pm and 6–10pm.

ISLAND NIGHTS IN SAVUSAVU

The expensive resorts provide nightly entertainment for their guests. Otherwise, there's not much going on in Savusavu after dark except at one local nightclub, which I have not had the courage to sample, and at three local drinking establishments, which I have. For a step back in time, visit **The Planter's Club** ⊛ (© **885 0233**), an ancient clapboard building near the western end of town. It's a friendly holdover from the colonial era, with a snooker table and a pleasant bar, where you can order a cold young coconut (add gin or rum, and you've got a genuine island cocktail). It's open Monday to Thursday from 10am to 10pm, Friday and Saturday 10am to 11pm, Sunday 10am to 8pm. You'll be asked to sign the club's register.

Yachties and the numerous expatriates who live here congregate at the wharf-side bars of the **Savusavu Yacht Club,** in the Copra Shed (© **885 0685**), and the nearby **Waitui Club** (© **885 0536**), upstairs at Waitui Marina. The yacht club is open Monday to Saturday from 10am to 10pm and Sunday from noon to 10pm. Waitui Club is open Monday to Thursday from 10am to 8pm, Friday and Saturday from 10am to 11pm.

2 Taveuni ⊛⊛⊛

One of my favorite places to hang out in Fiji, cigar-shaped Taveuni, the country's third-largest island, lies just 6.5km (4 miles) from Vanua Levu's eastern peninsula across the Somosomo Strait, one of the world's most famous scuba-diving spots. Although the island is only 9.5km (6 miles) wide, a volcanic ridge down Taveuni's 40km (25-mile) length soars to more than 1,200m (4,000 ft.), blocking the southeast trade winds and pouring as much as 30 feet of rain a year on the mountaintops and the island's rugged eastern side. Consequently, Taveuni's 9,000 residents (three-fourths of them Fijians) live in a string of villages along the gently sloping, less rainy but still lush western side. They own some of the country's most fertile and well-watered soil—hence Taveuni's nickname: The Garden Isle.

Thanks to limited land clearance and the absence of the mongoose, Taveuni is the best place in Fiji to explore the interior on foot. It still has all the plants and animals indigenous to Fiji, including the unique Fiji fruit bat, the Taveuni silktail bird, land crabs, and some species of palm that have only recently been identified. The **Ravilevu Nature Preserve** on the east coast and the **Taveuni Forest Preserve** in the middle of the island are designed to protect these rare creatures.

With dozens of fabulous dive sites nearby, including the Rainbow Reef and its Great White Wall, Taveuni also is the best place to explore Fiji's underwater paradise. The soft corals populating the reefs are regaining their brilliant colors after a coral-bleaching incident a few years ago.

The little airstrip and most of Taveuni's accommodations are at **Matei,** on the northeastern corner of the island facing the small, rugged islands of **Qamea** and **Matagi,** homes of two of my favorite little offshore resorts (see "Resorts on Qamea & Matagi Islands," later in this chapter).

GETTING TO TAVEUNI & GETTING AROUND

Both **Air Fiji** and **Sun Air** fly to Taveuni from Nadi, and Air Fiji has service from Suva. As we go to press, **Air Pacific** is planning to join them. The hotels send buses or hire taxis to pick up their guests.

> ⟨*Tips*⟩ **Don't Rent a Car**
>
> **Budget Rent-A-Car** (© 800/527-0700 or 888 0291; www.budget.com) has an agency on Taveuni, but I always hire a taxi and driver rather than a vehicle here. Taveuni's only road, which runs along the west and north coasts, is paved between Waiyevo and Matei, but elsewhere it's rough gravel, winding, often narrow, and at places carved into sheer cliffs above the sea. A taxi and driver cost about F$150 (US$90) for a full day, or about the same as a rental with insurance and gas.

The large ferries from Suva stop at Savusavu before arriving at Waiyevo, and the small *Amazing Grace* crosses the Somosomo Strait between Waiyevo and Buca Bay daily.

See "Getting to Savusavu" earlier in this chapter, and "Getting There & Getting Around" in chapter 4, for details.

Taxis don't ply the roads here, but your hotel staff can call one. I have been satisfied with **Taveuni Island Tours** (© 888 0221), **Nan's Taxi** (© 888 0705), and **Ishwar's Taxi** (© 888 0424). None of the taxis have meters, so negotiate for a round-trip price if you're going out into the villages and having the driver wait for you. The official fare from the airstrip is F$2 (US90¢) to Maravu Plantation and Taveuni Island resorts, F$17 (US$10) to Bouma Falls, and F$20 (US$12) to Navakoca (Qamea) Landing, or Waiyevo.

Local **buses** fan out from Waiyevo to the outlying villages about three times a day from Monday to Saturday. For example, a bus leaves Waiyevo for Bouma at 8:30am, 12:15pm, and 4:30pm. The one-way fare to Bouma is no more than F$4 (US$2.50). Contact **Pacific Transport** (© 888 0278) opposite Kaba's Supermarket in Nagara.

FAST FACTS: Taveuni

The following facts apply to Taveuni. If you don't see an item here, see "Fast Facts: Fiji" in chapter 4.

Currency Exchange **Colonial National Bank** has an office at Nagara (© 888 0433), but it does not have an ATM. It's open Monday to Friday 9:30am to 4pm.

Emergencies In an emergency phone © 917 for the **police**, © 911 for **fire** or **ambulance**. The **police station** (© 888 0222) is in the government compound.

Healthcare The **government hospital** (© 888 0222) is in the government compound in the hills above Waiyevo. To get there, go uphill on the road opposite the Garden Island Resort, then take the right fork.

Post Office The post office is in Waiyevo. It's open Monday to Friday 8am to 4pm, Saturday 8am to noon.

Safety Taveuni is relatively safe, but exercise caution if you're out late at night.

Water The tap water is safe to drink on Taveuni.

EXPLORING TAVEUNI

Taveuni's most famous sight is mountaintop **Lake Tagimaucia** (*Tangi*-maw-thia), home of the rare *tagimaucia* flower that bears red blooms with white centers. A shallow lake whose sides are ringed with mud flats and thick vegetation, it sits among the clouds in a volcanic crater at an altitude of more than 800m (2,700 ft.).

Bouma Falls are among Fiji's finest and most accessible waterfalls, and the area around them is included in the **Bouma National Heritage Park** (see below). Past Bouma at the end of the road, a sensational coastal hiking track begins at **Lavena** village and runs through the Ravilevu Nature Reserve.

By tradition, Taveuni's **Somosomo** village is one of Fiji's most "chiefly" villages; that is, its chief is one of the highest ranking in all of Fiji, and the big meeting house here is a prime gathering place of Fiji's influential Great Council of Chiefs. (Hence, Taveuni's coastal road is paved only from just east of the airstrip to Somosomo.) Adjoining Somosomo, the predominately Indo-Fijian **Nagara** village is the island's commercial center.

The administrative village of **Waiyevo** sits halfway down the west coast. A kilometer (½ mile) south, a brass plaque marks the **180th Meridian** of longitude, exactly halfway around the world from the Zero Meridian in Greenwich, England. In addition to the aptly named Meridian Cinema, the village of **Waikiki** sports a lovely 19th-century Catholic mission built to reward a French missionary for helping the locals defeat a band of invading Tongans.

BOUMA NATIONAL HERITAGE PARK ★★★

One attraction on everyone's list is **Bouma National Heritage Park** (© **888 0390**) on Taveuni's northeastern end, 18km (11 miles) from the airstrip, 37km (23 miles) from Waiyevo. The government of New Zealand provided funds for the village of Bouma to build trails to the three levels of **Bouma Falls.** It's a flat, 15-minute walk along an old road from the visitors center to the lower falls, which plunge some 180m (600 ft.) into a broad pool. From there, a trail climbs sharply to a lookout with a fine view of Qamea and as far offshore as the Kaibu and Naitoba islands east of Taveuni. The trail then enters a rain forest to a second set of falls, which are not as impressive as the lower cascade. Hikers ford slippery rocks across a swift-flowing creek while holding onto a rope. This 30-minute muddy climb can be made in shower sandals, but be careful of your footing. A more difficult track ascends to yet a third falls, but I've never followed it, and people who did have told me it isn't worth the effort.

Another trail, the **Vidawa Rainforest Walk,** leads to historic hill fortifications and more great views. Guides lead full-day treks through the rainforest, but you'll need to book at your hotel activities desk or call the visitor center (© **888 0390**) at least a day in advance. The hikes cost F$40 (US$24) per person.

𝄞 Moments Yesterday & Today

The 180th Meridian would have been the international date line (IDL) were it not for its dividing the Aleutians and Fiji into 2 days, and for Tonga's wish to be on the same day as Australia. Even so, I love to stand here on Taveuni with one of my feet in today, the other in yesterday.

The park is open daily from 8am to 5pm. Admission is F$8 (US$5) per person without a guide, F$15 (US$9) with a guide. See "Getting to Taveuni & Getting Around," above, for information about how to get here.

HIKING ✺✺✺

In addition to the short walks in the Bouma National Heritage Park (see above), three other treks are worth doing, depending on the weather. The relatively dry (and cooler) season from May to September is the best time to explore Taveuni on foot.

At the end of the road past the park, the **Lavena Coastal Walk** ✺✺✺ runs for 5km (3 miles) along a well-worn, easy to follow trail connecting Fijian villages, then climbs to **Wainibau Falls.** The last 20 minutes or so of this track are spent walking up a creek bed, and you'll have to swim through a rock-lined canyon to reach the falls (stay to the left, out of the current). The creek water is safe to drink, but you might want to bring your own supplies. Admission to the village and walking track is F$8 (US$5) per person.

Lavena village has one of Taveuni's best beaches and a lodge where hikers can overnight for F$25 (US$15) per person (© **923 9080,** and ask for Maria).

High in the center of the island, a track leads to **Lake Tagimaucia,** home of the famous flower that blooms from the end of September to the end of December. This crater lake is surrounded by mud flats and filled with floating vegetation. Beginning at Somosomo village, the hike to the lake takes about 8 hours round-trip. The trail is often muddy and slippery, and given the usual cloud cover hanging over the mountains by midmorning, you're not likely to see much when you reach the top. Only hikers who are in shape should make this full-day trek. An alternative is to take a four-wheel-drive vehicle up Des Voeux Peak for a look down at the lake. The drive is best done early in the morning, when the mountain is least likely to be shrouded in clouds. You must pay a F$5 (US$3) per person "custom fee" to visit the lake, which includes a guide. Your hotel will make the arrangements.

SCUBA DIVING ✺✺✺

The swift currents of the Somosomo Strait feed the soft corals on the Rainbow Reef and its White Wall between Taveuni and Vanua Levu, making this one of the world's most colorful and famous scuba-diving sites. Although bleached by unusually warm seawater in 1998, the soft corals are rebounding.

The Rainbow Reef and its Great White Wall are only 4 miles off Waiyevo, so the Garden Island Resort (see "Where to Stay on Taveuni," below) is the closest dive base, a 20-minute boat ride across the Somosomo Strait. The U.S. firm **Aqua-Trek** (© **800/ 541-4334** or 888 0286; www.aquatrek.com) owns the resort and has its dive base here. This five-star PADI operation has full equipment rental, NITROX, and teaches courses

---

⌒Tips It All Depends on the Tides

Because of the strong currents in the Somosomo Strait, dives on Taveuni's most famous sites must be timed according to the tides. You can't count on making the dives you would like if the tides are wrong when you're here. A very good friend of mine spent 10 days in the area and never did get out to the Rainbow Reef.

from beginner to dive master. Aqua-Trek's prices start at F$165 (US$99) for a two-dive excursion. PADI learn-to-dive courses cost F$720 (US$432).

Based at Taveuni Estates, a real estate development about 7km (4 miles) south of the 180th Meridien, Carl Fox's **Taveuni Estates Dive** (© **866/217-3438** or 888 0063; www.taveunidive.com) also is within reach of the Rainbow Reef, in addition to other top sites on Taveuni's southern end. It charges US$95 for a two-tank dive.

Farther away but still in easy range at the northern end of Taveuni is **Swiss Fiji Divers** (© **885 0586;** www.swissfijidivers.com), where Dominique Edgerter charges about F$150 (US$90) for a two-tank dive, and teaches PADI certification courses. Rental equipment is available. Also on the northern end is the Fijian-owned **Jewel Bubble Divers** (© **888 2080;** www.jeweldivers.com).

FISHING, GOLF, SWIMMING & OTHER OUTDOOR ACTIVITIES
The hotels and resorts will arrange all of Taveuni's outdoor activities, although you should book at least a day in advance.

FISHING   Two charter boats will take you in search of big game fish offshore: American John Llanes's **Makaira Charters** (© **888 0686;** makaira@connect.com.fj) and New Zealander Geoffrey Amos's **Matei Game Fishing** (© **888 0371**). They charge about US$300 for half a day, US$525 for a full day **for up to four fishermen or fisherwomen or fishers or whatever you want to call them.** Call for exact rates and for reservations, which are required.

GOLF & TENNIS   The real estate development known as **Taveuni Estates** has grass tennis courts and a scenic 9-hole golf course along the island's eastern shore. Reserve at the clubhouse (© **888 0044**), which serves lunch and has a bar. The fee for either sport is F$20 (US$12) per person. The clubhouse rents equipment.

SWIMMING, SNORKELING & KAYAKING   Because Taveuni is a relatively new island in geological terms, it doesn't have a great number of good swimming beaches. But the few it does have are first rate. The best is at Lavena village at the far end of the north shore road (see "Hiking," above). More convenient places to swim and snorkel are **Prince Charles Beach** and the lovely, tree-draped **Beverly Beach,** both south of the Matei airstrip. Keep a sharp eye peeled for sharks.

Some of the best do-it-yourself snorkeling is at the foot of the cliff off **Tramontu Bar & Grill** (see "Where to Dine on Taveuni," below), and the three little rocky islets off the north shore, near the airstrip, provided kelp from the nearby seaweed farms isn't drifting by. You can land on the islands for a bring-your-own picnic. **Coconut Grove Beachfront Cottages & Restaurant** (© **888 0328**), opposite the airstrip (see "Where to Stay on Taveuni," below), rents two-person ocean kayaks for F$30 (US$18) per half day, F$55 (US$33) all day. Owner Ronna Goldstein will prepare a picnic lunch with advance notice. **Jewel Bubble Divers** (© **888 2080;** www. jeweldivers.com) also rents kayaks for F$8 (US$5) an hour for a single, F$10 (US$6) for a two-seater.

If they aren't too busy with serious divers, most of Taveuni's scuba operators will take snorkelers along (see "Scuba Diving," above). For example, **Aqua-Trek** at the Garden Island Resort has snorkeling trips to Korolevu, a rocky islet off Waiyevo. The company will even take you snorkeling out to the Rainbow Reef, but book these trips well in advance.

Tips **Beware of "Jaws"**

Ancient legend says that Taveuni's paramount chief is Fiji's highest ranking because sharks protect the island from enemies. True or not, shark attacks are frequent here, so be extremely careful when you're swimming and snorkeling, and don't under any circumstances swim out to the edge of the reef.

You can also snorkel from a Fijian *bilibili* (bamboo raft) over the **Waitabu Marine Park** (© **888 0451**), a restored reef. These half-day ventures cost F$40 (US$24) including lunch, F$20 (US$12) for snorkeling only.

WHERE TO STAY ON TAVEUNI

With the exception of Garden Island Resort at Waiyevo, Taveuni's best accommodations are near the airstrip on the island's northeastern corner. A few small planes arrive and depart about 9:30am and again about 2:30pm, so it's not like you're staying under the flight path of an international airport. You can walk among the airstrip-area hotels and restaurants in no more than 20 minutes.

EXPENSIVE

Maravu Plantation Beach Resort & Spa ✿ *Value*   Although it has its own lovely beach across the road (a 5-min. downhill walk), this unusual retreat is set among 90 acres of palms on a former copra plantation. Most of the bures are laid out among grounds carefully planted with bananas, papayas, and a plethora of ginger plants and wild orchids. This plantation setting means the property can get warm and humid during the day. Built in the style of South Seas planters' cottages, the guest bungalows have thatch-covered tin roofs and reed or mat accents that lend a tropical ambience. Six units have a view of the sea. Situated about 5 minutes away from the main complex via wooden walkways, they also are the newest and most luxurious accommodations here, with outdoor Jacuzzis. Four honeymoon bures have four-person-size whirlpool tubs under their outdoor showers, while four more honeymoon suites feature two rooms, outdoor showers, Jacuzzis, and sun decks surrounded by rock privacy walls. Only the older, "planters bures" don't have outdoor showers, nor air-conditioners. With an emphasis on very good "nouvelle Fijian" cuisine, the dining room is under the high thatch roof and looks out to the lawns and a pool that's surrounded by an expansive deck. Wine lovers are in for a treat here, for owner Jochen Kiess, a former German lawyer, has accumulated a fine list. Since most of Maravu isn't directly on the beach, Jochen doesn't charge an arm and a leg, which makes it good value.

Postal Agency, Matei, Taveuni (1km/½ mile south of airstrip). © **866/528-3864** or 888 0555. Fax 888 0600. www. maravu.net. 20 units. US$130–US$340 per person double occupancy. Rates include full breakfast, airport transfers, most activities, and spa package. AE, DC, MC, V. **Amenities:** Restaurant; bar; outdoor pool; exercise room; spa; free bicycles; activities desk; limited room service; babysitting; laundry service. *In room:* A/C (most units), minibar, coffeemaker, hair dryer, no phone.

Taveuni Island Resort ✿✿   Once known as Dive Taveuni, this resort now relies on honeymooners for the bulk of its business (no kids under 15 here). If you are among these romantic souls, you're in for a very private, pampered stay with a fabulous view. You will be sorely disappointed if you expect to step out of your bungalow onto the beach, however, for this property sits high on a bluff overlooking Somosomo Strait, and you will have to climb down it to reach the sand. "Steep Descend (sic)

Please Mind Your Step," a sign at the top of the walkway warns. To compensate, a hill-top pool commands a stunning view over the strait, as do the central building and the guest bungalows. Six of the units are hexagonal models built of pine with side wall windows that let in the view and the breeze. The most stunning view of all is from the spacious deck of the Veidomoni bure—or you can take in the vista from its open-to-the-sea outdoor shower. All other units also have outdoor showers as well as separate sleeping and living areas. One deluxe unit has a separate bedroom, and the luxurious Matalau villa has two master bedrooms and its own private pool.

Postal Agency, Matei, Taveuni (1.5km/1 mile south of airstrip). © 866/828-3864 or 888 0441. Fax 888 0466. www.taveuniislandresort.com. 12 units. US$780 per person double, US$1,230–US$1,630 villa. Rates include meals and nonalcoholic beverages. AE, MC, V. Children under 15 not accepted. **Amenities:** Restaurant; bar; outdoor pool; spa; free bicycles; limited room service; laundry service. In room: A/C, minibar, coffeemaker, hair dryer.

Taveuni Palms ☀ This private little retreat in a coconut grove specializes in pampering guests in its two private bungalows, each of which has its own expansive deck, swimming pool, and small beach among the rocks and cliffs lining the coast here. Owners Tony and Kelly Acland have no restaurant and bar. Instead, the staff prepares and serves your meals in your own dining room, on your deck, down by the beach, or just about any place you choose. The bungalows have sea views from their perches above the shoreline. Each also has two air-conditioned bedrooms with king beds, a big-screen TV to play DVDs, and an outdoor shower, an intercom for ordering your next meal, and its own kayaks and snorkeling gear. Taveuni Palms has its own dive master, and you can have your massage or spa treatment down by the beach.

P.O. Box 51, Matei, Taveuni (1km/½ mile south of airstrip). © 888 0032. Fax 888 2445. www.taveunipalmsfiji.com. 2 units. US$960 double. Minimum 5-night stay required. Rates include meals, non-alcoholic beverages, airport transfers, most activities. AE, MC, V. **Amenities:** 2 outdoor pools; spa treatments; free kayaks; massage; babysitting; laundry service. In room: A/C, TV (DVDs only), kitchen, fridge, coffeemaker, hair dryer, no phone.

MODERATE
Coconut Grove Beachfront Cottages ★★★ (Value) Ronna Goldstein, who named
this little gem not for the palm trees growing all around it but for her hometown in Florida, has three bures set beside a fine little beach next to her restaurant (see "Where to Dine on Taveuni," below). Ronna lives here, and the restaurant is on her big, breezy front porch with a terrific view of the sea and offshore islets. You can dine here or down by the beach. Next door, her Mango cottage has an outdoor shower and a great sea view from its large front porch. Her Banana bure is somewhat smaller and lacks the great view, but it's right by the beach and is more private. It also has an outdoor shower. Almost on the beach, the Papaya bure is the smallest, but it's also the most private. Gracie, Ronna's friendly Doberman, is in charge of guest relations. Your children under 15 won't be petting Gracie, however, since they are not accepted here. Ronna provides free kayaks and snorkeling fins (bring your own mask), but you'll pay for a beachside massage. For the money, this is one of Fiji's great values.

Postal Agency, Matei, Taveuni (opposite airstrip). ©/fax 888 0328. www.coconutgrovefiji.com. 3 units. US$155–US$195 double. Rates include afternoon tea. 3-night minimum stay required. MC, V. No children under 15 accepted. **Amenities:** Restaurant; massage; babysitting; laundry service. In room: CD player, fridge, no phone.

INEXPENSIVE
Garden Island Resort ☀ (Value) Built as a Travelodge motel in the 1960s, this water-
side hotel is now operated by the San Francisco–based dive company Aqua-Trek, which has its Taveuni base here. Most of the clientele are divers since this is the closest hotel to the White Wall and its Rainbow Reef (a 20-minute boat ride away in normal

conditions), but the friendly staff welcomes everyone. There is no beach, but all rooms face a fine view over the Somosomo Strait to Vanua Levu. Each medium-size unit has a queen and a single bed, tropical-style chairs, a desk, and a tub-and-shower combo bathroom. All but the two rooms used as dormitories are air-conditioned (the dorms have ceiling fans). Opening to a strait-side pool, the dining room serves meals, which always include vegetarian selections, at reasonable prices. Guests and nonguests can rent kayaks and go on snorkeling trips to Korolevu islet offshore and even to the Rainbow Reef with Aqua-Trek. The hotel also arranges hiking trips and other excursions.

P.O. Box 1, Waiyevo, Taveuni (Waiyevo village, 11 km/7 miles south of airstrip). ℂ 800/541-4334 or 888 0286. Fax 888 0288. www.aquatrek.com. 28 units, 8 dorm beds. F$230 (US$138) double room, F$38 (US$23) dorm bed. Room rate includes breakfast; dorm rate does not. AE, MC, V. **Amenities:** Restaurant; bar; outdoor pool; watersports; limited room service; massage; babysitting; laundry service. *In room:* A/C (except in dorms), fridge, coffeemaker, hairdryer, safe.

Tovu Tovu Resort   Spread out over a lawn across the road from the lagoon, the Peterson family's simple bungalows have front porches, reed exterior walls, tile floors, ceiling fans, and bathrooms with hot-water showers. Three of them also have cooking facilities. The Vunibokoi Restaurant is here, and it's a scenic walk to Coconut Grove Restaurant and others near the airport (see "Where to Dine on Taveuni," below).

Postal Agency, Matei, Taveuni (1 km/½ mile east of airstrip). ℂ 888 0560. Fax 888 0722. www.tovutovu.com. 5 bungalows. F$85–F$95 (US$51–US$57) bungalow. AE, MC, V. **Amenities:** Restaurant; bar; bike and kayak rentals; laundry service. *In room:* Kitchen (in 3 units).

COTTAGE RENTALS

As in Savusavu, several expatriate landowners on Taveuni rent out their own homes when they're away, or they have cottages on their properties to let (see "Where to Stay in Savusavu," earlier in this chapter). If you rent one, be sure it's fully licensed by the Fiji government.

One owner who did not move here from someplace else is Fiji-born May Goulding, who has one cottage at **Todranisiga,** her property south of the airstrip. The land slopes through coconut palms from the road down to the top of a seaside cliff, from where her planter-style bungalow looks out over the Somosomo Strait. It has a double bed in its one room, and the bathroom opens to an al fresco shower—and I do mean al fresco, since nothing blocks you from the view, or the view from you! You'll spend most of your time out on the porch enjoying the breeze, taking in the view, and perhaps cooking a light meal on a gas camp stove out there. May charges F$155 (US$93) double. She does not accept credit cards, but she does run the generator from 4:30pm through the night (you'll need batteries for your iPod during daylight hours). Contact May at Postal Agency, Matei, Taveuni (ℂ 888 0680; makaira@connect.com.fj).

Another cottage with a view is American Roberta Davis's **Makaira By the Sea** (ℂ 888 0686; makaira@connect.com.fj), sitting on a cliff with a 180° view down over Prince Charles Beach and the sea. Built of pine and covered in thatch, the cottage has a queen bed, kitchen, porch, and both indoor and outdoor showers. Tramontu Bar & Grill is across the road (see "Where to Dine on Taveuni," below). Roberta also charges F$155 (US$93) double, with discounts for long stays. She does not accept credit cards.

Also be on the lookout for Jim and Robin Kelly's **Kakia Resort & Dive** (ℂ 888 1111; jimandrobinfiji@hotmail.com), a four-cottage complex they were completing during my recent visit.

CAMPING

Campers who like to sleep by the sea can find a beautiful (if not insect-free) site at **Beverly Campground** (✆ **888 0381**), on Beverly Beach about 1.5km (1 mile) south of the airstrip. Maravu Resort's beach is next door to one side, Jewel Bubbles dive base on the other. Large trees completely shade the sites and hang over portions of the lagoon-lapped shore. The ground has flushing toilets, cold-water showers, and a rudimentary beachside kitchen. Rates are about F$20 (US$12) per person. Bring your own tent.

WHERE TO DINE ON TAVEUNI

East of the airstrip, **Audrey's Island Coffee and Pastries** (✆ **888 0039**) really isn't a restaurant, it's American Audrey Brown's front porch. Audrey is known as Taveuni's best baker. Audrey's is open daily from 10am to 6pm. She doesn't accept credit cards.

Coconut Grove Restaurant 👁👁 INTERNATIONAL   American Ronna Goldstein consistently serves Taveuni's best fare at her little enclave, where she also rents cottages (see "Where to Stay on Taveuni," above). She offers breakfasts (her banana and papaya breads are fabulous) and salads, soups, burgers, and sandwiches for lunch. Dinner sees a variety of local seafood dishes, spicy Thai and mild Fijian curries (I love the Thai fish), and homemade pastas. Saturday night features a buffet and Fijian musicians. Dining is on Ronna's veranda, which has a great view of the little islands off Taveuni, making it a fine place not just for lunch or dinner but to sip a great fruit shake or juice while waiting for your flight.

Matei, opposite airstrip. ✆ **888 0328**. Reservations required by noon for dinner. Main courses F$15–F$25 (US$9–US$15). MC, V. Daily 8am–5pm and 6–9pm.

Tramontu Bar & Grill REGIONAL   The best thing about this open-air, Fijian-owned cafe is its spectacular perch atop a cliff overlooking the Somosomo Strait, which makes it a fabulous spot to have a cold drink while watching the sun set. The forgettable local fare consists of the usual curries, grilled steaks, and chicken stir-fries. If you decide to have dinner here, tell them a day in advance so they can acquire fresh lobster or fish; otherwise, don't eat seafood here.

Matei, south of airstrip. ✆ **888 2224**. Reservations required at dinner. Lunch F$15 (US$9); main courses F$18–F$30 (US$11–US$18). No credit cards. Mon–Thurs 11am–2pm and 6–9:30pm, Fri–Sun 10am–10pm. Bar daily 11am–10pm.

Vunibokoi Restaurant   On the front porch of the main house at Alan Petersen's Tovu Tovu Resort (see above), this plain but pleasant restaurant serves breakfast, lunch, and dinner, with a blackboard menu that features home-cooked Fijian, Indian, and Western fare. When I'm on Taveuni I never miss a Friday night buffet of Fijian lovo food, one of the most extensive in the islands. Sunday is roast night.

Matei, in Tovu Tovu Resort, 1km/ ½ mile east of airstrip. ✆ **888 0560**. Reservations recommended. Main courses F$12–F$20 (US$7–US$12). AE, MC, V. Daily 8am–2pm and 6–9pm.

3 Resorts on Qamea & Matagi Islands 👁👁👁

The northern end of Taveuni gives way to a chain of small, rugged islands that are as beautiful as any in Fiji. Their steep, jungle-clad hills drop to rocky shorelines in most places, but here and there little shelves of land and narrow valleys are bordered by beautiful beaches. The sheltered waters between the islands cover colorful reefs, making the area a hotbed for scuba diving and snorkeling.

Matangi Island Resort ★★★ *Value*   It's unfortunate that geography places this resort at the end of my coverage of Fiji, for Matangi is one of the best values in the South Pacific. It also ranks high because of proprietors Noel and Flo Douglas. Of English-Fijian descent, Flo's family owns all of hilly, 260-acre Matagi Island, a horseshoe-shaped remnant of a volcanic cone, where in 1987 they built their resort in a beachside coconut grove on the western shore. A main building whose deck hangs out over the lagoon takes full advantage of gorgeous sunset views of Qamea and Taveuni. At first the Douglases catered to low-budget Australian divers, but as their business grew, their clientele shifted to a mix of diving and nondiving American, Australian, and European adults (children under 12 are no longer accepted here). Honeymooners can escape to three romantic bures 20 feet up in the air, one of them actually in a shady Pacific almond tree. These units all have outdoor showers, as do some of the deluxe units down in the coconut grove beside the beach. You can also be taken to the spectacular half-moon beach in aptly named Horseshoe Bay and be left alone for a secluded picnic. Other nondiving activities include hiking, kayaking, bird-watching, sailing, windsurfing, and sportfishing. Except for a two-room villa at a far end of the property and the honeymoon bures, Matangi's bungalows are round, in the Polynesian-influenced style of eastern Fiji. Umbrella-like spokes radiating from hand-hewn central poles support reed-lined conical roofs. One bure is equipped for disabled guests.

P.O. Box 83, Waiyevo, Taveuni (Matagi Island, 20 min. by boat from Taveuni). © **888/628-2644** or 888 0260. Fax 888 0274. www.matangiisland.com. 14 units. F$792–F$1,884 (US$475–US$950) double. Rates include meals and all excursions and activities except scuba diving, water-skiing, and sportfishing. AE, DC, MC, V. Children under 12 not accepted. **Amenities:** Restaurant; 2 bars; spa; watersports; limited room service; massage; laundry service. *In room:* Minibar, coffeemaker, hair dryer, no phone.

Qamea Resort and Spa ★★★ *Value*   This luxury property has some of the most stunning bures and main building of any resort in Fiji. In the proverbial lagoonside coconut grove, this entire property shows remarkable attention to American-style comfort and Fijian detail. If I were to build a set for a South Seas movie, it would feature these bungalows covered by a foot-thick Fijian thatch. Spacious and rectangular, each has an old-fashioned screen door that leads out to a porch that's complete with a hammock strung between two posts. Each bure is partially reed lined and large enough to swallow the king-size bed, two oversize sitting chairs, a coffee table, and several other pieces of island-style furniture, some of it exquisitely handcrafted by the staff. Their bathrooms include outdoor showers. If you need more space, you can rent the split-level honeymoon bure, which is twice the size of the regular units, or one of two large, luxuriously appointed "premium villas," which have swimming pools sunken into their front porches. Qamea's centerpiece is a soaring, 16m (52-ft.) high priest's bure supported by two huge tree trunks. Orange light from kerosene lanterns hung high under the roof lends romantic charm for feasting on gourmet quality meals. There is no children's menu because no kids under 13 are accepted here.

P.O. Matei, Taveuni (Qamea Island, 15 min. by boat from Taveuni). © **866/867-2632** or 888 0220. Fax 888 0092. www.qamea.com. 14 units. US$650–US$995 bungalow. Rates include meals, airport transfers, all activities except diving, sportfishing and island tours. AE, MC, V. Children under 13 not accepted. **Amenities:** Restaurant; bar; outdoor pool; exercise room; spa; laundry service. *In room:* A/C, minibar, coffeemaker, hair dryer, iron (premium villas only), safe, phone (premium villas only).

7

Introducing French Polynesia

Tahiti has evoked the image of an idyllic tropical paradise since 1767, when canoe-loads of young *vahines* gave uninhibited, bare-breasted receptions to a British navy captain named Capt. Samuel Wallis and his crew on the HMS *Dolphin*. Sent in search of a mysterious southern continent, Wallis instead discovered Tahiti. It was the beginning of the world's long romance with the magical islands we know as French Polynesia.

Even today you are likely to encounter bare breasts on the beaches, for Tahiti and her sister islands are indeed French as well as Polynesian. Unlike other South Pacific countries, where the preaching of puritanical missionaries took deeper root, here you will discover a marvelous combination of both *joie de vivre* and *laissez-faire*. Add the awesome beauty of its islands and you'll quickly see why French Polynesia is one of the world's top honeymoon destinations.

Tahiti is both one of the most gorgeous and one of the most developed South Pacific islands. Don't be surprised when you take a freeway from the airport into the bustling capital of Papeete. Chic bistros and high-rise shopping centers long ago replaced Papeete's wooden Chinese stores, and glass-and-steel luxury resorts on the edge of town supplanted its cheap waterfront hotels. If you're into cities, Papeete will be up your alley. Even if you're not, Tahiti is worth seeing, especially its museums devoted to painter Paul Gauguin, the writer James Norman Hall, and to the islanders themselves.

Most visitors bypass these jewels and head to Moorea, Bora Bora, Huahine, and Raiatea. These high, mountainous islands are much less developed than Tahiti and even more blessed with the other-worldly peaks, multihued lagoons, and palm-draped beaches that have come to symbolize the South Pacific. The late James A. Michener thought Bora Bora was the most beautiful island in the world. I give that title to Moorea. It's all a matter of degree, for these are the world's most dramatically beautiful islands.

Out in the atolls of Rangiroa, Tikehau, Manihi, and Fakarava, you'll find marvelous snorkeling and diving in lagoons stocked with a vast array of sealife. As I wrote when suggesting a French Polynesian itinerary in chapter 3, the atolls may seem anticlimactic after the high islands, so come out here first.

1 French Polynesia Today: The Islands in Brief

French Polynesia sprawls over an area of 2 million square miles in the eastern South Pacific. That's about the size of Europe, excluding the countries of the former Soviet Union, or about two-thirds the size of the continental United States. The 130 main islands, however, consist of only 1,500 square miles, an area smaller than the state of Rhode Island. Only 245,500 or so souls inhabit these small specs.

THE ISLANDS IN BRIEF

The territory's five major island groups differ in terrain, climate, and to a certain extent, people. With the exception of the Tuamotu Archipelago, an enormous chain of low coral atolls northeast of Tahiti, most are "high" islands; that is, they are the mountainous tops of ancient volcanoes eroded into jagged peaks, deep bays, and fertile valleys. All have fringing or barrier coral reefs and blue lagoons.

THE SOCIETY ISLANDS   The most beautiful and most frequently visited are the **Society Islands,** so named by Capt. James Cook, the great English explorer, in 1769 because they lay relatively close together. These include **Tahiti** and nearby **Moorea,** which also are known as the Windward Islands because they sit to the east, the direction of the prevailing trade wind. To the northwest lie **Bora Bora, Huahine, Raiatea, Tahaa, Maupiti,** and several smaller islands. Because they are downwind of Tahiti, they also are called the Leeward Islands.

Moorea and Bora Bora are the most developed from a tourism standpoint. In fact, Bora Bora is French Polynesia's tourism dynamo, with more resorts than any other island. Although Huahine is almost as beautiful as Moorea and Bora Bora, it has only a handful of hotels and retains its old-Polynesian charm. The administrative center of the Leeward Islands, Raiatea lacks beaches, but the deep lagoon it shares with Tahaa makes it the sailing capital of French Polynesia. Tahaa has only recently opened to tourism, with one of French Polynesia's top resorts now sitting out on a small islet. Virtually unscathed by tourism, Maupiti has a few locally-owned pensions. It can be visited on a day trip from Bora Bora.

THE TUAMOTU ARCHIPELAGO   Across the approaches to Tahiti from the east, the 69 low-lying atolls of the **Tuamotu Archipelago** run for 1,159km (720 miles) on a line from northwest to southeast. The early European sailors called them the "Dangerous Archipelago" because of their tricky currents and because they virtually cannot be seen until a ship is almost on top of them. Even today they are a wrecking ground for yachts and interisland trading boats. Two of them, Moruroa and Fangataufa, were used by France to test its nuclear weapons between 1966 and 1996. Others provide the bulk of Tahiti's well-known black pearls. **Rangiroa,** the world's second-largest atoll and the territory's best scuba-diving destination, is the most frequently visited. Neighboring **Tikehau,** with a much smaller and shallower lagoon, also has a modern resort hotel, as does **Manihi,** the territory's major producer of black pearls. To the south, the reef at **Fakarava** encircles the world's third largest lagoon.

THE MARQUESAS ISLANDS   Made famous in 2002 by the *Survivor* television series, the **Marquesas** are a group of 10 high islands some 1,208km (750 miles) northeast of Tahiti. They are younger than the Society Islands, and because a cool equatorial current washes their coasts, protecting coral reefs have not enclosed them. As a result, the surf pounds on their shores, there are no encircling coastal plains, and the people live in a series of deep valleys that radiate out from central mountain peaks. The Marquesas have lost their once-large populations to 19th-century disease and the 20th-century economic lure of Papeete; today their sparsely populated, cloud-enshrouded valleys have an almost haunting air about them. Most visitors get to the Marquesas via *Aranui 3* cruises (see "Seeing the Islands by Cruise Ship & Yacht," later in this chapter). Only two of them—**Nuku Hiva** and **Hiva Oa**—have international-standard hotels.

THE AUSTRAL AND GAMBIER ISLANDS   The seldom-visited **Austral Islands** south of Tahiti are part of a chain of high islands that continues westward into the

The Society Islands & the Northern Tuamotus

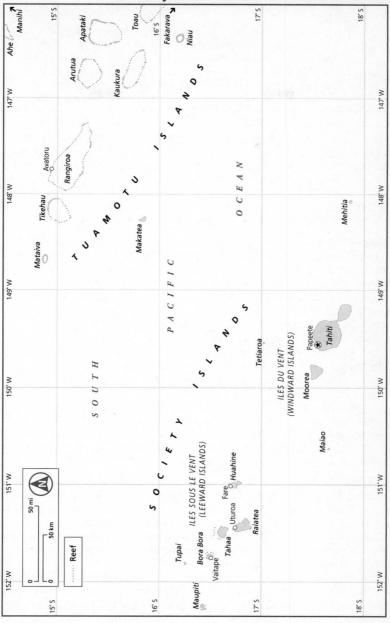

Ahe
Manihi
Apataki
Toau
Fakarava
Niau
Arutua
Kaukura

TUAMOTU ISLANDS

Avatoru
Rangiroa
Tikehau
Mataiva
Makatea

PACIFIC OCEAN

SOUTH

Tetiaroa
Papeete
Tahiti
Mehitia
Moorea

ILES DU VENT
(WINDWARD ISLANDS)

SOCIETY ISLANDS

Maiao

Huahine
Fare
Uturoa
Raiatea
Tupai
Bora Bora
Tahaa
Vaitape

ILES SOUS LE VENT
(LEEWARD ISLANDS)

Maupiti

N

50 mi
0
50 km
0

······ Reef

15° S
16° S
17° S
18° S
152° W
151° W
150° W
149° W
148° W
147° W

181

Impressions

It is no exaggeration to say, that to a European of any sensibility, who, for the first time, wanders back into these valleys—away from the haunts of the natives—the ineffable repose and beauty of the landscape is such, that every object strikes him like something seen in a dream; and for a time he almost refuses to believe that scenes like these should have a commonplace existence.
—Herman Melville, 1847

Cook Islands. The people of the more temperate Australs, which include Rurutu, Raivavae, and Tubuai, once produced some of the best art objects in the South Pacific, but these skills have passed into time. Far on the southern end of the Tuamotu Archipelago, the **Gambier Islands** are part of a semisubmerged, middle-aged high island similar to Bora Bora. The hilly remnants of the old volcano are scattered in a huge lagoon, which is partially enclosed by a barrier reef marking the original outline of the island before it began to sink. The largest of these remnant islands is Mangareva.

GOVERNMENT

French Polynesia is a "country" within the French system of overseas territories. France sends a high commissioner from Paris and controls foreign affairs, defense, justice, internal security, and currency. French Polynesians have considerable autonomy over their internal affairs through a 49-member Assembly, which selects a president, the country's highest-ranking local official. The Assembly decides all issues that are not reserved to the metropolitan French government.

Local voters also cast ballots in French presidential elections and choose two elected deputies and a senator to the French parliament in Paris (they will pick a second senator beginning in 2007). The city of Papeete and a few other *communes* have local police forces, but the French *gendarmes* control most law enforcement (they are as likely to be from Martinique as from Moorea).

Local politics breaks down generally into two camps: those who favor remaining French but with increased local autonomy (pro-autonomy), and those who seek complete independence from France (pro-independence). At press time the pro-independence party had the upper hand, albeit narrowly. See "French Polynesia Yesterday: History 101," below.

THE ECONOMY

French Polynesia has only two significant industries: tourism and black pearls. More than 200,000 visitors arrive in the islands each year, bringing in more than US$400 million in tourism earnings. Some US$125 million worth of pearls are exported annually, mostly to Japan. Vanilla, copra, coconut oil cosmetics (you will see the *Monoi* brand everywhere), and an elixir made from the *noni* fruit are minor exports. About 80% of all food consumed here is imported.

French Polynesia would be bankrupt were it not for more than 12€ billion (US$14 billion) poured in by Paris each year. That includes some 150€ million (US$180 million) a year from an economic restructuring fund, set up after France closed its nuclear testing facility in 1996, to foster self-sufficiency by developing the local infrastructure. The fund has paid for public works projects that have transformed the waterfronts in Papeete and on Raiatea, improved the roads, and built new schools, hospitals, and docks.

In addition, the local government set up highly favorable tax and investment laws, which have spurred hotel construction. Bora Bora has most of the new properties, but islands such as Tahaa and Fakarava also received major resorts for the first time. The emphasis has been on the high-end, however, which has done little to reduce the cost to visitors.

All this money translates into both a high standard of living (the minimum wage here is about US$1,100 a month plus benefits, compared to about US$850 without benefits in the U.S.) and high prices for everyone. If there is a saving grace for us visitors, it's the lack of tipping and no direct sales tax, which together can add 25% to your bill elsewhere.

2 French Polynesia Yesterday: History 101

Surely Capt. Samuel Wallis of HMS *Dolphin* could hardly believe his eyes in 1767 when more than 500 canoes greeted him at Matavai Bay on Tahiti. Many were loaded with pigs, chickens, coconuts, fruit, and topless young women "who played a great many droll and wanton tricks" on his scurvy-ridden crew.

The French explorer Louis Antoine de Bougainville was similarly greeted a year later. Bougainville stayed at Hitiaa only 10 days, but he took back to France a young Tahitian named Ahutoru, who became a sensation in Paris as living proof of Jean-Jacques Rousseau's theory that man was at his best a "noble savage." Indeed, Bougainville and Ahutoru contributed mightily to Tahiti's hedonistic image.

In 1769 Capt. James Cook arrived to measure the transit of the planet Venus across the face of the sun. If successful, his survey would enable navigators for the first time to measure longitude accurately on the earth's surface. Cook set up an observation point on a sandy spit on Tahiti's north shore, a locale he appropriately named Point Venus. His measurements were of little use, but Cook remained in Tahiti for 6 months. Cook used Tahiti as a base during two subsequent voyages, during which he discovered numerous islands and charted much of the South Pacific.

THE MUTINY ON THE *BOUNTY* Capt. William Bligh, one of Cook's navigators, returned to Matavai Bay in 1788 in command of HMS *Bounty* on a mission to procure breadfruit as cheap food for plantation slaves in Jamaica. One of Bligh's handpicked officers was a former shipmate, Lt. Fletcher Christian.

Bligh waited on Tahiti for 6 months until his cargo was ready. Christian and some of the crew apparently enjoyed the island's women and lifestyle so much that they mutinied on April 28, 1789, off the Ha'apai islands in Tonga. Christian set Bligh and 18 of his loyal officers and crewmen adrift with a compass, a cask of water, and a few provisions (they eventually returned to England after one of history's epic longboat voyages). Christian sailed the *Bounty* back to Tahiti, where he put ashore 25 other crewmembers who were loyal to Bligh. Christian, eight mutineers, their Tahitian wives, and six Tahitian men then disappeared.

Royal Navy's HMS *Pandora* eventually rounded up the *Bounty* crewmen still on Tahiti and returned them to England. Three were hung, four were acquitted, and three were convicted but pardoned; one of these three was Peter Heywood, who wrote the first English–Tahitian dictionary while awaiting court martial.

The captain of an American whaling ship that happened upon remote Pitcairn Island in 1808 was astonished when some mixed-race teenagers rowed out and greeted him not in Tahitian but in perfect English. They were the children of the mutineers, only one of whom was still alive.

Bligh collected more breadfruit on Tahiti a few years later, but his whole venture went for naught when the slaves on Jamaica insisted on rice.

THE FATAL IMPACT   The discoverers brought many changes to Tahiti, starting with iron, which the Tahitians had never seen. The Tahitians figured out right away that iron was much harder than stone and shells and that they could swap pigs, breadfruit, bananas, and the affections of their young women for it. So many iron nails soon disappeared from the *Dolphin* that Wallis restricted his men to the ship out of fear it would fall apart in Matavai Bay. A rudimentary form of monetary economy was introduced to Polynesia for the first time, and the English word *money* entered the Tahitian language as *moni*.

The *Bounty* mutineers hiding on Tahiti loaned themselves and their guns to rival chiefs, who for the first time were able to extend their control beyond their home valleys. With the mutineers' help, Chief Pomare II came to control half of Tahiti and all of Moorea.

Much more devastating European imports were diseases such as measles, influenza, pneumonia, and syphilis, to which the islanders had no resistance. Captain Cook estimated Tahiti's population at some 200,000 in 1769. By 1810 it had dropped to fewer than 8,000.

CONVERTS & CLOTHES   The opening of the South Pacific coincided with a fundamentalist religious revival in England. In 1797 members of the London Missionary

Sexy Skin

The United States isn't the only place where it's cool to have a tattoo. With their increasing interest in ancient Polynesian ways, many young Tahitian men and women are getting theirs—but not necessarily with modern electric needles.

The 18th-century explorers who arrived on Tahiti were amazed to find many Polynesians on Tahiti and throughout the South Pacific to be covered from face to ankle with a plethora of geometric and floral designs. In his journal, Capt. James Cook described in detail the excruciatingly painful tattoo procedure, in which natural dyes are hammered into the skin by hand. The repetitive tapping of the mallet gave rise to the Tahitian word *tatau,* which became *tattoo* in English.

Members of the opposite sex rejected anyone with plain skin, which may explain why members of Cook's crew were so willing to endure the torture to get theirs. At any rate, thus began the tradition of the tattooed sailor.

Appalled at the sexual aspects of tattoos, the missionaries stamped out the practice on Tahiti in the early 1800s. Although the art continued in the remote Marquesas and in Samoa, by 1890 there were no tattooed natives left in the Society Islands.

When a British anthropologist undertook a study of tattooing in 1900, the only specimen he could find was on the skin of a Tahitian sailor, who died in England in 1816. Before he was buried, an art-loving physician removed his hide and donated it to the Royal College of Surgeons.

Society (LMS) arrived in Tahiti to save the souls of the "heathens." They toiled for 15 years before making their first convert, and even that was only accomplished with the help of Chief Pomare II. The missionaries thought he was king of Tahiti, but in reality Pomare II was locked in battle to extend his rule and to become just that. By converting to Christianity, he won the missionaries' support, and with it, he quickly gained control of the entire island. The people then made the easy transition from their primary god Taaroa to the missionaries' supreme being. They put on clothes and began going to church.

THE TRICKED QUEEN   The Protestant missionaries enjoyed a monopoly until the first Roman Catholic priests arrived from France in the 1830s. The Protestants immediately saw a threat, and in 1836 they engineered the interlopers' expulsion by Queen Pomare IV, the illegitimate daughter of Pomare II who had succeeded to her father's throne.

When word of this outrage reached Paris, France demanded a guarantee that Frenchmen would thereafter be treated as the "most favored foreigners" in Tahiti. Queen Pomare politely agreed, but as soon as the warship left Papeete, she sent a letter to Queen Victoria, asking for British protection. Britain declined to interfere, which in 1842 allowed a Frenchman to trick several Tahitian chiefs into signing a document that in effect made Tahiti a French protectorate.

Queen Pomare retreated to Raiatea, which was not under French control, and continued to resist. On Tahiti, her subjects launched an armed rebellion against the French. This French-Tahitian war continued until 1846, when the last native stronghold was captured and the remnants of their guerrilla bands retreated to Tahiti Iti, the island's eastern peninsula. A monument to the fallen Tahitians now stands beside the round-island road near the airport at Faaa, the village still noted for its strong pro-independence sentiment.

Giving up the struggle, the queen returned to Papeete in 1847 and ruled as a figurehead until her death 30 years later. Her son, Pomare V, remained on the throne 3 more years until abdicating in return for a sizable French pension for himself, his family, and his mistress. In 1903 all of eastern Polynesia was consolidated into a single colony known as French Oceania. In 1957 its status was changed to the overseas territory of French Polynesia.

A BLISSFUL BACKWATER   French Polynesia remained an idyllic backwater until the early 1960s, except for periodic invasions by artists and writers. French painter Paul Gauguin gave up his family and his career as a Parisian stockbroker and arrived in 1891; he spent his days reproducing Tahiti's colors and people on canvas until he died in 1903 on Hiva Oa in the Marquesas Islands. W. Somerset Maugham, Jack London, Robert Louis Stevenson, Rupert Brooke, and other writers added to Tahiti's romantic reputation during the early years of the 20th century. In 1932 two young Americans—Charles Nordhoff and James Norman Hall—published *Mutiny on the Bounty*, which quickly became a bestseller. Three years later MGM released the first movie version, with Clark Gable and Charles Laughton in the roles of Christian and Bligh, respectively.

In 1942 some 6,000 U.S. sailors and marines quickly built the territory's first airstrip on Bora Bora and remained there throughout World War II. A number of mixed-race Tahitians claim descent from those American troops.

MOVIES & BOMBS   The sleepy years ended in 1960, when Tahiti's new international airport opened at Faaa. Marlon Brando and a movie crew arrived shortly thereafter to film

---

⌐Fun Fact **Picking Up a Few Extra Bucks**

Neither Clark Gable nor Charles Laughton came to Tahiti to film the 1935 version of *Mutiny on the Bounty*. While background scenes were shot on Tahiti, they performed on Catalina Island, off southern California. The Mexican actress Maria "Movita" Castenada, who played the chief's young daughter, was later married to Marlon Brando, star of the 1962 remake. A young actor named James Cagney, who was vacationing on Catalina at the time, picked up a few extra bucks by playing a sailor for a day.

---

an update of *Mutiny on the Bounty*. This new burst of fame, coupled with the ability to reach Tahiti overnight, transformed the island into a jet-set destination, and hotel construction began in earnest.

Even more changes came in 1963, when France established the *Centre d'Experimentation du Pacifique* and began exploding nuclear bombs on the Moruroa and Fangataufa atolls in the Tuamotus, about 1,127km (700 miles) southeast of Tahiti. A huge support base was constructed on the eastern outskirts of Papeete. Thousands of Polynesians flocked to Tahiti to take the new construction and hotel jobs, which enabled them to earn good money and experience life in Papeete's fast lane. The nuclear tests continued aboveground until 1974, then deep beneath the atolls until 1996. Their health repercussions are still being debated.

TO BE—OR NOT TO BE—INDEPENDENT In 1977 the French parliament created the elected Territorial Assembly with powers over the local budget. A high commissioner sent from Paris, however, retained authority over defense, foreign affairs, immigration, the police, civil service, communications, and secondary education.

Local politics have long centered on the question of whether the islands should have even more autonomy while remaining French, or whether they should become an independent nation. Politicians have been divided roughly into "pro-autonomy" and "pro-independence" camps. Neither side wants to give up all that money from Paris.

An additional grant of local control followed in 1984, and in 2004 the islands shifted status from an "overseas territory" of France to an "overseas country within the French republic." The local assembly gained increased powers over land ownership, labor relations, civil aviation, immigration, education, and international affairs (within the South Pacific, that is). The 2004 law also called for fresh assembly elections. In a surprise upset, a coalition led by Oscar Temaru, the mayor of independence-leaning Faaa, narrowly ousted long-time pro-autonomy President Gaston Flosse.

Temaru was in office less than 5 months before being toppled by Flosse, who ruled for only 4 months until special elections on Tahiti and Moorea removed him and returned Temaru to the presidency. It was an unsettling period for French Polynesia, but things are stable as we go to press. Temaru has predicted that his goal of complete independence from France will take as long as 20 years to achieve. In the meantime, he is encouraging economic development at home. The son of a Tahitian father and a Cook Islander mother, he also is improving relations with Tahiti's English-speaking neighbors. And he is insisting that schools from nurseries up teach English as well as French and Tahitian.

3 The Islanders

About 70% of French Polynesia's population of 245,500 or so are pure Polynesian. They are known as Tahitians, although persons born on the other islands do not necessarily consider themselves to be Tahitians and sometimes gripe about this overgeneralization. They are all called Tahitians because more than 70% of the territory's population lives on Tahiti, and because the Polynesian language originally spoken only on Tahiti and Moorea has become the territory's second official language (French is the other).

Of the 172,000 persons who live on Tahiti, some 130,000 reside in or near Papeete. No other village in the islands has a population in excess of 4,000.

THE TAHITIANS

Many Tahitians now refer to themselves as *Maohi* (the Tahitian counterpart of *Maori*), a result of an increasing awareness of their unique ancient culture. Their ancestors came to Tahiti as part of a great Polynesian migration that fanned out from Southeast Asia to much of the South Pacific. These early settlers brought along food plants, domestic animals, tools, and weapons. By the time Capt. Samuel Wallis arrived in 1767, Tahiti and the other islands were lush with breadfruit, bananas, taro, yams, sweet potatoes, and other crops. Most of the people lived on the fertile coastal plains and in the valleys behind them, each valley or district ruled by a chief. Wallis counted 17 chiefdoms on Tahiti alone.

TAHITIAN SOCIETY   Tahitians were highly stratified into three classes: chiefs and priests, landowners, and commoners. Among the commoners was a subclass of slaves, mostly war prisoners. One's position in society was hereditary, with primogeniture the general rule. In general, women were equal to men, although they could not act as priests.

A peculiar separate class of wandering dancers and singers, known as the *Arioi,* traveled about the Society Islands, performing ritual dances and shows—some of them sexually explicit—and living in a state of total sexual freedom. Family values were the least of their concerns; in fact, members immediately killed any children born into their clan.

The Polynesians had no written language, but their life was governed by an elaborate set of rules that would challenge modern legislators' abilities to reduce them to writing. Most of these rules were prohibitions known as *tabu,* a word now used in English as *taboo.* The rules differed from one class to another.

A HIERARCHY OF GODS   The ancient Tahitians worshipped a hierarchy of gods. At its head stood Taaroa, a supreme deity known as Tangaroa in the Cook Islands and Tangaloa in Samoa. *Mana,* or power, came down from the gods to each human, depending on his or her position in society. The highest chiefs had so much mana that they were considered godlike, if not actually descended from the gods.

Impressions

I was pleased with nothing so much as with the inhabitants. There is a mildness in the expression of their countenances which at once banishes the idea of a savage, and an intelligence which shows that they are advancing in civilization.

—Charles Darwin, 1839

Impressions

He had once landed [in the Marquesas], and found the remains of a man and a woman partly eaten. On his starting and sickening at the sight, one of Moipu's young men picked up a human foot, and provocatively staring at the stranger, grinned and nibbled at the heel.

—Robert Louis Stevenson, 1890

The Tahitians worshipped their gods on *maraes* (ancient temples or meeting places) built of stones. Every family had a small marae, which served the same functions as a chapel would today. Villages and entire districts—even islands—built large maraes that served not only as places of worship but also as meeting sites. Elaborate religious ceremonies were held on the large central marae. Priests prayed that the gods would come down and reside in carved tikis and other objects during the ceremonies (the objects lost all religious meaning afterward). Sacrifices were offered to the gods, sometimes including humans, mostly war prisoners or troublemakers. Despite the practice of human sacrifice, cannibalism apparently was never practiced in the Society Islands, although it was fairly widespread in the Marquesas.

The souls of the deceased were believed to return to Hawaiki, the homeland from which their Polynesian ancestors had come. In all Polynesian islands, the souls departed for it from the northwest corner of each island. That's in the direction of Taiwan, which a recent DNA study has indicated may be the origin of the Polynesians.

Sex & the Single Polynesian

The puritanical Christian missionaries who arrived in the South Pacific during the early 19th century convinced the islanders that they should clothe their nearly naked bodies. They had less luck, however, when it came to sex. To the islanders, sex was as much a part of life as any other daily activity, and they uninhibitedly engaged in it with a variety of partners from adolescence until marriage.

Even today, they have a somewhat laissez-faire attitude about premarital sex. Every child, whether born in or out of wedlock, is accepted into one of the extended families that are the bedrock of Polynesian society. Mothers, fathers, grandparents, aunts, uncles, and cousins of every degree are all part of the close-knit Polynesian family. Relationships sometimes are so blurred that every adult woman within a mile is known as a child's "auntie"—even the child's mother.

Male transvestitism, homosexuality, and bisexuality are facts of life in Polynesia, where families with a shortage of female offspring will raise young boys as girls. Some of these youths grow up to be heterosexual; others become homosexual or bisexual and, often appearing publicly in women's attire, actively seek out the company of tourists. In Tahitian, these males are known as *mahus;* in Samoan, *magus;* and in Tongan, *fakaleitis.*

THE CHINESE

The outbreak of the American Civil War in 1861 resulted in a worldwide shortage of cotton. In September 1862 an Irish adventurer named William Stewart founded a cotton plantation at Atimaono, Tahiti's only large tract of flat land. The Tahitians weren't the least bit interested in working for Stewart, so he imported a contingent of Chinese laborers. The first 329 of them arrived from Hong Kong in February 1865. Stewart ran into financial difficulties, which were compounded by the drop in cotton prices after the American South resumed production after 1868. His empire collapsed.

Nothing remains of Stewart's plantation at Atimaono (a golf course now occupies most of the land), but many of his Chinese laborers decided to stay. They grew vegetables for the Papeete market, saved their money, and invested in other businesses. Their descendants and those of subsequent immigrants from China now influence the economy far in excess of their numbers. They run nearly all of French Polynesia's grocery and general merchandise stores, which in French are called *magasins chinois,* or Chinese stores.

4 Languages

With the exception of some older Polynesians, everyone speaks **French,** the official language. **Tahitian** is quickly gaining ground as a coequal now that a pro-independence government is in power. **English** is also taught as a third language in most schools (and all of those operated by the Chinese community), and it's a prerequisite for getting a hotel job involving guest relations. You can converse in English with your hotel's professional and activities staff, but not necessarily with the housemaids.

Many young Tahitians are eager to learn English, if for no other reason than to understand the lyrics of American songs, which dominate the radio in French Polynesia. Accordingly, you can get by with English in shops, hotels, restaurants, and other businesses frequented by tourists. Once you get off the beaten path, however, an ability to speak what I call *Francais touristique*—tourist French, as in asking directions—will be very helpful if not outright essential. I really need my schoolbook French on Maupiti, and it came in handy in the Marquesas, too.

Not to fear: Tahitians are enormously friendly folk, and most will immediately warm to you when they discover you don't speak French, or that you speak it haltingly or with a pronounced English accent.

TAHITIAN PRONUNCIATION

If for no other reason, a little knowledge of Tahitian will help you correctly pronounce the tongue-tying place names here.

The Polynesian languages, including Tahitian, consist primarily of vowel sounds, which are pronounced in the Roman fashion—that is, *ah, ay, ee, oh,* and *ou,* not *ay, ee, eye, oh,* and *you,* as in English. Almost all vowels are sounded separately. For example, Tahiti's airport is at Faaa, which is pronounced Fah-*ah*-ah, not Fah. Papeete is Pah-pay-*ay*-tay, not Pa-pee-tee. Paea is Pah-*ay*-ah.

Some cultural activists advocate the use of apostrophes when writing Tahitian to indicate glottal stops—those slight pauses between some vowels similar to the tiny break between "Oh-oh!" in English. Apostrophes already appear in written Tongan and Samoan. Moorea, for example, is pronounced Moh-*oh*-ray-ah and is often spelled Mo'orea. Consequently, you may see Papeete spelled Pape'ete.

The consonants used in Tahitian are *f, h, m, n, p, r, t,* and *v.* There are some special rules regarding their sounds, but you'll be understood if you say them as you would in English.

USEFUL WORDS

To help you impress the locals with what a really friendly tourist you are, here are a few Tahitian words you can use on them:

English	Tahitian	Pronunciation
hello	**ia orana**	ee-ah oh-*rah*-na (sounds like "your honor")
welcome	**maeva**	mah-*ay*-vah
goodbye	**parahi**	pah-*rah*-hee
good	**maitai**	*my*-tie
very good	**maitai roa**	*my*-tie-*row*-ah
thank you	**maruru**	mah-*roo*-roo
thank you very much	**maruru roa**	mah-*roo*-roo *row*-ah
good health!	**manuia**	mah-*new*-yah
woman	**vahine**	vah-*hee*-nay
man	**tane**	*tah*-nay
sarong	**pareu**	pah-*ray*-oo
small islet	**motu**	*moh*-too
take it easy	**hare maru**	*ha*-ray *mah*-roo
fed up	**fiu**	few

5 Visitor Information & Entry Requirements

VISITOR INFORMATION

The best source of up-to-date information in advance is the territory's tourism promotion bureau: **Tahiti Tourisme,** B.P. 65, 98713 Papeete, French Polynesia (© **50.57.00;** fax 43.66.19; www.tahiti-tourisme.pf).

You can also contact Tahiti Tourisme's overseas offices or representatives:

- **United States:** 300 N. Continental Blvd., Suite 160, El Segundo, CA 90245 (© **310/414-8484;** fax 310/414-8490; www.tahiti-tourisme.com)
- **Australia:** Paramour Productions, 362 Riley St., Surry Hills, NSW 2010 (© **1300 655 563** toll free in Australia or 02/9281-6020; fax 02/9211-6589; www.tahiti-tourisme.com.au)
- **New Zealand:** 200 West Victoria St., Suite 2A (P.O. Box 106192), Auckland (© **09/368-5262;** fax 09/368-5263; www.tahiti-tourisme.co.nz)
- **United Kingdom:** BGB & Associates, 7 Westminster Palace Gardens, Artillery Row, London SW1P 1RL(© **20/7233-2300;** fax 20/7233-2301; www.tahiti-tourisme.co.uk)
- **France:** 28, bd. Saint Germain, 75005 Paris (© **01/55426434;** fax 01/55426120; www.tahiti-tourisme.fr)
- **Germany:** Travel Marketing Romberg, Swartzbachstrasse, 32 40822, Mettman bei Dusseldorf (© **2104 286672;** fax 2104 912673; www.tahititourisme.de)
- **Italy:** Aigo, Piazza Castello, 3 20 124 Milano (© **02/66-980317;** fax 02/66-92648; www.tahiti-turisme.it)
- **Chile:** Officina de turismo de Tahiti y sus islas, Av. 11 de Septiembre 2214, Of. 116, Casila 16057, Santiago 9 (© **251-2826;** fax 233-1787; www.tahiti-tourisme.cl)

• **Japan:** Tahiti Tourist Promotion Board, Tokyo City Air Terminal 2F 42-1, Nihonbashi-Hakozakicho, Chuo-ku, Tokyo 103-0015 (℃ **3/3639 0468;** fax 3/3665 0581; www.tahiti-tourisme.jp)

Once you're in Papeete, you can get maps, brochures, and other information at **Tahiti Manava** (℃ **50.57.12;** www.tahiti-manava.pf), in the cruise-ship welcoming center on the waterfront on boulevard Pomare at the foot of rue Paul Gauguin. See "Fast Facts: Tahiti," in chapter 8.

Local tourism committees have information booths on Moorea, Bora Bora, Huahine, and Raiatea (see the "Fast Facts" boxes in the following chapters).

Be sure to pick up the *Tahiti Beach Press,* a free weekly English-language newspaper that lists special events and current activities. Copies also are available in most hotel lobbies.

Useful websites include **www.airtahitimagazine.com**, with articles from Air Tahiti's in-flight magazine; **www.tahitisun.com**, with links to several other sites with a host of information about each island; **www.tahiti-explorer.com** and its affiliated **www.tahiti-guide.com**, with details about most resorts; **www.tahiti.com**, which has been around since 1994; the Moorea-based **www.tahitiguide.com**; and **www.polynesianislands.com**, with coverage of all the South Pacific islands. And you can see what other travelers have to say on the South Pacific travel talk boards at **www.frommers.com**.

If you plan to scuba dive, the Tahiti Diving Guide at **www.diving-tahiti.com** has general information and links to dive operators in all the islands.

ENTRY REQUIREMENTS

All visitors except French nationals are required to have a **passport** that will be valid for 6 months beyond their intended stay, as well as a **return or ongoing ticket.** French citizens must bring their national identity cards.

Citizens and nationals of the United States, Canada, New Zealand, Argentina, Bermuda, Brunei, South Korea, Croatia, Hungary, Japan, Malaysia, Mexico, Poland, the Czech Republic, Singapore, Slovakia, Slovenia, Uruguay, Bolivia, Chile, Costa Rica, Equador, Estonia, Guatemala, Honduras, Latvia, Lithuania, Nicaragua, Panama, Paraguay, and El Salvador may visit for up to 1 month without a visa.

Nationals of Australia, the European Union countries, Belgium, Luxembourg, Monaco, Switzerland, Andorra, the Vatican, Cyprus, Iceland, Liechtenstein, Malta, Norway, and St. Martin can stay up to 3 months without a visa.

Citizens from all other countries (including foreign nationals residing in the United States) must get a visa before leaving home. French embassies and consulates overseas can issue "short stay" visas valid for 1 to 3 months, and they will forward applications for longer visits to the local immigration department in Papeete. *Note:* Visas issued by French embassies and consulates do not entitle you to visit Tahiti without being stamped "*valable pour la Polynésie Française*"—valid for French Polynesia.

In the United States, the **Embassy of France** is at 4102 Reservoir Road NW, Washington, DC 20007 (℃ **202/944-6000;** www.info-france-usa.org). There are French consulates in Boston, Chicago, Detroit, Houston, Los Angeles, New York, Miami, San Francisco, and New Orleans.

No **vaccinations** are required unless you are coming from a yellow fever, plague, or cholera area.

Customs allowances are 200 cigarettes or 100 cigarillos or 50 cigars; 2 liters of liquor, Champagne, or wine; 50 grams of perfume, ¼ liter of eau de toilette; 500

grams of coffee and 100 grams of tea; and 30,000CPF (US$300) worth of other goods. Narcotics, dangerous drugs, weapons, ammunition, and copyright infringements (that is, pirated video- and audiotapes) are prohibited. Pets and plants are subject to stringent regulations (don't even think of bringing your pet).

6 Money

U.S. dollar and European euro notes (but not coins) are widely accepted as cash in the islands, although at less favorable exchange rates than at banks. The official currency is the **French Pacific franc (CFP),** which comes in coins up to 100CFP and in colorful notes ranging from 500CFP into the millions. The value of the CFP is pegged to the European euro at a rate of **1€** = 119.33CFP. That means the value of the CFP fluctuates against the U.S. dollar. I have seen US$1 worth as much as 170CFP and as little as 75CFP. Recently it has hovered around 100CFP per buck, so I have used the rate of **US$1 = 100CFP** (or 100CFP = US$1) to compute the equivalent U.S. dollar prices given in parentheses after the CFP prices in this book.

The local government wants to shift French Polynesia from the Pacific franc to the European euro, but this is unlikely to happen until 2007 or later.

HOW TO GET LOCAL CURRENCY   Banque de Polynésie, Banque Socredo, and Banque de Tahiti have offices on the main islands. See the "Fast Facts" in the following chapters for bank and ATM locations. This is essential since some of the smaller islands do not have ATMs. All banks charge at least 450CFP (US$4.50) per transaction to cash traveler's checks, regardless of the amount, so you should change large amounts each time to minimize this bite.

Automatic teller machines (ATMs) are not always reliable at giving cash or cash advances. I have found Banque Socredo's machines to be more reliable than the other banks'. Visa credit and check/ATM cards are more likely to work than the MasterCard version. Bring some cash or travelers checks with you just in case, and be prepared to put as many purchases as you can on your credit cards. The ATM operating instructions are given in both French and English. You will need your personal identification number (PIN) for both credit and debit cards. See "Money" in chapter 2 for more information.

You will probably get a better rate if you change your money in French Polynesia rather than before leaving home.

CREDIT CARDS   MasterCard and Visa are widely accepted on the most visited islands. American Express cards are taken only by the major hotels and car-rental firms

---

Tips Converting in Your Head

No decimals are used with Pacific franc units, so prices at first can seem even more staggering than they really are. The easiest way to convert in your head is to follow the lead of local residents, who think of 100CFP as US$1 and often express prices that way to visitors. If the price of something is 1,000CFP, they might say it costs US$10. Using their method, you can make a quick conversion without a calculator by thinking of 100CFP as US$1, 500CFP as US$5, 1,000CFP as US$10, and so on. That is, drop the last two zeros, then add or subtract the percentage difference between the actual rate and 100CFP. In the case of US$1 = 125CFP, for example, you would subtract 25%.

and by some restaurants. Don't count on using your Diners Club card except at the major hotels. Discover cards are not accepted in the islands.

7 When to Go—Climate, Holidays & Events

There is no bad time to go to French Polynesia, but some periods are better than others. The weather is at its best—comfortable and dry—in July and August, but this is the prime vacation and festival season. July is the busiest month because of the *Heiva Nui* festival (see "French Polynesia Calendar of Events," below). Hotels on the outer islands are at their fullest during August, the traditional French vacation month, when many Papeete residents head for the outer islands to get away from it all. In other words, book your air tickets and hotel rooms for July and August as far in advance as possible.

May, June, September, or October offer the best combination of weather and availability of hotel rooms.

CLIMATE

Tahiti and the rest of the Society Islands have a balmy tropical climate. Tropical showers can pass overhead at any time of the year. Humidity averages between 77% and 80% throughout the year.

The most pleasant time of year is the May through October austral winter or **dry season,** when midday maximum temperatures average a delightful 82°F (28°C), with early morning lows of 68°F (20°C) often making a blanket necessary. Some winter days, especially on the south side of the islands, can seem quite chilly when a strong wind blows from Antarctica.

November through April is the austral summer or **wet season,** when rainy periods can be expected between days of intense sunshine. The average maximum daily temperature is 86°F (30°C) during these months, while nighttime lows are about 72°F (22°C).

Average Daytime Temperatures in Tahiti

	Jan	Feb	Mar	Apr	May	June	July	Aug	Sept	Oct	Nov	Dec
Temp °F	80.6	80.8	81.3	80.8	79.5	77.4	76.5	76.3	77	78.1	79.3	79.9
Temp °C	27	27.1	27.4	27.1	26.4	25.2	24.7	24.6	25	25.6	26.3	26.6

The central and northern Tuamotus have somewhat warmer temperatures and less rainfall. Since there are no mountains to create cooling night breezes, they can experience desertlike hot periods between November and April. The Marquesas are closer to the equator, and temperatures and humidity tend to be slightly higher than in Tahiti. The climate in the Austral and Gambier islands is more temperate.

French Polynesia is on the far eastern edge of the South Pacific cyclone (hurricane) belt, and storms can occur between November and March.

For the local weather including current satellite images, visit **Meteo France's** official website at **www.meteo.pf.** You can see what the weather is like right now at **www.tahiti-nui.com,** which has live Web cams overlooking the Papeete waterfront and the Bora Bora Pearl Beach Resort.

PUBLIC HOLIDAYS

Like all Pacific Islanders, the Tahitians love public holidays and often extend them past the official day. For example, if Ascension Day falls on a Thursday, don't be surprised if some stores and even banks are closed through the weekend. Plan your shopping forays accordingly.

Public holidays are New Year's Day (government offices also are closed on Jan 2), Good Friday and Easter Monday, Ascension Day (40 days after Easter), Whitmonday (the 7th Mon after Easter), Missionary Day (Mar 5), Labor Day (May 1), Pentecost Monday (the 1st Mon in June), Bastille Day (July 14), Internal Autonomy Day (Sept 8), All Saints Day (Nov 1), Armistice Day (Nov 11), and Christmas Day.

Tahiti Tourisme publishes an annual list of the territory's leading special events on its website (see "Visitor Information & Entry Requirements," above).

FRENCH POLYNESIA CALENDAR OF EVENTS

January

Chinese New Year. Parade, musical performances, demonstrations of martial arts, Chinese dances, and handicrafts. Between mid-January and mid-February.

International Oceania Film Documentary Festival (FIFO). More than 100 films produced by Pacific islanders are shown and judged in Papeete. Last weekend.

February

Tahiti Moorea Marathon. Prizes worth up to US$15,000 entice some of the world's best runners to trot 42km (26 miles) around Moorea. Second Saturday.

March

Coming of the Gospel. Gatherings on Tahiti commemorate the anniversary of the arrival of the London Missionary Society. March 5.

May

Billabong Pro. World-class surfers compete on the waves off Teuhupo'o on Tahiti Iti. First 2 weeks.

June

Tahiti Nui Cup Regatta. Yachts sail among Raiatea, Tahaa, Huahine, and Bora Bora. First 10 days.

Miss Tahiti, Miss Heiva, Miss Moorea, and Miss Bora Bora Contests. Candidates from around the islands vie to win the titles. It is among the biggest annual events on outer islands. Early to mid-June.

Tahiti International Golf Open. Local and international golfers vie at Atimaono Golf Course, Tahiti. Mid-June.

July

Heiva Nui. ๛๛๛ This is the festival to end all festivals in French Polynesia. It was originally a celebration of Bastille Day on July 14, but the islanders have extended the shindig into a month-long blast (it is commonly called *Tiurai,* the Tahitian word for July). They pull out all the stops, with parades, outrigger canoe races, javelin-throwing contests, fire walking, games, carnivals, festivals, and reenactments of ancient Polynesian ceremonies at restored maraes. Highlight for visitors: An extraordinarily colorful contest to determine the best Tahitian dancing troupe for the year—never do the hips gyrate more vigorously. Airline and hotel reservations are difficult to come by during July, so book early and take your written confirmation with you. Last weekend in June through July.

August

Mini Fêtes. Winning dancers and singers from the *Heiva Nui* perform at hotels on the outer islands. All month.

September

Tourism Days. Islanders pay homage to overseas visitors, who get discounts. Last weekend.

October

Aitoman (Iron Man) Moorea Triathlon. Top-shape athletes swim, bike, and run on Moorea. www.tahiti triathlon.pf. First Saturday.

Hawaiki Nui Va'a. Outrigger canoe racing, the national sport, takes center stage as international teams race from Huahine to Raiatea, Tahaa, and Bora Bora over 3 days. www.hawaikinuivaa. pf. Early Oct.

Tahiti Carnival. Parades, floats, and much partying on the Papeete waterfront. Last week.

November

All Saints Day. Flowers are sold everywhere to families who put them on graves after whitewashing the tombstones. November 1.

December

Tiare Tahiti Flower Festival (The Tiare Days on Tahiti). Everyone on the streets of Papeete and in the hotels receives a *tiare Tahiti,* the fragrant gardenia that is indigenous to Tahiti. Dinner and dancing later. First week in December.

New Year's Eve. A big festival in downtown Papeete leads territory-wide celebrations. December 31.

---

8 Getting There & Getting Around

GETTING TO FRENCH POLYNESIA

Air Tahiti Nui, Air New Zealand, Air France, and **Hawaiian Airlines** fly between Tahiti and North America, with Air New Zealand and Air Tahiti Nui going on to Auckland, New Zealand, and Sydney, Australia. Air New Zealand and **Qantas Airways** fly between Sydney and Tahiti. Air France and Air Tahiti Nui link the islands to Japan. See "Getting There & Getting Around" in chapter 2 for details.

All international flights arrive at **Tahiti-Faaa International Airport** on Tahiti's northwest corner, about 11km (7 miles) from downtown Papeete. See "Arriving & Getting Around" in chapter 8 for information about the airport and local transportation on Tahiti.

GETTING AROUND
BY PLANE

Air Moorea (© 86.41.41; fax 86.42.99; www.airmoorea.com) provides shuttle service between Tahiti-Faaa International Airport and Temae Airport on Moorea. Its small planes (and I do mean small) leave Faaa on the hour and half-hour daily from 6 to 9am, then on the hour from 10am to 3pm, and on the hour and half-hour again from 4 to 6pm. Each plane turns around on Moorea and flies back to Tahiti. The fare is about 3,100CFP (US$31) each way. Air Moorea's little terminal is on the east end of Tahiti-Faaa International Airport (that's to the left as you come out of Customs). Air Moorea will take you from the airport to your Moorea hotel for 500CFP (US$5) each way, but *you must buy your transfer ticket in Papeete.* It is not available after you arrive on Moorea.

Air Moorea is owned by **Air Tahiti** (© 86.44.42; fax 86.40.99; www.airtahiti.pf), which provides daily flights between Papeete and all the main islands. It's wise to reserve your seats as early as possible.

One-way adult fares on the usual visitor's circuit (double the fare for round-trips between any two islands and halve the cost for children) are as follows:

Papeete to Moorea	4,200CFP (US$42)
Moorea to Huahine	14,400CFP (US$144)
Moorea to Bora Bora	20,700CFP (US$207)
Huahine to Raiatea	6,100CFP (US$61)
Raiatea to Bora Bora	7,000CFP (US$70)
Bora Bora to Papeete	17,600CFP (US$176)
Bora Bora to Rangiroa	26,600CFP (US$266)
Rangiroa to Papeete	17,700CFP (US$177)

Visitors can save by buying an **Air Tahiti Pass** over the popular routes. For example, the "Bora Bora Pass" permits travel over the popular Papeete–Moorea–Huahine–Bora Bora–Papeete route for about 34,700CFP (US$347), which is 10,300CFP (US$103) less than the full adult fares. The "Bora Bora–Tuamotu Pass" adds Rangiroa, Tikihau, and Manihi. Whether you save anything will depend on how many islands you plan to visit, so add up the regular fares and compare to the price of the passes. All travel must be completed within 28 days of the first flight, and other restrictions apply.

Air Tahiti's central downtown Papeete walk-in reservations office is at the corner of rue du 22 Septembre and rue du Maréchal Foche (© **47.44.00**). It also has an office in the Tahiti-Faaa International Airport terminal (© **86.41.84**).

Pack carefully and bring evidence of your international ticket with you because the **baggage limit** on both of these airlines is 20 kilograms (44 lb.) per person if you're connecting with an international flight within 7 days, but only 10 kilograms (22 lb.) per person if you're not. You will face a substantial extra charge for excess weight. You can leave your extra belongings in the storage room at your hotel or at Tahiti-Faaa International Airport (see "Arriving & Getting Around" in chapter 8).

Check-in times vary from 1 to 2 hours, so ask Air Tahiti when you should arrive at the airport.

An alternative to taking Air Tahiti's scheduled flights is to charter a plane and pilot from **Air Moorea, Air Tahiti, Air Archepels** (© **81.30.30**; www.airarchipels.com), or **Wan Air** (© **50.44.18**; www.wanair.pf). **Polynesia Helicopteres** (© **86.60.29**; heli.pacific@mail.pf) charters helicopters. When the total cost is split among a large enough group, the price per person could be less than airfare on a commercial airline.

BY FERRY TO MOOREA

Two companies—**Aremiti** (© **50.57.57**; www.aremiti.pf) and **Moorea Ferry** (© **86. 87.47** on Tahiti, or 56.34.34 on Moorea; www.mooreaferry.pf)—run ferries between

---

Tips The Best Seats & Something to Eat

It depends on the pilots and how much sightseeing they want to do, but usually you will have the best views of the islands by sitting on the left side of the Air Tahiti aircraft when you're flying from Papeete to the outer islands. Sit on the right side when returning to Tahiti. And make sure you have your camera and a lot of film and camera batteries at the ready.

Most hotel dining rooms open for breakfast at 7am and close by 9:30am, so if you're catching an early morning flight to another island, stock up on some munchies and something to drink the night before, and bring them along on the plane.

> ### *Moments* Breaking Into Tahitian Song
>
> I was on the last ferry from Moorea to Tahiti when a Tahitian passenger, obviously on his way home from work, started playing a guitar. Within seconds everyone onboard spontaneously began singing Tahitian songs. If you're lucky you'll be somewhere when that happens, for you'll be in for a very special moment.

the Papeete waterfront and Vaiare, a small bay on Moorea's east coast. It can seem like madness when the boats arrive and depart at the wharves, so take your time and be sure to get on one of the fast catamarans, which take 30 minutes to cover the 19km (12 miles) between the islands. The *Aremiti V,* the *Aremiti Ferry,* and the *Moorea Express* are all fast catamarans. Don't get on the *Moorea Ferry,* which can take an hour. The one-way fare on any ferry, whether fast or slow, is about 900CFP (US$9).

In general, one or another of them departs Papeete about 6am, 7:30am, 9am, noon, 1:30pm, 3pm, and 5pm, with extra voyages on Friday and Monday (Moorea is a popular weekend retreat for Papeete residents). I usually pick up a schedule at the ferry dock and carry it with me throughout my visit.

Buses meet all ferries except the midday departures from Papeete to take you to your hotel or other destination on Moorea for 300CFP (US$3) per person. From Vaiare, they take about 1 hour to reach the northwest corner of Moorea.

BY SHIP TO THE OUTER ISLANDS
You can go by ship from Papeete to Huahine, Raiatea, Tahaa, and Bora Bora, but it's neither the quickest nor most comfortable way to travel, nor the most reliable.

Once used as a Tahiti–Moorea ferry, the catamaran *Aremiti 4* (© **50.57.57;** www.aremiti.pf) is the fastest of the lot. It departs Papeete at 8am on Wednesday and Sunday for Huahine and Raiatea. It arrives in Huahine at noon, at Raiatea at 1:30pm. It then returns over the same route, arriving back at Papeete about 6pm on the same day. The *Aremiti 4* has airline-style seats and a bar but no cabins. One way fares from Papeete are about 4,770CFP (US$48) to Huahine, 5,500CFP (US$55) to Raiatea.

Two cargo ferries, the *Vaeanu* (© **41.25.35;** fax 41.24.34; torehiatetu@mail.pf) and the *Hawaiki Nui* (© **45.23.24;** fax 45.24.44; sarlstim@mail.pf), make three voyages a week. Both have passenger cabins. Usually they depart Papeete about 4pm, arrive at Huahine during the night, and go on to the other Leeward Islands the next day. They return from Bora Bora over the reverse route. Contact the ship owners for fares and schedules, which are at the mercy of the weather and condition of the ships.

Once in the Leeward Islands, you can make the voyage between Bora Bora and Raiatea on the *Maupiti Express* (© **67.66.69** on Bora Bora, 66.37.81 on Raiatea; maupitiexpress@mail.pf). This small, fast ferry departs Bora Bora for Tahaa and Raiatea at 7am on Monday, Wednesday, and Friday, returning to Bora Bora in the late afternoon. It stops at Tahaa in both directions. On Tuesday, Thursday, and Saturday it sails from Bora Bora to Maupiti, departing at 8:30am and returning in late afternoon. In other words, it's possible to make day trips from Bora Bora to Raiatea or Maupiti. Fares on either route are 2,500CFP (US$25) one-way, 3,500CFP (US$35) return.

Except for the excellent *Aranui 3,* which is as much cruise vessel as cargo ship (see "Seeing the Islands by Cruise Ship & Yacht," below), ships to the Tuamotu, Marquesas, Gambier, and Austral groups keep somewhat irregular schedules in terms of weeks or even months, not days. I once met a young Australian who took a boat to Rapa in the Austral Islands, expecting to return in a few weeks to Papeete. The ship broke down and went into the repair yard on Tahiti, stranding him for 3 months on Rapa, where he survived on coconuts and the generosity of local residents. Consequently I cannot recommend them. If you're interested, contact Tahiti Tourisme for a list of inter-island schooners, their fares, and approximate schedules from Tahiti Tourisme. You had best have a 3-month visa to stay in French Polynesia.

BY RENTAL CAR

Avis and Europcar have rental-car agencies (*locations de voiture* in French) on Tahiti, Moorea, Huahine, Raiatea, and Bora Bora. Hertz is present on Tahiti, Raiatea, and Bora Bora. See "Getting Around" in the following chapters for details.

A **driver's license** from your home country will be honored in French Polynesia.

Service stations are common on Tahiti, but only in the main villages on the other islands. Expect to pay about twice as much per gallon of gas as in the United States.

DRIVING RULES   Driving is on the right-hand side of the road, as in North America and continental Europe.

All persons in a vehicle **must wear seat belts.** If you drive or ride on a scooter or motorbike, **helmets** (*casques,* pronounced "casks") are mandatory.

Speed limits are 40kmph (24 mph) in the towns and villages and 80kmph (48 mph) on the open road. The limit is 60kmph (36 mph) for 8km (5 miles) on either side of Papeete. The general rule on the Rte. 5 freeway between Papeete and Punaauia, on Tahiti's west coast, is 90kmph (54 mph), although there is one short stretch going down a hill where it's officially 110kmph (66 mph).

Drivers on the main rural roads have the right of way. In Papeete, priority is given to vehicles entering from the right side, unless an intersection is marked with a traffic light or a stop or yield sign. This rule differs from those of most other countries, so be careful at all intersections, especially those marked with a *priorité à droite* (priority to the right) sign, and give way accordingly.

Drivers are required to **stop for pedestrians** on marked crosswalks, but on busy streets, don't assume that drivers will politely stop when you try to cross.

Traffic lights in Papeete may be difficult to see, since some of them are on the far left-hand side of the street instead of on the driver's side of the intersection.

9 Seeing the Islands by Cruise Ship & Yacht

The Society Islands are ideal grounds for cruise ships, since it's barely an hour's steam from Tahiti to Moorea, half a day's voyage on to Huahine, and less than 2 hours each among Huahine, Raiatea, Tahaa, and Bora Bora. That means the ships spend most days and nights at anchor in lovely lagoons, allowing passengers plenty of time to explore the islands and play in the water. Bear in mind, however, that you will see a lot more of the ship than you will of the islands.

Cruises could be an affordable way to see the islands in style, since the prices usually include all meals, wine with lunch and dinner, soft drinks, and most onboard activities. You might even find a deal including airfare to and from Tahiti.

Likewise, these are wonderful islands for chartering a yacht and setting sail on your own.

TAKING A CRUISE

ADVENTURES ON THE *ARANUI* ✷✷✷

The working cargo ship *Aranui 3* (© **800/972-7268** in the U.S. or 42.62.40 in Papeete; fax 43.48.89; www.aranui.com) is the most interesting way to visit the out-of-the-way Marquesas Islands. Outfitted for up to 200 passengers, this 386-foot freighter makes 15-day round-trips from Papeete to 6 of the 10 Marquesas Islands, with stops on the way at Fakarava and Rangiroa in the Tuamotus. While the crew loads and unloads the ship's cargo, passengers spend their days ashore experiencing the islands and islanders. Among the activities: picnicking on beaches, snorkeling, visiting villages, and exploring archaeological sites. Experts on Polynesian history and culture accompany most voyages.

Accommodation is in 10 suites, 12 deluxe cabins, 63 standard cabins, and dormitories. The suites and cabins all have private bathrooms. Suites and deluxe cabins have windows and doors opening to outside decks, and their bathrooms are equipped with bathtubs as well as showers. Standard cabins lack outside doors and have portholes instead of windows. The ship has a restaurant, bar, boutique, library, video lounge, and swimming pool.

The *Aranui's* primary job is to haul cargo, so it does not have stabilizers and other features of a luxury liner. In other words, do not expect the same level of comfort, cuisine, and service as on the other ships cruising these waters. If you only want to sit by the pool, eat prodigious quantities of fine food, and smoke cigars, the *Aranui* may not be your cup of tea. But for those of us who want to go places few people visit, and learn a lot in the process, then it is an excellent choice.

Fares for the complete voyage range from about US$1,980 for a dormitory bunk to US$4,950 per person for suites. All meals are included, but you have to pay your own bar bill and your airfare to and from Tahiti.

LUXURY ON THE *PAUL GAUGUIN* ✷✷

The 157m (513-ft.), 318-passenger *Paul Gauguin* (© **877/505-5370** or 904/776-6123 in the U.S., 54.51.00 in Papeete; www.rssc.com) is the most luxurious of Tahiti's cruise ships. It spends most of its year making 7-day cruises through the Society Islands, but occasionally extends to Rarotonga in the Cook Islands and to the Tuamotu and Marquesas islands. All of the ship's seven suites and about half of its 152 staterooms have private verandas or balconies (the least expensive lower-deck units have windows or portholes). All are luxuriously appointed with minibars, TVs and VCRs, direct-dial phones, and marble bathrooms with full-size tubs. Most have queen-size beds, although some have two twins. Per-person double-occupancy fares for the 1-week Society Islands cruises start at about US$1,800 per person.

A LOT OF COMPANY ON THE *TAHITIAN PRINCESS*

Operated by **Princess Cruises** (© **800/774-6237** or 904/527-6660; www.princess cruises.com), the 700-passenger *Tahitian Princess* makes 10-night voyages through French Polynesia and to Rarotonga in the Cook Islands. Formerly a Renaissance Cruises ship, this is the largest vessel operating in French Polynesia, so you won't have the same intimacy as on the other vessels. It's also the least expensive, with special fares sometimes offered during the slow seasons. Passengers can make use of a sun deck, swimming pool, fitness center, casino, cabaret lounge, two bars, and four restaurants. Shore excursions are offered, but unlike the *Paul Gauguin* and the *Wind Star,* the

---

Fun Fact Phoning Like a Local

In French Polynesia, the local phone numbers are presented as three two-digit numbers—for example, 42.29.17. If you ask someone there for a number, he or she will say it like this: *"quarante-deux, vingt-neuf, dix-sept"* in French or "forty-two, twenty-nine, seventeen" in English.

Tahitian Princess doesn't have a stern platform to support on-board watersports activities. Almost 70% of the 280 staterooms and 62 suites open to private terraces. Prices start at US$1,850 per person for an interior stateroom.

An identical vessel, the ***Pacific Princess,*** cruises part of the year in French Polynesia, then repositions to other ports, including Sydney, Australia, from where it sails through the western Pacific.

DINING IN THE LAGOON WITH BORA BORA CRUISES

Using smaller ships, **Bora Bora Cruises,** P.O. Box 40186, Papeete (© **45.10.66;** fax 45.10.65; www.boraboracruises.com), are more along the lines of Blue Lagoon Cruises in Fiji (see chapter 5). Its sleek, luxurious yachts, the *Tu Moana* and the *Tia Moana,* measure in at 69m (226-ft.) and can carry up to 60 passengers in 30 staterooms spread over three decks. They make 1-week cruises from Bora Bora to Huahine, Raiatea, and Tahaa. The boats are small enough to anchor closer to shore than the other ships here. Consequently, passengers enjoy extras such as breakfast served in the lagoon (that's right, you actually sit at tables in the water) and movies shown on a beach. Fares are 3,850€ (US$4,600) per person.

DIVING FROM THE *TAHITI AGGRESSOR*

Intermediate and advanced divers can explore the lagoons of Bora Bora, Huahine, Raiatea, and Tahaa on the live-aboard *Tahiti Aggressor* (© **800/348-2628;** fax 985/384-0817; www.aggressor.com). Owned and operated by the Louisiana-based Aggressor Fleet, this nine-cabin, 36m (106-ft.) catamaran makes 1-week cruises starting at Bora Bora. The cruises cost about US$3,000 per person.

FLY FISHING FROM THE *HAUMANA*

If you like to fish, you can cast your line from the *Haumana* (© **50 06 74;** fax 50.06.72; www.tahiti-haumana-cruises.com). This 33.5-meter (110-foot), 42-passenger catamaran specializes in 3-, 4-, and 7-night cruises on the calm, shallow lagoons of Rangiroa and Tikehau in the Tuamotus. Fishing is not the primary focus of the cruises, but this is one of the few vessels to carry rods, reels, and other gear. Although the *Haumana* is smaller than other ships here, its 21 air conditioned cabins all have large windows or portholes, queen beds, sofas or settees, minibars, TVs, VCRs, phones, and shower-only bathrooms with hairdryers. Rates range from US$2,130 to US$5,070 per person, double occupancy, including all meals, drinks, fishing, and kayak excursions.

CHARTERING A YACHT

If you are an experienced sailor, you can charter a yacht—with or without skipper and crew—and knock around some of the French Polynesian islands as the wind and your own desires dictate. The best place to start is Raiatea, which shares a lagoon with Tahaa, the only French Polynesian island which can be circumnavigated entirely within a protective reef. Depending on the wind, Bora Bora and Huahine are relatively easy blue-water trips away.

The Moorings ✮✮✮, a respected yacht charter company based in Florida (© 800/ 535-7289 or 727/535-1446; www.moorings.com), operates a fleet of sailboats based at **Apooti Marina** on Raiatea's northern coast (© **66.35.93;** fax 66.20.94; moorings@mail.pf). That's a few minutes' sail to Tahaa. Depending on the size of the boat—they range from 11m to 15m (36 ft.–50 ft.) in length—and the season, bareboat rates (that is, without skipper or crew) run about US$415 to US$1,480 per vessel per day. Provisions are extra. The agency will check you out to make sure you and your party can handle sailboats of these sizes; otherwise, you must pay extra for a skipper.

Sunsail Yacht Charters (© **800/327-2276** in the U.S., 60.04.85 on Raiatea; www.sunsail.com) has a fleet of 11m to 15m (36 ft.–50 ft.) yachts based at Faaroa Bay on Raiatea. Its bareboat rates range from about US$360 to US$1,200 a day per boat, depending on size and season, plus provisions, skipper, and cook if you need them.

The French-owned **Tahiti Yacht Charter** (© **45.04.00;** fax 45.76.00; www.tahiti yachtcharter.com) has 11m to 14m (36 ft.–49 ft.) yachts based at Papeete and Raiatea. It designs cruises throughout the territory, including lengthy voyages to the Tuamotus and Marquesas. Similar services are offered by **Archipel Croisiers** on Moorea (© **56.36.39;** fax 56.35.87; www.archipels.com).

10 Dining Out in French Polynesia

Unlike other South Pacific countries, French Polynesia has a plethora of excellent restaurants. I'm not fabricating when I say I've seldom had a really bad meal here. You are in for a special treat when ordering tomatoes and other locally-grown vegetables, for they will be as fresh as if they had come from your own garden.

Many visitors are shocked at the high prices on the menus of their resorts' dining rooms, and in the grocery stores. Most foodstuffs are imported, and except for sugar, flour, and a few other necessities, are subject to stiff duties. On the other hand, you won't have sales tax added to your bill, nor will you necessarily tip the wait staff, as in the United States. In other words, Americans will not have to add up to 25% to the cost of restaurant meals. When all is said and done, restaurant prices outside the resort dining rooms are comparable to those in large Western cities. (See below for how I save money on food here.)

LOCAL FARE: *MA'A TAHITI*

The Tahitians have adopted many Western and Chinese dishes, but they still consume copious quantities of *ma'a Tahiti* (Tahitian food), especially on Sunday. Like their Polynesian counterparts elsewhere, Tahitians still cook meals underground in an earth oven, known here as an *himaa*. Pork, chicken, fish, shellfish, leafy green vegetables such as taro leaves, and root crops such as taro and yams are wrapped in leaves, placed on a bed of heated stones, covered with more leaves and earth, and left to steam for several hours. The results are quite tasty, since the steam spreads the aroma of one ingredient to the others, and liberal use of coconut cream adds a sweet richness.

Many restaurants serving primarily French, Italian, or Chinese cuisine also offer Tahitian dishes. One you will see virtually everywhere is *poisson cru,* French for "raw fish". It's the Tahitian-style salad of fresh tuna or mahi-mahi marinated in lime juice, cucumbers, onions, and tomatoes, all served in coconut cream. Chili is added to spice up a variation known as Chinese poisson cru.

Most of Tahiti's big resort hotels have at least one *tama'ara'a* (Tahitian feast) a week, followed by a traditional, hip-swinging dance show (see the box "A Most Indecent Song & Dance" in chapter 8).

SNACK BARS AND *LES ROULOTTES*

Tahiti has two McDonald's, but locals still prefer their plethora of snack bars, which they call "snacks." You can get a hamburger and usually poisson cru, but the most popular item is the *casse-croûte,* a sandwich made from a crusty French baguette and ham, tuna, *roti* (roast pork), *hachis* (hamburger), lettuce, tomatoes, and cucumbers—or even spaghetti. A casse-croûte usually costs about 300CFP (US$3) or less.

Also in this category are *les roulottes*—or portable meal wagons. A friend of mine says he hates the idea of dining in a parking lot, but les roulottes are one of the best values here, with meals seldom topping 1,500CFP (US$15). They roll out after dark on most islands. The carnival-like ambience they create on the Papeete waterfront makes them a highlight of any visit to the city (see "Don't Miss *Les Roulottes"* in chapter 8).

MONEY-SAVING TIPS

Despite the high prices, you don't have to go broke dining here. In addition to finding the nearest "snack," here are some ways to eat well for the least money:

- Do not eat at the resort hotel dining rooms, which charge a premium for food and drink. For example, a graze of the breakfast buffet can easily cost 3,000CFP (US$30) or more per person. You can have a perfectly good breakfast for less than half that at a snack bar or patisserie.
- Likewise, do not buy a hotel meal package except on remote islands, where your resort's restaurant is your only choice. Dining out is as much a part of the French Polynesian experience as is snorkeling.
- Order breakfast from room service if you don't want to go out and your hotel restaurant serves only an expensive buffet. Room service menus usually are *a la carte,* meaning you can order individual items whose total may be much less than the full buffet price.
- Dine at *restaurants conventionné,* which get breaks on the government's high duty on imported alcoholic beverages. Wine and mixed drinks in these establishments cost significantly less than elsewhere. You can also order *vin ordinaire* (table wine) served in a carafe to save money. The chef buys good-quality wine in bulk and passes the savings on to you.
- Take advantage of *plats du jour* (daily specials), especially at lunch, and *prix-fixe* (fixed priced) menus, often called "tourist menus." These three- or four-course offerings are usually made from fresh produce direct from the market.
- Consider sharing a starter course. Unlike some American menus, which list the main course as an "entrée," here an entrée is the first course, and it is likely to be a more substantial serving than an American "appetizer." If you have a light appetite, an entrée could suffice as your only course, or you can share one with your mate or a friend. I discreetly glance at other tables to check portion sizes before ordering.
- Make your own snacks or perhaps a picnic lunch to enjoy at the beach. Every village has at least one grocery store. Fresh loaves of French bread cost about 55CFP (55¢) each, and most stores carry cheeses, deli meats, vegetables, and other sandwich makings, many imported from France. Locally brewed Hinano beers sell for about 200CFP (US$2) or less in grocery stores, versus 500CFP (US$5) or more at the hotel bars, and bottles of decent French wine cost a fraction of restaurant prices.

FAST FACTS: French Polynesia

The following facts apply to French Polynesia in general. For more specific information, see the "Fast Facts" sections in chapters 8 through 11.

American Express The territory's one full-service representative is in Papeete. See "Fast Facts" in chapter 8.

Bookstores Only Tahiti and Moorea have well-stocked bookstores (see "Fast Facts" in chapters 8 and 9). Many hotel boutiques sell colorful picture books of the islands.

Business Hours Although many shops in downtown Papeete stay open over the lunch period, general shopping and business hours are from 7:30 to 11:30am and from 2 to 5pm Monday to Friday, 8am to noon on Saturday. In addition to regular hours, most grocery stores also are open from 2 to 6pm Saturday and from 6 to 8am on Sunday.

Camera/Film Photographic film and color-print processing are widely available.

Climate See "When to Go—Climate, Holidays & Events," earlier in this chapter.

Clothing Evening attire for men is usually a shirt and slacks; women typically wear a long, brightly colored dress (slacks or long skirts help to keep biting sand flies away from your ankles). Women sunbathe topless at most beaches (although I saw more exposed bums than boobs during my recent visit). Shorts are acceptable during the day almost everywhere. Outside Papeete, the standard attire for women is the colorful wraparound sarong known in Tahitian as a *pareu*, which can be tied in a multitude of ways into dresses, blouses, or skirts.

Drug Laws Plenty of pot may be grown up in the hills, but possession and use of dangerous drugs and narcotics are subject to long jail terms.

Electricity Electrical power is 220 volts, 50 cycles, and the plugs are the French kind with two round, skinny prongs. Most hotels have 110-volt outlets for shavers only, so you will need a converter and adapter plugs for other appliances. Some hotels, especially those on the outer islands, have their own generators, so ask at the reception desk what voltage is supplied.

E-mail The only local Internet provider is **MANA** (© **50.88.88;** www.mana.pf). No international Internet service provider, such as AOL or Earthlink, has a local access number here. You can go to cybercafes on the main islands (see "Fast Facts" in chapters 8–11), and most hotels and resorts have computer terminals you can use—at a cost, of course. Many have ADSL connections, which are not as fast as DSL or cable access in the U.S. and other countries but are speedier than dial-up connections.

If you bring your laptop, you can easily dial up from your hotel room using MANA's "anonymous" service. When setting up a new Network Connection (see the "Configuring Your Laptop" box in chapter 2), type in **0,368888** as the local access telephone number (0 is the number used to reach an outside line in all hotels here). When you make your first connection, enter *both* your name and your password as **anonymous.** (If your first try fails, retype both in all capital letters.) MANA charges 85CFP (US85¢) per minute for access time, and the cost of the local call also will be billed to your room. The hotel may well add an additional charge, so it can become very expensive very quickly.

Embassies/Consulates The **United States** has a consular agent here (℃ **50.80.95;** fax 50.80.96; usconsular@mail.pf), whose main function is to facilitate local residents in applying for visas from the U.S. embassy in Suva, Fiji. Australia, Austria, Belgium, Chile, Denmark, Finland, Germany, Italy, Monaco, New Zealand, Norway, the Netherlands, South Korea, Sweden, and the United Kingdom have honorary consulates in Papeete. Tahiti Tourisme has their phone numbers (see "Visitor Information & Entry Requirements," earlier in this chapter).

Emergencies/Police If you are in a hotel, contact the staff. Otherwise, the emergency **police** phone number is ℃ **17** throughout the territory.

Etiquette Even though many women go topless and wear the skimpiest of bikini bottoms at the beach, the Tahitians have a sense of propriety similar to what you find in any Western nation. Don't offend them by engaging in behavior that would not be permissible at home.

Gambling You can play "Lotto," the French national lottery.

Healthcare Highly qualified specialists practice on Tahiti, where some clinics possess state-of-the-art diagnostic and treatment equipment; nevertheless, public hospitals tend to be crowded with local residents, who get free care. Most visitors use private doctors or clinics. English-speaking physicians are on call by larger hotels. Each of the smaller islands has at least one infirmary (see "Fast Facts" in chapters 9–11). American health insurance plans are not recognized, so remember to get receipts at the time of treatment.

Hitchhiking Thumbing rides is possible in the rural parts of Tahiti and on the outer islands. Women traveling alone should be extremely cautious.

Insects There are no dangerous insects in French Polynesia. The only real nuisances are mosquitoes and tiny, nearly invisible sand flies known locally as "no-nos," elsewhere as "no-seeums." They appear at dusk on most beaches here. Wear trousers or long skirts and plenty of insect repellent (especially on the feet and ankles) to ward off the no-nos. If you forget to bring insect repellent along, look for the Off or Dolmix Pic brands at the pharmacies.

Liquor Laws Regulations about where and when you can drink are liberal. Anyone over 18 can purchase alcoholic beverages, and some bars in Papeete stay open until the very wee hours on weekends. Official *conventionné* restaurants and hotels pay reduced duty on imported alcoholic beverages, so they will cost less there than at local bars and nightclubs.

Mail Letters usually take about a week to 10 days to reach overseas destinations in either direction. Mailing addresses in French Polynesia consist of post office boxes (*boîtes postales* in French, or B.P. for short) but no street numbers or names. Local addresses have postal codes, which are written in front of the city or town. (If you send a letter to French Polynesia from the U.S., do *not* put the postal code behind the name of the town; otherwise the U.S. Postal Service may dispatch it to a zip code within the United States.)

Maps Tahiti Tourisme distributes free maps of each island. Each weekly edition of the free *Tahiti Beach Press* carries artistic island and Papeete maps. Libraire

Vaima, a large bookstore in Papeete's Vaima Centre, sells several *cartes touristiques*. The most detailed map is *Tahiti: Archipel de la Société*, published by the Institut Géographique National. Although it dates to 1994 and doesn't include all new roads on Tahiti, it shows all the Society Islands in detail, including topographic features. The full-color *Guide Touristique de Tahiti et ses Isles* shows the precise locations of all hotels and pensions.

Newspapers/Magazines The *Tahiti Beach Press*, an English-language weekly devoted to news of Tahiti's tourist industry, runs features of interest to tourists and advertisements for hotels, restaurants, real estate agents, car-rental firms, and other businesses that cater to tourists. Establishments that buy ads in it give away copies free. The daily newspapers, *La Dépêche de Tahiti* and *Les Nouvelles*, are in French. Le Kiosk in front of the Vaima Centre on boulevard Pomare in Papeete sells some international newspapers and magazines.

Radio/TV French Polynesia has government-operated AM radio stations with programming in French and Tahitian. Several private AM and FM stations in Papeete play mostly American and British musical numbers in English; the announcers, however, speak French. Two government-owned television stations broadcast in French. Most hotels pick up a local satellite service, which carries CNN International in English. The government-owned radio and TV stations can be received throughout the territory via satellite. Moorea has an American-style cable system with CNN, ESPN, and HBO, all in English.

Safety Do not leave valuables in your hotel room or unattended anywhere. Street crimes against tourists are still rare, and you should be safe after dark in the busy parks along boulevard Pomare on Papeete's waterfront. Friends of mine who live here, however, don't stroll away from the boulevard after dark. For that matter, stay alert everywhere after dusk. Women should not wander alone on deserted beaches any time, since some Polynesian men may still consider such behavior to be an invitation for instant amorous activity.

Taxes Local residents do not pay income taxes; instead, the government imposes stiff duties on most imported goods, and levies a value-added tax (VAT, or *TVA* in French) on most goods and services, including restaurant and hotel bills. Only the TVA on set pearls is refundable in the European fashion (see "Shopping" in chapter 8). These taxes will not be added to your bills in the American fashion, but you will see the 10% tax tacked to your hotel bills and another 50CFP to 200CFP (50¢–$2) per night for the Tahiti, Moorea, and Bora Bora communes.

Telephone/Fax Direct international dialing is available to all telephone and fax numbers in French Polynesia. The international country code is **689**. There are no domestic area codes.

Public pay phones are located at all post offices and are fairly numerous elsewhere on Tahiti, less so on the other islands. You must have a *télécarte* to call from public pay phones (coin phones are history here). Digital read-outs on the phones tell you how many *unites* you have left on a card. The cards are sold at all post offices and by most hotel front desks and many shops in 1,500CFP, 2,000CFP, and 5,000CFP (US$15, US$20, and US$50) sizes.

To call overseas, dial **00,** then the country code (**1** for the U.S. and Canada), followed by the area code and phone number. Dial © **19** if you need assistance making an overseas call. For directory information (*service des renseignements*), dial © **12.** The operators speak English.

The direct-dial charge from French Polynesia to the U.S., Europe, Australia, and New Zealand is 103CFP (US$1.03) per minute. You can make them through your hotel, though with a surcharge, which can more than double the fee.

You can look up numbers online at **www.annuaireopt.pf** (it's in French).

You need a GSM cellphone for it to work in French Polynesia (see "The 21st Century Traveler," in chapter 2). You can rent a phone from **Vini** (© **48.13.13;** www.vini.pf). If you have a GSM phone, you can buy pre-paid SIM cards from stores displaying the Vini sign. The least expensive costs about 5,500CFP (US$55) and includes 30 minutes of outgoing calls (incoming are free). **CellularAbroad** (© **800/287-3020;** www.cellularabroad.com) of Santa Monica, CA, rents GSM phones and sells prepaid SIM cards for French Polynesia.

Time Local time in the most visited islands is 11 hours behind Greenwich Mean Time. I find it easier to think of it as 5 hours behind U.S. Eastern Standard Time or 2 hours behind Pacific Standard Time. Translated: When it's noon in California, it's 10am in Tahiti. When it's noon on the U.S. East Coast, it's 7am in Tahiti. Add 1 hour to the Tahiti time during daylight saving time.

The Marquesas Islands are 30 minutes ahead of the rest of the territory.

Since French Polynesia is on the east side of the international date line, Tahiti has the same date as the United States, the Cook Islands, and the Samoas, and is 1 day behind Australia, New Zealand, Fiji, and Tonga.

Tipping Despite inroads (credit card forms now have a "tip" line here), tipping is considered contrary to the Polynesian custom of hospitality. In other words, tipping is not expected unless the service has been truly beyond the call of duty. Some hotels accept contributions to the staff Christmas fund.

Water Tap water is consistently safe to drink only in Papeete and on Bora Bora. Well water in the Tuamotu islands tends to be brackish; rainwater is used there for drinking. You can buy bottled water at every grocery. The local brands Vaimato and Eau Royal are much less expensive than imported French waters.

Weights/Measures French Polynesia is on the metric system.

8

Tahiti

Large and abundant, Tahiti is the modern traveler's gateway to French Polynesia, just as it was for the late 18th-century discoverers who used it as a base to explore the South Pacific. In later years, the capital city, **Papeete,** became a major shipping crossroads. Located on Tahiti's northwest corner, the city curves around one of the region's busiest harbors.

There wasn't even a village where Papeete now stands until the 1820s, when Queen Pomare set up headquarters along the shore and merchant ships and whalers began using the harbor in preference to the less protected Matavai Bay to the east. A simple town of stores, bars, and billiard parlors sprung up quickly, and between 1825 and 1829 it was a veritable den of iniquity. It grew even more after the French made it their headquarters upon taking over Tahiti in 1842. A fire nearly destroyed the town in 1884, and waves churned up by a cyclone did severe damage in 1906. In 1914 two German warships shelled the harbor and sank the French navy's *Zélée.*

Papeete is a very different place today. Vehicles of every sort now crowd boulevard Pomare, the broad avenue along Papeete's waterfront, and the four-lane expressway linking the city to the trendy suburban districts of Punaauia and Paea on the west coast. Indeed, suburbs are creeping up the mountains overlooking the city and sprawling for miles along the coast in both directions. The island is so developed and so traffic-clogged that many Tahitians commute up to 2 hours in each direction on weekdays. Many are moving to Moorea, a mere 30-minute ferry ride away.

But there is a bright side to Tahiti's development: Using money from a post-nuclear-testing economic restructuring fund, Papeete has done a remarkable job in refurbishing its waterfront, including a cruise-ship terminal and a classy park where families gather and the city celebrates its festivals. It's a real treat now to walk along the promenade fronting this storied South Seas port.

Papeete's chic shops, busy Municipal Market, and lively mix of French, Polynesian, and Chinese cultures are sure to invigorate any urbanite. If you're looking for old-time Polynesia, on the other hand, you will find it on Tahiti's rural east and south coasts and especially on its peninsula, Tahiti Iti. Its three fine museums are reason enough for me to spend a day or two here.

Even if you plan to leave immediately for Moorea, Bora Bora, and the other less-developed islands, you will have to spend at least a few hours here, since all international flights land at Faaa on the northwest coast of this legendary and still very beautiful island.

1 Arriving & Getting Around

ARRIVING & DEPARTING

ARRIVING

All international flights arrive at **Tahiti-Faaa International Airport,** 7km (4 miles) west of downtown Papeete. Once you've cleared Customs, you will see a **visitor information booth** straight ahead. Start there for maps and other information. Group tour operators will be holding signs announcing their presence. Pick up some pocket money at **Banque de Polynésie,** to the left as you exit Customs, or at **Banque Socredo** to the right. Both have ATMs, and Banque Socredo has a machine that will change U.S. dollars and other major notes.

I have spent many an hour waiting for flights at the open-air, 24-hour **snack bar** to the right. There's a **McDonald's** next to Air Tahiti's domestic departure lounge, also to the right.

GETTING TO YOUR HOTEL   Unless you're on a package tour or your hotel has arranged a transfer, your only choice of transportation to your hotel between 10pm and 6am will be a **taxi.** Official fares from 8pm to 6am are 1,500CFP (US$15) to the hotels on the west coast; 2,500CFP (US$25) to downtown. Add 100CFP (US$1) for each bag.

If you arrive when they are running and are in good physical condition, you can haul your baggage across the parking lot in front of the terminal, climb the stairs to the main road, and flag down a local bus. If you're driving a rental car, take Route 1 west to the InterContinental Resort Tahiti, the Sofitel Maeva Beach, or Le Meridien Tahiti. Route 1 east passes the Sheraton Hotel Tahiti on its way to downtown Papeete. If you're going to downtown, watch for the Route 5 signs directing you to the express-way connecting Papeete to the west coast. See "Getting Around," below, for more information.

BAGGAGE STORAGE   Most hotels will keep your baggage for free. The airport's **baggage storage room** is in the parking lot in front of the international departures gate. It's the small building behind the pavilion where Tahitian women sell leis and flower crowns. Charges range from 640CFP (US$6.40) per day for regular-size bags to 1,100CFP (US$11) for large items such as surfboards and bicycles. The room opens 2 hours before every international flight departs. Regular hours are Monday 4am to 7pm, Tuesday to Thursday 5am to 11pm, Saturday 5am to 12:30am, Sunday and holidays 1pm to 12:30am. MasterCard and Visa credit cards are accepted.

DEPARTING

Check-in time for departing international flights is 3 hours before flight time; for domestic flights, be there 2 hours in advance. All of your bags must be screened for both international and domestic flights leaving Papeete. (There are no security proce-dures at the outer island airstrips.)

There is no airport departure tax for either international or domestic flights.

Note: There is no bank or currency exchange bureau in the international departure lounge, so change your money before clearing immigration.

GETTING AROUND

Except for the Route 5 expressway between Papeete and Punaauia, the island's highway system consists primarily of a paved road running for 116km (72 miles) around Tahiti Nui and halfway down each side of Tahiti Iti. From the isthmus, a road partially lined

Tahiti

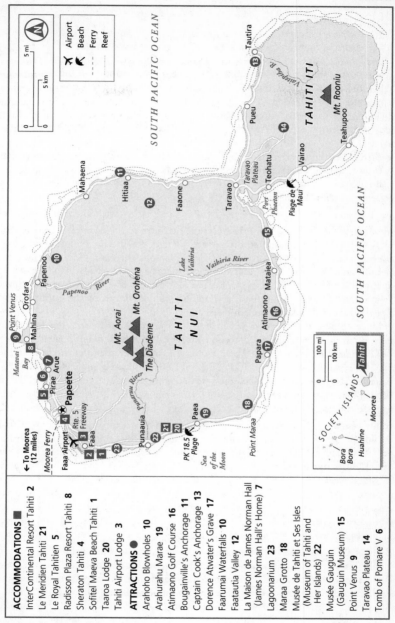

ACCOMMODATIONS ■
InterContinental Resort Tahiti **2**
Le Meridien Tahiti **21**
Le Royal Tahitien **5**
Radisson Plaza Resort Tahiti **8**
Sheraton Tahiti **4**
Sofitel Maeva Beach Tahiti **1**
Taaroa Lodge **20**
Tahiti Airport Lodge **3**

ATTRACTIONS ●
Arahoho Blowholes **10**
Arahurahu Marae **19**
Atimaono Golf Course **16**
Bougainville's Anchorage **11**
Captain Cook's Anchorage **13**
Dorence Atwater's Grave **17**
Faarumai Waterfalls **10**
Faatautia Valley **12**
La Maison de James Norman Hall
(James Norman Hall's Home) **7**
Lagoonarium **23**
Maraa Grotto **18**
Musée de Tahiti et Ses Isles
(Museum of Tahiti and
Her Islands) **22**
Musée Gauguin
(Gauguin Museum) **15**
Point Venus **9**
Taravao Plateau **14**
Tomb of Pomare V **6**

209

Impressions

Edward called for him in a rickety trap drawn by an old mare, and they drove along a road that ran by the sea. On each side of it were plantations, coconut and vanilla; now and then they saw a great mango, its fruit yellow and red and purple among the massy green of the leaves, now and then they had a glimpse of the lagoon, smooth and blue, with here and there a tiny islet graceful with tall palms.
                                    —W. Somerset Maugham, "The Fall of Edward Bernard," 1921

with trees heads up to the high, cool Plateau of Taravao, with pastures and pines that look more like provincial France than the South Pacific.

Be prepared to deal with numerous **traffic circles** in and near Papeete. You must give way to traffic already in the circles.

BY BUS

Although it might appear from the number of vehicles scurrying around Papeete that everyone owns a car or scooter, the average Tahitian gets around by local bus. Modern buses have replaced all but a few of Tahiti's famous *le trucks,* those colorful vehicles so named because the passenger compartments are gaily painted wooden cabins mounted on the rear of flatbed trucks. The last of them operate between downtown Papeete and Centre Moana Nui, a shopping complex south of the Sofitel Maeva Beach. Elsewhere look for modern buses.

Once upon a time le trucks would stop for you almost anywhere, but today you must catch them and the buses at official stops (called *arrêt le bus* in French).

The villages or districts served by each bus are written on the sides and front of the bus. **Fares** within Papeete are 130CFP (US$1.30) until 6pm and 200CFP (US$2) thereafter. A trip to the end of the line in either direction costs about 750CFP (US$7.50).

BUSES GOING WEST   The few remaining le trucks and all short-distance buses going west are painted red and white. They line up on rue du Maréchal-Foch behind the Municipal Market and travel along rue du Général-de-Gaulle, which becomes rue du Commandant-Destremeau and later route de-l'Ouest, the road that circles the island. Buses run along this route as far as the Centre Moana Nui (south of the Sofitel Maeva Beach) Monday to Friday at least every 30 minutes from 6am to 6pm, once an hour between 6pm and midnight. Except for le trucks serving tourists at the west coast hotels, there is irregular service on Saturday, none on Sunday. Trucks and buses labeled Faaa, Maeva Beach, and Outuamaru pass the airport and the Sheraton Hotel Tahiti and InterContinental Resort Tahiti.

BUSES GOING EAST   Short-distance buses going east are painted green and white. They line up in the block west of the Banque de Polynésie on boulevard Pomare, opposite the cruise ship terminal and near the Municipal Market and rue Paul Gauguin. They proceed out of town via avenue du Prince-Hinoi, passing the Le Royal Tahitien Hotel cutoff and the Radisson Plaza Resort Tahiti on their way to Pirae, Arue, and Mahina. They run frequently from 6am to 5pm as far as the Mahina. None runs at night, so you must rent a car or take a taxi to and from the Radisson and Le Royal Tahitien after dark and on weekends.

LONG-DISTANCE BUSES   Buses going in either direction to Tahiti's south coast and Tahiti Iti are painted orange and white. They line up next to the Manava Tahiti Visitors Bureau, on boulevard Pomare at rue Paul Gauguin. They run on the hour from 6am to noon Monday to Friday; there is only one afternoon trip, at 4:30pm back to the villages. They do not run nights or weekends.

BY TAXI

Papeete has a large number of taxis, although they can be hard to find during the morning and evening rush hours, especially if it's raining. You can flag one down on the street or find them gathered at one of several stations. The largest gathering points are on boulevard **Pomare near the market** (© 42.02.92) and at the **Centre Vaima** (© 42.60.77). Most taxi drivers understand some English.

Taxi fares are set by the government and are posted on a board at the Centre Vaima taxi stand on boulevard Pomare. Few cabs have meters, so be sure that you and the driver have agreed on a fare before you get in. Note that *all fares are increased by at least 20% from 8pm to 6am.* A trip anywhere within downtown Papeete during the day starts at 1,000CFP (US$10) and goes up 120CFP (US$1.20) for every kilometer after the first one during the day, 240CFP (US$2.40) at night. As a rule of thumb, the fare from the Papeete hotels to the airport or vice versa is about 1,700CFP (US$17) during the day; from the west coast hotels to the airport, about 1,000CFP (US$10). A trip to the Gauguin Museum on the south coast costs 10,000CFP (US$100) one-way. The fare for a 4-hour journey all the way around Tahiti is about 16,000CFP (US$160). Drivers may charge an extra 50CFP to 100CFP (50¢–US$1) per bag of luggage.

BY RENTAL CAR

Avis (© 800/331-1212 or 41.93.93; www.avis.com), **Hertz** (© 800/654-3131 or 42.04.72; www.hertz.com), and **Europcar** (© 800/227-7368 or 45.24.24; www.europcar.com) all have agencies on Tahiti. Europcar is slightly less expensive than the others, with rates starting at 1,850CFP (US$18.50) a day plus 41CFP (US41¢) per kilometer, or 8,600CFP (US$86) a day with unlimited kilometers. You get a better deal on the unlimited rate if you rent for more than 1 day. Collision damage waiver insurance costs an additional 1,500CFP (US$15) a day on the per-kilometer plans but is included in the unlimited kilometer rate.

The best local rental company is **Daniel Location de Voitures,** in the Faaa airport terminal (© 81.96.32; fax 85.62.64; daniel.location@mail.pf). Its unlimited kilometer rates start at 8,020CFP (US$80) per day.

DRIVING HINTS   In Papeete priority is given to vehicles entering an intersection from the right side. This rule does not apply on the four-lane boulevard Pomare along the waterfront, but be careful everywhere else because drivers on your right will expect

---

(Tips Around Tahiti by Bus?

Although you had to walk across the Taravao isthmus, it once was possible to circumnavigate Tahiti by le truck in 1 day. Today the long distance buses run only from 6am to noon weekdays, so it is virtually impossible. I recommend renting a vehicle or taking a guided tour to go around the island.

> **Tips Get Unlimited Kilometers If Driving Around Tahiti**
>
> If you rent a car, consider the unlimited kilometer rate if you intend to drive around Tahiti, since the round-island road is 114km (72 miles) long, not counting Tahiti Iti.

you to yield the right of way at intersections where there are no stop signs or traffic signals. Outside of Papeete, priority is given to vehicles that are already on the round-island road.

The main round-island road is a divided highway east and west of Papeete, which means that to make a left turn, you will have to turn around at the next traffic circle and drive back to your destination.

PARKING   Parking spaces can be as scarce as chicken teeth in downtown Papeete during the day. You must pay to park in most on-street spaces from 8am to 5pm Monday to Saturday, which costs 100CFP (US$1) per hour, payable by tickets sold at numerous shops and newsstands displaying signs saying **Parc Chec.** Put the *parc chec* ticket on the dashboard inside the vehicle, not outside under the windshield wiper, where it will be stolen. There are several municipal parking garages, including one under the Hotel de Ville (Town Hall); enter off rue Collette between rue Paul Gauguin and rue d'Ecole des Frères. Some large buildings, such as the Centre Vaima, have garages in their basements. Frankly, if I'm not staying downtown, I usually leave my car at the hotel and take a bus into the city during workdays.

FAST FACTS: Tahiti

The following facts apply specifically to Tahiti. For more information, see *"Fast Facts:* French Polynesia" in chapter 7.

American Express The American Express representative is **Tahiti Tours,** on rue Jeanne-d'Arc (© **54.02.50;** fax 42.25.15), across from the Centre Vaima in downtown Papeete. The mailing address is B.P. 627, 98713 Papeete, Tahiti, French Polynesia.

Bookstores **Librairie Vaima,** on the second level of the Centre Vaima (© **45. 57.57),** has some English-language novels and a wide selection of books on French Polynesia, many of them in English and some of them rare editions. It also has maps of the islands. **Le Kiosk** in front of the Centre Vaima sells the *International Herald Tribune, Time,* and *Newsweek,* as does **La Maison de la Presse,** on boulevard Pomare at Quartier du Commerce (© **50.93.93).**

Business Hours Although some shops stay open over the long lunch break, most businesses are open Monday to Friday from 8 to 11:30am and 2 to 5pm, give or take 30 minutes, since "flex hours" help alleviate Tahiti's traffic problem. Saturday hours are 8 to 11:30am, although some shops in the Centre Vaima stay open Saturday afternoon. The Papeete Municipal Market is a roaring beehive from 5 to 7am on Sunday, and many of the nearby general stores are open during those hours. Except for some small groceries, most other stores are closed on Sunday.

Camera/Film Film and 1-hour color print processing are available at several stores in downtown Papeete. One of the best is **Tahiti Photo,** in the Centre Vaima (℗ **42.97.34**), where you can get help in English.

Currency Exchange **Banque de Polynésie, Banque de Tahiti,** and **Banque Socredo** each has at least one branch with ATMs on boulevard Pomare and in many suburban locations where you can cash traveler's checks. See "Money" in chapter 7 for more information.

Drugstores **Pharmacie du Vaima,** on rue du Général-de-Gaulle at rue Georges La Garde behind the Centre Vaima (℗ **42.97.73**), is owned and operated by English-speaking Nguyen Ngoc-Tran, whose husband runs Pharmacie Tran on Moorea. Pharmacies rotate night duty, so ask your hotel staff to find out which one is open after dark.

E-mail Every hotel here has Internet access for its guests, but you will have more fun at American expatriate Nina Piermatti's **Tiki Soft Café,** on rue Paul Gauguin at the Rond Point de L'Est traffic circle (℗ **88.93.98**). Nina has computer terminals where you can check your e-mail while sipping a cup of French roast java or a glass of freshly squeezed fruit juice (or munching on a healthy salad or sandwich). Dial-up access costs 250CFP (US$2.50) for 15 minutes, 1,000CFP (US$10) for an hour, while high-speed or wireless laptop connects are 350CFP (US$3.50) for 15 minutes, 1,000CFP (US$10) per hour. Open Monday to Wednesday 8am to 8:30pm, Thursday and Friday 8:30am to 10:30pm. Nina has wine tasting here Wednesday from 5 to 8pm. Friday night is gay friendly.

Cybernesia Tahiti, on the second level of the Vaima Centre (℗ **85.43.67**), has both dial-up and wireless access for 20CFP (US20¢) for the first 10 minutes, 15 CFP (US15¢) per minute thereafter. It has English keyboards and the Skype telephone program on some of its computers, and it will burn your digital photos to CD. Open Monday to Friday 8am to 6pm, Saturday 9am to 4pm. **La Maison de la Presse,** on boulevard Pomare at Quartier du Commerce (℗ **50.93.93**), also has English keyboards. It charges 250CFP (US$2.50) for each 15 minutes online.

If you need to check your e-mail after dark, the **business center** at Faaa airport (℗ **83.63.88**) is open until midnight Monday to Saturday (from 8am Monday, Wednesday, and Friday; from 6am Tuesday, Thursday, and Saturday). It charges 300CFP (US$3) for 15 minutes, and it will put your photos on CDs.

Emergencies/Police Consult with your hotel staff. The **emergency police** telephone number is ℗ **17** (but don't expect the person on the other end of the line to speak English). The **central gendarmerie** is at the inland terminus of avenue Bruat (℗ **42.02.02**).

Eyeglasses Papeete has several opticians, including **Optique Vaima** (℗ **42.77. 54**) in the Centre Vaima.

Hairdressers/Barbers The staff of the beauty salons in the InterContinental Resort Tahiti speaks English.

Healthcare Both **Clinque Cardella** (℗ **42.80.10**), on rue Anne-Marie-Javouhey, and **Clinic Paofai** (℗ **43.77.00**), on boulevard Pomare, have highly trained specialists and some state-of-the-art equipment. They are open 24 hours.

Information **Tahiti Manava visitors bureau** (✆ **50.57.12;** www.tahiti-manava.pf), in the cruise-ship welcoming center on the waterfront on boulevard Pomare at the foot of rue Paul Gauguin, is open 7:30am to 5pm Monday to Friday, 1 to 4pm Saturday, 8am to noon on holidays. It's also open on Sunday if cruise ships are in port.

Laundry **Laverie Gauguin,** 64 rue Paul Gauguin (✆ **43.71.59**), at Pont de l'Est, has wash-dry-fold service for 2,200CFP (US$22) a load. Open Monday to Friday 7am to 5:30pm.

Libraries The **Office Territorial D'Action Culturelle (Territorial Cultural Center)** on boulevard Pomare, west of downtown Papeete (✆ **42.88.50**), has a small library of mostly French books on the South Pacific and other topics. Hours are 8am to 5pm Monday to Friday, except on Wednesday when it closes at 4pm.

Post Office The main post office is on boulevard Pomare a block west of the Centre Vaima. Open from 7am to 6pm Monday through Friday, 8 to 11am Saturday. The branch post office at the Tahiti-Faaa International Airport terminal is open from 6 to 10:30am and noon to 2pm Monday through Friday, and from 6am to 9am on Saturday, Sunday, and holidays.

Restrooms Both **Tahua Vaite** (the park by the cruise-ship terminal at rue Paul Gauguin) and **Place Toata** on the western end of downtown have free and clean public toilets.

Safety Papeete has seen increasing street crime in recent years. The busy parks on boulevard Pomare along the waterfront generally are safe, but be very careful if you wander onto the side streets after dark.

Telephone/Fax The main post office, the cruise-ship terminal, and Place Toata all have pay phones, where you can use a *télécarte* to make local and international calls. See "Fast Facts" in chapter 7 for more information about pay phones and international calls.

Water You can drink the tap water in Papeete and its nearby suburbs, which includes all the hotels, but not out in the rural parts of Tahiti. Bottled water is available in all grocery stores.

2 Exploring Tahiti

Tahiti is shaped like a figure eight lying on its side. The "eyes" of the eight are two extinct, eroded volcanoes joined by the flat Isthmus of Taravao. The larger, western part of the island is known as *Tahiti Nui* ("Big Tahiti" in Tahitian), and the smaller eastern peninsula beyond the isthmus is named *Tahiti Iti* ("Little Tahiti"). Together they comprise about 670km (416 square miles), about two-thirds the size of the island of Oahu in Hawaii.

Tahiti Nui's volcano has been eroded over the eons so that now long ridges, separating deep valleys, march down from the crater's ancient rim to the coast far below. The rim itself is still intact, except on the north side, where the Papenoo River has cut its way to the sea. The highest peaks, **Mount Orohena,** 2,206m (7,353 ft.), and

Mount Aora, 2,045m (6,817 ft.), tower above Papeete. Another summit, Mount Te Tara O Maiao, or the **Diadème,** which stands 1,308m (4,360 ft.), can be seen from the eastern suburb of Pirae but not from downtown.

With the exception of the east coast of Tahiti Iti, where great cliffs fall into the lagoon, and a few places where the ridges end abruptly at the water's edge, the island is skirted by a flat coastal plain. Tahiti's residents live on this plain, in the valleys, or on the hills adjacent to the plain.

THE TOP ATTRACTIONS

Arahurahu Marae ☆☆   Arahurahu is the only *marae*—an ancient temple or meeting place—in all of Polynesia that has been fully restored, and it is maintained like a museum. Although not nearly as impressive as the great lagoonside marae on Huahine and Raiatea (see chapter 11), this is Tahiti's best example of ancient Polynesian temples and meeting places, and its exhibit boards do a good job of explaining the significance of each part. For example, the stone pens near the entrance were used to keep the pigs to be sacrificed to the gods. Arahurahu is used for the reenactment of old Polynesian ceremonies during the July *Heiva Nui* celebrations.

Paea, 23km (14 miles) west of Papeete. No phone. Free admission. Open daily 24 hr.

Lagoonarium de Tahiti   If you won't be diving or snorkeling in the lagoons, then you will enjoy a visit to this underwater viewing room surrounded by pens containing reef sharks, sea turtles, and many colorful species of tropical fish. It's part of the Captain Bligh Restaurant and Bar (see "Where to Dine," later). The view of Moorea from here is terrific.

Punaauia, 12km (7 miles) west of Papeete. © **43.62.90.** Admission 500CFP (US$5) adults, 300CFP (US$3) children under 12. Daily 9am–5:30pm.

La Maison James Norman Hall (James Norman Hall's Home) ☆☆☆   This marvelous museum is a required stop for all of us who have ever dreamed of writing successful novels in a lovely lagoonside house. James Norman Hall lived most of his adult life here in Arue, now a suburb of Papeete. Hall was a U.S. army pilot in France during World War I, when he was shot down behind German lines and held prisoner. He met Charles Nordhoff in Paris shortly after the war, and together they wrote *The Lafayette Flying Corp,* the story of the American unit that fought for France before the U.S. entered the war. In 1920 they moved to Tahiti, where they sailed around on copra schooners and wrote *Faery Lands of the South Seas.* In 1932 they published *Mutiny on the Bounty,* the first of their three novels about the incident and its aftermath (*Men Against the Sea* and *Pitcairn's Island* are the others). It was turned into the 1935 movie starring Clark Gable and Charles Laughton, and the 1962 remake with Marlon Brando. Hall and Nordhoff penned several more books about the islands, including *Hurricane,* which also was turned into two movies.

Impressions

To those who insist that all picturesque towns look like Siena or Stratford-on-Avon, Papeete will be disappointing, but to others who love the world in all its variety, the town is fascinating. My own judgment: any town that wakes each morning to see Moorea is rich in beauty.

—James A. Michener, *Return to Paradise,* 1951

Hall and his wife, Sarah Teraireia Winchester Hall, lived their entire married lives here. Their family manages the home and has stocked it with his typewriter, original manuscripts, and tons of heirlooms and memorabilia. (One of the three Oscars won by his son, the late Hollywood cinematographer Conrad L. Hall, is here.) His office is adorned with photographs of him with Zane Grey, Robert Dean Frisbee, and other men-of-the-pen when they dropped by for visits. One of Hall's grandsons still lives on the property, so you will need permission to visit his grave on the hill above the house. Staff members lead 30-minute tours and sell coffee and soft drinks. The free parking lot is across the highway beside the lagoon; if coming from Papeete you'll have to turn around at the next traffic circle and come back to reach it.

Arue, 5½km (3¼ miles) east of Papeete. © **50.01.60.** www.jamesnormanhallhome.pf. Admission 600CFP (US$6). Tues–Sat 9am–4pm. Closed public holidays.

Marché Municipale (Municipal Market) ☆☆☆

An amazing array of fruits, vegetables, fish, meat, handicrafts, and other items are sold under the big tin pavilion of Papeete's bustling public market. Unwritten rules dictate that Tahitians sell fruits and traditional vegetables, such as taro and breadfruit, Chinese sell European and Chinese vegetables, and Chinese and Europeans serve as butchers and bakers. If your stomach can handle it, look for hogs' heads hanging in the butcher stalls. The market is busiest early in the mornings, but it's like a carnival here from 5 to 7am every Sunday, when people from the outlying areas of Tahiti, and even from the other islands, arrive to sell their produce. (*Note:* By 8am the pickings are slim.) A Tahitian string band plays during lunch at the upstairs snack bar, which purveys inexpensive island chow.

Papeete, between rue du 22 Septembre and rue François Cardella, 1 block inland from bd. Pomare. No phone. Free admission. Mon–Fri 5am–6pm, Sat 5am–1pm, Sun 4–8am.

Musée de Tahiti et Ses Isles (Museum of Tahiti and Her Islands) ☆☆☆

Set in a lagoonside coconut grove with a gorgeous view of Moorea, this ranks as one of the best museums in the South Pacific. On display is the geological history of the islands, including a terrific topographic map; their sea life, flora, and fauna; and the history and culture of their peoples. Exhibits are devoted to traditional weaving, tapa-cloth making, early tools, body ornaments, tattooing, fishing and horticultural techniques, religion and maraes, games and sports, warfare and arms, deaths and funerals, writers and missionaries (note the 1938 Tahitian Bible). Most, but not all, of the display legends are translated into English. Start in the air-conditioned exhibit hall to the left as you enter and proceed outside. Give yourself at least 30 minutes here, preferably an hour.

Punaauia, 15km (9 miles) west of Papeete. © **58.34.76.** Admission 600CFP (US$6) adults, free for children. Tues–Sun 9:30am–5:30pm. Turn toward the lagoon at the Total station and follow the signs.

Musée Gauguin (Gauguin Museum) ☆☆☆

This museum/memorial to Paul Gauguin, the French artist who lived in the Mataiea district from 1891 until 1893, owns a few of his sculptures, wood carvings, engravings, and a ceramic vase. It has an active program to borrow his major works, however, and one might be on display during your visit. Otherwise, the exhibits are dedicated to his life in French Polynesia. It's best to see them counterclockwise, starting at the gift shop, which sells excellent prints and reproductions of his works. The originals are in the first gallery. An interesting display in the last gallery shows who owns his works today. The museum has a lagoonside restaurant, although most visitors have lunch at the nearby Restaurant du Musée Gauguin, at PK 50.5 (see "The Circle Island Tour," below).

Fun Fact **Shipwrecked**

While researching the novel *Pitcairn's Island,* which he co-authored with Charles Nordhoff, James Norman Hall disappeared for several months in 1933 after being shipwrecked near Mangareva, between Tahiti and Pitcairn.

The museum is adjacent to the lush **Harrison W. Smith Jardin Botanique (Botanical Gardens),** which was started in 1919 by Harrison Smith, an American who left a career teaching physics at the Massachusetts Institute of Technology and moved to Tahiti. He died here in 1947. His gardens, which now belong to the public, are home to a plethora of tropical plants from around the world. This is the wettest part of Tahiti, so bring an umbrella.

Mataiea, 51km (32 miles) west of Papeete. *©* **57.10.58.** Museum admission 600CFP (US$6) adults, 300CFP (US$3) children 12–18. Gardens admission 600CFP (US$6), free for children under 12. Daily 9am–5pm.

Point Venus *🌺🌺🌺*   Capt. James Cook observed the transit of the planet Venus in 1769 at Point Venus, Tahiti's northernmost extremity. The low, sandy peninsula covered with ironwood (casuarina) trees is about 2km (1¼ miles) from the main road. Captains Wallis, Cook, and Bligh landed here after anchoring their ships offshore, behind the reef in Matavai Bay. Captain Cook made his observations of the transit of Venus across the sun in 1769 from a point between the black-sand beach and the meandering river that cuts the peninsula in two. The beach and the parklike setting around the white lighthouse, which was completed in 1868 (notwithstanding the 1867 date over the door), are popular for picnics. There is a snack bar, a souvenir and handicraft shop, and toilets.

Mahina, 10km (6 miles) east of Papeete. No phone. Free admission. Open daily 4am–7pm, snack bar and souvenir shop daily 8am–5pm.

WALKING TOUR   PAPEETE

Start:	Tahiti Manava visitors bureau
Finish:	Papeete Town Hall
Time:	2 hours
Best Time:	Early morning or late afternoon
Worst Time:	Midday, or Sunday when most establishments are closed

---

Begin at Tahiti Manava visitors bureau in Tahua Vaiete, the park by the cruise-ship dock, at the foot of rue Paul Gauguin. Stroll westward along Boulevard Pomare. Opposite the tuna boat dock stands Centre Vaima.

❶ Centre Vaima

The chic shops in Papeete's first shopping mall are a mecca for Papeete's French and European residents (the Municipal Market still attracts mostly Tahitians). The infamous Quinn's Bar stood in the block east of the Centre Vaima, where the Noa Noa boutique is now. The Centre Vaima takes its name from the Vaima Restaurant, everyone's favorite eatery in those days, which it replaced.

Across the four-lane boulevard from the Vaima is the wooden boardwalk along the Quay.

❷ The Quay

Cruising yachts from around the world congregate here from April to September, and resident boats are docked here all year. Beyond them, on the other side of the harbor, is **Motu Uta,** once a small natural island belonging to Queen Pomare but now home of the wharves and warehouses of Papeete's shipping port. The reef on the other side has been filled to make a breakwater and to connect Motu Uta by road to **Fare Ute,** the industrial area and French naval base to the right. The interisland boats dock alongside the filled-in reef, and their cargoes of *copra* (dried coconut meat) are taken to a mill at Fare Ute, where coconut oil is extracted and later shipped overseas to be used in cosmetics.

Walk west along the waterfront, past the main post office, next to which is Parc Bougainville.

❸ Parc Bougainville

This shady park next to the post office is named for the French explorer who found Tahiti a little too late to get credit for its discovery. Two naval cannons flank the statue of Bougainville: The one nearest the post office was on the *Seeadler,* Count von Luckner's infamous World War I German raider, which ran aground in the Cook Islands after terrifying the British and French territories of the South Pacific. The other was on the French navy's *Zélée.* Bougainville's statue stands between the guns.

Walk westward to the traffic circle at the foot of avenue Bruat.

❹ Place Jacques Chirac

Few projects exemplify Papeete's vast road improvements more than the big traffic circle, under which pass the four busy lanes of boulevard Pomare. On the harbor side, the semicircular-shaped park is known as Place Jacques Chirac, whose name created quite a stir because French tradition says not to name a public place after a living president. Underneath is a public parking garage. The park is the beginning of recent landfills, which have

replaced a black-sand beach that used to run west of here.

Keep going west along the waterfront, to rue l'Arthémise, where you can't miss the big beige church on the mountain side of the boulevard.

❺ Eglise Evangélique

An impressive steeple sits atop Eglise Evangélique, the largest Protestant church in French Polynesia. The local evangelical sect grew out of the early work by the London Missionary Society. Today the pastors are Tahitian. Outrigger canoe racing is Tahiti's national sport, and the *va'a*—those long, sleek vessels seen cutting the harbor during lunchtime and after work—used to be kept on a black-sand beach across the boulevard from the church. Today a section of the landfill across is reserved for them.

Continue west along boulevard Pomare for 6 more blocks. You'll see a few remaining stately old colonial homes across the boulevard. On the harbor side you will come to Place Toata.

❻ Place Toata

Another project funded by the economic restructuring fund, Place Toata is another park built on the landfill, and it is a favorite gathering place for office workers during the day and families at night. They come to stroll, take in the view, and dine at inexpensive snack bars. Place Toata's outdoor amphitheater hosts concerts all year (Joe Cocker played here recently) and the national dance competition during the huge *Heiva Nui* festival in July. Next door, on the banks of Tipaerui River, stands the **Office Territorial d'Action Culturelle,** Tahiti's cultural center and library.

 TAKE A BREAK
Comparable to *les roulottes* (see "Where to Dine," later in this chapter) but permanently here, Place Toata's open-air snack bars are great for cold drinks, ice cream cones, or even a complete lunch. There are clean public restrooms here.

Walking Tour: Papeete

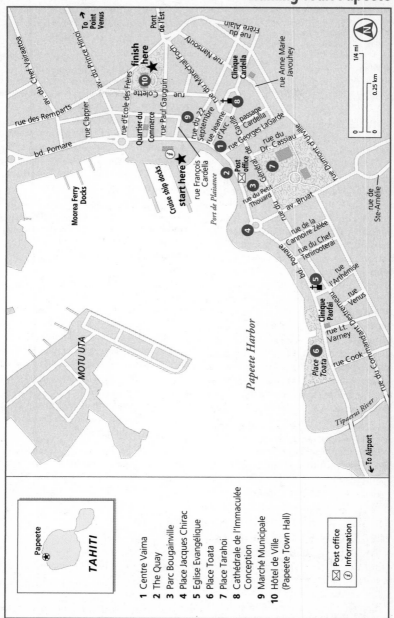

1 Centre Vaima
2 The Quay
3 Parc Bougainville
4 Place Jacques Chirac
5 Eglise Evangélique
6 Place Toata
7 Place Tarahoi
8 Cathédrale de l'Immaculée Conception
9 Marché Municipale
10 Hôtel de Ville (Papeete Town Hall)

⊠ Post office
ⓘ Information

Turn around and backtrack east on boulevard Pomare to Parc Bougainville (see number 3, above), cut through the park, and proceed through the park to the spacious grounds of Place Tarahoi.

❼ Place Tarahoi

Place Tarahoi, Papeete's governmental center, was royal property in the old days and site of Queen Pomare's mansion, which the French used as their headquarters after 1842. Her impressive home is long gone but is replicated by the Papeete Town Hall (see number 10, below). As you face the grounds, the buildings on the right house the French government and include the home of the president of French Polynesia. The modern building on the left is the Territorial Assembly. You can walk around hallways of the Assembly building during business hours. In front stands a monument to Pouvanaa a Oopa (1895–1977), a Tahitian who became a hero fighting for France in World War I and then spent the rest of his life battling for independence for his homeland. During the 1960s and '70s he spent 15 years in prison in France, but he returned home in time to see more local autonomy granted to the territory. In fact, his fellow Tahitians sent him back to Paris as a member of the French Senate.

Continue 2 more blocks along rue du Général-de-Gaulle, past the rear of Centre Vaima, to Cathédrale de l'Immaculée Conception.

❽ Cathédrale de l'Immaculée Conception

Tahiti's oldest Catholic church, Cathédrale de l'Immaculée Conception houses a series of paintings of the Crucifixion. Recently renovated, it's a cool, quiet, and comforting place to worship or just to contemplate.

Rue du Général-de-Gaulle becomes rue du Maréchal-Foch past the church. Follow it for a block. Bear left at rue Colette and continue until you come to *Marché Municipale*.

❾ Marché Municipale

Take a stroll under the large tin pavilion of Papeete's Municipal Market and examine the multitude of fruits and vegetables offered for sale (see "The Top Attractions," above).

After sampling the market and the marvelous handicraft stalls along its sidewalk and upstairs, walk along rue Colette 2 more blocks, until you come to Papeete Town Hall.

❿ Hotel de Ville (Papeete Town Hall)

This is a magnificent replica of Queen Pomare's mansion, which once stood at Place Tarahoi. This impressive structure, with its wraparound veranda, captures the spirit of the colonial South Pacific. This *Hôtel de Ville* or *Fare Oire* (French and Tahitian, respectively, for "town hall") was dedicated in 1990 by French President François Mitterand during an elaborate celebration. Walk up the grand entrance steps to catch a cool breeze from the broad balconies.

From here you can find your way back to Vaima Centre and some much-needed refreshment at its open-air cafes (see "Where to Dine," later).

THE CIRCLE ISLAND TOUR ✿✿

A **Circle Island Tour,** or a drive around Tahiti, is the best way to spend a day seeing the island's outlying sights and a bit of old Polynesia away from Papeete's bustle. It can be done even if you're staying on Moorea (take an early morning ferry over, a late afternoon boat back).

The road around the Tahiti Nui is 114km (72 miles) long. It's 54km (32 miles) from Papeete to Taravao along the east coast and 60km (40 miles) returning along the west coast. If your car has a trip meter, reset it to zero; if it doesn't, make note of the total kilometers on the odometer at the outset.

> **⌐Tips** **Avoid Rush Hour & Check on Road Work**
>
> If you drive yourself around Tahiti, avoid getting snarled in morning and evening weekday rush hours. Landslides between PK 44 and PK 45 on the east coast can close the round-island road, so ask the car rental agent or the staff at the Tahiti Manava visitors bureau if it is open all the way around.

On the land side of the road are red-topped concrete **kilometer markers** (*pointes kilomètres* in French, or *PK* for short). They tell the distance in kilometers between Papeete and the isthmus of Taravao. That is, the distance from Papeete to Taravao in each direction—not the total number of kilometers around the island. The large numbers facing the ocean are the number of kilometers from Papeete; the numbers facing you as you drive along are the number of kilometers you have to go to Papeete or Taravao, depending on your direction. Distances between the PKs are referred to in tenths of kilometers; for example, PK 35.6 would be 35.6km from Papeete.

For a more detailed description of the tour than I give here, buy a copy of Bengt Danielsson's *Tahiti: Circle Island Tour Guide*. French and English editions are available in the local bookstores.

THE NORTH & EAST COASTS OF TAHITI NUI

Proceeding clockwise from Papeete, you'll leave town by turning inland off Boulevard Pomare and following the broad **avenue du Prince-Hinoi,** the start of the round-island road.

FAUTAUA VALLEY, LOTI'S POOL & THE DIADEME   It's not worth the side trip, but at PK 2.5, a road goes right into the steep-walled Fautaua Valley and the **Bain Loti,** or Loti's Pool. Julien Viaud, the French merchant mariner who wrote under the pen name Pierre Loti, used this pool as a setting for his novel *The Marriage of Loti,* which recounted the love of a Frenchman for a Tahitian woman. Now part of Papeete's water-supply system, the pool is covered in concrete. Don't take any chances in this traffic, but try for a look up the valley to the **Diadème,** a rocky outcrop protruding like a crown from the interior ridge. (I think it looks like a single worn molar sticking up from a gum.) The road goes into the lower part of the valley and terminates at the beginning of a hiking trail up to the **Fautaua Waterfall,** which plunges over a cliff into a large pool 300m (985 ft.) below. The all-day hike to the head of the valley is best done with a guide (see "Golf, Hiking & Watersports," later).

TOMB OF POMARE V 🏛🏛   At PK 4.7 turn left at the sign and drive a short distance to a Protestant churchyard commanding an excellent view of Matavai Bay to the right. The tomb with a Grecian urn on top was built in 1879 for Queen Pomare. Her remains were removed a few years later by her son, King Pomare V, who abdicated in return for a French pension and later died of too much drink. Now he is buried there, and tour guides like to say the urn is not an urn at all but a liquor bottle, which makes it a monument not to Pomare V but to the cause of his death.

LA MAISON JAMES NORMAN HALL (JAMES NORMAN HALL'S HOME) 🏛🏛🏛   At PK 5.4, on the mountain side of the road just east of the small bridge, stands the home of James Norman Hall, coauthor with Charles Nordhoff of *Mutiny on the Bounty.* See "The Top Attractions," earlier.

Impressions

Look to the Northward, stranger / Just over the hillside there / Have you in your travels seen / A land more passing fair?

—James Norman Hall (on his tombstone)

ONE TREE HILL 👁👁   At PK 8, past the new Radisson Plaza resort, you'll come to the top of One Tree Hill, so named by Capt. James Cook because a single tree stood on this headland in the late 1700s. For many years it was the site of a luxury hotel, now closed. Pull into the roundabout at the entrance and stop for one of Tahiti's most magnificent vistas. You'll look down on the north coast from Matavai Bay to Papeete, with Moorea looming on the horizon.

POINT VENUS 👁👁👁   At PK 10, turn left at Super Marché Venus Star and drive to Point Venus, Tahiti's northernmost point, where Capt. James Cook observed the transit of the planet Venus in 1769 (see "The Top Attractions," earlier).

PAPENOO VALLEY   At PK 17.1, Tahiti's longest bridge crosses its longest river at the end of its largest valley at one of its largest rural villages—all named Papenoo. The river flows down to the sea through the only wall in Tahiti Nui's old volcanic crater. Opened since I was last here, a new cross-island road goes up the valley, literally through the mountains (via a tunnel), and down to Tahiti's south shore. Four-wheel-drive vehicles go into the valley on their rugged excursions (see "Safari Expeditions," later).

ARAHOHO BLOWHOLES   At PK 22, the surf pounding against the headland at Arahoho has formed overhanging shelves with holes in them. As waves crash under the shelves, water and air are forced through the holes, resulting in a geyser-like phenomenon. One shoots up at the base of a cliff on the mountain side of the road, but be careful because oncoming traffic cannot see you standing there. Pull into the overlook with free parking and toilets west of the curve. There's a snack bar across the road, and a black-sand beach is within sight.

***CASCADES DE FAARUMAI* (FAARUMAI WATERFALLS)** 👁👁   At PK 22.1, a sign on the right just past the blowhole marks a somewhat paved road that leads 1.5km (1 mile) up a small valley to the Cascades de Faarumai, Tahiti's most accessible waterfalls. The drive itself gives a glimpse of how ordinary rural Tahitians live in simple wood houses surrounded by bananas and breadfruit. Park near the stand of bamboo trees and take a few minutes to read the signs, which explain a romantic legend. Vaimahuta falls are an easy walk; Haamaremare Iti and Haamaremarerahi falls are a 45-minute climb up a more difficult trail. Vaimahuta falls plunge straight down several hundred feet from a hanging valley into a large pool. Bring insect repellent.

MAHAENA BATTLEFIELD   At PK 32.5, the Tahitian rebellion came to a head on April 17, 1844, when 441 French troops charged several times and many poorly armed Tahitians dug in near the village of Mahaena. The Tahitians lost 102 men and the French, 15. It was the last set battle of the rebellion.

BOUGAINVILLE'S ANCHORAGE 👁   At PK 37.6, a plaque mounted on a rock on the northern end of the bridge at Hitiaa commemorates Bougainville's landing. The French explorer anchored just offshore when he arrived in Tahiti in 1768. The two small islands on the reef, Oputotara and Variararu, provided slim protection against the prevailing trade winds, and Bougainville lost six anchors in 10 days trying to keep his ships off the reef. Tahitians recovered one and gave it to the high chief of Bora Bora, who in turn gave it to Captain Cook in 1777.

FAATAUTIA VALLEY   At PK 41.8 begins a view of Faatautia Valley, which looks so much like those in the Marquesas that in 1957 director John Huston chose it as a location for a movie version of *Typee,* Herman Melville's novelized account of his ship-jumping adventures among the Marquesans in the 1840s. The project was scrapped after another of Huston's Melville movies, *Moby Dick,* bombed at the box office. The uninhabited valley surely looks much today as it did 1,000 years ago.

TARAVAO   At PK 53, after passing the small-boat marina, the road climbs up onto the Isthmus of Taravao, separating Tahiti Nui from Tahiti Iti. At the top are the stone walls of Fort Taravao, which the French built in 1844 to bottle up what was left of the rebellious Tahitians on the Tahiti Iti peninsula. Germans stuck on Tahiti during World War II were interned there. It is now used as a French army training center. The village of Taravao with its shops, suburban streets, and churches has grown up around the military post. Its snack bars are a good place for a refueling stop.

TAHITI ITI

Tahiti Iti is much less sparsely populated and developed than its bigger twin, Tahiti Nui. Paved roads dead-end about halfway down its north and south sides. A series of cliffs plunges into the sea on Tahiti Iti's rugged east end. While the north shore holds historical interest, the south coast has Tahiti's best beach and its top surfing spot.

TARAVAO PLATEAU   If you have to chose one of three roads on Tahiti Iti, take the one by the school and stadium. It dead-ends high up into the rolling pastures of the Taravao Plateau. It begins at the traffic signal on the north coast road to Tautira and runs up through cool pastures reminiscent of rural France, with huge trees lining the narrow paved road. At more than 360m (1,200 ft.) high, the plateau is blessed with a refreshing, perpetually spring-like climate. Near the end of the road you'll come to the **Taravao Plateau Overlook,** where you'll have a spectacular view of the entire isthmus and down both sides of Tahiti Nui.

THE NORTH COAST TO TAUTIRA   The road on the north coast of Tahiti Iti goes for 18km (11 miles), to the sizable village of **Tautira,** which sits on its own peninsula. Captain Cook anchored in the bay off Tautira on his second visit to Tahiti in 1773. His ships ran aground on the reef while the crews were partying one night. He managed to get them off but lost several anchors in the process. One of them was found in 1978 and is now on display at the Museum of Tahiti and Her Islands, which we will come to on the west side of the island.

A year after Cook landed at Tautira, a Spanish ship from Peru named the *Aguila* landed here, and its captain claimed the island for Spain. It was the third time Tahiti had been claimed for a European power. He also put ashore two Franciscan priests. The *Aguila* returned a year later, but the priests had had enough of Tahiti and sailed back to Peru.

Impressions

It came upon me little by little. I came to like the life here, with its ease and its leisure, and the people, with their good-nature and their happy smiling faces.

—W. Somerset Maugham, "The Fall of Edward Bernard," 1921

(*Fun Fact* **R. L. S. Was Here**

Robert Louis Stevenson spent 2 months at Tautira in 1888, working on *The Master of Ballantrae,* a novel set not in Tahiti but in Scotland. Stevenson's mother was with him in Tautira. After she returned to London, she sent the local Protestant church a silver Communion service, which is still being used today. See chapter 13 for more about Stevenson's South Pacific adventures.

When you enter the village, bear left and drive along the scenic coast road as far as the general store, where you can buy a cold soft drink and snack.

THE SOUTH COAST TO TEAHUPOO   The picturesque road along the south coast of Tahiti Iti skirts the lagoon, passing through small settlements. Novelist Zane Grey had a deep-sea-fishing camp at PK 7.3, near the village of Toahotu, from 1928 to 1930. He caught a silver marlin that was about 4m (14 ft.) long and weighed more than 1,000 pounds—even after the sharks had had a meal on it while Grey was trying to get it aboard his boat. He wrote about his adventures in *Tales of Tahitian Waters.*

According to Tahitian legends, the demigod Maui once made a rope from his sister Hina's hair and used it to slow down the sun long enough for Tahitians to finish cooking their food in their earth ovens (a lengthy process). He accomplished this feat while standing on the reef at a point 8.5km (5 miles) along the south coast road. Beyond Maui's alleged footprints, now under the road, the Bay of Tapueraha provides the widest pass and deepest natural harbor on Tahiti. It was used as a base by a large contingent of the French navy during the aboveground nuclear tests at Moruroa atoll in the 1960s and 1970s. Some of the old mooring pilings still stand just offshore.

Reminiscent of the great Matira Beach on Bora Bora, *La Plage de Maui* (**Maui Beach**) ✿✿ borders the bay and is the best strip of white sand on Tahiti. Get out of the car and take a break at the lagoonside snack bar here. A cave, known as the *Caverne de Maui,* is a short walk inland.

Near Vairao village you'll pass the modern **IFREMER: *Le Centre Océanologique du Pacifique* (Pacific Oceanographic Center),** which conducts research into black pearl oysters, shrimp farming, and other means of extracting money from seawater. The buildings formerly were used for France's nuclear testing program.

The south coast road ends at **Teahupoo,** the famous *"village de surf,"* whose beachside park overlooks the big waves curling around Hava'a Pass. World-class boarders compete in the Billabong Pro tournament here every May. A footbridge crosses the Tirahi River, from where a trail begins along Tahiti Iti's rugged eastern shoreline. It's a strenuous and sometimes dangerous hike done only with a guide (see "Golf, Hiking & Watersports," later in this chapter).

THE SOUTH COAST OF TAHITI NUI

As you leave Taravao, heading back to Papeete along Tahiti's south coast, note that the PK markers begin to decrease the nearer you get to Papeete. The road rims casuarina-ringed Port Phaeton, which cuts nearly halfway across the isthmus. Port Phaeton and the Bay of Tapueraha to the south are Tahiti's finest harbors, yet European settlement and most development have taken place on the opposite side of the island, around Papeete. The shrimp you'll order for dinner come from the aqua farms in the bay's shallow waters.

Finds **Take a Break**

Sitting beside the sands of Maui Beach, **La Plage de Maui** snack bar (© 74.71.74) is a great place to stop for refreshment while taking in the gorgeous scenery, or perhaps a dip in the shallow lagoon. Owners Rose Wilkinson and Alain Corre, both veterans of the Sofitel la Ora on Moorea, offer reasonably priced burgers, steaks, *poisson cru* (marinated fish), ice cream, and other temptations. Open daily 10am to 6pm. No credit cards.

PAPAEARI   At PK 52 stands Tahiti's oldest village. Apparently the island's initial residents recognized the advantages of the south coast and its deep lagoons and harbors, for word-of-mouth history says they came through the Hotumatuu Pass in the reef and settled at Papeari sometime between A.D. 400 and 500. Robert Keable, author of *Simon Called Peter*, a best-selling novel about a disillusioned clergyman, lived here from 1924 until he died in 1928 at age 40. His home, now a private residence, stands at PK 55. Today Papeari is a thriving village whose residents often sell fruit and vegetables at stands along the road.

MUSEE GAUGUIN **(GAUGUIN MUSEUM)** ✵✵✵   At PK 51.2 is the entrance to the museum/memorial to Paul Gauguin, who lived near here from 1891 until 1893 (see "The Top Attractions," earlier). The museum sits in lush **Harrison W. Smith Botanical Gardens,** started in 1919 by American Harrison Smith. The museum and

The Moon & Six Million

In 1891 a marginally successful Parisian painter named Paul Gauguin left behind his wife and six children and sailed to Tahiti. He wanted to devote himself to his art, free of the chains of civilization.

Instead of paradise, Gauguin found a world that suffered from some of the same maladies as did the one from which he fled. Poverty, sickness, and frequent disputes with church and colonial officials marked his decade in the islands. He had syphilis, a bad heart, and an addiction to opium.

Gauguin disliked Papeete and spent his first 2 years in the rural Mataiea district, on Tahiti's south coast, where a village woman asked what he was doing there. Looking for a girl, he replied. The woman immediately offered her 13-year-old daughter, Tehaamana, the first of Gauguin's early teenage Tahitian mistresses. One of them bore him a son in 1899.

Tehaamana and the others figured prominently in Gauguin's impressionistic masterpieces, which brought fame to Tahiti but did little for his own pocketbook. After 649 paintings and a colorful career, immortalized by W. Somerset Maugham in *The Moon and Sixpence,* Gauguin died penniless in 1903.

At the time of his death, on Hiva Oa in the Marquesas Islands, a painting by Gauguin sold for 150 French francs. Today, on the rare occasion when one comes on the market, it fetches far in excess of $6 million.

gardens are open daily from 9am to 5pm. There's a snack bar here, but your best bet is to continue west.

VAIHIRIA RIVER AND VAIPAHI GARDENS   At PK 48, in the village of Mataiea, the main road crosses the Vaihiria River. The new cross-island road from Papenoo on the north coast terminates here. An 11km (7⅓ mile) track leads to **Lake Vaihiria,** at 465m (1,550 ft.) above sea level. It is Tahiti's only lake and is noted for its freshwater eels. Cliffs up to 900m (3,000 ft.) tall drop to the lake on its north side. Also in Mataiea is the lush *Jardin Vaipehi* (Vaipehi Gardens; no phone), a cool and refreshing spot with an oft-photographed waterfall and a bubbling natural spring. The garden is lush with elephant ears, tree ferns, ground orchids, jade vines, and other tropical vegetation. A planned renovation project is to emphasize its historical importance, since ancient Tahitian nobles followed the path to the springs in order to be spiritually purified.

ATIMAONO   At PK 41 begins the largest parcel of flat land on Tahiti, site of **Atimaono Golf Course,** French Polynesia's only links. Irishman William Stewart started his cotton plantation here during the American Civil War. Nothing remains of the plantation, but it was Stewart who brought the first Chinese indentured servants to Tahiti. See "Golf, Hiking & Watersports," below.

DORENCE ATWATER'S GRAVE   At PK 36, on the lagoon side of the road in Papara village, stands a Protestant church, under whose paved yard is buried Dorence Atwater, American consul to Tahiti after the Civil War. Captured while serving in the Union Army, Atwater was assigned to the hospital at the infamous Confederate prisoner-of-war camp at Andersonville, Georgia, where he surreptitiously recorded the names of Union soldiers who died in captivity. He later escaped and brought his lists to the federal government, thus proving that the Confederacy was keeping inaccurate records. His action made him a hero in the eyes of the Union Army. He later moved to the south coast of Tahiti, married a daughter of a chief of the Papara district, and at one time invested in William Stewart's cotton venture.

MARAA GROTTO   At PK 28.5, on Tahiti's southwest corner, the road turns sharply around the base of a series of headlands, which drop precipitously to the lagoon. Deep into one of these cliffs goes the Maraa Grotto, also called the Paroa Cave. It actually is two caves, both with water inside, and they go much deeper into the hill than appears at first glance. Park in the lot, not along the road, and enter at the gazebo to reach the larger of the two caves. A short trail leads from there to the smaller cave and a miniwaterfall.

Finds Take a Break

The circle island tour buses deposit their passengers for lunch at the lagoonside **Restaurant du Musée Gauguin,** at PK 50.5 (© **57.13.80**), which is worth a stop just for its phenomenal view of Tahiti Iti. The lunch buffet costs about 2,650CFP (US$27) per person Monday to Saturday, 3,500CFP (US$35) on Sunday. Sandwiches are available. Open daily noon to 3pm. A less expensive option is **Beach Burger** (© **57.41.03**), at PK 39, west of the golf course at Atimaono. In addition to burgers, it offers salads, steaks, Chinese fare, and pizzas. Open Sunday to Thursday 6am to 8pm, Friday and Saturday 6am to 9:30pm.

Moments **Watching the Sun Paint Moorea**

I was born to see sights, and no matter how many times I visit French Polynesia, I never tire of its incredible natural beauty. I always spend sunset of my first day at the InterContinental Resort Tahiti, on the west coast, depleting my camera battery as the sun paints another glorious red and orange sky over Moorea's purple ridges.

THE WEST COAST OF TAHITI NUI

North of Maraa the road runs through the Paea and Punaauia suburbs of Papeete. The west coast is the driest part of Tahiti, and it's very popular with Europeans, Americans, and others who have built homes along the lagoon and in the hills overlooking it and Moorea.

ARAHURAHU MARAE 🐟🐟   At PK 22.5 a small road on the right of Magasin Laut leads to a narrow valley, on the floor of which sits the restored Arahurahu Marae (see "The Top Attractions," earlier).

***MUSÉE DE TAHITI ET SES ISLES* (MUSEUM OF TAHITI AND HER ISLANDS)** 🐟🐟🐟   At PK 15.1, turn left at the gas station and follow the signs through a residential area to the lagoon and the *Musée de Tahiti et Ses Isles*, one of the South Pacific's best museums (see "The Top Attractions," earlier).

PUNARUU VALLEY   On a cloudless day you will have a view up the Punaruu Valley to the Diadème as you drive from the museum back to the main road. Power lines mar the view, but it's worth stopping to take a look. Tahitian rebels occupied the valley during the 1844–48 war, and the French built a fort to keep them there (the site is now occupied by a television antenna). Later the valley was used to grow oranges, most of which were shipped to California. Villagers sell the now-wild fruit at roadside stands during July and August.

The Route 5 expressway goes as far south as the Punaruu River, just north of the Tahiti Museum. Instead of taking the overpass onto the expressway, stay in the right lane to the traffic circle under the overpass. The first exit off the circle will take you up into the Punaruu Valley. The second exit leads to the Route 5 expressway. The third is Route 1, the old two-lane coast road, which will take you to the Lagoonarium.

LAGOONARIUM   At PK 11.4, the Captain Bligh Restaurant and Bar has a terrific view of Moorea and is home to *Le Lagoonarium de Tahiti,* an underwater viewing room (see "The Top Attractions," earlier).

After the Lagoonarium, Route 1 soon joins the four-lane Route 5 expressway, which passes shopping centers and marinas in Punaauia. It splits just before the Sofitel Maeva Beach. The left lanes feed into the Route 5 expressway, which roars back to Papeete. The right lanes take you along Route 1, the old road that goes past the west coast hotels and the Tahiti-Faaa International Airport before returning to town.

ORGANIZED TOURS AROUND THE COASTAL ROAD

Several companies offer tours along the coastal road around Tahiti Nui. They are a good way to see the island without hassling with traffic, and they are an especially fine way to spend your first day here, since you can see the island while recovering from jet lag.

> **Tips   Touring Tahiti from Moorea—& Vice Versa**
>
> You can take a circle-island tour or safari expedition of Tahiti if you're staying on Moorea. Catch an early flight or ferry to Papeete, go on the tour or safari expedition, and return to Moorea in the late afternoon. Let the tour companies know you're coming from Moorea when you make your reservation so they can meet you at the airport or ferry dock. If you do it yourself, the rental car companies will have a vehicle waiting on Tahiti. **Avis** (© **56.32.68** on Moorea) has special packages including air or ferry fares and a car on Tahiti, starting at 9,600CFP (US$96) via ferry and a 1-day rental.
>
> By the same token, I would spend a day on Moorea even if I had a short layover on Tahiti. You can easily arrange it yourself by ferry or plane, but you will need a rental vehicle on Moorea (Avis or Europcar will have one waiting for you at the Moorea airport or ferry dock). An alternative is to take a Moorea day tour, such as offered by **Tahiti Nui Travel** (© **54.02.00;** www.tahitinui travel.com). It charges between 10,300CFP and 14,100CFP (US$103–US$141), depending on whether you fly or take the ferry. Call or book at any hotel activities desk.

If one is scheduled when you are here, I recommend Tahiti Tourisme's *Le Tere Faati* tour, which takes you around the island via open-air le truck, with Tahitian musicians entertaining you all the way. It stops at waterfalls, a beach, Tautira, the Vapahi Garden, and in Paea. It may not, however, include the James Norman Hall, Gauguin, and Tahiti museums. These all-day excursions leave the *Office Territorial d'Action Culturelle* (Cultural Center) on boulevard Pomare at Place Toata at 8am, returning at 5:30pm. They cost just 2,000CFP (US$20) for adults, 500CFP (US$5) for children under 15. Check with your hotel activities desk or call **Tahiti Tourisme** (© **50.57.00**) to find out if one is scheduled, and to make reservations.

Also good is English-speaking William Leteeg's **Adventure Eagle Tours** (© **77.20. 03**). William takes you around in an air-conditioned van and lends his experiences growing up on the island to his commentaries. Others include **Tahiti Tours** (© **54. 02.50;** www.tahiti-tours.com), **Tahiti Nui Travel** (© **42.40.10;** www.tahiti-nui. com), and **Marama Tours** (© **50.74.74;** www.maramatours.com). They have reservations desks in several hotels. Expect to pay about 5,000CFP (US$50) for a half-day tour, 9,500CFP (US$95) for all day, plus entrance fees to the museums and other attractions and lunch, usually at the Restaurant du Musée Gauguin.

For a spectacular bird's-eye view of Tahiti or Moorea, take a 20-minute sightseeing ride with **Polynesia Hélicoptères** (© **86.60.29;** www.polynesia-helicopter.com). The flights cost an arm and a leg, but if you can afford it, they are well worth the expense.

SAFARI EXPEDITIONS ❀❀❀

So-called safari expeditions into Tahiti's interior offer a very different view of the island—and some spectacular views at that. Riding in the back of open, four-wheel-drive vehicles, you follow narrow, unpaved roads through Tahiti's central crater, usually via the breathtaking Papenoo Valley. Weather permitting, you'll ride up to 1,440 meters (4,800 feet) altitude on the sides of the island's steep interior ridge. The cool temperatures at the higher elevations are refreshing, as is a swim in a cold mountain stream.

Tips Pick a Clear Day

The safari expeditions do not go into the mountains when the weather is bad, and even if it's not raining, clouds atop the mountains can obscure what would otherwise be some fantastic views. It's best, therefore, to pick as clear a day as possible for this thrilling outing. Your best chance for that will be during the drier austral winter, June through early September.

Tahiti Safari Expedition (*©* **42.14.15;** www.tahiti-safari.com) has been the best since owner Patrice Bordes pioneered the concept in 1990. He charges about 5,500CFP (US$55) per person for a half-day trip, 9,500CFP (US$95) for a full day. Patrice usually stops at a restaurant in the Papenoo Valley, where you can buy lunch, or you can bring your own picnic. Don't forget your bathing suit, a towel, hat, sunscreen, insect repellent, and camera. These are popular trips with limited space, so reserve as early as possible at any hotel activities desk.

3 Golf, Hiking & Watersports

GOLF

The 18-hole, 6,255m (6,839-yd.) **Atimaono Golf Course,** PK 40.2 (*©* **57.43.41**), sprawls over the site of William Stewart's cotton plantation. A clubhouse, pro shop, restaurant, bar, locker rooms, showers, a swimming pool, a spa pool, and a driving range are on the premises. The club is open daily from 8am to dark. Greens fees are about 5,500CFP (US$55). The hotel activities desks can book all-day golf outings for about 24,000CFP (US$240) for one golfer, 35,000 (US$350) for two, including greens fees, equipment, lunch, and transportation to and from the course.

HIKING

Tahiti has a number of hiking trails, such as the cross-island Papenoo Valley–Lake Vaihiria route. Another ascends to the top of Mount Aorai, and another skirts the remote and wild eastern coast of Tahiti Iti. This is not the Shenandoah or some other American or New Zealand national park with well-marked trails, and the French gendarmes do not take kindly to rescuing some tourist who became lost trying to scale one of Tahiti's peaks. Downpours can occur in the higher altitudes, swelling the streams that most trails follow, and the nights can become bitterly cold and damp. Which side of the island is the rainy side can shift daily, depending on which way the wind blows. In addition, the quick-growing tropical foliage can quickly obscure a path that was easily followed a few days before. Permits are required to use some trails that cross government land.

Accordingly, always go with a guide or on organized hikes such as offered by **Tahiti Evasion** (*©* **56.48.77;** www.tahitievasion.com). This Moorea-based company has all-day treks into the Fautaua valley, home of Loti's Pool; the Orofero Valley on Tahiti's south coast; and to the top of Mt. Aorai, the island's third-highest peak. The treks start at 5,200CFP (US$52) per person. Hikes along the wild, uninhabited east coast of Tahiti Iti take 3 days and 2 nights of camping (call for prices). All except the Mt. Aorai climb are rated as easy walks. Tahiti Evasion will also organize hiking-and-watersports trips of up to 3 weeks throughout the islands.

You can also check with the **Tahiti Manava visitors bureau** in Papeete (© **50. 57.12;** www.tahiti-manava.pf) for the names of guides and hiking clubs.

WATERSPORTS

Based at the InterContinental Resort Tahiti, **Aquatica Dive Centre and Nautical Activities** (© **53.34.96**) offers the most comprehensive list of watersports activities, and you don't have to be an InterContinental guest to partake. Some sample prices: snorkeling gear rental, 2,000CFP (US$20); snorkeling trips, 4,000CFP (US$40); water-skiing, 4,500CFP (US$45); and kayak rental, 1,800CFP (US$18) per hour. A two-tank dive including equipment and a guide costs 11,000CFP (US$110); and introductory dive, 6,000CFP (US$60).

Most beaches on Tahiti have black volcanic sand, not the white variety most of us expect in the South Pacific. The most convenient of these is the public beach in front of **Le Royal Tahitien Hotel** (© **50.40.40**), in Pirae 4km (2½ miles) east of downtown (see "Where to Stay," below). There is some white sand among the pebbles at the **PK 18.5 Plage de Publique (Public Beach),** on the west coast at the Punaauia–Paea border. It has a restaurant and snack bar. The best beach of all is **Plage de Maui,** on Tahiti Iti (see "The Circle Island Tour," earlier).

Tahiti is famous for world-class surfing, especially Teuhupo'o on Tahiti Iti, home of the annual Billabong Pro championships in May. The best big waves crash on jagged reefs offshore, however, so you could be turned into hamburger meat if you've never surfed before. On the other hand, *Ecole de Surf Tura'i Mataare* **(Tahiti Surf School)** (© **41.91.37;** www.tahitisurfschool.info) teaches a half-day surfing and bodyboarding courses for 4,800CFP (US$48), or you can take private lessons for 12,000CFP (US$120). It's a good way to find out if you have what it takes to "hang ten."

4 Shopping

There's no shortage of things to buy in Tahiti, especially in Papeete. Black pearls and handicrafts are sure to tempt you. The selection and prices on some items may be better on Moorea.

If you just can't live without visiting a modern shopping mall, head for the **Centre Moana Nui,** on the main road in Punaauia about .5km (¼ mile) south of the Sofitel Maeva Beach. Here you'll find a huge Carrefour supermarket, several boutiques, a snack bar with excellent hamburgers, a hairdresser, a bar, banks with ATMs, and a post office (open Mon–Fri 8am–5pm, Sat 8am–noon). The local **Centre Artisinant** stands across the parking lot under a teepee-shaped roof (see "Handicrafts," below).

Duty-free shopping is very limited, with French perfumes the best deal. **Duty Free Tahiti** (© **42.61.61**), on the street-level waterside of the Centre Vaima, is the largest duty-free shop. Its specialties are Seiko, Lorus, and Cartier watches and Givenchy, Yves St. Laurent, Chanel, and Guerlain perfumes. The **airport departure lounge** has two duty-free shops.

BLACK PEARLS

Papeete has scores of *bijouteries* (jewelry shops) that carry black pearls in a variety of settings. Some stalls in Papeete's Municipal Market sell pearls, but give them a miss and buy yours from an experienced, reputable dealer. Most of these stores are in or around the Centre Vaima, along boulevard Pomare, and in the Quartier du Commerce, the narrow streets off boulevard Pomare between rue Paul Gauguin and rue d'Ecole des Frères north of the Municipal Market.

Your beginning point should be the **Musée de la Perle Robert Wan,** on the rue Jeanne d'Arc side of the Centre Vaima (℃ **45.21.22**). Named for Robert Wan, the man who pioneered the local industry back in the 1960s, this museum explains the history of pearls from antiquity, the method by which they are cultured, and the things to look for when making your selection. The museum is open Monday to Saturday from 9:30am to noon and from 1 to 4:15pm. Admission is 600CFP (US$6).

Adjoining the museum, **Tahiti Perles** (℃ **45.05.05**) carries only excellent-quality pearls and uses only 18-karat gold for its settings, so the prices tend to be high. Tahiti Perles has outlets on all the main islands.

On the second level of the Centre Vaima, **Sibani Perles Joallier** (℃ **41.36.34**) carries the jewelry line of Didier Sibani, another pioneer of the local industry. European-style elegance is the theme here and at the other Sibani outlets throughout the islands.

HANDICRAFTS

Although most of the inexpensive souvenir items sold here are made in Asia, many local residents, especially on the outer islands, produce a wide range of seashell jewelry, rag dolls, needlework, and straw hats, mats, baskets, and handbags. I love the *tivaivai,* colorful appliqué quilts stitched together by Tahitian women, who create their works using the same techniques their great-grandmothers were taught by early missionaries. You can also buy exquisite shell chandeliers like those adorning many hotel lobbies.

The most popular item by far is the cotton *pareu,* or wraparound sarong, which everyone wears at one time or another. They are screened, blocked, or printed by hand in the colors of the rainbow. The same material is made into other tropical clothing and various items, such as bedspreads and pillowcases. Pareus are sold virtually everywhere a visitor might wander.

The **Papeete Municipal Market** ✺✺✺ is the place to shop (see "The Top Attractions," above). It has stalls both upstairs and on the surrounding sidewalk, where local women's associations offer a wide selection of handicrafts at reasonable prices. The market is one of the few places where you can regularly find pareus for 1,000CFP (US$10), bedspreads made of the colorful tie-dyed and silk-screened pareu material, and tivaivai quilts. By and large, cloth goods are sold at the sidewalk stalls; those upstairs have a broader range of shell jewelry and other items.

Several villages have *centres artisanants,* where local women display their wares. The one in Punaauia, in the Centre Moana Nui parking lot south of the Sofitel Maeva Beach, is the best place to look for tivaivai quilts, which sell for about 35,000CFP (US$350).

For finer-quality handicrafts, such as woodcarvings from the Marquesas Islands, shell chandeliers, tapa lamp shades, or mother-of-pearl shells, try **Tamara Curios** (℃ **42.54.42**), on rue du Général-de-Gaulle in Fare Tony.

Impressions

It's a comfort to get into a pareu when one gets back from town . . . I should strongly recommend you to adopt it. It's one of the most sensible costumes I have ever come across. It's cool, convenient, and inexpensive.
—W. Somerset Maugham, "The Fall of Edward Bernard," 1921

Buying Your Black Pearl 🐚🐚🐚

French Polynesia is the world's largest producer of cultured black pearls. They are created by implanting a small nucleus into the shell of a live *Pinctada margaritifera,* the oyster used here, which then coats it with nacre, the same lustrous substance that lines the mother-of-pearl shell. The nacre produces dark pearls known as "black" but whose actual color ranges from slightly grayer than white to black with shades of rose or green. Most range in size from 10 millimeters to 17 millimeters (slightly less than a ½ in. to slightly less than ¾ in.).

Size, color, luster, lack of imperfections, and shape determine a pearl's value. No two are exactly alike, but the most valuable are the larger ones that are most symmetrical and have few dark blemishes, and whose color is dark with the shades of a peacock showing through a bright luster. A top-quality pearl 13 millimeters or larger will sell for $10,000 or more, but there are thousands to choose from in the $300 to $1,000 range. Some small, imperfect-but-still-lovely pearls cost much less.

So many pearls were being produced a few years ago that many small pearl farms closed. Competition is still fierce among the islands' shops, some of which (or their agents—commissioned tour guides and bus and taxi drivers) will bombard you with sales pitches almost from the moment you arrive. Even at the highest-end shops, discounting is *de rigeur*. Despite the general rule to avoid haggling in French Polynesia, you shouldn't pay the price marked on a pearl or a piece of jewelry until you have politely asked for a discount.

With most tourists now spending minimum time on Tahiti in favor of the other islands, you might find pearl prices in Papeete to be lower than on Moorea and Bora Bora. That's not always the case, so you should look in shops like **Ron Hall's Island Fashion Black Pearls** on Moorea and **Matira Pearls** on Bora Bora before making a purchase in Papeete (see "Shopping" in chapters 9 and 10). Your salesperson over there is more likely to speak English fluently.

You can get a refund of the 16% value added tax (TVA) included in the price of set pearls (but not on loose pearls). The TVA is not added after the purchase like an American sales tax, so you won't see it. Don't believe them if they say you can't get a refund because they've already taken the TVA off a reduced price. Truth is, they'll have to send the government 16% of whatever price you paid. Ask your dealer how to get your money back by sending them an official form after you have left the country (you can mail it after clearing Immigration at Faaa).

5 Where to Stay

If you want to stay in downtown Papeete instead of at the hotels I recommend below, try **Hotel Tiare Tahiti Noa Noa,** B.P. 2359, Papeete (© **50.01.00;** fax 43.68.47; hoteltiaretahiti@mail.pf), an upstairs, five-story facility on boulevard Pomare a block west of the Centre Vaima. It is simple but clean. The rooms are minimally furnished, however, and can be noisy, since most face directly onto the busy boulevard (request one on the upper floors, which are quieter and have better views from their slim balconies). The Chinese-accented **Hotel Le Mandarin**, B.P. 302, Papeete (℗ **50.33.50;** fax 42.16.32; www.hotelmandarin.com), is a bit shopworn, but it's in a somewhat quieter location on rue Collette opposite the Town Hall. My friend Dick Beaulieu likes to stay at Le Mandarin when he comes over from Fiji because it's business-oriented and close to most offices and many restaurants. Both charge between 15,000CFP and 17,000CFP (US$150–US$170) for a double room.

EXPENSIVE

InterContinental Resort Tahiti ★★★
This is the best all-around resort on Tahiti. Built in the 1960s as the Tahiti Beachcomber Travelodge, it was more recently named the InterContinental Tahiti Beachcomber Resort. Most folk here still call it "the Beachcomber," and many would like a return to its old, familiar name. It sits at Tataa Point on the island's northwest corner, from whence souls supposedly leapt to the ancient Polynesian homeland. Today planes leap into the air from the nearby airport at Faaa, although the jet noise seldom penetrates the rooms here. It has a range of accommodations, including smaller rooms dating from its original Travelodge incarnation, newer and more spacious "Panoramic" rooms, and overwater bungalows with unimpeded views of Moorea. Whatever the vintage, all units now are luxuriously appointed with the likes of canopy beds and marble bathrooms, and all have private patios or balconies with views of Moorea. The original overwater units are smaller than newer models on the resort's south end, which have separate sitting areas and steps leading from their decks into the lagoon. The resort doesn't have a natural beach, but bulkheads separate the sea from white imported sand. Or you can frolic in two pools—one in a large complex sitting lagoonside before the main building, or the other smaller pool with water cascading over its horizon (and apparently into the lagoon). The latter is adjacent to the romantic Le Lotus restaurant, one of Tahiti's best (see "Where to Dine," below). Features here include an all-night lobby bar, and the best watersports center on Tahiti. I love to stay here between jaunts to the outer islands because I can clean my dirty clothes in the free washers and dryers, a real money-saver given the exorbitant cost of laundry services (buy your soap powder before the boutique closes at 7pm).

B.P. 6014, 98702 Faaa (8km/5 miles west of Papeete). ℗ **800/327-0200** or 86.51.10. Fax 86.51.30. www.tahiti. interconti.com. 214 units. 34,800CFP–59,400CFP (US$348–US$594) double; 76,100CFP–84,000CFP (US$761–US$840) suite; 51,600CFP–74,400CFP (US$516–US$744) overwater bungalow. AE, DC, MC, V. **Amenities:** 2 restaurants; 2 bars; 2 outdoor pools; tennis courts; health club; Jacuzzi; watersports equipment rentals; concierge; activities desk; car-rental desk; salon; 24-hr. room service; 24-hr. business center w/high-speed Internet access; massage; babysitting; laundry service; coin-op washers and dryers. *In room:* A/C, TV, dataport, minibar, coffeemaker, hair dryer, iron, safe.

Le Meridien Tahiti ★★
Two blocks from the Museum of Tahiti and Her Islands, this luxury resort sits alongside one of Tahiti's few white-sand beaches. It's an excellent choice—provided you don't have to get to Tahiti-Faaa International Airport to catch a flight during the weekday morning traffic jam, when the usual 15-minute ride can take considerably longer. The Melanesian-inspired architecture is stunning, with swayback shingle roofs evoking the "spirit houses" of Papua New Guinea. Imported sand surrounding the wade-in pool compensates for the pebbly beach and shallow lagoon here. The best accommodations are 12 overwater bungalows, but note that

---

Tips   It Pays to Shop for Room Rates

Like many big hotels these days, those in French Polynesia adjust their room rates according to such factors as the season and how many guests they expect to have on a given day, and many offer Internet specials on their websites. Accordingly, their published "rack rates"—which I am compelled to give in this book—are nearly meaningless. For example, Le Meridien Tahiti recently offered an Internet special of 17,000CFP (US$170) a night for a standard room, less than half the published rack rate of 35,000CFP (US$350). In other words, it can pay bountifully to shop around. See "Tips on Accommodations" in chapter 2.

---

unlike most others, they have neither glass panels in their floors for fish-watching nor steps into the lagoon from their porches. The luxuriously appointed guest quarters have balconies, but try to get a north-facing unit for a Moorea view. Le Meridien provides complimentary le truck shuttles into Papeete twice a day and on two evenings a week. *Le Carré* is one of the best resort dining rooms in French Polynesia. A shopping center next door has a grocery store, hairdresser, pharmacy, post office, restaurants, and a patisserie for inexpensive breakfasts.

B.P. 380595, 98718 Punauuia (15km/9 miles south of Papeete, 8km/5 miles south of the airport). © **800/225-5843** or 47.07.07. Fax 47.07.08. www.lemeridien-tahiti.com. 150 units. 35,000CFP (US$350) double; 45,000CFP–85,000CFP (US$450–US$850) suite; 50,000CFP (US$500) bungalow. AE, DC, MC, V. **Amenities:** 2 restaurants; 2 bars; outdoor pool; tennis court; exercise room; watersports equipment rentals; concierge; activities desk; car-rental desk; wireless Internet access; 24-hr. room service; babysitting; laundry service. *In room:* A/C, TV, dataport, minibar, coffee maker, hair dryer, iron, safe.

Radisson Plaza Resort Tahiti ✦   This modern resort opened in 200 beside a beach of deep black sand on Matavai Bay, where the 18th-century explorers dropped anchor. A huge, turtle-shaped thatch roof covers most of the central complex, which holds a restaurant, bar, arts and crafts center, full-service spa, and a cozy library devoted to author James Norman Hall. Outside is a horizon-edge pool beside the beach. Currents create an undertow here, so heed the "Dangerous Sea" signs when swimming in the lagoon. Seven hotel buildings hold the accommodations, which include standard rooms, two-story town house–style "duplexes" (their upstairs bedrooms have their own balconies), suites, and—my favorites—rooms with hot tubs romantically placed behind louvers on their balconies. Furnishings and decor are tropical with a European flair. The Radisson sends a shuttle to downtown Papeete each morning and afternoon, but public buses do not run out here after 5pm, meaning you will need to rent a car or take a taxi to get to and from downtown after dark. All units have high-speed Internet ports, making this a very good bet for business travelers with expense accounts for rental cars. Like at Le Meridien Tahiti, rush-hour traffic can make for a long trek to the airport from here.

B.P. 14170, 98701 Arue (on Matavai Bay, 7km/4½ miles east of downtown). © **800/333-3333** or 48.88.88. Fax 43.88.89. www.radisson.com/aruefrp. 165 units. 32,000CFP–38,000CFP (US$320–US$380) double; 41,300CFP–42,600CFP (US$413–US$426) suite. AE, DC, MC. V. **Amenities:** restaurant; 2 bars; outdoor pool; exercise room; spa; Jacuzzi; watersports equipment rentals; activities desk; car-rental desk; business center; salon; 24-hr. room service; massage; babysitting; laundry service; concierge-level rooms. *In room:* A/C, TV, high-speed dataport, minibar, coffeemaker, hairdryer, iron, safe.

Sheraton Hotel Tahiti & Spa ✦✦   A 15-minute walk to downtown and a quick drive to the airport, this state-of-the-art hotel was built in 2000–01 on the site of the old Hotel Tahiti, whose massive thatched-roof public areas hosted many a local soiree.

With Tahiti's largest meeting space, the Sheraton still serves as one of the city's prime gathering places. Curving steps under a huge shell chandelier lead down to Quinn's Bar, an overwater dining room, and an expansive courtyard with restaurant and lagoonside swimming pool, which helps compensate for the lack of beach. A hot tub perched atop a pile of rocks beside the pool offers a terrific view of Moorea. Except for 10 suites, which have one or two bedrooms, the spacious units are virtually identical except for the vistas off their private balconies. "Superior" units directly face Moorea, but you actually pay less for them since they are slightly smaller than the "deluxe lagoon" units facing the open ocean or harbor (someone who's never been to Tahiti must have devised that policy). This is a good choice for a short layover when you don't need a beach. Top Dive, one of French Polynesia's best operators, has a base here.

B.P. 416, 98713 Papeete (1km/½ mile west of downtown, 6km/3½ miles east of the airport). ℂ 800/325-3535 or 86.48.48. Fax 86.48.40. www.starwoodtahiti.com. 200 units. 30,000CFP–37,000CFP (US$300–US$370) double; 55,000CFP–85,000CFP (US$550–US$850) suite. AE, DC, MC, V. **Amenities:** 2 restaurants; bar; outdoor pool; health club; exercise room; spa; concierge; activities desk; car-rental desk; wireless Internet access in public areas; salon; limited room service; massage; babysitting; laundry service. *In room:* A/C, TV, dataport, minibar, coffeemaker, hair dryer, iron, safe.

Sofitel Maeva Beach Tahiti   Recently given a thorough facelift, this mid-rise hotel was built in the 1960s to resemble a modern version of a terraced Mayan pyramid. It sits beside Maeva Bay and a gray-sand beach of the same name. The murky lagoon off the beach isn't as good for swimming and snorkeling as it is for anchoring numerous yachts, whose masts slice the beach's view of Moorea. Equipped with modern European amenities (the bright, lime-green bathrooms nearly blinded me), the smallish rooms open to balconies. Those on the upper floors on the north (or "beach") side have partial views of Moorea, while those on the garden side look south along Tahiti's west coast. The Maeva Beach often is featured in some of the least expensive package tours. While adequate if cost is a major consideration, don't expect the same amount of space, luxuries, or amenities as at the InterContinental Resort Tahiti or Le Meridien.

B.P. 6008, 98702 Faaa (7½km/4 miles west of Papeete). ℂ 800/763-4835 or 86.66.00. Fax 41.05.05. www.sofitel.com. 230 units. 29,500CFP–37,500CFP (US$295–US$375) double; 55,500CFP (US$555) suite. AE, DC, MC, V. **Amenities:** 2 restaurants; 2 bars; outdoor pool; tennis courts; watersports equipment rentals; concierge; activities desk; car-rental desk; limited room service; babysitting; laundry service. *In room:* A/C, TV, minibar, coffeemaker, hair dryer, iron, safe.

MODERATE

Le Royal Tahitien ⟨⟨ ⟨Value⟩   One of the top values in French Polynesia, this American-owned hotel is the only moderately priced place on the island with its own beach, a stretch of deep black sand from which its suburban neighbors fish and swim. And long-time Australian-born manager Lionel Kennedy (a die-hard baseball fan) and his English-speaking staff are Tahiti's best when it comes to friendly, personalized service. Sitting in an expansive lawn and lush garden traversed by a small stream, a swimming pool sports a Jacuzzi and a waterfall cascading over rocks. The spacious guest rooms are in contemporary two-story wood-and-stone buildings that look like an American condominium complex. Colorful bedspreads and seat cushions add a tropical ambience to the rooms, however, and the tropics definitely pervade the fine, moderately-priced restaurant under a 1937-vintage thatch ceiling. Both the beachside restaurant and adjacent bar are popular with local businesspeople. A local band plays on Friday and Saturday evenings. Your fellow guests are likely to be businesspersons living on the

Guesthouses & Family Accommodation

In general you will find a significant difference in quality between French Polynesia's moderate and inexpensive accommodations. Few establishments here are comparable in price or quality to the inexpensive motels found in abundance in the United States, Canada, Australia, and New Zealand.

The local government is encouraging the development of guesthouses and family pensions, of which there are a growing number. Many owners have used government-backed loans to acquire one-room guest bungalows with attached bathrooms. Although the bungalows are identical, the owners have added decorative touches, in some case quite tasteful, barely in others.

Tahiti Tourisme inspects these establishments and distributes lists of those it recommends (see "Visitor Information & Entry Requirements" in chapter 7). Many promote themselves through an organization known as **Haere-Mai,** whose website (www.haere-mai.pf) describes them.

Local families operate most of them, so if you decide to go this route, an ability to speak some French may be essential.

---

other islands and travelers who have made their own arrangements (that is, few groups stay here). It's very popular, so reserve as soon as possible. As with the Radisson Plaza (see above), you will need to rent a car or take a taxi if going downtown after dark, since the last local bus passes here about 5pm.

B.P. 5001, 98716 Pirae (4km/2½ miles east of downtown). © 818/843-6068 or 50.40.40. Fax 50.40.41. www.hotel royaltahitien.com. 40 units. 18,000CFP (US$180) double. AE, DC, MC, V. Take a Mahina bus or follow av. Prince Hinoi to the Total and Mobil stations opposite each other; turn around at next traffic circle and return; turn right to hotel. **Amenities:** Restaurant; bar; outdoor pool; Jacuzzi; laundry service. *In room:* A/C, TV, fridge, coffeemaker.

INEXPENSIVE

Taaroa Lodge   Avid surfer Ralph Sanford bought the two bungalows at his humble lagoonside establishment, in ritzy Paea, as prefabricated kits in New Zealand; hence, they are larger and have more character than the cookie-cutter *fares* found at most small family-run establishments here. And their porches present million-dollar views of Moorea, especially the one sitting beside the bulkhead along the lagoon. Each has a kitchen, TV, and ceiling fan. Behind them an A-frame chalet houses a room with a double bed downstairs and a six-bed dormitory in the loft. The communal kitchen stays busy, as do Ralph's free kayaks (bring your own snorkeling gear). Grocery stores and snack bars are short walks away. In my opinion, this is the top backpacker accommodation on Tahiti, even if you do have to stay at least 2 nights.

B.P. 498, 98713 Papeete (PK 18.2 in Paea). ©/fax 58.39.21. www.taaroalodge.com. 2 bungalows (w/bathroom), 1 room (w/bathroom), 6 dorm beds. 10,000CFP (US$100) bungalow; 6,000CFP (US$60) double room; 2,500CFP (US$25) dorm bed. Rates include breakfast. MC, V. 2-night minimum stay required. **Amenities:** Communal kitchen; free kayaks. *In room (bungalows only):* TV, kitchen, coffeemaker, no phone.

Tahiti Airport Lodge   Perched on the side of a hill in the Cité de l'Air housing development above the airport, Charlie and Margarite Bredin's simple but clean and friendly bed-and-breakfast commands a spectacular view of Moorea from its lovely, open-air guest lounge. Unfortunately you won't get this view from any of the rather dark rooms, which range from ample motel-size with king beds and private bathrooms down to tiny share-bathroom units barely big enough to accommodate a double bed.

All rooms have fans and electric mosquito deterrents, and all showers dispense hot water. The house is a steep, 5-minute climb from the round-island road, but Charlie will pick you up from the airport or the bus stop. Charlie and Margarite speak English as well as French.

B.P. 2580, 98713 Papeete (PK 5.5, opposite Tahiti-Faaa International Airport). © **82.23.68.** Fax 82.25.00. 10 units (4 w/bathroom). 6,000CFP–8,000CFP (US$60–US$80) double. Rates include breakfast and airport transfers. No credit cards. *In room:* No phone.

6 Where to Dine

Tahiti has a plethora of excellent French, Italian, and Chinese restaurants. The ones recommended below are but a few of many; don't hesitate to strike out on your own.

Downtown Papeete has a McDonald's at the corner of rue du Général-de-Gaulle and rue du Dr. Cassiau behind Centre Vaima, and there's a second on the main road in Punaauia. If you want to make your own meals or a picnic, the downtown **Champion** supermarket is on rue du Général-de-Gaulle in the block west of the Eglise Evangélique. On the west coast, head for the huge **Carrefour** supermarket in the Centre Moana Nui south of the Sofitel Maeva Beach.

Value Don't Miss *Les Roulottes*

Although prices in some hotel dining rooms and restaurants here can be shocking, you don't need to spend a fortune to eat reasonably well in French Polynesia. In fact, the best food bargains in Papeete literally roll out after dark on the cruise ship docks: portable meal wagons known as les roulottes.

Some owners set up charcoal grills behind their trucks and small electric generators in front to provide plenty of light for the diners, who sit on stools along either side of the vehicles. A few operate during the daytime, but most begin arriving about 6pm. The entire waterfront soon takes on a carnival atmosphere, especially on Friday and Saturday nights.

The traditional menu includes charbroiled steaks or chicken with french fries (known, respectively, as *steak frites* and *poulet frites)*, familiar Cantonese dishes, poisson cru, and *salade russe* (Russian-style potato salad, tinted red by beet-root juice) for 950CFP to 1,500CFP (US$9.50–US$15) per plate. Glassed-in display cases along the sides of some trucks hold actual examples of what's offered at each (not exactly the most appetizing exhibits, but you can just point to what you want rather than fumbling in French). You'll find just as many trucks specializing in crepes, pizzas, couscous, and waffles (*gaufres*). So many cruise-ship passengers and other tourists eat here that most truck owners speak some English.

Even if you don't order an entire meal at les roulottes, stop for a crepe or waffle and enjoy the scene.

Although they now have permanent homes, the open-air restaurants at **Place Toata,** on the western end of the waterfront, were born as roulottes, and they still offer the same fare and prices as their mobile siblings. They are open for lunch Monday to Saturday and for dinner Friday and Saturday.

EXPENSIVE

It was closed for vacation during my recent visit, but my foodie friend Dick Beaulieu did dine at **L'O à la Bouche** (*©* **45.29.76**), on Passage Carella behind the Vaima Centre. He has only one word to describe the Provençal lamb and *magret* of duck: "Superb!" Open for lunch Monday to Friday, dinner Monday to Saturday. Let me know what you think.

Auberge du Pacifique 🐟🐟🐟 TRADITIONAL FRENCH/TAHITIAN   This lagoonside restaurant has been among Tahiti's finest since 1974. Owner Jean Galopin was named a Maître Cuisinier (Master Chef) de France in 1987, in large part because of his unique blending of French and Tahitian styles of cooking. His *fafa* (chicken and taro leaves steamed in coconut milk) is in marked contrast with what comes out of a local *himaa* on Sunday afternoon. Jean has shared many of his techniques in a popular cookbook, *La Cuisine de Tahiti et des Iles*. The roof over his main dining room opens to reveal the twinkling stars above. Guests are welcome to visit the air-conditioned wine cellar and choose from among excellent French vintages. A special tourist menu features poisson cru and main courses such as a light mahimahi soufflé.

PK 11.2, Punaauia (3.7km/2¼ miles south of Sofitel Maeva Beach on the round-island road; take a Paea bus during the day, a taxi at night). *©* **43.98.30.** Reservations recommended, especially on weekends. Main courses 2,600CFP–4,000CFP (US$26–US$40); tourist menu 5,000CFP (US$50). AE, MC, V. Mon–Sat 11:30am–2:30pm and 6:30–10pm.

Captain Bligh Restaurant and Bar 🐟 TRADITIONAL FRENCH   One of Tahiti's last large thatched-roof buildings covers this restaurant beside the lagoon (you can toss bread crumbs to the fish swimming just over the railing). The food is not the best on the island, but you can't beat the old Tahitian charm. Specialties of the house are grilled steaks and lobster. Get here early to graze the all-you-can-eat lunchtime salad bar, which is so popular with locals that it quickly disappears. One of the island's top Tahitian dance troupes performs here Friday and Saturday nights after a seafood buffet—the 5,000CFP (US$50) per person price is excellent value compared to the resort hotels' buffets and dance shows. You can sample local food at the *ma'a Tahiti* buffet Sunday at noon. A pier goes out to the Lagoonarium here (see "The Top Attractions," earlier).

PK 11.4, Punaauia, at the Lagoonarium (3.9km/2⅓ miles south of Sofitel Maeva Beach on the round-island road; Paea buses go by it during the day; take a taxi at night). *©* **43.62.90.** Reservations recommended on weekends. Burgers 1,300CFP (US$13); lunch salad bar 1,700CFP (US$17); main courses 1,800CFP–3,400CFP (US$18–US$34). AE, MC, V. Tues–Sun 11am–2:30pm and 6:30–10pm; bar 9am–10pm.

Casablanca Cocktail Restaurant 🐟🐟 FRENCH/MEDITERRANEAN   Perched beside the yachts moored in Marina Taina, this casual restaurant is very popular with local residents, especially on weekends, when live music is featured (make Fri and Sat reservations at least 2 days in advance). Couscous on Wednesday night also draws a crowd. The main menu features French treatments of local seafood with some island twists. The menu is in French, but the friendly staff will help you decipher *le carte.* Try to get a table in one of the romantic gazebos out in the yard.

PK 9, Punaauia, at Marina Taina. *©* **43.91.35.** Reservations recommended. Main courses 2,600CFP–4,200CFP (US$26–US$42); fixed-price dinner 4,900CFP (US$49). AE, MC, V. Daily noon–2pm and 7–10pm. Heading south, turn right into marina after first traffic circle.

Le Lotus 🐟🐟🐟 FRENCH/CONTINENTAL   With two round, thatched-roof dining rooms extending over the lagoon and enjoying an uninterrupted view of Moorea,

> ## (Value) Dining with a Belle View
>
> I like to spend my last evening on Tahiti up at **Le Belvédère** (© **42.73.44**), for this innlike establishment has a spectacular view of the city and Moorea from its perch 600m (2,000 ft.) up in the Fare Ape Valley above Papeete. The restaurant provides round-trip transportation from your hotel up the narrow, one-lane, winding, switchback road that leads to it (I don't encourage anyone to attempt this drive in a rental car). Take the 5pm pickup so you'll reach the restaurant in time for a sunset cocktail. They'll drop you back at the airport if you're leaving tonight. The specialty of the house is fondue Bourguignonne served with six sauces. The 5,900CFP (US$59) fixed price includes three courses, wine, and transportation, so it is a reasonably good value. The quality of the cuisine doesn't match the view, however, so treat the evening as a sightseeing excursion, not as a fine dining experience. Reservations are required, and American Express, MasterCard, and Visa cards are accepted. Closed Wednesday.

Le Lotus has the best setting of any restaurant in the South Pacific. The widely spaced tables are all at the water's edge (a spotlight between the two dining rooms shines into the lagoon, attracting fish in search of a handout). The gourmet French fare and attentive but unobtrusive service more than live up to this romantic scene. Your choices will depend on which of Europe's top master chefs has accepted the resort's invitation to take a working vacation here. Whomever is in residence, you're in for a gastronomic delight.

In InterContinental Resort Tahiti, Faaa (7km/4 miles west of Papeete). © **86.51.10**, ext. 5512. Reservations highly recommended. Main courses 4,200CFP–5,000CFP (US$42–US$50). AE, DC, MC, V. Daily noon–2:30pm and 6:30–9:30pm.

Le Rubis ☆☆ TRADITIONAL FRENCH/REGIONAL Faux grape vines (*rubis* in French) hang from the ceilings of this casual but elegant restaurant, and the mat-lined walls are adorned with numerous paintings of wine bottles and vineyards. The decor will get you in the mood to select from one of Tahiti's most extensive lists of French vintages, many of them offered by the glass. The menu suggests a match for each item. Shrimp in a sweet, slightly curried coconut cream sauce is the star here, or you can opt for the same sauce over fresh tuna. Salmon in puff pastry and traditional French versions of steak, veal, lamb, and duck are all tasty.

16 rue Jeanne d'Arc, in Vaima Centre. © **43.25.55**. Reservations recommended. Main courses 2,000CFP–3,600CFP (US$20–US$36). AE, MC, V. Tues–Thurs 11am–2pm and 6–10pm, Fri 11am–2pm and 6pm–1am, Sat 6pm–2am, Sun 6–10pm.

MODERATE

L'Api'zzeria ☆ ITALIAN On a par with Lou Pescadou (see below) but with a garden setting, this restaurant in a grove of trees across from the waterfront has been serving very good pizza and pasta since 1968. I prefer a table outside under the trees rather than inside, which resembles an Elizabethan waterfront tavern accented with nautical relics. The food, on the other hand, is definitely Italian. Both large and small pizzas and tender steaks are cooked in a wood-fired oven. The menu also features spaghetti, fettuccine, lasagna, steak Milanese, veal in white or Marsala wine sauce, and grilled homemade Italian sausage.

Bd. Pomare, between rue du Chef Teriirooterai and rue l'Arthémise. € **42.98.30.** Pizzas and pastas 420CFP–1,750CFP (US$4.20–US$18); meat courses 1,500CFP–2,600CFP (US$15–US$26). MC, V. Mon–Sat 11:30am–10pm.

Les 3 Brasseurs FRENCH   The quality of its food tends to be up and down, but this sidewalk microbrewery is the nearest thing Papeete has to an American-style bar-and-grill. The sidewalk tables are fine for a cold one while waiting for the Moorea ferry at the docks across the boulevard. The tabloid menu is all in French, but wait staffers speak enough English to explain offerings. Choose from sandwiches, salads, roast chicken served hot or cold, and grilled steaks, mahimahi, tuna plain or with optional sauces. *Jarret de porc,* smoked ham hocks served with sautéed potatoes and sauerkraut, reminds me of the Southern soul food of my youth. The best deal here is the *croque brasseurs,* a ham sandwich served under melted Gruyère cheese and accompanied by a glass of beer and a green salad with excellent vinaigrette dressing, all for 900CFP (US$9).

Bd. Pomare, between rue Prince Hinoi and rue Clappier, opposite Moorea ferry docks. € **50.60.25.** Sandwiches and salads 900CFP–1,700CFP (US$9–US$17); main courses 1,300CFP–2,400CFP (US$13–US$24). MC, V. Daily 9am–1am.

Lou Pescadou ⭐ *Value* ITALIAN   A lively young professional clientele usually packs this quintessentially Italian trattoria (red-and-white–checked tablecloths, dripping candles on each table, Ruffino bottles hanging from every nook and cranny). They come for good, fresh, and tasty Italian fare at reasonable prices (be prepared to wait for a table). The individual-size pizzas are cooked in a wood-fire oven, and the excellent pasta dishes include lasagna and spaghetti and fettuccine under tomato, carbonara, and Roquefort sauces.

Rue Anne-Marie Javouhey at passage Cardella. € **43.74.26.** Pizzas and pastas 600CFP–1,050CFP (US$6–US$11); meat courses 1,650CFP–2,650CFP (US$17–US$27). MC, V. Mon–Sat 11:30am–2pm and 6:30–11pm. Take the narrow passage Cardella, a 1-block street that looks like an alley, directly behind Centre Vaima.

INEXPENSIVE

Le Cignalon/Pacific Burger *Value* PIZZA/SNACK BAR   Cost-conscious guests at Le Meridien Tahiti resort walk next door to Pacific Burger, the open-air snack bar side of this otherwise Italian restaurant, for good, reasonably priced salads, poisson cru, sashimi, pizzas from a wood-fired oven, burgers (beef, chicken, or fish), grilled rib-eye steaks, and fish with or without sauce. A big tarp covers plastic patio tables and chairs in front of the fast-food-style counter. The menu is in French and English. The Tahiti museum is a few blocks away, so this is a good place to stop for refreshment on your round-island tour.

PK 15, Punaauia. € **42.40.84.** Burgers 450CFP–850CFP (US$4.50–US$8.50); pizza 1,000CFP–1,500CFP (US$10–US$15); main courses 1,300CFP–2,300CFP (US$13–US$23). MC, V. Tues–Thurs 10am–3pm and 5:30–9pm; Fri–Sun 10am–3pm and 5:30–9:30pm (burgers and hot dogs only 3–5pm Sun).

Le Retrot FRENCH/ITALIAN/SNACKS   You'll find better food elsewhere, but this Parisian-style sidewalk cafe is Papeete's best place to rendezvous, or to grab a quick bite, a drink, or an ice cream while watching the world pass along the quay. A diverse selection of salads, sandwiches, pizzas, and pasta gets attention from the cafe crowd.

Bd. Pomare, front of Centre Vaima, on waterfront. € **42.86.83.** Salads, sandwiches, and burgers 450CFP–1,200CFP (US$4.50–US$12); pizza and pastas 800CFP–1,900CFP (US$8–US$19); main courses 1,800CFP–2,100CFP (US$18–US$21). AE, MC, V. Daily 6am–midnight.

L'Oasis du Vaima SNACK BAR   You'll find me having a small quiche or a tasty pastry with strong French coffee for breakfast at this kiosklike building on the southwest corner of Centre Vaima. In addition to dishing out ice cream and milkshakes to

---

⟨ *Fun Fact* **A Most Indecent Song & Dance**

The young girls whenever they can collect 8 or 10 together dance a very indecent dance which they call Timorodee singing most indecent songs and using most indecent actions in the practice of which they are brought up from their earliest Childhood.

—Capt. James Cook, after seeing his first Tahitian dance show in 1769

The Tahitian dances described by the great explorer in 1769 left little doubt as to the temptations that inspired the mutiny on the *Bounty* a few years later. At the time Cook arrived, the Tahitians would stage a *heiva* (festival) for almost any reason, from blessing the harvest to celebrating a birth. After eating meals cooked in earth ovens, they would get out the drums and nose flutes and dance the nights away. Some of the dances involved elaborate costumes, and others were quite lasciviously and explicitly danced in the nude or seminude, which added to Tahiti's reputation as an island of love.

The puritanical Protestant missionaries would have none of that and put an end to dancing in the early 1820s. Of course, strict prohibition never works, and Tahitians—including a young Queen Pomare—would sneak into the hills to dance. Only after the French took over in 1842 was dancing permitted again, and then only with severe limitations on what the dancers could do and wear. A result of these various restrictions was that most of the traditional dances performed by the Tahitians before 1800 were nearly forgotten within 100 years.

You'd never guess that Tahitians ever stopped dancing, for after tourists started coming in 1961, they went back to the old ways. Today traditional dancing is a huge part of their lives—and of every visitor's itinerary. No one goes away without vivid memories of the elaborate and colorful costumes, the thundering drums, and the swinging hips of a Tahitian *tamure* in which young men and women provocatively dance around each other.

The tamure is one of several dances performed during a typical dance show. Others are the *o'tea,* in which men and women in spectacular costumes dance themes such as spear throwing or love; the *aparima,* the hand dance, which emphasizes everyday themes, such as bathing and combing one's hair; the *hivinau,* in which men and women dance in circles and exclaim *"hiri haa haa"* when they meet each other; and the *pata'uta'u,* in which the dancers beat the ground or their thighs with their open hands. It's difficult to follow the themes without understanding Tahitian, but the color and rhythms (which have been influenced by faster, double-time beats from the Cook Islands) make the dances thoroughly enjoyable.

passersby at a sidewalk counter, it serves up varied goodies, from crispy *casse-croûtes* to two substantial *plats-du-jour* selections each day, on a covered dining terrace and in an air-conditioned dining room upstairs.

Rue du Général-de-Gaulle at rue Jeanne d'Arc (at the corner of Centre Vaima, opposite Cathédrale de l'Immaculée Conception). ℂ **45.45.01.** Sandwiches, burgers, quiches, small pizzas 350CFP–900CFP (US$3.50–US$9); meals 1,500CFP–2,000CFP (US$15–US$20). No credit cards. Mon–Sat 5am–5pm.

7 Island Nights

A 19th-century European merchant wrote of the Tahitians, "Their existence was in never-ending merrymaking." In many respects this is still true, for after the sun goes down, Tahitians like to make merry as much today as they did in the 1820s, and Papeete has lots of good choices for visitors who want to join in the fun.

TAHITIAN DANCE SHOWS 𝓻𝓻𝓻

Traditional Tahitian dancing isn't as indecent as it was in Captain Cook's day (see the box "A Very Indecent Dance," above), but seeing at least one show should be on your agenda. You'll have plenty of chances, since nightlife on the outer islands consists almost exclusively of dance shows at the resorts, usually in conjunction with a feast of Tahitian food.

Each of Tahiti's big resort hotels has shows at least 1 night a week. Not to be missed is the **Grande Danse de Tahiti** 𝓻𝓻𝓻 troupe, which usually performs at the InterContinental Resort Tahiti (ℂ **86.51.10**) on Wednesday, Friday, and Saturday evenings (the Sat night show is a re-enactment of the dance which seduced the crew of HMS *Bounty*). Call the resort to make sure. Another good place to catch a show is the **Captain Bligh Restaurant and Bar** (ℂ **43.62.90**), which usually has them on Friday and Saturday at 8:30pm. Expect to pay from 5,000CFP (US$50) for the show and dinner at the Captain Bligh to 8,500CFP (US$85) at the big resorts.

PUB CRAWLING

Papeete has a nightclub or watering hole to fit anyone's taste, from upscale private *(privé)* discotheques to down-and-dirty bars and dance halls where Tahitians strum on guitars while sipping on large bottles of Hinano beer (and sometimes engage in a fisticuffs after midnight). If you look like a tourist, you'll be allowed into the private clubs. Generally, everything gets to full throttle after 9pm (except on Sun, when most pubs are closed). None of the clubs are inexpensive. Expect to pay at least 1,000CFP (US$10) cover charge, which will include your first drink. After that, beers cost at least 500CFP (US$5), with most mixed drinks in the 1,000CFP to 1,500CFP (US$10–US$15) range.

The narrow rue des Ecoles is the heart of Papeete's mahu district, where male transvestites hang out. The **Piano Bar** (ℂ **42.88.24**) is the most popular of the "sexy clubs" along this street, especially for its late-night strip shows featuring female impersonators. It's open daily from 3pm to 3am. The multistory **Mana Rock Cafe,** at the corner of boulevard Pomare and rue des Ecoles (ℂ **48.36.36**), draws a more mixed crowd to its bars and discotheque (you can check your e-mail between sips here).

You're unlikely to be groped or get into a fight at **Le Royal Tahitien Hotel** in Pirae (ℂ **50.40.400**), which has a live band for dancing on Friday nights. The moderate-price seaside restaurant here has very good food for the money, so you can make Friday a dining-and-dancing evening. See "Where to Stay," earlier in this chapter.

Impressions

They have several negative comments on the beachcombing life in Tahiti: Not much cultural life. No intellectual stimulus. No decent library. Restaurant food is disgraceful . . . But I noticed that Saturday after Saturday they turned up at Quinn's with the most dazzling beauties on the island. When I reminded them of this they said, "Well, that does compensate for the poor library."
—James A. Michener, *Return to Paradise*, 1951

You don't have to pay to be entertained on Friday, which is "cruise ship day" on the Papeete waterfront. Arts and crafts are on display, and Tahitians make music, from 8am to 5pm at the Manava Tahiti tourist office, at the foot of rue Paul Gauguin. Tahitian bands perform afterwards out on Place Vaiate, by the cruise ship docks.

9

Moorea

Like most visitors to French Polynesia, I soon grab the ferry to Moorea, just 20km (12 miles) west of Tahiti. James Michener may have thought Bora Bora to be the world's most beautiful island, but Moorea is my choice. In fact, it's so stunningly gorgeous that I have trouble keeping my eye on the road here. Hollywood often uses stock shots of Moorea's jagged mountains, deep bays, and emerald lagoons to create a South Seas setting for movies that don't even take place here.

Geologists attribute Moorea's rugged, otherworldly beauty to a great volcano, the northern half of which either fell into the sea or was blown away in a cataclysmic explosion, leaving the heart-shaped island we see today. In other words, Moorea is only half its old self. The remaining rim of the crater has eroded into the jagged peaks and spires that give the island its haunting, dinosaur-like profile. Cathedral-like Mount Mouaroa—Moorea's trademark "Shark's Tooth" or "Bali Hai Mountain"—shows up on innumerable postcards and on the 100CFP coin.

Mount Rotui stands alone in the center of the ancient crater, its black cliffs and stovepipe buttresses dropping dramatically into Cook's Bay and Opunohu Bay, two dark blue fingers that cut deep into Moorea's interior. These mountain-shrouded bays are certainly among the world's most photographed bodies of water.

Perched high up on the crater's wall, the Belvédère overlooks both bays, Mount Rotui, and the jagged old crater rim curving off to left and right. Do not miss the Belvédère, for it is one of the South Pacific's most awesome panoramas.

With traffic choking Tahiti and Moorea only a 30-minute ferry ride away from Papeete, the island already is a bedroom community for its big sister. Still, it has maintained its Polynesian charm to a large extent. Its hotels and resorts are spread out enough that you don't feel like you're in a tourist trap, and the locals don't feel inundated by us. They still have time to stop and talk with visitors.

Most of Moorea's 15,000 or so residents live on its fringing coastal plain, many of them in small settlements where lush valleys meet a lagoon enclosed by an offshore coral reef. This calm blue lagoon makes Moorea ideal for swimming, boating, snorkeling, and diving. Unlike the black sands of Tahiti, white beaches stretch for miles on Moorea.

Impressions

From Tahiti, Moorea seems to have about 40 separate summits: fat thumbs of basalt, spires tipped at impossible angles, brooding domes compelling to the eye. But the peaks which can never be forgotten are the jagged saw-edges that look like the spines of some forgotten dinosaur.

—James A. Michener, *Return to Paradise*, 1951

GETTING AROUND 245

1 Getting Around

Where you stay and most of what you will want to see and do lie on Moorea's north coast, between the ferry wharf at **Vaiare** and the area known as **Haapiti** on the island's northwestern corner. A large Club Med dominated Haapiti until it closed in 2002, and locals still say "Club Med" when referring to this area.

All ferries from Papeete land at Vaiare, on Moorea's east coast 5km (3 miles) south of **Temae Airport** (see "Getting There & Getting Around," in chapter 7).

BY BUS   The only scheduled buses on Moorea are those which carry passengers to and from the morning and afternoon ferries at Vaiare. Tell the drivers where you're going; they will show you which vehicle is going to your hotel. The trip from Vaiare to the end of the line, at the old Club Med site, takes about 1 hour. The buses also return from the Petite Village shopping center in Haapiti to Vaiare prior to each departure. They stop at the hotels and can be flagged down along the road elsewhere. The one-way fare is 300CFP (US$3), regardless of direction or length of ride.

BY TAXI   Unless you catch a ferry bus or rent a vehicle, you're at the expensive mercy of Moorea's taxi owners, who don't run around looking for customers. The only **taxi stand** is at the airport (✆ **56.10.18**). It's staffed daily from 6am to 6pm. The hotel desks can call one for you, or phone **Pero Taxis** (✆ **56.14.93**), **Albert Tours** (✆ **56.13.53**), or **Justine Taxi** (✆ **77.48.26**). Make advance reservations for service between 6pm and 6am.

Fares are 800CFP (US$8) during the day, 1,700CFP (US$17) at night, plus 110CFP (US$1.10) per kilometer. They double from 8pm to 6am. Expect to pay about 2,000CFP (US$20) one-way from the ferry or airport to the Cook's Bay area, about 4,000CFP (US$40) one-way from the airport or Cook's Bay to the Haapiti area, less for stops along the way. Be sure that you understand what the fare will be before you get in.

BY RENTAL CAR & SCOOTER   Avis (✆ **800/331-1212** or 56.32.68; www.avis.com) and **Europcar** (✆ **800/227-7368** or 56.34.00; www.europcar.com) both have booths at the Vaiare ferry wharf and at several hotels. Although I usually rent from Avis, Europcar is the more widespread and slightly less expensive of the two, with unlimited-kilometer rates starting at 8,600CFP (US$86) a day. The local firm **Albert Rent-a-Car** (✆ **56.13.53**) is the least expensive, with unlimited-kilometer rates starting at 8,000CFP (US$80) for a day. Insurance is included in all rates, but gasoline is not.

In addition to automobiles, Avis also rents little "Fun Cars" (noisy contraptions with two seats and no top) and somewhat larger (and safer) open-air Be-Up vehicles. Both are fun to drive on sunny days. So are scooters, which Europcar and Albert rent starting at 4,800CFP (US$48) for 4 hours and 6,000CFP (US$60) for 24 hours, including gasoline, full insurance, and unlimited kilometers.

Making reservations for cars and scooters is a very good idea, especially on weekends, when many Tahiti residents come to Moorea.

BY BICYCLE   The 60km (36-mile) road around Moorea is relatively flat. The two major hills are on the west side of Cook's Bay and just behind the Sofitel Ia Ora Moorea (the latter is worth the climb, since it has a stupendous view of Tahiti). Some resorts have bikes for their guests to use, and **Europcar** (see above) rents mountain bikes for about 1,600CFP (US$16) for 8 hours, 2,000CFP (US$20) all day.

FAST FACTS: Moorea

The following facts apply specifically to Moorea. For more information, see "Fast Facts: French Polynesia" in chapter 7.

Bookstores **Kina Maharepa** (© **56.22.44**) in the Maharepa shopping center has English novels and magazines. **Supersonics** (© **56.14.96**) in Le Petit Village shopping center opposite the former Club Med carries some English-language magazines and newspapers.

Camera/Film The hotel boutiques, **Kina Maharepa** (© **56.22.44**) in the Maharepa shopping center, and **Supersonics** (© **56.14.96**) in Le Petit Village opposite the old Club Med all sell film.

Currency Exchange **Banque Socredo, Banque de Tahiti,** and **Banque de Polynésie** have offices and ATMs in or near the Maharepa shopping center. Banque de Polynésie has an ATM and a currency exchange machine but not an office in Le Petit Village shopping center in Haapiti. Accordingly, bring cash or travelers checks if you're staying on the northwest corner, or be prepared to put most of your expenditures on a credit card. Banks are open Monday to Friday from 8am to noon and 1:30 to 4:30pm.

Drugstores **Pharmacie Tran** (© **56.10.51**) is in Maharepa. The owner, Tran Thai Thanh, is a Vietnamese refugee who speaks English. It's open Monday to Friday from 7:30am to noon and 2 to 6pm; Saturday from 8am to noon and 3:30 to 6pm; and Sunday and holidays from 8 to 11am.

E-mail Every hotel has Internet access for its guests. In Cook's Bay, **Maria Tapas** restaurant (© **55.01.70**; www.mariatapas.com) has fast Internet access for 250CFP (US$2.50) for 15 minutes (see "Where to Dine," later). Computers are available Monday to Thursday 9am to 11pm, Friday 9am to 1am. In Haapiti, **Polynesian Arts** (© **56.22.00**), in Le Petit Village, also has fast access at 20CFP (20¢) a minute. Open Monday to Saturday 8:30am to 6pm. You can burn your digital photos onto CDs at either.

Emergencies/Police The emergency police telephone number is © **17**. The telephone number for the **gendarmerie** in Cook's Bay is © **56.13.44**. Local police have offices at **Pao Pao** (© **56.13.63**) and at **Haapiti** (© **56.10.84**), near where the Club Med was.

Eyeglasses **Optique Moorea,** in the Maharepa shopping center (© **56.55.44**).

Healthcare The island's **infirmary,** which has an ambulance, is at Afareaitu on the southwest coast (© **56.24.24**). Several doctors are in private practice; ask your hotel staff for a recommendation.

Information The **Moorea Visitors Bureau,** B.P. 1121, 98279 Papetoai (© **56. 29.09**; www.gomoorea.com), has an office at Le Petit Village shopping center in Haapiti. Open Monday to Thursday 8am to 4pm (more or less; they sometimes change). The bureau has an unstaffed booth at the Temae airport, where you can pick up maps and brochures any time.

Post Office Moorea's main post office is in the Maharepa shopping center. It's open Monday to Thursday 7:30am to noon and 1:30 to 4pm, Friday 7:30am to noon and 1:30 to 3pm, and Saturday 7:30 to 9:30am. A post office in Papetoai village is open Monday to Thursday from 7:30am to noon and 1:30 to 4pm, Friday from 7:30am to noon and 1:30 to 3pm, and Saturday from 8 to 10am.

Taxes Moorea's municipal government adds 100CFP to 150CFP (US$1–US$1.50) per night to your hotel bill. Don't complain: The money helps keep the island litter-free.

Water Tap water on Moorea is not safe to drink, so buy bottled water at any grocery store. Some hotels filter their water; ask if it's safe before drinking from the tap.

2 Exploring Moorea

The sights of Moorea may lack great historical significance, but the physical beauty of the island makes a tour—at least of Cook's and Opunohu bays and up to the Belvédère lookout—a highlight of any visit here. There are few places on earth this gorgeous.

As on Tahiti, the round-island road—about 60km (36 miles) long—is marked every kilometer with a PK post. Distances are measured between the intersection of the airport road with the main round-island coastal road and the village of Haapiti on Moorea's opposite side. In other words, the distances indicated on the PKs increase from the airport in each direction, reaching 30km near Haapiti. They then decrease as you head back to the airport.

THE CIRCLE ISLAND TOUR ✶✶✶

The hotel activities desks offer tours around Moorea and up to the Belvédère lookout in the interior. **Albert Tours** (✆ 56.13.53) and **Moorea Explorer** (✆ 56.12.86) have half-day round-island tours, including the Belvédère, for about 3,300CFP (US$33) per person. The tour buses all stop at one black pearl shop or another (guess who gets a commission when you buy the pearl of your dreams?). See "Shopping," later in this chapter, and "Buying Your Black Pearl," in chapter 8, before making a purchase.

TEMAE & MAHAREPA   Begin at the airstrip on Moorea's northeast corner. The airstrip is on the island's only sizable area of flat land. At one time it was a *motu*, or small island, sitting on the reef by itself. Humans and nature have since filled the lagoon except for Lake Temae, which you can see from the air if you fly to Moorea. A resort with Moorea's first golf course is being built here.

Head west from the round-island road/airport road junction.

Temae, 1km (½ mile) from the junction, supplied the dancers for the Pomare dynasty's court and is still known for the quality of its performers. Herman Melville

---

Fun Fact Pai's Spear

Tahitian lore says the legendary hero Pai made the hole in the top of Mount Tohiea when the god of thieves attempted to steal Mount Rotui in the middle of the night. Pai threw his spear from Tahiti and pierced Mount Tohiea. The noise woke up Moorea's roosters, whose commotion alerted the citizenry to put a stop to the dastardly plan.

spent some time here in 1842 and saw the famous, erotic *upaupa,* which he called the "lory-lory," performed clandestinely, out of sight of the missionaries.

The relatively dry north shore between the airport and the entrance to Cook's Bay is **Maharepa,** the island's commercial center. The road skirts the lagoon and passes the Moorea Pearl Resort & Spa and soon reaches the island's main shopping center.

COOK'S BAY 🐟🐟🐟   As the road curves to the left, you enter **Cook's Bay,** the finger-like body of water virtually surrounded on three sides by the jagged peaks lining the semi-circular "wall" of Moorea. The tall thumb with a small hole in its top is **Mount Tohiea.** Coming into view as you drive farther along the bay is **Mount Mauaroa,** Moorea's trade-mark, cathedral-like, "Shark's Tooth" mountain buttressed on its right by a serrated ridge.

Huddled along the beach at the head of the bay, the village of **Pao Pao** is the site of Moorea's public schools. The *Marché Municipale* **(Municipal Market)** is open Monday to Saturday from 5am to 5pm and Sunday from 5 to 8am. Unlike Papeete's market, this one has slim pickings; locals come here primarily to buy fresh fish. The paved road that seems to run through the school next to the bridge cuts through the valley between Cook's Bay and Opunohu Bay. It intersects with the main road between Opunohu Bay and the Belvédère lookout.

The small **St. Joseph's Catholic Church** sits on the shore on the west side of Cook's Bay, at PK 10 from the airport. Inside is a large mural that artist Peter Heyman painted in 1946 and an altar decorated with mother-of-pearl. From the church, the road climbs up the side of the hill, offering some fine views, and then descends back to the lagoon's edge.

Watch on the left for the road leading inland to *Jus de Fruits de Moorea* **(Moorea Fruit Juices)** (© 56.22.33), a factory and distillery which turns the island's produce into the Rotui juices and the potently alcoholic Tahiti Drink you will see in every gro-cery store. I like to refresh here by tasting the yummy fruit liqueurs. Every souvenir imaginable is for sale, too. Hours are Monday to Thursday 8:30am to 4:30pm, Friday and Saturday 8:30am to 3:30pm.

OPUNOHU BAY 🐟🐟🐟   Towering over you is jagged **Mount Rotui,** the huge green-and-black rock separating Moorea's two great bays. Unlike Cook's Bay, Opunohu is virtually devoid of development, a testament to efforts by local residents to maintain the natural beauty of their island (they have ardently resisted efforts to build a luxury resort and golf course here). As soon as the road levels out, you can look through the trees to yachts anchored in **Robinson's Cove,** one of the world's most photographed yacht anchorages. Stop here and put your camera to work.

JARDIN KELLUM   Near the cove, at PK 17.5, stands the bayside home and botan-ical garden of the late Medford and Gladys Kellum, an American couple that once owned all of Opunohu Valley. The Kellums arrived here in 1925, aboard his parents' converted lumber schooner, and they lived for 65 years in their clapboard colonial-style house. Their daughter, Marimari Kellum, lives here today and gives tours of the house and garden to groups who book in advance (© **56.18.52**).

Impressions

Seen for the first time by European Eyes, this coast is like nothing else on our workaday planet; a landscape, rather, of some fantastic dream.
—Charles Nordhoff and James Norman Hall, *Mutiny on the Bounty,* 1933

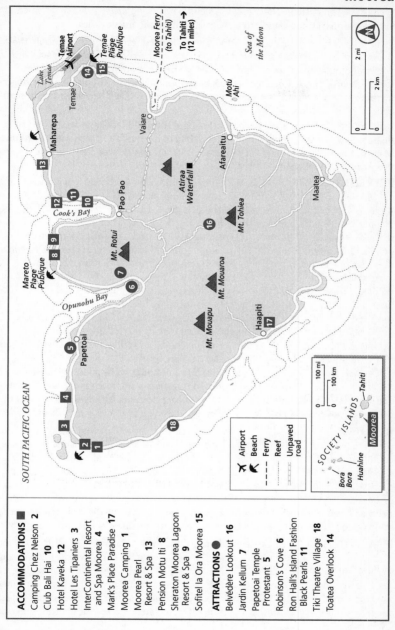

Moorea

Sea of
the Moon

Moorea Ferry (to Tahiti)
To Tahiti → (12 miles)

Temae Airport
Temae Plage Publique
Lake Temae
Temae
Maharepa
Vaiare
Motu Ahi
Afareaitu
Atiraa Waterfall
Maatea
Pao Pao
Cook's Bay
Mt. Rotui
Mt. Tohiea
Mareto Plage Publique
Mt. Mouaroa
Opunohu Bay
Mt. Mouapu
Haapiti
Papetoai
SOUTH PACIFIC OCEAN

N

2 mi
2 km
0 0

SOCIETY ISLANDS
Huahine
Bora Bora
Moorea
Tahiti
100 mi
100 km
0 0

Legend:
Airport
Beach
Ferry
Reef
Unpaved road

ACCOMMODATIONS ■
Camping Chez Nelson **2**
Club Bali Hai **10**
Hotel Kaveka **12**
Hotel Les Tipaniers **3**
InterContinental Resort and Spa Moorea **4**
Mark's Place Paradise **17**
Moorea Camping **1**
Moorea Pearl Resort & Spa **13**
Pension Motu Iti **8**
Sheraton Moorea Lagoon Resort & Spa **9**
Sofitel la Ora Moorea **15**

ATTRACTIONS ●
Belvédère Lookout **16**
Jardin Kellum **7**
Papetoai Temple Protestant **5**
Robinson's Cove **6**
Ron Hall's Island Fashion Black Pearls **11**
Tiki Theatre Village **18**
Toatea Overlook **14**

⎛Moments The View from Belvédère Lookout

If the view from Le Belvédère restaurant on Tahiti doesn't thrill me enough, the scene from the Moorea lookout of the same name certainly does. I never tire of standing at the base of that cliff and watching dramatic Mount Rotui separate the deep blue fingers of Cook's and Opunohu bays.

From the garden, the road soon curves right along a black-sand beach backed by shade trees and the Opunohu Valley at the head of the bay. The beach was turned into Matavai Bay on Tahiti for the 1983 production of *The Bounty*, starring Mel Gibson and Anthony Hopkins.

BELVÉDÈRE LOOKOUT 🕸🕸🕸   After the bridge by the beach, a paved road runs up Moorea's central valley through pasture land, across which Warren Beatty and Annette Benning strolled in their flop movie *Love Affair* (the scenes with Katherine Hepburn were filmed in the white house on the hill to your right). You can stop at *Lycée Agricole d'Opunohu* (**Opunohu Agricultural School**), on the main road (© **56.11.34;** www.formation-agricole-opunohu.org), to see vanilla and other plantations. It's open Monday to Friday 8am to 4:30pm, Saturday 9am to 12:30pm.

At the head of the valley the road climbs steeply up the old crater wall to the restored **Titiroa Marae,** which was part of a concentration of *maraes* and other structures. Higher up you'll pass an archery platform used for competition (archery was a sport reserved for high-ranking chiefs and was never used in warfare in Polynesia). A display in the main marae parking lot explains the history of this area. You can walk among the remains of the temples, now shaded by towering Tahitian chestnut trees that have grown up through the cobblestone-like courtyards.

The narrow road then ascends to **Belvédère Lookout,** whose awesome panorama of the valley and the bays on either side of Mount Rotui is unmatched in the South Pacific. You won't want to be without film or camera batteries here. There's a snack bar in the parking lot, so grab a cold drink or ice cream while you take in this remarkable vista.

PAPETOAI   Back on the coastal road, the sizable village of **Papetoai** was the retreat of the Pomare dynasty in the 1800s and the base from which Pomare I launched his successful drive to take over all of Tahiti and Moorea. It was also headquarters for the London Missionary Society's work throughout the South Pacific. The road to the right, past the new post office, leads to the octagonal **Papetoai Temple Protestant,** built on the site of a marae dedicated to Oro, son of the supreme Taaroa and the god of war. The original church was constructed in the 1820s, and although advertised as the oldest European building still in use in the South Pacific, the present structure dates from the late 1880s.

HAAPITI   From Papetoai, the road runs through the Haapiti hotel district on the northwest corner and then heads south through the rural parts of Moorea. Beginning in the 1970s, a 300-bungalow Club Med generated much business here, including Le Petit Village shopping center across the road. The area has been a bit depressed since the club closed in 2002. Still, this is your last chance to stop for refreshment before the sparsely populated southern half of Moorea. There are several choices here (see "Where to Dine," later in this chapter).

About 4km (2½ miles) beyond Club Med, look for the **Tiki Theatre Village** ⭐⭐⭐, a cultural center that consists of thatch huts on the coastal side of the road. It's the only place to see what a Tahitian village looked like when Captain Cook arrived, so pull in. See "Tiki Theatre Village," below, for details.

When the first Europeans arrived, the lovely, mountain-backed village of **Haapiti** was home of the powerful Marama family, which was allied with the Pomares. It became a center of Catholic missionary work after the French took over the territory, and it is one of the few villages whose Catholic church is as large as its Protestant counterpart. Stop here and look up behind the village for a view of Mount Mouaroa from a unique perspective.

THE SOUTH COAST   South of Haapiti, just as the road curves sharply around a headland, is a nice view of a small bay with the mountains towering overhead (there's no place to park on the headland, so stop and walk up for the view). In contrast to the more touristy north shore, the southeast and southwest coasts have retained an atmosphere of old Polynesia.

The village of **Afareaitu,** on the southeast coast, is the administrative center of Moorea, and the building that looks like a charming hotel across from the village church actually is the island's *mairie,* or town hall.

About half a kilometer (¼ mile) beyond the town hall, opposite an A-frame house on the shore, an unpaved road runs straight between several houses and then continues uphill to the **Atiraa Waterfall** ⭐⭐. Often called Afareaitu Waterfall, water plunges more than 32m (100 ft.) down a cliff, into a small pool. You can drive partway to the falls, then walk 20 minutes up a steep, slippery, and muddy trail. Wear shoes or sandals that have good traction if you make this trek, for in places the slippery trail is hacked into a steep hill; if you slip, it's a long way down to the rocks below. Villagers will be waiting at the beginning of the footpath to extract a small fee.

Beyond Afareaitu, the small bay of **Vaiare** is a beehive of activity when the ferries pull in from Papeete. On workdays commuters park their vehicles at least 1km (½ mile) in either direction from the wharf.

Atop the hill north of the Sofitel Ia Ora Moorea is the **Toatea Overlook** ⭐⭐⭐. Here you'll have a magnificent view of the hotel, the green lagoon flecked with brown coral heads, the white line of the surf breaking on the reef, the deep blue of the Sea of the Moon, and all of Tahiti rising magnificently from the horizon. There's a parking area at the overlook.

The unpaved road to the right at the bottom of the hill leads to the *Temae Plage Publique* (**Temae Public Beach**) ⭐⭐⭐, Moorea's finest stretch of public beach. Follow the left fork through the coconut grove to the lagoon. This is a continuation of the Sofitel Ia Ora Moorea's beach, except that here you don't have a staff to rake the leaves and coral gravel from the sand. Locals often sell snacks and souvenirs here, especially on weekends. Bring insect repellent if you do your beaching here.

Moments Tahiti in All Its Glory

My neck strains every time I cross the hill behind Moorea's Sofitel Ia Ora Moorea, for there across the Sea of the Moon sits Tahiti in all its green glory. What amazement the early explorers must have felt when those mountains appeared over the horizon!

Tiki Theatre Village ★★★

The best cultural experience in French Polynesia is at **Tiki Theatre Village,** at PK 31, or 2km (1¼ miles) south of old Club Med (© **55.02.50;** www.tiki village.pf). Built in the fashion of ancient Tahitian villages, this cultural center has old-style *fares* (houses) in which the staff demonstrates traditional tattooing, tapa-cloth making and painting, wood and stone carving, weaving, cooking, and making costumes, musical instruments, and flower crowns. There's even a "royal" house floating out on the lagoon, where you can learn about the modern art of growing black pearls.

Tiki Theatre Village will even arrange a traditional beachside wedding. The bride is prepared with flowery *monoi* oil like a Tahitian princess, and the groom is tattooed (with a wash-off pen). Both wear traditional costumes.

The village is open Tuesday to Saturday from 11am to 3pm. Admission and a guided tour costs 1,200CFP (US$12).

Not to be missed is the authentic Tahitian feast and dance show here on Tuesday, Wednesday, Friday, and Saturday nights. They pick you up from your hotel and deposit you on the beach for a rum punch and sunset. After the staff uncovers the earth oven, they take you on a tour of the village. A buffet of both Tahitian and Western foods is followed by an energetic 1½-hour dance show with some of the most elaborate yet traditional costumes to be seen in French Polynesia. The dinner and show cost 7,900CFP (US$79) per person, or you can come for the 9pm show for 3,900CFP (US$39). Kids 3 to 12 pay half price. Add 1,150CFP (US$12) for round-trip transportation.

3 Safari Expeditions, Lagoon Excursions & Dolphin-Watching

SAFARI TOURS ★★

You can see the sights and learn a lot about the island on a four-wheel-drive excursion through Moorea's mountainous interior. Every hotel activities desk will book you on one of these adventures. **Albert Tours** (© **56.13.53**) and **Moorea Explorer** (© **56. 12.86**) both have them. I've been with Alex and Gheslaine Haamatearii's **Inner Island Safari Tours** (© **56.20.09**), which will take you through the valleys, up to Belvédère Lookout, and then down to a vanilla plantation in Opunohu Valley. They explain the island's flora and fauna along the way. The best trips end with a drive around Moorea's south coast and a hike up to Atiraa Waterfall for a refreshing swim (see "The South Coast" under "The Circle Island Tour," above). Expect to visit a black pearl shop and Jus de Fruits de Moorea (see "Shopping" below). These half-day trips cost between 4,000CFP and 5,000CFP (US$40–US$50) per person.

In a variation on this theme, **Mahana ATV Tours** (© **56.20.44**) takes you on all-terrain vehicles into the Opunohu Valley.

LAGOON EXCURSIONS ★★★

The lagoon around Moorea is not as beautiful or diverse as Bora Bora's, but it's worth a day's outing. Most hotel activity desks will book you on a lagoon excursion, the best way to experience the magnificent setting. The full-day version of these excursions invariably includes a "motu picnic"—a lunch of grilled fresh fish, poisson cru, and salads served on a little islet (motu) out on the reef. Quite often the fresh fish is caught on the way. You'll have an opportunity to snorkel in the lagoon, and the staff will show you how to husk a coconut. Some of them also include shark- and ray-feeding, one of the most interesting and exciting things to do in the water here. Wear shoes you don't mind getting wet. The tours cost about 7,000CFP (US$70) per person.

Some lagoon excursions may take you to *Lagoonarium de Moorea,* on Motu Ahi off Afareaitu (© 78.31.15). Like its counterpart on Bora Bora (see chapter 10), you can snorkel in a fenced area with dolphins, small sharks, and other sealife. The islet also has a snack bar and scuba diving. You can get there yourself, since the transfer boat leaves from PK 8 in Afareaitu. Fares are 2,300CFP (US$23) adults, 1,500CFP (US$15) for children, including use of kayaks and snorkeling gear. It's open daily.

DOLPHIN-WATCHING 👫👫👫

One of the best things to do on Moorea is a dolphin- and whale-watching excursion led by American marine biologist **Dr. Michael Poole** (© **56.23.22** or **77.50.07;** www.drmichaelpoole.com). An expert on sea mammals and a leader in the effort to have French Polynesian waters declared a whale sanctuary, Dr. Poole will take you out beyond the reef to meet some of the 150 acrobatic spinner dolphins he has identified as regular Moorea residents. In calm conditions and if the animals are agreeable, you can don snorkeling gear and swim with them. You'll also be on the lookout for pilot whales that swim past year-round and giant humpback whales that frequent these waters from July to October. The half-day excursions cost about 7,000CFP (US$70) for adults, half price for kids, including pickup at most hotel docks. Make reservations in advance, and be prepared not to go if the sea isn't calm.

Among the many activities at the InterContinental Resort and Spa Moorea (see "Watersports," below) and by far the most popular for families is the **Moorea Dolphin Center** 👫👫 (© **55.19.48;** www.mooreadolphincenter.com). The intelligent sea mammals are sure to excite young and old alike. The animals live in a fenced area, although the center professes to be dedicated to their care and conservation. Kids 16 and older can join adults in snorkeling with the mammals in deeper water (all must be good swimmers) for 21,000CFP (US$210) per person. A 1-hour "dolphin discovery" excursion in shallow water costs 17,400CFP (US$174) per person. There's a 1-hour children's program (ages 5 to 11) which costs 10,800CFP (US$108) per kid, and there are family programs, too. They'll even take honeymooners on their own private encounter.

4 Fishing, Hiking, Watersports & Other Outdoor Activities

By the time you arrive Moorea may have a golf course, part of a resort being built at Temae. In the meantime, stay on Tahiti if you must play golf. Moorea has no public tennis courts, so pick a hotel that has them if tennis is important to you.

Most hotels have active watersports programs for their guests, such as glass-bottomed-boat cruises and snorkeling in, or sailing on, Moorea's lagoon.

The lagoon off Moorea's northwest corner is blessed with offshore motu, small islets where you can sunbathe, swim, and snorkel (but be beware of strong currents), and have lunch on **Motu Moea** (see "Where to Dine," later in this chapter). You can rent a boat to get over there from **Moorea Locaboat** (© 78.13.39), based next to Hotel Les Tipaniers, or take a transfer from **Tip Nautic** next door (© 73.76.73) for

700CFP (US$7) round-trip. Tip Nautic also rents snorkel gear for 500CFP (US$5) for half a day and kayaks starting at 500CFP (US$5) per hour, and it has water-skiing and dolphin-watching trips.

The most extensive array of sporting activities is at the **InterContinental Resort and Spa Moorea** (© 55.19.19), whose facilities can be used by both guests and visitors who are willing to pay. The facilities include scuba diving, parasailing (magnificent views of the bays, mountains, and reefs); water-skiing; wakeboarding; scooting about the lagoon and Opunohu Bay on jet skis; viewing coral and fish from Aquascope boats; walking on the lagoon bottom while wearing diving helmets; line fishing; and speedboat rentals. Nonguests can also pay to use the pool, snorkeling gear, tennis courts, and to be taken over to a small islet. Call the hotel for prices, schedules, and reservations, which are required.

FISHING   Chris Lilley, an American who has won several sportfishing contests, takes guests onto the ocean in search of big game catch on his *Tea Nui* (© 55.19.19, ext. 1903, or 56.15.08 at home; teanuiservices@mail.pf). You can go out for half a day for about 6,500CFP (US$65) per person, with a minimum of four required, or charter the boat for a whole day for about 66,000CFP (US$660). In keeping with South Pacific custom, you can keep the little fish you catch; Chris sells the big ones. Chris is based at the InterContinental Resort and Spa Moorea.

HIKING   You won't need a guide to hike from the coast road up the Opunohu Valley to Belvédère Lookout. Up and down will take most of a day. It's a level but hot walk along the valley floor and gets steep approaching the lookout. Bring lots of water. Several unmarked hiking trails lead into the mountains, including one beginning in Cook's Bay and ending on the east coast, another from the southwest coast across a pass and into Opunohu Valley. I would go with a guide on longer hikes up in the mountains. Moorea-based **Tahiti Evasion** (© 56.48.77; www.tahitievasion.com) has half-day treks to the archeological sites in the Opunohu Valley, across Three Coconuts Pass between the Belvédère and the south coast, and to the Afreaitu waterfall and the pierced Mt. Tohiea. Prices range from 4,000CFP to 6,000CFP (US$40–US$60) per person.

HORSEBACK RIDING   Landlubbers can go horseback riding along the beach and into the interior with **Ranch Opunohu Valley** (© 56.28.55). Rates are about 6,000CFP (US$60) for a 1½-hour ride.

SCUBA DIVING & SNORKELING   Although Moorea's lagoon is not in the same league with those at Rangiroa, Fakarava, or even Bora Bora, its outer reef has some decent sites for viewing coral and sea life. The island's best diving operator is **TOPdive** (© 56.17.32; www.topdive.com), with bases in Cook's Bay and at the Sheraton Moorea Lagoon Resort & Spa. Also excellent is Gilles Pétré's **Moorea Blue Nui Dive Center** (© 55.17.50; www.bluenui.com) at the Moorea Pearl Resort & Spa. On the northwest coast, the InterContinental Resort and Spa Moorea is home to **Bathy's Club Moorea** (© 55.19.19, ext. 1139), and **Scubapiti Moorea** (© 56.30.38) resides at Hotel Les Tipaniers. All charge about 7,500CFP (US$75) for one dive, including equipment (gauges are metric).

Sharing the lagoon with the Sofitel Ia Ora Moorea, the *Temae Plage Publique* **(Tamae Public Beach)** has some of the island's best snorkeling, and it's relatively safe. Also good is the lagoon around the motus off Haapiti, but watch out for strong currents coming in and out of the nearby reef passes.

Another favorite with locals for sunning and swimming is *Mareto Plage Publique* **(Mareto Public Beach),** in a coconut grove west of the Sheraton Moorea between the two bays. Go around the wire fence on the eastern end.

5 Shopping

THE SHOPPING SCENE

The island's commercial center is at **Maharepa,** where you'll find black-pearl shops, banks, grocery stores, hairdressers, the post office, and other services. The neocolonial buildings of **Le Petit Village** shopping center anchor the northwestern corner, where stores sell *pareus,* T-shirts, and souvenirs. **Supersonics** (© **56.29.73**) carries film, batteries, stamps, magazines, and other items. There's a grocery store.

Boutiques and art galleries are numerous on Moorea, but they come and go as frequently as their owners arrive from France, then decide to go home. The shops I mention below have been around for a while.

ART

Galerie van der Heyde   Dutch artist Aad van der Heyde has lived and worked on Moorea since 1964. One of his bold impressionist paintings of a Tahitian woman was selected for French Polynesia's 100CFP postage stamp in 1975, and his landscape of Bora Bora appeared on a 2004 stamp. Aad will sell you an autographed lithograph of the paintings. Some of his works are displayed on the gallery's garden wall. Aad has produced excellent videos of the islands and will gladly sell you a copy on DVD. He also has a small collection of pearls, wood carvings, *tapa* cloth, shell and coral jewelry, and primitive art from Papua New Guinea. East side of Cook's Bay. © **56.14.22.** Mon–Sat 8am–5pm.

Sculpture Par Woody   Woody Howard was studying horticulture at the University of Hawaii when he came to Moorea in 1982 to work on Hotel Bali Hai's plantation. Like so many others, he stayed. You can visit his lagoonside workshop and, if he's not off searching for driftwood, watch him carving award-winning images of dolphins, fish, Polynesian wildlife, and women. He also has a reasonably priced selection of black pearls. Papetoai, between village and InterContinental Resort and Spa Moorea. © **56.37.00** or 56.17.73. Mon–Sat 8am–5pm.

BLACK PEARLS

Moorea has more pearl shops than you can visit in a normal vacation. In fact, many of the stores will come looking for you, with offers of free transportation to and from your hotel or the cruise ship landing in Opunohu Bay, and tour operators are likely to deposit you at the shop offering the highest commission at the end of your excursion. Always shop around, and re-read the "Buying Your Black Pearl" box in chapter 8 before making your purchase.

Among several stores near the old Club Med site in Haapiti is **Tahia Collins** (© **55.05.00;** www.tahiacollins.com), formerly the Black Pearl Gem Company. Owner and chief designer Tahia Collins was a Miss Moorea and is a scion of the Albert Haring family (you will see the Albert name all over the island). Her husband, Marc Collins, was born in Hawaii of an American father and Tahitian mother. This is one of the more aggressive pearl shops on Moorea. Others worth visiting in this area are **Herman Perles** (© **56.42.79**) and **Pai Moana Pearls** (© **56.25.25**).

My favorites are on the other side of the island, to wit:

Eva Perles Eva Frachon, the French owner of this little shop, graduated from the University of Wisconsin at Oshkosh with a bachelor's degree in photography and art metals; thus, she does her own creative settings, and speaks American-style English. It's worth stopping to look at her selection of woodcarvings from the Marquesas. Maharepa, opposite the post office. ℂ 56.10.10. Mon–Sat 9:30am–5:30pm.

Ron Hall's Island Fashion Black Pearls ✸✸✸ (Value) Ron Hall sailed from Hawaii to Tahiti with the actor Peter Fonda in 1974; Peter went home, Ron didn't. Now Ron and his son, Heimata, run this air-conditioned Moorea retail outlet. It's worth a stop to see the antiques and old photos, including one of the infamous Quinn's Bar and a William Leeteg painting of a Tahitian *vahine* (Ron's wife and Heimata's mother, Josée, was herself a championship Tahitian dancer). In 15 minutes of "pearl school," you will learn the basics of picking a pearl. They will have your selection set in a mounting of your choice, their prices are fair, and they donate 10% of every pearl purchase to Dr. Michael Poole's dolphin and whale research (see "Dolphin-Watching," above). They also carry one of Moorea's best selections of bathing suits, aloha shirts, and T-shirts. East side of Cook's Bay. ℂ 56.11.06. Mon–Sat 9am–6pm.

6 Where to Stay

Most of Moorea's hotels and restaurants are grouped in or near Cook's Bay, or in the Haapiti district on the northwest corner of the island around the old Club Med site. With the exception of the Sofitel Ia Ora Moorea, those in or near Cook's Bay do not have the best beaches on the island, but the snorkeling is excellent and their views of the mountains are unsurpassed in the South Pacific. Those on the northwest corner, on the other hand, have generally fine beaches, lagoons like giant swimming pools, and unobstructed views of the sunset, but not of Moorea's famous mountains. The two areas are relatively far apart, so you might spend most of your time near your hotel unless you rent a vehicle or otherwise make a point to see the sights. An alternative is to split your stay between the two areas.

HOTELS IN THE COOK'S BAY AREA
EXPENSIVE
Moorea Pearl Resort & Spa ✸✸✸ Forget a great view here, since this multi-faceted resort faces the open ocean, and its 28 overwater bungalows block most of the sea view. Snorkeling is excellent here, however, especially from the decks of the 20 deluxe, overwater bungalows perched out on the edge of the clifflike reef. They and 18 beach bungalows with private pools in their courtyards are the pick of a mixed litter of accommodations. Some of the garden bungalows are stand-alone, while others are in less private duplex units. All bungalows are identical inside, with tasteful native wood accents, ceiling fans, king beds, and ample shower-only bathrooms. The least expensive units are 30 spacious hotel rooms in two-story blocks away from the lagoon. They all have king beds and balconies or patios, and eight family rooms add two single beds. Big thatch roofs cover a large dining room and pool-level bar, which hosts Tahitian dance shows twice a week. The smallish beach and big infinity swimming pool serve as centers for numerous outdoor activities.

B.P. 3410, 98728 Maharepa, Moorea. ℂ 800/657-3275 or 55.17.50. Fax 55.17.51. www.pearlresorts.com. 95 units. 25,000CFP–30,000CFP (US$250–US$300) double; 39,000CFP–62,000CFP (US$390–US$620) bungalow. AE, DC, MC, V. **Amenities:** 2 restaurants; bar; outdoor pool; spa; Jacuzzi; watersports equipment rentals; bike rentals; activities desk; car-rental desk; limited room service; massage; babysitting; laundry service. *In room:* A/C, TV, dataport, kitchen, minibar (bungalows only), fridge, coffeemaker, hair dryer, irons, safe.

Sheraton Moorea Lagoon Resort & Spa 🏝🏝   On the north coast about halfway between Cook's and Opunohu bays, this hotel is not particularly convenient to restaurants and activities, but it does provide shuttles to the Tiki Village Theatre and the Vaiare ferry dock. Two stunning, conical thatch roofs cover the reception area and a French restaurant overlooking a decent beach. Steps lead down to a beachside pool with its own sunken bar. You'll get some serious pampering in the resort's full-service Mandara spa. All the guest bungalows are identical except for their location. A Y-shaped pier—with its own sundowner bar—leads to half of them out over the lagoon. These all have glass floor panels for fish-viewing and decks with steps down into the clear, 4-foot-deep water. The others are situated in a coconut grove by the beach. Every unit is equipped with niceties such as CD players, complimentary snorkeling gear, plush robes, and claw-foot bathtubs, in addition to walk-in showers. The public areas and guest quarters here are the most luxurious on Moorea.

B.P. 1005, 98279 Papetoai, Moorea (between Cook's and Opunohu bays). © **800/325-3535** or 55.11.11 in Moorea. Fax 86.48.40. www.sheraton.com. 106 units. 34,400CFP–89,000CFP (US$344–US$890) bungalow. AE, DC, MC, V. **Amenities:** 2 restaurants; 3 bars; outdoor pool; 2 tennis courts; health club; spa; watersports equipment rentals; bike rentals; concierge; activities desk; car-rental desk; business center; 24-hr. room service; massage; babysitting; laundry service. *In room:* A/C, TV, CD player, dataport, minibar, coffeemaker, hair dryer, iron, safe.

Sofitel Ia Ora Moorea   On the island's northeast coast, this sprawling resort was built in the 1960s, and it was shuttered temporarily in 2005 for its first renovation since then. All its original bungalows were being replaced, and 19 new overwater units were being added—which set off demonstrations by local environmentalists opposed to damaging the reef. When it reopens in 2006 it will still sit beside one of the South Pacific's best lagoons and a long, lovely beach over which grape-leaf and casuarina trees hang. It's also the only hotel with a view of Tahiti, whose green, cloud-topped mountains seem to climb out of the horizon beyond the reef.

B.P. 28, Maharepa, Moorea (Temae, on the northeast coast facing Tahiti). © **800/763-4835**, 55.03.55, or 41.04.04 in Papeete. Fax 41.05.05. www.accorhotels.com. 129 units. Check the website for post-renovation rates. AE, DC, MC, V. **Amenities:** 2 restaurants; bar; outdoor pool; 2 tennis courts; watersports equipment rentals; bike rentals; activities desk; car-rental desk; massage; babysitting; laundry service. *In room:* A/C, TV, minibar, coffeemaker, hair dryer, iron, safe.

MODERATE

Club Bali Hai *(Value)*   The last property operated by Moorea's two surviving Bali Hai Boys (see the "The Bali Hai Boys" box, below), this basic hotel has an incredible view of Moorea's ragged mountains across Cook's Bay, a scene that epitomizes the South Pacific. Under a bayside thatch-roof, the Blue Pineapple restaurant serves breakfast and lunch (see "Where to Dine," below). It also is the scene for Muk McCallum's bring-your-own happy hours from 5:30 to 7pm Thursday to Tuesday, when he "talks story" about the good old days on Moorea. It's worth stopping by the club's Wednesday night Tahitian dance shows too. A swimming pool with a rock waterfall augments the manmade beach here. Half of the guest units are part of a time-share operation, but that means they come equipped with cooking facilities, which is a plus for budget-minded travelers. The overwater bungalows are the least expensive in French Polynesia, while the beachfront bungalows have huge bathrooms with gardens growing in them, another trademark of the Bali Hai Boys. Most other units are in one- or two-story motel-style buildings. All are simply but comfortably furnished. *Note:* Some units have air-conditioners in their bedrooms but not in their living areas, and the least expensive "budget units" do not have coffeemakers (bring your own coffee even

The Bali Hai Boys

Californians Jay Carlisle, Don "Muk" McCallum, and the late Hugh Kelley gave up their budding business careers as stockbroker, lawyer, and sporting goods salesman, respectively, and in 1960 bought an old vanilla plantation on Moorea. Instead of planting, they refurbished an old beachfront hotel that stood on their property. Taking a page from James Michener's *Tales of the South Pacific*, they renamed it the Bali Hai and opened for business in 1961. With construction of Tahiti-Faaa International Airport across the Sea of the Moon, their timing couldn't have been better. With Jay managing the money, Hugh building the resort, and Muk entertaining their guests, they quickly had a success on their hands. Travel writers soon dubbed them the "Bali Hai Boys."

Supplies and fresh produce weren't easy to come by in those days, so they put the old vanilla plantation to work producing chickens, eggs, and milk. It was the first successful poultry and dairy operation on the island.

Thank Jay, Muk, and Hugh for overwater bungalows—cabins sitting on pilings over the lagoon with glass panels in their floors so that we can watch the fish swim below. They built the world's first in 1968 on Raiatea. A novelty at the time, their romantic invention is now a staple at resorts well beyond French Polynesia.

if your unit does have one). This is good value if you don't need a phone in your room or other such luxuries. On the other hand, the view is worth a million bucks.

B.P. 8, 98728 Maharepa, Moorea. ℂ 56.13.68. Fax 56.13.27. www.clubbalihai.com. 44 units. US$100–US$115 double; US$185–US$245 bungalow. AE, DC, MC, V. **Amenities:** Restaurant (breakfast and lunch); bar; outdoor pool; activities desk; car-rental desk; coin-operated washers and dryers. *In room:* A/C, kitchen (except budget rooms), fridge, coffeemaker (except budget units), no phone.

Hotel Kaveka *Value* Another modest property with a fine view, this all-bungalow hotel sits behind a rock wall along the road, but its other side opens to Cook's Bay. Noted primarily for its fish burgers, the hotel's overwater Fisherman's Wharf enjoys the best view of any Moorea restaurant serving an international menu. The white-sand beach here is compact (a breakwater fronts most of the property), but snorkeling here is very good. The bungalows are made of timber with shingle roofs covering pandanus ceilings. Most have double and single platform beds and smallish, shower-only bathrooms. Two units have two double beds and much better bathrooms. All units have ceiling fans, and some (including beachfront bungalows) have air-conditioners. The least expensive lanai units lack porches. If your bungalow doesn't have one, you can rent TVs and fridges (as well as cellphones). The few-frills Kaveka often is the least expensive hotel offered in package trips to French Polynesia.

B.P. 373, 98728 Maharepa, Moorea. ℂ 56.50.50. Fax 56.52.63. www.hotelkaveka.com. 25 units. 11,500CFP–23,500CFP (US$115–US$235) double. AE, MC, V. **Amenities:** Restaurant; bar; watersports equipment rentals; laundry service. *In room:* A/C (some units), TV, no phone.

Pension Motu Iti Auguste and Dora Ienfa's little pension sits beside the lagoon about 800 meters (880 yards) west of the Sheraton Moorea Lagoon Resort & Spa.

They have no beach, only a bulkhead along the shore, but a pier goes to an overwater cabana for relaxing. Their five bungalows are clean, comfortable, and reasonably spacious, and they have a small dormitory over the main building. Their dining room serves breakfast, lunch, and dinner daily, although the food at Restaurant Aito next door is much more interesting (see "Where to Dine," below).

B.P. 189, 98728 Maharepa, Moorea (between Cook's and Opunohu bays). © **55.05.20**. Fax 55.05.21. www.pension motuiti.com. 5 units. 10,500CFP–12,000CFP (US$105–US$120) bungalow; 1,650CFP (US$17) dorm bed. AE, MC, V. **Amenities:** Restaurant; bar; free kayaks, canoes, snorkeling gear; babysitting; laundry service. *In room:* TV, no phone.

HOTELS ON THE NORTHWEST COAST
EXPENSIVE

InterContinental Resort and Spa Moorea ★★★ *Kids*   Although relatively isolated about 2.5km (1½ miles) east of the Club Med area, Moorea's best all-around resort has plenty to keep its house guests busy. The beach and sometimes murky lagoon here aren't Moorea's best, but the resort has the widest range of watersports activities on the island—all of them available both to guests and to nonguests who are willing to pay (see "Fishing, Hiking, Watersports & Other Outdoor Activities ," earlier in this chapter). A well-organized children's program makes this the best family vacation resort in French Polynesia. The airy central building with a shingle roof opens to a large pool area surrounded by an ample sunning deck. Most of the guest bungalows extend partially over the water from man-made islands. Although the construction style is European, mat walls and rattan furnishings lend tropical ambience. They also are air-conditioned, which the less expensive garden bungalows are not. A curving two-story building holds 52 spacious hotel rooms; they all have patios or balconies facing the beach, and their combination tub-showers are a rarity on Moorea. The Tahitian dance show on the beach is one of Moorea's most colorful.

B.P. 1019, 98279 Papetoai, Moorea (between Papetoai and Haapiti). © **800/327-0200** or 55.19.19. Fax 55.19.55. www.interconti.com. 52 units, 102 bungalows. 36,000CFP (US$360) double; 42,000CFP–80,700CFP (US$420–US$807) bungalow. AE, DC, MC, V. **Amenities:** Restaurant; bar; outdoor pool; tennis courts; spa; free snorkel gear, kayaks, canoes; watersports equipment rentals; bike rentals; children's programs; concierge; activities desk; car-rental desk; limited room service; babysitting; laundry service. *In room:* A/C, TV, minibar, coffeemaker, hair dryer.

MODERATE

Hotel Les Tipaniers ★★ *Value*   One of Moorea's best values, this friendly, French-owned establishment sits in a coconut grove beside the sandy beach that wraps around the island's northwestern corner. The widely spaced bungalows stand back in the trees, which gives the small complex an open, airy atmosphere. They also are far enough from the road to be quiet. The "standard superior" bungalows have L-shaped settees facing sliding glass doors to covered porches. Behind the settee a raised sleeping area supports a queen-size bed, and behind that, a fully tiled bathroom has a sizable shower and vanity space. To the rear of the property, other bungalows are equipped with kitchens and can sleep up to five persons. Also out back, a building houses four small hotel-style rooms equipped with twin beds (you can push them together), reading lights, and ample tiled bathrooms with showers. Okay for couples, these rooms are the least expensive yet comfortable place to stay on Moorea. Unlike the others, however, they do not have phones, fridges, or safes. All units here have ceiling fans but not air-conditioners. A very good restaurant with a deck over the beach is open daily for breakfast, lunch, and afternoon snacks. The hotel is also home to a terrific beach bar and an excellent Italian restaurant (see "Where to Dine," below). Guests can make free

---

> ### *Tips* Bring Travelers Checks, or Card It
>
> The only banking facility on Moorea's northwest corner is Banque de Polynésie's ATM in Le Petit Village shopping center, opposite the old Club Med site. Since you cannot be assured of withdrawing cash from the machine, and it's a long and expensive trip to the banks at Maharepa, bring travelers checks if you're staying in this area, or be prepared to put most of your expenditures on a credit card.

---

use of canoes and bicycles, or pay Tip Nautic for kayaking, water-skiing, motu trips, and diving with Scubapiti, which is based here.

B.P. 1002, 98279 Papetoai, Moorea (in Haapiti, east of old Club Med). ✆ 56.12.67. Fax 56.29.25. www.lestipaniers.com. 22 units. 6,900CFP (US$69) double; 13,950CFP (US$140) bungalow; 13,950CFP–15,950CFP (US$140–US$160) double w/kitchenette. AE, DC, MC, V. **Amenities:** 2 restaurants; 2 bars; watersports equipment rentals; canoes and bicycles; babysitting; laundry service. *In room:* Kitchen (6 units), fridge (18 units), safe (18 units).

INEXPENSIVE

Camping Chez Nelson   All guests share toilets, cold-water showers, and communal kitchen facilities at this campground and hostel in a beachside coconut grove about 200 yards west of the former Club Med. In addition to camping space on a shadeless lawn, basic accommodations here include small bungalows for couples, four blocks of small dorm rooms (two bunks each), and four other thatched-roof hostel bungalows down the road (and still on the beach).

B.P. 1309, 98279 Papetoai, Moorea (in Haapiti, west of old Club Med). ✆/fax **56.15.18.** www.camping-nelson.pf. 4 bungalows, 15 rooms, 20 dorm beds. 1,100CFP (US$11) per camper; 1,300CFP–1,600CFP (US$13–US$16) dorm bed; 3,800CFP–5,800CFP (US$38–US$58) double; 4,000CFP–4,700CFP (US$40–US$47) per bungalow. Lower rates for stays of more than 1 night. AE, DC, MC. V. *In room:* No phone.

Mark's Place Paradise   A cabinet maker from Idaho, Mark Walker moved to French Polynesia in 1980 and has put his skills to work on the creatively rustic units at this retreat beside a stream in the Haapiti Valley. No two alike, his units range in size from a honeymoon unit that has a TV with DVD player to one large enough for groups or use as a dormitory. Two studio rooms have TVs, kitchens, and private bathrooms. All others—including couples in the honeymoon unit plus campers and dorm residents—share toilets, showers, and the communal kitchen. Although he isn't on the beach, Mark's attention to his guests makes this an excellent place for budget-conscious travelers and backpackers.

B.P. 41, 98279 Papetoai, Moorea (at PK 23.5 in Haapiti valley). ✆ **56.43.02** or 78.93.65. www.marks-place-paradise.com. 5 bungalows (3 w/bathroom), 10 dorm beds, 25 tent sites. 6,000CFP–7,500CFP (US$60–US$75) bungalow; 1,500CFP–2,500CFP (US$15–US$25) dorm bed; 1,050CFP (US$11) per camper. MC, V. **Amenities:** Bike and kayak rentals. *In room:* TV, kitchen, no phone.

Moorea Camping   This establishment in a coconut grove has much more shade and a better beach for swimming than does Camping Nelson. A beachside pavilion covers picnic tables and a communal kitchen. A long plywood house—actually little more than a permanent tent—contains eight rooms with foam mattresses. One bungalow can accommodate up to four persons. The showers dispense cold water.

PK 27.5, Tiahura, Moorea (in Haapiti, west of old Club Med). ✆ **56.14.47.** Fax 56.30.22. einui@hotmail.com. 20 tent sites, 9 beds, 8 rooms, 5 bungalows. 1,100CFP–1,500CFP (US$11–US$15) per camper; 1,200CFP–1,800CFP

(US$12–US$18) dorm bed; 2,500CFP–3,800CFP (US$25–US$38) per person in rooms; 4,800CFP–5,800CFP (US$48–US$58) single or double per bungalow. Lower rates for stays of more than 1 night. No credit cards. **Amenities:** Bike rentals. *In room:* Kitchen (bungalows only), no phone.

7 Where to Dine

The restaurant scene changes quickly on Moorea, so I can only hope the ones I recommend below are still in business when you get here. As on Tahiti, you can save by eating at snack bars for breakfast, lunch, or an early dinner.

RESTAURANTS IN THE COOK'S BAY AREA

Nicely spiced pies come from the wood-fired oven at **Allo Pizza,** in Cook's Bay near the gendarmerie (② **56.18.22**). There are only two tables, so most folks carry out or call for delivery if they're staying between the Sofitel Ia Ora Moorea and the Sheraton Moorea. Prices range from 900CFP to 1,900CFP (US$9–US$19). Open Tuesday to Saturday 11am to 2pm and 5 to 9pm, Sunday 5 to 9pm.

EXPENSIVE

Le Sud ❧ SOUTHERN FRENCH   For a pleasant change of French pace, head to this little white house in the Maharepa shopping district for paella, Provençal-style fish dishes, and seafood pastas from *le sud* (the south) of France. The spices definitely reflect Spanish and Italian influences. The *plats du jour* here are very good value, especially at lunch. Torches contribute to romantic nighttime dining on the patio.

Maharepa. ② **56.42.95.** Reservations recommended. Main courses 1,900CFP–2,900CFP (US$19–US$29). MC, V. Tues–Sun 11am–2pm and 6:30–9:30pm.

MODERATE

Alfredo's ITALIAN/FRENCH   Gregarious French restaurateur Christian Boucheron, who worked at hotels in the Washington, D.C., suburbs for 19 years, will make you feel right at home in this old building, a short walk from the Club Bali Hai. In fact, many guests are Americans and other English-speaking visitors who come here as much for fun as food (local guitarist Ron Falconer usually plays and sings here Thurs and Sun nights).

Pao Pao, near Club Bali Hai. ② **56.17.71.** Reservations recommended. Pizzas 1,650CFP (US$17); main courses 1,650CFP–3,800CFP (US$17–US$38). MC, V. Daily 11am–2:30pm and 5:30–9:30pm.

Le Mahogany ❧❧ *Value* FRENCH/CHINESE   French chef François Courtien spent 30 years cooking at the former Hotel Bali Hai before joining Tahitian Blondine Agnia at her pleasant little dining spot next to the local gym. It's a favorite with local expatriates who appreciate value and friendly service. Polished mahogany tables, art-adorned walls, and a window opening to a garden provide tropical ambience. A rich avocado-and-shrimp cocktail is a good way to start. Daily specials feature the likes of Moorea-grown shrimp with curry or Provençal sauce, and shrimp and scallops in a puff pastry with a light cream sauce. The Cantonese main courses are better than those at any Chinese restaurant here. Or you can opt for the special tourist menu of a salad, mahimahi grilled or with meunière sauce, and ice cream for dessert. Otherwise, end with a *tarte tatin,* a caramelized apple pie served with vanilla ice cream.

Maharepa. ② **56.39.73.** Reservations recommended. Main courses 1,550CFP–2,950CFP (US$16–US$30); tourist menu 3,100CFP (US$31). MC, V. Thurs–Tues 11am–2:30pm and 6–9:30pm.

⌐Value Call for Transportation

Most Moorea restaurants will come get you or pay half if not all of your taxi fare if you make reservations for dinner. Although they restrict this service to nearby restaurants, depending on the size of your group, it pays to call ahead.

Restaurant Aito FRENCH/CORSICAN Extending out over the lagoon, this open-air cafe preserves the old South Seas ambience better than any other on Moorea. Adding to the charm are big *aito* (ironwood) trees growing through the deck and thatch roof (hence the restaurant's name). Owner Jean-Baptiste Cipriani grew up in Marseilles on the cooking of his Corsican ancestors, and he repeats some of those dishes here, including a luscious tomato sauce that requires 10 hours to prepare. You can dip your bread into some *very* spicy Corsican peppers while waiting. This isn't the cleanest place on Moorea, but it's a terrific spot for a lagoonside lunch, as many celebrity visits attest.

PK 13.1, west of Sheraton Moorea between Cook's and Opunohu bays. 🕐 **56.45.52.** Reservations recommended. Main courses 1,850CFP–2,600CFP (US$19–US$26). MC, V. Daily 7–9am, 11am–2:30pm, and 6–9pm.

INEXPENSIVE

Caraméline PATISSERIE/SNACKS A good choice for a cooked breakfast, this patisserie also offers a selection of pastries, crepes, pizzas, salads, omelets, quiches, burgers, sandwiches, fruit plates, ice cream, sundaes, and other goodies. The patio tables here are a relaxing spot to write a postcard.

Maharepa, next to the post office. 🕐 **56.15.88.** Breakfasts 650CFP–1,550CFP (US$6.50–US$16); snacks and light meals 400CFP–1,800CFP (US$4–US$18). MC, V. Daily 7am–5pm.

Maria Tappas *(Finds)* FRENCH/TEX-MEX You'll hear conversations being held in French, English, and Tahitian—sometimes all three simultaneously—at this lively pub, where the offspring of Moorea's many expatriate residents like to hang out. Happy hours from 6 to 7pm on Thursday and Friday and entertainment on Thursday and Saturday evenings really pack them in. Although Tex-Mex is the official specialty, I stick to burgers, salads, steaks, and French fare. Friendly owners Julie Berten and Herenui Teriitehau stock a wide selection of European beers. You can check your e-mail here every day except Saturday.

Cook's Bay, PK 6 in Kilupa Centre. 🕐 **55.01.70.** Reservations accepted. Most items 950CFP–2,100CFP (US$9.50–US$21). MC, V. Restaurant Mon–Thurs 11:30am–2:30pm and 6:30–9:30pm, Fri 11:30am–2:30pm and 6:30pm–1am, Sat 6pm–1am. Bar Mon–Thurs 9am–11pm, Fri 9am–1am, Sat 6pm–1am.

Snack l'Ananas Bleu (The Blue Pineapple) *(Value)* BREAKFAST/SNACKS Matahi Hunter's snack occupies what once was the sunken bayside bar at the Club Bali Hai, where you get a stupendous view of Cooks' Bay to go with your cooked or continental breakfast and lunches of big juicy beef, fish, or teriyaki burgers accompanied by french fries. Ice cream and fruit drinks provide relief from the midday heat. There's a seafood barbecue on Wednesday night following the Club's Tahitian dance show.

Pao Pao, in Club Bali Hai. 🕐 **56.12.06.** Breakfast 600CFP–1,500CFP (US$6–US$15); burgers and sandwiches 750CFP–1,550CFP (US$7.50–US$16); main courses 1,600CFP–2,000CFP (US$16–US$20). MC, V. Daily 7am–3pm.

Snack Rotui SNACK BAR   On the shore of Cook's Bay, this walk-up "snack" is run by a Chinese family, and for about 500CFP (US$5) you can get a *casse-croûte* sandwich, a soft drink, and a slice of delicious homemade cake. Forget the daily plate lunches, usually a Chinese dish with rice, which are prepared earlier in the day and served without refrigeration. A few tables under a roof beside the beach catch the breezes off the bay.

Pao Pao, west of the bridge at the head of Cook's Bay. (C) **56.18.16.** Sandwiches 140CFP–200CFP (US$1.40–US$2). No credit cards. Tues–Sun 7am–6pm.

RESTAURANTS ON THE NORTHWEST COAST

Even if you don't spend a day on the little islet off the northwest coast, you can pop over for a French or Tahitian lunch at **Motu Moea** ((C) **74.96.96**). Book at your hotel activities desk, since reservations are essential for a boat shuttle at 10am, noon, or 2pm daily. Roundtrip boat transfers cost about 1,000CPF (US$10), while main courses average about 2,000CFP (US$20). You'll be on your own out here, so follow the advice of the activity staff and don't swim in the pass between the islets. Expensive

Linareva Floating Restaurant and Bar FRENCH SEAFOOD   You'll pay a price to have dinner here, but Eric Lussiez's restaurant and bar is Moorea's most unusual: It occupies the original *Tamarii Moorea,* the first ferry to ply between Papeete and Moorea. Eric completely rebuilt the old vessel and outfitted the dining room with polished wood, large windows, and plenty of bright brass and other nautical decor. The menu changes with the availability of local seafood such as shark and emperor fish, most expertly prepared with traditional French sauces. Tour groups stop here for lunch, when prices run about half of those at dinner.

Haapiti (7km/4 miles south of old Club Med). (C) **55.05.66.** Reservations strongly recommended for dinner. Main courses 1,700CFP–3,850CFP (US$17–US$39); tourist menu 3,550CFP (US$36). MC, V. Daily 11am–3pm and 5–10pm.

MODERATE

Le Mayflower *Value* CASUAL FRENCH   This casual roadside restaurant draws mostly local residents, who rightly proclaim it to be Moorea's best for both food and value. The sauces are lighter than you will experience elsewhere, and there is always a vegetarian selection. I like to start with a salad of warm local shrimp over cool fresh greens. The house special—lobster ravioli in a cream sauce—is a worthy main choice, as are seafood pasta under pesto or the reliable shrimp in coconut curry. Mahimahi in a lobster sauce highlights a special tourist menu here.

Haapiti, west of old Club Med. (C) **56.53.59.** Reservations recommended. Main courses 1,650CFP–2,650CFP (US$17–US$27). AE, MC, V. Tues–Sun 11:30am–2pm and 6:30–10:30pm.

Tips Check Out Moorea's *Roulottes*

As on Tahiti, your best bet for inexpensive nighttime meals are the local roulottes (see "Where to Dine," in chapter 4). The best of these meal wagons, **Roulotte Jules & Claudine** at the municipal market in Pao Pao ((C) **56.25.31**), serves a mixed menu of poisson cru, chow mein, char-grilled steaks, chicken, and fish, but the best item is local shrimp in a tasty coconut curry sauce. Prices range from 800CFP to 1,500CFP (US$8–US$15). No credit cards. Open Monday to Saturday 6:30 to 8:30pm. You'll find another roulotte near the Petite Village shopping center in Haapiti.

Restaurant Les Tipaniers ✦✦ *Value* ITALIAN/FRENCH   This romantic, thatched-roof restaurant is popular with visitors and Moorea's permanent residents, who come here for delicious pizzas with a variety of toppings and homemade spaghetti, lasagna, tagliatelle, and gnocchi served with Bolognese, carbonara, or seafood sauce. French dishes include pepper steak and filets of mahimahi in butter or vanilla sauce. Discounted transportation is available for Haapiti-area hotel guests.

Haapiti, at Hotel Les Tipaniers, east of old Club Med. ✆ **56.12.67.** Reservations recommended. Pasta and pizza 1,000CFP–1,550CFP (US$10–US$16); main courses 1,850CFP–2,500CFP (US$19–US$25). AE, DC, MC, V. Daily 6:30–9pm.

INEXPENSIVE

Le Motu Pizza Grill SNACK BAR   You can get a steak with french fries at this open-air restaurant, but it's best for pizzas and hamburgers. Light fare includes salads, crepes, and soft ice cream, and a selection of soft drinks, beer, and wine.

Haapiti, opposite old Club Med. ✆ **56.16.70.** Burgers, sandwiches, and salads 500CFP–1,400CFP (US$5–US$14); pizza 1,050CFP–1,300CFP (US$11–US$13). MC, V (2,000CFP [US$20] minimum). Mon–Sat 9:30am–9pm, Sun 9:30am–3pm.

Les Tipaniers Restaurant de la Plage (Restaurant by the Beach) ✦ SNACK BAR/ITALIAN   Under a soaring thatch roof and opening to the lagoon, this is the best place in Haapiti for a lagoonside lunch or sunset cocktail. It offers a good selection of salads, some with fruit, and a big juicy burger. Or you can select one of the pastas that make Les Tipaniers' nighttime restaurant popular. Breakfast is served here.

Haapiti, at Hotel Les Tipaniers, east of old Club Med. ✆ **56.19.19.** Salads, sandwiches, burgers 550CFP–1,300CFP (US$5.50–US$13); pastas 1,000CFP–1,700CFP (US$10–US$17). AE, DC, MC, V. Daily 6:30–9:30am and noon–2:15pm (bar 6:30am–7pm).

8 Island Nights

The one required nighttime activity here is an authentic feast and dance show at **Tiki Theatre Village** (✆ **55.02.50**) in Haapiti. See the "Tiki Theatre Village" box, earlier in this chapter.

Moorea's major resorts also have Tahitian feasts and dance shows at least once a week. The most elaborate is the Saturday evening lagoonside show at the InterContinental Resort and Spa Moorea. Most charge 7,500CFP to 8,500CFP (US$75–US$85) per person for the dinner and dance show.

One notable exception is a free show at the **Club Bali Hai** (✆ **56.13.68**) every Wednesday at 6pm. It's followed by an a la carte seafood barbecue at Snack l'Ananas Bleu (The Blue Pineapple). Depending on what you order, dinner should cost about 2,500CFP (US$25). Reservations are required for the barbecue.

Moments   **Sunsets with Muk at Club Bali Hai**

If I'm on Moorea, you'll find me beside Cook's Bay at the **Club Bali Hai** (✆ **56. 13.68**) swapping yarns with Muk McCallum, one of the original Bali Hai Boys, Thursday to Tuesday between 5:30 and 7pm. Bring your own drinks (Muk usually hauls out a bucket of ice). This is one of the great vistas in the South Pacific; you'll want to become a modern Paul Gauguin in order to capture the changing colors of the bay, sky, and the jagged mountains.

Among the restaurants, **Maria Tapas** (© **55.01.70**) has entertainment on Thursday and Saturday evenings (expect a cover charge when bands perform unless you dine there), and Scottish-born guitarist Ron Falconer usually plays at **Alfredo's** (© **56.17.71**) on Thursday and Sunday.

See "Where to Stay" and "Where to Dine," earlier in this chapter.

10

Bora Bora

Because of its fame and extraordinary beauty, little Bora Bora is a playground for the well-to-do, occasionally the famous, and honeymooners blowing a wad. French Polynesia's tourist magnet, it has seen an explosion of hotel construction in recent years, with piers reaching out like tentacles to multitudinous overwater bungalows standing over its gorgeous lagoon. Some of the piers are so long that The Moorings has added them to its sailing charts as hazards to navigation!

Those of us who remember the island in its more natural state often bemoan that development has ruined it. But when I meet people who are here for the first time, they invariably are as blown away by Bora Bora as I was when I camped on a then-deserted Point Matira a few ions ago. If you look beyond the tourists hanging under parasails over the lagoon, you will appreciate why James A. Michener wrote that this is the world's most beautiful island.

Of course, there are more tourists here than on any other French Polynesian island, and some lovers now like to finish their honeymoons on more peaceful Tahaa or Huahine after the mile-a-minute pace here.

Lying 230km (143 miles) northwest of Tahiti, Bora Bora is a middle-aged island consisting of a high center completely surrounded by a lagoon enclosed by coral reef. It has a gorgeous combination of sand-fringed *motus* (small islets) sitting on the outer reef enclosing the multihued lagoon. In turn, the lagoon cuts deep bays into the high central island. Towering over it all is Bora Bora's trademark, the basaltic tombstone known as **Mount Otemanu** (725m/2,379 ft.). Standing next to it is the more normally rounded **Mount Pahia** (660m/2,165 ft.).

One of the best beaches in French Polynesia stretches for more than 3km (2 miles) around the flat, coconut-studded peninsula known as **Point Matira,** which juts out from the island's southern end.

Bora Bora is so small that the road around it covers only 32km (19 miles) from start to finish. All the 7,000 or so Bora Borans live on a flat coastal strip that quickly gives way to the mountainous interior.

Impressions

I saw it first from an airplane. On the horizon there was a speck that became a tall, blunt mountain with cliffs dropping sheer into the sea. And about the base of the mountain, narrow fingers of land shot out, forming magnificent bays, while about the whole was thrown a coral ring of absolute perfection. . . . That was Bora Bora from aloft. When you stepped upon it the dream expanded.

—James A. Michener, *Return to Paradise*, 1951

1 Arriving & Getting Around

ARRIVING

Bora Bora's airport is on **Motu Mute,** a flat island on the northwestern edge of the barrier reef. U.S. marines built the airstrip during World War II when Bora Bora was a major refueling stop on the America-to-Australia supply line.

You will see the lagoon close up soon after landing because all passengers are ferried across it from the airport. Some resorts send boats to pick up their guests (be sure to tell them your flight number when making your reservations). The major resorts have welcome desks in the terminal to greet you and steer you to the correct boat. It can be a tad confusing out on the dock, where baggage is unloaded. You do not want to end up on the wrong motu, so pay attention, and ask someone if you are not sure which boat is yours.

If your hotel does not send a boat, you will take Air Tahiti's launch to **Vaitape,** the only village and the center of most commerce. Buses will take you from Vaitape to your hotel. Get in the bus displaying the name of your hotel, or ask the drivers if you are not sure. Bus fares from Vaitape to the Matira Point hotel district are 500CFP (US$5).

See "Getting There & Getting Around" in chapter 7 for more information.

GETTING AROUND

There is no regularly scheduled public transportation system on Bora Bora. Buses do ferry passengers from Vaitape to the Matira hotel district on cruise-ship days, and anyone can catch a ride for 300CFP (US$3).

Some hotels on the main island shuttle their guests to Vaitape and back once or twice a day, but the frequency can vary depending on how many guests they have. Most resorts out on the islets run shuttle boats to Vaitape. Major exceptions are the Bora Bora Pearl Beach Resort, with shuttles that go to Chancelade on the northwestern corner; and Le Meridien Bora Bora, which sends its *navettes* to remote Anau village on the east coast. Take this into account if you plan to spend time on the main island.

BY RENTAL CAR, SCOOTER & BICYCLE   Europcar (✆ **800/227-7368** or 67.70.15; www.europcar.com) and a local firm, **Fare-Piti Rent a Car** (✆ **76.65.28**), have offices at Vaitape wharf. Rates at both start at 8,900CFP (US$89) a day for their smallest cars, including unlimited kilometers and insurance. Both rent open-air Fun Cars for about 8,900CFP (US$89) a day. Fare-Piti rents scooters for 7,500CFP (US$75) a day. Both have bicycles for about 1,700CFP (US$17) all day.

The 32km (19 miles) of road around Bora Bora are paved. Most of it is flat, but be very cautious on the unpaved portion, which climbs a steep hill. Always drive or ride slowly and carefully, and always be on the lookout for pigs, chickens, pedestrians, and especially dogs.

BY TAXI   No taxis patrol Bora Bora looking for passengers, but several firms have transport licenses, which means they can come get you if someone calls. The hotel desks and restaurants will do that for you, or you can phone **Léon** (✆ **70.69.16**), **Otemanu Tours** (✆ **67.70.49**), **Jacques Isnard** (✆ **67.72.25**), or **Dino's Land & Water Taxi** (✆ **79.29.65**). Fares between Vaitape and the Matira Point hotel district are at least 1,500CFP (US$15) from 6am to 6pm and 2,000CFP (US$20) from 6pm to 6am. A ride between Vaitape and Le Meridien Bora Bora's shuttle landing at Anau village costs 5,000CFP (US$50) anytime. (Add up your expected fares; it may be more economical to rent a vehicle.) The taxis aren't metered, so make sure you and the driver agree on a fare before setting out.

If you're staying at a resort on an islet and don't want to wait for the next boat shuttle, you can call **Dino's Land & Water Taxi** (© 79.29.65) or **Taxi Motu** (© 67.60.61). The ride to the main island costs about 2,500CFP (US$25).

FAST FACTS: Bora Bora

The following facts apply specifically to Bora Bora. For more information, see "Fast Facts: French Polynesia" in chapter 7.

Babysitters The hotels can arrange for English-speaking babysitters, or you can contact **Robin Teraitepo** at Chez Ben's (© 67.74.54).

Bookstores/Newstands **La Maison de la Press,** across the main road from the Vaitape wharf (© 60.57.75), carries *The International Herald Tribune* and *USA Today,* though not today's edition. It also sells film, camera batteries, and prepaid SIM cards for your cell phone.

Camera/Film **Jeanluc Photo Shop,** at the Vaitape wharf (© 72.01.23), offers professional photo services and overnight processing of color print film.

Currency Exchange **Banque de Tahiti, Banque Socredo,** and **Banque de Polynésie** have branches with ATMs in Vaitape.

Drugstores **Pharmacie de Bora Bora** (© 67.70.30), north of the town wharf in Vaitape, is open Monday through Friday from 8am to noon and 2:30 to 6pm, Saturday from 8am to noon and 5 to 6pm, Sunday and holidays from 9 to 11 am.

E-mail **L'Appetisserie,** in the Centre Commercial Le Pahia just north of the Vaitape wharf (© 67.78.88), has a computer terminal for e-mail, which costs 40CFP (40¢) per minute of online time. See "Where to Dine," later, for more about this pastry shop.

Emergencies/Police The emergency police telephone number is © **17**. The **gendarmerie** (© 67.70.58) is opposite the Vaitape wharf.

Healthcare The island's **infirmary** is in Vaitape (© 67.70.77), as is **Dr. Azad Roussanaly** (© 67.77.95).

Post Office The **Vaitape post office** is open Monday from 8am to 3pm, Tuesday through Friday from 7:30am to 3pm, and Saturday from 8 to 10am.

Restrooms Public restrooms in the small octagonal building on the Vaitape wharf are open sporadically during the day and not at all after dark. It can be a long wait for a shuttle boat back to your resort, so take preventive action as necessary.

Taxes Bora Bora's municipal government adds 100CFP to 150CFP (US$1–US$1.50) per night to your hotel bill.

Visitor Information The **Bora Bora Comité du Tourisme,** B.P. 144, Vaitape, Bora Bora (©/fax 67.76.36; info-bora-bora@mail.pf), has a visitor center in the large building on the north side of the Vaitape wharf. Open Monday to Friday, and on cruise-ship days, from 8:30am to 4pm.

Water Bora Bora has a huge desalinization plant, so the tap water is safe to drink. Most residents still drink bottled water, available at groceries.

Bora Bora

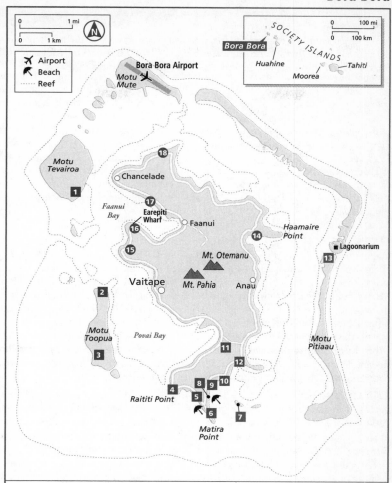

Map Legend:
- ✈ Airport
- ⚓ Beach
- ---- Reef

0 — 1 mi
0 — 1 km

SOCIETY ISLANDS
Bora Bora
Huahine
Moorea
Tahiti
0 — 100 mi
0 — 100 km

Map labels:
Motu Mute
Bora Bora Airport ✈
Motu Tevairoa
Chancelade
Faanui Bay
Earepiti Wharf
Faanui
Haamaire Point
Lagoonarium
Mt. Otemanu
Vaitape
Mt. Pahia
Anau
Motu Toopua
Povai Bay
Motu Pitiaau
Raititi Point
Matira Point

ACCOMMODATIONS ■

Bora Bora Lagoon Resort & Spa **2**
Bora Bora Nui Resort & Spa Luxury Collection **3**
Bora Bora Pearl Beach Resort **1**
Club Med Bora Bora **12**
Hotel Bora Bora **4**
Hotel Maitai Polynesia **8**

Hotel Matira **5**
InterContinental Le Moana Resort **6**
Le Meridien Bora Bora **13**
Novotel Bora Bora Beach Resort **9**
Rohutu Fare Lodge **11**
Sofitel Marara Bora Bora **10**
Sofitel Motu Bora Bora **7**

ATTRACTIONS ●

Aehautai Marae **14**
Marotetini Marae **16**
Old Hyatt Site **18**
U.S. guns **17**
U.S. wharf **15**

2 Exploring Bora Bora

THE CIRCLE ISLAND TOUR ⍟⍟

Because the round-island road is only 32km (19 miles) long, many visitors see it by bicycle (give yourself a full day), scooter, or car. Some of those sights mentioned below may not be easy to find, however, so consider taking a guided sightseeing tour around the island. **Otemanu Tours** (© **67.70.49**) still uses one of the traditional, open-air *le truck* vehicles, which adds an extra dimension to its trips. You can book them at any hotel activities desk. They charge about 3,000CFP (US$30) per person.

If you do it yourself, begin at the **wharf in Vaitape,** where there's a monument to French yachtsman Alain Gerbault, who sailed his boat around the world between 1923 and 1929 and lived to write a book about it (thus adding to Bora Bora's fame). From the wharf, head counterclockwise around the island. The road soon curves along the shore of **Povai Bay,** where mounts Otemanu and Pahia tower over you. Take your time along this bay; the views here are the best on Bora Bora. When you reach Bloody Mary's Restaurant, go out on the pier for a killer view back across the water at Mount Otemanu.

MATIRA BEACH   The road climbs the small headland, where a huge banyan tree marks the entrance to the Hotel Bora Bora on **Raititi Point,** then runs smoothly along curving **Matira Beach** ⍟⍟⍟, one of the South Pacific's finest. When the road curves sharply to the left, look for a narrow paved road to the right. This leads to **Matira Point,** the low, sandy, coconut-studded peninsula that extends out from Bora Bora's south end. Down this track about 50 yards is a **public beach** on the west side of the peninsula, opposite the InterContinental Le Moana Resort. The lagoon is shallow all the way out to the reef at this point, but the bottom is smooth and sandy. When I first came to Bora Bora, I camped for a week on Matira Point; the InterContinental Le Moana Resort is only one of many structures in what was then a deserted coconut grove completely surrounded by unspoiled beach.

THE EAST COAST   After rounding the point, you'll pass through the island's busy hotel and restaurant district before climbing a steep hill above the Club Med. A trail cuts off to the right on the north side of the hill and goes to the **Aehautai Marae,** one of several old temples on Bora Bora. This particular one has a great view of Mount Otemanu and the blue outlines of Raiatea and Tahaa islands beyond the motus on the reef.

You will go through a long stretch of coconut plantations before entering **Anau,** a typical Polynesian village with a large church, a general store, and tin-roofed houses crouched along the road.

The road goes over two hills at Point Haamaire, the main island's easternmost extremity, about 4km (2½ miles) north of Anau village. Between the two hills on the lagoon side of the road stands **Aehautai Marae,** a restored temple. Out on the point is **Taharuu Marae,** which has a great view of the lagoon. The Americans installed naval guns in the hills above the point during World War II.

THE NORTH AND WEST COASTS   On the deserted northeast coast you will ride through several miles of coconut plantations pockmarked by thousands of holes made by *tupas* (land crabs). After turning at the northernmost point, you pass a group of overwater bungalows and another group of houses, which climb the hill. Some of these are expensive condominiums; the others are part of a defunct project that was to have been a Hyatt resort. Across the lagoon are Motu Mute and the airport.

A Side Trip to Maupiti

French Polynesia's last outpost is **Maupiti,** a little jewel of an island 40km (25 miles) west of Bora Bora. Like its neighbor, the much smaller Maupiti consists of an outer reef and a horseshoe of sand-edged motus enclosing a clear lagoon around a high central island. Unlike Bora Bora, Maupiti has not a hint of modern tourism; in fact, its residents recently voted down a proposed resort. Consequently, it reminds me of Bora Bora when I first went there almost 30 years ago. Maupiti definitely is a throwback to old Polynesia when, among other things, very few locals spoke English.

The distinguishing landmark is **Hotu Parata,** a black basaltic cliff abruptly rising 165 meters (540 feet) above the wharf and Maupiti's only village. It's pockmarked with caves, which attract a multitude of nesting seabirds. On the western side is **Plage Tereia,** a gorgeous white-sand beach wrapping around a peninsula. Archaeologists have uncovered marae and petroglyphs dating to 850 A.D.

You can make a day trip to Maupiti on the fast ferry *Maupiti Express* (© **67.66.69;** maupitiexpress@mail.pf), which departs Bora Bora Tuesday, Thursday, and Saturday at 8:30am, arriving at Maupiti about 10:15am. It leaves Maupiti at 4pm and returns to Bora Bora about 5:30pm. Fares are 2,500CFP (US$25) one-way, 3,500CFP (US$35) round-trip. One caveat: The sole navigable pass into the Maupiti lagoon is narrow and bordered by a shifting sandbar upon which the surf breaks. If high waves come up, the Maupiti Express may be unable to return to Bora Bora. (Air Tahiti flies to and from Maupiti thrice weekly, from Raiatea.)

The road around Maupiti's central island is only 9.6km (5¾ miles) long, so you can easily see it in half a day via bicycle (you will negotiate only one hill). Local residents will be waiting at the wharf when the *Maupiti Express* docks to rent bikes for 1,000CFP (US$10) a day. Since the marae and petroglyphs are not marked and thus not easily found, consider taking a tour arranged by the *Maupiti Express* or **Maupiti Loisirs** (© **67.80.95**) for 2,000CFP (US$20).

Maupiti has several family-run pensions beside incredibly white-sand beaches out on the atoll-like reef islands. The best is **Pension Poe Iti** (© **67. 83.14** or 74.58.76; maupitiexpress@mail.pf), operated by Gerard and Josephine Sachet, owners of the *Maupiti Express.* Their four bungalows have air-conditioners, hot-water showers, and TVs with DVD players, making them the most luxurious I've seen at any pension in French Polynesia. If they do not have a vacancy, another good choice is **Pension Papahani** (© **60.15.35**), although friendly owners Denis and Vilna Tuheiava speak English scantly.

Other than the pensions, the only place to dine is the inexpensive **Snack Tarona** (© **67.82.46**), lagoonside in the village. It serves food Monday to Saturday from 10am to 1:30pm and 6 to 10pm.

Neither the pensions nor Snack Tarona accept credit cards because Maupiti does not have a bank. Bring cash.

Faanui Bay was used during World War II as an Allied naval base. It's not marked, but the U.S. Navy's Seabees built the concrete wharf on the north shore as a seaplane ramp. Just beyond the main shipping wharf at the point on the south side of Faanui Bay is the restored **Marotetini Marae,** which in pre-European days was dedicated to navigators. In his novel *Hawaii,* James Michener had his fictional Polynesians leave this point to discover and settle the Hawaiian Islands. Nearby are tombs in which members of Bora Bora's former royal family are buried. If you look offshore at this point, you'll see the only pass into the lagoon. The remains of two **U.S. guns** that guarded it stand on the hill above but are best visited on a safari tour (see "Safari Expeditions," below).

As you enter Vaitape, **Magasin Chin Lee** is a major gathering place for local residents. It's a good place to soak up some island culture while trimming your thirst with a cold bottle of Eau Royale.

3 Safari Expeditions & Lagoon Excursions

SAFARI EXPEDITIONS ⚔

The regular tours stick to the shoreline, but safari expeditions venture into the hills in open-air, four-wheel-drive vehicles for panoramic views and visits to the old U.S. Navy gun sites. Compared to safari expeditions on Moorea, Huahine, and Tahaa, which emphasize local culture as well as scenery, here they are more like scenic thrill rides. The journeys can be rough, so I do not recommend them for children, the elderly, or anyone prone to carsickness. The mountain roads are mere ruts in places, so you could become stuck if it has been raining.

For the time being, the Levard family's **Tupuna Four-Wheel-Drive Expeditions** (© **67.75.06**) is your only choice. Your last stop will be at The Farm, their black pearl operation (see "Shopping," below). The Levards charge 6,600CFP (US$66) per person. Book at any hotel activity desk.

LAGOON EXCURSIONS & SHARK FEEDING ⚔⚔⚔

Bora Bora has one of the world's most beautiful lagoons, and getting out on it, snorkeling and swimming in it, and visiting the islands on its outer edge are absolute musts. Although it's a widespread activity now, this is where **shark feeding** began. That is, your guide feeds reef sharks while you watch from a reasonably safe distance. Some conservationists have criticized shark feeding, but it is guaranteed to leave an indelible imprint on your memory.

Any hotel activity desk will book you an all-day excursion with one of several operators. My long-time favorite is Nono Levard's **Teremoana Tours** (© **67.71.38**), which everyone here calls Nono's Tours. You spend the day going around the lagoon in a speedy outrigger canoe. Depending on the weather, you will go snorkeling and watch a shark-feeding demonstration in the morning. You'll stop on a motu for swimming and a picnic lunch, then pet sting rays on your way home in the afternoon. Expect to pay about 8,000CFP (US$80) for a full-day outing.

If your all-day excursion doesn't feature it, you can still visit the **Bora Bora Lagoonarium** (© **67.71.34**), a fenced-in underwater area near Le Meridien Bora Bora. Here you can swim with (and maybe even ride) manta rays and observe sharks (which are on the other side of the fence here). The Lagoonarium has its own morning tour with shark-feeding and lunch on the motu, and an afternoon excursion with fish-watching. The morning excursion costs 7,800CFP (US$78), the afternoon tour is 6,600CFP (US$66), or you can do both for 11,000CFP (US$110).

You can rent a boat and explore the lagoon yourself, but I strongly suggest you know what you are doing, and that you understand how the color of the water tells its depth. You do not want to ruin your vacation by running onto a shallow reef. If you're still interested in renting a small craft, contact **Taxi Motu** (© **67.60.61**) at the Novotel Bora Bora Beach Resort or **Moana Adventure Tours** (© **67.61.41**), near the Hotel Bora Bora.

A much drier way to see the underwater delights is in the semisubmersibles *Spirit of Polynesia* (© **74.99.99** or 67.55.55; www.spiritofpacific.com) and *Aquascope Bora Bora* (© **67.61.92**). The half-submarines operate along the edges of the lagoon and along the reef outside the pass. The 50-minute voyages cost about 6,000CFP (US$60) for adults, about half for children 4 to 12. The transfer boats leave Vaitape wharf several times a day, but call for reservations.

4 Diving, Fishing & Watersports

SCUBA DIVING & SNORKELING 🕉🕉

Certified and noncertified divers alike can swim among the coral heads, sharks, large manta rays, eels, and some 1,000 species of colorful tropical fishes out in the lagoon here. Every resort has a scuba diving program. Both 30-minute introductory courses and one-tank lagoon dives cost about 7,500CFP (US$75), and open-water and night dives are priced at 9,000CFP (US$90).

Based adjacent to Hotel Bora Bora, friendly dive operators Michel and Anne Condesse offer morning, afternoon, and evening dives from their **Bora Diving Center** (© **67.71.84**; fax 67.74.83; www.boradive.com). They provide buoyancy compensators, fins, snorkels, wetsuits, regulators, and all other equipment (be prepared for the metric system; depth and pressure gauges display measurements in meters and kilograms). They also teach PADI certification courses. For non-divers, they offer "Aqua Safari" excursions, on which you walk on the bottom while wearing a diving helmet.

The island's other major dive operator, **TOPdive Bora Bora** (© **60.50.50**; fax 60.50.51; www.topdive.com), also has top equipment and some of the best dive boats in French Polynesia. Its base is on the northern outskirts of Vaitape.

Among the easily accessible snorkeling spots, the best is off the southern tip of Point Matira. You can walk to the outer reef from here, thus increasing your chances of seeing more fish than elsewhere. Next best are the reefs off the Hotel Bora Bora and the Sofitel Motu, but you need to stay there to fully enjoy them.

SPORTFISHING

For combined sailing and fishing, American Richard Postma's *Taravana* (© **72.39.99** or 67.77.79; www.taravana.com) is the world's first sail-powered luxury game-fishing boat. This 50-footer is available for day trips or charters to the other Leeward Islands, including Tupai, a small atoll northwest of Bora Bora. Sailing or fishing costs 90,000CFP (US$900) for a half day, to 120,000CFP (US$1,200) for a full day, including food but not alcoholic beverages. You can go on a nonfishing sunset cruise for about 6,500CFP (US$65) per person. Among Richard's first guests were actors Dennis Quaid and Meg Ryan (when they were still a couple). Former *Baywatch* star Pamela Anderson Lee came along later.

OTHER WATERSPORTS

Every hotel has some water toys for its guests to use, and hotel activities desks can arrange fishing, diving, and other watersports. You don't have to stay at the **Novotel**

Bora Bora Beach Club (✆ **60.59.50**) to use its equipment and facilities, but you do have to pay a fee. You can go water-skiing, sail on Hobie Cats, paddle canoes, and get a bird's-eye view of the lagoon while parasailing.

Matira Jet Tours (✆ **77.63.63**) has lagoon excursions by jet ski as well as inland tours by all-terrain vehicles. Many of those people riding above the lagoon went with **Bora Bora Parasail** (✆ **78.27.10**).

You can go day- or sunset sailing on the **Taaroa** catamaran (✆ **24.62.04**) for about 4,500CFP (US$45).

Based at Rohotu Fare Lodge (see "Where to Stay," below), **Bora Bora Kayaks** (✆ **70.77.99;** www.boraborakayak.com) rents one- and two-person sea kayaks ranging from 1,500CFP (US$15) for 1 hour to 6,500CFP (US$65) for a whole day. These quality boats were made in the United States and come equipped with snorkeling and fishing gear.

5 Shopping

Local artisans display straw hats, pareus, and other handicraft items at **Bora Bora I Te Fanau Tahi** (no phone), in the large hall at the Vaitape wharf. Open from 8:30am to 4pm Monday to Friday, and weekends when cruise ships are here.

Boutique Bora Bora   Catering to the cruise ship crowd, this store has more T-shirts and pareus than most others, plus it sells wood carvings, books, curios, calendars, and a few black pearls. It's a good place to stock up on Hinano beer glasses. Vaitape, opposite the ferry wharf. ✆ **67.79.72**. Daily 9am–5:30pm.

Boutique Gauguin   In a white house 1.5km (1 mile) north of Hotel Bora Bora, Boutique Gauguin is one of the larger stores here, offering a selection of handicrafts, clothing, black pearls, and curio items. This is the best place on Bora Bora to shop for prints of Paul Gauguin's paintings. Some of the pareus here are particularly artistic. Povai Bay. ✆ **67.76.67**. Daily 8am–5:30pm.

Matira Pearls ✫✫✫ *Value*   You will have ample opportunities to shop for black pearls here (Vaitape village alone has a dozen outlets), but this is my favorite. It's owned by Steve Fearon, whose family once had a piece of the Hotel Bora Bora, and whose brother, Tom Fearon, has a bungalow resort on Rarotonga in the Cook Islands (see "Where to Stay" in chapter 12). Steve's chief assistant is his son, Heirama, who graduated from Pepperdine University in California. Unlike some other stores, their customized settings emphasize the pearl, not the gold. Set and loose pearls start at $100. East side of Matira Point. ✆ **67.79.14**. Mon–Sat 9am–5:30pm; Sun 10am–5pm.

The Farm   You need to know about The Farm, since it's owned by the Levard family and thus you are likely to be deposited here after going on one of their safari excursions. Although the family's main black pearl farms are on Tahaa, they have about 10,000 oysters growing here, primarily to show you how pearls are grown, harvested, graded, and turned into jewelry. The final products are for sale in the **Bora Pearl Company,** the showroom here. It's worth a visit here to see how it's all done. Raititi Point, near Hotel Bora Bora. ✆ **70.06.65**. Daily 9am–6pm.

6 Where to Stay

Bora Bora has some of the South Pacific's finest—and most expensive—resorts, and it will have a few more of them by the time you get here. The **InterContinental Resort** and **Thalasso Spa Bora Bora** (www.boraboraspa.interconti.com), the **St. Regis Resort Bora Bora** (www.starwoodspacollection.com), and the **Four Seasons Bora Bora** (www.fourseasons.com) were due to open in 2006, all on the eastern motus. Their bungalows, amenities, and room rates should be over-the-top.

EXPENSIVE

Bora Bora Lagoon Resort & Spa 𝒦𝒦
Speedboats shuttle 23 times a day from the Vaitape wharf to this posh resort on the northern end of Motu Toopua, a hilly island facing the rounded peak of Mount Pahia (not Mount Otemanu's tombstone). The main building, under three interlocking thatch roofs, holds a reception area, a bar, and a gourmet restaurant. To the rear, an expansive stone deck surrounds one of French Polynesia's largest swimming pools, where you'll find another bar and daytime restaurant. Long piers with hand-carved railings lead to the 44 overwater bungalows, while the rest of the units sit ashore in tropical gardens. One is a two-bedroom villa well suited to well-heeled families. Three of the beachside bungalows—one of which has a Jacuzzi tub—interconnect to form suites. The luxurious units are so close together that you can overhear your neighbor's favorite TV show (not to mention certain amorous activities) unless you run your air-conditioner. For the most part, the accommodations do not live up to the resort's exceptional amenities. The unusual spa here has treatment rooms high up in a banyan tree.

B.P. 175, 98730 Vaitape, Bora Bora (on Motu Toopua, 1km/½ mile off Vaitape). ⓒ 800/860-4905 or 60.40.00. Fax 60.40.01. www.boraboralagoonresort.orient-express.com. 77 units. 395€–1,550€ (US$470–US$1,844) bungalow. AE, DC, MC, V. **Amenities:** 2 restaurants; 2 bars; large outdoor pool; 2 tennis courts; exercise room; spa; game room; watersports equipment rentals; concierge; activities desk; limited room service; laundry service. *In room:* A/C, TV, dataport, minibar, coffeemaker, hair dryer, safe.

Bora Bora Nui Resort & Spa Luxury Collection 𝒦𝒦𝒦
This sprawling resort occupies the southern end of hilly Motu Toopua, a 15-minute boat ride off Vaitape. Although this is the island's swankiest resort (for the time being, anyway), it faces west toward the sea, thus depriving its public areas and all but a handful of its bungalows of the typical Bora Bora view. They're called "horizon" bungalows here because they look over the sea to the horizon. Only the full-service spa, perched atop the islet's central ridge, looks at Mt. Otemanu. A beachside, two-level infinity swimming pool serves as the focal point of activities. It's backed by two public buildings, one with a large boutique and a casual, sand-floor restaurant offering very reasonably priced lunches and dinners. The other houses a fine-dining outlet, an air-conditioned library, and a fascinating photo collection of U.S. marines building the airstrip on Motu Mute during World War II. Spread out over 6.4 hectares (16 acres) and nearly a kilometer (½ mile) of lagoon (you'll soon learn to call for a golf-cart to take you to dinner), the 120 luxurious, suite-size units—84 of them overwater—are some of the largest in French Polynesia (again, for the time being). The overwater bungalows feature separate bedrooms, huge bathrooms with both tubs and walk-in showers, and big decks with privacy screens. Housed in a hillside hotel-style building, the "lagoon-view suites" are the least expensive units, and they interconnect to accommodate families. Top of the line are the huge royal suites. Unlike Bora Bora's other resorts, room rates here include full breakfast, which the staff will deliver by canoe to your overwater mansion.

B.P. 502, 98730 Vaitape, Bora Bora (on Motu Toopua, 1½km/1 mile off Vaitape). ⓒ 800/782-9488 or 60.32.00. Fax 60.32.01. www.boraboranui.com. 120 units. 73,800CFP–275,000CFP (US$738–US$2,750) bungalow; 62,000CFP–68,500CFP (US$620–US$685) suite. Rates include full breakfast. AE, DC, MC, V. **Amenities:** 2 restaurants; 2 bars; large outdoor pool; tennis courts; exercise room; spa; Jacuzzi; sauna; watersports equipment rentals;

bike rentals; children's programs; game room; concierge; activities desk; 24-hr. room service; massage; babysitting; laundry service. *In room:* A/C, TV, dataport, minibar, coffeemaker, hair dryer, iron, safe.

Bora Bora Pearl Beach Resort *₰₰*   The most traditionally Polynesian resort on Bora Bora, the Pearl Beach resides on Motu Tevairoa, the largest of the flat islets dotting the outer reef, and it has better views of Mount Otemanu across the lagoon than does the Bora Bora Lagoon Resort to its south (see above). Covered by interconnected conical thatch roofs, the open-air restaurant, main bar, and library stand on a raised earthen platform, which enhances their views over a large swimming pool to the lagoon and mountains. Guests can also enjoy splashing or snorkeling in the natural sand-bottom lagoon (the beach sand is subject to erosion, but dredges replenish it as needed). Gilles Pétré, one of French Polynesia's top dive operators, is in charge of the shop here (and all other Pearl resorts). Long, curving piers extend out to 50 overwater bungalows, which ooze Polynesian charm. The 15 premium units are worth paying extra for, because they are more private than the others and enjoy unimpeded views of Bora Bora. If privacy is more important than the sound of water lapping under your bungalow, consider one of the garden bungalows, which have private courtyards with sun decks and splash pools. If you bring the kids, opt for a beachside bungalow with a separate bedroom. An annoying drawback here is that the resort's shuttle boats land at Chancelade on Bora Bora's northwestern corner, an expensive taxi ride if you don't catch an infrequent shuttle bus to Vaitape.

B.P. 169, 98730 Vaitape, Bora Bora (on Motu Tevairoa, 1km/½ mile off Farepiti). (♪ **800/657-3275** or 60.52.00. Fax 60.52.22. www.pearlhotels.com. 80 units. 51,000CFP–85,000CFP (US$510–US$850) bungalow. AE, DC, MC, V. **Amenities:** 2 restaurants; 2 bars; outdoor pool; tennis court; exercise room; spa; watersports equipment rentals; game room; concierge; activities desk; limited room service; massage; babysitting; laundry service. *In room:* A/C, TV, dataport, minibar, coffeemaker, hair dryer, iron, safe.

Hotel Bora Bora *₰₰₰*   This venerable institution opened in 1961, but lost some of its Polynesian character a few years ago when the luxury-laden Amanresorts put more of an Asian imprint on the property. The thatched-roof central building has always been a key part of the resort's charm, and it still sits atop Point Raititi, a low headland overlooking the start of magnificent Matira Beach. Down below, one of the few real beach bars in the South Pacific rests right on those white sands. The comfortable Tahitian-style bungalows sit among the palm trees on the flat shoreline on either side of the headland. On the north, some of the 15 overwater bungalows are actually perched right on the reef's edge, where coral gives way to a deep blue lagoon (snorkeling off their porches is like flying off a canyon wall). A few others enjoy views of Mount Otemanu's tombstone across Povai Bay. Otherwise, the best units here are on the Matira side of the point; they lack the view but they share a much better beach and are more likely to be cooled by the trade winds. Most of the bungalows are relatively small compared to Bora Bora's other resorts, but not the hotel's huge L-shaped units known as "premium beach bungalows." Virtual houses, they all have separate bedrooms, and the "garden" versions even have their own small swimming pools, surrounded by rock walls for privacy. Furnishings throughout are top of the line, with some Oriental antique pieces here and there. All units have oak-trimmed claw-foot bathtubs in addition to showers. Avoid units next to the neighboring round-island road, which can send the noise of innumerable scooters into them at the crack of dawn. Also note that you will find no satisfaction here if you need to splash around in a swimming pool or watch TV in your room.

B.P. 1, 98730 Vaitape, Bora Bora (Matira Point, 7km/4½ miles from Vaitape). © 800/421-1490 or 60.44.11. Fax 60.44.22. www.amanresorts.com. 54 units. US$675–US$1,000. AE, DC, MC, V. **Amenities:** Restaurant; 2 bars; tennis courts; exercise room; watersports equipment rentals; bike rentals; game room; concierge; activities desk; car-rental desk; limited room service; massage; babysitting; laundry service. *In room:* A/C, stereo, dataport, minibar, coffeemaker, hair dryer, safe.

InterContinental Le Moana Resort 𝒜𝒜𝒜

On the eastern side of the Matira peninsula, this exclusive resort was until recently known as the InterContinental Bora Bora Beachcomber Resort (and, like its sibling in Tahiti, may revert back to the Beach-comber name). This is one of the older resorts here, although much improved over the years. Its bungalows, most of them overwater, are some of the most charmingly designed here. They were the first in which you could remove the tops of the glass coffee tables and actually feed the fish swimming in the turquoise lagoon below. Ashore, 11 beachside bungalows are less enchanting, but like the overwater units, they have Raiatea and Tahaa in their lagoon views. Two suites—one overwater, one ashore—have kitchenettes, making them suitable for families. Also beside the beach, a circular thatched-roof building houses the reception area, a lounge, and the restaurant and bar, both with outdoor seating. The airy, beachside dining room offers very fine French selections, with an emphasis on seafood.

B.P. 156, 98730 Vaitape, Bora Bora (east side of Matira Point). © 800/327-0200 or 60.49.00. Fax 60.49.99. www.interconti.com. 64 units. 113,900CFP (US$1,139) bungalow, 101,565CFP–259,300CFP (US$1,016–US$2,593) suite. AE, DC, MC, V. **Amenities:** Restaurant; bar; outdoor saltwater pool; spa; watersports equipment rentals; bike rentals; concierge; activities desk; car-rental desk; 24-hr. room service; massage; babysitting; laundry service. *In room:* A/C, TV, dataport, minibar, kitchens (suites only), coffeemaker, hair dryer, iron, safe.

Le Meridien Bora Bora 𝒜𝒜

Located on the northern tip of an atoll-like island stretching 10km (6 miles) along the southeastern side of the outer reef, this well-managed resort is both the busiest and the most unusual on Bora Bora. Most obvious is its Melanesian architecture, like its sister property on Tahiti (see "Where to Stay," in chapter 8). The architects also created a seawater-fed, lakelike lagoon, in which you can swim with endangered sea turtles, bred there as part of the resort's award-winning preservation program. Of the 100 identical guest units, 85 are built overwater. Only a few of these have views of Mt. Otemanu, whose tombstone is seen from its narrow end out here. Standing over waist-deep water, they are notable for their huge glass floors, which make it seem as if you're walking on air (maids cover the glass with carpets at evening turndown). All units here are smaller than those at Bora Bora's other resorts, however, and you could stumble over too much furniture for the space available. Ten otherwise identical "beach" bungalows actually sit beside the manmade lagoon, but most of them have fine views of Bora Bora. Since the shallow manmade lagoon is safe for swimming, they are better for families with small children. The broad, brilliantly white main beach here has its own bar. The hotel's launch shuttles to Anau village, from where a morning bus goes to Vaitape. Otherwise, it's an expensive taxi ride to town.

B.P. 190, 98730 Vaitape, Bora Bora (on Motu Pitiaau, 1km/½ mile off Anau village). © 800/225-5843 or 60.51.51. Fax 60.51.10. www.lemeridien.com. 100 units. 72,150CFP–94,350CFP (US$722–US$944). AE, DC, MC, V. **Amenities:** 3 restaurants; 2 bars; outdoor pool; spa; watersports equipment rentals; game room; concierge; activities desk; 24-hr. room service; babysitting; laundry service. *In room:* A/C, TV, dataport, minibar, coffeemaker, hair dryer, iron, safe.

Sofitel Marara Bora Bora

Italian movie producer Dino De Laurentis built this resort in 1977 to house star Mia Farrow and the crew working on his box-office bomb *Hurricane*. A beehive-shaped central building houses the restaurant and bar, both of which open to a walk-in swimming pool sunken into a deck built out over Matira Beach and the lagoon. The resort has the island's largest array of watersports activities, which it shares with the Novotel Bora Bora Beach Resort, its Accor Hotels sibling next door (the toys are available to both guests and nonguests). The overwater bungalows here have some of Bora Bora's largest decks, but some units stand so close to the round-island road that you will wonder if you're sleeping over the lagoon. Units numbered 51, 52, 62, 63, or 64 are the most private. Facing a curving beach of white sand, the land-based bungalows have views of Raiatea and Tahaa on the horizon. Guests here can dine at the Sofitel Motu (see below), but not partake of the activities there.

B.P. 6, 98730 Vaitape, Bora Bora (northeast of Matira Point). (C) 800/763-4835 or 41.04.04 in Papeete, or 60.55.00 on Bora Bora. Fax 41.05.05 or 67.74.03. www.sofitel.com. 64 units. 33,000CFP–78,00CFP (US$330–US$780). AE, DC, MC, V. **Amenities:** 2 restaurants; bar; outdoor pool; tennis court; watersports equipment rentals; bike rentals; concierge; activities desk; car-rental desk; limited room service; babysitting; laundry service. *In room:* A/C, TV, dataport, minibar, coffeemaker, hair dryer, iron, safe.

Sofitel Motu Bora Bora *⟨★★⟩*   More exclusive and private than its sister property, this intimate, adult-oriented resort sits on a rocky, one-hill motu and is a 3-minute boat ride from the Sofitel Marara. Guests here can take the free on-demand shuttle boat and use all of the Marara's facilities. Marara guests, on the other hand, are allowed out here only for lunch and dinner. Unlike any other Bora Bora resort, this one has a gorgeous, picture-postcard view of Mount Otemanu's tombstone face (most but not all units enjoy the view, so ask for one that does). Often-steep stone pathways lead up and downhill to the guest bungalows; for this reason, I don't recommend the Motu to disabled travelers or anyone who has trouble walking. Most of the luxurious if not overly spacious units are overwater. Those that are ashore extend on stilts from the side of the hill, rendering great lagoon views. The most expensive unit here is a large villa. Several small beaches offer hammocks and easy chairs, and one has a shower mounted on a tree. Children under 12 can stay at the Sofitel Marara but not here.

B.P. 516, 98730 Vaitape, Bora Bora (on Piti Uuuta, ½km/¼ mile off Matira Beach). (C) 800/763-4835 or 41.04.04 in Papeete, or 60.56.00 on Bora Bora. Fax 41.05.05 or 60.56.66. www.sofitel.com. 31 units. 43,500CFP–120,000CFP (US$435–US$1,200). AE, DC, MC, V. Children under 12 not accepted. **Amenities:** Restaurant; bar; watersports equipment rentals; activities desk; limited room service; massage; babysitting; laundry service. *In room:* A/C, TV, dataport, minibar, coffeemaker, hair dryer, iron, safe.

MODERATE

Club Med Bora Bora *⟨Value⟩*   Lush tropical gardens provide the setting for this Club Med beside a good beach in a little half-moon-shaped bay north of Matira Point. The focus of attention is a large thatched-roof beachside pavilion, which houses a reception area, bar, buffet-oriented dining room, and nightclub. Guests pay extra for scuba diving, but all meals (with wine) and a wide range of activities are included in the rates. Considering the prices elsewhere on Bora Bora, this makes Club Med a good value. The accommodations are in a mix of stand-alone and duplex bungalows and two-story, motel-style buildings. The beachfront bungalows are the preferred choice here, especially for honeymooners and others seeking privacy. The rooms are comfortably if not extravagantly furnished. If you don't have a roommate, one of the same sex may be assigned.

B.P. 34, 98730 Vaitape, Bora Bora (northeast of Matira Point). (C) 800/258-2633, 60.46.04, or 42.96.99 in Papeete. Fax 42.16.83. www.clubmed.com. 150 units. 17,700CFP (US$177) per person double; 21,240CFP–26,000CFP (US$212–US$260) per person bungalow. Rates include all meals, w/wine, and most activities. AE, DC, MC, V. **Amenities:** Restaurant; bar; tennis courts; bike rentals; activities desk; car-rental desk; salon; massage; coin-op washers and dryers. *In room:* A/C, TV, fridge, coffeemaker, hair dryer, safe.

Hotel Maitai Polynesia *Value* Like the nearby Novotel, this resort has hotel rooms, but here they climb a hill, giving upper floor units spectacular lagoon views. Unlike the Novotel, it also has beachside and overwater bungalows, which are among the more reasonably priced in French Polynesia. The bungalows are smaller than those at the more expensive resorts, but they are packed with Polynesian decor, and those overwater have glass floor panels for fish-viewing. The round-island road runs through the property, separating the beach and bungalows from the thatch-roofed main building and hotel rooms. Of its two restaurants, one sits beachside.

B.P. 505, 98730 Vaitape, Bora Bora (northeast of Matira Point). © 60.30.00. Fax 67.66.03. www.hotelmaitai.com. 74 units. 24,200CFP–35,500CFP (US$242–US$355) double; 39,000CFP–53,300CFP (US$390–US$533) bungalow. Higher rates June–Oct. AE, DC, MC, V. **Amenities:** 2 restaurants; 2 bars; watersports equipment rentals; bike rentals; activities desk; babysitting; laundry service. *In room:* A/C (hotel rooms only), TV, dataport, minibar, coffeemaker, hair dryer, safe.

Hotel Matira This is not so much a hotel as a collection of bungalows on and near the beach at the northern end of the Matira peninsula. Imported from Indonesia, the teak units have thatch roofs, porches on one corner, shower-only bathrooms, and pairs of double beds. You'll get a ceiling fan, fridge, and coffeemaker, but forget amenities like TVs, phones, and hair dryers. What you get here is essentially an unscreened cottage, so keep your insect repellent handy. The choice and most expensive models rest beside Matira Beach, while the others are back in the garden. Ask for a discount if you book directly.

B.P. 31, 98730 Vaitape, Bora Bora (on Matira Beach, south of Hotel Bora Bora). © 67.70.51. Fax 67.77.02. www.hotel-matira.com. 14 units. 21,000CFP–35,500CFP (US$210–US$355). MC, V. **Amenities:** Bike rentals. *In room:* Fridge, coffeemaker, no phone.

Novotel Bora Bora Beach Resort *Value* Opened in 2003, this modest but attractive property is one of the better values on the island, especially if you book it as part of a package. It sports a U-shaped tropical-style public building and an infinity swimming pool beside a palm-draped section of Matira Beach, where the Novotel shares a wide array of watersports with the Sofitel Marara next door. On the other side of the round-island road, the motel-style accommodations occupy two-story buildings dressed up in Tahitian thatch and bamboo that surround a lush courtyard with lily pond. The medium-size rooms are nicely trimmed with native woods and are comfortably furnished with a queen bed, a built-in settee which can double as a single bed, a desk, shower-only bath, and sliding doors opening to a patio or balcony. You can dine at the Sofitel Motu but not use the other facilities out there.

B.P. 943, 98730 Vaitape, Bora Bora (heart of Matira hotel district). © 800/221-4542 or 60.59.50. Fax 60.59.51. www.novotel.com. 80 units. 21,600CFP–28,800CFP (US$216–US$288) double. AE, MC, V. **Amenities:** Restaurant; bar; outdoor pool; watersports equipment rentals; activities desk; car rental desk; massage; laundry service. *In room:* A/C, TV, dataport, fridge, coffeemaker, hair dryer, safe.

INEXPENSIVE

On the peninsula leading to Matira Point, the pension-style **Chez Nono** (© 67.71.38; nono.levard@mail.pf) has six simple rooms, four bungalows, and an apartment. Rates start at 6,100CFP (US$61) double for a room, 15,000CFP (US$150) for a bungalow. Expect to share a bathroom here. Book early, since local French residents love its beachside location.

On a small part of Matira Beach in the hotel district, the no-frills **Village Temanuata** (© 67.75.61; www.temanuata.com) has 11 thatched-roof bungalows ranging from one room to family units with kitchens and sleeping lofts. They all have private bathrooms but few other amenities. Rates range from 13,700CFP to 15,900CFP (US$137–US$159).

Rohotu Fare Lodge *(Finds)*   Almost hidden by botanical gardens on the mountainside overlooking Povai Bay, this little lodge is the creation of Nir Shalev, an Israeli expatriate whom I met shortly after he first arrived on Bora Bora wearing a backpack in 1989. With teak floors and natural thatch roofs, his cleverly designed bungalows are for lovers, definitely not Puritans. In addition to suggestive paintings, statues, and other paraphernalia in the sleeping quarters, faucets in the outdoor bathrooms pour water from certain parts of nude statues. (After a night here, you may not be up to the 15-minute bike ride to Matira Beach!) Nir's two lagoon-view bungalows are more charming and have better vistas than his mountain-view unit. They all have ceiling fans, kitchens, decks with lounge furniture, and four-poster beds with mosquito nets. You will not have to leave here to enjoy a view of Mount Otemanu's tombstone face.

B.P. 400, 98730 Vaitape, Bora Bora (hillside in Povai Bay). *©* 70.77.99. www.rohotulodge.com. 3 units. 14,900CFP (US$149) bungalow. MC, V. **Amenities:** Kayak rentals; free bicycles. *In room:* Kitchen, coffeemaker, safe.

7 Where to Dine

EXPENSIVE

A French chef who came here to work at the Hotel Bora Bora took over the restaurant at the **Yacht Club Bora Bora** (*©* 67.70.69), on the lagoon about 1.5km (1 mile) north of Vaitape, after my recent visit. I have received highly favorable reports about his cooking.

Bloody Mary's Restaurant & Bar *(🌾🌾🌾)* SEAFOOD/STEAKS   Having a few drinks and a slab of barbecued fish at this charming structure is as much a part of the Bora Bora experience as is taking a lagoon excursion. Ceiling fans, colored spotlights, and stalks of dried bamboo dangle from a large thatch roof over a floor of fine white sand (stash your sandals in a foot locker and dine in your bare feet). The butcher-block tables are made of coconut-palm lumber, and the seats are sections of palm trunks cut into stools. Bloody Mary's is essentially an American-style barbecued fish and steak joint—which can be a welcome relief after a diet of lard-laden French sauces. You'll be shown the seafood and beef laid out on a bed of ice. (If it's offered, choose the mouthwatering teriyaki-style wahoo.) The chef will charbroil your selection to order and serve it with a salad, vegetables, and your choice of sauce on the side. Open all day, the cozy bar is cut from a beautifully polished litchi tree and is one of my favorite watering holes. The lunch menu consists of burgers, fish and chips, and salads, which are not served at dinner. You will have an evening of fun, as have the many famous faces posted on a board out by the road.

Povai Bay, 1km (½ mile) north of Hotel Bora Bora. *©* 67.72.86. Reservations strongly recommended. Lunch 950CFP–1,400CFP (US$9.50–US$14); dinner main courses 2,650CFP–3,200CFP (US$27–US$32). AE, MC, V. Mon–Wed and cruise ship days 11am–3pm; Mon–Sat 6–9pm. Bar Mon–Sat 9:30am–11pm. Closed Dec.

Kaina Hut *(🌾🌾)* FRENCH FUSION   Restaurateur Gilles Ricaud brings a fascinating combination of French cooking and fresh Polynesian ingredients to this romantic restaurant with a thatch roof and sand floor. This fusion is apparent in the signature dish, gnocchi made from breadfruit instead of potato and served with a light tomato sauce. Otherwise seafood with Asian influences predominates here. Lunch is served at an open-air snack bar by the lagoon across the main road.

Povai Bay, north of Hotel Bora Bora. (C) **71.20.73.** Reservations recommended. Main courses 2,800CFP–5,500CFP (US$28–US$55). MC, V. Wed–Mon 11am–5pm and 6–10pm.

La Villa Mahana *᪘᪘᪘* INTERNATIONAL   You will need one night for fun at Bloody Mary's, another for a romantic dinner at this little restaurant, Bora Bora's finest. Owner Damien Rinaldi Devio, an accomplished young Corsican-born chef, will get you started with a complimentary glass of champagne, perhaps laced with peach liqueur. I started with tuna *tartare exotique,* a luscious version of *poisson cru* with a sharp wasabi-accented sauce. My friends went on to mahimahi perfectly cooked with a subtle version of coconut curry sauce, while I opted for filet mignon with vanilla cream gnocchi. Both were outstanding. The fixed price menus for four or five courses will save money. The walls of this Mediterranean-style villa are adorned with the works of noted French Polynesian artist Garrick Yrondi, but Damien has only six tables, so consider calling or e-mailing for a reservation well before you get here (damien@ villamahana.com).

Povai Bay, behind Boutique Gauguin, 1½km (1 mile) north of Hotel Bora Bora. (C) **67.50.63.** Reservations required. Main courses 3,200CFP–3,600CFP (US$32–US$36); fixed-price dinners 8,500CFP–10,500CFP (US$85–US$105). AE, MC, V. Wed–Thurs 6–8pm. Closed Feb.

TOPdive Restaurant *᪘᪘* NEW FRENCH   A soaring thatch roof covers this excellent lagoonside restaurant north of Vaitape. The kitchen produces wonderful nouvelle cuisine renditions of fresh seafood. For example, you might start with a lobster salad with citrus vinaigrette. Shrimps and scallops in coconut curry sauce is my favorite main. The fixed-price *menu exotique* menu offers a choice of starters, a main course, and a dessert. You'll need both an appetizer and a main course here because the portions are as small as they are extraordinarily well presented.

Vaitape, 1km (½ mile) north of wharf. (C) **60.50.50.** Reservations recommended. Main courses 3,250CFP–6,850CFP (US$33–US$69); tourist menu 6,000CFP (US$60). AE, MC, V. Tues–Sun noon–2pm and 7–9pm. Bar daily 11:30am–9pm.

MODERATE

La Bounty *᪘* *Value* FRENCH/ITALIAN   This casual restaurant under a thatch roof provides some of the island's best pizza and other reasonably priced Italian (and French) fare. A pie makes an ample meal for one person or can be shared as an appetizer. The spaghetti and tagliatelle are tasty, too, with either smoked salmon, carbonara, Alfredo, Neapolitan, blue cheese, or seafood sauce. Steaks and fish are served under French sauces such as mustard or creamy vanilla. Pizzas are served quickly here, but everything else is prepared to order and takes longer. Whatever you choose, it will be excellent quality for the price.

Matira, between Hotel Maitai Polynesia and Bora Bora Beach Resort. (C) **67.70.43.** Reservations recommended. Pizza and pasta 1,500CFP–1,650CFP (US$15–US$17); main courses 1,500CFP–2,800CFP (US$15–US$28). MC, V. Tues–Sun 11:30am–2pm and 6:30–9pm.

INEXPENSIVE

In addition to Roulotte Matira (see below), other meal wagons roll out on and near the Vaitape wharf after dark. See "Don't Miss *Les Roulottes*" in chapter 8 for details about these inexpensive food wagons. You can get an inexpensive snack in Vaitape at **Bora Bora Burger,** next to the post office (no phone). Open Monday to Saturday from 8am to 5:30pm. No credit cards.

Chez Ben's SNACK BAR/PIZZA   Honeymooners from the nearby Hotel Bora Bora frequently wander to this lean-to across the road from a shady portion of Matira Beach, where Bora Bora–born Ben Teraitepo and his Oklahoma-born wife, Robin, have been offering American-style cooked breakfasts, lunches, and afternoon pick-me-ups since 1988. Ben's fresh tuna salad sandwiches, pizzas and pastas, unusually spicy poisson cru, tacos, and fajitas are homemade and substantial, although Ben and Robin's company is the main reason to hang out here. They will shoo the dogs and cats away if they bother you.

Matira, between Hotel Bora Bora and Matira Point. 🕐 67.74.54. Breakfast 600CFP–1,700CFP (US$6–US$17); sandwiches and salads 250CFP–1,900CFP (US$2.50–US$19); pizzas and meals 850CFP–1,350CFP (US$8.50–US$14). No credit cards. Daily 8am–5pm.

L'Appetisserie 𝒱𝒶𝓁𝓊𝑒 FRENCH/PASTRIES   I often have breakfast here, for this patisserie bakes excellent croissants, tarts, and quiches to go with strong French coffee. Also on the menu: sandwiches, pizzas by the slice, and a *plat du jour* at lunch. Order at the counter or at a table inside or on the shopping center sidewalk. You can use the computer terminal here to check your e-mail (see "Fast Facts: Bora Bora," earlier in this chapter).

North of the Vaitape wharf, in Centre Commercial le Pahia. 🕐 67.78.88. Breakfast 700CFP–2,400CFP (US$7–US$24); pastries and sandwiches 150CFP–1,050CFP (US$1.50–US$11); meals 1,650CFP (US$17). No credit cards. Mon–Sat 6am–6pm.

Roulotte Matira 🎯 𝒱𝒶𝓁𝓊𝑒 SNACK BAR   This is one of the best roulottes in French Polynesia, especially when owner Samuel Ruver cooks tandoori chicken and curries from recipes handed down by his East Indian father. Otherwise, he works at the gas grill to produce steaks and fish, both served with french fries. Anything with *legumes* will be a so-so Chinese-style stir-fry. You can get a continental breakfast here. Grab a white plastic table; there's wait service.

Matira, at the curve. No phone. Hamburgers 900CFP (US$9); main courses 1,000CFP–1,500CFP (US$10–US$15). No credit cards. Daily 6am–2pm and 6–10pm.

Snack Matira SNACK BAR   Right on Matira Beach and within hailing distance of Chez Ben's, this open-air snack bar is a favorite lunch and afternoon retreat of Bora Bora's French-speaking expatriates. It offers a roulotte-style menu of pizzas, salads, omelets, grilled steaks and fish, juicy burgers, and *casse-croûte* sandwiches, plus ice cream and milk shakes. The company is better at Chez Ben's, but not the lagoon view.

Matira, between Hotel Bora Bora and Matira Point. 🕐 67.77.32. Most items 300CFP–1,700CFP (US$3–US$17). No credit cards. Tues–Sun 10am–4pm.

8 Island Nights

As on Moorea, things are really quiet on Bora Bora after dark (this is, after all, one of the world's most romantic honeymoon hideaways, not a place to practice your dance steps). You might want to listen to a Tahitian band playing at sunset or watch the furious hips in a Tahitian dance show, which all the resorts have at least 1 night a week. The schedules change, so call ahead.

Even if you're not staying at the **Club Med Bora Bora** (🕐 60.46.04), you can dine there and watch the nightclub show staged by its staff. The full meal, wine, and show together cost about 6,100CFP (US$61). Call for reservations.

11

Huahine & the Other Islands of French Polynesia

Your French Polynesian experience will be much richer if you get off the usual Tahiti-Moorea–Bora Bora tourist trek and visit the less developed islands, where you will glimpse "the way Tahiti used to be," as they say in these parts. In this chapter I cover the islands which get just enough visitors to warrant resorts, but not so many to turn off the locals' marvelous warmth, joviality, and hospitality.

One example is Huahine, which I think is the third most beautiful island in French Polynesia (behind Moorea and Bora Bora). Although busy Bora Bora looms on the horizon, agriculture still far outweighs tourism on Huahine, and unless a cruise ship is in port, you'll have it almost to yourself.

Huahine is famous for its ancient archaeological sites, as is nearby Raiatea, historically the most important of all Polynesian islands and today the administrative center of the Leeward Islands. Except for cruise ship visits, neither Raiatea nor neighboring Tahaa are on the usual tourist circuit, primarily because neither has beaches. But the deep-water lagoon surrounding them is the territory's charter yacht center. You do not have to be a world-class sailor here, for you can spend a lazy week or more circumnavigating Tahaa without venturing onto the open ocean.

The atolls of the Tuamotus offer a very different kind of experience. This immense archipelago, stretching across the northeastern approaches to Tahiti, consists not of high, mountainous islands but of low-lying necklaces of islets enclosing crystal clear lagoons. You'll find excellent accommodations and French Polynesia's best scuba diving out on Rangiroa, Tikehau, Manihi, and Fakarava. You will also find drier and warmer climes than in the Society Islands, and sand so brilliantly white that it alone requires sunglasses in the midday sun.

As I have noted elsewhere, Huahine and Tahaa are popular as last stops for honeymooners, who like to "come down" here after the sometimes frantic pace on Bora Bora. On the other hand, I think you should go to the Tuamotus first, so as not to be "let down" after the awesome mountainous beauty of the Society Islands.

1 Huahine ★ ★

Pronounced Wa-*ee*-nee by the French (who never sound an H) and *Who*-a-hee-nay by the Tahitians (who always do), Huahine ranks with Easter Island and Raiatea (see below) as the three most important Polynesian archaeological sites. Here the ancient chiefs built a series of maraes on the shores of **Lake Fauna Nui,** which separates the north shore from a long, motulike peninsula, and on Matairea Hill above the lakeside village of **Maeva.** These have been restored, and informational markers explain their history and purposes.

Fun Fact **Say Hello to Dorothy**

Be sure to say Hello to Dorothy Levy, who runs the snack bar at the Huahine airport. Dorothy's Tahitian father came to Hollywood in the 1930s to work with Clark Gable on the original *Mutiny on the Bounty* movie. He later participated in the first film version of *Hurricane* with Dorothy Lamour, for whom he named this Dorothy.

Geographically, Huahine actually is two islands—Huahine Nui and Huahine Iti—enclosed by the same reef and joined by a short bridge. France did not annex Huahine until 1897, more than 50 years after it took over Tahiti, and its 5,500 residents are still independent in spirit. When the first Europeans arrived, Huahine was governed as a single chiefdom and not divided into warring tribes as were the other islands, and this spirit of unity is still strong. Pouvanaa a Oopa, the founder of French Polynesia's independence movement, hailed from here.

Of attraction to today's visitors are Huahine's Mooreaesque bays, clear lagoon, and lovely beaches. Baie Avea (Avea Bay), on the far southwestern coast of Huahine Iti, is fringed by one of the South Pacific's most glorious beaches. Another is right in the small hamlet of **Fare,** one of the region's best examples of what the South Seas were like in the days of trading schooners and copra planters.

GETTING AROUND HUAHINE

Huahine's airport is on the flat peninsula paralleling the north side of the island, 3km (2 miles) from Fare. Unless you have previously reserved a rental car or are willing to walk into Fare, take your hotel minibus. At other times, **Moe's Taxi** (✆ **72.80.60**) or **Enite's Taxi** (✆ **68.82.37**) will carry you around. Fares are about 600CFP (US$6) from the airport into Fare, about 2,500CFP (US$25) to the southern end of Huahine Iti.

Avis (✆ **800/230-4898** or 68.73.34; www.avis.com), **Europcar** (✆ **800/227-7368** or 68.82.59; www.europcar.com), and **Hertz** (✆ **800/654-3131** or 68.76.85; www.hertz.com) have agents in Fare. Avis charges about 7,500CFP (US$75) a day for a car. Europcar rents scooters for 6,200CFP (US$62) a day, bicycles for 2,000CFP (US$20) a day. On Huahine Iti, **Mara'amu Sailing School** (✆ **68.77.10**), at Pension Mauarii, rents scooters for 6,500CFP (US$65) a day and bicycles for 1,500CFP (US$15) a day.

Each district has **local buses,** which run into Fare at least once a day, but the schedules are highly irregular. If you take one from Fare to Parea, for example, you might not be able to get back on the same day.

FAST FACTS: Huahine

The following facts apply specifically to Huahine. For more information, see "Fast Facts: French Polynesia" in 7.

Currency Exchange **Banque Socredo** is in Fare, on the road that parallels the main street and bypasses the waterfront. **Banque de Tahiti** is on Fare's waterfront. Both have ATMs.

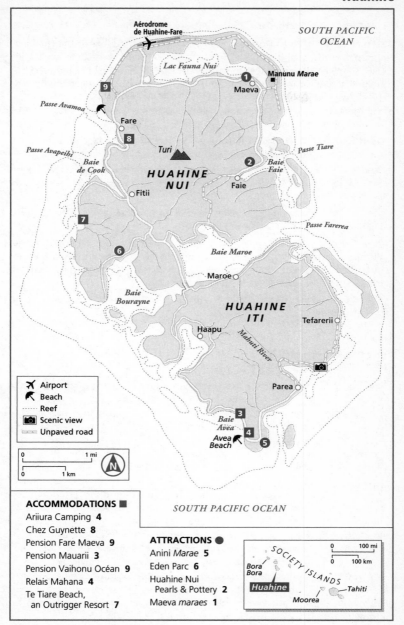

Aérodrome
de Huahine-Fare

*SOUTH PACIFIC
OCEAN*

Lac Fauna Nui

1 ○ Manunu *Marae* ■
Maeva

9 ◼

Passe Avamoa ↖

○ Fare

8 ◼

Turi ▲

Passe Tiare

2 ○ *Baie
Faie*

Passe Avapeihi

*Baie
de Cook*

**HUAHINE
NUI**

○ Fitii ○ Faie

7 ◼

Passe Farerea

6 ●

Baie Maroe

Maroe ○

*Baie
Bourayne*

**HUAHINE
ITI**

Tefarerii ○

Haapu ○

Mahuti River

📷

Parea ○

3 ◼

*Baie
Avea*

4 ◼

*Avea
Beach* ↖ **5** ●

✈ Airport
↖ Beach
⋯⋯ Reef
📷 Scenic view
▦ Unpaved road

0 ———— 1 mi
0 ———— 1 km
Ⓝ

SOUTH PACIFIC OCEAN

ACCOMMODATIONS ◼

Ariiura Camping **4**
Chez Guynette **8**
Pension Fare Maeva **9**
Pension Mauarii **3**
Pension Vaihonu Océan **9**
Relais Mahana **4**
Te Tiare Beach,
  an Outrigger Resort **7**

ATTRACTIONS ●

Anini *Marae* **5**
Eden Parc **6**
Huahine Nui
  Pearls & Pottery **2**
Maeva *maraes* **1**

0 ———— 100 mi
0 ———— 100 km

SOCIETY ISLANDS

Bora
Bora

Huahine

Moorea

Tahiti

Drugstore The pharmacist at the drugstore, on the main road between Fare and the airport, speaks English (© **68.80.90**). Open Monday to Friday 7:30am to noon and 2:30 to 5pm, Saturday 8am to noon, Sunday and holidays 8 to 9am.

E-mail You can pick up e-mail at **AO Api New World** (© **68.70.99**), upstairs over the Manava Huahine Visitors Bureau. Open Monday to Friday 8:30am to noon and 4 to 7:30pm. Access costs 15CFP (15¢) a minute.

Emergencies/Police The emergency **police** telephone number is © **17**. The phone number of the **gendarmerie** in Fare is © **68.82.61.**

Healthcare The **government infirmary** is in Fare (© **68.82.48**). Ask your hotel for the name of doctors and dentists in private practice.

Post Office The colonial-style post office is in Fare, on the bypass road north of the waterfront area. Hours are Monday to Thursday 7:30am to 3pm, Friday 7am to 2pm.

Restrooms There are public toilets on the Fare wharf opposite the visitors bureau, but don't expect them to be clean.

Visitor Information On Fare's main street opposite the wharf, **Manava Huahine Visitors Bureau** (©/fax **68.78.81**) is open Monday to Saturday from 8am to noon (more or less). Some local pensions and tour operators have banded together to host **www.iaorana-huahine.com**.

Water Don't drink the tap water on Huahine. Bottled water is available at all grocery stores.

EXPLORING HUAHINE
TOURING THE *MARAES* ✿✿✿

The village of **Maeva,** beside the pass where Lake Fauna Nui flows toward the sea, was a major cultural and religious center before Europeans arrived in the islands. All of Huahine's chiefly families lived here. More than 200 stone structures have been discovered between the lakeshore and **Matairea Hill,** which looms over Maeva, including some 40 maraes (the others were houses, paddocks, and agricultural terraces).

To see the maraes on your own, start west of Maeva village at the big reed-sided building known as **Fare Potee.** Flanked by maraes and extending out over Lake Fauna Nui, the present building is modeled after a large meeting house which stood here in 1925 but was later destroyed by a hurricane. Take time to read the historical markers outside, which expertly explain the history and use of the maraes. Fare Potee has been a museum in the past, and if it has reopened, you'll observe adzes (stone axes), fishhooks, and other artifacts uncovered during restoration work by Dr. Yoshiko H. Sinoto, the chairman of the anthropology department of the Bernice P. Bishop Museum in Honolulu. He restored this and many other maraes throughout Polynesia.

Six maraes and other structures (some were built as fortifications during the 1844–48 French-Tahitian war) sit on Matairea Hill. The track up the hill can be muddy and slippery during wet weather, and the steep climb is best done in early morning or late afternoon. Better yet, take a tour (see below).

Easier to reach, the large **Manunu Marae** stands on the beach about 1km (½ mile) across the bridge on the east end of Maeva. Follow the left fork in the road after crossing the bridge. The setting is impressive.

From the bridge you will see several stone **fish traps.** Restored by Dr. Sinoto, they work as well today as they did in the 16th century, trapping fish as the tide ebbs and flows in and out of the narrow passage separating the lake from the sea.

HISTORICAL TOURS

The most informative way to see the historical sites—and much of Huahine, for that matter—is with Paul Atallah of **Island Eco Tours** ⏤⏤⏤ (📞 **68.79.67;** www.island-eco-tours.com). Paul is an American who graduated from the University of Hawaii with a major in anthropology and a minor in Polynesian Island archaeology. He has lived in French Polynesia for more than a decade. His is more than a typical safari expedition, for he gives in-depth commentary about the Maeva marae and other historical sites. He charges 5,000CFP (US$50) for either morning or afternoon trips. The 4-hour trips depart daily at 8am and 1pm. He will pick you up at your hotel. Paul can also guide you to the maraes on Matairea Hill by special arrangement.

TOURING THE ISLAND

You can rent a vehicle and tour both parts of Huahine in half a day. The main roads around both islands are about 32km (20 miles) long and are paved. Be careful on the steep *traversière,* which traverses the mountains from Maroe Bay to Faie Bay on the east coast. (I would not ride a scooter or bicycle over this road). Heading clockwise from **Fare,** you skirt the shores of Lake Fauna Nui and come to the maraes outside Maeva village (see "Touring the *Maraes,*" above).

From Maeva the road heads south until it turns into picturesque Faie Bay. There you'll pass the landing for **Huahine Nui Pearls & Pottery** ⏤ (📞 **78.30.20;** www. huahinepearlfarm.com), a pearl farm and pottery studio (see "Shopping on Huahine," below). Once you're past Faie village at the head of the bay, the road starts uphill across the traversière (see above). At the top, you'll be rewarded with a view down across Mooreaesque **Maroe Bay,** which splits Huahine into two islands.

Turn right at the dead-end by the bay and drive west to the main west-coast road. Turn left and follow it across the bridge over the narrow pass separating Huahine Nui from Huahine Iti. A right turn past the bridge will take you along the winding west-coast road to **Avea Bay,** where Relais Mahana and Pension Mauarii (see "Where to Stay on Huahine," below) sit beside one of the South Pacific's greatest beaches. Either is an excellent place to stop for refreshment.

Sitting at the end of the peninsula at the south end of Huahine Iti, **Anini *Marae*** presents a glorious view of the island's southern coast. Nearby, **Parea** is one of Huahine's largest villages. From Parea you'll skirt the shoreline until you come to the village of **Tefarerii,** on the east coast. In between is a pull-off with a marvelous view

---

Tips Fruit Juice & an Exotic Lunch

On your way back to Fare from Huahine Iti, turn off the main road toward Bourayne Bay and drive 2km (1¼ mile) to **Eden Parc** (📞 **68.86.58;** www.eden parc.org), a lush tropical garden where you can get freshly squeezed fruit juice or enjoy an "exotic" lunch made from produce organically grown on the premises. It's a hot and steamy site, so get out your insect repellant. Open Monday to Saturday from 8am to 2pm.

over the reefs and sea. From there it's an easy drive to Maroe Bay. The large cruise ships land their passengers at Maroe village, on the south side of the bay.

VISITING THE OLD SOUTH SEAS IN FARE

The main village of **Fare** &&& (*Fa*-ray) is hardly more than a row of Chinese stores and a wharf opposite the main pass in the reef on the northwest shore, but it takes us back to the days when trading schooners were the only way to get round the islands. Even today trucks and buses arrive from all over Huahine with passengers and cargo when the interisland boats put in from Papeete. The rest of the time, Fare lives a lazy, slow pace, as people amble down its tree-lined main street and browse through the stores facing the town wharf. A monument on the waterfront designates it as Place Hawaiki, the starting point for October's big outrigger canoe race to Raiatea and Bora Bora.

Beginning at the Temarara restaurant and bar (see "Where to Dine," below), a pebbly promenade leads north along the waterfront to a sandy swimming beach, which has a daytime snack bar.

LAGOON EXCURSIONS

As on Moorea and Bora Bora, one of the most enjoyable ways to see the island is on a lagoon excursion including snorkeling and a picnic on an islet out on the reef. The biggest difference here is that with relatively few tourists around, you and your companions are likely to have the islet all to yourselves. The all-day excursion with **Huahine Nautique** (© 68.83.15; www.huahine-nautique.com) takes you by outrigger canoe through Maroe Bay and around Huahine Iti. You'll stop for snorkeling and a picnic featuring freshly made *poisson cru,* and you will observe shark-feeding before returning to Fare. Huahine Nautique's canoes have shade canopies, and the guides speak English as well as French. The excursions cost 8,000CFP (US$80) per person. **Poetaina Cruises** (**60.60.06**) charges about 7,500CFP (US$75) per person for its all-day trips, but I can't guarantee that you'll have shade on your outrigger. Don't be surprised if you visit Huahine Nui Pearls & Pottery (see "Touring the Island," above).

SAFARI EXPEDITIONS

As on most of the Society Islands, you can make four-wheel-drive expeditions into the mountains here. You will see a bit of the interior of Huahine Nui with Paul Atallah on his **Island Eco Tours** (see "Historical Tours," above), which I would take first. You will repeat seeing the Maeva maraes, but either **Huahine Land** (© 68.89.21), which is owned by American expatriate Joel House, or **Huahine Explorer** (© 68.87.33) will also take you to Huahine Iti on their half-day expeditions. Both charge about 5,000CFP (US$50) per person.

Moments **Sailboats & Sunsets at Fare**

I thoroughly enjoy strolling along the wharf, poking my head into the stores across the main street, observing the cruising yachts anchored in the harbor, and watching the boats come and go. With Raiatea, Tahaa, and Bora Bora resting on the western horizon, Fare is one of my favorite places to watch a sunset.

SWIMMING, SNORKELING, DIVING, & OTHER OUTDOOR ACTIVITIES

You don't have to leave Fare to find a fine little swimming and snorkeling beach; just follow the seaside promenade north past Restaurant Temarara. **Europcar** (© **68.82. 59**) rents snorkeling equipment for 400CFP (US$4).

Huahine's best, however, is the magnificent crescent of sand at **Avea Beach,** skirting Baie Avea on Huahine Iti. A hilly peninsula blocks the brunt of the southeast trade winds, so the speckled lagoon here is usually as smooth as glass. **Mara'amu Sailing School** (© **68.77.10**), at Pension Mauarii (see "Where to Stay on Huahine," below), rents Hobie Cats for 4,000CFP (US$40) for the first hour, 3,000CFP (US$30) for each additional hour, and power boats for 7,000CFP (US$70) for 4 hours. It also has power- and sailboat tours and will teach you to windsurf, kite surf, or ride a wake board.

Pacific Blue Adventure (© **68.87.21;** fax 68.80.71; www.divehuahine.com), Didier Forget's scuba-dive operation, has an office on the Fare wharf. Didier charges about 7,500CFP (US$75) for a one-tank dive, during which he might feed the sharks and pet the moray eels. Most dives are outside the reef or in Avapeihi Pass, Huahine's most famous site.

You can go for a half- or full-day cruise with Claude and Martine Bordier of **Sailing Huahine Voile** (©/fax **68.72.49;** www.sailing-huahine.com) on their *Eden Martin,* a 15m (50-ft.) yacht, which they sailed out from France in 1999. A half day of sailing costs about 5,500CFP (US$55) per person; a whole day, 10,000CFP (US$100). They also have sunset cruises for 4,800CFP (US$48) per person. The boat is also available for 1- or 2-week cruises in the Leeward or Tuamotu islands.

For lagoon or deep-sea fishing, contact **Huahine Marine Transports** (© **68.84.02;** hua.mar.trans@mail.pf), owned by American expatriate Rich Shamel, who has lived on Huahine for many years and who runs the transfer boats for Te Tiare Beach Resort (see "Where to Stay on Huahine," below). Rich charges US$800 for half a day and US$1,200 for a full day of fishing on his 11m (36-ft.) Hatteras sportfishing boat. He lives and works at the resort's transfer base, just across the bridge on the south side of Fare.

One of the best horseback riding operations in French Polynesia is **La Petite Ferme (The Little Farm;** © **68.82.98;** www.la-petiteferme.com), on the main road north of Fare, just before the airport turnoff. It has Marquesas-bred horses that can be ridden with English or Western saddles along the beach and around Lake Fauna Nui. Prices range from 5,000CFP (US$50) for 2 hours to 9,800CFP (US$98) for an all-day trail ride. The farm also has accommodations, from a dormitory to bungalows.

SHOPPING ON HUAHINE

You are not as likely to be pestered to buy black pearls on Huahine as on Tahiti, Moorea, and Bora Bora—another of Huahine's appealing attributes, in my opinion. One stop you should make is **Huahine Nui Pearls & Pottery** ✳ (© **78.30.20;** www. huahinepearlfarm.com), a pearl farm and pottery studio operated by American expatriate Peter Owen on a motu off Baie Faie (see "Touring the Island," above). Peter offers free tours daily from 10am to 4pm, with the boat leaving Faie Bay every 15 minutes. If you aren't going to the Tuamotus, this is a good place to see how black pearls are grown.

Local women sell shell jewelry, bedspreads, and other handicrafts at **Huahine Mata Aiai** (no phone), in a thatch building at the south end of the Fare waterfront. Also look into the small art galleries and other shops along here.

WHERE TO STAY ON HUAHINE
EXPENSIVE

Te Tiare Beach, an Outrigger Resort 🏝🏝🏝   Rudy Markmiller made a fortune in the overnight courier business in California and then spent more than a decade—and a sizable chunk of his loot—building this luxury resort, one of French Polynesia's finest. Although it's on the main island, guests are ferried here from Fare, which makes this seem like a remote offshore resort (never fear: a shuttle boat makes the 10-minute run to and from Fare every hour from 5:30am to 11pm). You will land at a thatched-roof, overwater structure housing the reception area, lounge, bar, and dining room serving excellent international cuisine. A long pier connects this central complex to a westward-facing, white-sand beach with gorgeous sunsets over Raiatea and Tahaa out on the horizon. The lagoon is not deep here, but it's still good for swimming and snorkeling over coral heads close to shore. You can use canoes, paddle boats, and kayaks, or cool off in a beachside swimming pool equipped with its own bar. Diving, sailing, fishing, picnicking on a *motu*, horseback riding, or touring the maraes costs extra. Jet skis and water-skiing are available but not in front of the resort.

The 41 spacious bungalows are as luxuriously appointed as any in French Polynesia. You won't have a fish-viewing glass panel in the floor, but you can step out to huge L-shaped decks, one half of them under the shade of thatch roofs. The decks also have privacy screens so your neighbors can't see you dining in the altogether, or whatever. Steps lead into the lagoon from the decks of the 11 "deep overwater" bungalows, which have spa tubs as well as showers in their bathrooms (all other units, including five "shallow overwater" models, have large showers). Six bungalows sit beside the beach, but the garden units (the least expensive here) don't have unimpeded views of the lagoon.

B.P. 36, 98731 Fare, Huahine (in Fitii District, 10 min. by boat from Fare). ℂ 888/600-8455 or 60.60.50. Fax 60.60.51. www.tetiarebeach.com. 41 units. 32000CFP–70,000CFP (US$320–US$700) double. AE, DC, MC, V. **Amenities:** Restaurant; 2 bars; outdoor pool; watersports equipment rentals; activities desk; car-rental desk; limited room service; massage, babysitting; laundry service. *In room:* A/C, TV, minibar, coffeemaker, hair dryer, iron (overwater only), safe.

MODERATE

Relais Mahana   This property offers one of the South Pacific's best beach-lagoon combinations, for it sits right on Avea Beach, the white sand stretching along the peninsula on Huahine's south end. A pier from the main building runs out over a giant coral head, around which fish and guests swim. Just climb down off the pier and swim with the fishes. I cannot tell you much about the accommodation, since a major renovation was upgrading it from *relais* to resort during my recent visit. The first stage, to be completed by 2007, aims to enlarge and improve the existing bungalows—heretofore lacking TVs, phones, and other amenities. An infinity pool and other features are to be added later. Be sure to check the website to see if it has reopened.

B.P. 30, 98731 Fare, Huahine (Avea Bay, Huahine Iti). ℂ 60.60.40. Fax 68.85.08. www.relaismahana.com. 28 units. 21,750CFP–31,000CFP (US$218–US$310). AE, DC, MC, V. **Amenities:** Restaurant; bar; watersports equipment

---

(*Fun Fact* **The Swimsuit Models Were Here**

Those extraordinarily beautiful women seen briefly—as in both time and clothing—at Te Tiare Beach Resort recently were here to model for the 2006 swimsuit issue of *Sports Illustrated* magazine.

rentals; bicycle rental; game room; activities desk; car-rental desk; babysitting; laundry service. *In room:* TV, data port, minibar, coffeemaker, iron, safe.

INEXPENSIVE

Two family-run pensions sit on the rocky shoreline between Fare and the airport. **Pension Fare Maeva** (© **68.75.53;** www.fare-maeva.com) is the more luxurious of the two, with a restaurant, swimming pool, and 10 modern bungalows. Rates range from 6,000CFP (US$60) for a unit without kitchen to 9,000CFP (US$90) for one with cooking facilities. **Pension Vaihonu Océan** (© **68.87.33;** www.iaorana-huahine. com) is more basic, with beach huts, a dorm, yard space for camping, and a two-story building holding two modern units. Rates start at 1,650CFP (US$17) for a dorm bed to 7,200CFP (US$72) for a modern duplex unit. Both accept MasterCard and Visa credit cards.

Chez Guynette *(Value)* Marty and Moe (*Mo-*ay) Temahahe (wife Marty is American; husband Moe is Tahitian) operate this friendly hostel across the main street from the Fare waterfront. A corridor runs down the center of the building to the kitchen and lounge at the rear. The simple but clean rooms and dorms flank the hallway to either side. The rooms are screened and have ceiling fans and their own bathrooms with hot-water showers. The dorms also have ceiling fans; they share two toilets and showers. Marty and Moe offer breakfast and lunch (sandwiches, burgers, salads, poisson cru on their street-side patio, plus wine and beer). It's the best place in Fare to slake a thirst and get into a good conversation—in English.

B.P. 87, 98731 Fare, Huahine (opposite the town wharf). © 68.83.75. chezguynette@mail.pf. 7 units (all w/bathroom), 8 bunks. 1,750CFP–2,000CFP (US$18–US$20) dorm bed; 5,400CFP–5,700CFP (US$54–US$57) double (higher rates apply to 1-night stays). MC, V. **Amenities:** Restaurant; bar. *In room:* No phone.

Pension Mauarii *(🟊)* Beautifully situated right on Avea Beach, this little pension may not offer all the comforts of home, but it oozes charm. Its buildings are constructed of thatch, bamboo, tree trunks, and other natural materials. Although cleverly designed, they seem to be slapped together, which adds to the ambience. Most units are in the tropical gardens, but the rooms open to a long porch right on the beach, as does the one beachside bungalow—my favorite here. All units have ceiling fans, but not all have bathrooms, and their windows aren't screened. The pension offers a host of waterborne activities. Unless the owners have moved it to the inland side of the road to make room for more bungalows, the restaurant here is the most charming on the island (see "Where to Dine on Huahine," below).

B.P. 473, 98731 Fare, Huahine (Baie Avera, Huahine-Iti). © 68.86.49. Fax 60.60.96. www.mauarii.com. 5 bungalows (3 w/bathroom), 4 rooms (2 w/bathroom). 7,500CFP (US$75) double; 10,000CFP–20,000CFP (US$100–US$200) bungalow. AE, MC, V. **Amenities:** Restaurant; bar; watersports equipment rentals; bike and rentals. *In room:* No phone.

CAMPING

You can pitch a tent or rent a rudimentary thatched-roof *fare* (cabin) at Cecèle and Upereto Bremond's **Ariiura Camping** (© **68.85.20** or 68.83.78), on the southern end of Avea Beach. The shoreline here has as many coral ledges and sand, but the shady grounds are appealing. Guests share a communal kitchen, tables under a thatch roof, toilets, and cold-water showers (don't expect a shower head). The cabins have either a double bed or two single beds and range from 4,500CFP to 5,000CFP (US$45–US$50), while tent sites are 1,250CFP (US$13) per person.

WHERE TO DINE ON HUAHINE

You will meet the locals having breakfast or lunch on the patio at **Chez Guynette.** You can also enjoy the fine dining room at **Te Tiare Beach, an Outrigger Resort,** though you will need to make reservations and pay 500CFP (US$5) for the boat ride there and back. See "Where to Stay on Huahine," above.

You'll find Huahine's *roulottes* on the Fare wharf. They're open for both lunch and dinner. See the "Don't Miss *Les Roulottes*" box in chapter 8.

Patisserie Fare (Value) BAKERY   Under a thatch lean-to roof extending from a house, this patisserie is my favorite place for a breakfast of fresh croissants, quiches, or a full American version. Lunch sees the appearance of fresh salads such as roast chicken with almonds, and country-style French potatoes and bacon.

Fare, main road north opposite post office. (✆ 68.77.19. Most items 250CFP–950CFP (US$2.50–US$9.50). No credit cards. Mon–Sat 6am–6pm.

Restaurant La Boussole FRENCH   Located in a house on Fare's south side, just beyond the Te Tiare Beach Resort's landing, this restaurant is Huahine's fine-dining outlet, casual though it may be. The menu features fondue Bourguignonne, magret of duck, and steaks and fish in traditional French sauces.

Fare, main road south of downtown. (✆ 68.88.62. Reservations recommended. Main courses 1,650CFP–2,800CFP (US$17–US$28). AE, MC, V. Tues–Sat 11:30am–2:30pm and 6:30–10pm.

Restaurant Mauarii FRENCH/TAHITIAN   Assuming the owners haven't taken leave of their senses and moved this restaurant across the road, it will still be sitting almost over the sand, with a great view southward along Avea Beach. It's a charmer, with a thatch-lined ceiling and tables hewn from tree trunks. Lunch-time sandwiches include a "Killer" baguette loaded with grilled fish and french fries (yes, in the sandwich) under your choice of vanilla or other sauces. For my money, this is a good place to sample Tahitian treats such as chicken with *ruru* (taro leaves) in coconut cream, or sample different dishes on a Polynesian platter. Ask for a menu in English if the friendly staff doesn't figure you out first.

Avea Beach, Huahine Iti (at Pension Mauarii). (✆ 68.86.49. Reservations recommended for dinner. Sandwiches and burgers 600CFP–1,200CFP (US$6–US$12); main courses 1,600CFP–3,200CFP (US$16–US$32). AE, MC. V. Daily noon–2pm and 6–8pm.

Restaurant Temarara (✿ FRENCH   Facing due west beside the lagoon at the north end of Fare's wharf, this restaurant is everyone's favorite place for a sundown cocktail during half-price happy hour from 5:30 to 6:30pm. The quality doesn't match the great view, but you can get a good beef or fish burger here as well as steaks and fish with French sauces. The coconut crumbed mahimahi is a spicy version of breaded fish. If offered, try the parrot fish with lemon butter.

Fare, north end of wharf. (✆ 68.89.31. Reservations accepted. Burgers 800CFP–900CFP (US$8–US$9); main courses 1,400CFP–2,200CFP (US$14–US$22). MC, V. Mon–Sat 9am–9pm (bar open all day, to 11pm Fri–Sat).

2 Raiatea & Tahaa (✿

The mountainous clump of land you can see on the horizon from Huahine or Bora Bora may appear to be one island, but it actually is two, Raiatea and Tahaa, which are enclosed by a single barrier reef. Cruising yachts can circumnavigate Tahaa without leaving the lagoon, and Huahine and Bora Bora are relatively easy hauls from here. Accordingly, this is French Polynesia's yacht-chartering center. There are no beaches on either Raiatea or Tahaa other than a few on islets out on the reef, and except for sailing and cruise-ship visits, tourism is not an important part of their economies, which are based on agricultural produce and, in the case of Raiatea, government salaries.

Raiatea, the largest of the Leeward Islands, is by far more important than Tahaa, both in terms of the past and the present. In the old days it was the religious center of all the Society Islands, including Tahiti. Polynesian mythology has it that Oro, the god of war and fertility, was born in **Mount Temehani,** the extinct flat-top volcano that towers over the northern part of Raiatea. **Taputapuatea,** on its southeast coast, was at one time the most important marae in the islands. Legend also has it that the great Polynesian voyagers who discovered and colonized Hawaii and New Zealand left from there. Archaeological discoveries have substantiated the link with Hawaii.

Today Raiatea (pop. 10,000) is still important as the economic and administrative center of the Leeward Islands. Next to Papeete, the town of **Uturoa** (pop. 4,000) is the largest settlement and is one of the most important transportation hubs in French Polynesia. Uturoa's waterfront has undergone a major transformation of late, with a big new cruise-ship terminal and welcome center now dominating the town wharf. Although most prefer anchoring offshore in order to use their watersports platforms, Uturoa is the only island port other than Papeete where the larger cruise ships spend their nights tied up to a wharf.

Tahaa (pronounced *Tah*-ah-ah) is much smaller than Raiatea in terms of land area, population (about 1,500), and the height of its terrain. It's a lovely island, with a few very small villages sitting deep in bays that cut into its hills. Tahaa has a few family-operated pensions, but other than sailors and guests at the super-luxurious Le Taha'a Private Island & Spa on one of its reef islets, few visitors see it, and most of those who do, see it on day tours from Raiatea.

GETTING AROUND RAIATEA & TAHAA

The Raiatea airstrip, 3km (2 miles) north of Uturoa, serves both islands. You have to rent a vehicle or take a taxi, for there is no regular public transportation system on either Raiatea or Tahaa.

Avis (© **800/230-4898** or 60.00.95; www.avis.com), **Europcar** (© **800/227-7368** or 66.34.06; www.europcar.com), and **Hertz** (© **800/654-3131** or 66.44.88; www.hertz.com) have rental-car offices here. Europcar's prices start at 9,400CFP (US$94) a day, including insurance and unlimited kilometers. It also rents scooters, bicycles, and open-air "Bugster" vehicles. Europcar also has an office at Tupuamu Wharf on Tahaa's west coast (© **65.67.00**), so you can take the ferry there, rent a car, and drive around the island. You must take a water taxi back to Uturoa.

There is a taxi stand near the cruise-ship terminal in Uturoa, or you can contact **René Guilloux** (© **66.31.40**), **Marona Teanini** (© **66.34.62**), or **Apia Tehope** (© **66.36.41**). Fares are about 600CFP (US$6) from the airport to town and 1,200CFP (US$12) to the Raiatea Pearl Resort.

The passenger ferry *Tamarii Tahaa* (© **65.67.10**) docks in front of the Champion store on Uturoa's waterfront and runs from there to Patio on Tahaa's northern coast. It departs from Uturoa Monday to Friday, usually at 10am and 4pm, Saturday at 11am. You had best make sure it will return to Uturoa on the same day it leaves. Fares are about 1,000CFP (US$10) one-way. **Dave's Tours** (© **65.62.42**) also runs a shuttle from Uturoa to Tahaa, departing Monday to Saturday at 9am, returning at 4:30pm. Fares are 1,500CFP (US$15) one-way, 2,500CFP (US$25) round-trip. **Water-taxi** service is available at the waterfront (© **65.66.64**); rides cost about 2,000CFP (US$20).

Fun Fact **Delicate Petals**

Found nowhere else except in Raiatea's mountains, the *tiare apetahi* is a one-sided white flower of the gardenia family. Legend says that its five delicate petals are the fingers of a beautiful Polynesian girl who fell in love with a prince but couldn't marry him because of her low birth. Just before she died, heartbroken, in her lover's arms, she promised to give him her hand to caress each day throughout eternity. At daybreak each morning, accordingly, the *tiare apetahi* opens its five petals.

FAST FACTS: Raiatea & Tahaa

The following facts apply specifically to Raiatea and Tahaa. For more information, see "Fast Facts: French Polynesia" in chapter 7.

Bookstores **Librairie d'Uturoa** (© 66.30.80) on the inland side of the main street, in the center of town, carries French books and magazines.

Currency Exchange French Polynesia's three banks have offices with ATMs on Uturoa's main street. There is no bank on Tahaa.

Drugstores **Pharmacie de Raiatea** (© 66.34.44) in Uturoa carries French products. Open Monday to Friday 7:30am to noon and 1:30 to 5:30pm; Saturday 7:30am to noon; Sunday 9:30 to 10:30am.

E-mail **ETS,** in the Gare Maritime on the Uturoa waterfront (© 60.25.25), has computers with Internet access for 15CFP (15¢) a minute. It's open Monday to Friday 7:30am to 5pm, Saturday 7:30am to noon. It will burn your digital photos to CDs.

Emergencies/Police The emergency police telephone number is © **17.** The telephone number of the **Uturoa gendarmerie** is © **66.31.07.** The **Tahaa gendarmerie** is at Patio, the administrative center, on the north coast (© 65.64.07).

Eyeglasses **Optique Te Mata Ore,** on Uturoa's main street (© **66.16.19).**

Healthcare Opposite the post office, the **hospital** at Uturoa (© 66.32.92) serves all the Leeward Islands. Tahaa has an **infirmary** at Patio (© 65.63.31). Drs. **Sonia Andreu** and **Pascal Diochin** (© 66.23.01) practice together on Uturoa's main street.

Information **Raiatea Manava** (© 60.07.77; fax 60.07.76; raiateainfo@mail.pf) has a visitor information office in the Gare Maritime on the waterfront. Open Monday to Friday 8am to 4pm, Saturday 8am to 3pm (Sunday 8am to 3pm when cruise ships are in port).

Laundry **Laverie Apetahi,** at Apooti Marina (© 66.28.36), will wash, dry, and fold your laundry for 363CFP (US$3.65) a kilo. Open Monday to Friday 8am to noon and 1 to 4:30pm.

Post Office The post and telecommunications office is in a modern building north of Uturoa on the main road (as opposed to a new road that runs along the shore of reclaimed land on the north side of town). It is open Monday to Thursday 7:30am to 3pm, Friday 7am to 2pm, and Saturday 8 to 10am.

Restrooms The Gare Maritime on the waterfront has clean restrooms.

Telephone There are *télécarte* phones on the waterfront and at the post and telecommunications office.

Water Don't drink the tap water on either Raiatea or Tahaa.

EXPLORING RAIATEA & TAHAA

Highlights of a visit here are visiting the ancient maraes, day trips to and around Tahaa, picnics on small islands on the outer reef, and four-wheel-drive excursions into the mountains.

VISITING THE *MARAE*

On the outskirts of Opoa village 29km (18 miles) south of Uturoa, the **Taputapuatea Marae** ✿✿✿ is the second most important archaeological location in all of Polynesia, behind only Easter Island. Legend says that Te Ava Moa Pass offshore was the departure point for the discovery and settlement of both Hawaii and New Zealand. The large marae on the site was actually built centuries later by the Tamatoa family of chiefs. Vying for supremacy, the Tamatoas mingled religion with politics by creating Oro, the ferocious god of war and fertility supposedly born on Mount Temehani, and by spreading his cult. It took almost 200 years, but Oro eventually became the most important god in the region. Likewise, the Tamatoas became the most powerful chiefs. They were on the verge of conquering all of the Society Islands when the missionaries arrived in 1797. With the Christians' help, Pomare I became king of Tahiti, and the great marae the Tamatoas built for Oro was soon left to ruin, replaced by the lovely Protestant church in nearby Opoa village.

The marae was restored in the 1960s, and more recently Tahiti Museum archaeologists discovered human bones under some of the structures, apparently the remains of sacrifices to Oro. The marae's huge *ahu,* or raised altar of stones for the gods, is more than 45m (150 ft.) long, 9m (30 ft.) wide, and 3.3m (11 ft.) tall. Flat rocks, used as backrests for the chiefs and priests, still stand in the courtyard in front of the ahu. The entire complex is in a coconut grove on the shore of the lagoon, opposite a pass in the reef, and legend says that bonfires on the marae guided canoes through the reef at night.

Taputapuatea is worth a visit not only for the marae itself but for the scenery there and along the way. The road skirts the southeast coast and follows Faaroa Bay to the mouth of the river, then back out to the lagoon.

On the west coast, 14.5km (9 miles) from Uturoa, **Taninuu Marae** also was dedicated to Oro. Stones bordering the foundation of the ancient chief's home bear petroglyphs of turtles. This is a place of Christian history, too, since the lovely white Eglise Siloama is one of the oldest churches in French Polynesia.

WALKING AROUND UTUROA

A number of Chinese stores still line the main street, but the center of activity in Uturoa is the glistening **Gare Maritime,** a cruise-ship terminal built with money from France's economic restructuring fund. You can't miss this big Mediterranean-style building, which houses restaurants, shops, the island's visitor information office, and public restrooms. Needless to say, the waterfront is busiest when a cruise ship arrives, and handicraft and souvenir vendors occupy a number of small thatch buildings next door.

Just north of downtown Uturoa, the street to the left as you face the gendarmerie leads to a trail that ascends to the television towers atop 291m (970-ft.) **Papioi Hill.** (Be sure to close the gates, which keep the cows out of the station.) From the top you can see Uturoa, the reef, and the islands Tahaa, Bora Bora, and Huahine. Another trail begins with a Jeep track about 200 yards south of the bridge, at the head of Pufau Bay on the northwest coast. It leads up to the plateau atop **Mount Temehani.** The mountain itself is actually divided in two by a deep gorge.

ORGANIZED TOURS

American anthropologist Bill Kolans of **Almost Paradise Tours** (© 66.23.64) has lived on Raiatea since sailing his boat down from Hawaii in 1979. He will take you to Taputapuatea and other archaeological sites in his van. Although Bill tends to wander a bit and doesn't like being interrupted, he provides informative commentary about the history and culture of the islands. His 3-hour island tour costs 4,500CFP (US$45) per person.

SAFARI EXPEDITONS ON RAIATEA & TAHAA

Either **Raiatea 4×4** (© 66.24.16) or **Jeep Safari Raiatea** (© 66.15.73) will take you via four-wheel-drive Jeep into Raiatea's interior, including a ride into the ancient crater of Mount Temehani, and they both stop at Taputapuatea Marae before heading back to Uturoa. These expeditions are less thrill ride and more oriented to history and culture than those on Bora Bora. I would opt for Raiatea 4×4, especially if the highly informative Ronnie Moufat is to be your guide. Each has two trips a day, requires reservations a day in advance, and charges about 4,500CFP (US$45) per person.

The mountains of Tahaa offer less dramatic scenery than on Raiatea, and the island lacks the historical importance of its big sister. Consequently, safari expeditions there include visits to **La Maison de Vanille** (© 57.61.92), which explains the cultivation and uses of vanilla (Tahaa's major product), and to a black pearl farm. I thoroughly enjoyed my expedition guided by the energetic and engaging Roselyne Atiniu of **Dave's Tours** (© 65.62.42), or you can go with **Vai Poe Tours** (© 65.60.83). Either will pick you up at Uturoa.

LAGOON EXCURSIONS

If you can put together your own group (because a minimum of four persons is required), you can take a variety of **lagoon excursions** and see firsthand the Raiatea-Tahaa lagoon, one of the most beautiful in French Polynesia. All trips include snorkeling, and most include picnics on tiny islets sitting on the outer reef; unlike the mainland of Raiatea and Tahaa, they have beautiful white-sand beaches. **Motu Toahotu** and **Motu Mahena** are equipped with restrooms and other facilities, for which the locals extract a 500CFP (US$5) per person entrance fee. **Dave's Tours** (© 65.62.42) will take you out from Uturoa.

Marie and Tony Tucker (she's French, he's South African) of **West Coast Charters** (© 66.45.39) have a complete tour around Tahaa with swimming, guided snorkeling

---

Tips **Avoid Cruise-Ship Days**

Unless you're on one of them, try to avoid visiting Raiatea when cruise ships are in port, since their passengers can monopolize all organized activities here.

over coral gardens, shark feeding, a pearl farm visit, and lunch for 7,500CFP (US$75) a person. Andrew Brotherson at **Manava Excursions** (© **66.28.26;** fax 66.28.26; maraud@mail.pf) charges 6,500CFP (US$65) per person for an all-day trip to Tahaa, including visits to a vanilla plantation and pearl farm, a picnic on a motu, and snorkeling over a coral garden. He also offers a half-day lagoon trip with a motu picnic for 1,500CFP (US$15) per person, and a boat trip up the Faaroa River and on to the Taputapuatea marae for 4,500CFP (US$45) per person.

DIVING, SAILING ✴✴✴ & HORSEBACK RIDING
The Moorings (© **800/535-7289** or 727/535-1446; www.moorings.com) and **Sunsail Yacht Charters** (© **800/327-2276** or 207/253-5400 in the U.S., or 60.04.85 on Raiatea; fax 66.23.19; www.sunsail.com) charter sailboats (see "Seeing the Islands by Cruise Ship & Yacht," in chapter 7). Both operators are based on Raiatea. If a boat is available, it can be chartered on a daily basis. Arrangements for longer charters ordinarily should be made before leaving home.

Raiatea may not have beaches, but the reef and lagoon are excellent for scuba diving, including descents of 50 to 80 feet above the wreck of the S.S. *Norby*, a three-masted Danish schooner which sunk off Uturoa in 1900. With bases at the Hawaiki Nui Hotel and at Apooiti Marina, **Hémisphère Sub Raiatea** (© **66.12.49;** fax 66.28.63; www.multimania.com/diveraiatea) takes divers on one-tank excursions for 6,500CFP (US$65).

You can go horseback riding with **Kaoha Nui Ranch** (© **66.25.46;** www. kaohanui.com), which charges 4,500CFP (US$45) for 2 hours, 6,500CFP (US$64) for half a day. The ranch also has accommodation for riders, lagoon excursions, and guided botanical walks.

SHOPPING IN UTUROA
The Gare Maritime on the waterfront has several black pearl and other shops, including **My Flower** (© **66.19.19**), where owner Flora Hart carries not just floral arrangements but excellent tapa drawings and wood carvings, some from the Marquesas Islands, others done in *hue papa'a* wood, a specialty of Raiatea's own carvers.

Other stores line the main street, where you will find the unique **Magasin Vanira** (© **66.30.06**). Owner Jeanne Chane—the *"préparatrice de vanille"*—makes many products from vanilla beans: extract, powder, even vanilla soup. The wonderful aroma alone makes it worth a visit.

WHERE TO STAY ON RAIATEA
Hawaiki Nui Hotel ✴ This hotel is of historical importance in its own right, for it was here in 1968 that Moorea's "Bali Hai Boys" built the world's first overwater bungalows (see the box in chapter 9). It was their way of compensating for the lack of a beach here. The hotel has gone through several name changes since its days as the Hotel Bali Hai Raiatea, but those bungalows still stand out on the edge of the reef. From them you can climb into the water and get the sensation of flying as you snorkel along its clifflike face. (Snorkel gear and kayaks are free for guests here.) It's also still Raiatea's best hotel. The friendly and helpful staffers speak English, but the ambience is definitely French these days. The land-based bungalows, some of which have two units under their thatch roofs, are either along the seawall or in the gardens beyond. The least expensive units are hotel rooms, which have the same amenities as the bungalows and are air-conditioned.

B.P. 43, 98735 Uturoa, Raiatea (2km/1¼ miles south of town). © 800/657-3275 or 66.20.23. Fax 66.20.20. www. pearlresorts.com. 32 units. 24,000CFP (US$240) double; 26,000CFP–46,000CFP (US$260–US$460) bungalow. AE, MC, V. **Amenities:** Restaurant; bar; outdoor pool; tennis court; bike rentals; activities desk; car-rental desk; babysitting; laundry service. *In room:* A/C (rooms only), TV, minibar, coffeemaker, hair dryer, safe.

Pension Manava   Roselyne and Andrew Brotherson rent two rooms in their house and have four bungalows in their gardens, across the road from the lagoon. The two rooms share a bathroom and the Brothersons' kitchen. The bungalows have corrugated tin roofs, screened louvered windows, double and single beds, and large bathrooms with hot-water showers. Two also have kitchens. Roselyne will cook breakfast and provide free dinner transportation to town on request.

B.P. 559, 98735 Uturoa, Raiatea (6km/3½ miles south of town). © 66.28.26. www.manavapension.com. 6 units. 4,700CFP (US$47) double (no bathroom); 7,000CFP (US$70) bungalow; 8,000CFP (US$80) bungalow w/kitchen. No credit cards. *In room:* Kitchen (2 units), no phone.

Sunset Beach Motel 🐟 *Value*   One of the best values in French Polynesia, this is not a motel but a collection of cottages in a coconut plantation on a peninsula sticking out west of the airport. The cottages sit in a row just off a palm-draped beach. The lagoon here is very shallow, but the beach enjoys a gorgeous westward view toward Bora Bora, and a long pier stretches to deep water (guests can paddle free kayaks from it). Of European construction rather than Polynesian, the bungalows are spacious, comfortably furnished, and have fully equipped kitchens and large covered verandas facing the sea. Part of the grove is set aside for campers, who have their own building with toilets, showers, and kitchen (bring your own tent). Manager Steeve "Moana" Boubée speaks English. There is no restaurant here, but you order breakfast in your bungalow.

B.P. 397, 98735 Uturoa, Raiatea (in Apooiti, 5km/3 miles northwest of Uturoa). © 66.33.47. Fax 66.33.08. www. raiatea.com/sunsetbeach. 22 units. 9,000CFP (US$90) double bungalow. 1,100CFP (US$11) per person camping. MC, V. **Amenities:** Free kayaks; rental bikes; laundry service. *In room:* TV, kitchen, no phone.

WHERE TO STAY ON TAHAA

Le Taha'a Private Island & Spa 🐟🐟🐟   When I was traveling by yacht back in 1977, we anchored near *Motu* Tautau, an islet on the reef off Tahaa's northwest coast, and went ashore to get an unsurpassed view of Bora Bora from its outer edge. There was nothing on Tautau then except palm trees, a brackish lake, and several million mosquitoes. Since 2002 the mossies have mostly resided on the sea side of the motu, while one of French Polynesia's most luxurious and architecturally creative resorts has occupied the lagoon shoreline. A 40-minute boat ride from the Raiatea airport, or 15 minutes by helicopter from Bora Bora, this Relais & Chateau–affiliated hotel sports the territory's most tastefully decorated bungalows. Most stand out over the hip-deep lagoon, where their large decks have privacy fences screening covered sitting areas under thatch roofs. Most face hilly Tahaa, but a few have views of Bora Bora through a shallow reef pass between Tautau and its neighboring motu. Ashore beside the brilliant white-sand beach, 12 villa suites are even larger and more private. They have living rooms, bedrooms, and courtyards with plunge pools hidden behind high rock walls. At the center of it all is a stunning two-story central building, where stairs built in a tree lead up to the main bar and casual gourmet restaurant with both indoor and outdoor tables, all with a view. The most romantic tables sit by themselves on extensions from the terrace. Or you can retire to the air-conditioned fine dining restaurant. The resort's infinity pool, a lunchtime restaurant and bar, and full-service spa are on one end of the property, thus removing most daytime activities from the vicinity of the bungalows. There's much to do here, from snorkeling to safari expeditions on Tahaa. This is the most remote resort in the Society Islands, so don't expect to run over to the mainland and save a few bucks on dinner. On the other hand, this is a marvelous place to chill after the rigors of Bora Bora.

B.P. 67, 98733 Patio, Tahaa (on *Motu* Tautau). ⓒ **800/657-3275** or 69.84.00. Fax 69.84.01. www.letahaa.com. 60 units. 90,000CFP–125,000CFP (US$900–US$1,250) bungalow. AE, DC, MC, V. **Amenities:** 2 restaurants; 2 bars; outdoor pool; tennis court; spa; Jacuzzi; watersports equipment rentals; concierge; activities desk; limited room service; massage; babysitting; laundry service. *In room:* A/C, TV, CD player, dataport, minibar, coffeemaker, hair dryer, safe.

WHERE TO DINE ON RAIATEA

Raiatea's inexpensive les roulottes congregate after dark near the Gare Maritime in the middle of Uturoa's business district. They stay open past midnight on Friday and Saturday.

Brasserie Maraamu *(Value* CHINESE/TAHITIAN   Before it moved into the Gare Maritime, this restaurant occupied a waterfront shack and was widely known for its simple but good Chinese dishes, poisson cru, and fried chicken and steaks served with french fries. The chow is still good, as witnessed by the number of local office workers who head here for lunch. Local business types like to hang out here over strong cups of morning coffee served in soup bowls, Chinese style.

In Gare Maritime, Uturoa waterfront. ⓒ **66.46.64.** Main courses 1,000CFP–1,800CFP (US$10–US$18). MC, V. Mon–Fri 7am–2pm and 6:30–9pm, Sat 10am–2pm.

Le Napoli ⓕ *(Finds* ITALIAN   A stack of firewood beside a pond (note the Tahitian eels swimming about) hints that the very good pizzas and steaks are cooked in a wood-fired oven in this open-air restaurant, which is dolled up with bamboo trim. The 15 varieties of pizza are all two-person size, so unless you are famished, forget the special tourist menu which adds poisson cru and a dessert.

Main road north of Uturoa, near airport. ⓒ **66.10.77.** Reservations recommended. Pizza and pasta 1,250CFP–1,450CFP (US$13–US$15); main courses 1,400CFP–2,000CFP (US$14–US$20). MC, V. Tues and Thurs–Sat 11am–2pm and 6:30–9pm, Wed and Sun 6:30–9pm.

Restaurant Quai des Pecheurs ⓕⓕ *(Value* FRENCH   Robert Cazenave, one of French Polynesia's top hotel managers, gave up the sheets-and-pillows business to turn this casual but chic restaurant into Raiatea's best place to dine. A big awning shades tables out on the Gare Maritime's plaza, where you can cool off with ice cream at a walk-up counter or slake a thirst at the bar. Robert's menu features fresh local seafood and New Zealand steaks. The tuna steak in a spicy Creole sauce is a pleasant diversion from familiar French choices. There's music for dancing on Friday nights and a Tahitian dance show on Saturday evenings. Call for free transportation from the Hotel Hawaiki Nui.

In Gare Maritime, Uturoa waterfront. ⓒ **66.43.19.** Reservations recommended for dinner. Main courses 1,400CFP–2,950CFP (US$14–US$30). AE, MC, V. Daily noon–2pm and 7–9pm (ice cream counter and bar 10am–11pm).

Snack Moemoea SNACKS/FRENCH/CHINESE   Predating the Gare Maritime by many years, this old corner storefront has tables both outside on the sidewalk and inside on the ground floor or on a mezzanine platform. It's another good place for breakfast, from croissants to omelets. The lunch menu includes *casse-croûte* sandwiches (a sandwich made on a crusty French baguette with any array of fillings), fine hamburgers, grilled fish and steaks, and Raiatea's best poisson cru. I love to slake my thirst here with an ice cold coconut.

Waterfront, Uturoa (in Toporo Bldg.). *© **66.39.84.*** Breakfast 600CFP–1,500CFP (US$6–US$15); sandwiches 400CFP–700CFP($4–US$7); main courses 1,300CFP–1,800CFP (US$13–US$18). No credit cards. Mon–Fri 6am–5pm, Sat 6am–2pm.

3 Rangiroa ★ ★

The largest and most often visited of the Tuamotu atolls, Rangiroa lies 312km (194 miles) northeast of Tahiti. It consists of a ring of low, skinny islets enclosing the world's second largest lagoon. At more than 70km (43 miles) long and 26km (16 miles) wide, it's big enough so that when you stand on one side of the lagoon, you cannot see the other. In fact, the entire island of Tahiti could be placed in Rangiroa's lagoon, with room to spare.

Like all the atolls, the islets here are so low—never more than 3m (10 ft.) above sea level, not including the height of the coconut palms growing all over them—that ships can't see them until they're a few kilometers away. For this reason, Rangiroa and its Tuamotu sisters are also known as the Dangerous Archipelago. Hundreds of yachts and ships have been wrecked on these reefs, either unable to see them until it was too late or dragged ashore by tricky currents.

Schools of dolphins usually play early mornings and late afternoons in Rangiroa's two navigable passes into its interior lagoon, both located on the north side. Currents of up to 6 knots race through the passes as the tides first fill the lagoon and then empty it during their never-ending cycle. Even at slack tide, watching the coral rocks pass a few feet under your yacht is a tense experience. Once inside the lagoon, however, you anchor in a huge bathtub whose crystal-clear water is stocked with an incredible variety of sea life (including a multitude of large sharks and manta rays).

Most visitors come to Rangiroa primarily for French Polynesia's best scuba diving, snorkeling, and fishing. Others venture across the lagoon to Rangiroa's islets, where they can literally get away from civilization at a very remote resort.

GETTING AROUND RANGIROA

Rangiroa's airstrip and most of its hotels and pensions lie on the main islet, a perfectly flat, 11km-long (7-mile) stretch of sand and palm trees on the north side of the lagoon. The airport is about equidistant from the village of Avatoru on the west end and Tiputa Pass, which separates the main island from Tiputa village, on the east. The hotels and pensions send buses or vans to meet their guests.

You can cross Tiputa Pass to Tiputa village via **Maurice Navette** (*© **96.67.09*** or 78.13.25), which operates water taxis daily from 6am to 5pm. Call or check with your hotel staff for schedules and fares.

Rangi Rent a Car is the local agent for **Europcar** (*© **800/227-7368*** or 96.08.28; www.europcar.com). It has an agency near Avatoru and a desk at the Hotel Kia Ora (see "Where to Stay on Rangiroa," below). Scooters and open-air "Fun Cars" (the most you'll need here) cost about 6,500CFP (US$65) for a day (which is longer than you'll need to see the islet). Bicycles rent for 1,500CFP (US$15) for half a day, 1,800CFP (US$18) for a full day. **Arehahio Locations** (*© **98.82.45***) in Avatoru rents scooters for 5,200CFP (US$52) a day, bicycles for 1,300CFP (US$13) a day.

Rangiroa's 11km-long (7-mile) main island actually consists of 7 islets separated by narrow reef passes. The only road crosses the passes over bridges, none of them with guardrails and some of them only one-lane wide. The pavement is uneven, adding to the need for constant caution when driving.

FAST FACTS: Rangiroa

The following facts apply specifically to Rangiroa. For more information, see "Fast Facts: French Polynesia" in chapter 7.

Currency Exchange **Banque Socredo** has an agency with an ATM in Avatoru post. It's open Tuesday, Wednesday, and Friday from 8am to noon; Monday and Thursday from 1:30 to 4:30pm. **Banque de Tahiti** also has a branch in Avatoru. It's open Monday and Friday 8 to 11am and 1 to 4pm, Tuesday and Thursday 8 to 11am.

Drugstore **Pharmacie de Rangiroa,** in Avatoru (℡ **93.12.35**), is open Monday to Friday 7am to 12:30pm and 2:30 to 6:30pm, Saturday from 7am to 12:30pm and 4:30 to 6:30pm, Sunday and holidays 10 to 11:30am.

Emergencies/Police The emergency **police** telephone number is ℡ **17**. The phone number of the **gendarmerie** on Rangiroa is ℡ **96.03.61**.

Healthcare **Dr. Guy Thirouard** has an office in Avatoru (℡ **96.04.44** or 96.04. 33). There are **infirmaries** at Avatoru (℡ **96.03.75**) and across the pass at Tiputa (℡ **96.03.96**).

Photographic Needs For film, check the boutique at the **Hotel Kia Ora.** You won't get overnight processing here.

Post Office The small post office in Avatoru is open Monday to Thursday from 7am to 3pm, Friday 7am to 2pm.

Telephone Public pay phones are at the post office in Avatoru and at the dock on the eastern end of the island. Residents in the Tuamotus tend to write their phone numbers in groups of three digits; that is, 960 375 instead of 96.03.75.

Water Except at the hotels, the tap water is brackish. Don't drink it.

LAGOON EXCURSIONS & SCUBA DIVING 𝄞𝄞𝄞

Except for walks around Avatoru and Tiputa, typical Tuamotuan villages with white-washed churches and stone walls lining the main streets, plan on either doing nothing or enjoying the fantastic lagoon. The hotels and pensions either have or can arrange lagoon excursions by boat. One favorite destination is the **Lagon Bleu (Blue Lagoon),** a small lagoon within the big lagoon on the far eastern side of the island. It's full of colorful corals and plentiful sea life. **Les Sables Rose (The Pink Sands),** on the eastern end, is another popular destination. These trips are not inexpensive—plan on paying 10,000CFP (US$100) or more for a full day's outing. You're looking at an hour's boat ride in each direction to reach the Blue Lagoon or The Pink Sands.

Close to home, snorkelers and scuba divers can **"ride the rip"** tide through the passes, one of the most exhilarating waterborne experiences French Polynesia has to offer. These so-called drift snorkeling trips cost about 5,000CFP (US$50) and are worth it—if you've got a strong heart.

The same operators also have **dolphin-watching** cruises, usually for about 3,000CFP (US$30) per person, but you can ride or walk to the public park at the western side of Tiputa Pass and watch them play for free.

The best **scuba diving** here is from December to March, when huge hammerhead sharks gather off Tiputa Pass for their mating season, and also between July and October, when the manta rays look for mates. You can see gray and black-tipped sharks all year. But be aware that dives here are deep and long compared to American standards, so bring a buddy and be prepared to stretch the limits of the dive tables in order to see the magnificent sea life. Divers must be certified in advance and bring their medical certificates.

Any of the hotels or pensions can arrange scuba dives. The best operators are **Blue Dolphins** (✆ **96.03.01;** www.bluedolphinsdiving.com), at the Hotel Kia Ora (see "Where to Stay on Rangiroa," below), and **Top Dive Rangiroa** (✆ **72.39.55;** www.topdive.com). Other operators here include **The Six Passengers** (✆ **96.02.60**), which allows only six divers on its boat at any one time; **Raie Manta Club** (✆ **96.04.80**); and **Rangiroa Paradive** (✆ **96.05.55**). One-tank day dives cost about 7,000CFP (US$70). Night dives are more expensive.

A WINERY & A BLACK PEARL FARM

Near Avarotu, **Cave de Rangiroa** (✆ **96.04.70;** www.vindetahiti.pf) is the tasting room for Vin de Tahiti (Tahiti Wines), French Polynesia's only vineyard and winery. The Carignan, muscat de Hambourg, and Italia varieties were first planted in a coconut grove out on an islet in 1999. You can take a half-day tour to the motu vineyard for 6,000CFP (US$60) per person, or just stay here in the *cave* and taste the results in air-conditioned comfort. Open Monday to Saturday 9am to 1pm and 3 to 6pm.

Rangiroa does not produce black pearls in the same quantity as Manihi, but you can visit **Gauguin's Pearl Farm,** west of the airport (✆ **93.11.30**), and see how it's done. For 5,000CFP (US$50) they will open an oyster and you get to keep any pearl inside. If there isn't one, they keep opening oysters until there is. It's like playing the lottery: You might win big; then again, you might not. Open Monday to Friday 8am to noon and 1 to 5pm, weekends 9am to noon and 3 to 5pm.

WHERE TO STAY ON RANGIROA

Hotel Kia Ora ★★   This romantic establishment in a huge coconut plantation has been Rangiroa's premier hotel for almost 3 decades. Its thatch-roofed buildings look like a lagoonside Polynesian village. White sand is hauled over from the ocean side of the island, but the beach still is a bit pebbly; however, a long pier reaches out into deep water for excellent swimming, snorkeling, and sunset watching, and there's a canoe-shaped swimming pool beside the lagoon. Ten bungalows sit over the reef and share the sunsets. Ashore stand two-story beachside bungalows with bedrooms downstairs and up, and one-story models with only the downstairs bedroom. These beach units have Jacuzzi tubs set in their partially covered front decks, but they have not one iota of privacy. Much better are three deluxe beach units with their own small pools and bathrooms with outdoor tubs. The much smaller original bungalows have also been spiffed up but they do not have window screens. As at most accommodations on Rangiroa, guests here are overwhelmingly European and Japanese.

B.P. 1, 98775 Tiputa, Rangiroa (3km/2 miles east of airport, near east end of island). ✆ **96.02.22.** Fax 93.11.17. www.hotelkiaora.com. 58 units. 30,000CFP–65,000CFP (US$300–US$650) double. AE, DC, MC, V. **Amenities:** Restaurant; bar; outdoor pool; tennis court; Jacuzzi; watersports equipment rentals; bike rentals; activities desk; car-rentals; massage; babysitting; laundry service. *In room:* A/C, dataport, fridge (stocked on request), coffeemaker, hair dryer, safe.

Kia Ora Sauvage   This outpost offers one of the South Pacific's most remote Robinson Crusoe–like escapes. Guests are transferred daily by a 1-hour speedboat ride from Hotel Kia Ora, which manages this retreat. Once you're out on tiny, triangle-shaped Avearahi motu, you will find a thatched main building, where the Tahitian staff cooks up the day's catch, often caught during the guests' lagoon excursions. Accommodation is in five comfortable bungalows built entirely of native materials. They have their own modern bathrooms, but they are not screened. Nor do they have electricity. Bring reef shoes, lots of insect repellent, and 60-factor sun block.

B.P. 1, 98775 Tiputa, Rangiroa (hotel is 1-hr. boat ride from airport). © 96.02.22. Fax 93.11.17. www.hotelkiaora. com. 5 units. 40,000CFP (US$400) double. Meals and drinks 7,600CFP (US$76) per person per day. Round-trip boat transfers cost 10,000CFP (US$100) per person. AE, DC, MC, V. **Amenities:** Restaurant; bar. *In room:* No phone.

Les Relais de Josephine *(★ (Value* You can watch the dolphins frolic in Tiputa Pass from this comfortable inn, the creation of Denise Thirouard, whose husband, Dr. Guy Thirouard, practices medicine in Avatoru (see "Fast Facts," above). The bungalows flank a Mediterranean-style villa with an expansive veranda overlooking the pass. Guests can relax there or in a lounge equipped with a TV, VCR, and CD player. At night the veranda turns into the Le Dolphin Gourmand restaurant, which serves excellent three-course French and Mediterranean meals. Furnished with reproductions of French colonial antiques, the bungalows have thatch roofs over solid white walls. Sliding doors open to the porches with high-quality wooden patio furniture. Neither the doors nor the prop-up windows are screened, but the queen-size beds are covered by mosquito nets. The substantial bathrooms have double sinks and walk-in showers. Do anything possible to get one of the three units beside the pass.

B.P. 140, Avatoru, Rangiroa. ©/fax **96.02.00.** http://relaisjosephine.free.fr/englis/indexuk.htm. 6 units. 14,300CFP (US$143) per person double occupancy. Rates include breakfast and dinner. AE, DC, MC, V. **Amenities:** Restaurant; bar; bike rentals; laundry service. *In room:* Coffeemaker, safe, no phone.

Novotel Rangiroa Beach Resort This modest but attractive resort sits beside a rocky stretch of lagoon shoreline west of the airport. Brilliant white sand has been brought in to make a sunbathing strip along the property. Opened in 2004, its 38 bungalows and main building (with restaurant and bar) are packed on limited land. The units here come either as individual bungalows or as duplex rooms, which are narrower than the bungalows. Both are tastefully decorated with tropical furniture and fabrics, and they have adequate bathrooms and front porches. You'll have much more room to roam at the Hotel Kia Ora, where you will pay about the same for a garden bungalow.

B.P. 17, 98775 Avatoru, Rangiroa. © **800/221-4542** or 93.13.50. Fax 93.13.51. www.novotel.com. 38 units. 24,600CFP–39,000CFP (US$246–US$390) bungalow. AE, MC, V. **Amenities:** Restaurant; bar; car and bike rentals; activities desk; massage; laundry service. *In room:* A/C, TV, dataport, fridge, coffeemaker, hairdryer, safe.

WHERE TO DINE ON RANGIROA

Non-guests are welcome at Les Relais de Josephine's Le Dolphin Gourmand restaurant (see above), where the three-course meals cost 3,950CFP (US$40) per person. Make your reservations before noon. Outsiders are welcome at the Hotel Kia Ora's dining room, too. You'll find a few inexpensive snack bars in Avatoru and at Tiputa Pass.

Restaurant Le Kai Kai FRENCH West of the airstrip and near the Novotel Rangiroa Beach Resort, this open-air restaurant with crushed coral floor and mat-lined ceiling is my favorite spot for a casual lunch or dinner. Midday sees a selection of omelets, salads, and *croques* (toasted sandwiches), while dinner turns to French fare with Polynesian ingredients, such as a Tuamotuan-style sautéed pork. Otherwise I stick with the mahimahi, wahoo, or other fresh fish. A special *prix fixe* dinner menu includes a starter of beef or tuna carpaccio, a main of shrimps in coconut curry sauce or a filet of beef, and a dessert, such as a Tahitian sundae with coconut and honey. Reserve for a 7pm pickup from your hotel.

Main road, west of airport. (C) **96.30.39.** Reservations recommended. Lunch sandwiches and omelets 400CFP–1,000CFP (US$4–US$10); main courses 1,200CFP–2,000CFP (US$12–US$20); fixed-price diner 3,400CFP (US$34). MC, V. Daily 11:30am–2pm and 6:30–9pm.

4 Tikehau 🖈

Separated from Rangiroa by a deep-water channel, Tikehau is much smaller and less developed. Its nearly circular lagoon, 26km (16 miles) across, is dotted with islets such as Ohihi, which has a pink-sand beach, and Puarua and Oeoe, the so-called Bird Islands, where noddy birds and snowy white fairy terns nest. The lagoon is no more than 30m (100 ft.) deep, which means it's unlikely to see big manta rays and sharks in here. A multitude of colorful tropical fish swim in the lagoon, which makes it great for snorkelers and novice divers, but Tikehau's best diving is in the ocean beyond the one passed in the reef.

Manihi Blue Nui Dive Center, based at the Tikehau Pearl Beach Resort (see below), is one of the best in French Polynesia, with top-of-the-line equipment and hard-topped boats with ladders. It charges about 7,500CFP (US$75) per one-tank dive, and it teaches PADI certification courses.

Famous for a riot of hibiscus, frangipani, bougainvillea, and other colorful flowers that seem to grow everywhere, Tikehau's only village, **Tuherahera,** is one of the most picturesque in the Tuamotus. It's also one of the wealthiest since the 400 or so residents here make more money by trapping and shipping fish to Papeete than they do from their four black pearl farms. You'll find grocery stores, a post office, and an infirmary in Tuherahera, but you won't find a bank.

WHERE TO STAY & DINE ON TIKEHAU

Tikehau Pearl Beach Resort 🖈🖈🖈 You may think you have made a horrible mistake as your transfer boat approaches, for rustic Tuamotu-style thatch disguises the luxuries awaiting at this resort, which occupies all of *Motu* Tiano, a small reef islet a 10-minute boat ride from the village and the airport. Other than a concrete patio separating the lagoonside pool from the conical-roofed dining room and bar, everything about it is *très* Polynesian, with beaucoup thatch, mats, and bamboo. Strong currents in a shallow pass rip in and out beneath some of the overwater bungalows here, which means you can't go swimming from their decks. Consequently, opt for one of the "premium" suites built over quieter water; they do have ladders leading into the lagoon. The beach here has more white sand than you'll find on Rangiroa and Manihi. Every unit is spacious and well appointed, and the beachside units have large outdoor bathrooms behind high rock walls. The bungalows aren't screened, but the staff closes the windows and turns on the electric mosquito repellents while you're at dinner. Ceiling fans and the trade winds usually provide plenty of ventilation, but opt for a premium overwater or deluxe beach bungalow if air-conditioning is important to you.

B.P. 20, 98778 Tuherahera, Tikehau. (C) **800/657-3275** or 50.84.54 for reservations, or 96.23.00. Fax 43.17.86 for reservations, or 96.23.01. www.pearlresorts.com. 37 units. 38,000CFP–75,000CFP (US$380–US$750) double. Meals 10,000CFP (US$100) per person per day. AE, DC, MC, V. **Amenities:** Restaurant; bar; outdoor pool; spa; free use of snorkeling gear, canoes, and kayaks; bike rentals; babysitting; laundry service. *In room:* A/C (in premium overwater and deluxe beach units), TV, minibar, coffeemaker, hair dryer, safe.

5 Manihi ★

Known for its black pearl farms, Manihi lies 520km (312 miles) northeast of Tahiti in the Tuamotus. At 30km (16 miles) long by 5.6km (4 miles) wide, the clear lagoon is not nearly as large—nor as deep—as Rangiroa's, but it's better for diving among colorful tropical fish, as opposed to the big rays and sharks that make diving at Rangiroa so exciting. That's not to say there are no sharks here; to the contrary, the lagoon seems infested. Tairapa Pass, the main entry into the lagoon, is wider and deeper than those at Rangiroa, but it has a strong enough current to make riding-the-rip snorkeling trips a highlight here.

French Polynesia's pearl farming industry began here in the late 1960s, and although many are now closed, the farms seem to sit atop nearly every coral head dotting the lagoon. Most of the workers stay in Turipaoa, the only village here. If you visit the village, head inland from the dock for 1 block, turn right, and walk to the pass, where there's a grocery store. From there walk along the seawall for a view of the outer reef. You'll pass a small, picturesque Catholic church.

Note: There is no bank on Manihi, and the airport does not have restrooms.

As at Tikehau, Gilles Petrie's **Manihi Blue Nui Dive Center,** based at the Manihi Pearl Beach Resort (see below), provides top-of-the-line PADI diving. It charges about 6,700CFP (US$67) per one-tank dive.

WHERE TO STAY & DINE ON MANIHI

Manihi Pearl Beach Resort ★★   This modern resort and the airstrip share a motu on the western end of Manihi's lagoon. Like at Rangiroa, the beach here is more pebbly than sandy, but guests can sun themselves on little islets equipped with palm trees and chaise lounges, or on a faux beach beside a lagoonside horizon pool. A thatch-roof bar adjacent to the pool is cozy and conducive to meeting your fellow guests. In addition to diving, activities include swimming, snorkeling (you can ride the rip tide through the pass), canoeing, visiting pearl farms and the village, lagoon and deep-sea fishing, spending a day on a deserted motu, and cruising at sunset. The prevailing trade winds can generate a choppy lagoon under the 19 overwater bungalows here. Both the overwater and beachside units have mat-lined walls, natural wood floors, ceiling fans hanging from thatch roofs, king-size beds, writing tables, ample shower-only bathrooms, and covered porches with two recliners. Each beachfront unit also has a hammock strung between two palm trees out front, and the beachfront unit bathrooms are outdoors behind high wooden walls. Although a majority of guests here are European couples, the English-speaking Tahitian staff makes Americans feel at home.

B.P. 1, 99711 Manihi. ☎ 800/657-3275 or 50.84.54 for reservations, or 96.42.73. Fax 43.17.86 for reservations, or 96.42.72. www.pearlresorts.com. 40 units. 28,000CFP–60,000CFP (US$280–US$600) double. Meals 10,000CFP (US$100) per person per day. AE, MC, V. **Amenities:** Restaurant; bar; outdoor pool; watersports equipment rentals; free bicycles; game room; activities desk; babysitting; laundry service. *In room:* A/C (in premium overwater bungalows), TV, dataport, minibar, coffeemaker, hair dryer, safe.

6 Fakarava

Fakarava rests in the northern Tuamotus southeast of Rangiroa and about 490km (300 miles) northeast of Tahiti. Its rectangular reef encloses French Polynesia's second largest lagoon, a 60km by 24km (37 × 15 mile) aquamarine jewel filled with such a rich variety of sealife that it has been designated as a United Nations nature preserve.

The resort, airstrip, and main village, **Rotoava,** sit at the atoll's northeastern end, near **Garuae Pass,** the widest in the Tuamotus. It's so wide and deep, that ships as large as the *Queen Elizabeth 2* (*QE2*) can safely enter the lagoon. From there a road—facetiously dubbed "rue Flosse" because former French Polynesian President Gaston Flosse paved part of it prior to a visit by French President Jacques Chirac in 2003—runs for 30km (18 miles) along one of the South Pacific's longest motus. A smaller pass and the ancient village of **Tetamanu,** site of an 1834-vintage Catholic church, lie at Fakarava's southeastern end, a 2-hour boat ride from the airport. Nondivers can spend a day on one of Fakarava's small islets surrounded by beaches of pink sand.

Rotoava village has a post office, infirmary, school, white-washed church, and two general stores, but no bank.

WHERE TO STAY & DINE ON FAKARAVA

Hotel Maitai Dream   A sister of the Hotel Maitai Polynesia on Bora Bora (see "Where to Stay," in chapter 10), this comfortable, unpretentious resort sits beside the lagoon, a 15-minute ride by *le truck* or boat from the airstrip. A pier extends from the central building out over the multihued lagoon, but there are no overwater bungalows. Instead, the 28 units sit along or facing the pebbly beach, and all of their front porches have lagoon views. Built of timber with peaked shingle roofs, they are spacious and comfortably furnished with king-size and single beds, desks, and ceiling fans, and their ample bathrooms feature open-air showers and their own outside entry. The restaurant features both indoor and outdoor tables and serves good French fare with Polynesian influences. Tahitians put on a dance show once a week. Kayaks, canoes, and snorkeling gear are free, but you'll pay for excellent lagoon excursions and diving.

B.P. 19, 98764 Fakarava (14km/8½ miles from airport). © **98.43.00.** Fax 98.43.01. www.hotelmaitai.com. 28 units. 44,000CFP–55,000CFP (US$440–US$550). Rates include all meals and airport transfers. AE, MC, V. **Amenities:** Restaurant; bar; free kayaks, canoes, snorkeling gear; scooter rentals; activities desk; laundry service. *In room:* TV, dataport, fridge, coffeemaker, hair dryer, safe.

12

Rarotonga & the Cook Islands

"**R**arotonga is cool," a French naval officer based in Papeete said to me. "It's like Tahiti—without the French."

He may have been jesting, but in many ways Rarotonga is a miniature Tahiti, and indeed without the French, since the Cook Islands are an independent country associated with New Zealand. Like Tahiti, it has jagged peaks and steep valleys surrounded by a flat coastal plain, white sandy beaches, an azure lagoon, and a reef extending about .5km (¼ mile) offshore.

Rarotonga's enchanting sister, Aitutaki, substitutes for Bora Bora in the Cook Islands. It is nearly surrounded by a large, shallow lagoon of multihued beauty and abundant sea life. Spending a day on the lagoon at this charming, atoll-framed outpost is a highlight of any visit here.

The Cook Islanders have more than beautiful islands in common with the people of French Polynesia, which lies some 900km (550 miles) to the east. Like the Tahitians, they enjoy having a good time, and this lust for happiness very quickly rubs off on visitors. They share about 60% of their native language with the Tahitians, and their lifestyles and religions were similar in the old days. In fact, many Tahitians and Cook Islanders are related. Like their Tahitian cousins, the people here have a keen interest in their eastern Polynesian past, and they are very good at explaining those old ways to those of us who visit them today.

In addition to Polynesian culture, the Cooks have enough activities to satisfy almost anyone, including snorkeling, shopping, sightseeing, and scuba diving. They have beaches of dazzlingly white sand, a friendly and fun-loving people who speak English, a variety of accommodations and restaurants in all price ranges, an excellent public transportation system, and some of the region's great bars and dance shows. Indeed, no other place in the South Pacific packs so much to see and do into such small islands—and at relatively reasonable prices, too.

1 The Cook Islands Today

The 15 Cook Islands are scattered between Tahiti and Samoa, in an ocean area about one-third the size of the continental United States, yet all together they comprise only 241 sq. km (93 sq. miles) of land—a third the size of New York City. Two-thirds of that is on Rarotonga, which is only 32km (20 miles) around. With only 21 sq. km (8 sq. miles), Aitutaki is a mere speck in comparison.

THE NATURAL ENVIRONMENT The Cook Islands are divided both geographically and politically into a Southern and a Northern Group. The nine islands of the Southern Group are high enough to have hills, but only Rarotonga is mountainous. All but one of the remote and infrequently visited Northern Group are low-lying atolls, with circles of reef and low coral islands enclosing central lagoons. The few residents in the Northern Group earn their living fishing and growing black pearls.

Impressions

If I could vacation on only one Pacific island I would choose Rarotonga. It's as beautiful as Tahiti, much quieter, much stuffier, and the food is even worse. But the climate is better and the natives are less deteriorated.
                                    —James A. Michener, *Return to Paradise,* 1951

Rarotonga's shoreline consists of a slightly raised sandy bar backed by a swampy depression, which then gives rise to the valleys and mountains. Before the coming of missionaries in 1823, Rarotongans lived on the raised ground beyond the swampy flats, which they used for growing taro and other wet-footed crops. They built a remarkable road, the *Ara Metua* (back road), paved in part with stones. The route ran from village to village, almost around the island. It still exists, although the paved round-island road now runs near the shore. The area between the two roads appears to be bush but is in fact heavily cultivated with a plethora of crops and fruit trees. Otherwise the vegetation is typically tropical. The mountains and hills are covered with native brush, while the valley floors and flat coastal plains are studded with coconut and banana plantations and a wide range of flowering trees and shrubs.

THE GOVERNMENT   The Cook Islands are an independent country in association with New Zealand, which provides for the national defense needs of the islands and renders substantial financial aid. Cook Islanders hold New Zealand citizenship, which means they can live there. New Zealanders, on the other hand, are not citizens of the Cook Islands and cannot live here without permission from the Immigration department. New Zealand has a representative—not an ambassador or consul—in Avarua. Although the Cook Islands technically are independent, their ties with New Zealand deprive it of a seat in the United Nations.

The Cook Islands have a Westminster–style parliament led by a prime minister chosen by members of the majority party. Parliament meets twice a year, in February and March and from July to September. There is also a House of Ariki (that is, hereditary chiefs), which advises the government on matters of traditional custom and land tenure.

THE ECONOMY   The economy in the Cook Islands is based on tourism (more than half of the country's gross domestic product), black pearls (its number-one export), and agriculture, mainly tropical fruit and fruit juices. Still, the country relies to a large extent on overseas aid and cash sent home by islanders living abroad. Many Cook Islanders have pulled up stakes and left for better employment, education, and health care in New Zealand, resulting in a decrease in the islands' population. The exodus has resulted in a shortage of labor, especially in the tourism industry (don't be surprised to see Australians and Fijians working alongside Cook Islanders at the major hotels).

2 The Cook Islands Yesterday: History 101

Legend has it that the first Polynesians arrived in the Cook Islands by canoe from the islands of modern-day French Polynesia about A.D. 1200, although anthropologists think the first of them may have come much earlier. In any event, they discovered the Cook Islands as part of the great Polynesian migrations that settled all of the South Pacific. Before Europeans arrived, feudal chiefs, known as *ariki,* ruled the islands. They owned all the land within their jurisdictions and held life-and-death power over their subjects. Like other Polynesians, the islanders believed in a hierarchy of gods and spirits, among them Tangaroa, whose well-endowed carved image is now a leading handicraft item.

The Spanish explorer Alvaro de Mendaña laid the first European eyes on the Cook Islands, sighting Pukapuka in 1595. As happened in so many South Pacific island groups, Capt. James Cook stumbled onto some of the islands during his voyages in 1773 and 1777; he named them the Hervey Islands. (A Russian cartographer changed the name to the Cook Islands in 1824.) Captain Cook sailed around the Southern Group but missed Rarotonga, which apparently was visited first by the mutineers of HMS *Bounty*, under Fletcher Christian (see "French Polynesia Yesterday: History 101," in chapter 7). There is no official record of the visit, but oral history on Rarotonga has it that a great ship arrived offshore about the time of the mutiny.

MORE MISSIONARIES   The man who claimed to have discovered Rarotonga was the Rev. John Williams of the London Missionary Society. Williams came from London to Tahiti in 1818 as a missionary, and he soon set up a base of operations on Raiatea in the Society Islands, from which he intended to spread Christianity throughout the South Pacific. On his way to Australia in 1821, Williams left two teachers at Aitutaki. By the time Williams returned 2 years later, they had converted everyone on Aitutaki.

Pleased with this success, Williams headed off in search of Rarotonga. It took a few weeks, during which he stopped at Mangaia, Mauke, Mitiaro, and Atiu, but he eventually found Rarotonga in July 1823.

Williams established churches in the villages of Ngatangiia, Arorangi, and Avarua, but he spent most of the next 4 years forcing the locals to build a new ship, *The Messenger of Peace,* which he eventually sailed west in search of new islands and more converts. Those of us who take a dim view of proselytizing would argue that the *Messenger of Peace* extracted a measure of revenge by delivering Williams to a cannibal's oven in Vanuatu. Whatever your opinion, his reputed bones were later recovered and reburied in Samoa (see chapter 13). Meanwhile, the missionaries he left behind quickly converted all of the islanders to his rock-ribbed version of Christianity.

On Rarotonga, the missionaries divided the land into rectangular parcels, one for each family. Choice parcels were set aside for the church buildings and rectories. Rarotongans moved down from the high ground near their gardens and became seaside dwellers for the first time. All land except church and government property is still communally owned; it can be leased but not sold.

Out of the seeds planted by Williams and the London Missionary Society grew the present-day Cook Islands Christian Church, to which about 60% of all Cook Islanders belong. The churches, many of them built of coral block in the 19th century, are the center of life in every village, and the Takamoa College Bible School that the missionaries established in 1837 still teaches in Avarua. The Cook Islands Christian Church owns the land under its buildings; the churches of all other denominations sit on leased property.

Fun Fact **On Her Merry Way**

When the 19th-century missionaries would shear a woman's locks for misbehaving, she would appear in public wearing a crown of flowers and continue on her merry way.

All in the Family

The missionaries weren't the only English folk to have a lasting impact on the Cook Islands.

In 1863 a farmhand from Gloucester named William Marsters accepted the job as caretaker of tiny, uninhabited Palmerston Island, an atoll sitting all by itself northwest of Rarotonga. He took his Cook Islander wife and her sister with him. A Portuguese sailor and his wife, a first cousin of Mrs. Marsters, joined them.

The Portuguese sailor skipped the island within a year, leaving his wife behind. Marsters then declared himself to be an Anglican minister and married himself to both his wife's sister and her first cousin.

Marsters proceeded to start three families, one with each of his three wives. Within 25 years, he had 17 children and 54 grandchildren. He divided the island into three parts, one for each clan, which he designated the "head," "tail," and "middle" families. He prohibited marriages within a clan (in a twist of logic, he apparently thought sleeping with your half-brother or half-sister apparently wasn't incest).

Obviously there was a lot of marrying outside the clans, for today there are thousands of Marsters in the Cook Islands and New Zealand. All trace their roots to Palmerston Island, though only 50 or so live there.

THE COMING OF THE KIWIS   It was almost inevitable that the Cook Islands would be caught up in a wave of colonial expansion that swept across the South Pacific in the late 1800s. The French, who had established Tahiti as a protectorate, wanted to expand their influence west, and in 1888 they sent a warship to Manihiki in what is now the Northern Group of the Cooks. Although the British had made no claim to the islands, locals quickly sewed together a Union Jack and ran it up a pole. The French ship turned away. Shortly thereafter the British declared a protectorate over the Cook Islands, and the Union Jack went up officially.

In 1901 Britain acceded to a request from New Zealand's prime minister, Richard Seddon, to include the Cook Islands within the boundaries of his newly independent country. In addition to engineering the transfer, Seddon is best remembered for his policy of prohibiting the Chinese—and most other Asians—from settling in the Cooks.

Otherwise, New Zealand, itself a former colony, never did much to exploit—or develop—the Cook Islands. For all practical purposes, the Cook Islands remained a South Seas backwater for the 72 years of New Zealand rule, with a brief interlude during World War II when U.S. troops built the airstrip on Aitutaki.

SIR ALBERT AND SIR GEOFF   The situation began to change after 1965, when the Cook Islands became self-governing in association with New Zealand. The first prime minister of the newly independent government was Sir Albert Henry, one of the South Pacific's most colorful modern characters. He ruled for a controversial 13 years, during which time his government enlarged Rarotonga's airport (Queen Elizabeth II was on hand for the grand opening) and built The Rarotongan Resort (now The Rarotongan Beach Resort & Spa). Although Sir Albert lost the national elections in 1978 and was later indicted for bribery, he remained highly popular. When he died in 1981, his body was taken around Rarotonga on the back of a pickup truck; the road was lined with mourners.

Dr. Tom Davis, a Cook Islander who had worked in the United States for NASA, succeeded Sir Albert. The premiership returned to Henry hands in 1989, with the victory of Sir Geoffrey Henry, Sir Albert's cousin. Sir Geoffrey's tenure is best remembered for the government-backed "Sheraton Hotel" project at Vaimaanga, on Rarotonga's south coast, which went unfinished after being caught up in a scandal in Italy. The project left the Cook Islands government seriously in debt. Although plans had been announced to resume work on the hotel as I write, the property has been caught up in a land dispute. Meantime, the unfinished buildings stand hauntingly like ancient ruins-in-the-making.

Succeeding governments have adopted probusiness policies, and despite a dip after the terrorist attacks of September 11, 2001, record numbers of tourists, more than half of them from New Zealand, have fueled the economy. The country has seen a boom of new resorts, motels, and bungalows.

3 The Cook Islanders

The Cook Islands have a population of 17,900, more or less since the figure fluctuates as some islanders move to New Zealand and others return. More than half reside on Rarotonga. A vast majority of the population is of pure Polynesian descent. In culture, language, and physical appearance they are closely akin to both the Tahitians and the Maoris of New Zealand. Only on Pukapuka and Nassau atolls to the far northwest, where the residents are more like the Samoans, is the cultural heritage significantly different.

Modern Cook Islanders have maintained the warmth, friendliness, and generosity that characterize Polynesians everywhere. Like their ancestors, they put great emphasis on family life. Within the extended family, a guiding principle remains share and share alike, and no one ever goes without a meal or a roof over his or her head. In fact, they may be generous to a fault: Many of the small grocery stores they run reputedly stay on the verge of bankruptcy.

Although not a matriarchy, Cook Islands culture places great responsibility on the wife and mother. Women are in charge of the section of land upon which their families live. They decide which crops and fruit trees to plant, they collect the money for household expenses, and, acting collectively and within the churches, they decide how the village will be run. When the mother dies, the land passes jointly to her children.

The burial vaults you see in many front yards are the final resting places of the mothers who built the houses. Their coffins are sealed in concrete vaults both for sanitary reasons and because to shovel dirt on a woman's dead body is to treat her like an animal.

Tips Why Hurry?

Cook Islanders live by the old Polynesian tradition known as "island time." The clock moves more slowly here, as it does in other South Pacific islands. Everything will get done in due course, not necessarily when you want it done. In other words, service can be slow by Western standards. But why hurry? You're on vacation.

(Likewise, striking a live woman is the quickest way for a Cook Islands man to wind up in prison.) The survivors care only for the graves of persons they knew in life, which explains the many overgrown vaults. Eventually, when no one remembers their occupants, the tops of the old vaults are removed and the ground is plowed for a new crop.

In addition to those who are pure Polynesian, a significant minority in the Cook Islands are of mixed European-Polynesian descent. There are also a number of New Zealanders and Australians plus a few Americans and Europeans, most of whom live on Rarotonga. There are very few Chinese or other Asians here.

4 Language

Nearly everyone in the Cook Islands speaks English, which is an official language along with Cook Islands Maori, a Polynesian language similar to Tahitian and New Zealand Maori. A little knowledge of the latter is helpful, primarily because nearly all place names are Maori.

Cook Islands Maori has eight consonants and five vowels. The vowels are pronounced in the Roman fashion: *ah, ay, ee, oh, oo* instead of *a, e, i, o, u* as in English. The consonants used are *k, m, n, p, r, t,* and *v*. These are pronounced much as they are in English. There is also *ng*, which is pronounced as the *ng* in "ring." The language is written phonetically; that is, every letter is pronounced. If there are three vowels in a row, each is sounded. The name of Mangaia Island, for example, is pronounced "Mahn-gah-*ee*-ah."

Generally, Cook Islanders speak English to visitors, but here are some helpful expressions with pronunciations:

English	Maori	Pronunciation
hello	**kia orana**	*kee*-ah oh-*rah*-nah
goodbye	**aere ra**	ah-*ay*-ray rah
thank you	**meitaki**	may-ee-*tah*-kee
how are you?	**peea koe**	*pay*-ay-ah *ko*-ay
yes	**ae**	*ah*-ay
no	**kare**	*kah*-ray
good luck	**kia manuia**	*kee*-ah mah-*nu*-ee-ah
European person	**Papa'a**	pah-*pah*-ah
wraparound sarong	**pareu**	*pah*-ree-oo
keep out	**tapu**	*tah*-poo
small island	**motu**	*moh*-too

5 Visitor Information & Entry Requirements
VISITOR INFORMATION
The helpful staff of the **Cook Islands Tourism Corporation** provides information upon request. The address is P.O. Box 14, Rarotonga, Cook Islands (✆ **29-435;** fax 21-435; www.cook-islands.com). The main office and visitors center is west of the traffic circle, in the heart of Avarua. It's open Monday to Friday 8am to 4pm. Other offices are:

- **North America:** 17880 Skypark Circle, Suite 250, Irvine, CA 92614 (✆ **949/ 476-4086;** fax 949/476-4088; usamanager@cook-islands.com)

- **New Zealand:** 1/127 Symonds St. (P.O. Box 37391), Parnell, Auckland (© **09/ 366-1199;** fax 09/309-1876; nzmanager@cook-islands.com)
- **Australia:** P.O. Box 20, Guildord, NSW 2161 (© **02/9955-0446;** fax 02/ 9955-0447; ausmanager@cook-islands.com)
- **United Kingdom:** Nottcut House, 36 Southwark Bridge Rd., London SE1 9EU (© **020/7202-6369;** fax 020/7202-6369; ukmanager@cook-islands.com)
- **Germany:** Petersburgstrasse 94, 10247 Berlin (© **30/4225-6027;** fax 30/4225-6286; europemanager@cook-islands.com)

When you get to Rarotonga, stop by the visitor center and pick up brochures and other current information, especially Jason's *What's On in the Cook Islands* (www. jasons.com) and the *Cook Islands Sun,* two free tourist publications that are full of facts, advertisements, and excellent maps of the islands. The daily newspapers, the *Cook Islands News* and the *Cook Islands Herald,* provide radio and TV schedules, weather forecasts, shipping information, and advertisements for island nights and other entertainment.

ENTRY REQUIREMENTS

Visas are not required for visitors, who can stay for 31 days if they have valid passports, onward or return air tickets (they will be examined at the immigration desk upon arrival), and sufficient funds. New Zealand citizens do not need passports to enter the Cook Islands, but they do need them to reenter New Zealand. Extensions are granted on a month-to-month basis for up to 5 more months; apply at the Immigration Department near the airport in Avarua. Visitors intending to stay more than 6 months must apply in advance from their home country to the **Principal Immigration Officer,** Ministry of Labour and Commerce, P.O. Box 61, Rarotonga, Cook Islands (© **29-363**).

Customs allowances are 2 liters of spirits or wine, 200 cigarettes or 50 cigars, and NZ$250 (US$113) in other goods. Arriving passengers can purchase items from the duty-free shop and change money before clearing Immigration. Firearms, ammunition, and indecent materials are prohibited, as are live animals, including pets (they will be placed in quarantine until you leave the country). Personal effects are not subject to duty. All food and other agricultural products must be declared and will be inspected.

6 Money

Although the local government mints some unusual coins, the New Zealand dollar is the medium of exchange in the Cook Islands. At the time of this writing, one New Zealand dollar is worth about US65¢. The exchange rate fluctuates, so check the business sections of most daily newspapers or find the present rate on currency conversion websites such as **www.xe.com**.

Fun Fact **Tangaroa & Her Highness**

One side of the famous Cook Islands dollar coin bears the likeness of the Polynesian god of fertility, Tangaroa—including his private part. On the other side is the image of Queen Elizabeth II, who was reportedly not at all pleased about sharing the coin with the uninhibited Tangaroa.

The New Zealand Dollar & the U.S. Dollar

At this writing, **NZ$1** = approximately **US65¢** (or **US$1 = NZ$1.45**), the rate of exchange used to calculate the U.S. dollar prices given in this chapter. Since the U.S. dollar has fluctuated in recent years, this rate may change by the time you visit. Use the following table only as a guide:

NZ$	US$	NZ$	US$
.25	.16	15	9.75
.50	.33	20	13.00
.75	.49	25	16.25
1	.65	30	19.50
2	1.30	35	22.75
3	1.95	40	26.00
4	2.60	45	29.25
5	3.25	50	32.50
6	3.90	75	48.75
7	4.55	100	65.00
8	5.20	125	81.25
9	5.85	150	97.50
10	6.50	200	130.00

HOW TO GET LOCAL CURRENCY   **Westpac Bank, ANZ Bank,** and the **Bank of the Cook Islands** have offices west of the traffic circle on the main road in Avarua. Westpac and ANZ have ATMs. Banking hours are Monday to Friday 9am to 3pm (4pm at ANZ Bank). **GlobalEX,** in Mana Court west of the traffic circle (© **29-907**), changes currency and travelers checks, often at better rates than the banks.

CREDIT CARDS   American Express, MasterCard, and Visa are widely accepted by hotels and restaurants on Rarotonga and Aitutaki. Only the major hotels and car-rental firms accept Diner's Club cards. Discover cards are not accepted anywhere in the islands. If you're going to Aitutaki or another outer island, you can use credit cards at the larger hotels and some restaurants, but not everywhere. Therefore, carry cash or small-denomination traveler's checks.

7 When to Go

THE CLIMATE

Rarotonga and Aitutaki, which are about as far south of the equator as the Hawaiian Islands are north of it, enjoy a tropical climate. Even during the summer months of January and February, the high temperatures on Rarotonga average a comfortable 84°F (29°C), although there can be hot, humid, and sticky summer days. The climes are much more pleasant during the winter, from June to August, when the average high drops to 77°F (25°C), and the ends of Antarctic cold fronts can bring a few downright chilly nights. It's a good idea to bring a light sweater or jacket for evening wear during the winter months.

December through April is both the cyclone (hurricane) and rainy season. There always is a chance that a cyclone will hit during these months (three struck almost back-to-back early in 2005), but most of the rain comes in short, heavy cloudbursts that are followed by sunshine. Rain clouds usually hang around Rarotonga's mountain peaks, even during the dry season (June to Aug).

In short, there is no bad time weatherwise to visit the Cook Islands, although the shoulder months of April, May, September, and October usually provide the best combination of sunshine and warmth.

HOLIDAYS & SEASONS

Legal holidays are New Year's Day, Anzac (Memorial) Day (Apr 25), Good Friday, Easter Monday, the Queen's Birthday (first Mon in June), Gospel Days (last Mondays in July and Oct), Constitution Day (Aug 4), National Gospel Day (Oct 26), Aitutaki Gospel Day (Oct 27, Aitutaki only), Christmas Day, and Boxing Day (Dec 26). Note that government offices and many businesses are closed on Monday if a holiday falls on a weekend.

The busiest season is from late June through August, when New Zealanders and Australians escape their own winters. Make hotel reservations early for these months. Many Cook Islanders live in New Zealand and come home for Christmas; you can easily get a room, but airline seats are hard to come by during that holiday season.

THE COOK ISLANDS CALENDAR OF EVENTS

April

Anzac Day. Cook Islanders killed in the two World Wars are honored with parades and church services. April 25.

Dancer of the Year Contest ✷✷. This is one of the South Pacific's great traditional dance competitions; villages from all over the country send their young people to Rarotonga to compete for the coveted Dancer of the Year award. Begins mid-April.

August

Constitution Week/Cultural Festival Week ✷✷✷. Honoring the attainment of self-government on August 4, 1965, this celebration is highlighted by parades and sporting events. Begins August 4.

October

Edgewater Round Rarotonga Road Race. Marathoners race completely around Rarotonga—all 32km (20 miles) of it. First week in October.

Tivaevae Exhibition. Traditional and modern quilts are showcased in a month-long show. Mid-October to mid-November.

Gospel Day. Honors the arrival of the first missionaries and features outdoor religious plays known as *nuku*. Last Sunday in October.

⌐Moments Swinging Hips

I never visit the Cook Islands without watching the hips swing at a traditional dance show. Take my word for it: Had the crew of HMS *Bounty* seen the dancing on Rarotonga instead of Tahiti, even Captain Bligh might have mutinied. The best times to see the best dancing come during the Dancer of the Year contest and during Constitution Week.

November

All Souls Day. Colorful decorations and evening programs are held to remember deceased loved ones. November 1.

Tiare Week Festival. Shops and offices are ablaze with fresh floral arrangements, leading up to a beauty contest and parade of flower-covered floats. Mid- to late November.

8 Getting to Rarotonga & Getting Around

GETTING THERE

Air New Zealand flies directly to Rarotonga from Los Angeles, Tahiti, Fiji, and Auckland. Its flights from and to Los Angeles stop for an hour or so in Tahiti, less than 2 hours away; accordingly, the Cook Islands can easily be combined with a visit to French Polynesia. **Polynesian Blue** has service from Sydney and Auckland. For details, see "Getting There & Getting Around" in chapter 2.

ARRIVING   The small terminal at **Rarotonga International Airport,** the country's only gateway, is 2km (1⅓ miles) west of Avarua. Westpac Pacific Banking's terminal office is open 1 hour before and after all international flights; it has windows both inside and outside the departure lounge, but it does not have an ATM. Small shops in the departure lounge sell handicrafts, liquor, cigarettes, and stamps. Arriving passengers can purchase duty-free items before clearing Immigration.

Representatives of all the hotels and hostels will be waiting outside Customs to usher you to your transportation.

DEPARTING   **Raro Tours** (© **25-325**) begins picking up departing passengers about 2 hours before each international flight. Your hotel or guest house can reserve a seat for you and tell you when it will arrive at your accommodation. Before clearing Immigration you must pay a **departure tax** of NZ$30 (US$20) for adults, NZ$15 (US$10) for children between the ages of 2 and 12, in New Zealand currency at Wespac Bank's airport booth, or in advance at the bank's Avarua office. No tax is imposed for domestic departures.

GETTING AROUND THE COOK ISLANDS

Air Rarotonga (© **22-888;** www.airraro.com) is the country's only airline, and it's a good one. It has several flights per day (one on Sun) to Aitutaki and one per weekday to Atiu, Mauke, Mangaia, and Mitiaro. Regular one-way fares are about NZ$200 (US$130) to Aitutaki, slightly less to the other islands in the Southern Group. You can save with Air Rarotonga's discounted fares, which can be as little as NZ$300 (US$195) round-trip to Aitutaki.

Don't forget to reconfirm your return flight.

GETTING AROUND RAROTONGA

BY BUS   When people say "catch the bus" on Rarotonga, they mean the **Cook's Island Bus** (© **25-512**), which is actually two big yellow "Cook's Passenger Transport" buses that leave the Cook's Corner shopping center in Avarua going clockwise and counterclockwise around the island, respectively. Clockwise buses depart on the hour from Avarua Monday to Saturday from 7am to 4pm, Sunday from 8am to noon. Counterclockwise buses depart once an hour Monday to Friday beginning at 8:25am. Each takes 50 minutes to circle the island. There's less frequent, one-bus evening service Monday to Saturday from 6 to 10pm (to 1:30am on Friday night). The tourist

Rarotonga

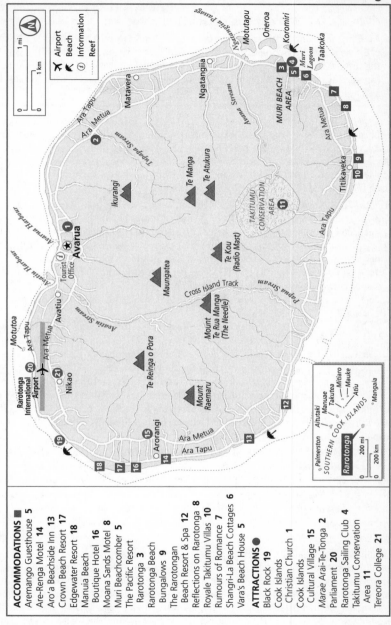

ACCOMMODATIONS ■
Aremango Guesthouse **5**
Are-Renga Motel **14**
Aro'a Beachside Inn **13**
Crown Beach Resort **17**
Edgewater Resort **18**
Manuia Beach
  Boutique Hotel **16**
Moana Sands Motel **8**
Muri Beachcomber **5**
The Pacific Resort
  Rarotonga **3**
Rarotonga Beach
  Bungalows **9**
The Rarotongan
  Beach Resort & Spa **12**
Reflections on Rarotonga **8**
Royale Takitumu Villas **10**
Rumours of Romance **7**
Shangri-La Beach Cottages **6**
Vara's Beach House **5**

ATTRACTIONS ●
Black Rock **19**
Cook Islands
  Christian Church **1**
Cook Islands
  Cultural Village **15**
Marae Arai-Te-Tonga **2**
Parliament **20**
Rarotonga Sailing Club **4**
Takitumu Conservation
  Area **11**
Tereora College **21**

317

Tips How to Save If You're Going to Aitutaki

Air Rarotonga and local travel agencies such as **Island Hopper Vacations** (✆ 22-026; www.islandhoppervacations.com) will book hotels and most activities on the other islands free of charge. If you are going to Aitutaki, for example, you can save as much as NZ$100 (US$65) by buying a package that includes airfare and accommodations.

---

publications available from the Cook Islands Tourism Corporation have the schedules, or ask your hotel receptionist when a bus will pass. Regardless of the length of the ride, daytime fares are NZ$3 (US$1.95) one-way, NZ$5 (US$3.25) round-trip. You can buy 1-day passes for NZ$10 (US$6.50) or a 10-ride book of tickets for NZ$20 (US$13). The buses cost NZ$5 (US$3.25) at night.

BY RENTAL CAR & SCOOTER   I usually rent a vehicle from Arthur Pickering and his friendly crew at **Budget Rent-A-Car** (✆ 800/527-0700 or 20-895; www.budget.co.ck), the largest company here. The main Budget office is in Avarua, a block off the main road, or you can rent at a booth next to the police station in Avarua and at desks at the Edgewater Resort Hotel, the Rarotongan Resort Hotel & Spa, and at Muri Beach. Cars start at NZ$60 (US$39) per day with unlimited kilometers. Budget delivers and drops off at the hotels or airport.

The Pickering family also owns the local **Avis** franchise (✆ 800/331-1212 or 21-901; www.avis.co.ck), which also is good.

Other local rental companies include **Rarotonga Rentals** (✆ 22-326; www.rarotongarentals.co.ck), **Island Car & Bike Hire** (✆ 27-632 or 55-278; www.islandcarhire.co.ck), **BT Rentals** (✆ 23-586), and **Fun Rentals** (✆ 22-426; www.funrentals.co.ck). The latter rents open-air, tricycle-like Fun Cars.

Cook Islanders are as likely to travel by motorbike or scooter as they are by automobile. **Polynesian Bike Hire Ltd.** (✆ 20-895) and the companies mentioned above all rent motorbikes and scooters on a daily or weekly basis. Rates start at about NZ$25 (US$16) per day. Polynesian Bike Hire Ltd. and Budget Rent-A-Car share offices (see above).

Driver's Licenses   You must have a valid **Cook Islands driver's license** before operating any motorized vehicle. To get one, go to Police Headquarters (on the main road just west of the Avarua traffic circle), present your valid overseas license, and pay NZ$10 (US$6.50). If you want to rent a motorbike or scooter, and you aren't licensed to drive them at home, you have to take a driving test and pay an additional NZ$5 (US$3.25). All drivers must be at least 21 years old. The license desk is open Monday to Friday 8am to 3pm, Saturday and Sunday 8am to noon. (The laminated license with your photo makes a nice souvenir.)

Driving Regulations   Driving is on the **left side** of the road, as in the United Kingdom, Australia, and New Zealand. The speed limit is 40kmph (24 mph) in the countryside and 20kmph (12 mph) in Avarua and the villages. Gasoline (petrol) is available from service stations in Avarua, at the 24-hour Oasis Energy service station west of the airport terminal, and at some village shops. The road around the island is paved but somewhat rough; always be on the alert for dogs, chickens, potholes, pigs, and tourists on motor scooters.

BY BICYCLE   There are no hills on the round-island road, so touring by bicycle (or *push bikes,* as they're called here) is a pleasure. Several hotels have bicycles available for their guests to use. **Polynesian Bike Hire Ltd.** (*C* **20-895**), **Tipani Rentals** (*C* **22-327**), and **BT Rentals** (*C* **20-331**) rent them for NZ$8 (US$5) per day. The latter is at Muri Beach.

BY TAXI   A number of cars and minibuses scurry around Rarotonga with TAXI signs on top. Service is available daily from 7am to midnight and whenever international flights arrive. As a rule of thumb, taxi fares should be about NZ$2 (US$1.30) per kilometer, but the drivers are free to set their rates at will. Negotiate a fare before you get in. To call a taxi, phone **A's Taxi** (*C* **27-021**), **Ngatangiia Taxi** (*C* **22-238**), **BK Taxi** (*C* **20-019**), or **Muri Beach Taxi** (*C* **21-625**).

BY SHIP   *Adventures in Paradise,* the 1950s television series, may have glorified the South Pacific copra schooners that plied the South Seas, trading corned beef and printed cotton for copra, but to put it bluntly, you can't count on getting anywhere in the Cook Islands by ship these days.

FAST FACTS: Rarotonga

American Express There is no American Express representative in the Cook Islands.

Babysitters Contact your hotel reception desk.

Baggage Storage Most hotels and motels will keep your bags for free.

Bookstores **Bounty Bookshop** (*C* **26-660**), next to the main post office in Avarua, and the **Cook Islands Trading Corporation (C.I.T.C.)** (*C* **22-000**), on the waterfront, both sell paperback novels, maps of Rarotonga and Aitutaki, and books about the Cook Islands and the South Pacific in general.

Business Hours Most shops on Rarotonga are open Monday to Friday from 8am to 4pm and Saturday from 8am to noon. Some small grocery stores in the villages are open in the evenings and for limited hours on Sunday. Most government offices are open Monday to Friday from 8am to 4pm.

Camera/Film A reasonable selection of color-print film is available at many shops in Avarua. One-hour processing of color-print film is available at **Cook Islands Trading Corporation (C.I.T.C.)** (*C* **22-000**), on the waterfront. Color slides are sent to New Zealand for processing.

Clothing Dress in the Cook Islands is informal. Shorts of respectable length (that is, not of the short-short variety) can be worn during the day by both men and women, but beach attire should stay at the beach. Nudity is illegal, as is topless sunbathing, though some European women do it anyway. The colorful wraparound *pareu* is popular with local women. Evenings from May to September can be cool, so trousers, skirts, light jackets, sweaters, or wraps are in order after dark. The only neckties to be seen are at church on Sunday.

Currency Exchange See "Visitor Information & Entry Requirements" and "Money," earlier in this chapter.

Drug Laws Dangerous drugs and narcotics are illegal; possession can land you in a very unpleasant jail for a very long time.

Drugstores **C.I.T.C. Pharmacy** (© 29-292), in the C.I.T.C. shopping center west of the traffic circle, and **Cook Islands Pharmacy** (© 27-577), east of the traffic circle, dispense prescription medications and carry toiletries. Cook Islands Pharmacy has a small outlet at Muri Beach (© 27-587), which will send your prescription into town. The clinics on the outer islands have a limited supply of prescription medications.

Electricity Electricity is 230 volts, 50 cycles, so converters are necessary in order to operate U.S. appliances. The plugs, like those of New Zealand and Australia, have two angled prongs, so an adapter will also be needed. If your appliances or the table lamps in your room don't work, check to see whether the switch on the wall outlet is turned on.

E-mail Most accommodations have Internet access for their guests. In Avarua, **Telecom Cook Islands** (© 29-680; www.telecom.co.ck) has access in its main office (see "Telephone & Fax," below) and in its **TelePost** outlet in the C.I.T.C. shopping center (© 29-940). The main office is open 24 hours a day. TelePost is open Monday to Friday 8am to 4:30pm, Saturday 8:30am to noon. Access at both costs NZ$6 (US$4) for 30 minutes. At Muri Beach, **Dougie's Internet Cafe** (© 27-242) charges NZ$10 (US$6.50) per hour. It's open daily from 9am to 8pm, Sunday from noon to 6pm.

If you brought your Wi-Fi–capable laptop, you can get online at **hot spots** in Telekom's two offices (see above) and at Avatiu Harbour, the airport, The Rarotongan Beach Resort & Spa, the Edgewater Resort, and the Pacific Resort. More hot spots are being added all the time; look for the black-and-white bull's-eye signs. You must buy a prepaid wireless access card, available from Telekom and many shops. The cards start at NZ$15 (US$10) for 100 megabytes of downloaded data (they're priced by the amount of data moved, not access time), which I found more than sufficient to check my e-mail and do my Internet banking over 10 days.

Or you can sign up for a snail's pace "Temporary Oyster" dial-up account at Telecom's main office. There's a one-time NZ$25 (US$16) connection fee, plus NZ$7 (US$4.50) per hour spent online, which can be billed to your major credit card. You also must post a NZ$500 (US$325) bond against a credit card. In addition, your hotel will tack on the cost of the local phone calls and, quite likely, a surcharge. Sign up in the customer service office, which is open Monday to Friday 8am to 4pm.

Embassies/Consulates The New Zealand government has a representative, whose office is at the traffic circle in Avarua, but no other foreign government maintains an embassy or consulate here. In case of a problem, seek advice from the travel facilitation and consular officer in the **Ministry of Foreign Affairs** (© 20-507). The U.S. embassy in Wellington, New Zealand, has jurisdiction.

Emergencies/Police The emergency number for the **police** is © 999; for an **ambulance** or the **hospital,** © 998; for **fire,** © 996. The nonemergency **police** number is © 22-499.

Eyeglasses **Cook Islands Optics** (© 26-605), in the Mana Court shopping center, west of the traffic circle.

Firearms Don't even think about it—they're illegal.

Gambling There are no gambling casinos in the Cook Islands, but you can bet on the Australian and New Zealand lotteries at the C.I.T.C. shopping center.

Hairdressers/Barbers **BELT Hair Beauty Nails,** opposite the airport terminal (© **24-122**).

Healthcare The **hospital,** behind the golf course (© **22-664,** or 998 in case of emergency), has a 24-hour emergency room. Ask your hotel to recommend a doctor in private practice.

Hitchhiking It's not illegal, but hitchhiking is frowned upon by the government.

Insects There are no poisonous insects in the Cook Islands. Mosquitoes are plentiful, especially during the summer months and in the inland areas. Insect repellent and mosquito coils can be bought at the pharmacies and most village shops.

Laundry/Dry Cleaning **Snowbird Laundry & Dry Cleaners** has 1-day laundry and dry cleaning service at its main plant in Arorangi (© **20-952**) and a small laundry opposite Avatiu Harbour (© **21-952**). It will pick up and deliver if you or your hotel staff call in advance.

Libraries The **Cook Islands Library and Museum,** in Avarua near the Cook Islands Christian Church (© **26-468**), is open Monday to Friday 9am to 1pm, Saturday 9:30am to 1pm, with additional hours on Tuesday from 4 to 8pm. The library has a fine collection of works on the South Pacific, including many hard-to-find books.

Liquor Laws The legal drinking age is 18. Bottled liquor, beer, and wine are available from several stores. Bars and nightclubs close promptly at midnight Saturday. Hotel bars can sell alcoholic beverages to their guests all day Sunday, and restaurants can resume service on Sunday at 6pm.

Maps The best readily available maps of the islands are in the tourist publications Jason's *What's On in the Cook Islands* and the *Cook Islands Sun.* Get copies at the Cook Islands Tourism Corporation office (see "Visitor Information," above) or at most hotels.

Newspapers/Magazines Two local newspapers, the **Cook Islands News** (www.cookislandsnews.com) and the **Cook Islands Herald** (www.ciherald.co.ck), contain local, regional, and world news; radio and TV schedules; shipping schedules; a weather map for the South Pacific; and notices of local events, including advertisements for "island nights" at the hotels. Copies are available at the Bounty Bookshop and the large C.I.T.C. shopping center in the center of Avarua.

Post Office **Cook Islands Post** is located at the traffic circle in Avarua. Hours are Monday to Friday 8am to 4pm, Saturday 8am to noon. There's a branch office opposite Titikaveka College on Rarotonga's south coast, which is open Monday to Friday 8am to noon and 1 to 3:30pm. Each of the other islands has a post office. There is no mail delivery, so every address includes a post office box.

Radio/TV Rarotonga has one AM radio station and one FM radio station. Programming is in both English and Maori. Two TV channels broadcast news, entertainment, and innumerable rugby games.

Safety The streets here are safe. Burglaries and other property thefts have increased in recent years, however, so don't leave valuables in your hotel room or your belongings untended elsewhere.

Taxes The government imposes a **value-added tax (VAT),** which is included in the price of most goods and services. You should ask if the VAT is included in the rates quoted by the hotels and hostels, or whether it will be added to your bill when you leave. Unlike in Europe, the VAT here is not refunded at the end of your visit. The **departure tax** on international flights is NZ$30 (US$20) for adults, NZ$15 (US$10) for children, which you can pay at the airport or in advance at Westpac Bank in Avarua.

Telephone/Fax Direct-dialed calls can be made into the Cook Islands from most parts of the world. The country code is **682.** There are no local area codes.

International telephone calls and fax messages can be made or sent from most hotels or from **Telecom Cook Islands,** on the street between the C.I.T.C. shopping center and the Cook's Corner shopping center in Avarua (© **29-680;** www.telecom.co.ck or www.yellowpages.co.ck for business phone numbers). The Telecom office is open 24 hours daily.

The least expensive way to make both local and international calls is from a pay phone using a Kia Orana **prepaid card.** Cards are sold in NZ$5, NZ$10, NZ$20, and NZ$50 denominations (the equivalent of US$3.25, US$6.50, US$13, and US$32.50) at Telecom post offices and many shops. For international calls, dial © **00** followed by the country code (which is **1** for the U.S. and Canada) and the number you're trying to reach. A digital readout tells you how much money you have left during the call and warns you when to put in a fresh card. International calls cost NZ$2.14 (US$1.40) per minute to North America, NZ$3.20 (US$2.10) to the United Kingdom and Europe. Rates to Australia and New Zealand are NZ$1.04 (US68¢) during the day, NZ79¢ (US51¢) at night.

Some long-distance carriers have access numbers their customers can dial from within the Cook Islands to have international calls billed to their credit or prepaid cards, including **AT&T** (© **09111**) and **MCI** (© **09121**). You'll pay the regular local call charges on top of the international rates if you dial them from your hotel room.

You do not need a card to dial © **010** for local **directory assistance,** © **015** for an **international operator,** © **017** for **international directory assistance,** or © **1-407-333** to make an **international collect call.**

See "Emergencies/Police," above, for **emergency numbers.**

Telecom Cook Islands sells pre-paid SIM cards for unlocked GSM **cellphones,** starting at NZ$20 (US$13). Incoming calls are free, but outgoing air time counts NZ$1.99 (US$1.30) a minute against the cost of the card. See "The 21st-Century Traveler" in chapter 2.

Time Local time is 10 hours behind Greenwich Mean Time. That's 2 hours behind California during standard time, 3 hours behind California during daylight saving time. The Cook Islands are on the east side of the international date line, which puts them in the same day as the United States and a day behind New Zealand and Australia.

Tipping Tipping is considered contrary to the Polynesian way of life and is frowned upon.

Water Generally, the water on Rarotonga is safe to drink from the tap. It is filtered but not treated and can become slightly muddy after periods of heavy rain. If in doubt, boil it in the electric "jug" in your hotel room. Many hotels have their own filtration systems, and you can buy bottled water at most grocery stores and village shops. The tap water on Aitutaki is not safe to drink.

Weights/Measures The Cook Islands use the metric system.

9 Exploring Rarotonga

The Cook Islands' capital can be seen on foot, since this picturesque little South Seas town winds for only a mile or so along the curving waterfront between Avarua and Avatiu, its two harbors. Virtually every sight and most of the shops sit along or just off the main around-the-island road, which for this mile passes through town as the divided Te Ara Maire Nui (Marine Drive).

A STROLL AROUND AVARUA

Let's start at the traffic circle in the heart of town at Avarua Harbour, which is both the beginning and end of the round-island road. The rusty carcass on the reef offshore belonged to the **SS *Maitai*,** a trading ship that went aground here in 1916. At the circle is the modern courthouse. To the west, the low-slung structure with a large veranda houses a restaurant, several shops, and **The Banana Court,** once one of the South Pacific's most infamous watering holes (see "Island Nights on Rarotonga" later in this chapter). The building actually began life as a hotel.

From the traffic circle, walk east to the modern **Beachcomber, Ltd.** *ＦＦ*. This pearl and handicraft shop occupies a coral-block building erected in 1843 as a school for missionary children. The local legislative council met here from 1888 to 1901, but by 1968 it was condemned as unsafe. It was restored to its present grandeur in 1992 (see "Shopping on Rarotonga," later).

In a shady parklike setting across the road stands **Taputapuatea *Marae*** and the restored palace of Queen Makea Takau Ariki. Don't enter the grounds without permission, for they are *tabu* to us commoners. The palace was reputedly a lively place when Queen Makea was around in the 19th century.

Facing the palace grounds across the road running inland is the **Cook Islands Christian Church** *ＦＦＦ*. This whitewashed coral block structure was constructed in 1855. Just to the left of the main entrance is the grave of Sir Albert Henry, the late prime minister. A bust of Sir Albert sits atop the grave, complete with shell lei and flower crown. Robert Dean Frisbie, an American-born writer and colorful South Seas character, is buried in the inland corner of the graveyard, next to the road. (See "Recommended Reading" in chapter 2.)

To the right, near the end of the road, is the **Cook Islands Library and Museum** *ＦＦ* (© 26-468). The museum is small but well worth a visit to see its excellent examples of Cook Islands handicrafts; a canoe from Pukapuka built in the

Impressions

I have hunted long for this sanctuary. Now that I have found it, I have no intention, and certainly no desire, ever to leave it again.
        —Robert Dean Frisbie, *The Book of Puka-Puka*, 1928

old style, with planks lashed together; the island's first printing press (brought to Raro-tonga by the London Missionary Society in the 1830s and used until the 1950s by the government printing office); and the bell and compass from the *Yankee,* a world-famous yacht that in 1964 wrecked on the reef behind the Beachcomber, where its for-lorn skeleton rusted away for 30 years. The library and museum are open Monday to Friday 9am to 1pm, Saturday 9:30am to 1pm, and on Tuesday also from 4 to 8pm. Admission is NZ$2 (US$1.30).

Farther up the inland road past the **Avarua School** stands **Takamoa Theological College,** opened in 1842 by the London Missionary Society. The original **Takamoa Mission House** still sits on the campus.

Walk a block east on Makea Tinerau Road in front of the library and museum to the **Sir Geoffrey Henry National Cultural Centre** (also known as *Te Puna Korero*), the country's showplace, built in time for the 1992 South Pacific Festival of the Arts. The large green building houses the Civic Auditorium, and the long yellow structures contain government offices as well as the **National Museum** and **National Library** (© **20-725**). Exhibits at the National Museum feature contemporary and replicated examples of ancient crafts. The museum is open Monday to Friday from 9am to 4pm. Admission is by donation. The library is open when school is in session, Monday and Wednesday noon to 8pm and Tuesday, Thursday, and Saturday 9am to 4pm.

Opposite the national museum is the **Tupapa Sports Ground.** Like other South Pacific islanders formerly under New Zealand or Australian rule, the Cook Islanders take their rugby seriously. Although much of the action has shifted to the stadium at Tereora College behind the airport, Tupapa may still see a brawl or two on Saturday afternoons.

Walk back to the main road, turn left, and head to downtown. You can take a break at one of the restaurants or snack bars along the way. From the traffic circle west is a lovely stroll, either by the storefronts or along the seafront promenade. At the west end of town, stroll through **Punanga Nui Market,** where vendors sell clothing and sou-venirs (see "Shopping on Rarotonga," later) and food stalls offer take-out food that you can munch at picnic tables under the shade of casuarinas whispering in the wind.

End your tour at **Avatiu Harbour,** which is Rarotonga's commercial port (the small anchorage at Avarua is strictly a small-boat refuge). **The CocoBar** (© **20-340**), under a large thatch cabana at the harbor, is the perfect place to recover with ice-cold refreshment.

THE CIRCLE ISLAND TOUR

Traveling completely around Rarotonga and seeing the sights should take about 4 hours, with the help of a motor; allow a full day if you go by bicycle. A better idea is to take the guided tour offered by the **Cook Islands Cultural Village** (see "Cultural Experiences," below). Book at any hotel activities desk. You can do the circle island tour independently by car or motorbike, but you'll miss the informative commentary. Here's what you'll see, traveling clockwise from Avarua.

THE NORTH COAST

About 1km (½ mile) past the Kii Kii Motel, signs mark a small dirt road to the right. It leads to the *Marae* **Arai-Te-Tonga,** one of the most sacred spots on the island. Before the coming of Europeans, these stone structures formed a *koutu,* or royal court. The investiture of high chiefs took place here amid much pomp and circumstance. Offerings to the gods and the "first fruits" of each season were also brought here and presented to the local ariki, or chief. The basalt investiture pillar, the major remaining structure, stands slightly offset from a rectangular platform about 3.5m (12 ft.) long, 2m (7 ft.) wide, and 20cm (8 in.) high. Such temples, or maraes, are still considered sacred by some Cook Islanders, so don't walk on them.

The ancient Ara Metua road crosses by Arai-Te-Tonga and leads south a few yards to a small marae on the banks of **Tupapa Stream.** A trail follows the stream up to the peaks of Mounts Te Ikurangi, Te Manga, and Te Atukura, but these are difficult climbs; it's advisable to make them only with a local guide.

THE EAST COAST

Back on the main road, **Matavera** village begins about 2km (1¼ miles) beyond Tupapa Stream. Notable for the picturesque Cook Islands Christian Church and graveyard on the mountain side of the road, it's worth a stop for a photograph before continuing on to historic **Ngatangiia** village. Legend has it that a fleet of canoes left Ngatangiia sometime around A.D. 1350 and sailed off to colonize New Zealand, departing from a point across the road from where the Cook Islands Christian Church now stands in the center of the village. The canoes left on their voyage through **Ngatangiia Passage,** which lies between the mainland and **Motu Tapu,** a low island.

Ngatangiia also had its day in the sun in the early 1800s, when it was the headquarters of Charles Pitman, a missionary who came with the Rev. John Williams and later translated *The Pilgrim's Progress* into Cook Islands Maori. Unlike many of his fellow missionaries, Pitman carefully avoided becoming involved in local politics or business, and he objected strongly when Williams forced the Cook Islanders to build *The Messenger of Peace.* The **courthouse** across from the church was the first one built in the Cook Islands.

The shore at Ngatangiia, with three small islands sitting on the reef beyond the lagoon, is one of the most beautiful parts of Rarotonga. An old **stone fish trap** is visible underwater between the beach and the islands. Such traps were quite common throughout eastern Polynesia: Fish were caught inside as the tide ebbed and flowed through Ngatangiia Passage.

South of Ngatangiia begins magnificent **Muri Beach** 𝕮𝕮𝕮. Sailboats glide across the crystal-clear lagoon, the island's best for boating.

THE SOUTH COAST

The Cook Islands Christian Church in the village of **Titikaveka** was built in 1841 of coral blocks hand-cut from the reef (almost a mile away) and carried to the building site. Offshore, the **Titikaveka Lagoon** 𝕮𝕮𝕮 is the deepest on the island and has the best snorkeling. There are several public parks along the beach; the one opposite the Seventh-day Adventist church has restrooms.

⌐*Tips* Take a Fruit Break

You can pull off the road, take a dip, and grab a fresh fruit juice or a smoothie at **Fruits of Rarotonga,** near The Little Polynesian (✆ **21-509**). This country store also sells jams, chutneys, relishes, and other fruit products, and it'll keep your bag while you're in the water. Open Monday to Friday 7:30am to 5pm, Saturday 9am to 5pm.

Finds **Take a Shrimp Break**

Another good place to stop is the **Saltwater Cafe** (℃ 20-020), on the south coast exactly halfway around the island from Avarua. Carey and Ake Hosea Winterford have created a coffeehouse atmosphere here, and they indeed serve excellent coffee. They offer breakfast all day plus lunchtime burgers, fish and chips, and outstanding local freshwater shrimp in a curry sauce. The beach is across the road. Open Monday to Friday 8am to 3:30pm, Sunday 10am to 3:30pm.

Above the village, a part of the mountain is preserved in its natural state by the **Takitumu Conservation Area** (℃ 29-906; kakerori@tca.co.ck). The area is the only home of the unique and endangered kakerori (*Pomarea dimidiata*), a sparrow-size yellowish bird that is native to Rarotonga. The conservation program has raised the kakerori population from 29 in 1989 to more than 130 today. Rangers lead nature walks in the forest. Call for times, prices, and reservations.

From Takitumu, the road runs along the south coast and passes the late Albert Henry's white beachside home, now home to the Queen's representative. **Mount Te Rua Manga,** the rock spire also known as "The Needle," can be seen through the palms from the main road between Liana's Restaurant and The Rarotongan Beach Resort & Spa. Assuming that construction hasn't resumed, you also will pass what looks like a modern ruin; it's the site of the highly controversial Sheraton Hotel project.

THE WEST COAST

The road turns the island's southwestern corner at Aroa, home of The Rarotongan Beach Resort & Spa, and heads along the west coast to the low white walls of **Arorangi,** the coastal community founded by the missionary Aaron Buzacott in 1828. Arorangi replaced the old inland village, Puaikura, where the Tahitian missionary Papeiha went to teach Christianity after he had converted all of Aitutaki. Papeiha is buried in the yard of Arorangi's Cook Islands Christian Church, built in 1849. According to Polynesian legend, the canoes that left Ngatangiia in the 1300s stopped in Arorangi before heading off west to New Zealand. There is no reef passage near Arorangi, but the story enables the people on both sides of Rarotonga to claim credit for colonizing New Zealand.

The flat-topped mountain behind Arorangi is **Mount Raemaru.** Another legend says that mighty warriors from Aitutaki, which had no mountain, stole the top of Raemaru and took it home with them. There is a steep and somewhat dangerous trail to the top of Mount Raemaru.

The area north of Arorangi is well developed with hotels, restaurants, and shops. The shore just before the golf course is known as **Black Rock** because of the volcanic outcrop standing sentinel in the lagoon offshore. According to ancient Maori belief, the souls of the dead bid farewell to Rarotonga from this point before journeying to the fatherland, which the Cook Islanders called Avaiki.

There are two ways to proceed after passing the golf course. The main road continues around the west end of the **airport** runway (be careful; there are more road accidents on this sharp curve than anywhere else on Rarotonga). The New Zealand government built the original airstrip during World War II. It was enlarged to handle jumbo jets, and Queen Elizabeth II officially opened the new strip in 1974. The **Parliament** building is located on the shore about halfway along the length of the runway.

Parliament meets from February to March and from July to September. Visitors can observe the proceedings from the gallery.

The other way to return to Avarua from Black Rock is to turn right on the first paved road past the golf course and then left at the dead-end intersection onto the Ara Metua, or "back road." Located about halfway to town, **Tereora College** was established as a mission school in 1865. An international stadium was built on the college campus for the 1985 South Pacific Mini Games held on Rarotonga and is now the site of rock 'em, sock 'em rugby games on Saturday afternoons from June through August.

SAFARI EXPEDITIONS

Hooking up with **Raro Safari Tours** ⭐⭐ (© **23-629** or 61-139) is the best way to see the island's mountainous interior without hiking. In fact, you'll get better views down over the reef and the sea from these four-wheel-drive vehicles than you will on foot. The open-air trucks go up the Avatiu Valley on some unbelievably narrow tracks. Guides give often humorous commentary about the native flora and its uses, about ancient legends, and about what life was like in the old days when Rarotongans lived up in the valleys instead of along the coast. The 3½-hour tours depart Monday to Friday at 9am and 1:30pm, Sunday at noon. They cost NZ$60 (US$39) per adult, half for kids 6 to 12.

CULTURAL EXPERIENCES ⭐⭐⭐

Given their use of English and their pride in their culture, the Cook Islanders themselves offer a magnificent glimpse into the lifestyle of eastern Polynesia. They are more than happy to answer questions put to them sincerely by inquisitive visitors. Some of them also do it for money, albeit in a low-key fashion, by offering some of the finest learning experiences in the South Pacific. Unless you sit on the beach and do nothing, you won't go home from the Cook Islands without knowing something about Polynesian culture, both of yesteryear and the present.

COOK ISLANDS CULTURAL VILLAGE ⭐⭐⭐

Plan an early visit to the **Cook Islands Cultural Village** (© **21-314**), on the back road in Arorangi, for it will enable you to understand what you will see during the rest of your stay here. The village consists of thatch huts featuring different aspects of life, such as the making of crafts, cooking, and even dancing. Guests are guided through the huts and then enjoy a lunch of island-style foods, music, and dancing. The tour begins Monday to Friday at 10am. Cost for the entire morning and lunch is NZ$64 (US$42), including transportation to and from the village. The Cultural Village also does its own half-day circle island historical tour; it costs NZ$60 (US$39) and includes transfers and lunch. A full day combining the village tour, lunch, and a trip around the island costs NZ$90 (US$59) including transfers.

⌒Moments Learning a Little Culture

One of my fondest South Pacific memories was exploring Rarotonga with the entertaining and highly informative Exham Wichman, who once led the best round-island tours. He told me much of what this chapter has to say about the Cook Islanders' lifestyle. Today you can learn about local culture with the terrific Cook Islands Cultural Village's tour.

(Moments **Magnificent Harmony**

Nearly everyone in the Cook Islands puts on his or her finest white straw hat and goes to church on Sunday morning. Many visitors join them, for even though most sermons are in Maori, the magnificent harmony of Polynesian voices in full song will not soon be forgotten. Families have been worshipping together in the same pews for generations, but the ushers are accustomed to finding seats for tourists. Cook Islanders wear their finest to church, including neckties, but visitors can wear smart casual attire.

Sunday morning services at Rarotongan village churches usually begin at 10am; buses leave the hotels at 9:30am. Reserve at the activities desk, or just show up at any church on the island.

PA'S NATURE WALKS 🌺🌺🌺

The best way to explore Rarotonga's mountainous interior on foot is in the company of a blond, dreadlocked Cook Islander named **Pa** (© 21-079), who leads mountain and nature walks. Along the way he points out various wild plants, such as vanilla, candle nuts, mountain orchids, and the shampoo plant, and explains their everyday and medicinal uses in the days before corned beef and pharmacies. Pa's Cross-Island Mountain Walk costs NZ$55 (US$36) for adults, NZ$30 (US$20) for children under 12, while Pa's Nature Walk goes for NZ$55 (US$36) for adults, NZ$25 (US$16) for children under 12. Wear good walking or running shoes and bring a bathing suit (for a dip in an ancient pool once used by warriors). The nature walk takes 3½ hours. See "Fishing, Hiking, Diving & Other Outdoor Activities," below, for information about the cross-island hike. Reserve at any hotel activities desk, or call the phone number above.

10 Fishing, Hiking, Diving & Other Outdoor Activities

With tourism as its main business, Rarotonga has enough sporting and other outdoor activities to occupy the time of anyone who decides to crawl out of a beach chair and move the muscles. A couple of activities, such as Pa's Mountain Trek, are mentioned above, in "Cultural Experiences."

BOATING & SAILING   **Captain Tama's AquaSports** (© 27-350) is located at the Rarotonga Sailing Club on Muri Beach, where the lagoon is the island's best spot for swimming, snorkeling, and boating. The outfit rents a variety of watersports equipment, including beach kayaks, sailboats, Windsurfers, canoes, and snorkeling gear. Rental rates range from NZ$5 (US$3.25) for an hour's use of a one-person kayak to NZ$25 (US$16) to rent a Windsurfer for 1½ hours. You get a free beginner's Windsurfer lesson (on a simulator) with a rental or pay NZ$35 (US$23) for a full course. Captain Tama's is open daily from 8am to 5pm.

FISHING   There have been some world-class catches of skipjack tuna (bonito), mahimahi, blue marlin, wahoo, and barracuda in Cook Islands waters. If the sea is calm enough for them to leave Rarotonga's relatively unprotected harbors, charter boats start deep-sea fishing as soon as they clear the reef. Several boat owners will take you out, but I recommend Elgin and Sharon Tetachuk's **Seafari Charters** (© 20-328) and Wayne Barclay and Jenny Sorensen's **Pacific Marine Charters** (© 21-237), which have ship-to-shore radios and safety equipment. They charge about NZ$135

(US$88) per person for half a day's fishing, one of the lowest rates in the South Pacific. They like to have a day's notice, which you can probably give in person at the **Cook Islands Game Fishing Club** (© 21-419), whose clubhouse is beside the lagoon 1km (½ mile) east of the traffic circle. Whether you fish or not, you'll be welcome to have snacks and drinks at the club while taking in the view and swapping tall tales.

Don't expect to keep your catch; fresh fish are expensive here and will be sold by the boat operator. Bring your camera or camcorder.

GOLF   Visitors can take their shots at the radio towers and guy wires that create unusual obstacles on the 9 holes of **Rarotonga Golf Club** (© 22-062). The course was once located on what is now the Rarotonga International Airport, but had to move when the runway was expanded. It now lies under Rarotonga's radio station antennae (balls that hit a tower or wire can be replayed). Greens fees are NZ$15 (US$10). Rental equipment and drinks are available in the clubhouse, where "a reasonable standard of dress" is required. The club is open Monday through Saturday 8am until dark.

HIKING   There are a number of hiking trails on Rarotonga, but the most popular by far is the **Cross-Island Track** ✿✿✿ from Avarua to the south coast. A landslide had closed the track during my recent visit, but if it has reopened (check with the Cook Islands Tourism Corporation), it's the best hike in the South Pacific. The trail begins in the Avatiu valley and follows the stream high up to the base of Mount Te Rua Manga (*The Needle*). It's a very steep and often slippery climb, but the trail is well marked. The best way to do it is with **Pa's Cross-Island Mountain Walk** (see "Cultural Experiences," above).

HORSEBACK RIDING   Both adults and children will enjoy gentle rides along the beach and up to Wigmore's Waterfall with **Aroa Pony Trek** (© 25-415). The 2½-hour rides cost NZ$50 (US$33) for grownups, NZ$30 (US$20) for kids. Age and weight restrictions apply.

LAGOON EXCURSIONS   **Captain Tama's Aquasports** (© 27-350), at the Rarotonga Sailing Club on Muri Beach, has glass-bottom boat excursions on Muri Lagoon which include fish-feeding, snorkeling, and a barbecue lunch on one of the small offshore islands. Captain Tama charges NZ$60 (US$39).

RUNNING & JOGGING   The Hash House Harriers organization meets once a week for a fun run and sponsors an annual Round Rarotonga Road Run in October. Really, all one has to do for a jog on Rarotonga is to run down the road or beach.

SCUBA DIVING   Rarotonga's lagoon is only 1m to 3m (4 ft.–10 ft.) deep, but a shelf extends about 200m (650 ft.) beyond the fringing reef until it precipitously drops to more than 3,600m (12,000 ft.). Depths along the shelf range from 10m to 70m (30 ft.–200 ft.). There are canyons, caves, tunnels, and many varieties of coral. Visibility usually is in the 30m to 60m (100 ft.–200 ft.) range. Two wrecks—a 30m (100 ft.) fishing boat and a 45m (150 ft.) cargo ship—sit in depths of 24m (80 ft.) and 18m (60 ft.), respectively. Best of all for money-conscious travelers, the diving fees here are the lowest in the South Pacific.

Dive Rarotonga (© 21-873; fax 21-837; www.diverarotonga.com), **Cook Island Divers** (© 22-483; fax 22-484; www.cookislandsdivers.com), **The Rarotongan Dive Centre** (© 20-238; www.rarotongandivecentre.co.ck) on the west coast, and **Pacific Divers** (©/fax 22-450; www.pacificdivers.co.ck) on Muri Beach charge about NZ$60

⌒Tips The Best Swimming & Snorkeling

Getting into the water has to have high priority during a visit to Rarotonga. The lagoon is deep enough for snorkeling off most hotels at high tide, but you'll do better walking on the west coast reef when the tide's out. The best spot for snorkeling (and the only one at low tide) is the Titikaveka lagoon on the southeast coast. If you're not staying at Rarotonga Beach Bungalows or the Moana Sands Beachfront Hotel (see "Where to Stay on Rarotonga," below), you can snorkel off the nearby Fruits of Rarotonga shop (see the box "Take a Fruit Break," earlier). Muri Lagoon off Rarotonga Sailing Club is the best spot for boating.

Most hotels have snorkels, fins, and masks for their guests to use for free. You can rent them from the **Edgewater Resort** (℃ 25-435) or from **Dive Rarotonga** (℃ 21-873) on the west coast, or from **Captain Tama's AquaSports** (℃ 27-350) at the Rarotonga Sailing Club on Muri Beach. Cost is NZ$10 (US$6.50) a day.

(US$39) per one-tank dive, including equipment. They also teach PADI certification courses.

TENNIS   The tennis center at the **Edgewater Resort** (℃ 22-034) has two lighted, beachside Astro Grass courts, where pro Malcolm Kajer gives private lessons for NZ$30 (US$20) per hour. You can rent court time here for NZ$15 (US$10) per hour (Edgewater guests can play for free). Racquet rentals and balls are available.

11 Shopping on Rarotonga

The country's number one export is **black pearls,** most of them produced at Manihiki and Penrhyn atolls in the Northern Group. You'll be offered pearls at small shops and even by street vendors, but stick to dealers who are members of the local Pearl Guild, including those I recommend below. By and large, you will pay less for loose and set black pearls here than in French Polynesia.

There is a fine assortment of **handicrafts** to choose from here. Particularly good if not inexpensive are the delicately woven *rito* (white straw hats), which the women wear to church on Sunday, and the fine Samoan-style straw mats from Pukapuka in the Northern Group. Carvings from wood are plentiful, as is jewelry made from shell, mother-of-pearl, and pink coral. The most popular woodcarvings are small totems that represent the exhibitionist Tangaroa; they might be more appropriate for the nightstand than the coffee table.

Rarotonga is one of the region's best places to shop for **tropical clothing,** especially colorful cotton pareus, shirts, blouses, and dresses. Some of the works are more artistically creative than those in French Polynesia, especially one-of-a-kind pareus and women's apparel.

For years the Cook Islands government has earned revenue from the sale of its **stamps** to collectors and dealers overseas. The **Philatelic Bureau,** next to Cook Islands Post, at the traffic circle in Avarua, issues between three and six new stamps each year. All are highly artistic and feature birds, shells, fish, flowers, and historical events and people, including the British royal family.

I recommend some of the best stores, but you'll find many more in Avarua.

Beachcomber, Ltd.   This upscale establishment is worth a stop just to see the beautiful renovation of its 1843-vintage coral-block school house (see "A Stroll Around Avarua," earlier in this chapter). Owned by Bergman & Sons (see below), it has an excellent selection of black pearls, either loose or in exquisite settings designed and produced in the atelier behind the store. You'll also find high-quality handicrafts here, including woodcarvings, marvelous *tivaevae* quilts, and exquisite rito hats. One section is devoted to paintings and other works by local artists. Avarua, east of traffic circle. © **21-939.** Mon–Fri 9:30am–4pm, Sat 9:30am–noon.

Bergman & Sons (The Pearl Shop) 🐟🐟   Mike and Marge Bergman and sons Trevor and Ben helped to pioneer the pearl industry in the Cook Islands, and their two shops (plus Beachcomber Ltd.) are the place to see Rarotonga's largest selection of natural and cultured pearls, whether loose or incorporated into jewelry. Avarua, in Cook's Corner, and next to Banana Court. © **21-902.** Mon–Fri 10am–4pm, Sat 9:30am–noon.

Island Crafts 🐟🐟🐟   This large store next to Westpac Bank has been Rarotonga's best place to shop for handicrafts since 1943. It has the island's largest selection— including pieces from other parts of the South Pacific—and a wide choice of carved wooden Tangaroa tikis in various sizes. You can even buy a 9-karat gold pendant of the well-endowed god. The shop carries some black pearls, some set as pendants and earrings. Avarua, in Centrepoint Building. © **20-919.** Mon–Fri 8am–5pm, Sat 8:30am–1pm.

Maui Pearls (Paka's Pearls) 🐟🐟 *Value*   Cook Islander Paka Worthington attended American University in Washington, D.C. He obviously stopped at the shops owned by his friends Ron Hall on Moorea and Steve Fearon on Bora Bora (see "Shopping" in chapters 9 and 10), for these two outlets bear a lot of similarities with those fine stores. Specialties here are tension-set designs (where tension instead of a hole secures the pearl in place) and enhancers, which let you clip the pearl and setting on any chain, or even a white pearl necklace. Avarua, at C.I.T.C. shopping center. © **26-064.** Mon–Fri 9am–5pm, Sat 9am–1pm.

Perfumes of Rarotonga   Although their plant is at Matavera on the east coast, this showroom in the Cook's Corner shops displays perfumes, soaps, body lotions, shampoos, and other aromatic products from frangipani, gardenia, coconut, and other tropical flowers and plants. Avarua, in Cook's Corner shops. © **24-238.** Mon–Fri 9am–5pm, Sat 9am–1pm.

Punanga Nui Market *Value*   The vendor stalls in this waterfront municipal market are the best places to look for tie-dyed bedspreads and tablecloths. You can also find good prices on T-shirts, although some may be Chinese-made cottons that will shrink (buy a size larger than you usually wear). Saturday morning is market day here—the best time to shop. Avatiu Harbour. No phone. Mon–Fri 8am–5pm, Sat 8am–1pm.

TAV Ltd. 🐟🐟   Check out Ellena Tavioni's workshop for one of the island's best selections of block-printed swimwear, sundresses, and other items for men, women, and children. Ellena pioneered block printing here, and she exports her clothing to the

---

Tips **Do Some Homework & Shop Around**

Anyone interested in buying black pearls should do some research beforehand, perhaps starting with excellent articles in the August 1985 and June 1997 issues of *National Geographic*. Also see "Buying Your Black Pearl" in chapter 8. And don't buy without shopping around to compare quality, settings, and prices.

United States, Europe, the United Kingdom, and the high-end boutiques in Fiji. Here she has Rarotonga's best selection in this lovely style. Her workshop can alter items for free or make them for you from scratch. Avarua, on 2nd road inland behind Lotus China Restaurant. ✆ 21-802. Mon–Fri 8am–4pm, Sat 8am–noon.

12 Where to Stay on Rarotonga

Rarotonga is blessed with too many accommodations for me to list them all here, I regret to say. Since most of us desire to stay on the beach during our vacations, I have primarily confined my recommendations to waterfront locations.

I have organized the accommodations in accordance with Rarotonga's three hotel districts: **Muri Beach,** on the southeast coast; **Titikaveka,** on the south coast; and the **west coast**. Marvelous Muri Beach and its shallow lagoon have more activities than the others. Titikaveka also has a great beach, and its lagoon is the deepest and best for snorkeling on Rarotonga. The prevailing southeast trade winds, however, can make both areas chilly during the austral winter months of June through August. By the same token, these same winds provide nature's air-conditioning during the warmer summer months. You get glorious sunsets on the west coast, which the mountains shield from the prevailing trade winds, thus making the west somewhat drier than Muri Beach. The lagoon off the west coast tends to be very shallow, especially at low tide.

ACCOMMODATIONS AT MURI BEACH
EXPENSIVE

The Pacific Resort Rarotonga ☛ Although it needs some improvements to its restaurant and funky beachside bar, this resort sitting in junglelike grounds alongside Muri Beach comes closest of any Rarotonga property to capturing the appearance and ambience of French Polynesia's small resorts. The luxurious "villas" have two bedrooms, private entertainment areas, full kitchens, laundry facilities, minibars, and TVs with DVD players. Most other units are in one- and two-story buildings on either side of a stream crossed by foot bridges. More bungalow-like, the beachside and beachfront suites give the impression of having your own cottage. Six beachfront units in a two-story building are the largest and most expensive of the hotel-style rooms; their patios and porches are the only ones here which directly face the lagoon. Sitting near the round-island road, the swimming pool is almost an afterthought here.

P.O. Box 790, Rarotonga. ✆ **20-427.** Fax 21-427. www.pacificresort.com. 56 units, 7 houses. NZ$500–NZ$850 (US$325–US$553) double; NZ$980–NZ$1,660 (US$637–US$1,079) villa. Rates include continental breakfast. AE, DC, MC, V. **Amenities:** Restaurant; bar; outdoor pool; watersports equipment rentals; bike rentals; activities desk; car-rental desk; limited room service; massage; babysitting; laundry service; coin-op washers and dryers. *In room:* A/C, TV/DVD (some units), kitchen (in villas), fridge, coffeemaker, hair dryer, iron, safe.

Reflections on Rarotonga ☛☛ Some of the island's swankiest digs are the two thatched-roof, luxuriously furnished beachfront units at this establishment, a sister of Rumours of Romance (see below). Built town house–style and mirror images of each other, the two beachfront units have small, private pools as well as both upstairs and downstairs decks with lagoon views. Downstairs features a comfortable living room, full kitchen, and bedroom with its own large bathroom complete with bidets and his-and-her fixtures. Upstairs is another spacious bedroom and private bath, making this an excellent share choice for two couples (forget families, since no children under 18 are accepted here). The "waterfall villa" is smaller but has the same amenities; it opens to a coconut grove next door. All units have complimentary kayaks and snorkeling gear. Being contiguous, the units here do not provide maximum privacy.

P.O. Box 592, Rarotonga. (✆ 23-703. Fax 23-702. www.reflections-rarotonga.com. 3 units. NZ$500–NZ$1,000 (US$325–US$650) double. AE, MC, V. Children under 18 not accepted. **Amenities:** Free use of kayaks and snorkeling gear; laundry service. *In room:* A/C, TV/DVD, dataport, kitchen, coffeemaker, hair dryer, iron, safe.

Rumours of Romance 🖈🖈 Built town house-style along the lines of Reflections on Rarotonga (see above), these five units, all with two bedrooms, are even more luxurious, especially the central honeymoon suite. It has a movie theater with wall-size projection system, and its bathroom comes with a unique, glass-paneled shower under skylights. The highlights here are each unit's private garden with Jacuzzi tub and pond-like swimming pool. All units also have beachside decks with barbecue grills. Each also has a full kitchen, since there is no restaurant here. The two units on each end of the complex are less expensive since they are not directly on the beach. Kayaks and snorkeling gear are free here. You will have maximum luxuries here, but like Reflections on Rarotonga, you do not get the charm or privacy of your own self-standing bungalow.

P.O. Box 308, Rarotonga. (✆ 22-551. Fax 29-740. www.rumours-rarotonga.com. 5 units. NZ$750–NZ$1,200 (US$488–US$780). AE, MC, V. Children under 18 not accepted. **Amenities:** Outdoor pools (in units); Jacuzzi (in units); free use of kayaks and snorkeling equipment; car rentals; coin-op washers and dryers. *In room:* A/C, TV, dataport, kitchen, coffeemaker, hairdryer, iron, safe.

MODERATE

Muri Beachcomber 🖈 *Value* *Kids* This friendly motel sits right on Muri Beach, a short walk from The Pacific Resort, Sails Restaurant & Bar, and The Flame Tree restaurant. Ten of the one-bedroom, full-kitchen units are in five duplex buildings built of brown timber, with yellow peaked roofs that evoke the tropics. They form two courtyards, each opening to the beach. These spacious units have French doors leading from both living rooms and bedrooms to covered verandas. Children under 12 are allowed only in the larger family units, which stand away from the beach but next to the pool, making it easy for parents to keep an eye on the kids from their shady verandas. The largest of these is a two-bedroom unit atop the motel's office. The deluxe Watergarden Villas have stucco exteriors and huge wraparound verandas that make them look like coral-block colonial houses. Although they are behind and across a lily pond from the beachside units, they are more private and have phones, TVs, and DVD players.

P.O. Box 379, Rarotonga. (✆ 21-022. Fax 21-323. www.beachcomber.co.ck. 18 units, 3 houses. NZ$255–NZ$290 (US$166–US$189) double; NZ$355 (US$231) house. AE, DC, MC, V. **Amenities:** Outdoor pool; bike rentals; babysitting; laundry service; coin-op washers and dryers. *In room:* A/C, TV/DVD (in villas), kitchen, coffeemaker, hair dryer, iron (in villas), safe, no phone (except in villas).

Shangri-La Beach Cottages These adults-only cottages at Muri Beach line up in an L-shape in a beachfront yard with outdoor pool. The sailing club, The Pacific Resort Rarotonga, and the Muri restaurants are short walks away. The tropically attired cottages, which are of modern construction, have both showers and two-person whirlpool tubs. Screened doors and windows let in lots of light and fresh air. A counter separates the kitchen from the sleeping area, which has a queen-size bed. Ask about discounts if you book more than 30 days in advance.

P.O. Box 146, Rarotonga. (✆ 22-779. Fax 24-683. www.shangri-la.co.ck. 12 units. NZ$165–NZ$300 (US$107–US$195) double. MC, V. 4-night minimum stay required. Children under 18 not accepted. **Amenities:** Outdoor pool; free use of kayaks and snorkeling equipment. *In room:* A/C, TV, kitchen, coffeemaker, hair dryer.

INEXPENSIVE

Aremango Guesthouse   This is a good choice for cost-conscious travelers who can't get into Vara's Beach House (see below). The Tairea family constructed this peaked-roof building specifically with backpackers in mind. A central hallway runs between the relatively spacious rooms, which have ceiling fans, screened windows, and two or three single beds that couples can push together. The communal kitchen is large enough so that everyone gets a cupboard, and the shared bathrooms have hot-water showers and are fully tiled (as are all the floors here). Muri Beach is a short walk away.

P.O. Box 714, Rarotonga. ℂ 24-362. Fax 24-363. aremango@oyster.net.ck. 10 units (none w/bathrooms). NZ$40 (US$26) double; NZ$18 (US$12) dorm bed. No credit cards. *In room:* No phone.

Vara's Beach House ⟨⟩   One of the most popular backpackers' hostels in the entire South Pacific, Vara's is usually packed with as many as 200 young travelers jammed into dorms, five rooms, four studio suites, and two small cabins right on Muri Beach, or in five houses up on the hill across the road. The studio suites have kitchens, private bathrooms, and balconies, which make them suitable for any budget traveler regardless of age. The original beach house, a lagoonside dorm, and the five houses all have communal kitchens, toilets, and showers.

P.O. Box 434, Rarotonga. ℂ 23-156. Fax 22-619. www.varas.co.ck. 29 units (15 w/bathroom), 2 cabins (both w/bathroom), 50 dorm beds (shared bathrooms). NZ$48 (US$31) double room; NZ$120 (US$78) apartment; NZ$20 (US$13) dorm bed. Higher rates for stays shorter than 4 nights. MC, V. **Amenities:** Snorkeling gear rentals; bicycle and scooter rentals; coin-op washing machines. *In room:* Kitchens (studio suites only), no phone.

ACCOMMODATIONS AT TITIKAVEKA

The Little Polynesian (ℂ 24-280; www.littlepolynesian.com) was undergoing a massive renovation during my recent visit. Check progress on the website, because the "Little Poly" sits in a coconut grove beside Rarotonga's most picturesque beach and next to the deepest waters of Titikaveka Lagoon.

EXPENSIVE

Rarotonga Beach Bungalows ⟨⟩⟨⟩ ⟨Value⟩   The five charming bungalows at this little complex next door to the Moana Sands Beachfront Hotel and the Paw Paw Patch Restaurant & Bar (see below) are the most Tahitian on Rarotonga, and with good reason. They were designed and built by Tom Fearon, whose family was involved with the Hotel Bora Bora in the 1970s; who lived most of his adult life in French Polynesia; whose brother, Steve Fearon, operates Matira Pearls on Bora Bora (see chapter 10); and whose Cook Islander wife, Tere, is on the staff of James Norman Hall's Home on Tahiti (see chapter 8). Tere's twin sister, Luckey, looks after the guests here, so this is very much a family affair. The spacious bungalows have thatch-covered roofs lined inside with colorful pareu cloth, ceiling fans, walls of woven split bamboo, living rooms with sitting areas and full kitchens, air-conditioned bedrooms with king-size beds and televisions, and 18-foot-wide front porches with teak furniture. Borrowing from the original Bali Hai hotels in French Polynesia, Tom installed bathrooms with outdoor showers almost surrounded by gardens. Each unit has complimentary snorkeling gear and two kayaks for use in Titikaveka Lagoon, Rarotonga's best. The choice beachfront bungalows sit high enough off the ground to give unimpeded lagoon views. Complimentary tropical breakfast is served in a comfortable, open-air lounge. Don't expect grass here; the grounds are all pure white sand—a la Bora Bora, of course. Children under 12 aren't allowed here.

> **Tips   Renting a Beach House**
>
> With so many residents deserting the Cook Islands for New Zealand in recent years, a multitude of houses are now for rent, ranging from simple bungalows to deluxe villas. Many of the hotels I recommend consist entirely of "self-contained" (that is, with kitchens) bungalows, or they have beach houses in their inventories. If you want a place all to yourself, contact **Ocean Side Villa** (©/fax **28-776**; hwong@oyster.net.ck) or **Rarotonga Realty** (© **26-664**; fax 26-665; www.rarorealty.co.ck).

P.O. Box 3045, Rarotonga. © **27-030.** Fax 27-031. www.rarotongabeachbungalows.com. 5 units. NZ$445–NZ$495 (US$289–US$322) double. Rates include tropical breakfast. DC, MC, V. Children under 12 not accepted. **Amenities:** Free kayaks and snorkeling gear; laundry service. *In room:* A/C (in bedroom), TV (in bedroom), kitchen, coffeemaker, hair dryer, safe.

Royale Takitumu Villas   Another establishment catering to couples, and especially to honeymooners, this very private property (you won't see a sign by the road) sits in a coconut grove with lily ponds beside a white-sand beach and Titikaveka Lagoon. With stucco walls and thatch-covered roofs, the villas are spacious and comfortable, although they lack the Tahitian charm of those at Rarotonga Beach Bungalows or the luxurious furnishings and private pools at Reflections on Rarotonga (see above). Their bathrooms come equipped with bidets and whirlpool tubs. The six units directly facing the beach are preferable to the lagoon-view models. The beachfront honeymoon units are the most private, since they sit at the ends of the complex. Their bedrooms as well as living rooms open to furnished porches, which face the beach but not their neighbors. There's no restaurant here, but chefs will prepare private meals in your bungalow. The staff hosts weekly get-to-know-you breakfasts and poolside cocktail parties.

P.O. Box 1031, Titikaveka. © **24-682.** Fax 24-683. www.royaletakitumu.com. 10 units. NZ$495–NZ$545 (US$322–US$354) double. AE, DC, MC, V. Children under 15 not accepted. **Amenities:** Outdoor pool; free use of kayaks and snorkeling equipment; limited room service; laundry service. *In room:* A/C, kitchen, coffeemaker, hair dryer, iron, safe.

MODERATE
Moana Sands Beachfront Hotel   Right on the beach at the deepest part of Titikaveka Lagoon, this three-story, motel-like structure has 12 rooms on its first two levels and five new suites on the top floor. Each has a balcony or patio facing the lagoon, a ceiling fan, a cane table and chairs, a tiled shower-only bathroom, bright flower-print drapes and spreads, and a kitchenette with a fridge and microwave oven. The more spacious top-floor suites add TVs, DVD players, and glass-enclosed showers. Some units have single beds in addition to queens; others have only a queen-size bed. The Paw Paw Patch Restaurant & Bar, one of Rarotonga's best, is here.

P.O. Box 1007, Rarotonga. © **26-189.** Fax 22-189. www.moanasands.co.ck. 17 units. NZ$235–NZ$280 (US$153–US$182) double. Rates include tropical breakfast. MV, V. **Amenities:** Restaurant; bar; free use of kayaks and snorkeling equipment; scooter rentals; limited room service; massage; babysitting; laundry service. *In room:* A/C, TV (suites only), coffeemaker, hair dryer, safe.

ACCOMMODATIONS ON THE WEST COAST
EXPENSIVE
Crown Beach Resort ★★   Three hurricanes which struck back-to-back early in 2005 caused many properties here to not just repair but to improve. None did more

upgrades than the Crown Beach, which emerged as Rarotonga's top small full-service hotel. You will be greeted over marble floors in a thatched-roof building holding reception, an air-conditioned exercise room, and a business center. From there pathways lead through a sandy coconut grove to a swimming pool—with rock waterfall—beside Oceans bar and restaurant, serving breakfast and lunch, and a full-service spa. The best of the bungalows, or "villas" as they are known here, are the beachfront units with hot tubs on their covered front porches. Others face the swimming pool, while the least expensive are garden units between reception and Oceans restaurant. All units have separate bedrooms. Honeymooners and romance-seeking couples make up the bulk of the guests, although you can bring children under 18 with advance permission. The fine Windjammer Restaurant resides by the road here (see "Where to Dine on Rarotonga," below).

P.O. Box 738, Rarotonga. ✆ **23-953**. Fax 23-951. www.crownbeach.com. 22 units. NZ$399–NZ$620 (US$259–US$403). Rates include tropical breakfast. AE, MC, V. Children under 18 accepted by request only. **Amenities:** 2 restaurants; 2 bars; outdoor pool; exercise room; spa; free use of kayaks, canoes, snorkel gear; business center; limited room service; massage; laundry service. *In room:* A/C, TV/DVD players, dataport, kitchen, coffeemaker, hairdryer, iron, safe.

Manuia Beach Boutique Hotel ✵

This intimate little establishment has 20 rooms in 10 duplex bungalows set rather close together on a narrow rectangle of beachfront land. Tropical foliage helps give the garden units some semblance of privacy, but the six beachfront units definitely are the choice here. They have king-size beds, as opposed to queens, and a view of the reef across an infinity-edge swimming pool. Sliding glass doors lead to semiprivate wooden verandas on all units. Angled shower stalls in one corner and lavatories in another maximize space in the rather small bathrooms. Each garden unit has both a queen and a single bed. None of the rooms have kitchens, but you can amble down to the Right on the Beach Restaurant (see "Where to Dine on Rarotonga," below) and dig holes in its white-sand floor while enjoying a meal or snack. The facilities here do not live up to the "boutique hotel" claim, but the staff will call you by your first name while providing excellent service.

P.O. Box 700, Rarotonga. ✆ **22-461**. Fax 22-464. www.manuia.co.ck. 20 units. NZ$370–NZ$540 (US$241–US$351). Rates include tropical breakfast, a bottle of champagne, and afternoon tea. AE, MC, V. Children under 12 not accepted. **Amenities:** Restaurant; bar; outdoor pool; bike rentals; limited room service; laundry service. *In room:* A/C, fridge, coffeemaker, hair dryer, safe.

The Rarotongan Beach Resort & Spa ✵✵ *(Kids)*

After years of neglect by the government, which built it in 1977 on the island's choice hotel site beside Aroa Beach, Rarotonga's flagship resort continues to undergo a remarkable transformation under its present owner, Tata Crocombe, a Cook Islander who graduated from Harvard Business School. Under his tutelage, it has gone from rundown to Rarotonga's best large resort. There's something for everyone here, including a full-service spa for grownups, a children's program to keep youngsters both entertained and informed, and a host of activities for all ages. A poolside stone patio and a large lagoonside deck sit beside the beach, while a swimming pool with a waterfall also draws daytime attention. The resort also has Rarotonga's widest range of accommodation, from regular hotel rooms to a romantic honeymoon bungalow with a huge outdoor bathroom (it's in the middle of the property, but a high fence provides privacy). If you're not honeymooning, the choice units are the "deluxe beachfront junior suites," which occupy one-story buildings staggered to make them seem like bungalows. Four of these have two bedrooms, a kitchen, and a private sundeck on their rooftops. Each has a bathroom with a whirlpool bathtub in addition to an outdoor shower, and their sliding front doors open to wooden decks facing the beach. Although they couldn't be enlarged, the existing hotel rooms—in two-story buildings—have been vastly improved over their original versions. This is especially true of the "beachfront junior suites," which have been draped with tropical woods and mat walls (they are reserved for adults except when antipodean families invade during busy school holiday periods). The other units here are regular hotel rooms, about two-thirds of them facing the beach. A few have been turned into two-bedroom garden suites with kitchens and whirlpool bathtubs. Every room in the resort has either a patio or a balcony.

P.O. Box 103, Rarotonga. ✆ 800/481-9026 or 25-800. Fax 25-799. www.rarotongan.co.ck. 156 units. NZ$380–NZ$520 (US$247–US$338) double; NZ$545–NZ$725 (US$354–US$471) suite. AE, DC, MC, V. **Amenities:** 3 restaurants; 2 bars; outdoor pool; 2 tennis courts; spa; watersports equipment rentals; bike rentals; children's programs; game room; activities desk; car-rental desk; business center; limited room service; babysitting; laundry service; coin-op washers and dryers. *In room:* A/C, TV/DVD, CD player, kitchen (in some suites), minibar, coffeemaker, hair dryer, iron, safe.

MODERATE

Aro'a Beachside Inn Jim Bruce gave up his travel tour business in Hawaii and in 2001 moved to Rarotonga, where he built this modest little resort. The best feature here is his Shipwreck Hut, a bar and outdoor lounge beside Aroa Beach, the same stretch of white sand wrapping around The Rarotongan Beach Resort & Spa to the south. The hut hosts barbecues and evening entertainment (reservations are required). The accommodations here are in modern one- and two-story buildings, with the best and more expensive units sitting by the beach. All are spacious and have kitchens.

P.O. Box 2160, Arorangi. ✆ 22-166. Fax 22-169. www.aroabeach.com. 11 units. NZ$220–NZ$350 (US$143–US$228). Minimum stay 4 nights. MC, V. Children under 12 not accepted. **Amenities:** Restaurant; bar; free use of bicycles, kayaks, snorkeling gear; laundry service. *In room:* TV, dataport, kitchen, coffeemaker, hairdryer.

Edgewater Resort The Edgewater has the most units of any resort on the island, and like The Rarotongan Beach Resort & Spa (see above), it draws many visitors on package tours. Although thick tropical foliage helps make the grounds—just 1.6 beachside hectares (4 acres)—seem less crowded, you won't have nearly as much room to roam here. Several concrete two- and three-story block structures hold most of the rooms. Each has a bougainvillea-draped patio or balcony. Rooms in the 400 and 500 blocks are closest to the beach and farthest from the restaurant, bar, and swimming pool, which can be crowded and noisy when the house is full. Farther removed and much better appointed are the more expensive beachfront suites. The majority of these have whirlpool tubs in their spacious bathrooms. Their balconies or patios open directly to the sandy beach, which the main part of the property doesn't enjoy, since rocks line most of the shore in front of the pool and expansive patio space for sunning and sitting.

P.O. Box 121, Rarotonga. ✆ 25-435. Fax 25-475. www.edgewater.co.ck. 250 units. NZ$205–NZ$450 (US$133–US$292) double. AE, MC, V. **Amenities:** 2 restaurants; 3 bars; outdoor pool; 2 tennis courts; spa; bike rentals; game room; activities desk; car-rental desk; limited room service; massage; babysitting; laundry service; coin-op washers and dryers. *In room:* A/C, TV, fridge, coffeemaker, hair dryer, iron (some units), safe (some units).

INEXPENSIVE

Are-Renga Motel This good budget choice is located in the village of Arorangi. The entire property enjoys a beautiful view of the mountains, and a path leads to the beach through a churchyard across the road. The Estall family runs this basic but clean establishment, and the spaciousness of their units makes up for a complete lack of frills. Nine units are in a motel-like block at the rear of the property. An older building beside an ancient breadfruit tree has six units in which the bedroom is separated from the living and cooking area by a curtain; the three upstairs apartments share a large veranda, and a patio does double duty for the three apartments downstairs. All units have cooking facilities.

P.O. Box 223, Rarotonga. © 20-050. Fax 29-223. arerenga@oyster.net.ck. 15 units. NZ$60 (US$39) double; NZ$20 (US$13) per person shared unit. No credit cards. *In room:* Kitchen, no phone.

13 Where to Dine on Rarotonga

Once a culinary wasteland, Rarotonga is now blessed with some good and interesting restaurants. Most make use of fresh fish caught offshore by the country's small longline fishing fleet. You'll see broadbill sailfish, swordfish, and other species offered alongside the usual tuna and mahimahi found everywhere in the South Pacific.

Like the hotels, above, I have arranged the restaurants by geographic location on Muri Beach, Titikaveka, and the west coast, plus in the town of Avarua, where you will do your shopping and bar-hopping.

WHERE TO DINE ON MURI BEACH

Cafe Oma SNACK BAR   This inexpensive cafe in a three-store shopping center in front of Vara's Beach House serves omelets, French toast, crepes, and fried eggs and bacon for breakfast, then opens at lunch for burgers, salads, and fish and chips. You can get decent coffee and a refreshing fruit smoothie here.

Muri Beach, front of Vara's Beach House. © 29-613. Most items NZ$3.50–NZ$11 (US$2.25–US$7). No credit cards. Daily 8–11am and noon–3pm.

The Flame Tree ⊛ INTERNATIONAL   Within walking distance of The Muri Beachcomber and The Pacific Resort Rarotonga, this is one of the island's more interesting restaurants. Although it has slipped somewhat since its days under founder Sue Carruthers (see Tamarind House Restaurant & Bar, below), it still calls on the cuisine

---

Cook Islands Chow

Like their counterparts throughout Polynesia, in pre-European days the Cook Islanders cooked all their food in an earth oven—known here as an *umu*—and they still do for special occasions. The food (*umukai*) is as finger-licking good today as it was hundreds of years ago, although it's now eaten with knives and forks rather than fingers during "Island Nights" at Rarotonga's hotels, which include Cook Island dance shows (see "Don't Miss an Island Night," below). The hotels provide a wide assortment of salads and cold cuts for those who are not particularly fond of taro, arrowroot, and *ika mata* (the local version of poisson cru—fish marinated in lime juice and mixed with coconut milk and raw vegetables).

Get a schedule of island nights from Cook Islands Tourism Corporation. Also check the daily *Cook Islands News* (especially the Thursday and Friday editions) or with the hotels to find out when the feasts are on. Most buffets cost about NZ$55 (US$36). Some of them may charge a small admission fee to see the dance show if you don't have dinner.

> **_Tips_ Make a Reservation**
>
> Most Rarotongan restaurants are small, so reservations are almost essential at all of them. Folk tend to dine early here, too, so don't show up after 8pm if you haven't booked a table.

of India and other Asian countries to offer a range of very tasty selections. The signature dish is fish, shrimp, and mussels in a mild coconut curry sauce. Smoking is allowed only outside, not inside the converted house.

Muri Beach, north of The Pacific Resort (11km/6½ miles from Avarua). © 25-123. Reservations recommended. Main courses NZ$19–NZ$38 (US$13–US$25). MC, V. Daily 6–9pm (bar to 11pm).

Sails Restaurant & Bar &&& INTERNATIONAL   Occupying the main floor of the Rarotonga Sailing Club, this airy, nautically decorated restaurant offers a variety of salads, sandwiches, and "island fries"—sweet potato, taro, and banana. At dinner the chef turns his attention to fresh fish and vegetables, plus mussels and steaks flown in from New Zealand. You might be offered tuna marinated in Cajun spices, a nicely seasoned version of Thai rare beef salad, or vegetarian lasagna. Weekend afternoons are especially lively here; club members gather to sail their radio-controlled miniature yachts out on the lagoon.

Muri Beach, in Rarotonga Sailing Club, between The Pacific Resort and Muri Beachcomber. © 27-349. Reservations strongly recommended for dinner. Lunch NZ$14–NZ$20 (US$9–US$13); main courses NZ$28–NZ$32 (US$18–US$21). AE, MC, V. Mon–Sat 11am–9pm; Sun 10:30am–9pm.

WHERE TO DINE IN TITIKAVEKA

Maire Nui Gardens & Cafe & _Value_ SALADS/SANDWICHES   You won't appreciate Hinano MacQuarie's sophisticated cafe from the road, but wait until you walk around the thatched-roof building to the big veranda and its terrific vista of the green mountains rising beyond the flowery botanical gardens. It's the perfect spot to break a round-island tour or stop in for breakfast, a light lunch, an afternoon snack, a fruit smoothie, or a cup of espresso, cappuccino, or fresh mint tea. Hinano's breakfast offerings include muffins, fresh fruit, and omelets. You'll have more choices from her lunch-and-afternoon blackboard menu. The pineapple-lemon meringue cheesecake is well worth the calories.

Titikaveka, opposite The Little Polynesian. © 22-796. Most items NZ$6.50–NZ$15 (US$4.25–US$10). No credit cards. Mon–Fri 9am–4pm.

Paw Paw Patch Restaurant & Bar & INTERNATIONAL   This sophisticated cafe with an open kitchen and both indoor and outdoor seating brings a glimpse into local cuisine. The "Paw Paw Catch" of fresh fish seared and served under Hollandaise sauce over a bed of onions, coconut milk, and _rukau_ (taro leaves) is a bit unusual to novice tongues, but it's a fine example of Cook Islander home cooking. Otherwise the menu tends to more familiar steaks, fish, pastas, and Thai-style chicken or vegetable curry. Be sure to check the daily specials board. The beachside Sunday night barbecue here is the best on the island (come early for happy hour from 6 to 7pm). Note that the Paw Paw is open for breakfast and dinner but not for lunch.

Titikaveka, in Moana Sands Beachfront Hotel. © 27-189. Reservations recommended for dinner. Breakfast NZ$7.50–NZ$14 (US$5–US$9); main courses NZ$23–NZ$28 (US$15–US$18). Sunday barbecue buffet NZ$30 (US$20). MC, V. Daily 8–10:30am and 6–9pm.

WHERE TO DINE ON THE WEST COAST

Right on the Beach Restaurant ★★★ INTERNATIONAL   Unless you are very short in stature, you will have to stoop to get under the thatch-covered roof over this charming, sand-floored beachside restaurant. The food is not the best on Rarotonga, but the South Seas ambience makes it worth an evening, especially on Wednesday and Saturday when it offers an island night buffet and Cook Islands dance show. The regular menu offers Fijian-style curries, seared rare tuna, braised lamb shanks, steaks, chops, and a catch of the day (pass on the parrotfish). This is one of my favorite places on Rarotonga for a cocktail.

Arorangi, in Manuia Beach Boutique Hotel. (*) **22-461**. Reservations recommended. Main courses NZ$19–NZ$36 (US$12–US$24). AE, MC, V. Daily 7:30am–9pm.

Vaima Restaurant & Bar INTERNATIONAL   Lots of islandy ambience prevails at this bamboo-clad beachside restaurant, one of the better choices here. It offers a wide range of tastes, including spicy vegetarian curry. Always check the daily blackboard specials, which will feature the freshest fish. There are a few tables on a veranda facing the beach plus picnic tables out by the sand.

Takitimu (1km/½ mile east of The Rarotongan Beach Resort). (*) **26-123**. Reservations recommended. Main courses NZ$23–NZ$31 (US$15–US$20). MC, V. Thurs–Tues 6:30–9pm.

Windjammer Restaurant ★★★ ECLECTIC   During my recent visit chef Daniel Forsyth and partner Maire Porter, both of Cook Island descent but trained in New Zealand, were making this air-conditioned roadside restaurant at the Crown Beach Resort one of the best in Rarotonga. The octagonal pine building may lack Polynesian charm, but the widely spaced tables provide the island's most elegant dining, and the wait staff renders excellent service. Marie's family owns the local meat importer, so you will be served only top-grade lamb and aged steaks, plus fresh local fish. I started with a delightful warm seafood salad with a lemon dressing, and loved the aged rib-eye filet with a pink peppercorn sauce. Vegetarians get at least two choices every night, perhaps a veggie risotto. There's a limited list of very good New Zealand and Australian wines. You won't go wrong here or at the Tamarind House (see below).

Arorangi, between Manuia Beach Boutique Hotel and Edgewater Resort. (*) **23-950**. Reservations recommended. Main courses NZ$25–NZ$31 (US$16–US$20). MC, V. Wed–Mon 5:30–9pm.

WHERE TO DINE IN AVARUA

The Bus Stop Shop, a 7-Eleven-style convenience store opposite the Cook's Corner bus stop ((*) **22-787**), carries very good pastries, meat pies, and packaged sandwiches, as well as groceries. Open Monday to Friday 7:30am to 6pm, Saturday 7:30am to 4pm. If you get the late-night munchies, **Oasis Energy,** on the main road west of the airport ((*) **22-145),** is open all the time for sandwiches, salads, meat pies, coffee, groceries, and gasoline.

Blue Note Café SNACK BAR/REGIONAL   A fine place to take a town break and watch the traffic along the waterfront, this open-air snack bar occupies one end of the veranda of the Banana Court building. Breakfast is served all day, as are espresso, ice cream, milkshakes, and exotic cocktails. Sandwiches and big burgers are made to order for lunch. You can also try chicken or lamb curry, fish and chips, smoked fish, or barbecue pork.

Avarua, at the traffic circle. (*) **23-236**. Breakfast NZ$8.50–NZ$17 (US$5.50–US$11); sandwiches, salads, and burgers NZ$10–NZ$18 (US$6.50–US$12); meals NZ$14–NZ$18 (US$9–US$12). MC, V. Mon–Tues and Sat 8am–6pm; Wed–Fri 8am–9pm; Sun 8am–4pm.

> **Tips Sunday Night Roasts & Barbecues**
>
> Sunday is traditional New Zealand roast night on Rarotonga, and it's also pop-
> ular for beach barbecues. Keep your eye out for money-saving roast and bar-
> becue specials offered by many restaurants.

The Cafe ☆☆ SALADS/SANDWICHES/SNACKS   Neil Dearlove's cafe/coffee
house, which would grace Auckland's trendy Parnell district, is my favorite place to
grab a papaya muffin and a latte (known as a "flat white" in this part of the world)
before striking out on my rounds of Avarua. And when I have finished my walk, I
often retire here and select from daily specials or a panini-style sandwich. Lots of natural wood and big canvas patio umbrellas hung from the ceiling create an outdoorsy
ambience. Neil roasts his own coffee.

Avarua, east of traffic circle. ℂ 21-283. Breakfast NZ$4.50—NZ$13 (US$3—US$8); sandwiches and salads
NZ$10—NZ$17 (US$6.50—US$11). AE, MC, V. Mon—Fri 8:30am—4pm, Sat 8:30am—12:30pm.

Cafe Salsa ☆ *Finds* SNACK BAR   This storefront cafe with sidewalk tables rivals
The Cafe as Avarua's trendiest place for breakfast and lunch. You might start your day
with smoked marlin hash topped by poached eggs—or if that's too exotic, regular eggs
Benedict. Lunch sees salads, individual-size pizzas, and sandwiches on warm-from-
the-oven foccacia. An iced coffee (iced by a scoop of vanilla ice cream) will cool you
down after shopping, and live music at midday Saturday is a good excuse to linger in
town before hitting the beach.

Avarua, in CITC Centre. ℂ 22-215. Most items NZ$8—NZ$18 (US$5—US$12). MC, V. Mon—Fri 8am—9:30pm, Sat
8am—2pm.

Tamarind House Restaurant & Bar ☆☆☆ *Finds* INTERNATIONAL   Sue Cur-
ruthers, who grew up in Kenya and founded The Flame Tree restaurant here (see
above), and partner Robert Brown renovated this 1920s seaside home and turned it
into Rarotonga's top place to dine. Not only will you enjoy the first-rate food, but you
will have an ocean view, since most tables are on the veranda or covered patio out front
(it's terrifically romantic at night). You can begin your day with a late breakfast featuring Sue's marvelous corn fritters with tomato, guacamole, and sour cream. She offers
the fritters at lunch along with a wide variety of salads, including Indonesian *gado
gado* with a spicy peanut sauce. She expands her globe-trotting menu at dinner, with
the likes of a south Indian curry, Balinese pork, and Burmese tamarind fish with lime
and chili. Less adventurous tongues can choose from steaks, seafood ragout, or fish
and chips. I never visit Rarotonga without dining here.

Avarua, 1.5km (1 mile) east of traffic circle. ℂ 26-487. Reservations recommended at dinner. Breakfast
NZ$4.50—NZ$18 (US$3—US$12); lunch NZ$12—NZ$24 (US$7.50—US$15); dinner main courses NZ$20—NZ$34
(US$13—US$22). AE, MC, V. Tues—Sat 10:30am—9pm (bar until 11pm), Sun 9am—3pm and 6—8pm.

Trader Jack's Bar & Grill ☆☆☆ SEAFOOD   You won't be on Rarotonga long
before you hear about New Zealander "Trader Jack" Cooper's harborside joint, one of
the South Pacific's best bars and one of Rarotonga's top places to dine. Floor-to-ceiling windows on three sides open to the water and give nearly everyone in the dining
area a view of the harbor, the reef, and the sea and sunsets beyond. Outside, a square
bar dispenses libation and snacks. A regular printed menu plays second fiddle to the
chalkboard specials, which feature the freshest fish served on the island (Jack owns

Rarotonga's fish processing plant, and thus gets the pick of the day's catch). His big seller is a seafood catch for two persons, including fish, shrimp, scallops, oysters, marinated mussels, and smoked marlin and salmon with dipping sauce.

Avarua, waterfront at traffic circle. ☏ 26-464. Reservations recommended for dinner. Burgers and snacks NZ$9.50–NZ$14 (US$6–US$9); main courses NZ$19–NZ$25 (US$12–US$17). AE, MC, V. Mon–Sat noon–10pm. Bar Mon–Thurs and Sat 11am–midnight, Fri 11am–2am. Closed New Year's Eve.

Whatever! Bar *(Finds* This is not a restaurant so much as an upstairs deck where the staff barbecues burgers, steaks, chicken, and fish on a gas grill, which you eat at picnic tables with umbrellas. There's nothing fancy at all, except the view along the north coast of Rarotonga. Most people come up here to slake a thirst at the bar, especially on Friday and Saturday nights, when it's on the pub-crawling circuit (see "Island Nights on Rarotonga," below). To get here, follow the driveway from the bridge at the traffic circle.

Avarua, at the traffic circle. ☏ 22-299. Burgers NS$5 (US$3.25); main courses NZ$17-NZ$27 (US$11-US$17). MC, V. Tues-Thurs and Sat noon-midnight; Fri noon-2am.

14 Island Nights on Rarotonga

Cook Islanders are some of the most fun-loving folks you will meet in the South Pacific, and you can easily catch their spirit. Every evening except Sunday is a party night—especially Friday when the pubs stay open until 2am (they close promptly when the Sabbath strikes at Saturday midnight). As with their Tahitian cousins, the infectious sound of the traditional drums starts everyone dancing.

If Rarotongans aren't performing in a show (see the "Don't Miss an Island Night" box), they seem to be dancing with each other at some of the most colorful bars in the South Pacific. No one ever explained to me why they call their tour-de-bars a pub *crawl,* although I assume it's because crawling is the method of travel after too many locally brewed Cook's Lagers. However you get around, you can pub crawl yourself or take a Friday **nightlife bus tour,** which your hotel will book. The NZ$25 (US$16) fare is worth not having to drive home after 2am.

The Friday night crawl begins—and often ends—at **Trader Jack's Bar & Grill** *✸✸✸* (☏ 26-464) at Avarua's old harbor, one of the best bars in all of the South Pacific. The island's affluent movers and shakers start boozing here after work.

Heading east, you can grab an outdoor beer and an ocean view at **Whatever! Bar** (☏ 22-299). It's behind **TJ's** (☏ 24-722), a disco which draws a sometimes raucous young crowd. The Trader Jack's folk then wander into the **Stair Case Restaurant & Bar** (☏ 22-254), an upstairs restaurant that has rock-and-roll music for dancing after 10pm and an island night show once a week.

Backtracking to the traffic circle, you'll come to **The Banana Court** (☏ 23-397), which for several generations was *the* place to do your drinking, dancing, and fighting. It's now *the* big place to be on Wednesday night. Down the side street in Cook's Corner shops, the miniature **Hideaway Bar** (☏ 20-340) attracts a mature crowd of drinkers.

At Avatiu Harbour, **The CocoBar** (☏ 20-340) is the second best joint for grownups (after Trader Jack's). The bar is under a big thatch roof; the bands play in the backyard. From there you can head west to **The Nu Bar** (☏ 26-141) and the **RSA Club** (☏ 20-590), where the country's military veterans welcome everyone to drink and dance.

Don't Miss an Island Night ✮✮✮

A New Zealander once told me, only slightly tongue-in-cheek, that all Cook Islanders are deaf because they grow up 3 feet from drums you can hear from 3 miles away.

Danced to the heart-thumping beat of those deafening drums, their hip-pulsating *tamure* is very much like that in Tahiti, except it tends to be faster (which I found hard to believe until I saw it with my own eyes) and even more suggestive (which I had even more trouble believing). Indeed, dancing is high in the hearts of all Cook Islanders, and it shows every time the drums begin. Their costumes generally aren't as colorful as those in Tahiti but are as likely to be made of leaves and other natural materials as dyed synthetic fabrics.

Unadulterated Cook Islands dancing is best seen during the annual **Dance Week** in April or during the **Constitution Week** celebrations in late July and early August. If you can't be here then, you must make do with an "Island Night" feast and show—or two, or three—at the hotels. Indeed, one hotel or another will have a feast and show every night except Sunday. Although the hotel dance shows are tailored for tourists, the participants go at it with infectious enthusiasm.

Get a schedule of island nights from Cook Islands Tourism Corporation, or check the daily *Cook Islands News,* especially the Thursday and Friday editions, and make your reservations early. Also ask the locals where the top troupes are performing.

15 Aitutaki ✮✮✮

The farther you get from the South Pacific's international airports, the more likely you are to find an island and a way of life that have escaped relatively unscathed by the coming of Western ways—remnants of "old" Polynesia. Although it is quickly developing as a tourist destination, this is still true of Aitutaki.

Lying 225km (140 miles) north of Rarotonga, Aitutaki is often referred to as "the Bora Bora of the Cook Islands" because it consists of a small, hilly island at the apex of a triangular barrier reef lined with skinny flat islands. This reef necklace encloses one of the South Pacific's most colorful lagoons, which appears at the end of the flight up from Rarotonga as a turquoise carpet spread on the deep blue sea. The view from the air is memorable.

The lagoon sides of the uninhabited, coconut-studded small islands out on the reef have some of the South Pacific's most beautiful white-sand beaches. They're perfect for a snorkel-and-picnic excursion, Aitutaki's prime attraction.

The first European to discover the lagoon was Capt. William Bligh in 1789, a few weeks before the mutinous crew of HMS *Bounty* set him adrift off Tonga.

GETTING TO AITUTAKI

Air Rarotonga (© **22-888** on Rarotonga, or 31-888 on Aitutaki; www.airraro.com) flies to and from Aitutaki Monday to Saturday. It also offers day trips for about

---

Fun Fact **Dropping Their Rocks**

Legend has it that in the beginning Aitutaki was completely flat, but then its warriors sailed to Rarotonga and stole the top of Mount Raemaru. Pitched battles were fought on the way home, and the warriors dropped some of their rocks into the sea: Black Rock, on Rarotonga's northwest point; Rapota and Moturakau islands, in the south of Aitutaki's lagoon; and the black rocks along Aitutaki's west coast. In the end, the Aitutakian warriors were victorious, and the top of Raemaru is now **Mount Maungapu,** the highest point on Aitutaki, at 122m (407 ft.).

NZ$400 (US$260), which includes round-trip airfare and a lagoon excursion with a barbecue lunch (see "Lagoon Excursions," below). Regular round-trip fare is about NZ$380 (US$208), but it usually is less expensive to fly at midday or at night. The early morning and late afternoon flights are often filled with day-trippers, and thus are more expensive.

Air/hotel packages to Aitutaki also can result in savings. Check with Air Rarotonga or **Island Hopper Vacations** (© 22-026; www.islandhoppervacations.com), which specializes in outer island packages.

The airport is about 7km (4 miles) from most hotels and guesthouses, most of which pick up their guests who have reservations. The airline provides **airport transfers** for NZ$10 (US$6.50) each way.

Ask the hotel desk to reconfirm your return to Rarotonga. **Air Rarotonga's** office is in Ureia village, just north of Arutanga (© 31-888).

GETTING AROUND AITUTAKI

There is no **public bus transportation** system on Aitutaki, but you can call **Pacifica Taxi** (© 31-220).

All hotels and guest houses can arrange **car, scooter, and bike rentals,** or you can call **Rino's Rentals** (© 31-197), north of Arutanga, or **Popara Rentals** (© 31-735), on the mainland near the Aitutaki Lagoon Resort & Spa. Both have cars starting at NZ$65 (US$42) a day, scooters for NZ$25 (US$16) per day, and bikes for NZ$8 (US$5) per day. **Josie's Beach Lodge** (© 31-659), also near the Aitutaki Lagoon Resort & Spa, rents scooters for that same price.

FAST FACTS: **Aitutaki**

Currency Exchange **ANZ Bank** has a small agency and an ATM at Mango Traders, near The Pacific Resort Aitutaki. The office is open Monday to Friday 9am to 3pm. **Westpac Bank** has an office and ATM at the post office in Arutanga. It's open Monday and Thursday 9:30am to 3pm.

E-mail You can get online (slowly and expensively) at **SpiderCo Internet Lounge** south of the Pacific Resort Aitutaki (© 31-780). It's open Monday to Saturday 8am to midnight, Sunday 6 to 9pm.

Emergencies In case of emergency, contact your hotel staff. The **police station** is in Arutanga (© 31-015).

Healthcare Medical and dental treatment and prescription medications are available at the island's **hospital** (✆ 31-002), near Arutanga.

Post Office The post office at Arutanga is open Monday to Friday 8am to 4pm.

Radio/Television The national radio and television stations can be received here.

Safety See "Fast Facts: Rarotonga," earlier in this chapter, for general warnings and precautions.

Telephone/Fax The communications counter at the post office is open Monday to Friday from 8am to 4pm. It does not accept credit cards, but you can use Kia Orana prepaid calling cards.

Visitor Information Cook Islands Tourism Corporation's Aitutaki visitor information office is on Sir Albert Henry Drive near the wharf (✆ 31-767). It's open Monday to Friday 9am to 3pm.

Water Don't drink the tap water on Aitutaki unless you are sure it comes from a rainwater catchment, and boil it even if it does.

EXPLORING AITUTAKI

Aitutaki has much less to offer ashore than does Rarotonga. The best way to see it is on a guided walking tour with **Aitutaki Walkabout Tours** (✆ 31-757; www.aitutaki-walkabout.com), on which your guide will explain local flora and fauna, and you will visit local farms to see how crops are grown. These half-day tours cost NZ$40 (US$26) per person. If you're not up to walking, the same company's **Aitutaki Discovery Safari** will drive you around the island in a four-wheel-drive vehicle, stopping at historical and scenic sights. It costs NZ$50 (US$33) per person.

The central island is dotted with the coconut, pineapple, banana, and tapioca plantations that are worked by most of the island's 2,100 residents. Aitutaki is a major supplier of produce and seafood to Rarotonga.

The administrative center, most of the shops, and the main wharf are on the west side of the island at **Arutanga** village, where a narrow, shallow passage comes through the reef. Trading boats cannot get through the pass and must remain offshore while cargo and passengers are ferried to land on barges. The late Sir Albert Henry was born and raised on Aitutaki, and the divided road to the wharf is named for him and his wife, Elizabeth (one lane for Sir Albert and one lane for Lady Elizabeth).

Just south of the post office in Arutanga stands the **Cook Islands Christian Church,** the country's oldest church, built in 1839 of coral and limestone. The monument in front is to John Williams, the exploring missionary who came to Aitutaki in October 1821, and to Papeiha, the Tahitian teacher who came with him and converted the entire island. The interior of the church is unusual in that the altar is on one side rather than at one end. Worshippers from each village sit together during services, but visitors can take any vacancy during services at 10am on Sunday. An anchor suspended from the ceiling is a symbol of hope being a sure and steadfast anchor, as in Hebrews 6:19.

A network of mostly paved roads fans out from Arutanga to **Viapai** and **Tautu** villages on the east side and to the airport on a flat hook at the northern end of the island. About 1,000 American servicemen—with considerable help from the local residents—built the large airstrip during World War II. Many present-day Aitutakians reportedly trace their lineage to those Americans.

Tips **Don't Get Burned**

The boats all have canopies, but bring a hat and plenty of high-powered sunscreen on your Aitutaki lagoon outing—and use it! The sun out there on the water can blister you, even if you're under a canopy.

According to ancient legend, the first Polynesians to reach Aitutaki came in through **Ootu Pass,** on the eastern side of the lagoon between the airport and **Akitua** island, site of today's Aitutaki Lagoon Resort & Spa (see "Where to Stay on Aitutaki," below). They were led by the mighty warrior and navigator Ru, who brought 4 wives, 4 brothers, and a crew of 20 young virgins from either Tubuai or Raiatea (the legend varies as to which one) in what is now French Polynesia. Akitua island, where they landed, was originally named *Urituaorukitemoana,* which means "where Ru turned his back on the sea."

LAGOON EXCURSIONS ✿✿✿

The main reason to come to Aitutaki is to spend at least a day on the lagoon and one of the small islands out on the reef. The standard day trip begins at 9am and ends about 4pm. The boats spend the morning cruising and fishing on the lagoon. Midday is spent on one of the reef islands, where guests swim, snorkel, and sun while the crew cooks the day's catch and the local vegetables. The itinerary changes from day to day depending on the weather and the guests' desires.

A common destination is **Tapuaetai (One Foot) Island** and its adjacent sandbar, known as Nude Island (for its lack of foliage, not clothes). One Foot got its name when an ancient chief prohibited his subjects from fishing there on pain of death. One day the chief and his warriors saw two people fishing on the reef and gave chase. The two were a man and his young son. They ran onto the island, the boy carefully stepping in his father's footprints as they crossed the beach. The son then hid in the top of a coconut tree. The chief found the father, who said he was the only person fishing on the reef. After a search proved fruitless, the chief decided it must have been rocks he and his men saw on the reef. He then killed the father. Ever since, the island has been known as Tapuaetai (in the local dialect, *tapuae* means footprint, and *tai* is one).

Those dark things that look like cucumbers on the bottom of the lagoon are *bêches-de-mer* (sea slugs). Along with sandalwood, they brought many traders to the South Pacific during the 19th century because both brought high prices in China. Sea slugs are harmless—except in China, where they are considered to be an aphrodisiac.

As noted in "Getting to Aitutaki," above, Air Rarotonga has day trips from Rarotonga, which include lagoon excursions. Several operators also have full-day lagoon cruises Monday to Saturday. The oldest and still best is **Bishop's Lagoon Cruises** (© 31-009; fax 31-493; bishopcruz@aitutaki.net.ck). It goes to One Foot Island, where it has erected a beach bar. **Teking Tours** (© 31-582; tekiing@aitutaki.net) goes to a sand bar, where you'll have lunch sitting at umbrella tables in the lagoon. It also has champagne brunch and sunset tours. **Kia Orana Tours** (© 31-442; kcruises@aitutaki.net) uses a smaller boat to visit Maina Island, on the southwestern corner of the lagoon. All charge about NZ$65 (US$42) per person for the all-day excursions, including lunch.

BOATING, GOLF, HIKING & SCUBA DIVING

BOATING   You can rent kayaks at **Samade on the Beach** (© 31-526), on the lagoon north of the Aitutaki Lagoon Resort & Spa, for NZ$10 (US$6.50) per hour to NZ$20 (US$13) per day. Instead of going south to the resort at the Y intersection, follow the dirt track to the west.

GOLF   Golfers who missed hitting the radio antennae and guy wires on the Rarotonga course (see above) can try again at the 9-hole course at the **Aitutaki Golf Club,** on the north end of the island between the airport and the sea. Balls hit onto the runway used to be playable, but broken clubs and increasing air traffic put an end to that. You can rent equipment at the clubhouse. The club has neither a phone nor regular hours, but the hotels and guesthouses can arrange rentals and tee times. Members are more likely to volunteer to mow the greens between May and August than during the wetter summer months.

HIKING   Hikers can take a trail to the top of **Mount Maungapu,** Aitutaki's highest point, at 124m (410 ft.). It begins across from the Paradise Cove Guest House, about 1 mile north of The Pacific Resort Aitutaki. The trail starts under the power lines and follows them uphill for about a mile. The tall grass is sharp and can be soaked after a rain, but the track is usually well tramped and should be easy to follow. Nevertheless, wear trousers. The view from the top includes all of Aitutaki and its lagoon. Sunrise and sunset are the best times.

SCUBA DIVING & SNORKELING   The lagoon here is too shallow for scuba diving, so the sites are over the edge of the reef. Divers and snorkelers can go with Neil Mitchell of **Aitutaki Scuba,** P.O. Box 40, Aitutaki (© **31-103;** fax 31-310; scuba@aitutaki.net.ck), or Onu Hewett of **Bubbles Below** (© **31-537;** www.diveaitutaki.com). Both charge about NZ$95 (US$62) per one-tank dive.

The best place to don mask, snorkel, and fins on the mainland is off the north end of the short runway at the airport, near the radio antenna. You can swim right out to the reef's edge here at high tide, but observe the usual cautions.

WHERE TO STAY ON AITUTAKI
Like Rarotonga, Aitutaki has seen a "beach bungalow" boom in recent years. Indeed, everyone with lagoonside land seems to have put up bungalows to rent. **Samade on the Beach** and **Ranginui's Retreat,** below, are two of the better examples.

EXPENSIVE
Aitutaki Lagoon Resort & Spa ✹✹✹   Another property nursed back to health by Tata Crocombe, owner of The Rarotongan Beach Resort & Spa, this excellent resort is reached by boat across Ootu Pass to Akitua, a sandy, tadpole-shaped islet south of the airport. The ocean surf breaks on one side of Akitua, where the beach has been replenished. On the other, the magnificent lagoon laps a white-sand beach, off which a channel has been dredged for swimming. The choice—and most expensive—units here are overwater bungalows endowed with Polynesian charm. Although the lagoon off their decks is not as deep or as clear, their amenities are on par with most overwater units in French Polynesia. Their rears sit on land, and each has an outdoor shower in a private garden. Next best, and the farthest apart (and therefore most private), are the deluxe beachfront bungalows, each of which has a raised sleeping area behind a sofa-equipped lounge that opens through sliding, wooden louvered doors to a lagoonside deck. Other units date from the early 1970s. Some have been remodeled to make them more modern, but they have solid walls on one side, which affords privacy at the expense of ventilation (air-conditioners and ceiling fans calm the heat, but they operate only when you're in your room). The open-air, thatched-roof restaurant and beachside bar serve good regional fare. A spa offers full-service pampering.

P.O. Box 99, Aitutaki (on Akitua Island, 2km/1 mile south of airport, 9km/5½ miles from Arutanga). ℂ **800/481-9026** or 31-201. Fax 31-202. www.aitutakilagoonresort.com. 36 units. NZ$512–NZ$1,409 (US$333–US$916) bungalow. AE, DC, MC, V. **Amenities:** 2 restaurants; 2 bars; outdoor pool; spa; watersports equipment rentals; free kayaks and snorkel gear; scooter rentals; rental bikes; limited room service; babysitting; laundry service. In room: A/C, TV/DVD, dataport, minibar, coffeemaker, hair dryer, iron, safe.

Are Tamanu Beach Village 𝕉𝕉

This "village" is two beachside bungalow complexes separated by a coconut grove beside a powdery white-sand beach stretching along the entire northwestern shore of the island. It's the creation of Mike and Stuart Henry, two grandsons of the late Prime Minister Sir Albert Henry. They merged their two bungalow complexes—the former Are Tamanu and Manea Beach Hotel—into this one operation. Both parts have their own swimming pools and bars, while one sports Te Vaka Bar & Grill, a roadside restaurant. The spacious guest bungalows face courtyards that terminate at the beach. Some units have a separate bedroom, while others are one-room bungalows. Each has a king-size bed, a full kitchen, and a shower-only bathroom. The more expensive bungalows are on the beach.

P.O. Box 59, Aitutaki (on west coast, 3km/2 miles from airport). ℂ **31-810.** Fax 32-816. www.aretamanu.com. 22 units. NZ$350–NZ$495 (US$228–US$322) bungalows. Rates include continental breakfast. AE, MC. V. Children under 12 not accepted. **Amenities:** Restaurant; 2 bars; 2 outdoor pools; free use of bikes and snorkeling equipment; coin-op washers and dryers. In room: A/C, kitchen, coffeemaker, hair dryer, safe.

Etu Moana 𝕉𝕉

On a hillside terminating at a white-sand beach, this adult-oriented property is the creation of Jo-Anne and Jim Brittijn, a Canadian-Dutch couple. Jim is both an avid sailor and a carpenter, as witnessed by his skilled nautical cabinetry, which lends many yacht touches to these comfortable bungalows. Each unit has a porch with a settee built into one side, a king-size bed facing the lagoon, a full kitchen, a bathroom with walk-in shower, and another shower outside in a small courtyard. The units are grouped around an attractive swimming pool, although the best are beside the lagoon. The complex has no restaurant, but refreshment is available at a poolside honesty bar, and Are Tamanu Village and The Pacific Resort are close at hand.

P.O. Box 123, Aitutaki (west coast, 3km/2 miles from airport). ℂ **31-458.** Fax 31-459. www.etumoana.com. 8 units. NZ$405–NZ$450 (US$263–US$293). Rates include breakfast. AE, MC, V. Children under 12 not accepted. **Amenities:** Bar; outdoor pool; scooter rentals; free bikes, kayaks, snorkeling gear; laundry service. In room: A/C, TV, dataport, kitchen, coffeemaker, hairdryer, iron, safe.

The Pacific Resort Aitutaki 𝕉𝕉𝕉

This romantic, architecturally stunning sister of the Pacific Resort Rarotonga ranks with the Aitutaki Lagoon Resort & Spa as the best full-service hotels in the Cook Islands. Reception, shops, and restaurant—under a conical thatch roof—sit atop a headland overlooking a shallow but colorful lagoon. Steps lead from there down to an infinity swimming pool, daytime bar, and a white-sand beach strewn with some of the big black rocks the legendary Aitutaki warriors reputedly dropped while stealing the top of Rarotonga's Mount Raemaru (see "Dropping Their Rocks," earlier in this chapter). Lined up facing the lagoon are the resort's 13 beachfront bungalows. Comparable to bungalows found at top-end resorts in Fiji and French Polynesia, these spacious units have thatch-covered roofs, fans hanging from mat-lined ceilings, hardwood floors, king beds plus built-in settees, large bathrooms with double sinks and glass-enclosed showers, and front porches facing the beach. While the beachfront bungalows give direct access to the lagoon, the stars here are the six suites and three one-bedroom villas cleverly hidden among the rocks and old-growth tropical forest on the headland. You'll have to climb down steps to reach the beach, but these thatched-roof, stucco-sided units are much more private, and they all have both outdoor as well as indoor showers. Asian decor and furniture, including some antique pieces, make this resort seem as much Oriental as South Seas.

P.O. Box 90, Aitutaki (1km/½ mile north of Arutanga). ℭ **31-720.** Fax 31-719. www.pacificresort.com. 22 units. NZ$760–NZ$1,330 (US$494–US$865) bungalow. AE, DC, MC, V. **Amenities:** Restaurant; 2 bars; outdoor pool; free kayaks, rowboats, and snorkel gear; car, scooter, and bike rentals; limited room service; babysitting; laundry service. *In room:* A/C, TV, CD player, dataport, minibar, coffeemaker, hair dryer, iron, safe.

MODERATE

Samade on the Beach   These trellis-trimmed bungalows sit behind Samade on the Beach restaurant (see "Where to Dine on Aitutaki," below), where guests are served complimentary breakfast. Built of pine with cathedral ceilings under tile roofs, they are rather plain but well-equipped. Each is air-conditioned and has a ceiling fan. They also have kitchen sinks and counter space but no cooking facilities. Lounge chairs on a section of the white-sand beach are reserved for guests, who can get free use of kayaks. Although the units are a bit overpriced, the restaurant and beach setting make this a relaxing and friendly place to stay.

P.O. Box 75, Aitutaki (on east coast, near Ootu Pass). ℭ **31-526.** www.samadebeach.com. 12 units. NZ$285 (US$185) double. Rates include breakfast. MC, V. **Amenities:** Restaurant; bar; free use of kayaks; scooter and bicycle rentals. *In room:* A/C, TV, fridge, coffeemaker, hairdryer, no phone.

INEXPENSIVE

Aitutaki's least expensive backpacker lodging is at **Josie's Beach Lodge** (ℭ **31-659**), a tin-roof house with a screened veranda a few steps from Ootu Pass between the mainland and the Aitutaki Lagoon Resort & Spa, and within walking distance of Samade on the Beach restaurant and bar (see below). Its five rooms range from NZ$25 to NZ$50 (US$16–US$33) double per night. You can get breakfast at Josie's, but you cannot use your credit card.

Ranginui's Retreat   This no-frills bungalow complex sits on the beach across Ootu Pass from the Aitutaki Lagoon Resort & Spa (see above). You can also walk to Samade on the Beach (see "Where to Dine on Aitutaki," below). Although modest, the wooden bungalows here hold queen beds and sofas, kitchens with microwave ovens, and adequate bathrooms with glass-enclosed showers. Each has a porch with lagoon view. There's a small pool, and guests get free use of kayaks to explore the lagoon.

P.O. Box 8, Aitutaki (2km/1 mile south of airport, 9km/5½ miles from Arutanga). ℭ **31-657.** Fax 31-658. www.ranginuis.com. 7 units. NZ$120–NZ$160 (US$78–US$104) bungalow. MC, V. **Amenities:** Small outdoor pool; bike and scooter rentals; free use of kayaks; laundry service. *In room:* TV (3 units), kitchen, coffeemaker, no phone.

Rino's Beach Bungalows   These clean, comfortable New Zealand–style rooms and apartments sit beside the beach between Arutanga and the Pacific Resort. The duplex apartments open to decks by the beach, and the standard rooms are in two-story buildings just behind them. The beachside honeymoon unit by the beach is smaller but more private than the others. Three larger apartments are on the other side of the road. All units have kitchens, table fans, and walls of wood paneling and concrete blocks painted white, although flowered fabrics lend an islandy touch. Although not as charming, they are more spacious than most other beach bungalows here, and you can walk to the main villages.

P.O. Box 140, Aitutaki (Ureia Village, on west coast .5km/¼ mile north of Arutanga). ℭ **31-197.** Fax 31-559. rinos@ aitutaki.net.ck. 11 units. NZ$85 (US$55) double room; NZ$120–NZ$255 (US$78–US$166) apt. MC, V. **Amenities:** Car, bike, and scooter rental; coin-op washers and dryers. *In room:* Kitchen, coffeemaker, no phone.

WHERE TO DINE ON AITUTAKI

Some Aitutaki restaurants will come and get you at your hotel and take you back after dinner, so be sure to ask about free transportation when you make reservations.

Cafe Tupuna 🏵 REGIONAL   After a career as dressmaker, florist, and artist (her floral paintings adorn the walls), Tupuna Hewett opened this sand-floor charmer in an open-air addition to her home in the middle of the main island. Her blackboard menu depends on what the local fishermen have caught, plus tender steaks from New Zealand. For starters or a light meal, try her spicy version of *ika mata* (marinated raw fish) in half a coconut shell. For a main course, opt for the parrotfish cooked in banana leaves. This is the one place you will want to have dinner on Aitutaki.

Tautu Rd., in center of island. ℂ **31-678.** Reservations recommended. Main courses NZ$28–NZ$30 (US$18–US$20). MC, V. Mon–Sat 6–9pm. Turn inland at the post office, bear right at the roundabout at the top of the hill, bear left after the hospital and Mormon church, turn right at the sign to restaurant on left.

Samade on the Beach 🅥🅐🅛🅤🅔 REGIONAL   On Ootu Beach, a 5-minute walk from the Aitutaki Lagoon Resort & Spa, this lagoonside restaurant has a white-sand floor under a big tin roof lined with coconut mats, setting the stage for hearty local-style meals. Indeed, this is a poor person's version of the famous Bloody Mary's Restaurant & Bar on Bora Bora. There's nothing fancy about the chow, but the fish and chips don't get any fresher. The name Samade is from the owners, Tongan Sam Vakalahi and his Cook Islander wife, Adrianne. They serve breakfast all day and rent kayaks and other toys, and they should have 12 well-equipped beach bungalows by the time you arrive. Tuesday sees Aitutaki's most authentic island night, and the Sunday afternoon barbecue draws throngs of both locals and visitors.

Ootu Beach, north of Aitutaki Lagoon Resort & Spa (turn west at the Y intersection). ℂ **31-526.** Reservations recommended. Main courses NZ$17–NZ$25 (US$11–US$17). MC, V. Daily 7am–9pm.

Tuano's Garden Cafe 🏵🏵 REGIONAL   This is not really a cafe but the home of Tuano and Sonja Raela, who grow the vegetables and fruits they use in their spiced coconut bread, papaya soup, breadfruit chips, and fruit plates. They have no set menu, only daily specials culled from their plantation and the lagoon. Try the grilled mahimahi served with chilled cucumbers and mango chutney. Dinner depends on what fish have been caught that day, but always includes a choice for vegetarians. Tuano and Sonja grow and roast their own coffee, which makes a perfect afternoon snack with a slice of coconut cake. For NZ$35 (US$23) per person they will take you on a guided tour by van of their organic plantation (you will get to sample their in-season fruit.)

Amuri, on west coast. ℂ **31-950.** Reservations required at dinner. Sandwiches and cakes NZ$5.50–NZ$11 (US$3.50–US$7); main courses NZ$27–NZ$40 (US$17–US$26). No credit cards. Mon, Wed, Fri 3–5pm and 6–9pm.

ISLAND NIGHTS ON AITUTAKI

Island Night feasts and dance shows usually take place Monday and Friday at the **Pacific Resort Aitutaki,** Tuesday at **Samade on the Beach;** Thursday at the **Coconut Crusher Bar** (ℂ 31-283), off the main road north of the Pacific Resort; Saturday at the **Aitutaki Lagoon Resort & Spa** (see "Where to Stay on Aitutaki," above). I like the Tuesday show at Samade on the Beach, one of the more locally authentic feasts.

13

Samoa

The scenic 31km (19 mile) drive from Faleolo Airport into the historic capital of Apia provides a fitting introduction to Samoa. Here in this cultural storehouse, which was once known as Western Samoa, the Polynesian lifestyle known as *fa'a Samoa*—The Samoan Way—remains alive and well. On one side of the road lies an aquamarine lagoon; on the other, coconut plantations climb gentle slopes to the volcanic ridge along the middle of Upolu, the main island.

Along the shore sit hundreds of Samoan *fales* (houses), their big turtle-shaped roofs resting on poles, their sides open to the breeze and to passersby. Their grass trimmed and their borders marked with boulders painted white, expansive lawns make the route seem like an unending park. Samoans wrapped in *lava-lavas* shower under outdoor faucets and sit together in their fales. Only the dim glow of television screens coming from beneath tin roofs rather than thatch

remind us that a century has passed since Robert Louis Stevenson lived, wrote, and died here in Samoa.

Even the town of Apia harkens back to those bygone South Seas days. Although landfills have extended the shoreline, government high-rises now stand on the waterfront, and traffic lights blink at several corners, many old white clapboard buildings still sleep along Beach Road, just as they did when Stevenson stepped ashore here in 1889. Compared with the hustle and bustle of Papeete in French Polynesia, or with the congestion and tuna canneries of Pago Pago in nearby American Samoa, life in Apia is slow and easy.

If you go with an eye to exploring the culture as well as visiting some of the South Pacific's most beautiful and undeveloped beaches, Samoa will enchant you just as it did Stevenson, Maugham, and Margaret Mead, all of whom found plenty to write home about.

1 Samoa Today

The Samoa Islands, which include the independent nation of Samoa and the territory of American Samoa, stretch for some 480km (300 miles) across the central South Pacific, about 2,000km (1,200 miles) west of Tahiti and 4,000km (2,600 miles) southwest of Hawaii. The nine western islands are in Samoa; the others are in American Samoa.

GEOGRAPHY Independent Samoa, which many people still call Western Samoa, has a land area of 2,800 sq. km. (1,090 sq. miles), two-thirds of which are on **Savai'i,** the largest Polynesian island outside Hawaii and New Zealand. A series of volcanoes on a line running east to west formed **Upolu,** about 63km (39 miles) long and 21km (13 miles) wide. It's considerably smaller than Savai'i, 21km (13 miles) to the west,

> **Tips** **Both Share *Fa'a Samoa***
>
> Although American ways have made a serious impact in neighboring American
> Samoa (see chapter 14), the people there share fa'a Samoa with their relatives
> here in Samoa. Much of the background information in this chapter, therefore,
> applies equally to both.

but some 75% of Samoa's population lives on Upolu. Although geologically younger
than Upolu, Savai'i in many ways is the most "old Polynesia" of any island I include
in this book. It has no towns, and its villagers live very much by fa'a Samoa.

The tops of two small volcanoes, **Apolima** and **Manono** islands sit in the Apolima
Strait between the two main islands. Locals like to claim that James A. Michener was
inspired by Apolima and Manono to create the mysteriously romantic island of Bali
Ha'i in his *Tales of the South Pacific*. (Michener said in a television interview, however,
that he got the idea from a cloud-draped island off Espiritu Santo in Vanuatu, where
he spent much of World War II.)

GOVERNMENT   An independent nation since 1962, Samoa is ruled by a Parliament made up of 47 members, of whom 45 are *matais,* or chiefs. Only matais could
vote for candidates for these seats until
1991, when universal suffrage was
enacted. Part-Samoan and non-Samoan
citizens elect two non-matai members.
There are two parties: the Human
Rights Protection party and the Christian Democratic party.

The titular head of state since independence has been Malietoa Tanumafili
II, one of Samoa's four paramount
chiefs. He will hold the job for the rest of
his life. Parliament will choose his successor from among Samoa's four paramount chiefs. That person will serve not
for life but for a term of 5 years.

> **Impressions**
>
> *Imagine an island with the most
> perfect climate in the world, tropi-
> cal yet almost always cooled by a
> breeze from the sea. No malaria or
> other fevers. No dangerous snakes
> or insects. Fish for the catching, and
> fruits for the plucking. And an earth
> and sky and sea of immortal loveli-
> ness. What more could civilization
> give?*
>
> —Rupert Brooke, 1914

ECONOMY   Samoa's only exports of any magnitude are fresh fish, *copra* (dried
coconut meat), coconut cream, kava, noni juice, and beer (try a German-style Vailima
brew while you're here). Tourism is of increasing importance, with Aggie Grey's
Lagoon, Beach Resort & Spa opening in 2005, and a big Warwick resort slated to be
built by 2007. There is some light manufacturing, including cigarettes and garments.
Although there has been significant economic growth and development in recent
years, mainly in and around Apia, foreign aid and remittances sent home by Samoans
living elsewhere keep the country out of bankruptcy. With the minimum wage here
at S$2 (US67¢) an hour, several thousand Samoans regularly live and work in Amer-
ican Samoa, where they earn at least US$3 an hour. Some 20% of the country's gross
domestic product is attributable to remittances from Samoans living elsewhere.

2 Samoa Yesterday: History 101

Archaeologists believe that Polynesians settled in the Samoa Islands about 3,000 years ago. Their great migration halted here for some 1,000 years before voyagers went on to colonize the Marquesas, Society Islands, and other island groups farther east. Thus the Samoas are known as the "Cradle of Polynesia."

The universe known by the early Samoans included Tonga and Fiji, to which they regularly journeyed, often waging war. Tongan invaders ruled the Samoas between A.D. 950 and 1250, and there still is a strong rivalry between the two nations—especially on the rugby field.

The first European to see the Samoas was Dutchman Jacob Roggeveen, who in 1722 sighted the Manu'a Islands in what is now American Samoa. The first Europeans to land in Samoa were part of a French expedition under Jean La Pérouse in 1787. They came ashore on the north coast of Tutuila in American Samoa and were promptly attacked by Samoan warriors. Twelve members of the landing party and 39 Samoans were killed during the skirmish.

The Rev. John Williams, who roamed the South Pacific in *The Messenger of Peace,* landed the first missionaries in Samoa in 1830. European-style settlements grew up at Apia on Upolu and on the shores of Pago Pago Bay on Tutuila. German businessmen had established copra plantations on Upolu by the late 1850s. When steamships started plying the route between San Francisco and Sydney, the U.S. Navy negotiated a treaty with the chiefs of Tutuila in 1872 to permit the U.S. to use Pago Pago as a coaling station. The U.S. Congress never ratified this document, but it served to keep the Germans from penetrating into Eastern Samoa, as American Samoa was then known.

COLONIALISM ARRIVES   The Germans gained the upper hand over today's independent Samoa by staging a coup in 1887, backed up (unofficially) by German gunboats. They governed through Malietoa, one of the islands' four paramount chiefs. One of his rivals, Mataafa, lost a bloody rebellion in 1888 and was exiled.

Continuing unrest turned into a major international incident—fiasco is a better word—when the United States, Britain, and Germany sent a total of seven warships to Apia in March of 1889. A hurricane arrived unexpectedly, and only a British warship got out of the way. Of the rest, four were sunk, two others were washed ashore, and 146 lives were lost. (A newspaper story of the time is mounted in the lounge of Aggie Grey's Hotel & Bungalows in Apia.)

In December 1889 an agreement was signed in Berlin under which Germany was given today's independent Samoa, the United States was handed Eastern Samoa, and Britain created a protectorate over Tonga. The two Samoas were split apart and swept into the colonial system. The Germans in Samoa proceeded to make fortunes from their huge, orderly copra plantations.

Fun Fact **White-Skinned Sky Busters**

To the Samoans, the first Europeans to visit their shores seemed to have come through the slit that separated the sky from the sea. Thus they named these strange people *papalagi* (sky busters). Shortened to *palagi* (pah-*lahng*-gee), the name now means any Westerner with white skin.

Fun Fact **The Teller of Tales**

The salvage crews were still working on the hulks of the British, American, and German warships sunk in Apia's harbor by a hurricane in 1889 when a thin, tubercular writer arrived from Scotland.

Not yet 40 years old, Robert Louis Stevenson was already famous—and wealthy—for such novels as *Treasure Island* and *Dr. Jekyll and Mr. Hyde*. He arrived in Samoa after traveling across the United States and a good part of the South Pacific in search of a climate more suitable to his ravaged lungs. With him were his wife, Fanny (an American divorcée 11 years his senior), his stepmother, and his stepson. His mother joined them later.

Stevenson intended to remain in Apia for only a few weeks while he caught up on writing a series of newspaper columns. He and his entourage stayed to build a mansion known as Vailima on the slopes of Mount Vaea, overlooking Apia, where he lived lavishly and wrote more than 750,000 published words. He learned the Samoan language and translated "The Bottle Imp," his story about a genie, into it. It was the first work of fiction translated into Samoan.

Stevenson loved Samoa, and the Samoans loved him. Great orators and storytellers in their own right, they called him *Tusitala*, the "Teller of Tales."

On December 3, 1894, almost 5 years after he arrived in Apia, Stevenson was writing a story about a son who had escaped a death sentence handed down by his own father and had sailed away to join his lover. Leaving the couple embraced, Stevenson stopped to answer letters, play cards, and fix dinner. While preparing mayonnaise on his back porch, he suddenly clasped his hands to his head and collapsed. He died not of tuberculosis but of a cerebral hemorrhage.

More than 200 grieving Samoans hacked a "Road of the Loving Hearts" up Mount Vaea to a little knoll below the summit, where they placed him in a grave with a perpetual view overlooking Vailima, the mountains, the town, the reef, and the sea he loved. Carved on his grave is his famous requiem:

This be the verse you grave for me:
Here he lies where he longed to be;
Home is the sailor, home from the sea,
And the hunter home from the hill.

A KIWI BACKWATER   German rule came to an abrupt end with the outbreak of World War I in 1914, when New Zealand sent an expeditionary force to Apia, and the German governor surrendered. The Germans were interned for the duration of the war, and their huge land holdings were confiscated. New Zealand remained in charge until 1962, initially under the League of Nations and then under the United Nations.

The New Zealand administrators did little in the islands except keep the lid on unrest, at which they were generally successful. In 1929, however, the Mau Movement created an uprising. The movement was crushed when New Zealand constables fired on a crowd of protestors outside the government building in Apia, killing nine.

When opposition to colonialism flared up in the United Nations 20 years later, a Legislative Assembly of matais was established to exercise a degree of internal self-government. A constitution was drafted in 1960, and the people approved it and their own independence a year later by referendum. On January 1, 1962, Samoa became the first South Pacific colony to regain its independence from the Western powers.

Samoa remained a backwater during most of its career as a colony and trusteeship territory. Only during World War II did it appear on the world stage, and then solely as a training base for thousands of Allied servicemen on their way to fight the Japanese. Tourism increased after the big jets started landing at Pago Pago in the 1960s, but significant numbers of visitors started arriving only after Samoa's Faleolo Airport was upgraded to handle large aircraft in the 1980s.

3 The Samoan People

About 177,000 people live in independent Samoa, the vast majority of them full-blooded Samoans. They are the second-largest group of pure Polynesians in the world, behind only the Maoris of New Zealand.

Although divided politically in their home islands, the people of both Samoas share the same culture, heritage, and, in many cases, family lineage. Despite the inroads that Western influences have made—especially in American Samoa—they are a proud people who fiercely protect their old ways.

"Catch the bird but watch for the wave" is an old Samoan proverb that expresses the approach followed in the islands. This conservative attitude is perhaps responsible for the extraordinary degree to which Samoans have preserved fa'a Samoa while adapting it to the modern world. Even in American Samoa, where most of the turtle-shaped thatch fales have been replaced with structures of plywood and tin, the firmament of the Samoan way lies just under the trappings of the territory's commercialized surface.

The showing of respect permeates Samoans' lives. They are by tradition extremely polite to guests, so much so that some of them tend to answer in the affirmative all questions posed by a stranger. The Samoans are not lying when they answer wrongly; they are merely being polite. Therefore, visitors who really need information should avoid asking questions that call for a yes or no answer.

THE *AIGA*

The foundation of Samoan society is the extended family unit, or *aiga* (pronounced ah-*eeng*-ah). Unlike the Western nuclear family, an aiga can include thousands of relatives and in-laws. In this communal system, everything is owned collectively by the aiga; the individual has a right to use that property but does not personally own it. In a paper prepared for the government of American Samoa by the Pacific Basin Development Council, it states: "the [Samoan] attitude toward property is: if you need something which you don't have, there is always someone else who has what you need."

At the head of each of more than 10,000 aigas is a matai (*mah*-tie), a chief who is responsible for the welfare of each member of the clan. The matai settles family

---

Tips Keep an Eye on Your Camera

As is the case throughout the South Pacific islands, traditional Samoan custom is at odds with Western concepts of ownership. You may notice the difference directly when a camera or other item left unattended suddenly disappears.

disputes, parcels out the family's land, and sees that everyone has enough to eat and a roof over his or her head. Although the title matai usually follows bloodlines, the family can choose another person—man or woman—if the incumbent proves incapable of handling the job.

Strictly speaking, Samoans turn all money they earn over to their matai, to be used in the best interest of the clan. The system is being threatened, however, as more and more young Samoans move to the United States or New Zealand, earn wages in their own right, and spend them as they see fit. Nevertheless, the system is still remarkably intact in both Samoas. Even in Samoan outposts in Hawaii, California, Texas, and Auckland (which collectively have a larger Samoan population than do the islands), the people still rally around their aiga, and matais play an important role in daily life.

Land ownership is a touchy subject here. About 11% of the land here is freehold, which Samoan citizens can buy and sell. Non-Samoans can lease freehold and communal property, but they cannot buy it outright.

ORGANIZATION & RITUAL

Above the aiga, Samoan life is ruled by a hierarchy of matais known in English as high-talking chiefs, high chiefs, and paramount chiefs, in ascending order of importance. The high-talking chiefs do just that: talk on behalf of the high chiefs, usually expressing themselves in great oratorical flourishes in a formal version of Samoan reserved for use among the chiefs. The high chiefs are senior matais at the village or district level, and the paramount chiefs can rule over island groups. The chiefly symbol, worn over the shoulder, is a short broom that resembles a horse's tail.

The conduct and relations between chiefs are governed by strict rules of protocol. Nowhere is ritual more obvious or observed than during a kava (pronounced *'ava* in Samoan) ceremony. The slightly narcotic kava brew is made by crushing the roots of the pepper plant *Piper methysticum* (see the "'Grog' Etiquette" box in chapter 4). In the old days the roots were chewed and spit into the bowl by a chief's virgin daughter. (Forget the wisecracks about there being no virgin daughters these days; that method of kava preparation disappeared in the face of modern notions of hygiene.)

MISSIONARIES & MINISTERS

Like other Polynesians, the Samoans in pre-European days worshipped a hierarchy of gods under one supreme being, whom they called Le Tagaloa. When the London Missionary Society's Rev. John Williams arrived in 1830, he found the Samoans willing to convert to the Christian God. He and his Tahitian teachers brought a strict, puritanical version of Christianity. His legacy can be seen both in the large white churches

---

Tips How to Drink Kava

During a Samoan kava ceremony, coconut shells are scooped into a large wooden bowl of the gray liquid, which looks like mud and tastes like sawdust. The host passes a cup to one person at a time. When you get yours, hold the cup straight out with both hands, and say *"Manuia"* (Good health) before gulping most of it down in one swallow. Save a little to toss on the floor mats before handing the cup back to your host. And remember, this is a solemn occasion—not a few rounds at the local bar.

Tips **Wonderful Harmony**

Even if you can't understand the sermon, the sound of Samoans singing hymns in harmony makes going to church here a rewarding experience.

---

that dominate every settlement in all the Samoa Islands and in the fervor with which the Samoans practice religion today.

About a third of all Samoans are members of the Congregational Christian Church, a Protestant denomination that grew out of the London Missionary Society's work. Independent Samoa almost closes down on Sunday, and things come to a crawl on the Sabbath even in more Westernized American Samoa. Swimming on Sunday is tolerated in both countries only at the hotels and, after church, at beaches frequented by overseas visitors.

Christianity has become an integral part of fa'a Samoa, and every day at about 6:30pm each village observes *sa,* 10 minutes of devotional time during which everyone goes inside to pray, read Scripture, and perhaps sing hymns. A gong (usually an empty acetylene tank hung from a tree) is struck once to announce it's time to get ready, a second time to announce the beginning of sa, and a third time to announce that all's clear. It is permissible to drive on the main road during sa, but it's not all right to turn off into a village or to walk around.

MISS MEAD STUDIES SAMOAN SEX
Despite their ready acceptance of much of the missionaries' teaching, the Samoans no more took to heart their puritanical sexual mores than did any other group of Polynesians. In 1928 Margaret Mead, then a graduate student in anthropology, published her famous *Coming of Age in Samoa,* which was based on her research in American Samoa. She described the Samoans as a peaceable people who showed no guilt in connection with ample sex during adolescence, a view that was in keeping with practices of Polynesian societies elsewhere. Some 55 years later, New Zealand anthropologist Derek Freeman published *Margaret Mead and Samoa: The Making and Unmaking of an Anthropological Myth,* in which he took issue with Mead's conclusions and argued instead that Samoans are jealous, violent, and not above committing rape. The truth may lie somewhere in between.

The Samoans share with other Polynesians the practice of raising some boys as girls, especially in families short of household help. These young boys dress as girls, do a girl's chores around the home, and often grow up to be transvestites. They are known in Samoan as *fa'afafines.*

RULES OF CONDUCT
You should be aware of several customs of this conservative society. A briefing paper prepared by the Pacific Basin Development Council for the American Samoan Office of Tourism gives some guidelines that may be helpful:

- In a Samoan home, don't talk to people while standing, and don't eat while walking around a village.
- Avoid stretching your legs straight out in front of you while sitting. If you can't fold them beneath you, then pull one of the floor mats over them.
- If you are driving through a village and spot a group of men sitting around a fale with their legs folded, it's probably a gathering of matais to discuss business. It's

> ### Tips Don't Wear Skimpy Clothing
>
> Don't wear bathing suits, short shorts, halter tops, hip-huggers, or other skimpy clothing away from the beach or hotel pool. Although shorts of respectable length are worn by young Samoan men and women in Apia and Pago Pago, it is considered very bad form for a Samoan to display his or her traditional tattoos, which cover many of them from knee to waist. Even though Samoan women went bare-breasted before the coming of Christianity, going topless is definitely forbidden today. Traditional Samoan dress is a wraparound lava-lava (sarong) that reaches below the knee on men and to the ankles on women.

polite not to drive past the meeting place. If going past on foot, don't carry a load on your shoulders or an open umbrella.

- If you arrive at a Samoan home during a prayer session, wait outside until the family is finished with its devotions. If you are already inside, you will be expected to share in the service. If you go to church, don't wear flowers.

- Whenever possible, consult Samoans about appropriate behavior and practices. They will appreciate your interest in fa'a Samoa and will take great pleasure in explaining their unique way of life.

Finally, should you be invited to stay overnight in a Samoan home, let them know at the beginning how long you will stay. Upon leaving, it's customary to give a small gift known as a *mea alofa*. This can be money—between $5 and $10 a day per person—but make sure your hosts understand that it is a gift, not a payment.

Most Samoan villages charge small **custom fees** to visitors who want to use their beaches or swim under their waterfalls. These usually are a dollar or two and are paid by local residents from other villages as well as by tourists.

In all cases, remember that almost everything and every place in the Samoas is owned by an aiga, and it's polite to ask permission of the nearby matai before crossing the property, using the beach, or visiting the waterfall. They will appreciate your courtesy in doing so.

4 The Samoan Language

Although English is an official language in both Samoa and American Samoa and is widely spoken, Samoan shares equal billing and is used by most people for everyday conversation. It is a Polynesian language that's somewhat similar to Tahitian, Tongan, and Cook Islands Maori, but with some important differences.

The vowels are pronounced not as in English (*ay, ee, eye, oh,* and *you*) but in the Roman fashion: *ah, ay, ee, oh,* and *oo* (as in kanga*roo*). All vowels are sounded, even if several of them appear next to each other. The village of Nu'uuli in American Samoa, for example, is pronounced "New-u-u-lee." The apostrophe that appears between the vowels indicates a glottal stop—a slight pause similar to the tiny break between "Oh-oh!" in English. The consonants *f, g, l, m, n, p, s, t,* and *v* are pronounced as in English, with one major exception: The letter *g* is pronounced like "ng." Therefore, aiga is pronounced "ah-*eeng*-ah." Pago Pago is pronounced "Pango Pango" as in "pong."

Here are some words that may help you win friends and influence your hosts:

English	Samoan	Pronunciation
hello	**talofa**	tah-*low*-fah
welcome	**afio mai**	ah-*fee*-oh my
good-bye	**tofa**	tow-*fah*
good health	**manuia**	mah-*new*-yah
please	**fa'amolemole**	fah-ah-*moly*-moly
man	**tamaloa**	tah-mah-*low*-ah
woman	**fafine**	fah-*fini*
transvestite	**fa'afafine**	fah-fah-*fini*
thank you	**fa'afetai**	fah-*fee*-tie
kava bowl	**tanoa**	tah-*no*-ah
good	**lelei**	lay-*lay*
bad	**leaga**	lay-*ang*-ah
happy/feast	**fiafia**	fee-ah-*fee*-ah
house	**fale**	fah-*lay*
wraparound skirt	**lava-lava**	lava-lava
dollar	**tala**	tah-*lah*
cent	**sene**	say-nay
high chief	**ali'i**	ah-*lee*-ee
small island	**motu**	mo-*too*
white person	**palagi**	pah-*lahng*-ee

Many words in Samoan—as in most modern Polynesian languages—have English roots. Take the word for corned beef, *pisupo* (pee-*soo*-poh). The first Western canned food to reach Samoa was pea soup. *Pisupo,* the Samoan version of pea soup, was adopted as the word for corned beef, which also came in cans. Corned beef was and still is much more popular than pea soup.

5 Visitor Information & Entry Requirements

VISITOR INFORMATION

The friendly staff of the **Samoa Tourism Authority,** P.O. Box 2272, Apia, Samoa (© **63-500;** fax 20-886; www.visitsamoa.ws), have free brochures, maps, and other publications available at their office in a handsome Samoan fale on the harbor side of Beach Road, east of the Town Clock. The bureau is open Monday to Friday 8am to 4:30pm, Sat 8am to noon.

The visitors bureau has offices in:

- **Australia:** Level 5, 12 Butler Rd., Hurtsville NSW 2220 (© **02/9324-5050;** fax 02/9603-7579; samoa@ozemail.com.au)
- **New Zealand:** Level 1, Samoa House, 283 Karangahape Rd. (P.O. Box 68423), Newton, Auckland (© **09/379-6138;** fax 09/379-8154; samoa@samoa.co.nz)
- **United Kingdom:** Marketing Services Ltd., High Holburn House, 52034 High Holburn, London VC1V 6RB (© **20/7242-3231;** fax 20/7243-3131; info@ super@ps.com)

The bell captain's desk at **Aggie Grey's Hotel & Bungalows** (see "Where to Stay on Upolu," later) also has brochures and other information. Young visitors gather at the **Travellers' Lounge** (© **22-144** or 29-629; www.greenturtletours.com), which provides information and Internet access as well as selling ice cream and Green Turtle Tours, which is headquartered here.

ENTRY REQUIREMENTS

Except for American Samoans, no visa or entry permit is required for visitors who intend to stay 60 days or less and who have a valid passport, a return or ongoing airline ticket, and a place to stay in Samoa. Those who want to stay longer must apply, before arrival, to the **Immigration Office,** Government of Samoa, P.O. Box 1861, Apia, Samoa (© **20-291;** www.samoaimmigration.gov.ws).

Vaccinations are not necessary unless you're arriving within 6 days of being in an infected area.

Customs exemptions for visitors are 200 cigarettes, 1 liter of liquor, and their personal effects. Firearms, ammunition, illegal drugs, and indecent publications are prohibited. Plants, live animals, or products of that nature, including fruits, seeds, and soil, will be confiscated unless you have prior permission from the Samoa government's Department of Agriculture and Forest. All incoming baggage is X-rayed.

6 Money

Samoa uses the *tala* (pronounced tah-*lah;* the Samoans' way of saying dollar), which is broken down into 100 *sene* (cents). Although most people will refer to them as dollars and cents when speaking to visitors, you can avoid potential confusion by making sure they mean dollars and not talas. The official abbreviation for the currency is SAT, but I have used the more common **S$** in this chapter. Samoa's major hotels and some other firms quote their prices in U.S. dollars. U.S. dollar prices are given in this book as **US$.**

The **exchange rate** has been about S$3 for each US$1 (S$1=US33¢) for several years, so I have used that rate for the conversions in this chapter. You can find the present rate on **www.xe.com**.

HOW TO GET LOCAL CURRENCY   **ANZ Bank, Westpac Bank Samoa,** and **National Bank of Samoa** have offices on Beach Road in Apia. ANZ and Westpac both have ATMs in Apia, and ANZ has one at Faleolo Airport and one at Salelologa on Savai'i. **GlobelEX** will exchange currency and travelers checks at its office on Beach Road. Banking hours are Monday to Wednesday 9am to 3pm, Thursday and Friday 8:30am to 3pm. Westpac and GlobelEX are open on Saturday 8 to 11am for foreign currency transactions.

> **Tips Get Rid of Your *Talas***
>
> Since the Samoan tala is virtually worthless outside the independent nation of Samoa (and that includes American Samoa), don't even think of buying any before you get here. Be sure to change your leftover talas back to another currency before leaving Samoa. Use them to pay your hotel bill or change them at the airports.

The banks also have offices in the baggage claim area at Faleolo Airport, which are open when international flights arrive and depart, and there's an ATM outside in the main concourse.

CREDIT CARDS   American Express, Visa, MasterCard, and Diner's Club credit cards are accepted by the major hotels and car-rental firms, and many restaurants

The Samoan Tala & U.S. Dollar

Usually S$1 = approximately US33¢ (or US$1 = approximately S$3), the rate of exchange used to calculate the U.S. dollar prices given in this chapter. This rate may change by the time you visit, so use the following table only as a guide:

S$	US$	S$	US$
.25	.08	15.00	5.00
.50	.17	20.00	6.67
.75	.25	25.00	8.33
1.00	.33	30.00	10.00
2.00	.67	35.00	11.66
3.00	1.00	40.00	13.32
4.00	1.33	45.00	15.00
5.00	1.67	50.00	16.65
6.00	2.00	75.00	25.00
7.00	2.33	100.00	33.00
8.00	2.66	125.00	42.00
9.00	3.00	150.00	50.00
10.00	3.33	200.00	66.00

accept MasterCard and Visa. Discover cards are not accepted. When traveling outside Apia and to Savai'i, you should carry enough cash to cover your anticipated expenses.

7 When to Go

THE CLIMATE

The Samoas enjoy a humid tropical climate, with lots of intense sunshine, even during the wet season (Dec–May). Average daily high temperatures range from 83°F (28°C) in the drier and somewhat cooler months of June through September to 86°F (30°C) from December to April, when midday can be hot and sticky. Evenings are usually in the comfortable 70s (21°C–26°C) all year-round.

EVENTS

Duffers from around the South Pacific descend on Apia in early January for the **Head of State's Birthday** celebrations, which include a golf tournament. **Easter Week** sees

Impressions

Day after day the sun flamed; night after night the moon beaconed, or the stars paraded their lustrous regimen. I was aware of a spiritual change, or perhaps rather a molecular reconstitution. My bones were sweeter to me. I had come home to my own climate, and looked back with pity on those damp and wintry zones, miscalled the temperate . . . I am browner than the berry: only my trunk and the aristocratic spot on which I sit retain the vile whiteness of the north.

—Robert Louis Stevenson, 1891

> **Fun Fact Rise of the *Palolo***
>
> Dawn after the full moon in October sees thousands of Samoans out on the reefs with buckets to snare the wiggling *palolo,* a coral worm which comes out to mate only then. Actually, the rear ends of the worms break off and swim to the surface, spewing eggs and sperm in a reproductive frenzy which last only a few hours. Pacific islanders consider the slimy palolo to be their caviar.

various religious observances, including hymn singing and dramas. **Independence Day** in early June features dances, outrigger-canoe races, marching competitions, and horse racing. The country's biggest event is the **Teuila Festival** 🐦🐦 during the first week of September (www.teuilafestival.ws). It features a variety of entertainment, including canoe races, dance competitions, traditional games, a floral parade, handicraft demonstrations, and the **Miss Samoa** beauty pageant. The second Sunday in October is observed as **White Sunday,** during which children go to church dressed in white, lead the services, and are honored at family feasts. **Christmas week** is celebrated with great gusto.

The **Samoa Tourism Authority** posts the precise dates and the schedules for these events on its website, **www.visitsamoa.ws**.

HOLIDAYS

Offices and schools are closed January 1 and January 2 for New Year's; Good Friday and Easter Monday; April 25 as Anzac Day, to remember those who died in the two World Wars; the Monday after the second Sunday in May as Mothers' Day of Samoa; June 1 through June 3, for the annual Independence Celebrations; the first Monday in August as Labour Day; the Monday after the second Sunday in October, in honor of the preceding White Sunday; Christmas Day; and December 26 as Boxing Day.

8 Getting There & Getting Around

GETTING THERE

Air New Zealand has a weekly nonstop flight between Los Angeles and Apia. It also has non-stop and one-stop (in Tonga) service from Auckland. **Polynesian Blue,** a joint venture between the Samoan government and Virgin Blue, connects the country with Auckland and Sydney. **Air Pacific** flies between Apia and Fiji. **Polynesian Airlines** flies a small, propeller-driven plane between Samoa and Tonga (it's a long, noisy flight compared to jet aircraft). A less direct way to get to Apia is on **Hawaiian Airlines,** which flies between several West Coast cities and Honolulu, thence to Pago Pago in American Samoa. Connections to Samoa can then be made on **Polynesian Airlines'** small planes. See "Getting There & Getting Around" in chapter 2 for details.

Flights into and out of the Samoas are often packed with Samoans leaving and returning to the islands, so reserve a seat as soon as possible.

The **Samoa Shipping Corporation** (🕭 **20-935;** www.samoashipping.com) operates a ferry between Apia and Pago Pago in American Samoa. It usually departs Apia on Wednesday at midnight, arriving in Pago Pago at 8am on Thursday. The return voyage departs Pago Pago at 4pm Thursday, arriving at Apia at midnight. Fares range from S$75 (US$25) for a seat to S$100 (US$33) for a cabin.

The Samoa Islands

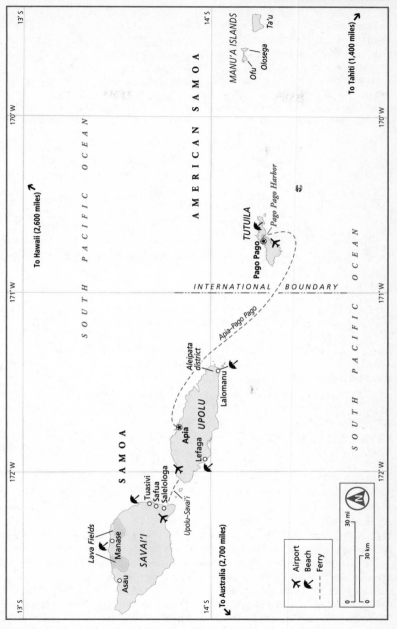

ARRIVING & DEPARTING

All international flights arrive at **Faleolo Airport,** on the northwest corner of Upolu about 32km (19 miles) from Apia. There are duty-free shops and two currency exchange windows in the baggage claim area, or you can wait until you've cleared Customs and use ANZ Bank's ATM in the main concourse.

Transportation from the Faleolo Airport is by taxi or by buses which meet all international flights (you will be astounded by how many passengers and their baggage can be crammed into one of these vehicles). The bus ride officially costs S$12 (US$4) each way. The government-regulated taxi fare into town is S$40 (US$13), but make sure you and the driver agree on the fare.

Shuttle buses also transport passengers from the Apia hotels to Faleolo Airport for departing international flights. They arrive at the hotels at least 2 hours before departure time. Be sure to tell your hotel what flight you are leaving on; otherwise, the bus could leave you behind.

Everyone over 12 years old must pay a S$40 (US$13) **departure tax** before leaving the country. Get your boarding pass and pay in Samoan currency at one of the banks in the main concourse, or after clearing Immigration if the banks aren't open.

There is no bank in the departure lounge, so change your leftover talas before clearing Immigration. Remember, Samoan currency cannot be exchanged outside the country, even in American Samoa.

GETTING AROUND
BY PLANE

Polynesian Airlines (© **800/264-0823** or 22-737; www.polynesianairlines.com) flies several times a day between Faleolo Airport and Maota Airstrip, near Salelologa on the southeastern corner of Savai'i. The round-trip Faleolo–Savai'i fares is about S$95 (US$31).

BY FERRY

Two passenger and automobile ferries shuttle between Mulifanua Wharf on Upolu and Salelologa on Savai'i every 2 hours Monday to Saturday from 6am to 4pm, Sunday 10am to 4pm. The *Lady Samoa* is larger, faster, and more comfortable than its smaller, open-air companion, with which it alternates trips. Plan on about 90 minutes each way. The one-way fare is S$9 (US$3). Local buses leave regularly from the Apia market and pass Mulifanua Wharf on their way to Pasi O Le Vaa. Taxi fare to the wharf is S$50 (US$17); bus fare is S$2 (US67¢). For more information, ask at the visitors bureau or contact the **Samoa Shipping Corporation** (© **20-935;** www.samoa shipping.com), on Beach Road opposite the main wharf.

BY RENTAL CAR

Budget Rent-A-Car (© **800/527-0700** or 20-561; www.budget.com) is the only international company with an agency here.

The largest and best firm here is **Funway Rentals,** on Beach Road opposite the main wharf (© **22-045;** fax 25-008; www.funwayrentals.ws). A variety of vehicles start at about S$150 (US$50) a day, including insurance and unlimited kilometers. Owner Sonny Ah Kuoi has almost as many deals as he does cars, however, so give him a call or just walk in. "We're for people who hate to waste money," he says.

If Funway doesn't have a vehicle available, check with **Apia Rentals** (© **24-244**), **Blue Pacific Car Hire** (© **22-668**), **Juliana's Rentals** (© **23-009**), **Samoana Rentals** (© **28-460**), and **Southpac Rentals** (© **22-074**).

The car-rental firms will arrange to pick you up at Faleolo Airport, usually at an extra charge, if you have reservations. Insurance policies do not cover damage to the vehicles' undercarriages, which may occur on some rocky, unpaved roads. Depending on your own insurance policies, you might also want to buy optional personal accident coverage, which covers you and your passengers.

The main roads on both islands are paved and in good condition, but only Funway Rentals will allow you to drive on unpaved roads or take a rented vehicle on the ferry to Savai'i. Don't count on buying gasoline outside Apia.

DRIVING RULES   You **drive on the right-hand side of the road,** as in the U.S., Canada, and Europe. You must stop for pedestrians in crosswalks and not exceed the speed limits of 35 mph on the open road or 25 mph in Apia and the villages.

Visitors are required to get a local **driver's license** from the Ministry of Transport (© **21-611**), on Beach Road opposite the Old Apia Market. There is a S$10 (US$3.35) fee. Bring your home license. No test is required.

BY BUS

Green Turtle Tours (© **22-144** or 29-629; www.greenturtletours.com) sends a 15-seat van around Upolu and another around Savai'i each day. Timed to connect to the ferries between the two islands, they depart Apia on Upolu and Salelologa on Savai'i at 8am and circle each island, clockwise on Upolu, counterclockwise on Savai'i. Each circuit takes all day. The van's primary duty is to haul backpackers between beach fale complexes, but you can make a day tour for S$90 (US$30), or buy a pass permitting unlimited rides for S$170 (US$57). Call or drop by the Green Turtles' headquarters at the **Traveller's Lounge** on Beach Road west of Aggie Grey's Hotel & Bungalows.

Samoa has a system of "aiga buses" which take passengers around the islands. The main **bus station** is behind the Old Apia Market on Beach Road, but the buses stop at the New Market before leaving town. They have the names of their villages written on the front. The first buses usually leave their villages between 5 and 7am, with the last departure between 2 and 2:30pm. They turn around in Apia and go back to the villages. The last departure from town is about 4:30pm. They do not run on Saturday afternoon or Sunday.

The Samoa Tourism Authority has schedules and fares. Here are the destinations most often visited, followed by the names of the village buses that go there:

To Robert Louis Stevenson Museum: Vaoala, Si'umu.
To Sinalei and Coconut Beach resorts: Si'umu.
To Fagali'i Airport: Fagali'i-uta.
To Piula Cave Pool: Falefa or Saoluafata.
To Return to Paradise Beach: Lefaga.

To Papase'a Sliding Rocks: Se'ese'e.

To Faleolo Airport: Faleolo, Pasi o le Vaa.

To Muliafanua Wharf: Pasi o le Vaa.

The Si'umu bus is the only one that goes all the way to the south coast via the Cross Island Road.

In general, 50 sene (US15¢) will take you around Apia and into the hills above the town. The maximum fare is about S$4 (US$1.35) to the most distant villages and to Mulifanua Wharf, where the Savai'i ferries land on Upolu's western end (see "Savai'i," later in this chapter).

BY TAXI

Apia has no shortage of taxis. The easiest way to get one is to hail a cab along Beach Road. You can also ask your hotel desk, or call **Central Taxi** (© 23-600), **Silver Star Taxis** (© 21-770), **Marlboro Taxis** (© 20-808), **Vailima Taxis** (© 22-380), **Heini Taxis** (© 24-431), and **Town Taxis** (© 21-600). They have stands at the Town Clock on Beach Road and nearby on Vaea Street. **Town Taxis** also has a stand at the airport.

The cabs do not have meters, but official **fares** are posted at the Samoa Tourism Authority. In general, S$2 (US65¢) will take you around Apia and its hotels. One-way fares are S$6 (US$2) from Apia to Vailima; S$40 (US$13) to Faleolo Airport; S$50 (US$17) to Mulifanua Wharf; S$35 (US$12) to Coconuts Beach Club and Sinalei Reef resorts; S$46 (US$15) to Lefaga and Return to Paradise Beach; and S$22 (US$7) to Piula College and Cave Pool.

FAST FACTS: Samoa

American Express There is no American Express representative in Samoa.

Baggage Storage The hotels will store your extra gear for free.

Bookstores **Aggie's Gift Shop** (© 22-880), next to Aggie Grey's Hotel & Bungalows on Beach Road, carries books on Samoa and the South Pacific and a few paperback novels.

Business Hours Most shops and government offices are open Monday to Friday from 8am to noon and 1 to 4:30pm, Saturday from 8am to noon. Except for the major hotels, the only businesses open on Sunday are the scores of mom-and-pop grocery shops in Apia and some villages.

Camera/Film **Image Lab,** on Convent Street west of Vaea Street (© 28-053).

Clothing Lightweight, informal summer clothing is best throughout the year, although a light sweater or wrap could come in handy for evening wear from June through September. Men can wear shorts and shirts almost anywhere, but women should stick to modest, knee- and shoulder-covering dresses away from the hotels and should never wear bathing suits or skimpy clothing away from the beach or pool. Topless or nude bathing is outlawed. Outside Apia most Samoans still wear wraparound lava-lavas, which come well below the knees of men and to the ankles on women.

Drugstores **Samoa Pharmacy** (© 22-595) and **Apia Pharmacy** (© 22-703) are both on Beach Road west of the Town Clock.

Electricity Electricity in Samoa is 240 volts, 50 cycles, and most plugs have angled prongs like those used in New Zealand and Australia. Aggie Grey's Hotel & Bungalows and the Kitano Tusitala Hotel supply 110-volt current for electric shavers only; you need a converter and adapter plugs for other American appliances.

Embassies/Consulates The **U.S. Embassy** (© **21-631**) is in the ABC House on Beach Road west of the Town Clock. New Zealand and Australia both have high commissions here.

E-mail You can check your e-mail at **CSL,** at Vaea and Convent streets (© **24-149**); **Lesamoa.net,** across the street in the Lotemanu Centre (© **20-926**); and **Traveller's Lounge,** on Beach Road west of Aggie Grey's Hotel & Bungalows (© **22-144**). Expect to pay about S$2 (US65¢) for 10 minutes.

Emergencies/Police The emergency phone numbers are © **995** for police, © **994** for fire, and © **996** for an ambulance. The **police station** (© **22-222**) is on Ifi'ifi Street, inland from the prime minister's office.

Eyeglasses Try the **National Hospital** (see "Healthcare," below).

Gambling There are no casinos in Samoa, but you can play the local lottery at its office on Vaea Street.

Hairdressers/Barbers **Double D'z Unisex Salon** is at Aggie Grey's Hotel & Bungalows (© **23-277**).

Healthcare The best doctors are at the **MedCen Private Hospital,** a modern facility on the Cross Island Road (© **26-519**). The government-run **National Hospital,** on Ifi'ifi Street in Apia (© **21-212**), has an outpatient clinic open daily from 8am to noon and from 1 to 4:30pm. Ask your hotel staff to recommend a dentist if you need one.

Insects There are no dangerous insects in Samoa, and the plentiful mosquitoes do not carry malaria. Bring a good insect repellent with you, and consider burning mosquito coils at night.

Libraries **Nelson Memorial Public Library,** on Beach Road at the Town Clock (© **21-028**), is open Monday to Thursday 9am to 4:30pm, Friday 8am to 4pm, Saturday 8:30am to noon.

Liquor Laws The legal drinking age is 18. Except for a prohibition of Sunday sale of alcoholic beverages outside the hotels or licensed restaurants, the laws are fairly liberal. Bars outside the hotels can stay open Monday to Saturday until midnight. Spirits, wine, and beer are sold at private liquor stores.

Maps The **Samoa Tourism Authority** distributes a one-sheet collection of maps of Upolu, Savai'i, and Apia town. See "Visitor Information & Entry Requirements," earlier in this chapter.

Newspapers/Magazines The daily **Samoa Observer** (www.samoaobserver.ws) carries local and world news.

Post Office The main SamoaTel post office is on Beach Road, east of the Town Clock (© **23-480**). Hours are Monday to Friday 9am to 4:30pm.

Radio/TV Samoa has two broadcast television stations. Many homes on Upolu's north shore can receive the American Samoan channels, one of which has commercial shows, the other Public Broadcasting System programs and live news from the United States. The government also operates two AM radio stations, on which most programming is in Samoan. The world news is rebroadcast from Radio Australia and Radio New Zealand several times a day. Three privately owned FM stations broadcast lots of music.

Safety Although street crimes are rare here, remember that the communal property system still prevails in the Samoas, and items such as cameras and bags left unattended may disappear. Women should not wander alone on deserted beaches. Samoans take the Sabbath seriously, and there have been reports of local residents tossing stones at tourists who drive through some villages on Sunday. If you plan to tour by rental car, do it during the week.

Taxes Samoa imposes a 12.5% General Services Tax, which is included in restaurant and bar bills and is added to the cost of some other items, including rental cars, but be sure to ask if your hotel has included the tax in its room rates. Also, an airport departure tax of S$40 (US$13) is levied on all passengers over 12 years of age leaving Samoa from Faleolo Airport. No tax is imposed on domestic flights or on the ferry to Pago Pago.

Telephone/Fax International calls can be directly dialed into Samoa from most parts of the world. The international country code is **685.**

SamoaTel (www.samoatel.ws) operates both the post office and the landline phone system here. It has pay telephones around Apia and in post offices in the villages. You will need a **prepaid phonecard** to make calls; buy them at post offices and most small shops. A digital readout will tell you how much money you have left on your card. Station-to-station calls to North America cost about S$4.50 (US$1.50) per minute. Calls to Australia and New Zealand are about half that amount.

The number for directory assistance is ✆ **933**; for the international operator, ✆ **900**; for international directory assistance, ✆ **910**; and for the domestic long-distance operator, ✆ **920.**

Telecom Samoa (✆ **26-081**; www.telecomsamoa.ws), in the Lotumanu Centre at the corner of Vaea and Convent streets, rents cell phones for S$5.60 (US$1.85) a day, but you must buy prepaid time cards to use them. Samoa is switching from analog to GSM, so you will be able to buy a prepaid SIM card for your unlocked GSM phone. See "The 21st Century Traveler," in chapter 2.

Time Local time in Samoa is 11 hours behind GMT. That means it's 3 hours behind Pacific Standard Time (4 hr. behind during daylight saving time). If it's noon standard time in California and 3pm in New York, it's 9am in Apia. During daylight saving time in California and New York, it's 8am in Samoa. Samoa is east of the international date line; therefore, it shares the same date with North America and is 1 day behind Tonga, Fiji, Australia, and New Zealand. Remember that if you are going on to those countries or will be arriving in Samoa from one of them.

Tipping Tipping is discouraged as being contrary to the traditional way of life. One exception is the practice of throwing money on the dance floor to show appreciation of a show well performed.

Water All tap water should be boiled before drinking. Safe bottled water is produced locally and is available at most grocery stores.

Weights/Measures Samoa is officially on the metric system, but in their everyday lives, many residents still calculate distances by the British system used in American Samoa and in the United States. Speed limits are posted in miles per hour, and the speedometers of many local vehicles (most of which have the steering wheels on the left side, in the American and European fashion) show both miles per hour and kilometers per hour.

9 Exploring Apia & the Rest of Upolu

The town of Apia sits midway along the north coast of Upolu, which makes it a centrally located base from which to explore the main island. The Cross Island Road runs 23km (14 miles) from town, across the range of extinct volcanoes that form Upolu, thereby bringing the south coast within easy reach of town.

THE TOP ATTRACTION

Robert Louis Stevenson Museum & Grave ✸✸✸   When Robert Louis Stevenson and his wife, Fanny, decided to stay in Samoa in 1889 (see the "Teller of Tales" box, earlier in this chapter), they bought 314 acres of virgin land on the slopes of Mount Vaea above Apia and named the estate **Vailima**—or "Five Waters"—because five streams crossed the property. They cleared about 8 acres and lived there in a small shack for nearly a year. The U.S. historian Henry Adams dropped in unannounced one day in 1890 and found them dressed in lava-lavas and doing dirty work about their hovel. To Adams, the couple's living conditions were repugnant. Their Rousseauian existence didn't last long, however, for in 1891 they built the first part of this magnificent mansion.

When it was completed, the big house had five bedrooms, a library, a ballroom large enough to accommodate 100 dancers, and the only fireplace in Samoa. The Stevensons shipped 72 tons of furniture from England, all of which was hauled the 3 miles from Apia on sleds pulled by bullocks. A piano sat in one corner of the great hall, in a glass case to protect it from Samoa's humidity. Among their possessions were a Rodin nude presented to Stevenson by the sculptor himself, a damask tablecloth from Queen Victoria, and a sugar bowl used by both Robert Burns and Sir Walter Scott.

The Stevensons' lifestyle matched their surroundings. Oysters were shipped on ice from New Zealand, Bordeaux wine was brought by the cask from France and bottled

Moments Expecting R. L. S. to Walk In

Anyone who has ever put words on paper or a computer screen will feel a sense of awe when reading Robert Louis Stevenson's requiem carved on his grave up on Mount Vaea overlooking Apia. The climb isn't easy, but it's worth it if you have a single literary bone in your body. The museum is one of the finest literary shrines I've ever seen: You almost expect Stevenson to walk in at any second, so much does Vailima look like it did when he was alive.

at Vailima, and 1840 vintage Madeira was poured on special occasions. They dressed formally for dinner every evening—except for their bare feet—and were served by Samoans dressed in tartan lava-lavas, in honor of the great author's Scottish origins.

Vailima and this lavish lifestyle baffled the Samoans. As far as they could tell, writing was not labor; therefore, Stevenson had no visible way of earning a living. Yet all this money rolled in, which meant to them that Stevenson must be a man of much *mana*, the mysterious power which Polynesians believed descended directly from heaven to their chiefs (the higher the chief, the more the mana). He was also a master at one of their favorite pastimes—storytelling—and he took interest in their own stories, as well as their customs, language, and politics. When the followers of the defeated Mataafa were released from prison, they built a road from Apia to Vailima in appreciation for Stevenson's support of their unsuccessful struggle against the Germans. And when he died in 1894, they cut the "Road of the Loving Hearts" to his grave on Mount Vaea overlooking Vailima.

> **Impressions**
>
> *Our place is in a deep cleft of Vaea Mountain, some six hundred feet above the sea, embowered in a forest, which is our strangling enemy, and which we combat with axes and dollars.*
>
> —Robert Louis Stevenson, 1890

Stevenson's wife, Fanny, died in California in 1914, and her ashes were brought back to Vailima and buried at the foot of Robert's grave. Her Samoan name, Aolele, is engraved on a bronze plaque.

Samoa's head of state lived in Vailima until hurricanes severely damaged the mansion in 1990 and 1991. Since then, an extraordinary renovation has returned it to its appearance when Stevenson lived here—without the Rodin. A sitting room matches exactly that seen in a photo made of Fanny on a chair. Another photo of Stevenson dictating is hung in his library, where he stood at the time.

The "Road of the Loving Hearts" leading to **Stevenson's Grave** passes a lovely cascade that Stevenson turned into a swimming pool. A short, steep trail to the grave takes about 30 strenuous minutes; a longer but easier path takes about an hour. Mount Vaea is best climbed in the cool of early morning.

Vailima, on the Cross Island Rd., 5km/3 miles south of Apia. (C) 20-798. Admission S$15 (US$5) adults, S$5 (US$1.65) children under 11. Mon–Fri 9am–3:30pm, Sat 8am–noon. Guided tours Mon–Fri 1pm.

A STROLL THROUGH APIA

Like most South Pacific towns, Samoa's capital and only town has expanded from one small Samoan village to include adjacent settlements and an area of several square miles, all of which is now known collectively as Apia, the name of the village where Europeans first settled. The old villages have given their names to the many neighborhoods of the sprawling metropolitan area, and much to the confusion of us visitors, the locals identify locations by neighborhood names instead of streets. The Apia area now has a population in excess of 50,000.

Most points of interest lie along **Beach Road,** the broad avenue curving along the harbor. A waterfront promenade extends along one side and churches, government buildings, and businesses line the other.

We start our walking tour of downtown at **Aggie Grey's Hotel & Bungalows,** on the banks of the Vaisigano River. This famous hotel and its founder are stories unto

Apia

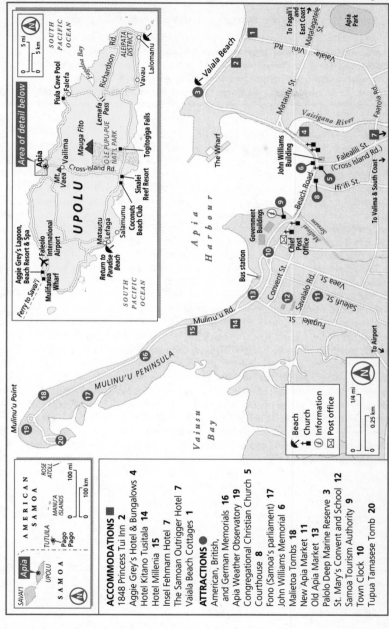

ACCOMMODATIONS ■

1848 Princess Tui Inn **2**
Aggie Grey's Hotel & Bungalows **4**
Hotel Kitano Tusitala **14**
Hotel Millenia **15**
Insel Fehmarn Hotel **7**
The Samoan Outrigger Hotel **7**
Vaiala Beach Cottages **1**

ATTRACTIONS ●

American, British,
  and German Memorials **16**
Apia Weather Observatory **19**
Congregational Christian Church **5**
Courthouse **8**
Fono (Samoa's parliament) **17**
John Williams Memorial **6**
Malietoa Tombs **18**
New Apia Market **11**
Old Apia Market **13**
Palolo Deep Marine Reserve **3**
St. Mary's Convent and School **12**
Samoa Tourism Authority **9**
Town Clock **10**
Tupua Tamasese Tomb **20**

> **Tips Start Early By Watching the Police Band Parade**
>
> Apia can be brutally hot at midday, so the best time to walk around it is right
> after the **Samoa Police Brass Band** marches along Beach Road (daily between
> 7:30 and 8am) to Government House, where it raises the national flag. It's
> worth watching the cops in their white helmets, light blue uniforms, and lava-
> lavas. If you take photos, don't get between the band and the flagpole.

themselves, which are recounted in "Where to Stay on Upolu," later in this chapter.
From Aggie's, head west, or to the left as you face the harbor.

The two large churches on the left are both Protestant, legacies of the Rev. John
Williams, for whom the modern high-rise office building at the corner of Falealili
Road is named. On the waterfront across Beach Road stands the **John Williams
Memorial** to this missionary who brought Christianity to Samoa and many more
South Pacific islands. Williams's bones are reputedly buried beneath the clapboard
Congregational Christian Church, directly across Beach Road from the memorial.
The missionary was killed and eaten on Erromango in what now is Vanuatu; the story
has it that his bones were recovered and buried here.

The clapboard, colonial-style **Courthouse** at the corner of Ifi'ifi Street formerly
housed the Supreme Court and Prime Minister's office, before they moved into the
big high-rise buildings across the road. In colonial times, it was headquarters of the
New Zealand trusteeship administration and site of the Mau Movement demonstration and shootings in 1929.

Upstairs in the Courthouse, the small but interesting **Museum of Samoa** (© 63-
444) is worth a brief look. It's open Monday to Friday noon to 4pm. Admission is free.

When he came to Samoa, Robert Louis Stevenson first stayed in the old clapboard
building where **Sails Restaurant and Bar** now makes its home. With several other
bars and restaurants, this block is the center of dining and drinking in Apia. The
Marist Brothers' Primary School is on the banks of Mulivai Stream. Across the bridge
stands **Mulivai Catholic Cathedral,** begun in 1885 and completed some 20 years
later. Farther along, the imposing **Matafele Methodist Church** abuts the stores in the
Wesley Arcade. According to a monument across Beach Road, Tongan Chief Saivaaia
brought Methodism to Samoa in 1835.

The remains of the German warship *Adler* are buried under the reclaimed land,
now the site of two huge, fale-topped government office buildings, built in the mid-
1990s with foreign aid from China. On the water side of Beach Road stands a memorial to the Samoans who fought alongside the New Zealanders during World War II.

The center of modern Apia's business district is the **Town Clock,** the World War I
memorial at the foot of Vaea Street. Across the street, the **Chan Mow & Co.** building is a fine example of late South Seas colonial architecture; its arches and red-tile
roof make it look almost Spanish. Between the clock and the water stands a large
Samoan fale known as **Pulenu'u House,** where local residents can be seen lounging
or eating their lunches. Facing the clock, **Nelson Memorial Public Library** is named
for Olaf Nelson, son of a Swedish father and Samoan mother. Olaf Nelson was exiled
to New Zealand in 1928 for his leadership role in the Mau Movement.

Continuing west on Beach Road, you come to the sprawling **Old Apia Market.**
Once the vegetable market, this large covered space is now home to flea-market stalls

where you can find items ranging from sandals to toothpaste. One area is devoted to handicraft vendors, and you can stop and watch local women weaving *pandanus* mats, hats, and handbags. This is a good place to shop for woodcarvings and *tapa* cloth (called *siapo* here; see "Shopping," later). I haven't had the stomach for such local fare since my days as a young backpacker, but the food stalls along the market's water side are the cheapest (and dirtiest) places in town to get a meal.

Fugalei Street, which leaves Beach Road across from the market, goes to the airport and the west coast. Walk down it a block, and turn left and go east on Convent Street past picturesque **St. Mary's Convent and School.** At the next corner, turn right on Saleufi Street and walk inland 2 blocks to the **New Apia Market,** a modern, tin-roofed pavilion where Samoan families sell a wide variety of tropical fruits and vegetables, all of which have the prices clearly marked (there is no bargaining). Like everywhere else in the islands, the market is busiest on Saturday morning.

THE MULINU'U PENINSULA

Beyond the market, Beach Road becomes Mulinu'u Road, which runs about a mile to the end of **Mulinu'u Peninsula,** a low arm separating Apia Harbour to the east from shallow Vaiusu Bay on the west. About halfway out on the peninsula stand the **American, British, and German Memorials,** one dedicated to the German sailors who died in the 1889 hurricane, one dedicated to the British and American sailors who were drowned during that fiasco, and one to commemorate the raising of the German flag in 1900.

The Mulinu'u Peninsula is home of the **Fono,** Samoa's parliament. The new Fono building sits opposite a memorial to Samoa's independence, the two separated by a wide lawn. The Fono's old home is next to the road in the same park. A tomb on the lawn holds the remains of Iosefa Mataafa, one of the paramount chiefs.

Beyond the Apia Yacht Club stand the tombs of the Malietoa family of paramount chiefs, which makes this the **burial grounds** of Samoa's incumbent "royalty." At the end of the paved road, a dirt path goes left past a gravel quarry to the **tombs** of Tuimalaeali'ifano and Tupua Tamasese, two other paramount chiefs. At the end of the peninsula you'll find the **Apia Weather Observatory,** originally built by the Germans in 1902 (they apparently learned a costly lesson from the unpredicted, disastrous hurricane of 1889).

EXPLORING UPOLU

To travel along the roads of Upolu away from Apia is to see Polynesia relatively unchanged from the days before the Europeans arrived in the islands. Bring your swimming gear, for you'll also visit some of the South Pacific's most stunningly beautiful beaches.

⟨Moments⟩ Walking in Apia

A Hollywood set designer would be hard-pressed to top Apia as an old South Seas town. I love to stroll along the promenade fringing the perfect half-moon curve of Beach Road and let the old churches and clapboard government buildings tell me how things used to be. Locals fishing or idling the time away along the seawall tell me what's going on today.

> **Tips Don't Leave Apia Without a Map**
>
> If you're driving around the island, be sure to bring a map, available from the Samoa Tourism Authority (see "Visitor Information & Entry Requirements," earlier in this chapter).

THE NORTHEAST COAST: APIA TO ALEIPATA

One of the most popular sightseeing tours makes a loop from Apia to the long, magnificent white beaches of Aleipata District on Upolu's eastern end. Most of Upolu is a volcanic shield that slopes gently to the sea, but because the eastern portion is older—and therefore more eroded and rugged than the central and western areas—this spot has the island's most dramatic scenery.

The East Coast Road follows the shore for 26km (16 miles) to the village of Falefa, skirting the lagoon and black-sand surf beaches at Lauli'i and Solosolo. Look for **Piula College,** a Methodist school on a promontory overlooking the sea about 3.3km (2 miles) before Falefa. Turn in at the playing field and drive around to the school on the right. Park there and follow the steps down to the freshwater **Piula Cave Pool** 🐟🐟. Bring snorkeling gear to swim through an underwater opening at the back of the pool into a second chamber. The cave pool is open from 8am to 4:30pm Monday through Saturday; admission is S$3 (US$1). There is a rudimentary changing room for visitors. No alcoholic beverages are allowed on the grounds.

Situated to the left of the bridge beyond Falefa village, **Falefa Falls** are especially impressive during the rainy season. The road then climbs toward 285m (950 ft.) **Le Mafa Pass** in the center of the island, with some great views back toward the sea. Another rugged, winding road to the left just before the pass dead-ends at picturesque **Fagaloa Bay,** once a volcanic crater that exploded to seaward, leaving a mountain-clad bay cutting deep into the island. Although paved, the Fagaloa Bay road is steep and winding, so drive with caution.

Once you're over the pass, the main road crosses a bridge. Just beyond, an unmarked road goes to the right and cuts through the forests down to the south coast. We will come back this way, road conditions permitting, but for now go straight ahead on the **Richardson Road.** Once a bush path, this paved road crosses a refreshingly cool high plateau and skirts **Afulilo Lake,** formed by the country's hydroelectric dam.

LALOMANU BEACH 🐟🐟🐟

From Afulilo Lake, the road gently descends into **Aleipata,** an enormously picturesque district. As you turn the corner to the south coast, stop at the overlook on the small promontory overlooking **Lalomanu Beach** 🐟🐟🐟, one of the most gorgeous in the South Pacific. Your photos from here will be among the best you'll take in Samoa, for the view includes a clifflike escarpment behind a narrow shelf of land bordered by a long, white-sand beach. Four small islands offshore enliven the view, and on a clear day you can see the jagged blue outline of American Samoa on the horizon.

There's not enough space at Lalomanu for a village, but a collection of rustic **beach fales,** available for camping, stands on these sands (see "Beach *Fales* at Aleipata," later in this chapter).

Keep going along the southeast shore to Vavau village, where the paved Le Mafa Pass Road begins (don't take the road to the left; it dead-ends at a river). Le Mafa Pass Road climbs steadily uphill to a viewpoint overlooking 53m (175 ft.) **Sopo'aga Falls** ☆. The villagers have built a small park on a cliff overlooking the deep and narrow gorge, complete with picnic tables and toilets. They charge S$5 (US$1.65) per vehicle, but that's a small price to pay for this view.

THE CROSS ISLAND ROAD

The Cross Island Road runs for 23km (14 miles) from the John Williams Building on Beach Road in Apia to the village of Si'umu on the south coast. Along the way it passes first the Robert Louis Stevenson Museum at Vailima and then the **Malololeilei Scenic View,** a park on the eastern side of the road. Pull off here and take the short walks to views over Apia, the sea, and a waterfall. Back on the road, you'll later pass the modern, nine-sided **House of Worship,** one of six Baha'i Faith temples in the world. Open for meditation and worship, the temple was dedicated in 1984. An information center outside the temple makes available materials about the Baha'i Faith.

After passing the temple, the road winds through cool, rolling pastures. Near the top of the island, a rough road leads off the Cross Island Road westward to the new **Lake Lanoto'o National Park.** The 400-hectare (1,000-acre) preserve is home to rare endemic bird species, including the red-headed parrot finch and the crimson-crowned fruit dove. Lake Lanoto'o, Samoa's largest lake, is filled with goldfish introduced by German settlers in the 19th century. Unless and until the often muddy trail is improved, it will take at least an hour to hike into the park, a feat best done with a guide (see "Watersports, Golf & Other Outdoor Activities," below). For more information contact the Ministry of Natural Resources and Environment (☎ **23-800;** www.mnre.gov.ws).

On your way down to the south coast, watch on the right for a parking area overlooking **Papapai-tai Waterfalls,** which plunge 90m (300 ft.) into one of the gorges that streams have cut into central Upolu's volcanic shield. Of the many waterfalls on Upolu, Papapai-tai is the most easily seen.

THE SOUTHWEST COAST ☆☆

A left turn at the end of the Cross Island Road in Si'umu village on the south coast leads to **O Le Pupu-Pue National Park** and the **Togitogiga National Forest** ☆. The park contains the best remaining tropical rain forest on Upolu, but you'll have to hike into the valley to reach it. Some 51 species of wildlife live in the park: 42 species of birds, 5 of mammals, and 4 of lizards. Lovely **Togitogiga Falls** is a short walk from the entrance, from where a trail to **Peapea Cave** also begins. It's a 2-hour round-trip hike to the cave, which is a lava tube (it's dangerous to enter during heavy rains). Another walking trail leads seaward to arches cut by the surf into the south coast. **Mount Le Pu'e,** in the northwest corner of the park, is a well-preserved volcanic cinder cone. The park and reserve are open daily during the daylight hours, and there's no admission fee. Contact the Ministry of Natural Resources and Environment (☎ **23-800;** www.mnre.gov.ws) for more information.

⌒Tips A Refueling Stop

You can refuel your body at **Boomerang Creek Beach Resort** (☎ **40-358**), which offers inexpensive meals and libation in its lattice-trimmed restaurant overlooking the beach a Lalomanu. It also rents bikes, kayaks, and snorkeling gear.

Moments **A Day on a Beautiful Beach**

A Sunday afternoon at one of the South Pacific's most beautiful beaches is on my agenda every time I come here. Return to Paradise Beach, where Gary Cooper filmed the movie by the same name, is what all beaches should be like: surf breaking around black rock outcrops, palm trees draped over white sand. But I'm also enamored of Aiepata Beach at Lalomanu, where a clifflike mountain provides a backdrop and offshore islands enhance the sea view.

Heading west from Si'umu, the road soon passes the Sinalei and Coconuts Beach Club resorts and then the nearby **Togo Mangrove Estuary,** a tidal waterway that's alive with birds, flowers, bees, and other wildlife.

Some of Upolu's most beautiful beaches await on the southwest coast, particularly in the Lefaga district. One of these is at the village of **Salamumu.** Farther on the south coast road, Matautu village boasts **Return to Paradise Beach** 𝒜𝒜𝒜. Palms hang over this marvelous sandy beach punctuated by large boulders that confront the breaking surf. It gets its name from the movie starring Gary Cooper that was filmed here in 1951. The S$5 (US$1.65) per-person custom fee charged by Matautu village is well worth it.

From Matautu the main road winds across the island to the north coast.

ORGANIZED TOURS

Based at the two Aggie Grey's hotels, **Samoa Scenic Tours** (ⓒ **22-880;** www.samoa scenictours.com) offers a variety of tours that stop for photographs and a swim at beautiful beaches and waterfalls. A half-day Apia township tour will take you around town and up to the Robert Lewis Stevenson Museum for S$40 (US$13) per person. A morning excursion goes to Piula Cave Pool and Falefa Falls for the same price. A full-day trip goes to either Lalomanu or Lefaga (Return to Paradise) beaches for S$110 (US$37). Another full-day excursion goes out to Manono Island, for about S$115 (US$38). On Sunday a half-day outing heads to Matavera beach on the southwest coast, with juice and towels included for S$46 (US$15) per person. Each day's offerings are written on a notice board in the lobby at Aggie's.

Oceania Travel & Tours, at the Hotel Kitano Tusitala (ⓒ **24-443;** www.oceania-travel.ws), and **Island Hopper Vacations** (ⓒ **26-940;** www.islandhoppervacations.com) have similar excursions.

The more backpacker-oriented **Green Turtle Tours** (ⓒ **22-144** or 29-629; www.greenturtletours.com) has half-day Apia sightseeing and a full-day around Upolu tour. On the island tour you ride Green Turtle's 15-seat van, which circles Upolu clockwise once a day. Green Turtle also offers a half-day Samoa Wilderness trip, on which you visit a Samoan village for a cultural demonstration and local-style lunch. Each tour costs S$90 (US$30) per person. Green Turtles' headquarters is at the **Traveller's Lounge** on Beach Road west of Aggie Grey's Hotel & Bungalows.

ENVIRONMENTAL TOURS

In addition to Green Turtle Tours, Dr. Steve Brown and his Samoan wife, Funealii Sooaemalelagi, also operate **Ecotour Samoa** (ⓒ **22-144;** www.ecotoursamoa.com). Leading proponents of nature-sensitive sustainable tourism, the Browns have a number of 1- to 7-day tours that explore the wildlife and fauna of such places as the Mount Vaea rain forest, remote Fagaloa Bay, the south coast estuaries and wetlands, Monono

Island, and Lake Lanoto'o. They also have expeditions to Savai'i and to American Samoa National Park (see chapter 14). You must book the multi-day excursions in advance, but you can check with the Browns at their headquarters, in the Traveller's Lounge on Beach Road west of Aggie Grey's Hotel & Bungalows, to see if space is available.

10 Watersports, Golf & Other Outdoor Activities

Most watersports are headquartered at Aggie Grey's Lagoon, Beach Resort & Spa near the airport, and on the south coast at Sinalei Reef Resort & Spa and Coconuts Beach Club (see "Where to Stay on Upolu," below). You need not be a guest to partake of the activities, since everyone must pay.

At Aggie's, **Aqua Samoa Watersports** (© **45-611,** ext 5017) offers jet- and water-skiing, banana boat rides, wake- and kite boarding, Hobie Cat sailing, snorkeling trips, scuba diving, and game fishing.

Based at Sinalei but also serving Coconuts Beach Club, **Liquid Motion** (© **64-381;** www.liquidmotion.ws) has scuba diving and PADI certification courses, snorkeling trips, game fishing, and sunset cruises. It also rents single- and double kayaks.

GOLF   In a sports complex at Tuanaimato, in the highlands southwest of Apia, the **Faleata Golf Course** (© **23-964**) has 18 holes, a driving range, and golf cart rental. Greens fees are S$20 (US$6.65). The **Royal Samoan Golf Club** (© **20-120**) has a 9-hole course at Fagali'i, on the eastern side of Apia, and visitors are welcome to use the facilities. Call the club's secretary for greens fees and starting times. **Sinalei Reef Resort** (© **25-191**) on the south coast has a 9-hole course (see "Where to Stay on Upolu," below).

HIKING   Upolu has a number of very good hiking trails. The most picturesque is the Coastal Trail in **O le Pupu-Pue National Park** (see "Exploring Apia & the Rest of Upolu," earlier in this chapter). This relatively flat track runs along the top of the park's sea cliffs and has some spectacular views. Another trail in the park goes through rainforests to the Peapea cave. The most exciting track leads to Lake Lanoto'o in the new **Lake Lanoto'o National Park** (see "The Cross Island Road," above). This difficult hike takes at least an hour in and out and is best done with a guide or group, such as offered by **Eco Tours Samoa** (see "Environmental Tours," above).

KAYAKING   As part of his **Ecotour Samoa** (©/fax **22-144** or 25-993; www.eco toursamoa.com), Dr. Steve Brown will take you sea kayaking to Manono Island. These trips are usually part of his environmentally friendly tour packages (see "Environmental Tours," above).

You can also go on guided day tours or overnight expeditions to Manono Island with **Island Explorer** (© **32-663** or 777-1814; www.islandexplorer.ws). Mats Arvidsson, a Swede who lives in Samoa, operates this company. He needs at least 1 day's advance notice.

SWIMMING & SNORKELING   The best swimming and snorkeling is on the beaches of Aleipata and the southwest coast (see "Exploring Apia & the Rest of Upolu," earlier in this chapter). In town, just east of the main wharf, canyons in the reef at **Palolo Deep Marine Reserve** ⚓ (© **26-942**) make for good snorkeling without having to leave town. The snorkeling is best at high tide, when you can swim rather than walk across the reef to the deep-water canyons. Don't expect to see colorful coral here; it's best for sealife. The small sandy beach is good for sunning at any tide. This city park has changing rooms, and it rents snorkeling gear. Admission is S$2 (US65¢). The reserve is open daily from 8am to 6pm.

You of strong bottom can slip down the waterfall known as **Papase'a Sliding Rocks** into a dark pool. Take a taxi or the Se'ese'e village bus. The rocks are about 2 kilometers (1¼ miles) from the paved road; the bus driver may go out of his way to take you there, but you will have to walk back to the bus route. The villagers extract a S$2 (US65¢) custom fee per person.

Another popular outing away from Apia is to **Piula Cave Pool** and the outlying beaches. See "Exploring Apia & the Rest of Upolu," earlier in this chapter, for details.

11 Shopping

Although not in the quantity you'll find in Tonga, Samoans turn out excellent handmade baskets, sewing trays, purses, floor mats, napkin rings, place mats, and fans woven from pandanus and other local materials, plus some woodcarvings.

Except for the Old Apia Market, which is open all day, the stores below observe regular business hours (see "Fast Facts: Samoa," earlier in this chapter).

Aggie's Gift Shop 🐦 This hotel gift shop has Apia's best selection of handicrafts and Samoan products such as sandalwood soap, small bags of kava, and watercolors by local artists. The handicrafts include shell jewelry and siapo cloth, carved wooden war clubs, ceremonial kava bowls, and high-talking chiefs' staffs (known as *tootoo*). Clothing items include hand-screened lava-lavas, T-shirts, shorts, and dresses. The shop also carries books about the Samoas and has a snack bar just inside the front door. Beach Rd., next to Aggie Grey's Hotel & Bungalows. ✆ 22-880.

Mr. Lavalava Harry Paul has been encouraging Samoans to resume making handicrafts. His shop carries some of the resulting works: bone fishhooks, carved war clubs, spears, hair clasps and ukuleles made from coconut shells, and orators' staffs and "horses tails" of the type carried by high-talking chiefs. He also has imported handicrafts from Tonga, Fiji, and other South Pacific islands. Fungulei Rd., 3 blocks south of Beach Rd. ✆ 25-080.

Old Apia Market Once the town's vegetable market, this giant shed is now a crowded and very active flea market, with vendors selling everything from cosmetics to shoes (local wags say it's better stocked than Apia's regular stores because some goods may have been slipped past Customs on their way from American Samoa). Your best buys here are fine mats and other Samoan handicrafts; in fact, you can even watch local women at work in their stalls. The other handicraft shops usually have better-quality pieces, but you might find an exceptional one here. Especially look for the merchant who sells intricately carved *tanoa* (kava) bowls. Beach Rd., west of Town Clock. No phone.

12 Where to Stay on Upolu

ACCOMMODATIONS IN APIA
MODERATE

Aggie Grey's Hotel & Bungalows 🐦🐦🐦 Although they are focusing much attention on Aggie Grey's Lagoon, Beach Resort & Spa (see below), the family of the late Aggie Grey is making sure that the hotel has the same warm, friendly atmosphere Aggie instilled when she opened it in 1943 (see the "Hot Dogs & Hamburgers" box, below). Aggie's Gift Shop next door shows what this venerable hotel looked like before the fire

Fun Fact Hot Dogs & Hamburgers

Back in 1919, a young woman of British and Samoan descent named Agnes Genevieve Grey opened the Cosmopolitan Club on a point of land where the Vaisigano River flows into Apia Harbour. It was just a small pub, catering to local businessmen and the occasional tourists who climbed off the transpacific steamers stopping in Apia.

And then in 1942 the U.S. Marines landed to train for the South Pacific campaigns against the Japanese. Aggie Grey started selling them much-appreciated hot dogs and hamburgers. Quickly her little enterprise expanded into a three-story clapboard hotel, with a bar at ground level, a dining room on the next, and rooms to rent on the third. Many of those young marines, including future U.S. Secretary of State George Shultz, left Samoa with fond memories of Aggie Grey and her hotel.

Another serviceman who came to Aggie's was a U.S. naval historian named James A. Michener. Everyone in Samoa believes Michener used Aggie as the role model for Bloody Mary, the Tonkinese woman who provided U.S. servicemen with wine, song, and other diversions in his *Tales of the South Pacific*.

Although her hotel grew after the war to include more than 150 rooms, Aggie always circulated among her guests, making them feel at home. Everyone sat down family style when taking a meal in the old clapboard building on Beach Road, and afterward they all moseyed over for coffee in the lounge. Afternoon tea was a time for socializing and swapping gossip from places far away. And on fiafia nights, when the feasts were laid out, Aggie herself would dance the graceful Samoan *siva*.

Like Robert Louis Stevenson before her, the Samoans revered Aggie Grey. They made her the only commoner ever to appear on a Samoan postage stamp. And when she died in 1988 at the age of 90, Head of State Malietoa Tanumafili II and hundreds of other mourners escorted her to her final resting place in the hills above Apia.

marshal ordered the old clapboard building closed. Now a modern but Victorian-style building fronting Beach Road houses the reception area, the air-conditioned Le Tamarina restaurant (see "Where to Dine in Apia," later in this chapter), the open-air Brando Bar facing the harbor, a coffee shop, and two floors of modern rooms and suites with private verandas overlooking Apia Harbour. In some ways this modern facility has made Aggie's two hotels in one, for its rooms are designed primarily for business travelers (children under 12 cannot stay in this wing), and its presidential suites are fit for potentates. The property out back is more like a resort, with its large, exquisite Old Fale beside the swimming pool with a palm tree growing out of an islet in the middle. Guests can still take their meals under the great turtle-shaped roof or wander over to the bar for a cold Vailima beer and a chat with friendly strangers. The efficient staff prepares feasts and barbecues in astounding quantity, as in Aggie's day, especially during the Wednesday night *fiafias* (see "Island Nights on Upolu," later).

The older hotel rooms out back are housed in modern, stone-accented, two-story buildings that ramble through a garden so thick with tropical vegetation that it's easy to get lost trying to find your way from one unit to another. They are comfortable and have both air-conditioners and good natural ventilation. Each has a veranda or balcony. My favorites are the much more charming individual VIP fale bungalows topped by turtle-shaped roofs. Each of these spacious units bears the name of one of Aggie's famous past guests, such as actors Gary Cooper, William Holden, and Marlon Brando. They have old-fashioned touches like fold-down ironing boards.

P.O. Box 67, Apia (Beach Rd., on the waterfront). © 800/448-8355 or 22-880. Fax 23-626. www.aggiegreys.com. 181 units. US$115–US$155 double, US$260–US$310 suite. AE, DC, MC, V. **Amenities:** 3 restaurants; bars; outdoor pool; exercise room; children's programs; concierge; activities desk; business center; salon; 24-hr. room service; babysitting; laundry service. In room: A/C, TV, minibar, fridge, coffeemaker, hair dryer, iron.

Hotel Kitano Tusitala   Built in 1974 by the government and named the Tusitala in honor of Robert Louis Stevenson, this hotel is now owned by Kitano, a Japanese construction company. The public areas are in three Samoan-style fales with huge turtle-shaped roofs. They ring a tropical garden featuring a children's wading pool, from which water falls down two levels into a larger adult swimming pool. The rooms are all in five two-story motel-style buildings grouped beyond the swimming pools. Superior and special units facing the pool are in much better condition than the standard rooms, which have a certain 1970s charm to them, if you can call it that. All units have a sliding glass door opening onto either a private patio or balcony. They are air-conditioned, but you won't feel any cross-ventilation unless you leave the back door open.

A bar and lounge in one of the open-air fales stands next to the pool, as does a daytime snack bar. Another of the three big common buildings houses Stevenson's Restaurant (with portraits of R. L. S. himself). The hotel's Seaview Restaurant, across the main driveway, proffers good Western and Japanese fare accompanied by a harbor view.

P.O. Box 101, Apia (Beach Rd., Mulinu'u Peninsula). © 800/448-8355 or 21-122. Fax 23-652. www.kitano.ws. 94 units. S$280–S$450 (US$93–US$150) double, S$500–S$800 (US$167–US$267) suite. AE, DC, MC, V. **Amenities:** 4 restaurants; 3 bars; outdoor pool; 2 tennis courts; activities desk; business center; limited room service; babysitting; laundry service; coin-op washers and dryers. In room: A/C, TV, fridge, coffeemaker, hair dryer, iron (in superior rooms).

Insel Fehmarn Hotel   This modern, well-kept motel sits on the side of the hill above Apia. Some rooms enjoy views of town and the reef from their balconies, especially those on the third (top) floor. Most of the identical rooms in this beige concrete block structure have two double beds, chairs, tables, tiled shower-only bathrooms, and kitchenettes. Some executive rooms have one king bed, and one suite has a separate bedroom. It's popular with business travelers looking for kitchen-equipped accommodations. Giodanno's Cafe & Pizzeria is across the road (see "Where to Dine in Apia," below).

P.O. Box 3272, Apia (on Cross Island Rd., 2km/1¼ miles uphill from Beach Rd.). © 23-301. Fax 22-204. www.insel fehmarnsamoa.com. 54 units. US$98–US$150 double, US$264 suite. Rates include breakfast. AE, DC, MC, V. **Amenities:** Restaurant; bar; outdoor pool; 2 tennis courts; business center; laundry service; coin-op washers and dryers. In room: A/C, TV, kitchen, coffeemaker.

INEXPENSIVE

1848 Princess Tui Inn   Most of the units in this historic and charming colonial house (see "The Legendary 'Queen Emma,'" in this section) are the original bedrooms. Although accommodations are basic by today's standards, fans hang from their high ceilings, and mosquito nets cover their beds, most queen size. The choice units are on the front of the house; their windows face the sea across the road. One of these and a larger family unit have private bathrooms. Two rooms with six beds each serve as dormitories, one reserved for females. A modern concrete block building next door holds four "cottage" rooms; these lack charm and share a bathroom, but they are air-conditioned. All guests share a communal kitchen. No smoking in the rooms here.

P.O. Box 9595, Apia (Vaiala Beach, 1.3km/1 mile east of Main Wharf). ✆ 23-342. Fax 22-451. www.princesstui.ws. 12 units (7 without bathroom), 12 dorm beds. US$37–US$51 double; US$14 dorm bed. Rates include breakfast. AE, MC, V. **Amenities:** Activities desk; laundry service. *In room:* A/C (cottage units); no phone.

Hotel Millenia *Value* This attractive three-story colonial-style hotel opened at the beginning of the new millennium in 2001, but it takes its name from two of its owners; thus the spelling and the pronunciation: Mel-ay-*nee*-ah. Sitting across Beach Road from Apia Harbor, the property looks and feels more like an inn than a hotel, given its large, comfortable guest lounge and veranda on the second floor. Both of these have sea views, as do some of its deluxe units, one of which opens to a front balcony. These are preferable to the standard units on the ground level and four kitchen-equipped units in a rear wing. Although most of the interior walls are of New Zealand pine, wicker chairs and bright bedspreads lend a tropical ambience. A ground floor restaurant with outdoor seating serves good regional fare at breakfast, lunch, and dinner, and the bar has free snacks and reduced drink prices during happy hour Friday from 4:30 to 7pm.

P.O. Box 214, Apia (Beach Road, Mulinu'u Peninsula). ✆ 28-284. Fax 28-285. www.hotelmilleniasamoa.com. 19 units. US$69–US$103 double; US$138 suite. MC, V. **Amenities:** Restaurant; bar; laundry service. *In room:* A/C, TV, kitchen (4 units), fridge.

The Samoan Outrigger Hotel Claus Hermansen liked what he saw so much during a visit to Samoa that he gave up a banking career in Denmark to live here and start this little hotel. There's a reading area and TV lounge with a billiards table in the great room of this colonial-style house, and to the rear is a pleasant communal kitchen and dining area. The best equipped rooms are on the ground floor. They have their own entrances, air-conditioners, patios, toilets, and cold-water showers. A family unit can sleep up to five persons. The dormitories here actually are four beach fales (see the "Beach *Fales* at Aleipata" box, below), which sit out in the backyard along with an above-ground pool. All rooms have fans as well as mosquito nets over their beds. Claus's hostel has been spotlessly clean throughout my recent visits. Giodanno's Cafe & Pizzeria is a short walk away.

P.O. Box 1922, Apia (Cross Island Rd., 1km/½ mile south of Beach Rd). ✆ 20-042. Fax 30-722. www.outrigger.netfirms. com. 11 units (4 without bathroom), 4 fales w/12 dorm beds. S$100–S$160 (US$33–US$53) double; S$45 (US$15) dorm bed. Rates include continental breakfast. MC, V. *In room:* A/C (5 units), fridge (5 units), no phone (5 units).

Vaiala Beach Cottages *Value* Located across the street from Vaiala Beach, these comfortable and airy bungalows share a yard with frangipani, crotons, and other tropical plants. Except for the tropical furnishings and decor, such as cane furniture and woven floor mats, the bungalows are all identical: a full kitchen with stainless-steel sink, a bedroom with either one double or two twin beds, a spacious bathroom with a shower that dispenses hot water, and a narrow balcony off a bright living room. They are built of pine, including the varnished interior walls. The living rooms have ceiling fans hanging over the sitting area, but the large, screened, louvered windows and sliding doors leading to the balconies usually allow the trade winds to cool the house without such assistance. Rental kayaks, snorkel gear, and tennis rackets are available.

P.O. Box 2025, Apia (Vaiala Beach, 1.5km/1 mile east of Main Wharf). ✆ 22-202. Fax 22-008. www.samoana.org/ vaiala. 7 units. US$68 double. MC, V. **Amenities:** Laundry service. *In room:* Kitchen, coffeemaker, no phone (5 units).

ACCOMMODATIONS AT THE BEACHES

Aggie Grey's Lagoon, Beach Resort & Spa ✿✿✿   Between the airport and Mulifanua Wharf on Upolu's northwestern corner, this sprawling beachside resort is the Grey family's latest contribution to Samoa. They copied many features from their historic in-town hotel and transposed them here, including fold-down ironing boards in each room and a duplicate of the huge Samoan fale restaurant and its weekly fiafia night (on Thurs here). As in town, complimentary afternoon tea is served; here it's offered in the courtyard between the big fale and a fine dining restaurant. The resort carries out an old South Seas theme, with Bloody Mary's Lagoon & Courtyard Bar honoring James A. Michener's famous character. Meanwhile, the Solent Flying Boat Bar pays homage to the amphibious planes which were Samoa's only air link to the world until the 1950s. The airy central building opens to a large beachside swimming pool complex with a swim-up bar. The guest quarters are in two-story buildings flanking the central complex. These buildings all face westward, so each unit espies Savai'i and Apolima islands as well as often glorious sunsets. Tropical furniture lends ambience to the spacious, well-equipped rooms, as does a lagoon-matching green-and-blue color scheme. Eight family units have two bedrooms. A century-old church has been restored as the resort's wedding chapel. Treatment rooms at the full-service Manaia Polynesian Spa are in private bungalows in a stand of old-growth tropical forest. The spa also has a state-of-the-art exercise room, a boutique, and its own bar. The watersports center here offers a wide range of activities.

P.O. Box 67, Apia (1km/.6 mile west of airport). ℂ **45-611.** Fax 45-626. www.aggiegreys.com. 140 units. US$180–US$190 double; US$400 suite. AE, DC, MC, V. **Amenities:** 2 restaurants; 4 bars; outdoor pool; 18-hole golf course; 2 tennis courts; exercise room; spa; Jacuzzi; watersports equipment rentals; children's program; concierge; activities desk; car-rental desk; 24-hr. room service; massage; babysitting; laundry service. *In room:* A/C, TV, dataport, minibar, fridge, coffeemaker, hairdryer, iron, safe.

Coconuts Beach Club ✿   Former Hollywood show-biz lawyers Barry and Jennifer Rose developed this resort on a piece of land abutting the Togo Mangrove Estuary (mosquitoes can be plentiful here at times). They chopped down enough of this dense growth for lagoon-facing bungalows and a two-story, motel-style block of eight rooms reached by treehouselike stairs. Later they added two luxuriously appointed hexagonal overwater bungalows with floor-to-ceiling glass walls and coffee tables with see-through tops for looking into the lagoon. Ashore, the spacious villas (one has two bedrooms and three baths, others have two bathrooms), garden suites, and "royal beach villas" have rustic looks without giving up luxuries. The beach fales and villas have outdoorsy bathrooms with showers pouring down rock walls into sunken tubs. The "Treehouse" hotel rooms have oval bathtubs and 7m (24 ft.) covered patios or balconies. Lots of natural wood creates unusual accents, such as tree limbs used as posts for the king-size beds, towel racks in the baths, and legs for coffee tables.

The open-sided thatch restaurant has a bar directly beside the beach. Specialties include fresh seafood, especially local lobster and mud crabs from the nearby mangrove estuary. Erosion has wiped away much of the beach here, so a rock breakwater fronts most of the property. You can walk around the breakwater, however, and swim out to a lava wall, which creates a good snorkeling area. A gecko-shaped pool with a gecko tile mosaic bottom sits just behind the breakwater but away from the main building. No kids under 3 are accepted here. There should be a spa here by the time you make your travel plans.

Fun Fact Beach *Fales* at Aleipata ⟨★★★⟩

"Where in the South Pacific can I rent a little grass shack by the beach?" people often ask me. The answer is here in Samoa, and it's known as a **beach fale.**

Although included in many accommodation listings, most of these rustic little structures belong in the camping category. They are miniature Samoan fales, with oval thatch roofs covering open-air platforms, and most provide mosquito nets, foam mattresses, and pull-down canvas or colorful plastic sides to afford some privacy and protection against the elements. Guests share communal toilets and cold-water showers in separate buildings.

The best on Upolu are beside the great Lalomanu Beach, 1 hour by car from Apia on Upolu's southeastern corner (see "Exploring Apia & the Rest of Upolu," earlier in this chapter). Directly on that beach, **Taufua Beach Fales** (© 41-051; www.samoabeachfales.com) and **Litia Sini's Beach Resort** (© 41-050) actually have wood sides on some of their fales, and Taufua has a beachside restaurant and bar. Expect to pay about S$55 (US$18) per person for an open fale, S$70 (US$23) for one with pull-down sides, including breakfast and dinner.

Nestled at the base of the cliff in adjacent Saleapaga, Steve and Ana Harrison's **Boomerang Creek Beach Bungalows** (© 40-358 or 73-202; www.boomerangcreek.ws) is the fanciest of the lot. It has two bars dispensing libation and a pleasant hillside restaurant, where you can order sandwiches, steaks, local lobster, and other simply prepared fare from a blackboard menu. Its fales—eight on the beach, seven on the mountain side of the road—are fully enclosed and much better equipped than the others. They cost S$40 to S$75 (US$13–US$25) double. Boomerang Creek rents snorkel gear, kayaks, and bikes, and it will arrange fishing charters, boat trips to nearby islands, and mountain hikes. You can get a Samoan-style massage here, too.

P.O. Box 3684, Apia (in Si'umu, 30 min. south of Apia; turn right at end of Cross Island Rd.). © 800/726-6268 or 24-849. Fax 20-071. www.coconutsbeachclubsamoa.com. 22 units. US$199–US$229 double; US$259–US$599 bungalow. Rates include minibar. AE, MC, V. No children under 3 accepted. **Amenities:** Restaurant; 2 bars; outdoor pool; spa; free use of watersports equipment; free use of bikes; activities desk; babysitting; laundry service. *In room:* A/C, minibar (in bungalows), fridge, coffeemaker, hairdryer, safe, no phone.

Sinalei Reef Resort & Spa ⟨★⟩   A tad more reserved than Coconuts Beach Club, this resort sits on a rise overlooking the lagoon. A path leads down to a magnificent crescent-shaped beach—backed by the proverbial palm grove—which separates it from Coconuts. Three spacious bungalows open to this beach; they can interconnect to form Sinalei's presidential suite. There's a second, more private beach area, where reside five fales, one a honeymoon unit with a swimming pool set into its front porch. The other guest bungalows are up on the hill and flank the central buildings, which gives some of them fine sea views. They are of European construction, with peaked shingle roofs and glass walls across the front. Some also have separate bedrooms and hot tubs set in their verandas. The beach and honeymoon fales lack air-conditioners, but they do have ceiling fans. A group of three open, Samoan-style thatched-roof buildings comprise the central complex, one each covering reception and gift shop, dining room, and bar. The bar opens to a lovely hilltop pool with a waterfall and huge lava rocks at its edge, but thick foliage obscures the sea view. At the end of a pier, a second restaurant overlooks freshwater welling up from a spring beneath the lagoon. You can indulge in the spa, participate in a wide range of watersports, and practice your game on the resort's 9-hole golf course.

P.O. Box 1510, Apia (in Si'umu, 30 min. south of Apia). © 25-191. Fax 20-285. www.sinalei.com. 25 units. US$190–US$1,500 bungalow. Rates include full breakfast, afternoon tea, town shuttle daily. AE, MC, V. Children under 12 not accepted. **Amenities:** 2 restaurants; 2 bars; outdoor pool; 9-hole golf course; 2 tennis courts; spa; watersports equipment rental; limited room service; laundry service. *In room:* A/C (except in beachside units), fridge, coffeemaker, hair dryer, safe.

13 Where to Dine in Apia

Start thinking seafood here, for a small but thriving local fishing industry means Apia is second only to Rarotonga in the South Pacific as a place to dine on fresh fish, especially yellowfin tuna (great for sashimi) and light, flaky mahimahi (known here as *masi masi*). Tropical lobsters are available here, too, although not in the numbers harvested in Tonga.

After you've sampled the places I recommend below, you can explore the area around Sails Restaurant & Bar on Beach Road. This "restaurant row" has several choices, plus Apia's largest concentrations of bars.

McDonald's is on Vaea Street, a block inland from the Town Clock. It's the only restaurant here open until 11pm Saturday to Thursday, until 1am Friday.

Cappuccino Vineyard 🌟🌟 COFFEE HOUSE/SNACKS This chic sidewalk cafe—it would be at home in New York or Sydney—is the best place in Apia to stop in for a cappuccino, an espresso, or a latte made from freshly roasted beans. For breakfast you can accompany it with yogurt or a pastry. Sashimi, steamed oysters, salads, sandwiches, and big American burgers appear about midday. Hang around Tuesday, Thursday, and Saturday evenings for live island music. The best tables are under umbrellas out on the pedestrian mall beside the high-rise ACB House on Beach Road.

Beach Rd., in ACB House mall west of Town Clock. © 22-049. Breakfast S$11–S$15 (US$3.50–US$5); snacks S$12–S$15 (US$4–US$5). No credit cards. Mon–Sat 7am–11pm.

Giodanno's Cafe & Pizzeria 🌟 *Value* PIZZA/PASTA Follow your nose around the take-out counter to Alex Stanley's romantic courtyard, where patio tables with candles sit under a breadfruit and other tropical trees. Small- or large-size pizzas come with a choice of several toppings. Pasta dishes consist of lasagna with beef sauce or spaghetti under Bolognese, marinara, carbonara, or a spicy vegetarian sauce. With jazz on the speaker system, this is a very popular establishment with local expatriate residents.

Cross Island Rd., opposite Hotel Insel Fehmarn. © 25-985. Reservations recommended. Pizzas S$15–S$35 (US$5–US$12); pasta S$22–S$32 (US$7.25–US$11). MC, V. Tues–Sat 3–10pm, Sun 5–9pm.

Gourmet Seafood & Grille *Value* SEAFOOD/STEAKS You can start your day with fresh fruit pies and muffins at this popular local establishment, which would win all awards for charm in the inexpensive-restaurant category anywhere. Large tree trunks hold up the roof, under which fishnets form a ceiling. Buoys and other nautical items add to the atmosphere. There's nothing gourmet here, but the hallmark is fresh fish. You'll get a monstrous slab of grilled mahimahi, most likely caught earlier

> ## (Tips) Don't Miss a *Fiafia*
>
> Like other islanders, the Samoans gave up the use of pottery at least 1,000 years before the Europeans arrived in the South Pacific. As did their fellow Polynesians, they cooked their foods in a pit of hot stones, which the Samoans call an *umu*. When it had all steamed for several hours, they threw back the dirt, unwrapped the delicacies, and sat down to a *fiafia*.
>
> Favorite side dishes were fresh fruit and *ota* (fish marinated with lime juice and served with vegetables in coconut milk, in a fashion similar to poisson cru in Tahiti). If you happen to be in Samoa on the 7th day after the full moon in late October or early November, the meal may include the coral worm known as palolo.
>
> **Aggie Grey's Hotel & Bungalows** (© 22-880) consistently has the best fiafia, traditionally on Wednesday night. Don't miss the exciting fire dance over and around the swimming pool. The same show is repeated on Thursday at **Aggie Grey's Lagoon, Beach Resort & Spa,** with the fire dance on the beach. The **Hotel Kitano Tusitala** (© 21-122) usually has its fiafia on Friday. **Coconuts Beach Club** (© 24-849) does its on Saturday. Check with them to make sure. Expect to pay about S$55 (US$18) per person. You'll pass a long buffet table loaded with European, Chinese, and Samoan dishes. After stuffing down the food, you get to watch a show of traditional Samoan dancing.

in the day, served with french fries and a salad. You can also get fish and chips, and New Zealand steaks. Get here early before the locals scarf down all of Apia's best *oka* (marinated raw fish with coconut cream and vegetables).

Convent St., 2 blocks behind Central Post Office. © 24-625. Breakfast S$5–S$14 (US$1.65–US$4.50); burgers S$6.50–S$11 (US$2–US$3.50); main courses S$9–S$28 (US$3–US$8). No credit cards. Mon–Sat 7am–10pm. Go inland at the post office, turn left at intersection to restaurant on left.

Le Tamarina Restaurant ★★ INTERNATIONAL   Tropical plants and furnishings lend appropriate atmosphere to this elegant, air-conditioned dining room with a view of Apia from the ground floor of Aggie's. Slacks and dresses are required for evening meals, which feature local and New Zealand produce in a variety of preparations. You may see veal saltimbocca, Pacific smoked salmon, or rack of lamb in an herb crust. The best night to dine here is on Saturday, when a seafood buffet is loaded with fresh local fish, crab, and lobsters, plus morsels flown in from New Zealand waters; it's a steal at S$70 (US$23) per person.

Beach Rd., in Aggie Grey's Hotel & Bungalows. © 23-626. Reservations recommended. Main courses S$40–S$52 (US$14–US$18). AE, DC, MC, V. Mon–Sat 6:30–10pm.

Sails Restaurant and Bar ★★★ SEAFOOD/STEAKS   I first met Ian and Lyvia Black, a charming Australian-Samoan couple, when they were expertly managing hotels in Fiji. In 1996 they returned to Samoa and converted the second floor of this historic clapboard store—the first place Robert Louis Stevenson lived when he arrived here in 1889—into one of the South Pacific's most charming restaurants. Be sure to reserve a table on the front porch above Beach Road, where you'll get a view over the white-and-blue railing to Apia Harbour. The creamy lobster bisque loaded with chunks of lobster is out of this world. For a main course, move on to citrus fish poached in lime and white wine. You can order a breakfast of eggs and bacon all day. Lunch features salads, sandwiches, and burgers, and Ian and Lyvia keep the bar open all day for drinks, the second best cappuccino in town, and snacks (including Commodore Sashimi). Nautical decor and jazz on the speakers add to the relaxed, friendly atmosphere. Dine early here on Friday and Saturday nights, before the bars next door strike up their noisy bands.

Beach Rd., between Ifi'ifi St. and Mulivai Stream. © 20-628. Reservations recommended for dinner. Breakfast S$20 (US$6.65); lunch S$13–S$35 (US$4.50–US$12); main courses S$30–S$55 (US$10–US$18). AE, DC, MC, V. Mon–Sat 9am–11pm, Sun 6–11pm.

14 Island Nights on Upolu

Samoa is no different from the other Polynesian countries in that watching a traditional dance show as part of a feast night (in Samoa called a fiafia) is a highlight of any visit. Samoan dance movements are graceful and emphasize the hands more than the hips; the costumes feature more siapo cloth and fine mats than flowers. While the dances are not as lively nor the costumes as colorful as those in Tahiti and the Cook Islands, they are definitely worth seeing. See "Don't Miss a *Fiafia*," above.

PUB CRAWLING   Sunday through Thursday nights are relatively quiet in Apia. But on weekends everyone with an itch to drink, dance, and socialize heads down Beach Road, hitting one pub after another. Most of these have live bands on Friday (the biggest night) and Saturday. Thanks to citizens outraged by bars opening in residential neighborhoods, pubs legally must close at midnight throughout the week (none are open on Sunday). As a practical matter, some of them keep right on going into the wee hours, especially on Friday night.

Start with a cocktail or cold Vailima beer in the Brando Bar at **Aggie Grey's Hotel & Bungalows,** then head west along Beach Road to Apia's version of restaurant row. You'll come to the slapped-together facade and worse-than-plain furniture at **Lighthouse Bar & Grill** (© 22-691), one of the more popular bars in town with both locals and expatriate residents. You can look right into this open-air establishment. On one side of Sails Restaurant and Bar is **Bad Billy's Bar** (© 30-258) and **Blue Lagoon Bar & Grill** (© 30-298). On the other is **On the Rocks** (© 20-093), where you can actually have a good conversation at the sidewalk tables. From there everyone heads west to the **RSA Night Club** (© 20-171), where Samoa's military veterans throw open a welcome to everyone with a few talas to pay for the rock band.

Cappuccino Vineyard (© 22-049) is the most civilized place to have a drink on Saturday night while listening to cool island music—but get here before the music stops at 10pm. See "Where to Dine in Apia," above.

15 Savai'i ★★★

Although it lacks first-rate accommodations, you will wish you had stayed longer on Savai'i. Green mountains rise out of the sea and into the clouds across the 21km-wide (13 mile) Apolima Strait that separates it from Upolu. Savai'i is half again as large as Upolu, yet it has only a quarter as many people as its smaller and more prosperous sister. On Savai'i, rural Samoan life is very much like it always has been. People reside in villages mainly along the east and south coasts.

The northern part of Savai'i has practically deserted lava fields and forests. The last major eruption from its 470 volcanic craters occurred between 1905 and 1911. According to geologist Warren Jopling (see "Organized Tours" under "Exploring Savai'i," below), there's a cycle of activity of about 150 years, so the next eruption should be due in another half century.

The other attractions on Savai'i are its long, white beaches, especially on the north side around the village of Manase, where you'll find some of Samoa's most popular beach fales.

GETTING THERE & GETTING AROUND

Air service to Savai'i is provided by **Polynesian Airlines,** while the **Samoa Shipping Corporation** operates two ferries between Mulifanua Wharf on Upolu and Salelologa, the commercial center on Savai'i. See "Getting There & Getting Around," earlier in this chapter.

You can organize a trip to Savai'i yourself, but the easiest way is to contact one of the tour operators in Apia (see "Organized Tours," earlier in this chapter). For example, **Oceania Travel & Tours** (© 24-443; www.oceania-travel.ws) has day trips for about S$300 (US$100) by ferry, S$350 (US$116) by plane, including breakfast and tour. It also has 2-day, 1-night packages.

Ecotour Samoa (©/fax 22-144 or 25-993; www.ecotoursamoa.com) has 2- and 3-day expeditions around Savai'i, with an emphasis on exploring the volcanic craters, lava fields, wetlands, and rain forests. See "Environmental Tours," earlier in this chapter, for more information about this company.

Taxis meet the planes and ferry. One-way fare from Maota Airstrip to Safua on the east coast is S$15 (US$5). From the ferry wharf to the east-coast hotels costs S$8 (US$2.65) one-way. The one-way fare is F$60 (US$20) to Manase, and S$100 (US$33) to Asau village, 89km (55 miles) on the opposite side of Savai'i.

Local **buses** going around the east and north coasts to Manase meet the 8am and noon ferries arriving from Upolu. The fare to Manase is S$4 (US$1.35).

Savai'i Car Rentals (© 51-392; fax 51-291; cars@samoa.ws) rents cars and SUVs for about S$165 (US$55) per day. A deposit of S$350 (US$117) is required. You can pay by MasterCard or Visa, although the company reluctantly takes credit cards. The round-island road is completely paved.

EXPLORING SAVAI'I

Unless you have a week or more and plenty of energy, you should take a guided tour of this large and sparsely populated island with little public transport and few road signs. Even then, you'll need 3 days to see all of the readily accessible sights and have no time for the beach.

ORGANIZED TOURS ✿✿✿

Guided by Warren Jopling, a retired Australian geologist who has lived on Savai'i for many years and knows it like the back of his hand, **Safua Tours** (© 51-271; fax 51-272) is absolutely the best way to see the island. Warren is a font of information, especially about the desertlike lava fields. He will tailor any tour to suit your interests. It will take an energetic full day to see most of the sights, with half the day spent going along the east and north coasts, the other half along the south shore. His full-day excursions cost S$120 (US$40) for two people, if you book directly and not through a travel agent. Reservations are required. Although Warren will meet you at the ferry wharf, he prefers that you come over to Savai'i the day before your tour and stay at the Safua Hotel (see "Where to Stay & Dine on Savai'i," below).

THE EAST & NORTH COASTS

Leaving the Safua Hotel, the east-coast road soon passes a memorial to the Rev. John Williams, then goes up a rise to **Tuasivi,** the administrative center of the island and site of the hospital and police station. From there it drops to **Faga** and **Siufaga,** two long, gorgeous beaches. Many villages along this stretch have bathing pools fed by freshwater that runs down underground from the mountains. Only the south side of Savai'i has rivers and streams. Rainwater seeps into the porous volcanic rock elsewhere and reappears as springs along the shoreline.

Mount Matavanu last erupted between 1905 and 1911, when it sent a long lava flow down to the northeast coast, burying villages and gardens before backing up behind the reef. Today primitive ferns primarily populate the desertlike **Matavanu lava field.** The flow very nearly inundated the village of **Mauga,** which sits along the rim of an extinct volcano's cone. The villagers play cricket on the crater floor. Past Mauga is the **Virgin's Grave,** a hole left around a grave when the lava almost covered a nearby church. The steeple still sticks out of the twisted black mass. The villagers charge S$3 (US$1) to visit the grave.

The north-coast road past the lava fields is picturesque but holds little of interest other than gorgeous tropical scenery.

On the north coast, the village of **Manase** has a gorgeous white-sand beach, which has made it the beach fale capital of Savai'i (see "Where to Stay & Dine on Savai'i," below). It also has a **Turtle Conservatory,** where you can swim with the turtles in freshwater pools—after paying a S$5 (US$1.65) custom fee.

THE SOUTH COAST

On the south coast near Vailoa, on the Letolo Plantation, stands the ancient ruin known as **Pulemelei Mound** *⚘⚘*. This two-tiered pyramid 72m (240 ft.) long, 58m (193 ft.) wide, and 14m (48 ft.) high is the largest archaeological ruin in Polynesia. It is similar to the ceremonial temples, or *maraes,* in French Polynesia and the Cook Islands, but it is so old (more than 1,000 years) that the Samoans no longer have legends explaining its original function. Shortly before his death in 2002, Thor Heyerdahl, of *Kon Tiki* fame,

---

Manono & Apolima

You will pass the small islands of **Manono** and **Apolima** on the trip across the Apolima Strait to Savai'i. The top of an extinct volcano, Apolima is the more scenic of the two. Its picturesque beachside village of Apolima-tui sits inside the crater that collapsed on one side, causing the island's half-moon shape. Small boats shuttle between Apolima Island and the village of Apolima-uta on Upolu's western end. Boats to Manono leave from Mulifanua Wharf. **Samoa Scenic Tours** (© **22-880**) at Aggie Grey's Hotel & Bungalows operates popular day trips to Manono and its beautiful surrounding reef, and **Ecotour Samoa** (©/fax **22-144** or **25-993**; www.ecotoursamoa. com) has sea-kayaking expeditions to Manono (see "Exploring Apia & the Rest of Upolu," earlier in this chapter).

> ### *Moments* Browsing Through a Living Museum
>
> You won't believe your eyes when you tour the desolate lava fields of Savai'i with retired Australian geologist Warren Jopling. Having lived on Savai'i for many years, Warren is an expert on Samoan customs and lifestyles (everyone on the island knows him). Touring with Warren is like browsing through a living geological and cultural museum.

visited the mound and organized an archaeological expedition, which cleared the pyramid of vegetation. More work was scheduled in 2006. A narrow dirt track, which passes Olemoe Waterfall, ends some 300 meters (300 yards) from the mound. A steep and often muddy track leads down to the waterfall.

From the mound, the south-coast road continues to **Gautavai Waterfall,** a lovely black-sand beach at Nu'u, and the geyserlike **Taga Blowholes** on the island's southernmost point.

SCUBA DIVING & SNORKELING

The reefs off the north shore of Savai'i provide bountiful sealife for snorkelers to view, but beware of strong currents near the reef passes. Scuba divers can find some relatively unexplored sites here, most no more than a 10-minute boat ride from shore. One of them is a missionary ship, which sank on the reef in 1881.

A young French couple, Fabien and Flavia Lebon, of **Dive Savai'i** (© 59-6022; www.divesavaii.com), opposite Le Lagoto Beach Resort (see below), charge S$150 (US$50) for a two-tank dive, and they teach PADI open-water courses for S$1,000 (US$333). They also have guided snorkeling trips for S$60 (US$20) per person, or they will rent snorkeling gear to do-it-yourselfers for S$30 (US$10) a day.

WHERE TO STAY & DINE ON SAVAI'I

Le Lagoto Beach Resort *&*   Kuki and Sara Retzlaff have cottagelike fales and rooms in a two-story, European-style house at the end of their shady property, which has the best view of any Savai'i hotel from its lovely beachside perch (*lagoto* means sunset in Samoan). One fale has a separate bedroom and a great view from its front porch. Each unit is equipped with a queen-size bed with a mosquito net, a kitchenette, a fan, a TV, and a bathroom with hot-water showers. The Retzlaffs also serve breakfast, lunch, and dinner in a screened Samoan-style fale with a beachside deck. It's the best restaurant on Savai'i. They provide complimentary kayaks and canoes for guests to explore a marine reserve offshore. Dive Savai'i has its base here (see above). The Retzlaffs may expand their operation by building larger and modern fales.

P.O. Box 34, Fagamalo (Lelepa village, 45km/28 miles north of ferry wharf). © 58-189. Fax 58-249. www.lelagoto. ws. 7 units. US$99 double. Rates include tropical breakfast. AE, MC, V. **Amenities:** Restaurant; bar; free use of snorkeling equipment and canoes. *In room:* TV, kitchen.

Safua Hotel   This rustic hotel is known not so much for the quality of its accommodations as for its owner, Moelagi Jackson, who holds several chiefly titles and often represents Samoa at international conferences, especially those dealing with women's rights. Her main fale holds a bar and dining room, where most travelers have breakfast before setting out to tour the island. Family-style meals feature Samoan favorites such as chicken curry and whole fish in ginger. The fales scattered about the lawn are of clapboard construction, with front porches, screened windows, basic electric lights, and bathrooms with cold-water showers. Don't be surprised to hear a catfight or the grunts of pigs running loose at night. The Safua will arrange village accommodation for US$35 per person, including meals.

P.O. Box 7088, Salelologa, Savai'i (in Safua village, 6.5km/4 miles north of wharf). ℂ **51-271**. Fax 51-272. safuahotel@ lesamoa.net. 12 units. US$70 fale. Rates include all meals. AE, MC, V. **Amenities:** Restaurant; bar. *In room:* No phone.

Stevenson's at Manase This eclectic resort has a dining room and bar beside a beach of brilliant white sand just west of Manase village. The best units here are five air-conditioned bungalows (they call them villas here) by the beach. Leaf exteriors and siapo-lined ceilings make these houses look rustic, but they are relatively modern, and they have outdoor hot-water showers enclosed by rock walls. Across the road, 19 small-ish, motel-style rooms occupy what appear to be converted shipping containers; one of these plain rooms has an air-conditioner. Guests have free use of paddle boats, canoes, and snorkeling gear, but at low tide the lagoon is too shallow for such diversions.

P.O. Box 210, Apia (at Manase village, 48km/30 miles north of ferry wharf). ℂ/fax **58-219**. 33 units (10 without bathroom). S$120 (US$40) double; S$250 (US$83) bungalow. Rates include breakfast. MC, V. **Amenities:** Restaurant; bar; watersports. *In room:* A/C (bungalows and 1 room), no phone.

BEACH *FALES* AT MANASE ✿✿✿

Like Upolu, Savai'i has scores of beach fales. The best share the brilliant white-sand beach with Stevenson's at Manase (see above). Many of its 34 fales at **Tanu Beach Fales** (ℂ/fax **54-050**) sit right by the lagoon, and the others are in a grove of tropical trees. They all have electric lights, mosquito nets, linen, mattresses, pillows, and pull-down side mats for privacy. A central Samoan fale provides a lounge and dining area, and guests can also wander into the owner's traditional Samoan fale. Guests share cold-water showers. There's a communal kitchen and grocery shop, or you can walk to Stevenson's for lunch or dinner. Musicians entertain several nights a week here, and Tanu has island tours in its own bus. Rates are S$60 (US$20) per person, including breakfast and dinner. No credit cards.

On the same beach but in the middle of Manase village, **Jane's Beach Fales,** Post Office, Fagamalo (ℂ/fax **54-066;** sbec@samoa.ws), are a bit more luxurious—if that word can be applied to these rustic accommodations. Her 24 fales are larger than Tanu's. Each is about half front porch, half bedroom; they are thus much more pri-vate, and you can lock them. Most of her fales sit among palms and breadfruit trees on a lawn, as opposed to sand at Tanu, but one of them actually sits on stilts above the lagoon. Although it can get breezy it is the most private and romantic. Another has a kitchen and its own bathroom. The others share toilets, cold-water showers, and a communal kitchen. A restaurant here serves simple local-style meals daily and stages a fiafia on Friday or Saturday night. Jane charges S$50 (US$17) per person per night, including breakfast and dinner, but she does not accept credit cards.

14

American Samoa

One of the prime reasons to visit American Samoa is to see Tutuila, one of the South Pacific's most dramatically beautiful islands, and you'll get an eyeful of gorgeous scenery on the 11km (7-mile) ride from the airport at Tafuna into the legendary port of Pago Pago. But first you will see the effects of American dollars, for the area around the airport is a bustling suburb with shopping centers and a modern multiscreen cinema. You will see that the road is crowded with automobiles and buses and are patrolled by policemen in big American-style cruisers. It's little wonder, therefore, that many visitors view American Samoa as crowded, littered, run-down, and ruined by commercialism.

Yet the physical beauty of this little island competes favorably with the splendor of Moorea and Bora Bora in French Polynesia. Once the road clears the shopping area at Nu'uuli, it twists and turns along the rocky coastline. At places it rounds the cliffs of headlands that drop down to the sea; at others it curves along beaches in small bays backed by narrow valleys. All the way, the surf pounds on the reef. When you make the last turn at Blount's Point, you'll behold green walls dropping precipitously into Pago Pago Harbor.

Just try to ignore the mountain of rusting shipping containers and the two smelly tuna canneries on the shore of the harbor.

Despite the obvious inroads of Western ways and American loot, the local residents still cling to *fa'a Samoa,* the ancient Samoan way of life (see "The Samoan People," in chapter 13). While many young American Samoans wear Western clothes and speak only English, often with a pronounced Hawaiian or Californian accent, in the villages the older folk still converse in Samoan and abide by the old ways.

This also is the scene of the first American national park below the equator. Although it has yet to be developed, you can hike its trails and explore some of American Samoa's phenomenal beauty close up.

1 American Samoa Today

The seven islands of American Samoa are on the eastern end of the 483km-long (300 mile) Samoa Archipelago. Together they comprise a land area of 200 sq. km (77 sq. miles), almost half of which belong to **Tutuila,** the slender remains of an ancient volcano. One side of Tutuila's crater apparently blew away, almost cutting the island in two. This created the long, bent arm of **Pago Pago Harbor,** one of the South Pacific's most dramatically scenic spots.

Fewer American Samoans live in their home islands than reside in the United States. The expatriate American Samoans have been replaced at home by their kindred from independent Samoa and by some Tongans, who have swelled the population to about 65,000, up from 30,000 in the 1990s.

GOVERNMENT   American Samoa is the only U.S. territory south of the equator. American Samoans are "non-citizen nationals" of the United States. Although they carry American passports, have unrestricted entry into the United States, and can serve in the U.S. armed forces, they cannot vote in U.S. presidential elections.

The U.S. Department of the Interior has jurisdiction over American Samoa, but American Samoans elect their own governor and members of the lower house of the Fono, their bicameral legislature. In accordance with Samoan custom, local chiefs pick members of the local senate. The Fono has authority over the budget and local affairs, although both the governor and the U.S. Department of the Interior can veto the laws it passes. American Samoans also elect a nonvoting delegate to the U.S. House of Representatives in Washington, D.C.

The territorial government's annual budget is considerably larger than that of independent Samoa, which has a population some three times larger. Washington provides about half the government's revenue. Some 80% of the taxes raised locally go to pay more than 5,100 government employees, about 42% of the local workforce. They earn an average of almost US$8 an hour, the highest in the South Pacific outside of French Polynesia.

ECONOMY   Together the local government and the two tuna canneries employ about 80% of the local workforce. The canneries account for some 80% of the territory's private sector product. About 70% of their 4,700 workers are from nearby Samoa (they earn an average hourly wage of US$3.60, nearly three times what they can make at home). The aging canneries have survived for more than 50 years because of tax credits and duty-free access to the United States. Their existence is threatened since the tax credits expire at the end of 2006, and the same free trade advantages are being extended to canneries in other countries. Tourism is a minuscule part of the economy. Most visitors arrive on large cruise ships that infrequently put into Pago Pago for a day.

2 History 101

As friendly as American Samoans are today, their ancestors did anything but warmly welcome a French expedition under Jean La Pérouse, which came ashore in 1787 on the north coast of Tutuila. Samoan warriors promptly attacked, killing 12 members of the landing party, which in turn killed 39 Samoans. The site of the battle is known as **Massacre Bay.** La Pérouse survived that incident, but he and his entire expedition later disappeared in what is now the Solomon Islands.

In 1872, the U.S. Navy negotiated a treaty with the chiefs of Tutuila to permit it to use Pago Pago as a coaling station. The agreement helped keep the Germans out of Eastern Samoa, as present-day American Samoa was then known.

In 1900 the chiefs on Tutuila ceded control of their island to the United States, and the paramount chief of the Manu'a Group of islands east of Tutuila did likewise in 1905. Finally ratified by the U.S. Senate in 1929, those treaties are the legal foundation for the U.S. presence in American Samoa.

ON THE DOLE   From 1900 until 1951, U.S. authority in Samoa rested with the U.S. Navy, which maintained the refueling station at Pago Pago and for the most part let the local chiefs conduct their own affairs. Tutuila became a training base for U.S. servicemen during World War II, but things quickly returned to normal after 1945. Control of the territory was shifted from the navy to the U.S. Department of the Interior in 1951.

> **Fun Fact Unfriendly Fire**
>
> During World War II a Japanese submarine surfaced off Tutuila and lobbed a few shells ashore. Ironically, their target was a store owned by Frank Shimasaki, the island's only resident of Japanese descent.

The Department of the Interior did little in the islands until 1961, when *Reader's Digest* magazine ran an article about "America's shame in the South Seas." The story took great offense at the lack of roads and adequate schools, medical care, water and sewer service, and housing. The U.S. federal government reacted by paving the roads and building an international airport, water and electrical systems, the then-modern Rainmaker Hotel, and a convention center. A 1.5km (½ mile) -long cable was strung across Pago Pago Harbor to build a television transmitter atop 480m (1,610 ft.) Mount Alava, from which education programming was beamed into the schools.

For fear of losing all that federal money, American Samoans were reluctant to tinker with their political relationship with Washington during the 1960s and 1970s, when other South Pacific colonies were becoming independent. The United States offered local autonomy, but they refused. They changed minds in the mid-1970s, when an appointed governor was very unpopular, and elected their own governor for the first time in 1977.

3 Visitor Information & Entry Requirements

VISITOR INFORMATION

The **American Samoa Office of Tourism**, P.O. Box 1147, Pago Pago, AS 96799 (© **699-9411;** fax 699-9414; www.amerikasamoa.info), has offices inconveniently located in Tafuna, near the airport. The office is open Monday to Friday from 8am to 4pm.

The **Delegate from American Samoa to the U.S. Congress** also dispenses some tourist information. The address is U.S. House of Representatives, Washington, DC 20515 (© **202/225-8577**).

ENTRY REQUIREMENTS

Except for Samoans, New Zealanders, and a few others, entry permits are not required for stays of up to 30 days. American citizens and nationals need valid passports or certified birth certificates (forget the birth certificate and bring your passport). Everyone else needs a valid passport and a ticket for onward passage. Women more than 6 months pregnant are not allowed entry.

Immunizations are not required.

Customs allowances are 1 liter of liquor or wine and one carton of cigarettes. Illegal drugs and firearms are prohibited, and pets are quarantined. U.S. citizens get larger customs allowances for purchases made in American Samoa than they do elsewhere in the South Pacific, provided that they have been in the territory for at least 48 hours (see "What You Can Take Home," in chapter 2).

4 Money

United States currency is used in American Samoa. Samoan *tala* are not accepted, nor can they be exchanged here.

HOW TO GET LOCAL CURRENCY   The **Bank of Hawaii** and the **ANZ Amerika Samoa Bank,** both in Fagatogo, are open Monday to Friday 9am to 3pm. Both have ATMs at their main offices, and ANZ has one in Pago Plaza, the shopping center at the head of the harbor.

CREDIT CARDS   American Express, Visa, MasterCard, and Diners Club are accepted by the hotels, car-rental firms, and airlines. Otherwise, it's best to carry cash to cover your anticipated expenses. No one here accepts Discover.

5 When to Go

CLIMATE

"It did not pour, it flowed," wrote W. Somerset Maugham in his 1921 short story "Rain," the famous tale of prostitute Sadie Thompson, who seduces a puritanical missionary while stranded in American Samoa. This description, however, applies mainly to Pago Pago, which, because of its location behind appropriately named Rainmaker Mountain, gets an average of over 500cm (200 in.) of rain per year. The rest of American Samoa enjoys a typically tropical climate, with lots of very intense sunshine even during the wet season from December to April. Average daily high temperatures range from 83°F (28°C) in the drier and somewhat cooler months of June through September to 86°F (30°C) from December to April, when midday can be hot and sticky. Evenings are usually in the comfortable 70s (21°C–26°C) all year-round.

EVENTS & HOLIDAYS

The biggest celebration is on April 17, when **American Samoa Flag Day** commemorates the raising of the Stars and Stripes over Tutuila in 1900. The second Sunday in October is observed as **White Sunday;** children attend church dressed in white and are later honored at family feasts.

   Public holidays are New Year's Day, Martin Luther King Jr. Day (third Mon in Jan), President's Day (third Mon in Feb), Good Friday, American Samoa Flag Day (Apr 17), Memorial Day (last Mon in May), the Fourth of July, Labor Day (first Mon in Sept), Columbus Day (second Mon in Oct), Veteran's Day (Nov 11), Thanksgiving (fourth Thurs of Nov), and Christmas Day.

6 Getting There & Getting Around

GETTING THERE

FROM SAMOA   Polynesian Airlines (© **800/644-7659** in the U.S., 22-737 in Apia, or 633-4331 in Pago Pago; www.polynesianairlines.com) and **Inter Island Airways** (© **42-580** in Samoa, 699-5700 in American Samoa; www.interislandair.com) both fly between Faleolo Airport in Samoa and Pago Pago several times a day. Round-trip adult fares are about S$330 (US$109) if purchased in Apia, US$121 plus taxes if bought in American Samoa.

   For the adventurous, a relatively modern ferry, the *Lady Naomi,* makes the 8-hour voyage between Pago Pago and Apia at least once a week, usually leaving the main wharf in Apia at 11pm on Wednesday and departing Pago Pago's marine terminal at 4pm on Thursday for the return voyage. Tickets should be bought at least a day ahead of time. One-way tickets purchased in Apia cost S$75 (US$25) for a seat, S$100 (US$33) for a cabin. The *Lady Naomi* is operated by the **Samoa Shipping Corporation,** whose ticket office is on Beach Road, opposite the main wharf in Apia

> **Tips Reconfirm Your Return Flight at the Airport**
>
> Right after you land at Pago Pago, go to the airline's office and reconfirm your
> return flight. This is especially important if you're flying back to Apia on the
> last flight of the day.

(© 20-935; www.samoashipping.com). The American Samoa agent is **Polynesia
Shipping Services** (© 633-1211). Because the trade winds prevail from the southeast, the trip going west with the wind toward Apia is usually somewhat smoother.

FROM OTHER COUNTRIES   The only international carrier serving American
Samoa is **Hawaiian Airlines,** which flies from several U.S. West Coast cities to Pago
Pago, with a change of planes at its base at Honolulu. Otherwise, you can fly to Faleolo Airport in Samoa on **Air New Zealand, Air Pacific,** or **Polynesian Blue,** and then
connect to Pago Pago. For more information, see "Getting There & Getting Around,"
in chapter 2.

ARRIVING & DEPARTING   **Pago Pago International Airport** is near the village
of Tafuna, about 11km (7 miles) west of Pago Pago. Taxi fare is about US$10 from
the airport to Pago Pago. The "Tafuna" local buses stop at the airport terminal on their
way into Pago Pago. Bus fare is US50¢.

A US$3 departure tax is included in the ticket price.

GETTING AROUND
Inter Island Airways (© 42-580 in Samoa, 699-5700 in American Samoa;
www.interislandair.com), the local carrier, flies to the Manu'a Islands, but don't count
on it. The territory has had trouble keeping a domestic airline recently.

BY RENTAL CAR   The only international car-rental firm in American Samoa is
Avis (© 800/331-1212 or 699-4408; www.avis.com), which rents air-conditioned
models for US$55 to US$65 per day, including unlimited mileage, plus an optional
US$10 for insurance. Local firms include **Sir Amos** (© 633-4554), **Friendly**
(© 699-7186), and **Dollar Rental Car** (© 633-7716; dollarrentalcar@yahoo.com).
The latter is not affiliated with the international rental company of the same name.

Your valid home driver's license will be honored in American Samoa. **Driving is on
the right-hand side of the road,** and traffic signs are the same as those used in the
United States. The speed limit is 15 mph in the built-up areas and 25 mph on the
open road.

BY BUS   Gaily painted *aiga* buses prowl the roads from early morning until sunset
every day except Sunday. Basically they run from the villages to the market in Pago
Pago and back, picking up anyone who waves along the way. Some buses leave the
market and run to Fagasa on the north coast or to the east end of the island; others
go from the market to the west. None goes from one end of the island to the other,
so you'll have to change at the market in order to do a stem-to-stern tour of Tutuila.
Most drivers are helpful, so just ask how far they go in each direction. Fares are
between US50¢ and US$1 per ride.

BY TAXI   There are **taxi stands** at the **airport** (© 699-1179) and at the **Pago Pago
market** (no phone). None of the taxis have meters, so be sure to negotiate the fare
before driving off. The fares should be about US$1 per mile.

FAST FACTS: American Samoa

American Express There is no American Express representative in American Samoa.

Baggage Storage The hotels will store your extra gear for free.

Business Hours Normal shopping hours are Monday to Friday 8am to 5pm and Saturday from 9am to noon. Government offices are open Monday to Friday 8am to 4pm.

Clothing Lightweight, informal summer clothing is appropriate all year, with a light sweater or wrap for evenings from June through September. Young American Samoans have adopted Western-style dress, including jeans and shorts of respectable length, although the traditional wraparound *lava-lava* is still worn by many older men and women. In keeping with Samoan custom regarding modesty, visitors should not wear bathing suits or other skimpy clothing away from the hotels. Women must confine their bikini tops to the beach.

Drugstores See "Healthcare," below.

Electricity American Samoa uses 110-volt electric current and plugs identical to those in the United States.

E-mail **DDW Internet Cafe,** in Pago Plaza at the head of the bay (✆ **633-5297**), has Internet access for US$3 for 15 minutes, US$5 for 30 minutes, US$10 for an hour. See "Where to Dine," later in this chapter.

Embassies/Consulates Independent Samoa and the Republic of Korea have consulates, and the Republic of China (Taiwan) maintains a liaison office in Pago Pago, primarily to assist the Korean and Taiwanese crews of the tuna boats unloading their catches at the tuna canneries.

Emergencies The emergency telephone number for the **police, fire department,** and **ambulance** is ✆ **911.** In a medical emergency, you can call or go to **Lyndon B. Johnson Tropical Medical Center** (see "Healthcare," below). The **police station** (✆ **633-1111**) is in Fagatogo, across the *malae* (open field) from the Fono.

Eyeglasses **Pacific Vision Center,** in Pago Plaza at the head of the harbor (✆ **633-1076**).

Firearms Guns are tightly controlled, and permits are required.

Gambling There are no casinos or other organized forms of gambling in American Samoa. Money is wagered at very popular bingo games.

Healthcare The **Lyndon B. Johnson Tropical Medical Center** (✆ **633-5555** for emergencies, or 633-1222) in Faga'alu west of Pago Pago (turn off the main road at Tom Ho Chung's store) handles the territory's medical and dental services. The outpatient clinic is open 24 hours daily. Frankly, you will get much better treatment in Apia (see "Fast Facts: Samoa" in chapter 13).

Insects There are no dangerous insects in American Samoa, and the plentiful mosquitoes do not carry malaria.

Libraries   The **Feleti-Barstow Public Library** (© 633-5816), in the government buildings in Utulei, is open Monday to Wednesday and Friday 9am to 5pm, Tuesday and Thursday 9am to 7pm, and Saturday 10am to 2pm.

Liquor Laws   There are no unusual laws to worry about. The minimum drinking age is 21.

Maps   The best map of the territory is in the brochure published by the National Park of American Samoa (see below). The American Samoa Office of Tourism distributes a sheet of maps (see "Visitor Information & Entry Requirements," above).

Newspapers/Magazines   The daily *Samoa News* (www.samoanews.com) is the dominant newspaper here. The *Samoa Post* and the *American Samoan Tribune* also appear.

Post Office   The U.S. Postal Service's main post office is in Fagatogo. Regular U.S. domestic postage rates apply, and first-class and priority letters and packages go by air between American Samoa and the United States. Unless you pay the first-class or priority mail rate, however, parcel post is sent by ship and will take several weeks to reach Hawaii or the U.S. mainland. The post office is open Monday to Friday 7:30am to 3:30pm, Saturday 9am to noon. The zip code for Pago Pago is **96799.**

Radio/TV   The transmitters atop Mount Alava are used during the day to send educational TV programs to the territory's public schools and to transmit CNN and live sporting events. At night they broadcast two channels of U.S. network entertainment programs. The broadcasts can be seen 129km (80 miles) away, on eastern Upolu in Samoa. Many homes in American Samoa also have cable television. The territory has three FM radio stations, which transmit American network news broadcasts on the hour.

Safety   Street crime is not a serious problem in American Samoa except late at night around Pago Pago Harbor. Fa'a Samoa and its rules of communal ownership are still in effect, however, so it's wise not to leave cameras, watches, or other valuables unattended or in your rental car.

Taxes   The US$3 airport departure tax is included in ticket prices. There is no sales tax, but an invisible import tax of 5% is imposed on most merchandise (it's much stiffer on tobacco and alcoholic beverages).

Telephone/Fax   Telephone calls can be dialed directly into American Samoa from most parts of the world. The territory's international country code is **684.**

Pay phones are the same type used throughout the United States. The number for directory assistance is © **411.** For emergencies, dial © **911.**

The easiest way to call home from here is to buy a prepaid **Blue Sky card,** available at many shops. You can use these cards from any phone as you would a prepaid card at home. Several international companies have access numbers here, including **AT&T** (© **633-2872**), **MCI** (© **633-2624**), **Sprint** (© **633-1000**), **GTE/Verizon** (© **633-1706**), and **Hawaii Verizon** (© **633-2482**).

You can also place overseas calls at **American Samoa Telecommunications Authority (SamoaTelCo),** diagonally across the Fagatogo malae from the Fono building. It is open 24 hours daily.

Blue Sky (℗ 699-2759; www.bluesky.as), which has offices in Pago Plaza and in the Lafou shopping center on the main road in Nu'uli, rents cell phones for US$25 a week plus air time. You can also buy a prepaid SIM card for your own unlocked GSM phone.

Time The local time in American Samoa is the same as in independent Samoa: 11 hours behind Greenwich Mean Time. That's 3 hours behind Pacific Standard Time (4 hr. behind during daylight saving time). In other words, if it's noon standard time in California and 3pm in New York, it's 9am in Pago Pago. If daylight saving time is in effect in the United States, it's 8am in American Samoa.

American Samoa is east of the international date line and shares the same date with North America, 1 day behind Tonga, Fiji, Australia, and New Zealand.

Tipping Although this is a U.S. territory, officially there is no tipping in American Samoa. A lot of American Samoans have lived in the United States, however, so the practice is not exactly uncommon.

Water The tap water is treated and is safe to drink except during periods of heavy rain.

Weights/Measures American Samoa is the only country or territory in the South Pacific whose official system of weights and measures is the same as that used in the United States—pounds and miles, not the metric system of kilograms and kilometers.

7 Exploring American Samoa

A STROLL THROUGH PAGO PAGO

Although the actual village of Pago Pago sits at the head of the harbor, everyone considers Pago Pago to be the built-up area on the south shore of the harbor, including Fagatogo, the government and business center. The harbor is also called the Bay Area. Despite development that has come with economic growth of the territory, Pago Pago still has much of the old South Seas atmosphere that captivated W. Somerset Maugham when he wrote "Rain" in the 1920s.

A stroll through the Pago Pago area should take about 2 hours. Begin at **Sadie's by the Sea Hotel** on the east end of the inner harbor, actually in the village of Utulei (see "Where to Stay," later in this chapter). Just across the main road from the hotel, a set of concrete steps climbs to **Government House,** the clapboard mansion built in 1903 to house the governor of American Samoa. The mansion is not open to the public, but there is a nice view from the top of the steps looking back over the hotel and across the harbor to flat-top Rainmaker Mountain.

Back on the main road heading north toward town, you walk past a mountain of shipping containers that stand idle on the main wharf. Beyond the busy port terminal and opposite the post office is the **Jean P. Haydon Museum** (℗ 633-4347), in an old iron-roofed building that was once the U.S. Navy's commissary. The museum has been undergoing a lengthy renovation, so it might not be open when you arrive. If it is, you'll find exhibits on Samoan history, sea life, canoes, kava making, and traditional tools and handicrafts, including the finely woven mats that have such great

Pago Pago

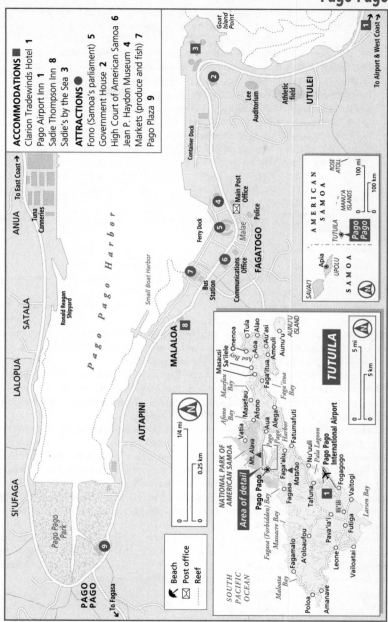

ACCOMMODATIONS ■
Clarion Tradewinds Hotel **1**
Pago Airport Inn **1**
Sadie Thompson Inn **8**
Sadie's by the Sea **3**

ATTRACTIONS ●
Fono (Samoa's parliament) **5**
Government House **2**
High Court of American Samoa **6**
Jean P. Haydon Museum **4**
Markets (produce and fish) **7**
Pago Plaza **9**

Goat Island Point

To Airport & West Coast →

UTULEI

Lee Auditorium

Athletic field

Container Dock

To East Coast →

ANUA

Tuna Canneries

SATALA

Ronald Reagan Shipyard

LALOPUA

SI'UFAGA

Pago Pago Harbor

Small Boat Harbor

Ferry Dock

Main Post Office

Malae

Police

FAGATOGO

Communications Office

Bus Station

MALALOA

AUTAPINI

PAGO PAGO

↙ To Fagasa

Pago Pago Park

Beach
⊠ **Post office**
····· **Reef**

N
0   1/4 mi
0   0.25 km

AMERICAN SAMOA

ROSE ATOLL

MANU'A ISLANDS

TUTUILA

Pago Pago

SAVAI'I

Apia

UPOLU

SAMOA

N
0   100 mi
0   100 km

TUTUILA

SOUTH PACIFIC OCEAN

NATIONAL PARK OF AMERICAN SAMOA

Area of detail

Mt. Alava

Pago Pago

Fagasa (Forbidden) Bay

Massacre Bay

Fagamalo
A'oloaufou
Leone
Vailoatai
Poloa
Amanave

Maloata Bay

Vatia
Afono
Masefau
Masefau Bay
Afono Bay

Aua
Pago Pago Harbor
Faga'alu
Matafao
Fagasa

Nu'uuli
Pala Lagoon
Pago Pago International Airport

Tafuna
Ili'ili
Futiga
Pava'ia'i

Alega
Fatumafuti
Fogagogo
Vaitogi

Larsen Bay

Fagaitua
Fagaitua Bay

Faga'itua

Amouli
Au'asi
Aoa
Alao
Tula
Onenoa

Masausi
Sa'ilele
Aoa Bay

AUNU'U ISLAND

Aunu'u

MANU'U ISLAND

N
0   5 mi
0   5 km

399

> **Tips**   **Seeing American Samoa as a Day Trip from Apia**
>
> You can see American Samoa as a 1-day side trip from independent Samoa. The easiest way is to buy a package from **Oceania Travel & Tours,** at the Kitano Tusitala Hotel in Apia (© **24-443**; fax 22-255; www.oceania-travel.ws). The US$250 per-person fee includes round-trip airfare, a guided tour of Tutuila island, and lunch. Oceania's American Samoa office is above the main post office in Pago Pago (© **633-1172**).
>
> To do it yourself, fly early in the morning from Apia to Pago Pago. Go immediately to the airline's office and reconfirm your afternoon return flight, then pick up a rental car (there is too much to see here to rely on the local bus system or even a taxi). Drive into Pago Pago and take the stroll described in "Exploring American Samoa," above. Drive out to the eastern end of the island, then backtrack to Pago Pago and have lunch. If you have time in the afternoon, drive out to the western end. Catch the last flight back to Apia.

value in Samoa and Tonga. Normal hours are Monday to Friday 9am to 3pm, except on holidays. Admission is free, but donations are accepted.

Every Samoan village has a **malae,** or open field, and the area across from the museum is Fagatogo's. The chiefs of Tutuila met on this malae in 1900 to sign the treaty that officially established the United States in Samoa. The round modern building across the road beside the harbor is the **Fono,** American Samoa's legislature; the visitors' galleries are open to the public. The ramshackle stores along the narrow streets on the other side of the malae were Pago Pago's "downtown" for half a century, although like any other place under the Stars and Stripes, much business is now conducted in suburban shopping centers. On the malae, the **American Samoa Archives Office** occupies the old stone jail that was built in 1911.

Just beyond the malae on the main road stands the **Judicial Building,** home of the **High Court** of American Samoa (everyone calls it the Court House). The big white clapboard building with columns looks as if it should be in South Carolina rather than the South Pacific. Across the road on the waterfront stands **Fagatogo Plaza,** a modern shopping center. In marked contrast to Fagatogo Plaza are the **produce and fish markets** a few yards farther on. They are usually poorly stocked, and when they do have produce, it most likely comes by ferry from Samoa. The markets also serve as the bus terminal.

Continuing north along the harbor, you soon come to the historic **Sadie Thompson Building,** where W. Somerset Maugham stayed in the 1920s. Now home to the Sadie Thompson Inn and restaurant (see "Where to Stay" and "Where to Dine," below), it is the best place in town for lunch before touring the island.

A TOUR OF TUTUILA
THE NORTH COAST OF TUTUILA
A paved road turns off the main highway at Spenser's Store in Pago Pago village and leads up **Vaipito Valley,** across a ridge, and down to Fagasa, a village huddled beside

picturesque Fagasa, or **Forbidden Bay,** on Tutuila's north shore. The road is steep but paved all the way, and the view from atop the ridge is excellent. The track up Mount Alava begins on the saddle (see "National Park of American Samoa," below). Legend says that porpoises long ago led a group of three men and three women to safety in Fagasa Bay, which has long been a porpoise sanctuary.

THE EAST SIDE OF TUTUILA

The 29km (18 mile) drive from Pago Pago to the east end of Tutuila skirts along the harbor, past the canneries and their fishy odor, and then winds around one headland after another. Watch particularly for **Pyramid Rock** and the **Lion's Head,** where you can wade out to a small beach. (Never go in the water anywhere here unless the locals are already swimming there.).

From Aua, at the foot of Rainmaker Mountain, a switch-backing road runs across Rainmaker Pass (great views from up there) to the lovely north-shore village of **Vatia,** on a bay of the same name. If you're going to venture off the main road, this is the place to do it. The north-shore coastal road runs through National Park of Samoa land and is the only way to visit the park without hiking (see "National Park of American Samoa," below). World War II pillboxes still dot the beach here. At the north end of Vatia Bay sits the skinny, offshore rock formation known as **The Cockscomb,** one of Tutuila's trademarks.

Another paved road leaves Faga'itua village and climbs to a saddle in the ridge, where it divides. The left fork goes down to Masefau Bay; the right goes to Masausi and Sa'ilele villages. Near the east end, a road from Amouli village cuts across Lemafa Saddle to **Aoa Bay** on the north coast.

To my eye, the southeastern coast road is the most scenic in American Samoa. The route twists and turns from one gorgeous little bay to the next, most of them with villages beside white-sand beaches. **Aunu'u Island** will be visible from the main road as you near the east end of Tutuila. The top of a small volcanic crater, Aunu'u has a village near a famous pink quicksand pit. Motorboats leave for it from the small-boat harbor at Au'asi, opposite it on the southeast coast.

Alao and **Tula** villages on the east end of Tutuila are the oldest settlements in American Samoa. They face a long, gorgeous surf beach, but be careful of the undertow from waves driven by the prevailing southeast trade winds. The road turns the northwestern point and climbs precipitously over a mountain ridge and down to **Onenoa,** a picturesque village tucked in a little bay. You'll have a fine view of the north shore and the Cockscombs as you descend into Onenoa.

THE WEST SIDE OF TUTUILA

You saw some of Tutuila's rugged coast on the drive from the airport west of Pago Pago, including the **Flower Pot,** a tall rock with coconut palms growing on its top sitting in the lagoon. About halfway from the airport to The Rainmaker Hotel, an inland road (at Tom Ho Chung's store) leads to the **Lyndon B. Johnson Tropical Medical Center** in the Faga'alu Valley. If you feel like taking a hike, take the left fork in the road past the medical center, and when the pavement ends, follow the track to **Virgin Falls.** It's not the easiest walk, but the falls have a nice pool beneath them. Allow several hours for this sweaty outing.

The **airport** sits on the island's only sizable parcel of relatively flat land, and the main road west from there cuts through rolling hills and shopping centers until emerging on the rugged west end.

Tips **A Fascinating Pit Stop**

Ramshackle bars by the beach are part of the South Seas lore, but few of these establishments actually exist these days. One that does is **Tisa's Barefoot Bar** on Alega Beach (© **622-7447**). This funky joint looks slapped together because it actually is. The owners put it together from driftwood, scrap lumber, well-worn tables, and whatever else they could find lying around. Libation is served daily from 11am to 7pm, with seafood dinners afterward by advance reservation only. You can go snorkeling and swimming here at high tide, and you can pay your bill at any tide with your American Express, MasterCard, or Visa.

At Pava'ia'i village a road goes inland and climbs to the village of A'oloaufou, high on a central plateau. A hiking trail leads from the village down the ridges to the north coast. From here it drops to A'asutuai on **Massacre Bay,** where Samoans attacked the La Pérouse expedition in 1787. The French have put a monument there to the members of the expedition who were slain by Samoan warriors. Do not undertake this hike unless you have experience on mountain trails, and if you do go, take plenty of water to drink.

Back on the main road, head west and watch for a sign on the left marking the turn to the villages of Illi'ili and Vaitogi. Follow the signs to **Vaitogi,** and when you're in the village, bear right at the fork to the beach. Take the one-lane track to the right along the beach, past some graves and the stone remains of an old church, and up a rocky headland through pandanus groves. When you reach the first clearing on the left, stop the car and walk over to the cliff. According to legend, Vaitogi once experienced such a severe famine that an old blind woman and her granddaughter jumped off this cliff and were turned into a shark and a turtle. Today the villagers can reputedly chant their names, and the turtle and the shark will appear. The view of the south coast from **Turtle and Shark Point,** with the surf pounding the rocks below you, is superb.

The Rev. John Williams chose the picturesque village of **Leone,** which sits on a white-sand beach in a small bay, as his landing place on Tutuila in 1830, and it became the cradle of Christianity here. There is a monument to Williams in the village. The road beside the Catholic church leads about 2.5km (1½ miles) to **Leone Falls,** which has a freshwater pool for swimming (but as in the equally religious Samoa, never on Sun).

The road from Leone to the western end of the island winds in and out of small bays with sandy beaches and climbs spectacularly across a ridge to Poloa village on the northwest coast.

8 National Park of American Samoa

The **National Park of American Samoa** was authorized by the U.S. Congress in 1988. Although its facilities have been slow in coming (little has been developed except a few rough hiking trails), the park has amassed some 10,000 pristine acres—3,000 of them on Tutuila and another 6,000 in the Manu'a Islands. In all, they protect some beautiful shoreline, magnificent beaches, cliffs dropping into the sea, colorful reefs, and rainforest reaching to serrated, mist-shrouded mountain peaks.

Unlike other U.S. National Parks, in which the federal government buys property outright, here the National Park Service has leased the land from the villages for 50 years, thereby protecting both the natural environment and traditional Samoan ownership customs.

Because development is ongoing, you should stop by the **Park Visitors Center,** in the Pago Plaza shopping center at the head of the bay, or contact them at NPAS, Pago Pago, AS 96799 (© **633-7082;** fax 633-7085; www.nps.gov/npsa). The center has exhibits that explain Samoa's prehistory.

On Tutuila, the park starts along the ridge atop Mount Alava and drops down sharp ridges and steep valleys to the north coast. It includes The Cockscomb off the north coast and the scenic Amalau Valley, near the picturesque north-shore village of Vatia, where you can see many of Samoa's native bird species plus flying foxes (fruit bats). See "A Tour of Tutuila," above, for directions to Vatia.

Hikers can scale 480m (1,600 ft.) Mount Alava via a trail that begins in the Fagasa Pass and ascends steeply through the rainforest. It's a 3-hour walk uphill along a seldom used four-wheel-drive track, and it takes about 2 hours to get back down, but you'll be rewarded with a view over the entire Pago Pago Harbor and most of Tutuila Island. It's one of the most spectacular vistas in the South Pacific, if not the world. Be sure to take plenty of water.

An easier hike follows the paved road between Afono and Vatia on the north shore. This route skirts cliffs and beaches, and you'll have a view of the Cockscomb offshore. Birds, bats, and land crabs will keep you company.

Rory West of **North Shore Tours** (© **644-1416** or 733-3047) has various expeditions to the north coast, including hiking, camping, and fishing trips. Prices start at US$25 per person.

9 Where to Stay

If you are a bed-and-breakfast type, check out Marvin and Tai Leach's **Sliding Rock Resort,** P.O. Box 2001, Pago Pago, AS 96799 (© **688-7553;** fax 688-1567; www.slidingrockresort.com), and Isabel and Dean Hudson's **Le Falepule,** P.O. Box 4179, Pago Pago, AS 96799 (© **633-5246;** fax 633-5648; www.american.samoa-hotels.com/le-falepule/Index.html).

Clarion Tradewinds Hotel 🦋🦋   Located in an area known as Ottoville west of the airport, this plantation-style property is very good. It would be terrific were it beside a beach instead of this inland setting. You won't be entirely without a place to swim and sun here, for a gleaming white marble floor leads through the two-story reception area to an outdoor pool in a landscaped courtyard to the rear of the three-story, stucco building. Guest quarters include Taupou rooms with two double beds, Manaia rooms with king beds, Maitai suites with king beds and dining tables, and Plaza suites with a separate bedroom. Some have patios or balconies. Teak furniture and sleigh- or four-poster beds lend a bit of elegance throughout. The restaurant and bar reside in a separate building.

P.O. Box 999, Pago Pago, AS 96799 (Ottoville Rd. off Airport Rd., 2.5km/1½ miles west of airport). © **699-1000.** Fax 699-1010. www.tradewinds.as. 104 units. US$135–US$150 double, US$165–US$240 suite. Rates include limousine airport transfers. AE, MC, V. **Amenities:** Restaurant; coffee shop; bar; outdoor pool; exercise room; car-rentals; salon; limited room service; laundry service. *In room:* A/C, TV, high-speed dataport, fridge (stocked on request), coffeemaker.

(**Tips** **Staying with a Samoan Family**

The National Park of American Samoa (see above) operates a **homestay pro-gram** known as *Fale, Fala Ma Ti*, in which it matches visitors seeking inexpensive accommodation with local families willing to take in paying guests. Some are Western-style houses; others are Samoan beach *fales* like those in independent Samoa. The Samoan hospitality will more than make up for the simple accommodation. Prior arrangements are required.

Pago Airport Inn   In a village setting west of the airport, this two-story motel is a more basic and less expensive alternative to the Clarion Tradewinds Hotel (see above). The dark motel-style rooms open to veranda-like walkways across the front of the white stucco building. The units are simple but clean. Each is equipped with a double or two single beds, cable TV mounted on the wall, a desk and chairs, and a tiled shower-only bathroom. A restaurant is open for breakfast and lunch only. It's a 15-minute walk to the island's McDonald's and Kentucky Fried Chicken outlets, but consider renting a car.

P.O. Box 783, Pago Pago, AS 96799 (Tafuna, 3 min. from airport). ℂ **699-6333.** Fax 699-6336. www.pago airportinn.com. 19 units. US$99 double. Rates include airport transfers. AE, MC, V. **Amenities:** Restaurant (breakfast and lunch); laundry service. *In room:* A/C, TV, fridge, coffeemaker, hair dryer, iron.

Sadie's by the Sea   I cannot tell you much about this hotel, since it had not yet fully opened during my recent visit. Nevertheless, I am sure it will be worthy of consideration since it is being developed by Tom and Ta'aloga Drabble, who did a terrific job with the Sadie Thompson Inn (see below). Sadie's by the Sea actually is two completely refurbished wings of the original Rainmaker Hotel, which opened in 1965 as an InterContinental hotel but which had gone steadily downhill in recent times. The wings sit by a good swimming beach, and their rooms have sea views. The complex will have a restaurant, bar, and swimming pool by the end of 2006. Meantime, guests are being provided with complimentary breakfast, and a shuttle runs to Sadie's Restaurant and Bar. There will be a website; search for Sadie's by the Sea.

P.O. Box 3222, Pago Pago, AS 96799 (Goat Island Point, at entrance to harbor). ℂ **699-5714.** Fax 699-2083. 46 units. US$135–US$150. AE, DC, MC, V. **Amenities:** Restaurant; bar; outdoor pool; kayak rentals; car rentals; limited room service; laundry service; coin-op washers and dryers. *In room:* A/C, TV, dataport, fridge, hairdryer, iron.

Sadie Thompson Inn 🏨🏨   This historic wooden structure was a rooming house when W. Somerset Maugham stayed here in the 1920s, and it provided the setting for his famous short story "Rain." Present-day owners Tom and Ta'aloga Drabble have turned it into this comfortable inn. Each named for a character in "Rain," the units are upstairs over Sadie's Restaurant and Bar (see "Where to Dine," below). The best for my money is a suite at the front of the building with a view of the harbor and Rainmaker Mountain. One of the suites has a separate bedroom, and two have large bathrooms with whirlpool tubs and showers. Most of the eight standard rooms are on the back of the building, but two others open to a long open-air passageway with harbor view.

P.O. Box 3222, Pago Pago, AS 96799 (in Pago Pago). ℂ **633-5981.** Fax 633-5982. www.sadiethompsoninn.com. 14 units. US$135–US$195. Rates include airport transfers. AE, DC, MC, V. **Amenities:** Restaurant; bar; limited room service; laundry service. *In room:* A/C, TV, high-speed dataport, minibar, coffeemaker, hair dryer, iron.

10 Where to Dine

The food doesn't match the harbor view, but a decent place to refresh during your walking tour of Pago Pago is the inexpensive **Waterfront Restaurant** (© **633-1199**), in the Fagatogo Square shops opposite the High Court. It offers pizzas, fried chicken, sandwiches, hamburgers, hot dogs, nachos, fish and chips, and daily specials such as fried fish with rice and gravy, a fattening local favorite. Open Monday to Friday 6am to 5pm, Saturday 6am to 3pm. No credit cards.

The DeLuxe Cafe *Value* AMERICAN   I usually stop for breakfast at this modern, American-style cafe complete with Leatherette booths. The walls are adorned with large paintings of Samoan wildlife both in and out of the sea, which adds a touch of sophistication. Among the eye-openers are fresh fruit plates and banana pancakes. Lunch sees a collection of American-style soups, salads, sandwiches, burgers, and fried chicken, shrimp, and fish.

Nu'uuli, on main rd. east of airport. © **699-4000**. Breakfast US$4–US$9; lunch US$5–US$15. AE, MC, V (US$10 minimum purchase). Mon–Sat 7am–2pm, Sun 9am–2pm.

Don't Drink the Water (DDW) Cafe AMERICAN   You can check your e-mail while having breakfast or lunch at this friendly cafe in the Pago Plaza shopping center at the head of the harbor. The hearty chow is all American: pancakes, omelets, burgers (including veggie patties), grilled sandwiches, steaks, and grilled or fried fish. The owners moved this cafe from Apia where you can't drink the water; hence its name.

Pago Pago, in Pago Plaza. © **633-5297**. Breakfast US$2.50–US$6.50; lunch US$2.50–US$12. MC, V. Mon–Fri 7am–2:30pm (Internet cafe to 4pm), Sat 7am–12:30pm.

Rubbles Tavern AMERICAN/MEXICAN   It's a long way from town, but this friendly air-conditioned pub is a good place to cool off while you're waiting for the last plane back to Apia. Except for the bamboo lining the walls of one dining room and the mat panels and huge Samoan war canoe rudder adorning the other, Rubbles could be in any Western city. You can even watch live contests on the two TVs that show sporting events behind the long bar. The fare includes salads, nachos, burgers, sandwiches, chicken wings, and grilled steaks and fish.

Nu'uuli, on main rd. in Nu'uuli Shopping Center (west of airport turnoff). © **633-4403**. Burgers, sandwiches, and salads US$8–US$11; main courses US$7.50–US$25. AE, MC, V. Mon–Sat 10am–11pm (bar open later), Sun 10am–2pm.

Sadie's Restaurant and Bar ✦ AMERICAN   This pleasant, American-style restaurant on the ground floor of the Sadie Thompson Inn is the most refined and best place to dine in American Samoa. You can get cooked or continental breakfasts; lunches of burgers, sandwiches, salads, and a few mains such as fish and chips; and dinners ranging from beef Wellington to steamed Alaska crab legs with drawn butter. Freshest is the daily catch, served either grilled, poached, or Cajun style. The attractive bar next door is decorated with posters advertising the various movies based on Somerset Maugham's "Rain." Wednesday is *fiafia* night, with a buffet and Samoan dance presentation.

Pago Pago, in Sadie Thompson Inn. © **633-5981**. Reservations recommended for lunch and dinner. Breakfast US$6.50–US$14; lunch US$8.50–US$20; main courses US$22–US$37. AE, DC, MC, V. Daily 6–10:30am, 11am–3pm, and 6–10pm (bar later).

15

The Kingdom of Tonga

Thanks to a quirk of humankind and not of nature, the international date line swings eastward from its north–south path down the middle of the Pacific Ocean just enough to make the last Polynesian monarch the first sovereign to see the light of each new day. When King Taufa'ahau Tupou IV of Tonga greets the dawn and looks out on his realm from the veranda of his whitewashed Victorian palace, he sees a country of low but extremely fertile islands, of gorgeous sandy beaches, and of colorful coral reefs waiting to be explored.

His nation is protected—but was never ruled—by a Western power. Like Samoa to the north, Tonga has managed to maintain its Polynesian culture in the face of modern change. The Tonga Visitors Bureau is spot on when it says the kingdom "still remains far away from it all; still different, still alone, and to the joy of those who find their way to her—essentially unspoiled."

While this description is true of the perfectly flat main island Tongatapu, it is even more applicable to Vava'u and Ha'a-pai. Vava'u is a group of hilly islands whose fjordlike harbor makes it one of the South Pacific's most popular yachting destinations. The low islands of the Ha'a-pai group seem to have changed little since the crew of HMS *Bounty* staged their mutiny just offshore in 1789. Visiting Vava'u is extremely pleasant to the eyes, and you should make every effort to see it and its multitudinous islets.

Along with my taste for adventure, I make sure to bring my sense of humor to Tonga. You may need yours, too, for things don't always go according to plan here. This is, after all, the poorest country covered in this book. The local airlines might not come to get you, the electricity might suddenly quit working, and the tap water might be turned off during your lukewarm shower (not that you can drink it when it's running). You'll see multitudes of dogs, chickens, and even pigs almost everywhere, even wandering the streets of Nuku'alofa, the capital. But if you take the unexpected quirks of humankind with a smile, you will thoroughly enjoy your time in Tonga, during which you will get a most fascinating glimpse into the way things used to be out here.

1 Tonga Today

When you drive from the airport into **Nuku'alofa,** the nation's capital, you can see why the country's main island is named **Tongatapu (Sacred Garden).** Every bit of it not occupied by a building or by the road is under cultivation with bananas, tapioca, taro, yams, watermelons, tomatoes, squash, and a plethora of other fruits and vegetables. The Tongans might be generally poor in terms of material wealth, but they own some of the South Pacific's most fertile and productive land. There just isn't much of it.

Impressions

Nature, assisted by a little art, nowhere appears in a more flourishing state than at this Isle.

—Capt. James Cook, 1773

GEOGRAPHY   The kingdom consists of 170 islands, 36 of them inhabited, scattered over an area of about 259,000 sq. km (100,000 sq. miles), an area about the size of Colorado. The amount of dry land, however, is only 697 sq. km (269 sq. miles). That's smaller than New York City.

Tonga has three major island groups. Tongatapu and its neighbor, the smaller **'Eua,** comprise the southernmost group. About 155km (96 miles) north are the islands of **Ha'apai,** where Fletcher Christian led the mutiny on the *Bounty.* About 108km (67 miles) beyond Ha'apai, beautiful **Vava'u** reigns as the kingdom's sailing heaven. Even farther north are the remote **Niuas Islands,** but you won't be going up there.

The largest island in the kingdom, Tongatapu, has about a third of the country's land area and about two-thirds of its population. It's a flat, raised atoll about 65km (40 miles) across from east to west and 32km (20 miles) across from north to south at its longest and widest points. In the center a sparkling lagoon is now unfortunately void of most sea life.

Most of the islands here are raised coral atolls. The exceptions are the Niuas and, in Ha'apai, the active volcano Tofua and its sister volcanic cone, Kao. Geologists say that the weight of the growing Ha'apai volcanoes has caused the Indo-Australian Plate to sag like a hammock, thereby raising Tongatapu and 'Eua on the south end of the Tongan chain and Vava'u on the north end. As a result, the sides of Tongatapu and Vava'u facing Ha'apai slope gently to the sea, and the sides facing away from Ha'apai end in cliffs that fall into the ocean.

GOVERNMENT   Tonga technically is a constitutional monarchy, although in many respects the king is head of a system of hereditary Polynesian chiefs who happen to have titles derived from England. The king picks his own Privy Council of advisors and appoints nine cabinet members and the governors of Ha'apai and Vava'u. With a few exceptions they are nobles. The cabinet members and the governors hold 11 of the 30 seats in the Legislative Assembly. Of the 19 other members of the assembly, the nobles choose 10 from among their ranks, leaving 9 to be elected by the taxpaying commoners.

It would be an understatement to say that the royal family has a hand in every important decision made in Tonga; in fact, very little gets done without the royal family's outright or tacit approval or involvement.

With more Tongans living abroad, and those at home being exposed more and more to news of the world, the monarchy has been under increasing pressure to move to a democracy. Observers say this is not likely to happen as long as King Taufa'ahau Tupou IV—now in his late 80s—is on the throne.

ECONOMY   Tourism is an important component of Tonga's economy but of minuscule size when compared to Fiji and French Polynesia. Tonga has few natural resources other than its fertile soil and the fish in the sea within its exclusive economic zone. The world markets for its exports—fresh fish, vanilla, kava, bananas, coconut oil, pineapples, watermelons, tomatoes, squash, and other vegetables—have been unstable and depressed at times in recent years. Money sent home by Tongans living overseas is a major source of foreign exchange. Nevertheless, Tonga is the poorest of the countries covered in this book.

2 History 101

Polynesians found and settled these islands sometime around 500 B.C. on their long migration across the South Pacific. Around A.D. 950, according to a myth, the supreme Polynesian god (known here as Tangaloa) came down to Tongatapu and fathered a son by a lovely Tongan maiden. Their son, Aho'eitu, thus became the first Tui Tonga—king of Tonga—and launched one of the world's longest-running dynasties.

The first *tuis* ruled from Niutoua village on the northwest corner of Tongatapu. They moved to Lapaha on the shore of the island's interior lagoon about 800 years ago, to take advantage of a safer anchorage for the large, double-hulled war canoes they used to extend their empire as far as Fiji and Samoa. At that time, a deep passage linked the lagoon to the sea; it has been slowly closing as geological forces raise the island and reduce the entrance to the present shallow bank.

Over time, the tui became more of a figurehead, and his power was dispersed among several chiefs, all of them descendants of the original tui. For centuries the rival chiefs seemed to stop warring among themselves only long enough to make war on Fiji and Samoa. The chiefs were fighting in 1798 when missionaries from the London Missionary Society landed on Lifuka in Ha'apai. Two of the missionaries were killed. The rest fled to Sydney, leaving Tonga to the heathens.

EUROPEANS ARRIVE   Although Dutch explorers had sighted Tonga in the 17th century, the missionaries knew of the islands from the visits of British Captains Samuel Wallis, James Cook, and William Bligh in the late 1700s. During his third voyage in 1777, Captain Cook was feted lavishly on Lifuka by a powerful chief named Finau I. Cook was so impressed by this show of hospitality that he named the Ha'apai group "The Friendly Islands," the modern kingdom's motto. Unbeknownst to Cook, however, Finau I and his associates apparently plotted to murder him and his crew, but they couldn't agree among themselves how to do it before the great explorer sailed away.

Captain Bligh and HMS *Bounty* visited Lifuka in 1789 after gathering breadfruit in Tahiti. Before he could leave Tongan waters, however, the famous mutiny took place near the island of Ha'afeva in the Ha'apai group.

Some 20 years later Chief Finau II of Lifuka captured a British ship named the *Port au Prince,* stealing all of its muskets and ammunition, setting it on fire, and brutally slaughtering all but one member of its crew. The survivor was a 15-year-old Londoner named Will Mariner. He became a favorite of the chief, spent several years living among the Tongans, and later wrote a four-volume account of his experiences. He told

---

(*Fun Fact* **Stop It!**

Legend says that Tonga's frequent earth tremors are caused when the Polynesian goddess Havea Hikule'o moves around in her underground lair. Tongans customarily stomp the shaking ground to get her to stop whatever she's doing down there.

Impressions
The good natured old Chief interduced [sic] me to a woman and gave me to understand that I might retire with her, she was next offered to Captain Furneaux but met with a refusal from both, tho she was neither old nor ugly, our stay here was but short.

—Capt. James Cook, 1773

how the Tongans mistook 12,000 silver coins on the *Port au Prince* for gaming pieces they called *pa'angas*. The national currency today is known as the pa'anga.

The arrival of the Wesleyan missionaries on Lifuka in the 1820s coincided with the rise of Taufa'ahau, a powerful chief who converted to Christianity in 1831. With their help, he won a series of domestic wars. By 1845 he had conquered all of Tonga and declared himself to be the new Tui Tonga.

ROYALTY ARRIVES Taufa'ahau took a Christian name and became King George I of Tonga. In 1862 he made his subordinate chiefs "nobles," but he also freed the commoners from forced labor and instituted the policy of granting each adult male a garden plot in the countryside and a house lot in town. He created a Privy Council of his own choosing and established a legislative assembly made up of representatives of both the nobles and commoners. This system was committed to writing in the Constitution of 1875, which still is in effect today. The legislative assembly is known now as Parliament.

King George I died in 1893 at the age of 97, thus ending a reign of 48 years. His great-grandson, King George II, ruled for the next 25 years and is best remembered for signing a treaty with Great Britain in 1900, which turned Tonga's foreign affairs over to the British and prevented any further encroachments on Tonga by the Western colonial powers. Consequently, the Kingdom of Tonga was never colonized.

King George II died in 1918 and was succeeded by his daughter, the 6-foot-2-inch Queen Salote (her name is the Tongan transliteration of Charlotte). For the next 47 years Queen Salote carefully protected her people from Western influence, even to the extent of not allowing a modern hotel to be built in the kingdom. She did, however, come to the world's attention in 1953, when she rode bareheaded in the cold, torrential rain that drenched the coronation parade of Queen Elizabeth II in London (she was merely following Tongan custom of showing respect to royalty by appearing uncovered in their presence). She later hosted Queen Elizabeth II and Prince Philip in Nuku'alofa.

Queen Salote died in 1965 and was succeeded by her son, the present King Taufa'ahau Tupou IV. Then in his late 40s, he set about bringing Tonga into the modern world. On the pretext of accommodating the important guests invited to his elaborate coronation scheduled for July 4, 1967, the International Dateline Hotel was built on Nuku'alofa's waterfront, and Fua'amotu Airport on Tongatapu was upgraded to handle jet aircraft. Tourism had arrived, albeit modestly.

DEMOCRACY DOESN'T ARRIVE The king and his government have had their problems, thanks to more and more of his commoner subjects going overseas to work in the Western democracies. Meanwhile those at home have become better educated and more aware of what's going on both in Tonga and in the rest of the world. In the late 1980s a group of commoners founded *Kele'a,* a newspaper published without the king's input. The paper created a ruckus almost from its first issue by revealing that some government ministers had rung up excessive travel expenses on trips abroad.

More scandals followed, including news that the government was selling Tongan passports to overseas nationals (which explains Tonga's growing Chinese population). Incensed, several hundred Tongans marched down Nuku'alofa's main street in a peaceful protest, and they established the Tonga Human Rights Democracy Movement. A recent scandal included the 2001 loss of some US$20 million of Tonga's overseas trust fund through a questionable investment by the official Court Jester (actually an American businessman).

In 2005, Tonga's civil servants went on strike demanding better pay. The protest went on for 6 weeks until the government agreed to raise wages by as much as 60%. As we went to press, it has announced plans to slice the government work force in half, which caused a new round of protests.

Lacking clairvoyance, I cannot predict what future course Tongan politics will take. Most observers believe the monarchical system will stay intact as long as King Taufa'ahau Tupou is on the throne. Crown Prince Tupuoto'a has indicated that reforms will come when he becomes king.

3 The Tongans

The population of Tonga is estimated at 100,000 (no one knows for sure). Approximately 98% of the inhabitants are pure Polynesians, closely akin to the Samoans in physical appearance, language, and culture.

As in Samoa, the bedrock of the Tongan social structure is the traditional way of life—*faka Tonga*—and the extended family. Parents, grandparents, children, aunts, uncles, cousins, nieces, and nephews all have the same sense of obligation to each other as is felt in Western nuclear families. The extended-family system makes sure that no one ever goes hungry or without a place to live.

THE TONGAN SYSTEM   The extended family aside, some striking differences exist between Tonga, Samoa, and the other Polynesian islands. Unlike the others, in which there is a certain degree of upward mobility, Tonga has a rigid two-tier caste system. The king and 33 "Nobles of the Realm"—plus their families—make up a privileged class at the top of society. Everyone else is a commoner, and although commoners can hold positions in the government (a commoner member of parliament was recently named as acting prime minister), it's impossible for them to move up into the nobility even by marriage. Titles of the nobility are inherited, but the king can strip members of the nobility of their positions if they fail to live up to their obligations (presumably including loyalty to the royal family).

Technically the king owns all the land in Tonga, which in effect makes the country his feudal estate. Tonga isn't exactly like the old European feudal system, however.

Moments Seeing His Highness Arrive

Being an American and therefore not particularly enamored of royalty, I nevertheless enjoy watching King Taufa'ahau Tupou IV being chauffeured around his kingdom in the back seat of his big black SUV and being given the royal treatment whenever he arrives somewhere.

Although the nobles each rule over a section of the kingdom, they have an obligation to provide for the welfare of the serfs rather than the other way around. The nobles administer the villages, look after the people's welfare, and apportion the land among the commoners.

TONGAN DRESS   Even traditional dress reflects the Tongan social structure. Western-style clothes have made deep inroads in recent years, especially among young persons, but many Tongans still wear wraparound skirts known as *valas*. These come to well below the knee on men and to the ankles on women. To show their respect for the royal family and to each other, traditional men and women wear finely woven mats known as *ta'ovalas* over their valas. Men hold these up with waistbands of coconut fiber; women wear decorative waistbands known as *kiekies*. Tongans have ta'ovalas for everyday wear, but on special occasions they break out mats that are family heirlooms, some of them tattered and worn. The king owns ta'ovalas that have been in his family for more than 500 years.

Tongan custom is to wear black for months to mourn the death of a relative or close friend. Since Tongan extended families are large and friends numerous, almost everyone in traditional Tonga dress wears black.

RELIGION   Tongans quickly converted to Christianity in the old days—apparently an easy transition, as Tongan legend holds that their own king is a descendant of a supreme Polynesian god and a beautiful earthly virgin. Today about half of all Tongans belong to the Free Wesleyan Church of Tonga, founded by the early Methodist

---

Fun Fact **What Day Is It?**

Theoretically, the international date line should run for its *entire length* along the 180th meridian, halfway around the world from the prime meridian, the starting point for measuring international time. If it followed the 180th meridian precisely, however, most of the Aleutian Islands would be a day ahead of the rest of Alaska, and Fiji would be split into 2 days. To solve these problems, the date line swings west around the Aleutians, leaving them in the same day as Alaska. In the South Pacific, it swerves east between Fiji and Samoa, leaving all of Fiji a day ahead of the Samoas.

Since Tonga and Samoa lie east of the 180th meridian, both countries should logically be in the same day. But Tonga wanted to have the same date as Australia and New Zealand, so the line was drawn arbitrarily east of Tonga, putting it 1 day ahead of Samoa.

To travelers, it's even more confusing because the time of day is the same in Tonga and Samoa. When traveling from one to the other, only the date changes. For example, if everyone is going to church at 10am on Sunday in Tonga, everyone's at work on Saturday in Samoa.

Tonga's Seventh-day Adventists, who celebrate the Sabbath on Saturday but work on Sunday, have taken advantage of this abnormality to avoid running afoul of Tonga's tough Sunday blue laws. In God's eyes, they say, Sunday in Tonga really is Saturday. Accordingly, Tonga is the only place in the world where Seventh-Day Adventists observe their Sabbath on Sunday.

⌐ *Fun Fact* **Buried with Banners**

Tongans of all religions bury their dead in unique cemeteries set in groves of frangipani trees. The graves are sandy mounds decorated with colorful flags, banners, artificial flowers, and seashells.

---

missionaries and headed by the king. The Free Church of Tonga is an offshoot that is still allied with the Methodist synods in Australia and New Zealand. There are also considerable numbers of Roman Catholics, Anglicans, Seventh-Day Adventists, and Mormons. Church services are usually held at 10am on Sunday, but very few of them are conducted in English. St. Paul's Anglican Church, on the corner of Fafatehi and Wellington roads, usually has communion in English on Sunday at 8am. The royal family worships at 10am in Centenary Church, the Free Wesleyan Church on Wellington Road, a block behind the Royal Palace.

The red national flag has a cross on a white field in its upper corner to signify the country's strong Christian foundation.

As was the case throughout Polynesia, the Tongans accepted most of the puritanical beliefs taught by the early missionaries but stopped short of adopting their strict sexual mores. Today Tongan society is very conservative in outlook and practice in almost every aspect of life except the sexual activities of unmarried young men and women.

As is true elsewhere in Polynesia, Tongan families without enough female offspring will raise boys as they would girls. They are known in Tongan as *fakaleitis* (like a woman) and live lives similar to those of the *mahus* in Tahiti and the *fa'afafines* in the Samoas. In Tonga they have a reputation for sexual promiscuity and for persistently approaching Western male visitors in search of sexual liaisons.

4 Language

The official language is Tongan, but English is taught in the schools and is widely spoken in the main towns. Tongan is similar to Samoan. One major difference between them is the enormous number of glottal stops (represented by an apostrophe in writing) in the Tongan tongue. These are short stops similar to the break between "Oh-oh" in English.

Every vowel is pronounced in the Latin fashion: *ah, ay, ee, oh,* and *oo* (as in kangaroo) instead of *ay, ee, eye, oh,* and *you* as in English. The consonants are sounded as they are in English.

An extensive knowledge of Tongan will not be necessary for English-speakers to get around and enjoy the kingdom, but here are a few words you can use to elicit smiles from your hosts and to avoid the embarrassment of entering the wrong restroom:

English	Tongan	Pronunciation
hello	**malo e lelei**	*mah*-low ay *lay*-lay
welcome	**talitali fiefia**	tah-lay-*tah*-lay fee-ay-*fee*-ah
how do you do?	**fefe hake?**	*fay*-fay *hah*-kay?
fine, thank you	**sai pe, malo**	*sah*-ee pay, *mah*-low

good-bye	'alu a	ah-*loo* ah
thank you	malo	*mah*-low
how much?	'oku fiha?	*oh*-koo *fee*-hah?
good	lelei	lay-*lay*-ee
bad	kovi	*koh*-vee
woman	fefine	fay-*feen*-ay
man	tangata	tahn-*got*-ah
house	fale	*fah*-lay
transvestite	fakaleiti	fah-ka-*lay*-tee

The Friendly Islands Bookshop on Taufa'ahau Road carries language books, and the Tonga Visitors Bureau on Vuna Road distributes a brochure of Tongan phrases.

5 Visitor Information & Entry Requirements

VISITOR INFORMATION

The friendly staff has many brochures, maps, and other materials available at the **Tonga Visitors Bureau (TVB),** P.O. Box 37, Nuku'alofa, Kingdom of Tonga (© 21-733; fax 23-507; www.tongaholiday.com). The office is on Vuna Road near the International Dateline Hotel. Especially good are the bureau's brochures on Tongan dancing, handicrafts, archaeology, construction skills, and a walking tour of central Nuku'alofa. A stop by the "TVB" is a must before setting out to see the country. Hours are Monday to Friday 8:30am to 4:30pm and Saturday 9am to noon.

Other sources of information are:

- **North America:** Tonga Consulate, 360 Post St., Suite 604, San Francisco, CA 94108 (© **415/781-0365;** fax 415/781-3964; www.tongaconsul.org)
- **Australia:** Tonga Visitors Bureau, 642 King St., Newton, NSW 2042 (© **02/9519-97009;** fax 02/9519-9419)
- **New Zealand:** Tonga Visitors Bureau, P.O. Box 24-054, Royal Oak, Auckland (© **09/634-1519;** fax 09/636-8973)
- **United Kingdom:** Tonga High Commission, 36 Molyneux St., London W1H 6AB (© **0207 245828;** fax 0207 239074)

Once you're in Nuku'alofa, **Friends Tourist Center,** on Taufa'ahau Road between Wellington and Salote roads (© **26-323**), is another good source of information. Owned by Paul Johansson, a Tongan who lived overseas for many years, it arranges tours of the islands and has Internet access (see "Fast Facts: Tonga," later in this chapter).

ENTRY REQUIREMENTS

Visas are not required for bona fide visitors from the United States, Canada, Australia, New Zealand, the United Kingdom, and most European and South Pacific island countries. They are permitted to stay for up to 1 month, provided they have a valid passport, and proof of adequate funds. You cannot board a plane flying into Tonga unless you have a ticket out of the country.

If in doubt about whether citizens of your country need visas, contact the **Immigration Department,** Hale Salote Kolofo'ou, Nuku'alofa (© **26-970;** fax 26-977; www.pmo.gov.to).

Applications for stays of longer than 30 days must be made to the principal immigration officer in Nuku'alofa.

Vaccinations are required only if you have been in a yellow fever or cholera area within 2 weeks prior to arrival in Tonga.

CUSTOMS Visitors are allowed to bring in 500 cigarettes and 2.25 liters of spirits or 4.5 liters of wine, as well as personal belongings in use at the time of arrival. Pets, dangerous drugs, indecent materials, firearms, and ammunition are prohibited, and foodstuffs must be declared and inspected. Arriving visitors can buy duty-free merchandise at Fua'amotu Airport after clearing Immigration but before going through Customs.

6 Money

The Tongan unit of currency is the **pa'anga,** which is divided into 100 **seniti.** The pa'anga is abbreviated in this book as **T$.** Most Tongans refer to "dollars" and "cents" when doing business with visitors, meaning pa'angas and senitis.

At the time of writing, T$1 was worth about US50¢, or US$1=T$2. The equivalent U.S. dollar prices given in parentheses are based on this rate of exchange. The rate is not published in major newspapers, but it is usually within a few cents of the Australian dollar's worth against the U.S. dollar. You can find the pa'anga exchange on currency conversion websites such as **www.xe.com**.

Tongan coins bear the likeness of the king on one side and such items as bananas, chickens, and pigs on the other.

HOW TO GET LOCAL CURRENCY **ANZ Bank,** at the corner of Railway and Salote roads near the market, is open Monday to Friday 9am to 4pm and Saturday from

The Pa'anga & the U.S. Dollar

At this writing, T$1 = approximately US50¢ (or US$1 = approximately T$2), the rate of exchange used to calculate the U.S. dollar prices given in this chapter. This rate may change by the time you visit, so use the following table only as a guide.

T$	US$	T$	US$
.25	.13	15	7.50
.50	.25	20	10.00
.75	.38	25	12.50
1	.50	30	15.00
2	1.00	35	17.50
3	1.50	40	20.00
4	2.00	45	22.50
5	2.50	50	25.00
6	3.00	75	37.50
7	3.50	100	50.00
8	4.00	125	62.50
9	4.50	150	75.00
10	5.00	200	100.00

8:30 to 11:30am. **Westpac Bank of Tonga,** at the waterfront end of Taufa'ahau Road, Nuku'alofa's main street, is open Monday to Friday 9am to 3:30pm and Saturday 8:30 to 11:30am. Both banks have ATMs. ANZ also has an ATM at the airport. You may get a better rate for cash and travelers checks at **GlobelEX/Western Union,** on Taufa'ahau Road. It's open Monday to Friday 8:30am to 4:30pm, Saturday 8:30am to 12:30pm.

CREDIT CARDS   The major hotels, car-rental firms, travel agencies, and Royal Tongan Airlines accept American Express, Diners Club, MasterCard, and Visa credit cards. Some restaurants and other businesses accept MasterCard or Visa; some may add 4% or 5% to your bill for doing so. It's a good idea to ask first if you want to charge your purchases. Leave your Discover card at home.

7 When to Go

THE CLIMATE

Tongatapu is far enough south of the equator to have cool, dry, and quite pleasant weather during the austral winter months (July–Sept), when temperatures range between 60°F and 70°F (15.5°C–21°C). However, the ends of occasional cold fronts from the Antarctic and periods of stiff southeast trade winds can make it seem even cooler during this period. During the summer (Dec–Mar), the high temperatures can reach above 90°F (32°C), with evenings in the comfortable 70s (21°C–26°C). A sweater, jacket, or wrap will come in handy for evening wear at any time of the year.

The islands get about 180 centimeters (70 in.) of rainfall a year, the majority of it falling during the summer months. Vava'u to the north tends to be somewhat warmer and slightly wetter than Tongatapu.

Tonga is in the southwestern Pacific cyclone belt, and hurricanes are possible from November to April. There will be ample warning if one bears down on the islands while you're there.

FESTIVALS & EVENTS

The largest annual festival is **Heilala,** which coincides with the King's Birthday on July 4. Nuku'alofa goes all out for a week of dance and beauty competitions, parades, sporting matches, band concerts, marching contests, yacht regattas, parties, and the lovely Night of Torches on the waterfront. Tongans living overseas like to come home for Heilala, so hotel reservations should be made well in advance. Vava'u stages its own version of Heilala early in May.

The Tonga Visitors Bureau keeps track of festival dates.

HOLIDAYS

Public holidays in Tonga are New Year's Day, Good Friday and Easter Monday, Anzac (Memorial) Day (Apr 25), Crown Prince Tupouto'a's birthday (May 4), Independence Day (June 4), the King's Birthday (July 4), Constitution Day (Nov 4), King Tupou I Day (Dec 4), Christmas Day, and Boxing Day (Dec 26).

⌒Tips Avoid Royal Funerals

There's no way to plan for it, but you do not want to be in Tonga if a key member of the royal family dies. The entire country virtually shuts down for a lengthy period of mourning.

---

8 Getting to Tonga & Getting Around

GETTING THERE

Air New Zealand flies between Los Angeles and Tonga at least once a week, with a brief stop in Samoa. Those flights go on to Auckland and return over the same route. **Air Pacific** connects Tonga to its flights to Fiji from Los Angeles, Australia, and New Zealand. **Polynesian Blue** flies to Tonga from Auckland and Sydney. **Polynesian Airlines** flies a small, propeller-driven plane between Tonga and Apia.

No flights go into, or out of, Tonga on Sunday, when local airports are closed.

For more information, see "Getting There & Getting Around," in chapter 2.

ARRIVING & DEPARTING   Except for the few international flights destined for Vava'u, most land at **Fua'amotu Airport** on Tongatapu, 24km (14 miles) or a 30-minute drive from Nuku'alofa. The terminal has currency exchange counters, an ATM, a duty-free shop, a snack bar, and a small handicraft outlet. International passengers can purchase duty-free liquor and cigarettes after clearing Immigration but before going through Customs.

Transportation from the airport into Nuku'alofa is by hotel minibuses or taxi. The bus ride to town costs T$10 (US$5). The one-way taxi fare into Nuku'alofa is about T$25 (US$13); the drivers will be happy to take U.S., New Zealand, or Australian currency.

A **departure tax** of T$25 (US$13) is charged of all passengers leaving on international flights. You pay it in Tongan currency at Fua'amotu Airport, at a separate booth outside Immigration. There is no departure tax for domestic flights.

There is no currency exchange facility in the departure lounge, so swap your money before clearing Immigration.

GETTING AROUND

BY PLANE

Domestic air service has been in a state of flux since the government-owned Royal Tongan Airlines folded in 2004. As I write, two carriers are operating here—**Peau Vava'u** (© 28-325; www.peauvavau.to) and **Airlines Tonga** (© 24-506; www.airlines tonga.com)—but indications were that the government might grant a monopoly to one of them. For the time being, both fly from Tongatapu to Ha'apai and Vava'u. The one-way fare from Tongatapu to Vava'u was about T$450 (US$225), and to Ha'apai, about T$300 (US$150).

Given this uncertainty, I get a local in-bound tour operator, such as **Pacific Travel Marketing** (© 28-304; sales@pacifictravelmarketing.afe.to) or **Teta Tours** (© 23-690; tetatour@kalianet.to), to make my arrangements.

BY RENTAL CAR

Avis (© 800/331-1212 or 21-179; www.avis.com; avis@tonfon.to) has an office on Taufa'ahau Road. Rates range from T$80 to T$130 (US$40–US$65) per day, including unlimited kilometers. **E. M. Jones Travel** (© 23-422 or 29-858; www.kalianet.to/emjones), also on Taufa'ahau Road, rents cars starting at T$50 (US$25) per day, including unlimited mileage. Both have a limited supply of cars, so reserve as soon as you can.

Gasoline (petrol) costs about double what you pay in the United States.

Before you can officially drive in Tonga you must obtain a **local driver's license** from the central police station (© 21-222), on Wellington Road just off Taufa'ahau

Nuku'alofa

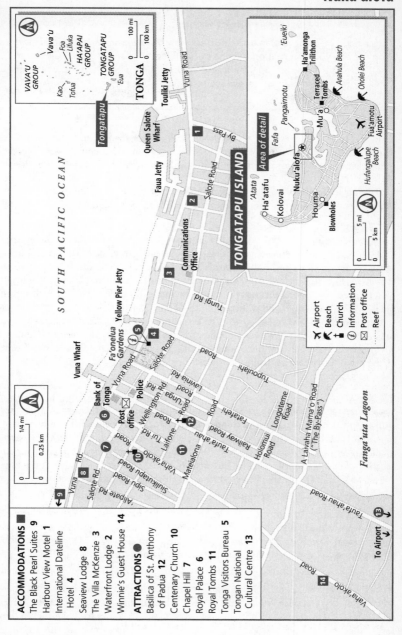

ACCOMMODATIONS ■
The Black Pearl Suites **9**
Harbour View Motel **1**
International Dateline
Hotel **4**
Seaview Lodge **8**
The Villa McKenzie **3**
Waterfront Lodge **2**
Winnie's Guest House **14**

ATTRACTIONS ●
Basilica of St. Anthony
of Padua **12**
Centenary Church **10**
Chapel Hill **7**
Royal Palace **6**
Royal Tombs **11**
Tonga Visitors Bureau **5**
Tongan National
Cultural Centre **13**

SOUTH PACIFIC OCEAN

TONGA

VAVA'U
GROUP

Vava'u
Foa
Lifuka
HA'APAI
GROUP

Kao
Tofua
TONGATAPU
GROUP
'Eua

Tongatapu

TONGATAPU ISLAND

'Eueiki
Ha'amonga
Trilithon
Anahula Beach
'Atata
Pangaimotu
Fafa
Mu'a
Terraced
Tombs
Oholei Beach
Fua'amotu
Airport
Nuku'alofa
Hufangalupe
Beach
Ha'atafu
Kolovai
Houma
Blowholes

Area of detail

✈ Airport
⌐ Beach
✝ Church
ⓘ Information
☒ Post office
---- Reef

Queen Salote Wharf
Toūliki Jetty
Vuna Road
By Pass
Faua Jetty
Salote Road

Communications
Office

Tungi Rd.

Fa'onelua
Gardens
Yellow Pier Jetty
Vuna Wharf

Bank of
Tonga
Post
office
Police
Vuna Road
Salote Road
'Unga Road
Wellington Rd.
Lavinia Rd.
Fatafehi
Tupoulahi
Road
Longoteme Road
A Laivaha Mama'o Road
("The By-Pass")

Taufa'āhau Road
Railway Road
Mateialona
Laifone
Tui Rd.
Vaha'akolo Road
Holomui Road
Siupate Road
Suilikutapu Road
'Alipate Rd.
Salote Rd.
Vuna Rd.

Fanga'uta Lagoon

To Airport
Vaha'akolo Road
Taufa'āhau Road

417

(Tips Don't Miss Your Flight Home

It's a good idea not to plan on flying back from Vava'u or Ha'apai to Nuku'alofa on the day your international flight is scheduled to take you home. Give yourself at least a day's cushion, just in case the local airline has an unexpected cancellation. And remember to always reconfirm your return flight as soon as possible.

Road in Nuku'alofa. Enter on the Railway Road side of the building. You will need your home driver's license and T$18 (US$8.75). It's a somewhat cumbersome process, so bring your sense of humor, or better yet, rent from Avis, which will get your license for you.

Driving in Tonga is on the left-hand side of the road. Speed limits are 65kmph (39 mph) on the open road and 40kmph (24 mph) in towns and villages.

BY TAXI

Taxis are plentiful in Nuku'alofa, although most are in poor condition (sometimes I think Tonga is where old cars go to die). They usually gather near Maketi Talamahu at the corner of Salote and Railway roads in Nuku'alofa, but you can flag them down anywhere. They aren't all identified as taxis except for their license plates, which begin with the letter T. Among the many firms are **Fiemalie Taxis** (© 24-270), **Wellington Taxis** (© 24-844), or **Holiday Taxis** (© 25-655 or 25-169).

Fares are T$3 (US$1.50) in town. The taxis have no meters, so make sure you and the driver agree on just how much the fare will be. The fares are doubled on Sundays, when taxis are officially permitted only to take passengers to church and back (some of them will carry tourists from their hotels or guesthouses to the wharf in order for them to get to the offshore islands).

BY BUS

Local buses operate Monday to Saturday during regular business hours (that is, they stop at 5pm). They use the **Vuna Road waterfront** as their terminal. Town buses stop in front of the Tonga Visitors Bureau; long-distance ones stop in front of the government buildings. They fan out from there to all parts of Tongatapu, but there are no reliable schedules. Simply ask the bus drivers at the market where they are going. About T$2 (US$1) will take you to the end of the island in either direction.

BY BICYCLE

Tongatapu is virtually flat, making it an ideal island for bicycling. "Pushbikes" can be rented from **Niko's Bike Rental** (© 878-4832) on the Vuna waterfront near the International Dateline Hotel. One-speed models cost T$2 (US$1) per hour, T$8 (US$4) for a full day. Open Monday to Saturday 9am to 5pm.

BY FERRY

It's not for everyone, but the **Shipping Corporation of Polynesia** (© 21-699) operates weekly ferry service from Nuku'alofa to Ha'apai and Vava'u. It usually leaves Nuku'alofa 1 day a week at 5:30pm and takes about 16 hours to make the 262km (163 mile) trip to Vava'u, stopping at Lifuka in the Ha'apai group on the way. The ship then turns around and arrives back in Nuku'alofa late the next afternoon. The one-way fare between Nuku'alofa and Vava'u is T$60 (US$30) for deck passage.

Tips **Watch Out for the Crown**

When driving in Tonga, be alert for pigs, dogs, horses, and chickens, and pull over for policemen on motorcycles escorting the king in his big black sport utility vehicle bearing license plates with no numbers, only a crown.

Tofa Ramsay Shipping (*©* 21-326) operates a daily ferry to 'Eua, departing from the Faua Jetty Monday to Saturday at 1:30pm, returning from 'Eua Monday to Friday at 5:30pm. Fare is T$15 (US$7.50) each way.

FAST FACTS: Tonga

American Express American Express has no representative in Tonga.

Bookstores **Friendly Islands Bookshop,** on Taufa'ahau Road near the Pacific Royale Hotel (*©* 23-787), carries greeting cards made from *tapa* cloth, paperback books, postcards, international news magazines, week-old Australian newspapers, books about Tonga and the rest of the South Pacific, and a sheet of maps of Tonga.

Business Hours In general, Tonga's shops are open Monday to Friday from 8am to 1pm and 2 to 5pm, Saturday from 8am to noon. Government offices are open Monday to Friday from 8:30am to 12:30pm and 1:30 to 4:30pm.

Camera/Film **Foto Fix,** on Taufa'ahau Road south of Wellington Road (*©* 23-466), sells Kodak and Fuji film and provides 1-hour color film processing.

Clothing It's against the law for men as well as women to appear shirtless in public. While Western men—but definitely not women—can swim and sunbathe shirtless at the hotel pools and beaches frequented by visitors, you will see most Tongans swimming in a full set of clothes. Accordingly, visitors should not wear bathing suits or skimpy attire away from the hotel pools or beaches frequented by foreigners (and that includes showing off your pierced naval and your lower back tattoo). Summer clothing is in order during most of the year, but a sweater, jacket, or wrap should be taken for evening wear throughout the year.

Currency Exchange See "Money," earlier in this chapter.

Drug Laws A drug-sniffing dog roams the baggage claim area at the airport, so don't even think about bringing illegal narcotics or dangerous drugs into Tonga.

Drugstores See "Healthcare," below.

Electricity Electricity in Tonga is 240 volts, 50 cycles, and the plugs are the heavy, angled type used in Australia and New Zealand. You will need a converter and adapter plug to operate American appliances.

E-mail **Friends Tourist Center** (*©* 26-323), on Taufa'ahau Road between Salote and Wellington roads, has Internet access Monday to Friday 8am to 10pm, Saturday 8:30am to 7:30pm.

If you brought your laptop, you can get a temporary Internet access account at **Tonga Communications Corp.** (© **23-499**), on Salote Road at Takaunove Road. There's a T$35 (US$17) setup fee plus T$23 (US$12) for 2 hours of access over 1 month, or T$46 (US$23) for a month's unlimited access. Go into the accounting office, which is open Monday to Friday 8:30am to 12:30pm and 1:30 to 4pm. See "The 21st Century Traveler" in chapter 2 for information on how to configure your computer.

Embassies/Consulates The nearest U.S. embassy is in Suva, Fiji. Consular offices in Tonga are the **Australian High Commission** (© **21-244**), the **New Zealand High Commission** (© **21-122**), and the **People's Republic of China Embassy** (© **24-554**).

Emergencies/Police The emergency telephone number for the **police, fire department,** and **hospital** is © **911.** The main **police station** (© **21-222**) is on Salote Road at Railway Road.

Eyeglasses **Vaiola Hospital** (© **21-200**) is the only place to get glasses fixed or replaced. See "Healthcare," below.

Firearms Guns are illegal in Tonga.

Gambling There is no casino or other form of organized gambling in Tonga.

Hairdressers The **International Dateline Hotel** has a hair salon (see "Where to Stay on Tongatapu," later in this chapter.

Healthcare **Vaiola Hospital** (© **21-200**) provides medical, dental, and optical service, but it's considerably below the standards you're used to. The outpatient clinics are open from 8:30am to 4:30pm daily. German-trained Dr. Heinz Betz practices at the **German Clinic & Pharmacy,** on Vahiaholo Road at Uelingi-toni Road, 1 block behind the Royal Palace (© **22-736**). **Vaiola Hospital** provides dental service in Nuku'alofa; the outpatient clinics are open from 8:30am to 4:30pm daily.

Hitchhiking It's not against the law, but Tongans are not particularly accustomed to picking up strangers.

Insects There are no dangerous insects in Tonga, and the mosquitoes do not carry malaria. Vava'u, warmer and more humid than Tongatapu, tends to have more mosquitoes and has tropical centipedes that can inflict painful stings if touched; watch your step if walking around with bare feet.

Laundry/Dry Cleaning **Savoy Dry Cleaners,** on Fatefehi Road (© **878-3314**), has 1-day laundry and dry-cleaning service. Open Monday to Friday 8am to 5pm, Saturday 8am to 2pm.

Liquor Laws The legal drinking age is 18. Licensed hotels can sell alcoholic beverages to their guests 7 days a week; otherwise, sale is prohibited from midnight Saturday to midnight Sunday. Royal beer is brewed here (Ikale is the higher-quality export brand).

Maps Free maps of Nuku'alofa, Tongatapu, and Vava'u are available at the Tonga Visitors Bureau.

Newspapers/Magazines All the local newspapers are published in Tongan. *Matangi Tonga* is a fine English-language monthly magazine edited by the noted Tongan writer and publisher Pesi Fonua. It has features about the kingdom and its people. **Friendly Islands Bookstore** (see "Bookstores," above) carries international newspapers and magazines.

Post Office The **Nuku'alofa Post Office** is at the corner of Taufa'ahau and Salote roads. It's open Monday to Friday 8:30am to 4pm. Many Tongan stamps in the shape of bananas and pineapples are collectors' items.

Radio/TV The government-owned radio station, A3Z (Radio Tonga), broadcasts in both the AM and FM bands. Most programming on the AM station is in Tongan, although the music played is mostly U.S., Australian, or British popular tunes. The news in English is relayed from the BBC or Radio Australia several times a day. One privately owned FM station in Nuku'alofa plays popular music.

Tonga has two over-the-air television channels, one owned by the government, the other with predominately Christian programming (which is to say, fundamentalist American preachers raising money while haranguing the faithful). They can be received only on Tongatapu and 'Eua. **Tonfon**, a communications company headed by the crown prince, provides the BBC and a few other channels on its cable TV service in Nuku'alofa; the TV set in your hotel probably will receive them.

Safety Robberies and break-ins are on the increase here, although crimes against tourists so far have been rare. It's a good idea to be on the alert if you walk down dark streets at night. Remember that the communal property system still prevails in the kingdom. Items such as cameras and bags left unattended might disappear, so take the proper precautions. Women should not wander alone on deserted beaches.

Taxes The government adds a 15% "consumption" tax to the price of *everything* purchased in Tonga, including hotel rooms. The tax is added to most bills in the American fashion and included in the price in others. All passengers on international flights pay a departure tax of T$25 (US$13) in Tongan currency.

Telephone/Fax Calls can be dialed directly into Tonga from most areas of the world. The international country code is **676.**

Calls can be placed from any phone using a prepaid Phonecard, which can be bought at many shops and at the **Tonga Communications Corporation (TCC),** on Salote Road at the corner of Takaunove Road, which has phones in private booths. TCC is open Monday to Saturday 8am to 10:30pm, Sunday 10am to 10:30pm. Direct-dial calls to anywhere in the world cost about T80¢ (US40¢) a minute during the day, T68¢ (US34¢) on weekends, making Tonga by far the least expensive place in the South Pacific from which to call home.

The number for directory assistance is ℂ **910** or ℂ **919,** and the number for the international operator is ℂ **913.**

Tonfon Mobile Center, at Salote and Fatafehi roads opposite the market (ℂ **872-0090**), sells prepaid SIM cards for your unlocked GSM cell phone, starting at T$5 (US$2.50). Tonfon also has a booth at the airport.

Time Local time in Tonga is 13 hours ahead of Greenwich Mean Time. It's in the same day as Australia, New Zealand, and Fiji, and a day ahead of the United States, the Samoas, the Cook Islands, and French Polynesia. Translated, Tonga is 3 hours behind the U.S. West Coast during standard time (4 hr. behind during daylight saving time)—and 1 day ahead. If it's noon on Tuesday in Tonga, it's 3pm Pacific Standard Time on Monday in Los Angeles and 6pm Eastern Standard Time on Monday in New York.

Tipping Although it has gained a foothold, tipping is officially discouraged in Tonga because it's considered contrary to the Polynesian tradition of hospitality to guests. One time gratuities are encouraged is during Tongan dance shows, when members of the audience rush up to the female dancers and stick notes to their well-oiled bodies.

Water Although the government proclaims the tap water in the main towns to be chlorinated and thus safe, I don't know anyone who drinks it. Because it comes from wells in the limestone bedrock, it's very hard (laden with minerals) and doesn't easily rinse off soap and shampoo. Bottled water is available at most grocery stores in Nuku'alofa.

Weights/Measures Tonga uses the metric system.

9 Exploring Tongatapu

The government and most businesses and tourist activities are in Nuku'alofa (pop. 25,000 or so), but there is much to see outside town, including some of the South Pacific's most important and impressive archaeological sites. You'll need about half a day to stroll around Nuku'alofa and see its sights and a full day to tour the island—half a day on the eastern end, another half to see the west.

THE TONGAN NATIONAL CULTURAL CENTRE ★★★

Make time to visit the **Tongan National Cultural Centre** (ⓒ 23-022), one of the South Pacific's best cultural expositions. Located on Fanga'uta Lagoon about 1.5km (1 mile) south of Nuku'alofa on Taufa'ahau Road, the center's turtle-roof, Tongan *fale*-style buildings house displays of the kingdom's history, geology, and handicrafts. In fact, artisans work daily on their crafts and sell their wares to visitors. In other words, you can see how Tonga's remarkable handicrafts are made, which should help as you later scour the local shops for good buys. The center is open Monday to Friday 9am to 4pm. Admission is T$3 (US$1.50) for adults, T$1 (US50¢) for children. Special displays feature demonstrations of carving, weaving, tapa making, food preparation, a kava ceremony, and dancing. The dinners and dance shows on Tuesday and Thursday nights are not to be missed (see "Island Nights on Tongatapu," later in this chapter).

A STROLL THROUGH NUKU'ALOFA

Before starting out to see Nuku'alofa, drop by the Tonga Visitors Bureau office on Vuna Road and pick up a copy of the brochure "Walking Tour of Central Nuku'alofa." A morning's stroll around this interesting town will be time well spent, for in many respects it's a throwback to times gone by in the South Pacific.

Although there are no street-name posts, the visitors bureau has put up signs that give general directions to the main sights. In addition, Nuku'alofa is more or less laid out on a grid, so you shouldn't have trouble finding your way around. It's also flat, with no hills to climb.

Fun Fact **The Queen's Robe & Tui Malila**

A highlight at the Tongan National Centre is the long robe Queen Salote wore at the coronation of Queen Elizabeth II in 1953. Another is the carcass of Tui Malila, the Galapagos tortoise Capt. James Cook reputedly gave the Tui Tonga in 1777. The beast lived until 1968.

Start at the **Tonga Visitors Bureau** and walk west along Vuna Road toward the heart of town. The park with a children's playground on the left as you leave the Visitors Bureau is known as **Fa'onelua Gardens.** The modern three-story building before Railway Road houses many government ministries.

Turn left on Railway Road. The small colonial-era wooden structure on the left in the first block serves as both the **Court House** and **parliament** when it meets from June to September. Both court and parliament sessions are open to the public. Now return to Vuna Road and turn left.

Vuna Wharf, at the foot of Taufa'ahau Road, Nuku'alofa's main street, was built in 1906, and for some 60 years most visitors to Tonga debarked from ships that tied up here. A railroad once ran through town along Railway Road to transport copra and other crops to Vuna Wharf.

Directly across Vuna Road from the wharf is the low **Treasury Building.** Constructed in 1928, it's a fine example of South Pacific colonial architecture. Early in its life it housed the Tongan Customs service and the post office as well as the Treasury Department.

The field to the west of the wharf is the **Pangai,** where royal feasts, kava ceremonies, and parades are held.

Overlooking the Pangai and surrounded by towering Norfolk pines is the **Royal Palace** ✸✸✸. The king lives in a modern mansion out on the lagoon shore these days, but he still conducts business and entertains dignitaries in this white Victorian building with gingerbread fretwork and gables under a red roof. The palace was prefabricated in New Zealand, shipped to Tonga, and erected in 1867. The second-story veranda was added in 1882.

Now walk up Taufa'ahau Road past **Raintree Square,** appropriately shaded by the huge rain tree in front of the modern Westpac Bank of Tonga. The park benches at the base of the tree are a local gathering place. Across the street stands the colonial-style **Prime Minister's Office** with its quaint tower.

Turn right at the post office on Salote Road. The **Nuku'alofa Club** on the left, about halfway down the block, is another holdover from the old South Pacific: It's a private club where Tonga's elite males gather to relax over a game of snooker and a few Australian beers.

The next block of Salote Road runs behind the Royal Palace. You can look over the backyard fence and observe the royal geese. Turn right on Vaha'akolo Road and walk along the west side of the palace toward the sea. The highest point on Tongatapu, **Chapel Hill** (or Zion Hill) to the left, part of the Royal Estate, was a Tongan fort during the 18th century and the site of a missionary school opened in 1830 and a large Wesleyan church built in 1865. The school, **Sia'atoutai Theological College,** is now located 6.5km (4 miles) west of Nuku'alofa. The church has long since been torn down.

When you get to the water, look back and take your photos of the palace framed by the Norfolk pines.

Picturesque **Vuna Road** runs west from the palace, with the sea and reef on one side and stately old colonial homes on the other. The house at the end of the first block was the home of a Tongan noble who on several occasions in the 1800s went to England, where he stayed with friends in Newcastle; accordingly, he named the house **Niukasa.** The British High Commissioner's residence, in the second block, sports a flagpole surrounded by four cannons from the *Port au Prince,* the ship captured and burned by the Tongans at Ha'apai in 1806 after they had clubbed to death all its crew except young Will Mariner. King George I had two wives—not concurrently—and both of them are buried in casuarina-ringed Mala'e'aloa Cemetery, whose name means "tragic field." The clapboard house at the end of the next block is known as **Ovalau** because it was built in the 1800s at Levuka, the old capital of Fiji on the island of Ovalau, and was shipped to Tonga in the 1950s.

Turn inland at the corner, walk 2 blocks on 'Alipate Road, take a left on Wellington Road, and walk 2 blocks east to **Centenary Church.** Just before the church, the large wooden building with a widow's walk atop it was reputed to have been built about 1871 by the Rev. Shirley W. Baker, a missionary who had much influence over King George I. Members of the Free Wesleyan Church of Tonga constructed Centenary Church between 1949 and 1952. While construction was going on, the town was divided into sections that fed the workers three meals a day on a rotating basis. The amount of money spent on the building was about T$80,000 (US$40,000); the actual value of the materials and labor was many times that amount. The church seats about 2,000 persons, including the king and queen, who worship here on Sunday mornings.

Tips **How to Survive Sunday in Tonga**

A clause in Tonga's constitution declares, "The Sabbath Day shall be sacred in Tonga forever and it shall not be lawful to work, artifice, or play games, or trade on the Sabbath." The penalty for breaking this stricture is 3 months in jail at hard labor. Although hotels can cater to their guests on the Sabbath, almost everything else comes to a screeching halt. Stores are closed, airplanes don't fly, most taxis don't operate, and most restaurants other than those in the hotels don't open. Tongans by the thousands go to church and then enjoy family feasts and a day of lounging around in true Polynesian style.

So how do the rest of us survive without "artificing" on Sunday? You can start by worshiping with the royal family at 10am in the Centenary Church on Wellington Road. Tongan men wear neckties to church, but tourists get by without if they're neatly dressed. Women should wear dresses that cover the shoulders and knees.

Even before church, many of us visitors—and many a Westernized Tongan, too—head for one of the offshore resorts, where we can get a meal, some libation, and a legal swim. You will find me having a few cold ones out at Pangaimotu Island Resort, where even the bachelor Crown Prince Tupuoto'a has been known to while away a Sunday afternoon. See "Island Excursions, Watersports & Other Outdoor Activities," below.

Turn right past the church and proceed inland on Vaha'akolo Road. Past the church is **Queen Salote College,** a girls' school named for a wife of King George I and not for his great-great-granddaughter, the famous Queen Salote.

Turn left at the first street, known as Laifone Road, and walk along a large open space to your right. Since 1893 this area has been known as the **Royal Tombs** ⚜⚜. King George I, King George II, Queen Salote, and most of their various wives and husbands are buried at the center of the field. At the corner of Tu'i Road stands the **Free Wesleyan Church of Tonga.** Built of coral block in 1888, it is a magnificent example of early Tongan church architecture.

On Taufa'ahau Road, behind this open expanse stands the modern **Queen Salote Memorial Hall,** the country's national auditorium.

On the other side of Taufa'ahau Road, opposite the Royal Tombs, rises the tent-shaped **Basilica of St. Anthony of Padua,** the first basilica built in the South Pacific islands. On the ground level are the Loki Kai Cafeteria (more commonly known as Akiko's Restaurant; see "Where to Dine on Tongatapu," later) and the 'Utue'a Public Library.

Now follow **Taufa'ahau Road** toward the waterfront. On this main street, you'll pass shop after shop, some of them carrying handicrafts and clothing. Between Wellington and Salote roads, an old house now provides the setting for the **Langafonua Women's Association Handicraft Center** (see "Shopping on Tongatapu," below). The clapboard house was built by William Cocker, a local merchant, for his five daughters, who lived in New Zealand but spent each winter in Nuku'alofa.

Turn right on the next street—Salote Road—and walk past the police station on the left to **Maketi Talamahu** in the second block, the lively produce market where vendors sell a great variety of fresh produce, ranging from huge taro roots and watermelons to string beans and bananas. Tongatapu's climate is cool enough during the winter months that both European and tropical fruits and vegetables grow in great bounty. Upstairs, several stalls carry handicraft items, such as tapa cloth and straw baskets and mats.

After looking around the market and perhaps munching on a banana or sipping a fresh young coconut, continue walking east. In the next block is Fa'onelua Gardens; walk through it to the Tonga Visitors Bureau, where you began your tour and can end it.

TOURING TONGATAPU

Most visitors see Tonga's main island in two parts: first the eastern side and its ancient archaeological sites, and then the western side for its natural spectacles. You can do these on your own via rental car or go with one of the local tour operators (see "Organized Tours," below). Either way, pick up a copy of the visitors bureau's "The Capital Places Tour," which covers the entire island.

THE EASTERN TOUR

Take Taufa'ahau Road out of Nuku'alofa, making sure to bear left on the paved road. If you want to see tropical birds in captivity, watch for the signs on the right-hand side of the road directing you to the **Bird Park** and follow the dirt track about 3km (1¾ miles). There you will find the **Tongan Wildlife Centre** ⚜⚜ (© 29-449), which has a fine collection of colorful birds from Tonga and other South Pacific islands. They are kept in cages carefully planted with native vegetation. A star is the Tongan megapode, a native only of Niuafo'ou in the Niuas islands; it buries its eggs in volcanic vents where the temperature is a constant 95°F (35°C), and then flies away, never to see its offspring. Admission is T$3 (US$1.50). The center is open daily 9am to 5pm.

Now backtrack to the main road and turn right toward the airport. Keep left, especially at Malapo (where the road to the airport goes to the right), and follow the Tonga Visitors Bureau's excellent signs, which will show you the way to **Mu'a.** When the road skirts the lagoon just before the village, watch for the stone-and-brass monument marking **Captain Cook's Landing Place** *☙☙*. The great British explorer landed and rested under a large banyan tree here when he came ashore in 1777 to meet with Pau, the reigning Tui Tonga. He attended the traditional presentation of first fruits marking the beginning of the harvest season. The banyan tree is long gone.

The next village is **Lapaha** *☙☙*, seat of the Tui Tonga for 6 centuries, beginning about A.D. 1200. All that remains of the royal compound is a series of *langa,* or ancient terraced tombs, some of which are visible from the road. A large sign explains how the supreme Polynesian god Tangaloa came down from the sky about A.D. 950 and sired the first Tui Tonga. The last Tui Tonga, who died in 1865, after being deposed by King George I in 1862, is buried in one of the tombs. The 28 tombs around Lapaha and Mu'a are among the most important archaeological sites in Polynesia, but none of them have been excavated. Walk down the dirt road near the sign to see more of the tombs.

From Lapaha, follow the scenic paved road along the coast until reaching the **Ha'a-monga Trilithon** *☙☙☙*, near the village of Niutoua on the island's northeast point, 32km (19 miles) from Nuku'alofa. This huge archway, whose lintel stone is estimated to weigh 35 tons, is 4.75m (16 ft.) high and 5.75m (19 ft.) wide. Tradition says it was built by the 11th Tui Tonga about A.D. 1200, long before the wheel was introduced to Tonga. It serves as the gateway to the royal compound. The present King Taufa'ahau Tupou IV advanced a theory that it was used not only as an entrance but also for measuring the seasons. He found a secret mark on top of the lintel stone and at dawn on June 21, 1967, proved his point. The mark pointed to the exact spot on the horizon from which the sun rose on the shortest day of the year. You can stand under this imposing archway and ponder just how the ancient Tongans got the lintel stone on top of its two supports; it's the same sense of wonderment you feel while looking at Stonehenge in England or contemplating the great long-nosed heads that were carved and somehow erected by those other Polynesians far to the east of Tonga, on Easter Island.

The paved road ends at **Niutoua,** but a narrow dirt track proceeds down the east coast. **Anahulu Beach** has a cave with limestone stalactites near the village of Haveluliku. A gorgeous sand beach begins here and runs to **Oholei Beach.** 'Eua Island is visible on the horizon.

On the way back to Nuku'alofa you can take a detour to **Hufangalupe Beach** on the south coast for a look at a large natural bridge carved out of coral and limestone by the sea.

THE WESTERN TOUR

Proceed out of Nuku'alofa on Mateialona Road and follow the Visitors Bureau signs to the **Blowholes** *☙☙* near the village of Houma on the southwest coast. At high tide the surf pounds under shelves, sending geysers of seawater through holes in the coral. These are the most impressive blowholes in the South Pacific, and on a windy day the coast for miles is shrouded in mist thrown into the air by hundreds of them working at once. Lime sediments have built up circular terraces like rice paddies, around each

Moments **High & Dry Above the Blowholes**

Having crossed the Pacific several times in U.S. Navy ships and sailed across it once in a small boat, I am acutely aware of the power of the sea. It's strangely comforting to watch it explode through the blowholes on Tongatapu's south coast. Maybe it's because I know those waves can't get me up there on dry land.

hole, and the local women come just before dusk to gather clams in the pools formed by the rings. There is a park with benches and a parking area at the end of the road near the blowholes, but you'll need shoes with good soles to walk across the sharp edges of the top shelf to get the best views. This area once was an underwater reef, and corals are still very much visible, all of them now more than 15m (50 ft.) above sea level. (Look for what appear to be fossilized brains; they are appropriately named brain corals.) The blowholes are known in Tongan as *Mapu'a a Vaea,* "the chief's whistle."

From Houma, proceed west toward the village of Kolovai, and watch for the trees with strange-looking fruit. The sounds you hear and the odors in the air are coming from what appear to be black fruit hanging on the trees. In reality, these are **flying foxes,** a bat with a foxlike head found on many islands in the Pacific. Nocturnal creatures, they spend their days hanging upside down from the branches of trees like a thousand little Draculas awaiting the dark, their wings like black capes pulled tightly around their bodies. They don't feed on blood but on fruit; hence they are known as fruit bats. On some islands they are considered a delicacy. In Tonga, however, where they live in trees throughout the villages of Kolovai and Ha'avakatolo, they are thought to be sacred, and only members of the royal family can shoot them. Legend says that a Samoan princess gave the first bats to a Tongan navigator.

Near the end of the island is **Ha'atafu,** site of an offshore reef preserve. The first missionaries to land in Tonga came ashore at the end of the peninsula on the northwest coast, and a sign now marks the spot at the end of the road. They obviously got their feet wet—if they were not inadvertently "baptized"—wading across the shallow bank just offshore.

You've now toured Tongatapu from one end to the other. Turn around and head back to town.

ORGANIZED TOURS

Several companies have half- and full-day tours around Nuku'alofa and the rest of the island, including **Teta Tours** (**✆ 23-690**) and **Friendly Islander Explorer** (**✆ 29-910**). You should reserve any of these tours at least a day in advance. Half-day tours cost about T$20 (US$10) per person; whole-day tours of the entire island, T$40 (US$20).

10 Island Excursions, Watersports & Other Outdoor Activities

ISLAND EXCURSIONS ★★★ You will have a much wider choice of watersports activities on Vava'u (see "Vava'u" later in this chapter). Here they are concentrated in the huge lagoon on Tongatapu's north shore, especially at resorts on the small islets off Nuku'alofa. In fact, the most popular way to spend a day—particularly a very slow Sunday in Tonga—is swimming, snorkeling, sunbathing, dining, or just hanging out

---

Fun Fact **Tap-Tap-Tap**

That tap-tap-tap sound you hear in many villages is the tattoo of hammers flattening bark of the paper mulberry tree into Tongan tapa cloth.

---

at the flat, small islands of Pangaimotu, Fafa, or 'Atata, each of which has a resort just a few miles off Nuku'alofa. These little beachside establishments have restaurants and bars, too.

Pangaimotu Island Resort ☆☆ (© 23-759) on Pangaimotu is the oldest and closest of the offshore resorts, and it's my favorite by far. Virtually hanging over a lovely beach, its main building oozes slapped-together, old South Seas charm. Its boat usually leaves Faua Jetty on Vuna Road at 10 and 11am Monday to Saturday, and at 10, 11am, noon, and 1pm on Sunday. They return at 3, 4, and 5pm Monday to Saturday, and at 3, 4, 5, and 6pm on Sunday. Round-trip fare is T$15 (US$7.50) adults, T$7.50 (US$3.75) children 6 to 12, free for kids under 6. Once there, a chalkboard menu offers burgers and sandwiches, and owner Earle Emberson serves icy cold brews from an ice box behind the bar. There's a children's playground.

Fafa Island Resort (© 22-800), a German-owned, Robinson Crusoe–like establishment, operates its own sailboat from Faua Jetty daily at 11am. Round-trip transfers and lunch cost T$50 (US$25).

Royal Sunset Island Resort ☆ (© 21-155) on 'Atata, the farthest from Nuku'alofa, charges T$58 (US$29), including transfers and lunch.

See "Where to Stay on Tongatapu," below, for more information about these offshore resorts.

GOLF   You won't be playing any golf on Sunday, but you can every other day at the flat 9-hole **Manamo'ui Golf Course,** home of the Tonga Golf Club. The tour desk at the International Dateline Hotel (© 21-411) can arrange equipment rentals and tee times on this somewhat-less-than-challenging course, which is on the main road between the airport and town.

SAILING   In addition to the charter yachts based in Vava'u (see "Vava'u," later in this chapter), **Sailing Tonga** ☆☆☆ (© 21-254; www.sailingtonga.com) has the 15m (51 ft.) yacht *Impetuous* that's available for charter anywhere in Tonga. It's one of the best ways to explore the more remote islands in the Ha'apai group. This crewed craft has three cabins, each with its own head (restroom) with shower. Rates start at US$410 per person per day for two people, and decrease to US$170 per person per day if six people go. The skipper, cook, and provisions are included.

SCUBA DIVING & SNORKELING   Although diving off Tongatapu plays second fiddle to diving off Vava'u, the reefs offshore have some colorful coral and a great variety of sea life. Herbert Keller's **Deep Blue Diving Centre,** on Vuna Road at Faua Jetty (©/fax 23-379; www.deep-blue-diving.to), has dives to Hakaumana'o and Malinoa Reef Reserves, two protected underwater parks, and to nearby 'Eua Island, which has one of the largest underwater caves in the South Pacific (the entry is 28m/85 ft. deep). A two-tank dive costs about T$120 (US$60), including all equipment. Nondivers can go on many of his diving trips for T$35 (US$18), including equipment. Herbert also has a 50-foot-long live-aboard dive boat.

Moments **Lazing Away Sunday on an Islet**

I usually stay very busy when I'm in Tonga to revise this guide, but I am forced by law to put it aside and relax on Sunday. I like to spend my day doing nothing except eating, drinking, and lazing in the sun at one of the little resorts off Nuku'alofa.

11 Shopping on Tongatapu

Tonga is the best place in the South Pacific to shop for extraordinary Polynesian handicrafts, such as tapa cloth, mats, carvings, shell jewelry, and other exquisite items. Your large laundry basket will take at least 3 months to get home via ship if you don't send it by air freight or check it as baggage on your return flight, but the quality of its craftsmanship will be worth the wait.

Tapa cloth and finely woven *pandanus* mats are traditional items of clothing and gifts in Tonga, and the women of the kingdom have carried on the ancient skills, not only out of economic necessity but also out of pride in their craft. Collectively they produce thousands of items each day, every one made by hand and no two exactly alike. Pick up a copy of the Tonga Visitors Bureau's brochure "Tongan Handicrafts" for an excellent description of how tapa cloth is made from the bark of the paper mulberry tree, and the process by which women weave baskets, mats, and other items from natural materials.

It's fun to browse around the handicraft stalls on the second level of **Maketi Talamahu** on Salote Road, where you can occasionally find an excellent basket or other item, especially at the branch of The Art of Tonga (see below).

Except for tobacco products and liquor, Tonga has little to offer in the way of duty-free shopping.

The Art of Tonga 🌴🌴🌴   This sophisticated store carries excellent baskets, tapa, coral jewelry, and both whale- and fish-bone scrimshaw, but the best items are the works of owner Sitiveni "Steve" Fehoko, one of Tonga's most talented wood carvers. He has another outlet in Talamahu Market, and he owns **Fehoko Art Creation,** a small shop on Vuna Road near the domestic wharf. He accepts MasterCard and Visa credit cards and will ship your purchases. Taufa'ahau Rd., in Fund Management Building between Wellington and Lafone roads. ✆ **27-667.** Mon–Fri 8:30am–5pm, Sat 8:30am–2pm.

Blue Banana Studios 🌴   This is the best place in town for hand-painted sarongs and T-shirts as well as watercolors on tapa, all by Sune, Shane, and Chris Egan, a family of artists. The Egans also carry Tahitian black pearls and some very clever Christmas cards. Taufa'ahau Rd., in Fund Management Building between Wellington and Lafone roads. ✆ **22-662.** Mon–Fri 9am–5pm, Sat 9am–noon.

Catholic Women's League Handicraft Centre   This little waterfront shop carries locally made baskets, tapa, carvings, and shell jewelry. It's not as well stocked as the Langafonua center (see below), but you might find an excellent piece here. Vuna Rd., opposite Faua Jetty. ✆ **27-524.** Mon–Fri 9am–5pm.

Kalia Handicrafts (FIMCO)   This retail outlet of the Friendly Islands Marketing Cooperative (FIMCO) gets a large variety of baskets, mats, tapa, shell jewelry, and other handicrafts. You can pay with American Express, MasterCard, and Visa credit cards, and the staff will pack and ship your purchases home. Taufa'ahau Rd., opposite Air New Zealand. © 23-155. Mon–Fri 8am–5pm, Sat 8am–noon.

Langafonua Women's Association Handicraft Centre ᡮᡮ This terrific (and quite charming) shop in the colonial house on Taufa'ahau Road was founded by Queen Salote in 1953 in order to preserve the old crafts and provide a market for them. It has an excellent collection, and some items may be priced somewhat lower than elsewhere. It does not accept credit cards; the shop will pack your purchases but not ship them. Taufa'ahau Rd., second block inland. © 21-014. Mon–Fri 8:30am–4:30pm, Sat 8:30am–noon.

12 Where to Stay on Tongatapu

If an expensive, superluxurious vacation or honeymoon is your primary reason for coming to the South Pacific, go to Fiji or French Polynesia, not to Tonga. There are no luxury resorts at all in Tonga, although there are comfortable hotels and island hideaways from which to choose. Tonga is more of a developing nation than any other South Pacific country or territory, so don't set your expectations too high. On the other hand, most hotels here are inexpensive.

ACCOMMODATIONS IN NUKU'ALOFA

The Black Pearl Suites ᡮ Built by Tongans living in the United States, this two-story clapboard building facing the lagoon has some of the best hotel rooms and suites in Tonga, even if their furniture is a bit overwrought, and the decor a tad gaudy in places. Downstairs units were on the drawing board when I stayed here; meantime, the units are upstairs and are entered through The Black Pearl Restaurant (see "Where to Dine on Tongatapu," below). Sharing space with the restaurant and bar, a guest lounge has more heavy furniture and a large-screen TV for watching movies and rugby, Tonga's national sport. Two of the units are large "executive suites" with large TVs, four-poster king beds, over-sized sofas, wet bars, kitchen table and chairs, and a mezzanine with sofa. Although called suites, the other units are standard hotel rooms with sleigh beds, desks, and combination tub-shower bathrooms. The neighborhood is primarily residential, thus peaceful and quiet.

P.O. Box 2913, Nuku'alofa (in Sopu, on Vuna Road, 2.5km/1.5 miles west of Royal Palace). © 28-393. Fax 28-432. www.blackpearlsuites.to. 10 units. T$160–T$300 (US$80–US$150). MC, V. **Amenities:** Restaurant; bar; laundry service. *In room:* A/C, TV, minibar, fridge, coffeemaker, iron, safe.

Harbour View Motel *(Value* Clean and good value, this three-story concrete building offers a variety of simple rooms, from budget to a penthouse suite. The latter

---

Tips Watch Out for Fake *Tapa* & Shoddy Carvings

Be careful when shopping for paintings on tapa cloth, since some unscrupulous artisans have been using real paper instead of real bark from the paper mulberry tree. Avoid men who approach you on the street and attempt to sell shoddy woodcarvings and black coral jewelry; they fall into the same category as the "sword sellers" of Fiji (see chapter 4). Also be sure you get what you paid for; that is, purchase handicraft items already made and on display rather than ordering for future production and delivery after you have left Tonga. In other words, stick to reputable shops such as those recommended in the section above.

occupies all of the third floor and is the largest hotel room in Tonga. It features windows on three sides, a TV, a wet bar, two king-size beds, and a spacious bathroom with a Jacuzzi tub. On the second floor, reasonably spacious deluxe rooms are equipped with TVs, refrigerators, and bathrooms. Three budget rooms and two standard units share bathrooms. The budget units all have phones but none of them has a TV or air-conditioner. This is a walk-up establishment with external stairways leading to verandas on each floor. The location opposite the commercial wharf is not particularly scenic or convenient to downtown, and noise from the Billfish Bar and Restaurant filters in on weekend nights, but some of Nuku'alofa's better restaurants are within easy walks. Continental breakfast is available in the lobby.

P.O. Box 83, Nuku'alofa (Vuna Rd., opposite Queen Salote Wharf). ✆ 25-488. Fax 25-490. harbvmtl@kalianet.to. 13 units (6 without bathroom). T$70–T$180 (US$35–US$90) double. MC, V. **Amenities:** Bar; laundry service; coin-op washers. *In room:* A/C (in some units), TV (in some units), fridge (in some units), coffeemaker, hair dryer (penthouse only), iron (penthouse only).

International Dateline Hotel
Built in time for the king's coronation in 1967, this is Tonga's largest and most widely known place to stay. Its Chinese owners have renovated all of the public areas and added a three-story wing holding 50 modern units. Most of these are moderately spacious standard rooms with balconies, either a king bed or two doubles, and somewhat cramped bathrooms with combination tub-showers. Executive suites add a living room with sofa and easy chairs, and their bathrooms are somewhat larger than in the standard units. The royal suite has two bedrooms, two bathrooms, and an office. Cherry wood furniture from China lends more of an Asian than Pacific ambience to all the new units. Do not let the front desk or a tour operator put you in 1 of the 76 rooms in the two original wings, which have not been renovated. In other words, stay in one of the new units—or somewhere else. The Dateline is Nuku'alofa's prime place for meetings, conventions, and other functions. The property enjoys a choice location facing the harbor across Vuna Road on Nuku'alofa's waterfront, a few blocks from downtown, and it's the only hotel on Tongatapu with spacious grounds featuring a swimming pool.

P.O. Box 39, Nuku'alofa (Vuna Rd. at Tupoulahi Rd., on the waterfront). ✆ 23-411. Fax 23-410. www.datelinehotel.com. 126 units. T$105–T$253 (US$53–US$127) double, T$218–T$517 (US$109–US$259) suite. AE, MC, V. **Amenities:** 2 restaurants; 2 bars; outdoor pool; activities desk; salon; limited room service; massage; babysitting; laundry service. *In room:* A/C, TV, minibar, coffeemaker.

Seaview Lodge 🏝🏝
Some of Nuku'alofa's best rooms are here at the fine Seaview Restaurant (see "Where to Dine on Tongatapu," below). Three of these spacious, light, and airy units are upstairs over the restaurant and have balconies with fine views across Vuna Road to the lagoon; they are the choice here. Two other upstairs units face inland over the gardens. Six more units in a building to the side of the restaurant lack any view. Each unit here is equipped with a TV and a VCR, a ceiling fan over a king-size bed, and a spacious bathroom with European-style, glass-enclosed showers with large heads. Six other less attractive but still comfortable units are in another building next door. Business travelers keep this place busy, so book as early as possible. The Seaview Restaurant is open to lodge guests for breakfast. You will get a good night's sleep here, since this quiet location is well away from Nuku'alofa's noisy bars.

P.O. Box 268, Nuku'alofa (Vuna Rd. west of Royal Palace). ✆ 23-709. Fax 26-906. www.tongaholiday.com/seaview.htm. 12 units. T$110–T$155 (US$55–US$78) double. AE, MC, V. **Amenities:** Restaurant; bar; laundry service. *In room:* A/C, TV, dataport, minibar, coffeemaker.

The Villa McKenzie 🌴🌴   This charming one-story colonial clapboard home on the waterfront is one of the South Pacific's best bed-and-breakfasts. A central hallway is flanked on one side by a large lounge room (equipped with TV and VCR), an old-fashioned dining room, and a huge country kitchen. To the other side, the four rooms all have tongue-in-groove walls, and mosquito nets hang over their double or single beds. Owners Kim and Jude Brabant have tea, coffee, and soft drinks available around the clock in the kitchen. The town's expatriate movers and shakers turn up here for snacks and kava in the rear garden Friday evenings. This clean and comfortable choice oozes old South Seas charm, so book as early as possible.

P.O. Box 1892, Nuku'alofa (Vuna Rd., at Tungi Rd.). ℂ/fax **24-998**. www.tongavilla.com. 5 units. T$145 (US$73) double. Rates include full breakfast. MC, V. **Amenities:** Laundry service. *In room:* A/C, dataport.

Waterfront Lodge   Taking a page from the Seaview Lodge's book, owners G. P. and Daniella Orbassano have eight units above their Waterfront Cafe (see "Where to Dine on Tongatapu," below). The moderately spacious rooms all have high ceilings with fans, polished oak floors, a king-size bed, tropical furniture including desks, shower-only bathrooms, and sliding doors opening to balconies trimmed with plantation-style fretwork. Units on the front of the building with sea views are the most expensive and preferable, although they are subject to the beat of loud music from a bar next door on weekends. Guests can purchase breakfast at the Waterfront Cafe downstairs.

P.O. Box 1001, Nuku'alofa (Vuna Rd., opposite domestic wharf). ℂ **25-260.** Fax 28-059. www.waterfront-lodge.com. 8 units. T$110–T$140 (US$55–US$70) double. AE, MC, V. **Amenities:** Restaurant; bar; massage; laundry service. *In room:* A/C, dataport, fridge, coffeemaker, hair dryer, safe.

Winnie's Guest House *Finds*   While The Villa McKenzie is a commercial operation (see above), here you share a typical Tongan home with the charming Mrs. Winnie Santos. Two of her rooms have twin beds, the other four have double beds. The rooms are screened, but all beds have mosquito nets anyway. Guests share three toilets, three showers, the kitchen, the large living room, and an enclosed veranda for reading and connecting to the Internet. The backyard offers a picnic table and a barbecue grill. The house is not air-conditioned, but on most days a breeze cools things off. Winnie's is in a residential neighborhood behind Vaiola Hospital; local buses pass in front.

P.O. Box 3049, Nuku'alofa (Vaha'akolo Rd., behind the hospital). ℂ **25-215.** winnies@tonfon.to. 6 units (none w/bathroom). T$40 (US$20) per person. Rates include tropical breakfast. MC, V. *In room:* No phone.

OFFSHORE RESORTS

Fafa Island Resort 🌴   German Rainer Urtel has stocked his little resort, on a 17-acre atoll-like island studded with coconut palms, with bungalows made entirely of natural materials. They have a rustic South Seas charm that attracts a clientele in search of a Robinson Crusoe–like experience, albeit one with most of the comforts of home. Two deluxe fales have refrigerators and two bedrooms. The push-out windows aren't screened, so each of the platform beds has a mosquito net. The bungalows all have front porches, over two of which are romantic "honeymoon" sleeping lofts with lagoon views. All of the toilets, lavatories, and showers are in fenced-enclosed courtyards. Complimentary morning coffee and tea are delivered to the units, and the dining room in a beachside central building features excellent seafood. Guests can use snorkeling gear for free; they pay extra for Windsurfers, Hobie Cats, and trips to an uninhabited island for snorkeling.

P.O. Box 1444, Nuku'alofa (Fafa Island, 10km/6 miles off Nuku'alofa). © **22-800**. Fax 23-592. www.fafa.to. 13 units. US$183–US$240 double. Meal plans US$65 per person per day. Round-trip transfers US$46 per person. AE, DC, MC, V. **Amenities:** Restaurant; bar; free use of snorkeling gear; watersports equipment rental; limited room service; massage; babysitting; laundry service. *In room:* Fridge, no phone.

Pangaimotu Island Resort Unless I were backpacking, I wouldn't stay at Earle and Ana Emberson's lively little joint, but you will find me out here on Sunday afternoons, when it's packed with tourists, local expatriate residents, and Westernized Tongans. Wait until you see one of the South Pacific's most charming pubs: a rickety lagoonside shack where Earle plays jazz compact discs and serves up ice-cold beer from a huge chiller behind the bar. Meanwhile, his staff whips up full meals or burgers and sandwiches served on an adjacent sundeck hanging haphazardly over a lovely beach. You can swim and snorkel in one of the safest lagoons in Tonga. Earle's basic guest fales are built of natural materials. Each has separate sitting and sleeping areas, a platform double bed with a mosquito net, and a simple bathroom with a cold-water shower. All the fales face the beach. Dorm beds are in a larger communal fale. Dorm dwellers and campers share communal cold-water showers, toilets, and kitchen facilities. There's a small store that dispenses groceries.

Private Bag 49, Nuku'alofa (Pangaimotu Island, 3km/2 miles off Nuku'alofa). © **15-762**. Fax 17-257. www. pangaimotu.to. 4 units, 12 dorm beds. T$90 (US$45) double bungalow; T$25 (US$13) dorm bed; T$10 (US$5) per person camping. Round-trip transfers T$15 (US$7.50). MC, V. **Amenities:** Restaurant; bar. *In room:* No phone.

Royal Sunset Island Resort This Italian-owned resort shares small, tadpole-shaped 'Atata Island with a native Tongan village. One of the South Pacific's finest beaches swings around their end, the "tail" of the tadpole, and the surrounding lagoon attracts swimmers, snorkelers, scuba divers, and anyone who loves to fish. Whales often play offshore from June through October. Two large shingle-roofed fales house a dining room and a triangular sunken bar, which opens to a pool surrounded by a deck that's dotted with lawn tables and umbrellas. About half the basic but comfortable guest bungalows face the prevailing southeast trade winds; these can be chilly from June to August but provide nature's air-conditioning during the warmer months of December to March. The others face the lagoon, but they have a much better beach, plus views of the royal sunsets. A few bungalows are minisuites—one room with a sitting area and tea-and-coffee facilities—and a few units have kitchens. Guests can use snorkeling gear, kayaks, sailboats, and Windsurfers for free, and they can pay to water-ski, sport fish, and scuba dive (you must be certified in advance).

P.O. Box 960, Nuku'alofa ('Atata Island, 10km/6 miles off Nuku'alofa). ©/fax **21-254**. www.royalsunset.to. 24 units. T$182–T$218 (US$91–US$109) double. Meals T$75 (US$38) per person per day. Round-trip transfers T$60 (US$30) per person. AE, DC, MC, V. **Amenities:** Restaurant; bar; outdoor pool; babysitting; laundry service. *In room:* Kitchen (some units), fridge, coffeemaker, no phone.

13 Where to Dine on Tongatapu

Nuku'alofa is blessed with a few restaurants that serve Continental cuisine of remarkably high quality for such a small and unsophisticated town. Expatriates, especially from Germany and Italy, operate most of them. This also means a high turnover factor because not all expatriates stay in the islands forever. The establishments listed below were open when I was here recently. There may be more by the time you arrive—or these may be gone.

Tips **Dine Like a Tongan**

Like most Polynesians, the Tongans in the old days cooked their food over hot rocks in a pit—an *umu*—for several hours. Today they roast whole suckling pigs on a spit over coals for several hours (larger pigs still go into the umu). The dishes that emerge from the umu are similar to those found elsewhere in Polynesia: pig, chicken, lobster, fish, octopus, taro, taro leaves cooked with meat and onions, breadfruit, bananas, and a sweet breadfruit pudding known as *faikakai-lolo,* all of it cooked with ample amounts of coconut cream. Served on the side are *ota ika* (fish) and *vasuva* (clams), both marinated in lime juice.

The best place to sample Tongan food is during the evening buffets and dance shows at the **Tongan National Centre** (© **23-022**). Others are the **International Dateline Hotel** (© **23-411**) and the **Good Samaritan Inn** (© **41-022**). See "Island Nights on Tongatapu," below, for details.

MODERATE

Billfish Bar and Restaurant INTERNATIONAL   Primarily a socializing and drinking spot (see "Island Nights on Tongatapu," below), the Billfish nevertheless serves good pub fare, especially fish and chips. Also acceptable are the spicy pepper steaks and fresh fish steamed with fresh herbs and coconut milk. For lunch you can opt for burgers, sandwiches, fish and chips, and grilled chops. Booze and food are served under a thatch-lined, lean-to roof, and there are dining tables in a gazebo to one side. The crushed coral floor helps create a tropical ambience. Sunday is roast night here.

Vuna Rd., opposite Queen Salote Wharf. © **24-084.** Reservations accepted. Lunch T$7–T$23 (US$3.50–US$12); burgers T$12–T$28 (US$6–US$14); main courses T$23–T$39 (US$12–US$20). MC, V. Mon–Fri noon–2pm and 6–10:30pm, Sat 6–10:30pm, Sun 6–9:30pm. Bar open Mon–Thurs noon–10:30pm, Fri noon–2am, Sat 6pm–midnight.

The Black Pearl Restaurant 𝒜 INTERNATIONAL   With a lagoon view from its upstairs location in The Black Pearl Suites, this restaurant is one of the more pleasant places to dine here. The ambience is casual yet refined, and the staff provides some of Tonga's most attentive table service. The chef on duty when I stayed here had trained in the U.S., thus was familiar with what I call *nouveau* American cooking—that is, the creative use of various spices and flavors. Although steaks are the biggest seller, I was impressed with her grilled snapper topped with spicy salsa, sautéed onions, and sour-cream sauce. Start with a salad such as chicken cashew in honey mustard sauce with fresh fruits. The best tables are out on the porch. The Black Pearl Suites guests can have breakfast here.

Vuna Rd. (in The Black Pearl Suites, Vuna Rd., 2.5km/1.5 miles west of Royal Palace). © **28-393.** Reservations recommended at dinner. Main course T$25–T$49 (US$13–US$25). MC, V. Daily 7–10am, noon–2pm, and 6–10pm.

Friends Cafe 𝒜𝒜𝒜 COFFEE HOUSE/CAFE   This outstanding coffee shop and cafe provides a delightfully modern oasis in Taufa'ahau Road's dusty business scene. Locally grown beans create great cappuccino, espresso, and latte. You can also eat the town's best cakes and pastries, luscious fruit plates, and made-to-order sandwiches at the counter, then sip or dine inside or out on the side patio while listening to jazz or classical music on the sound system. A blackboard menu offers specials such as quiche and salad and braised lamb shanks in tomato sauce. Late afternoon and evening offerings include sandwiches, cakes, pastries, and main courses such as lobster Polynesia-style and pan-fried snapper.

Taufa'ahau Rd., between Salote and Wellington rds. ✆ **21-284.** Reservations accepted at dinner. Breakfast T$5.50–T$15 (US$2.25–US$7.50); sandwiches T$5.50–T$10 (US$2.25–US$5); main courses T$15–T$30 (US$7.50–US$15). AE, MC, V. Mon–Fri 7:30am–10pm, Sat 8am–7:30pm.

La Terrazza ITALIAN   Upstairs in a converted house facing Faua Jetty, this restaurant has tables outside on the large, open-air front porch, the *terrazza*. In Italian fashion, you'll start with a choice of antipasti or pasta, followed by a fish or meat main course. Best is the tuna in "crazy water"—a Neapolitan-style sauce of hot olive oil drizzled with white wine, garlic, and fresh tomatoes.

Vuna Rd., at Faua Jetty. ✆ **25-393.** Reservations recommended. Pasta T$13–T$19 (US$6.50–US$9.50); main courses T$26–T$29 (US$13–US$15). AE, MC, V. Daily noon–2pm and 6:30–10:30pm.

Seaview Restaurant 𝕽𝕽𝕽 CONTINENTAL   This pleasant establishment in a colonial-style house west of the Royal Palace serves the best cuisine in Tonga. The fresh tropical lobster—especially served *au natural* with only butter, or house-style with crushed pepper—is outstanding, as are pepper steak and other dishes made with quality meats imported from New Zealand. Start with a chilled seafood cocktail and finish with homemade German pastries for dessert. Top seats are on the screened porch, which has a sea view across Vuna Road.

Vuna Rd., 3 blocks west of Royal Palace. ✆ **23-709.** Reservations recommended. Main courses T$31–T$43 (US$16–US$21). AE, MC, V. Mon–Fri 6–10pm.

Waterfront Cafe 𝕽𝕽 INTERNATIONAL   This stylish creation of Daniella Orbessano, an Italian who once worked on Princess Cruises's ships, is the next best place for Italian fare here. The restaurant is on the ground floor of her Waterfront Lodge, and the best tables are out on the long veranda fronting the colonial-style building. You can choose from homemade pastas, freshly caught fish, and tender steaks. Many wines from Australia, New Zealand, and Italy are available by the glass.

Vuna Rd., opposite Faua Jetty. ✆ **24-962.** Reservations recommended Thurs and Fri. Burgers T$14 (US$7); main courses T$14–T$38 (US$7–US$19). AE, MC, V. Tues–Fri 8:30–10am and 5–10pm, Sat–Sun 8–10am and 5–10:30pm.

INEXPENSIVE

Akiko's Restaurant (Loki Kai) 𝒱𝑎𝑙𝑢𝑒 EUROPEAN/CHINESE   Known as Akiko's in honor of its former Japanese owner, this plain but spotlessly clean establishment provides sandwiches and a selection of plain and simple European and Chinese selections that are marvelous bargains. No alcoholic beverages are served here.

Taufa'ahau Rd., in Basilica of St. Anthony of Padua. ✆ **25-339.** Sandwiches T$2 (US$1); meals T$2.50–T$7 (US$1.25–US$3.50). No credit cards. Mon–Fri 11am–3pm.

Pizzeria Little Italy 𝕽𝕽 𝒱𝑎𝑙𝑢𝑒 PIZZA   Angelo Crapanzano, who learned his trade as a pizza chef in Milan, Italy, scurries around the open kitchen in this unusual restaurant: It's a genuine, thatched-roof Tongan fale, but empty Ruffino wine bottles dangle from the support posts, and hats of every imaginable description adorn the walls. Don't be in a hurry, for everything is made from scratch, including the pizza dough. Pastas and main courses are on the menu, too, but this is primarily a pizza place.

Vuna Rd., 5 blocks west of Royal Palace. © **21-053.** Reservations recommended. Pizzas T$12–T$18 (US$6–US$9); pastas T$14–T$20 (US$7–US$10); main courses T$21–T$32 (US$11–US$16). MC, V. Mon–Fri noon–2pm and 6:30–10:30pm, Sat 6:30–10:30pm.

14 Island Nights on Tongatapu

You go to the movies here at the modern **Star Cinema,** on Taufa'ahau Road (© **28-771**). The three daily movies are more likely to be action flicks (in which language is of secondary importance) than dramas. Tickets cost T$4.50 (US$2.25).

TONGAN DANCE SHOWS *★★★* As in Samoa, traditional **Tongan dancing** emphasizes fluid movements of the hands and feet instead of gyrating hips, as is the case in French Polynesia and the Cook Islands. There is also less emphasis on drums and more on the stamping, clapping, and singing of the participants. The dances most often performed for tourists are the *tau'olunga,* in which one young woman dances solo, her body glistening with coconut oil; the *ma'ulu'ulu,* performed sitting down by groups ranging from 20 members to as many as 900 for very important occasions; the *laklaka,* in which rows of dancers sing and dance in unison; and the *kailao,* or war dance, in which men stamp the ground and wave war clubs at each other in mock battle.

The best place to see it is at **Tongan National Centre** *★★★* (© **23-022**), which stages a full Tongan-style feast complete with a traditional kava welcoming ceremony and dance show Tuesday and Thursday evenings. What makes the evening special is an explanation, in English, of what each dance represents. Cost is T$25 (US$13), including transportation. Book by 4:30pm.

Another good choice is the Friday night feast at the **Good Samaritan Inn** (© **41-022**), on the beach 18km (11 miles) west of Nuku'alofa. They offer an extensive buffet of Tongan and Western foods, followed by a dance show beside the lagoon. The meal and show costs about T$25 (US$13), plus T$10 (US$5) for round-trip transportation from town if you need it. Reservations are advised.

You'll also have a chance to see Tongan dancing on Wednesday night in Nuku'alofa at the **International Dateline Hotel** (© **23-411**), where floor shows start around 9pm after a buffet-style dinner.

PUB CRAWLING Because all pubs and nightclubs must close at the stroke of midnight Saturday, Friday is the busiest and longest night of the week in Tonga. That's when some establishments stay open until 2am. Many Tongans start their weekends at one of the local bars and then adjourn to a nightclub for heavy-duty revelry.

Clubs change in popularity quickly here, so it's best to ask around to learn which ones are drawing the crowds. You can avoid drunken fights by doing your drinking at the **Billfish Bar and Restaurant,** where a squad of security guards keep order, and at the **Waterfront Cafe,** which does not have live bands, thus encouraging conversation. Both are on Vuna Road opposite Queen Salote Wharf (see "Where to Dine on Tongatapu," above).

15 Vava'u *★★★*

The crown jewel of this little kingdom, Vava'u lies approximately 260km (163 miles) north of Tongatapu. It's one of the South Pacific's great yachting centers and one of this region's most unusual destinations.

Often mispronounced "Va-vow" (it's "Va-*va*-oo"), the group consists of one large, hilly island shaped like a jellyfish, its tentacles trailing off in a myriad of waterways

---

⌐Tips Don't Forget to Reconfirm

It's imperative to reconfirm your return flight to Tongatapu as soon as possible after arriving on Vava'u. The staff at your hotel can take care of this for you, or drop by the airlines' offices on the main street in Neiafu.

---

and small, sand-ringed islets. In the middle, the magnificent fjordlike harbor known as **Port of Refuge** ranks as one of the finest anchorages in the South Pacific. From its picturesque perch above the harbor, the main village of **Neiafu** (pop. 5,000) evokes scenes from the South Seas of yesteryear.

To the south of Neiafu, the reef is speckled with 33 small islands, 21 of them inhabited. The others are spectacularly beautiful little dots of land upon which Robinson Crusoe would fit right in. The white beaches and emerald lagoon are unsurpassed in their beauty.

When you see these protected waterways, you'll know why cruising sailors love Vava'u. But this is heaven not just to sailors but to any watersports enthusiast. Getting out on the water for a day is easy. If you like walking on unspoiled white beaches on uninhabited islands, swimming in crystal-clear water, and taking boat rides into mysterious caves cut into cliffs, you'll like Vava'u, too.

Vava'u is the most seasonal destination in the South Pacific. Virtually asleep for 6 months of the year, it comes alive during the yachting season from May to October, when more than 500 boats can be in port at any one time. This is also the time of year when humpback whales migrate from the Antarctic to frolic in Tongan waters. This is the best place in the region to get out and see them up close and personal.

As with Savai'i in Samoa, you will wish you had stayed longer in this most beautiful and enchanting part of Tonga.

GETTING TO VAVA'U & GETTING AROUND
GETTING THERE
For the time being, **Peau Vava'u** (© 28-325; www.peauvavau.to) and **Airlines Tonga** (© 24-506; www.airlinestonga.com) fly between Tongatapu to Vava'u (see "Getting to Tonga & Getting Around," earlier in this chapter). **Lupepa'u International Airport** is on the north side of Vauau'u, about 7km (4 miles) from Neiafu. Most hotels will pick up their guests, including the Paradise International Hotel, whose bus provides airport transfers to anyone else for T$5 (US$2.50). You can take a taxi to Neiafu for about T$15 (US$7.50).

The ferries from Nuku'alofa land in Neiafu at Uafu Lahi, which everyone calls the "Big Wharf." From there you can walk or take a taxi ride to your hotel or guesthouse. If you're on foot, turn right on the main street to reach the center of town and the accommodations.

The road from the airport dead-ends at a T-intersection atop the hill above the wharf. The main street runs from there in both directions along the water, with most of the town's stores and government offices flanking it.

GETTING AROUND
You can explore all of Neiafu on foot, but public transportation to the outlying areas of Vava'u is limited. If you book an excursion, ask about the availability of transportation to and from the event.

> **Fun Fact The Road of the Doves**
>
> The government used convicted adulteresses to help build the main road in Neiafu; hence, its Tongan name is Hale Lupe—"The Road of the Doves." There are no street signs, but the Tonga Visitors Bureau's helpful signs point the way to most establishments and points of interest.

Adventure Backpackers Lodge (✆ **70-955**) rents mountain bikes for T$20 (US$10) a day. See "Where to Stay on Vava'u," below.

Taxis are not metered, so be sure you determine the fare before getting in. **Falepiu Taxi** (✆ **70-671**) has a stand opposite the Westpac Bank of Tonga; **Liviela Taxi** (✆ **70-240**) is opposite the Bounty Bar; **J. V. Taxi** (✆ **70-136** or 70-157) is opposite Adventure Backpackers; and **Lopaukamea Taxi** (✆ **70-153**) is opposite the market. Fares are T$3 (US$1.50) in town, or you can hire one for about T$15 (US$7.50) per hour, but be sure to negotiate a fare in advance.

Buses and pickup trucks fan out from the market in Neiafu to various villages, but they have no fixed schedule and are not a reliable means of transport. If you take one, make sure you know when and whether it's coming back to town.

FAST FACTS: Vava'u

If you don't see an item here, check "Fast Facts: Tonga," earlier in this chapter, or just ask around. Vava'u is a very small place where nearly everyone knows everything.

Currency Exchange **ANZ Bank** and **Westpac Bank of Tonga** are both on the main street in Neiafu and have ATMs. Banking hours are Monday to Friday 9am to 4pm, with Westpac also open Saturday 8 to 11am.

E-mail **Cafe Tropicana**, on the main street in Neiafu (✆ **71-322**), has Internet access at T$3 (US$1.50) for 15 minutes. See "Where to Dine on Vava'u," below. Down by the harbor, **Aquarium Adventures** (✆ **71-493**) has faster access for T$12 (US$6) an hour. It's open Monday to Saturday 8am to 8:30pm.

Emergencies/Police The telephone number for the **police** is **70-234.**

Healthcare **Dr. Alfredo Carafa** (✆ **70-607**), an engaging Italian, has a private clinic and pharmacy next to Westpac Bank of Tonga. The clinic is open Monday to Friday 9am to 2pm; the pharmacy, Monday to Friday 8:30am to 12:30pm, Saturday 8:30 to 10:30am. The government has a **small hospital** in Neiafu.

Information The **Tonga Visitors Bureau** (✆ **70-115**; fax 70-666; tvbvv@kalianet. to) has an office on the main road in Neiafu. Check there for lists of local activities while you're in town. The staff can also help arrange road tours of the island and boat tours of the lagoon. The office is open Monday to Friday 8:30am to 4:30pm. The address is P.O. Box 18, Neiafu, Vava'u.

Laundry **CocoNet Internet Cafe**, down by the harbor (✆ **71-311**), will wash, dry, and fold your laundry for T$10 (US$5) per load.

Post Office The post office opposite the wharf is open Monday to Friday from 8:30am to 4pm.

Telephone Tonga Communications Corporation next to the post office is open 24 hours a day, 7 days a week for domestic and long-distance calls. It also has a card phone (there's one next to Westpac Bank of Tonga, too).

Water Don't drink the tap water.

EXPLORING VAVA'U

Be sure to take a walk along Port of Refuge from Paradise International Hotel into town, a stroll of about 15 minutes.

The flat-top mountain across the harbor, **Mo'unga Talau,** at 204m (675 ft.), is the tallest point on Vava'u and part of a Tongan national park. A hike to the top takes about 2 hours round-trip. To get there, turn inland a block past the Westpac Bank of Tonga on the airport road, and then turn left at the Old Market. This street continues through the residential area and then becomes a track, with rope handles in places. The turnoff to the summit starts as the track begins to head downhill. It's a steep climb and can be slippery in wet weather. The Tonga Visitors Bureau maintains the trail, so ask there before making this trek.

The hotels will arrange **sightseeing tours** of the island, or check with **Aquarium Adventures,** down by the harbor in The Moorings complex (© 71-493). They have half-day tours for T$35 (US$18) or full-day outings for T$90 (US$45). You will see lovely scenery of the fingerlike bays that cut into the island, visit some beautiful beaches, and take in the sweet smell of vanilla—the principal cash crop on Vava'u—drying in sheds or in the sun.

BOAT TOURS ✿✿✿

The absolute best thing to do in Vava'u is to take a boat tour out on the fabulous fjords for a day of swimming, snorkeling, and exploring of the caves and uninhabited islands.

The typical tour follows Port of Refuge to **Swallows Cave** on Kapa Island and then to **Mariner's Cave** (named for Will Mariner, the young Englishman captured with the *Port au Prince* in 1806) on Nuapapu Island. Both of these have been carved out of cliffs by erosion. Boats can go right into Swallows Cave for a look at the swallows flying in and out of a hole in the cave's top. Swimmers with snorkeling gear and a guide can dive into Mariner's Cave. Both caves face west and are best visited in the afternoon, when the maximum amount of natural light gets into them. Most trips also include a stop at one of the small islands for some time at a sparkling beach and a swim over the reefs in crystal-clear water.

Every hotel and guest house here can arrange boat tours, or you can drop by **Sailing Safaris** (© 70-650; www.sailingsafaris.com), which has all-day snorkeling trips to the caves and islets. Or you can rent a powerboat or sailboat and go where you please. Boats cost about T$200 (US$100) a day, T$250 (US$125) with a skipper. The skipper is worth having on a day trip, since he will take you to the caves and then stand by the boat while you explore.

SAILING 🐠🐠

The waterfront at the base of the hill in Neiafu is home to more than 30 charter yachts that you can rent for as many days as you can afford. Most Americans who visit Tonga, in fact, come here to explore Vava'u in a chartered yacht. You can spend your time sailing from one tiny islet to another in these calm waters. There are dozens of gorgeous beaches off which to anchor, and there are several restaurants to visit at night.

The Moorings 🐠🐠🐠 (© **800/534-7289** or 70-016; www.moorings.com), the Florida-based pioneer of chartering sailboats in the Caribbean, has one of its two South Pacific bases here. It requires that you be qualified to handle sailboats of the size it charters, and the staff will check out your skills before turning you loose. If you don't qualify, you can hire a skipper or guide at extra cost. Boats range in length from 10m to 15m (31 ft.–51 ft.) and in price from about US$400 to US$990 a night per boat for bareboat charters (that is, you hire the "bare" boat and provide your own skipper and crew). Prices are more expensive during the May to October high season, but that's far and away the best time to be here. A skipper will cost another NZ$200 (US$130) per day. The Moorings will do your shopping and have the boat provisioned with food and drink when you arrive.

You can rent small sailing dinghies for T$25 (US$13) per hour or T$125 (US$63) for all day from **Aquarium Adventures** (© **70-493**), on the waterfront in The Moorings complex. These little boats were once used as dinghies by The Moorings' yachts. Aquarium Adventures is operated by Ben and Lisa Newton, a young American couple who sailed their own yacht to Vava'u and stayed. They also offer jet-boat tours, waterskiing, and other watersports activities, and they have an Internet cafe on premises.

WHALE-WATCHING 🐠🐠🐠

Humpback whales breed in the waters off Vava'u from June to October, and going out to see them highlights a visit during that season. Other whale-watching destinations such as Hawaii won't allow you to swim with the whales, but you can here, albeit under very tightly controlled conditions. Local operators say there's a 50% to 60% chance you'll get to snorkel among the whales and a 90% chance of seeing them during the season.

Almost everyone here with a boat goes out to see the whales, including the fishing charter craft mentioned below. The most experienced operator is Allan Bowe's **Whale Watch Vava'u** (© **70-747**; www.whalewatchvavau.com). In fact, Allan practically launched whale-watching in Vava'u. He charges T$150 (US$75) per person. These are all-day voyages, and the sun can be brutal, so come prepared.

FISHING, KAYAKING & SCUBA DIVING

As noted above, Vava'u has a very busy yachting and whale-watching season from May to October. Some of the activities mentioned below operate only during this period and then clear out of Tonga entirely during the hurricane season from November to April. It's best to ask in advance whether any particular activity is available when you will be here.

⌒Moments **The Ghost of Will Mariner**

Every time I pop my head out of the water in Mariner's Cave, I swear I can see the ghost of the young Englishman Will Mariner, who wrote a best-selling book about being held captive here in the early 19th century.

FISHING   The waters off Vava'u hold a large number of sizable blue marlin, sailfish, yellowfin and dogtooth tuna, mahimahi, and other species, and you can charter one of several boats here to go get 'em.

New Zealanders Keith and Pat McKee of *Kiwi Magic* (℗/fax **70-441;** kiwifish@kalianet.to) take visitors offshore for a full day of sport-fishing, and snorkelers can go along by arrangement. The McKees operate year-round, as do their fellow Kiwis, Henk and Sandra Gross of *Target One* (℗/fax **70-647;** www.invited.to/target1) and Jeff and Janine Le Strange of the *Hakula* (℗ **70-872;** fax 70-875; www.fishtonga.com). They all charge about US$400 per day, including bait, tackle, and lunch. A minimum of three persons must be on board. Most of them do whale-watching trips during the season. The Stranges will put you up at their **Hakula Lodge,** on the edge of Neiafu.

KAYAKING   Yachties aren't the only ones who can enjoy the multitude of protected waterways here. Kayakers can, too. **Friendly Islands Kayak Company** (℗ **70-173;** fax 70-173 or 22-970; www.fikco.com), a New Zealand firm, operates the **Adventure Centre** south of the Paradise International Hotel. It rents sea kayaks and conducts guided tours. It has 5-, 9-, and 11-day trips through the islands, using double- and single-seat kayaks. The tours range from US$845 to US$1,995 per person and should be arranged in advance.

Several firms rent kayaks, including **Adventure Backpackers Lodge** (℗ **70-955**), the **Paradise International Hotel** (℗ **74-744**), and the two diving operators mentioned below. Expect to pay about T$30 (US$15) a day.

SCUBA DIVING   There's good diving in these clear waters, especially since you don't have to ride on a boat for several hours just to get to a spot with colorful coral and bountiful sea life. In Port of Refuge, divers can explore the wreck of the copra schooner *Clan McWilliam,* sunk in 1906.

The Dutch–New Zealander couple Huib and Sybil Kuilboer of **Beluga Diving** (℗/fax **70-327;** www.belugadivingvavau.com) and the New Zealand–based **Dolphin Pacific Diving** (℗/fax **70-292;** www.academydivers.co.nz) offer two-tank dives for about T$140 (US$70), including tanks and weight belts.

SHOPPING

As noted earlier in this chapter, Vava'u produces some of the finest handicrafts in Tonga. The establishments listed below will pack and ship your purchases home. Also look in the small jewelry shops along the main street for baskets, mats, wood carvings, and other items. The best place to shop is **Langafonua Handicrafts,** the Vava'u branch of Langafonua, the women's handicraft organization founded by Queen Salote (see "Shopping on Tongatapu," earlier in this chapter). Here it's in a Tongan fale adjacent to the Tonga Visitors Bureau. It carries a good variety of baskets, mats, wood carvings, and other items at reasonable prices.

WHERE TO STAY ON VAVA'U

Several islets out in the lagoon have small, low-key establishments with restaurants and bars frequented by yachties, who drop anchor and go ashore for some food and libation. Some of these, such as Mounu Island Resort (see below), also have accommodations.

Adventure Backpackers Lodge   In the center of Neiafu's commercial strip, Sandra and Henk Gross's excellent lodge for both backpackers and other cost-conscious travelers has a marvelous view of Port of Refuge from its communal kitchen and lounge with TV. Three of the nine rooms have private bathrooms. Although it doesn't, room 6 has windows on two sides and opens to the big veranda across the water-side of the building, which makes it preferable to the others. Two units in a separate build-ing are more private, but they lack good ventilation. One is a family-size unit with a double bed and two twins. Everyone else shares four toilets and four showers.

Private Bag 3, Neiafu, Vava'u (main st. next to Royal Tongan Airlines). (℃ 70-955. Fax 70-647. www.visit vavau.com/backpackers. 9 units (6 without bathroom), 6 dorm beds. T$48–T$88 (US$24–US$44) double; T$24 (US$12) dorm bed. MC, V. **Amenities:** Bicycle rentals; complimentary washers and dryers. *In room:* No phone.

Mounu Island Resort 🏝🏝 The long-time dream of New Zealanders Allan and Lyn Bowe, this little resort sits beside a wraparound beach of deep white sand on Mounu ("Bait Fish" in Tongan), an atoll-like, 2.4-hectare (6-acre) islet near the south-ern end of Vava'u's outer islands. Cruising yachties moor their boats near the colorful corals and row their dinghies ashore to imbibe and dine on freshly caught seafood in the Bowes' main building, a lovely mat-lined Tongan fale right on the beach. Their widely spaced guest fales are rustic but charming, with futon beds covered with mos-quito nets (which are necessary because the windows aren't screened), rattan easy chairs and glass-topped coffee tables, bathrooms with hot-water showers, and front porches facing the lagoon. Solar power generates the electricity, and rain provides all the fresh water here. You can swim, snorkel, kayak, fish, go on village visits, and observe seabirds at a nearby breeding colony. This is a very popular retreat during the June-to-October whale-watching season, when Allan operates Whale Watch Vava'u (see "Whale-Watching," above). It's a fine place to unwind after a week or two on a charter yacht any time of year.

Private Box 7, Neiafu, Vava'u (Mounu Island, 25 min. by speedboat from Neiafu). (℃ 70-747. Fax 70-493. www.mounuisland.com. 4 units. US$175–US$200 double. Meals US$70 per person per day. Transfers US$45 per per-son. MC, V. **Amenities:** Restaurant; bar; watersports; Internet access; laundry service. *In room:* No phone.

Paradise International Hotel Perched on a grassy ridge overlooking Port of Refuge and a short walk from Neiafu, this is one of the more comfortable hotels in Tonga, although it's getting a little long in the tooth. A large central building houses the reception area, a business center, bar, and restaurant. Next to it on a grassy lawn, a pool offers a panoramic view of the harbor below. A path leads down to the water's edge, where the hotel has its own pier and kayaks for rent. The large rooms, in one- and two-story buildings, are devoid of any tropical charms except the views from their balconies (the most expensive units have unimpeded views of Port of Refuge). They have various bed combinations, recliner chairs, coffee tables, and ample, American-style bathrooms with tub-and-shower combos.

P.O. Box 11, Neiafu, Vava'u (east end of Neiafu). (℃ 74-744. Fax 70-184. www.tongahost.com. 48 units. US$55–US$99. AE, DC, MC, V. **Amenities:** Restaurant; bar; outdoor pool; watersports; business center; limited room service; massage; babysitting; laundry service. *In room:* A/C, fridge, coffeemaker.

Puataukanave International Hotel The tongue-twisting *Puataukanave* means "hibiscus" in Tongan, but locals call this new property simply "Pua's Hotel." The restaurant and a building with 14 of the rooms sit right beside the Port of Refuge in the middle of Neiafu. With their balconies facing the water, rooms in this building are worth the extra money. These have gleaming tile floors, double beds, desks, and ample bathrooms with glass-enclosed corner showers. The less expensive economy rooms are in a building to the rear; they have only partial views of the Port of Refuge, and two of them lack air-conditioners. A wing has both simple rooms and dormitories aimed

---

Tips **A Tongan Feast at the Beach**

If you missed a Tongan feast in Nuku'alofa or you just liked it so much you want to go to another, head for **Hinakauea Beach Feast** (📞 **12-288**), which takes place Thursday on lovely Lisa Beach. It costs T$30 (US$15) per person. Inquire at the Paradise International Hotel or the Tonga Visitors Bureau.

---

at backpackers and low-budget divers. These units are devoid of amenities, and none has a view. In other words, they are much less attractive than the airy units at Adventure Backpackers (see above). It lacks charm, but is the most convenient and modern hotel on Vava'u.

P.O. Box 24, Neiafu, Vava'u (heart of town). 📞 **71-002.** Fax 70-080. tfpel@hotmail.com. 35 units, 20 dorm beds. T$80–T$204 (US$40–US$102) double; T$45–T$55 (US$23–US$28) double backpacker room; T$25–T$30 (US$13–US$15) dorm bed. AE, MC, V (5% card fee). **Amenities:** Restaurant; bar; outdoor pool; tennis court; bike rentals; laundry service. *In room:* A/C (33 units), TV, minibar, kitchen (super deluxe units).

Tongan Beach Resort   This isolated resort sits beside a lovely narrow channel south of Port of Refuge, giving guests their own swimming beach and jumping-off point for scuba diving, kayaking, and other watersports. The main building here is an open Tongan fale that houses a restaurant whose menu varies each day, depending on the catch, the emphasis being on fresh seafood. A sand-floored bar is in its own fale next door. The comfortable, motel-like guest rooms flank the main complex. They are of New Zealand–style construction and furnishings. Each has tile floors, ceiling fans, a dressing area, one queen and one single bed, and shower-only bathrooms.

P.O. Box 104, Neiafu, Vava'u (on 'Utungake Island, 8.8km/5½ miles from Neiafu, 14.5km/9½ miles from airport via dirt rd. and causeway). 📞/fax **70-380.** www.thetongan.com. 12 units. US$130–US$160 double. Meals US$52 per person per day. Round-trip airport transfers US$26. MC, V. **Amenities:** Restaurant; bar; free use of kayaks and snorkeling gear; bicycle rentals; laundry service. *In room:* Fridge, coffeemaker, no phone.

WHERE TO DINE ON VAVA'U

The Neiafu waterfront was undergoing many changes during my recent visit, including improvements to its restaurants and bars. One to check out is **'Ana's Waterfront Cafe** (📞 **70-664**), in front of a lighted cave in the cliff ('Ana is not a woman's name; it means "cave" in Tongan). Another good place to have a drink is the **Bounty Bar & Cafe** (📞 **70-576**), which has great views overlooking Port of Refuge from Neiafu's main street.

Cafe Tropicana 🍴 COFFEE SHOP   A knock-off of Friends Cafe in Nuku'alofa, this local version of Starbucks has a great view of Port of Refuge from its patio out back. Coffees, teas, juices, pastries, sandwiches, small pizzas, quiches, and salads are on the menu. The meal-size bowl of mildly spicy Thai-style noodle soup will keep you going. You can check your e-mail here, but you can't smoke, even outside on the patio.

Neiafu, main st. in heart of town. 📞 **71-322.** Breakfast T$5–T$15 (US$2.50–US$7.50); sandwiches and snacks T$5.50–T$15 (US$2.75–US$7.50). MC, V. Mon–Fri 7am–6pm, Sat 7am–2pm.

The Dancing Rooster 🍴 SEAFOOD   Swiss chef Gunter Schnell came here to cook at the Paradise International Hotel, married a local girl, settled down, and opened this little restaurant in the backyard of their home opposite the Catholic church. You won't have a water view here. Gunter should have named it "The Dancing

Lobster," for he's very good with fresh tropical lobsters. They're best whole with garlic butter, but he also dices them for salads or stir-fries.

Neiafu, main st. opposite Catholic church. ℭ **70-886**. Reservations recommended. Main courses T$25–T$50 (US$13–US$25). MC, V (plus 5%). Mon–Sat 11am–10pm.

Mermaid Bar & Grill SNACKS/SEAFOOD Operated by Sailing Safaris, this open-air restaurant beside the harbor is the most popular place in Neiafu for breakfast, sandwiches, burgers, salads, pizzas, and dinner choices including grilled lobster, steaks, and fish (check the specials board for today's catch). For lunch try the lobster salad. The Mermaid usually packs in local expatriates and passing yachties, especially during happy hour from 4 to 7pm.

Neiafu, main st. on the water next to Sailing Safaris Marine Center. ℭ **70-730**. Reservations recommended for dinner July–Aug. Breakfast T$6–T$17 (US$3–US$8.50); salads, sandwiches, and burgers T$7–T$20 (US$3.50–US$10); main courses T$20–T$50 (US$10–US$25). MC, V. Daily 8am–9pm (bar until midnight).

ISLAND NIGHTS ON VAVA'U

Bands play from June through August at the **Paradise International Hotel** (ℭ **70-211**), and all year at **Tonga Bob's Cantina** (ℭ **70-285**), an open-air waterfront joint near the western end of Neiafu. Otherwise, there's not much to do except hang out with all the expatriates and yachties down at The Mermaid on the waterfront (see "Where to Dine on Vava'u," above).

16 Ha'apai

Off the beaten path, Ha'apai is central in both Tonga's geography and history. In the middle of the kingdom, 155km (96 miles) north of Nuku'alofa and 108km (67 miles) south of Vava'u, Ha'apai consists of numerous small, atoll-like islands scattered across the sea. Linked by a causeway, **Lifuka** and **Foa** are the largest and the only ones you can visit without being on a sailboat. On the horizon to their west sits the active volcano **Tofua,** where puffs of steam spew from the rim above its crater lake, and the perfectly shaped cone of its inactive neighbor, **Kao.**

It was on Lifuka that Capt. James Cook was so impressed with the Tongans' hospitality in 1773 and 1777 that he named the group the "Friendly Islands." Fletcher Christian and the *Bounty* mutineers cast Capt. William Bligh adrift in a longboat off Tofua in 1789. In 1806 the locals ransacked the British privateer *Port-au-Prince,* killing all of its crew except the young Will Mariner, who lived to write about his adventure. Tonga's first Wesleyan missionaries arrived here in the 1820s. With their help, the converted local chief Taufa'ahau captured the rest of Tonga. The Rev. Shirley Baker, who dominated King George during his later years, is buried on Lifuka in **Pangai,** Ha'apai's only town.

Today Lifuka and the other islands seem much as they must have been when King George moved his capital to Tongatapu. You'll find some great beaches and fine scuba diving here, but there's not much else to do except relax, explore Pangai's historical sights, and go diving. In other words, it's a fine place to get away from it all.

GETTING TO HA'APAI & GETTING AROUND

As I write, **Peau Vava'u** (ℭ **28-325;** www.peauvavau.to) and **Airlines Tonga** (ℭ **24-506;** www.airlinestonga.com) were flying from Tongatapu to **Salote Pilolevu Airport,** on Lifuka's northern end. The airline's buses will take you from the airport 5km

(3 miles) south to Pangai. The **Shipping Corporation of Polynesia** (© **21-699** in Nuku'alofa) operates weekly ferry service from Nuku'alofa to Ha'apai. See "Getting to Tonga & Getting Around," earlier in this chapter.

EXPLORING LIFUKA

Begin your visit at the local **Tonga Visitors Bureau (TVB)** branch, in the government compound on Palace Road (© **60-733**), which distributes free maps of the island and a very helpful "Strolling Through Lifuka" brochure (you can pick these up at the TVB in Nuku'alofa, too). The post office, infirmary, Tonga Communications Corporation, and other offices are in the compound.

Check with Australian **Trevor Gregory,** owner of Mariners Bar & Cafe (© **60-374**), about guided walking tours of town. See "Where to Dine on Ha'apai," below.

Easily explored on foot, the town of Pangai spreads out from **Taufa'ahau Wharf,** on the western, lagoon side of Lifuka. Europeans settled north of the wharf and built colonial-style houses, a clapboard hotel, and a cemetery, where the **Rev. Shirley Baker Monument** is a major site today. In those days, the king resided in an impressive palace that stood at the inland end of Palace Road. The incumbent king stays at a much more modest **Royal Palace** on the lagoon, south of the wharf.

South of town, the tiered **Olovehi Tomb** was constructed of limestone in the late 1700s for the eldest sister of the high chief. The chiefly **Bathing Well at 'Ahau** nearby was dug as an inverted cone to stabilize the porous bedrock. Trees in the bottom provided privacy.

Captain Cook sailed past the **Huluipaongo Tomb,** built on the southern end of Lifuka by harsh chiefs who were notorious for making their subjects work on this and other mounds. Stones for those projects were taken from the **Holopeka Beach Quarry,** northeast of town on Lifuka's ocean side.

SCUBA DIVING ✸✸ & OTHER WATERSPORTS

The largest underwater caves and canyons in the South Pacific beckon divers to the fish-filled seas surrounding these islands. Based at the Sandy Beach Resort (see "Where to Stay on Ha'apai," below), **Ocean Blue Adventures** (© **60-369;** www.tonga-dive.com) charges about US$90 for two boat dives, including tanks and weights.

WHERE TO STAY ON HA'APAI

The pick of the basic, low-budget accommodations here is **Fifita Guesthouse** (© **60-213;** fax 60-374; mariners@kalianet.to) over Mariner's Cafe in the middle of Pangai (see "Where to Dine on Ha'apai," below). A simple, shared-bathroom, double room costs about T$35 (US$18). No credit cards.

Sandy Beach Resort ✸✸   This resort is aptly named, for it sits beside one of the South Pacific's great beaches, a glorious curving stretch of white sand that faces west, toward Tofua and Kao on the horizon. And unlike so many beaches in the islands, at this one you can swim and snorkel at all tides. You can have a meal or a cold drink while taking in this view from the central building's big concrete veranda. Of modern construction but with Tongan style, each light, airy bungalow has a porch facing the beach and is equipped with a cool tile floor, either a double or two single beds, and an ample bathroom with a tiled hot-water shower. Each bungalow also has its own hammock and a thatch cabana out by the beach. To provide privacy, the bungalows are staggered and have a solid wall on the side facing their nearest neighbor. Guests can take nature walks, watch a culture show, and catch a daily shuttle to Pangai. You'll pay extra for diving, horseback riding, boat trips, and tennis at the local Mormon church (bring your own racquet and balls). The resort is closed December and January.

P.O. Box 61, Pangai, Ha'apai (north end of Foa Island). *C*/fax **60-600**. www.tongaholiday.com/accommodation/ hotels/haapai/sandybeach.php. 12 units. US$122 bungalow. Rates include airport transfers. AE, MC, V. Children under 16 accepted on request only. Closed Dec 1–Feb 1. **Amenities:** Restaurant; bar; free use of snorkeling gear, kayaks, and bikes; laundry service. *In room:* Fridge, coffeemaker, no phone.

WHERE TO DINE ON HA'APAI

The Mariners Cafe REGIONAL   Australian Trevor Gregory sailed to Ha'apai on a yacht and liked it so much he returned to open the town's only restaurant. A tin roof covers the wooden chairs and white plastic tables. There's nothing fancy here—burgers, curries, steaks, chops, stir fries, and fish and chips—but the company's friendly and informative.

Fau Rd., Pangai. *C* **60-374**. Lunch T$3–T$10 (US$1.50–US$5); dinner T$10–T$20 (US$5–US$10). MC, V. Mon–Sat 8am–8pm.

Appendix:
The South Pacific in Depth

As you have seen in the preceding chapters, each South Pacific island group has its own history, culture, language, geography, and geology. That is the nature of such a far-flung region, where hundreds or thousands of miles separate one island from the next. On the other hand, the islands have many things in common. Their indigenous peoples are descended from Polynesians and Melanesians who migrated here several millennia ago. Many of their traditions and customs are the same, but with local quirks that have developed over the eons. Nowhere are the local variations as evident as in the Polynesian languages, which are similar but differ from one group to the next.

The following tells what the islands and islanders have in common.

1 A Shared History

Islanders had been living on their tiny outposts for thousands of years before Europeans had the foggiest notion that the Pacific Ocean existed. Even after Vasco Nuñez de Balboa crossed the Isthmus of Panama and discovered this largest of oceans in 1513, and Ferdinand Magellan sailed across it in 1521, more than 250 years went by before Europeans paid much attention to the islands that lay upon it.

VENUS IN A GRASS SKIRT The South Pacific came to Europe's attention during the latter half of the 18th century, when a theory came into vogue that an unknown southern land—a *terra australis incognita*—lay somewhere in the southern hemisphere. It had to exist, the theory went, for otherwise the unbalanced earth would wobble off into space. King George III of Great Britain took interest in the idea and in 1764 sent Capt. John Byron (the poet's grandfather) to the Pacific in HMS *Dolphin*. Although Byron came home empty-handed, King George immediately dispatched Capt. Samuel Wallis in the *Dolphin*. Wallis had no luck finding the unknown continent, but in 1767 he stumbled upon a high, lush island known as Tahiti.

Less than a year later, the Tahitians similarly welcomed French explorer Louis Antoine de Bougainville. So enchanted was Bougainville by the Venus-like quality of Tahiti's women that he named their island New Cythère—after the Greek island of Cythera, associated with the goddess Aphrodite (Venus).

Bougainville brought a Tahitian home with him. Parisians saw the man as proof of Rousseau's theory that man at his best lived an uninhibited life as a noble savage.

CAPTAIN COOK'S TOURS After Wallis arrived back in England, the Lords of the Admiralty put a lieutenant named James Cook in command of a converted collier and sent him to Tahiti. A product of the Age of Enlightenment, Cook was a master navigator, a mathematician, an astronomer, and a practical physician who became the first ship captain to prevent scurvy among his crewmen by feeding them fresh fruits and vegetables. His ostensible mission was to observe the transit of Venus—the planet, that is—across the sun, an astronomical event that would not occur again until 1874. If measured from widely separated points on the globe, the astronomical event would enable scientists for the first time to determine longitude on the earth's surface. Cook's second, highly secret mission was to find the elusive southern continent.

Cook's measurements of Venus were somewhat less than useful, but his observations of Tahiti, made during a stay of 6 months, were of immense importance in understanding the "noble savages" who lived there.

Cook went on to discover the Society Islands northwest of Tahiti and the Australs to the south, and then fully explored the coasts of New Zealand and eastern Australia. After nearly sinking his ship on the Great Barrier Reef, he left the South Pacific through the strait between Australia and Papua New Guinea, which he named for his ship, the *Endeavor*. He returned to London in 1771.

During two subsequent voyages, Cook visited Tonga and discovered several other islands, among them what are now Fiji, the Cook Islands, Niue, New Caledonia, and Norfolk Island. His ships were the first to sail below the Antarctic Circle. On his third voyage in 1778–79, he traveled to the Hawaiian Islands and explored the northwest coast of North America until ice in the Bering Strait turned him back. He returned to Hawaii, where on February 14, 1779, he was killed in a skirmish with the islanders.

With the exception of the Hawaiians who smashed his skull, Captain Cook was revered throughout the Pacific. He treated the islanders fairly and respected their traditions. The Polynesian chiefs looked upon him as one of their own. So revered was Capt. Cook that today you'll find Cook's Bay, Cooktown, Cook Strait, any number of Captain Cook's Landing Places, and an entire nation named for this explorer.

MUTINY ON THE *BOUNTY* Based on reports by Cook and others about the abundance of breadfruit, a head-size, potato-like fruit that grows on trees throughout the islands, a group of West Indian planters asked King George III if he would be so kind as to transport the trees from Tahiti to Jamaica as a cheap source of food for the slaves. The king dispatched Capt. William Bligh, who had been one of Cook's navigators, in command of HMS *Bounty* in 1787. One of Bligh's officers was a former shipmate named Fletcher Christian.

Their story is one of history's great sea yarns. The *Bounty* was late arriving in Tahiti, so Christian and the crew frolicked on Tahiti for 6 months, waiting for the next breadfruit season. They obviously enjoyed the affections of young Tahitian women as well as the balmy climate, for on April 28, 1789, on the way home, they overpowered Bligh off Tonga. After setting the captain and his loyalists adrift, Christian and eight other mutineers, along with their Tahitian wives and six Tahitian men, disappeared with the ship. Bligh and his men miraculously rowed the *Bounty's* longboat some 4,830km (3,000 miles) to the Dutch East Indies, where they hitched a ride back to England. The Royal Navy then rounded up the *Bounty* crewmen left on Tahiti.

Christian's whereabouts remained a mystery until 1808, when a U.S. whaling ship discovered the last surviving mutineer on remote Pitcairn Island. The mutineers, after landing there in 1789, had burned and sunk the *Bounty*. Their descendants still live on Pitcairn and elsewhere in the South Pacific.

See "French Polynesia Yesterday: History 101" in chapter 7 for more on the mutiny.

GUNS & WHISKEY The U.S. ship that found the mutineers' retreat at Pitcairn was one of many whalers roaming the South Pacific in the early 1800s.

(Fun Fact Recovering the *Bounty's* Rudder

Sunk by the mutineers in 1789, HMS *Bounty* remained in its watery grave until it was discovered by a *National Geographic* expedition in the 1950s. The *Bounty's* rudder is now on display at the Fiji Museum in Suva.

Their ruffian crews made dens of iniquity of many ports, such as Lahaina and Honolulu in Hawaii, Papeete and Nuku Hiva in what is now French Polynesia, and Levuka in Fiji. Many crewmen jumped ship and lived on the islands, some of them even casting their lots—and their guns—with rival chiefs during tribal wars. With their assistance, some chiefs were able to extend their power over entire islands or groups of islands.

Along with the whalers came traders in search of sandalwood, pearls, shells, and the sea cucumbers known as *bêches-de-mer,* which they traded for beads, cloth, whiskey, and guns and then sold in China. Some established stores became the catalysts for Western-style towns. The merchants brought more guns and alcohol to people who had never used them before. They also put pressure on local leaders to coin money, which introduced a cash economy where none had existed before. Guns, alcohol, and money had far-reaching effects on the easygoing, communal traditions of the Pacific Islanders.

Diseases brought by the Europeans and Americans were even more devastating. The Polynesians had little, if any, resistance to such ailments as measles, influenza, tuberculosis, pneumonia, typhoid fever, and venereal disease. Epidemics swept the islands and killed the majority of their inhabitants.

While the traders were building towns, other arrivals were turning the bush country into plantations: cotton in Tahiti, sugar in Fiji, coconuts everywhere. With the native islanders disinclined to work, Chinese indentured laborers were brought to a cotton plantation in Tahiti

in the 1860s. After it failed, some of the Chinese stayed and became farmers and merchants. Their descendants now form the merchant class of French Polynesia. Something similar happened in Fiji, where East Indians were brought to work the sugar plantations.

BRINGING THE WORD OF GOD

The reports of the islands by Cook and Bougainville may have brought word of noble savages living in paradise to some people in Europe; to others, they heralded heathens to be rescued from hell. So while alcohol and diseases were destroying the islanders' bodies, a stream of missionaries arrived on the scene to save their souls.

The "opening" of the South Pacific coincided with a fundamentalist religious revival in England, and it wasn't long before the London Missionary Society (LMS) was on the scene in Tahiti. Its missionaries, who arrived in 1797, were the first Protestant missionaries to leave England for a foreign country. They chose Tahiti because there "the difficulties were least."

Polynesians, already believing in a supreme being at the head of a hierarchy of lesser gods, quickly converted in large numbers. As an act of faith, the puritanical missionaries demanded the destruction of all *tikis,* which they regarded as idols. (As a result, today most Polynesian tikis carved for the tourist souvenir trade resemble those of New Zealand, where the more liberal Anglican missionaries were less demanding.) The missionaries in Polynesia also insisted that the heathen temples (known as *maraes*) be torn down.

Many have now been restored, however, and can be visited.

Roman Catholic missionaries made less puritanical progress in Tahiti after the French took over in the early 1840s, but for the most part the South Pacific was the domain of rock-ribbed Protestants. The LMS extended its influence west through the Cook Islands and the Samoas, and the Wesleyans had luck in Tonga and Fiji. Today, thanks to those early missionaries, Sunday is a very quiet day throughout the islands.

COLONIALS TAKE CHARGE
Although Captain Cook laid claim to many islands, Britain was reluctant to burden itself with such far-flung colonies, beyond those it already had—Australia and New Zealand. Accordingly, colonialism was not a significant factor in the history of the South Pacific islands until the late 19th century. The one exception was France's declaring a protectorate over Tahiti in 1842.

This situation changed half a century later, when imperial Germany colonized the western islands of Samoa in the 1890s (at the same time that novelist Robert Louis Stevenson arrived to live there). Britain took over Fiji and agreed to protect the Kingdom of Tonga from takeover by another foreign power; France moved into New Caledonia; and the United States stepped into the eastern Samoan islands, which became known as American Samoa. Britain also claimed the Cook Islands, but they were later annexed by newly independent New Zealand. Thus, within a period of 30 years, every South Pacific island group except Tonga became an official colony.

After World War I, when Germany was stripped of its colonies, New Zealand took over in Western Samoa. Otherwise, the colonial structure in the South Pacific remained the same, politically, until the 1960s.

Large Australian companies, such as Burns Philp and Carpenters, built up island trading and shipping empires based on the exchange of retail goods for copra and other local produce, and Australia and New Zealand to this day dominate finance in most islands outside the French and U.S. territories.

BASES, ROADS & AIRSTRIPS
The South Pacific leaped onto the front pages in World War II. Although fighting took place only in Papua New Guinea and the Solomon Islands, many other islands played supporting roles. Airstrips and training bases were built all over the South Pacific; many airfields are still in use today. Out-of-the-way islands, such as Bora Bora and Aitutaki, became refueling stops, and the Samoas and Fiji were invaded by thousands of U.S. Marines and GIs preparing for the fighting farther west and north. Entire communities with modern infrastructures were built in weeks—only to be abandoned almost overnight when the war ended.

CHIEFS, MINISTERS & NUCLEAR BOMBS
Colonialism began to crumble in the South Pacific when New Zealand granted independence to Western Samoa in 1962. Three years later, it gave complete local autonomy to the Cook Islands. Fiji became independent of Great Britain in 1970.

All these young nations have governments based on the Westminster parliamentary system, with wrinkles tailored to fit their citizens' traditions. Almost everywhere, a council of chiefs advises the

---

Impressions
It would have been far better for these people never to have known us.
—Capt. James Cook, 1769

modern-style ministers on custom and tradition. Fiji's bloodless military coups of 1987, which overthrew that country's first Indo-Fijian-dominated government, shocked observers because it directly opposed this democratic tradition. Fiji has since adopted a constitution that provides for an elected parliament.

Of the old colonial powers, only the United States and France remain.

Between 1966 and 1992, the French exploded 210 nuclear weapons in the Tuamotu Archipelago, about 1,208km (750 miles) southeast of Tahiti, first in the air and then underground. Led by New Zealand, where French secret agents sank the Greenpeace protest ship *Rainbow Warrior* in 1985, many South Pacific island nations vociferously complained about the blasts. That same year, the regional heads of government, including the prime ministers of New Zealand and Australia, adopted the Treaty of Rarotonga, calling for the South Pacific to become a nuclear-free zone. After a lull, French Pres. Jacques Chirac decided in 1995 to resume nuclear testing, a move that set off worldwide protests, a day of rioting in Papeete, and a Japanese tourist boycott of French Polynesia. After six underground explosions, the French halted further tests, closed its testing facility, and signed the Treaty of Rarotonga.

2 The Islanders

Early European explorers were astounded to find the far-flung South Pacific islands inhabited by peoples who shared similar physical characteristics, languages, and cultures. How had these people—who lived a late Stone Age existence and had no written languages—crossed the Pacific long before Christopher Columbus had the courage to sail out of sight of land? Where had they come from? Those questions baffled European explorers, and continue to intrigue scientists and scholars today.

THE FIRST SETTLERS

The late Thor Heyerdahl drifted in his raft *Kon Tiki* from South America to French Polynesia in 1947, to prove his theory that the Polynesians came from the Americas. Bolstered by DNA studies linking the Polynesians to Taiwan, however, experts now believe the Pacific Islanders have their roots in eastern Asia. The accepted view is that during the Ice Age a race of humans known as Australoids migrated from Southeast Asia to Papua New Guinea and Australia, when those two countries were joined as one land mass. Another group, the Papuans, arrived from Southeast Asia between 5,000 and 10,000 years ago. Thousands of years later, a lighter-skinned race known as Austronesians pushed the Papuans out into the more eastern South Pacific islands.

The most tangible remains of the early Austronesians are remnants of pottery, the first shards of which were found during the 1970s in Lapita, in New Caledonia. Probably originating in Papua New Guinea, Lapita pottery spread east as far as Tonga. Throughout the area it was decorated with geometric designs similar to those used today on Tongan tapa cloth.

Lapita was the only type of pottery in the South Pacific for a millennium. Apparently, however, the Lapita culture died out some 2,500 years ago. By the time European explorers arrived in the 1770s, gourds and coconut shells were the only crockery used by the Polynesians, who cooked their meals underground and ate with their fingers off banana leaves. Of the islanders covered in this book, only the Fijians still make pottery using Lapita methods.

MELANESIANS

The islands settled by the Papuans and Austronesians are known collectively as

Impressions
You who like handsome men would find no shortage of them here; they are taller than I, and have limbs like Hercules.
—Paul Gauguin, 1891

Melanesia, which includes Papua New Guinea, the Solomon Islands, Vanuatu, and New Caledonia. Fiji is the melting pot of the Melanesians to the west and the Polynesians to the east.

The name Melanesia is derived from the Greek words *melas,* "black," and *nesos,* "island." The Melanesians in general have features more akin to sub-Saharan Africans: brown-to-black skin, flat or hooked noses, full lips, and wiry hair. But interbreeding among the successive waves of migrants resulted in many subgroups with varying physical characteristics. That's why the Fijians look more African American than Polynesian. Their culture, on the other hand, has many Polynesian elements, brought by interbreeding and conquest.

POLYNESIANS

The Polynesians' ancestors stopped in Fiji on their migration from Southeast Asia but later pushed on into the eastern South Pacific. Archaeologists now believe that they settled in Tonga and Samoa more than 3,000 years ago and then slowly fanned out to colonize the vast Polynesian triangle.

These extraordinary mariners crossed thousands of miles of ocean in double-hulled canoes capable of carrying hundreds of people, animals, and plants. They navigated by the stars, the wind, the clouds, the shape of the waves, and the flight pattern of birds—a remarkable achievement for a people who had no written languages.

Their ancestors fought each other with war clubs for thousands of years, and it stands to reason that the biggest, strongest, and quickest survived (many

modern Polynesians have become professional football and rugby players). The notion that all Polynesians are fat is incorrect. In the old days, body size did indeed denote wealth and status, but obesity today is more likely attributable to poor diet. On the other hand, village chiefs are still expected to partake of food and drink with anyone who visits to discuss a problem; hence, great weight remains an unofficial marker of social status.

POLYNESIAN SOCIETY Although Polynesians frequently experienced wars among their various tribes, generally their conflicts were not as bloody as those in Fiji. Nor were their wars as likely to end with cannibalistic orgies at the expense of the losers as in Fiji and Melanesia, where cannibalism was widely practiced.

Polynesians developed highly structured societies. Strong and sometimes despotic chiefdoms developed on many islands. The royal family of Tonga continues a line of leaders who were so powerful in the 1700s that they conquered much of Fiji, where they installed Polynesian customs, including their hereditary chief system. Melanesians are more likely to choose their "big men" by consensus rather than ancestry.

In some places, such as Tahiti, the Polynesians developed a class system of chiefs, priests, nobility, commoners, and slaves. Their societies emphasized elaborate formalities. Even today ceremonies featuring kava—that slightly narcotic drink so loved in the islands—play important roles in Samoa, Tonga, and Fiji. Everyday life was governed by a system based on *tabu,* a list of things a person could or couldn't do, depending on

Impressions

Now the cunning lay in this, that the Polynesians have rules of hospitality that have all the force of laws; an etiquette of absolute rigidity made it necessary for the people of the village not only to give lodging to the strangers, but to provide them with food and drink for as long as they wished to stay.
—W. Somerset Maugham, 1921

his/her status. Tabu and its variants *(tapu, tambu)* are used throughout the South Pacific to mean "do not enter"; from them derives the English word *taboo.*

Western principles of ownership have made inroads, but by and large everything in Polynesia and Fiji—especially land—is owned communally by families. In effect, the system is pure communism at the family level. If your brother has a crop of taro and you're hungry, then some of that taro belongs to you. The same principle applies to a can of corned beef on a shelf in a store, which helps explain why islander-owned grocery shops often teeter on the brink of bankruptcy. It also explains why you should keep an eye on your valuables.

Although many islanders would be considered poor by Western standards, no one in the villages goes hungry or sleeps without a roof over his or her head. Most of the thatch roofs in Polynesia today are actually bungalows at the resort hotels; nearly everyone else sleeps under tin. It's little wonder, therefore, that visitors are greeted throughout the islands by friendly, peaceable, and extraordinarily courteous people.

THE OLD GODS   Before the coming of Christian missionaries in the 1800s, the Fijians believed in many spirits in the animist traditions of Melanesia. The Polynesians, however, subscribed to the idea of a supreme spirit, who ruled over a plethora of lesser deities who in turn governed the sun, fire, volcanoes, sea, war, and fertility. Tikis were carved of stone or wood to give each god a home (but not a

permanent residence) during religious ceremonies, and stone maraes were built as temples and meeting places for the chiefs. Sacrifices—sometimes human—were offered to the gods.

LANGUAGES

Like their DNA, linguists have traced the islanders' languages to present-day Taiwan. They belong to the Austronesian family of languages spoken from Madagascar, off the coast of Africa, to Easter Island, off the coast of South America. No other group of ancient languages spread to so much of the earth's surface.

Today, the Polynesian islanders speak similar languages from one major island group to another. For example, the word for "house" is *fale* in Tongan and Samoan, *fare* in Tahitian, *'are* in Cook Islands Maori, *hale* in Hawaiian, and *vale* in Fijian. Without having heard the other's language, Cook Islanders say they can understand about 60% of Tahitian, and Tongans and Samoans can get the gist of each others' conversations.

Thanks to the American, British, New Zealand, and Australian colonial regimes, English is an official language in the Cook Islands, both Samoas, and Fiji. It is spoken widely in Tonga. French is spoken alongside Tahitian in French Polynesia, although English is understood among most hotel and restaurant staffs.

FEASTS FROM UNDERGROUND OVENS

Whether called an "island night" in the Cook Islands, *fiafia* in the Samoas, or *meke* in Fiji, traditional feasts and dance shows are essential after-dark ingredients throughout the South Pacific. Before the Europeans arrived, the typical South Pacific diet consisted of bananas, coconuts, and other fruits. Staples were starchy breadfruit and root crops, such as taro, arrowroot, yams, and sweet potatoes. The reefs and lagoons provided abundant fish, lobsters, and clams to augment the meats provided by domesticated pigs, dogs, and chickens. Taro leaves and coconut cream served as complements. Corned beef has replaced dog on today's menu; otherwise, these same ingredients still make up the menus.

Like their ancestors, who had no crockery, today's islanders prepare their major meals in an earth oven, known as *himaa* in Tahiti, *lovo* in Fiji, and *imu* or *umu* elsewhere. Individual food items are wrapped in leaves, placed in the pit on a bed of heated stones, covered with more leaves and earth, and left to steam for several hours. The results are quite tasty, with the steam spreading the aroma of one ingredient to the others.

When the meal has finished cooking, the islanders uncover the oven, unwrap the food, and, using their fingers, set about eating their feast of *umukai* (island food) in a leisurely and convivial manner. Then they dance the night away.

3 The Islands & the Sea

A somewhat less-than-pious wag once remarked that God made the South Pacific islands on the 6th day of creation so He would have an extraordinarily beautiful place to rest on the 7th day. Modern geologists have a different view, but the fact remains that the islands and the surrounding sea are possessed of heavenly beauty and a plethora of life forms.

HIGH, LOW & IN BETWEEN

The Polynesian islands were formed by molten lava escaping upward through cracks in the earth's crust as it has crept slowly northwestward over the eons, thus building great seamounts. Many of these—called "high islands"—have mountains soaring into the clouds. In contrast, pancake-flat atolls were formed when the islands sank back into the sea, leaving only a thin necklace of coral islets to circumscribe their lagoons and mark their original boundaries. In some cases, geologic forces have once again lifted the atolls, forming "raised" islands whose sides drop precipitously into the sea. Still other, partially sunken islands, are left with the remnants of mountains sticking up in their lagoons.

The islands of Tonga and Fiji, on the other hand, were created by volcanic eruptions along the collision of the Indo-Australian and Pacific tectonic plates.

Fun Fact **Jotting It Down**

No Polynesian language was written until Peter Heywood jotted down a Tahitian vocabulary while awaiting trial for his part in the mutiny on the *Bounty* (he was convicted but pardoned). The early missionaries who later translated the Bible into Tahitian decided which letters of the Roman alphabet to use to approximate the sounds of the Polynesian languages. These tended to vary from place to place. For example, they used the consonants *t* and *v* in Tahitian. In Hawaiian, which is similar, they used *k* and *w*. The actual Polynesian sounds are somewhere in between.

Although the main islands are quiet today, they are part of the volcanically active and earthquake-prone "Ring of Fire" around the Pacific Ocean.

FLORA & FAUNA

Most species of plants and animals native to the South Pacific originated in Southeast Asia and worked their way eastward across the Pacific, by natural distribution or in the company of humans. The number of native species diminishes the farther east one goes. Very few local plants or animals came from the Americas, the one notable exception being the sweet potato, which may have been brought back from South America by voyaging Polynesians.

PLANTS   In addition to the west-to-east differences, flora changes according to each island's topography. The mountainous islands make rain from the moist trade winds and thus possess a greater variety of plants. Their interior highlands are covered with ferns, native bush, or grass. The low atolls, on the other hand, get sparse rainfall and support little other than scrub bush and coconut palms.

Ancient settlers brought coconut palms, breadfruit, taro, paper mulberry, pepper (*kava*), and bananas to the isolated midocean islands because of their usefulness as food or fiber. Accordingly, they are generally found in the inhabited areas of the islands and not so often in the interior bush.

With a few indigenous exceptions, such as the *tiare* (Tahiti gardenia) and Fiji's *tagimaucia*, tropical flowers also worked their way east in the company of humans. Bougainvillea, hibiscus, allamanda, poinsettia, poinciana (the flame tree), croton, frangipani (plumeria), ixora, canna, and water lilies all give colorful testament to the islanders' love for flowers of every hue in the rainbow. The aroma of the white, yellow, or pink frangipani is so sweet it's used as perfume on many islands.

ANIMALS & BIRDS   The fruit bat, or "flying fox," and some species of insect-eating bats are the only mammals native to the South Pacific islands. The early settlers introduced dogs, chickens, pigs, rats, and mice. There are few land snakes or other reptiles in the islands. The notable exceptions are geckos and skinks, those little lizards that seem to be everywhere. Don't go berserk when a gecko walks upside-down across the ceiling of your bungalow. They are harmless and actually perform a valuable service by eating mosquitoes and other insects.

The number and variety of species of bird life also diminishes as you go eastward. Most land birds live in the bush away from settlements and the accompanying cats, dogs, and rats. For this reason, the birds most likely to be seen are terns, boobies, herons, petrels, noddies, and others that earn their livelihoods from the sea. Of the introduced birds, the Indian myna exists in the greatest numbers. Brought to the South Pacific early in the 20th century to control insects, the myna quickly became a noisy nuisance in its own right. Mynas are extremely adept at stealing the toast off your breakfast table.

THE SEA

The tropical South Pacific Ocean teems with sea life, from colorful reef fish to the horrific Great White sharks featured in *Jaws,* from the paua clams that make tasty chowders in the Cook Islands to the deep-sea tuna that keep the canneries going at Pago Pago.

More than 600 species of coral—10 times the number found in the Caribbean—form the great reefs that make the South Pacific a divers' mecca. Billions of tiny coral polyps build their own skeletons on top of those left by their ancestors, until they reach the level of low tide. Then they grow outward, extending the edge of the reef. The old skeletons are white, while the living polyps present a

> **Tips   Be Careful What You Touch**
>
> Most island countries have tough laws protecting their environment, so *do not deface the reef*. You could land in the slammer for breaking off a gorgeous chunk of live coral to take home as a souvenir. The locals know what they can and cannot legally take from under the water, so buy your souvenir coral in a handicraft shop.

rainbow of colors. Corals grow best and are most colorful in the clear, salty water on the outer edge or in channels, where the tides and waves wash seawater along and across the reef. A reef can grow as much as 2 inches a year in ideal conditions. Although pollution, rising seawater temperature, and a proliferation of crown-of-thorns starfish have greatly hampered reef growth—and beauty—in parts of the South Pacific, there still are many areas where the color and variety of corals are unmatched.

A plethora of tropical fish and other marine life fill most of the lagoons, which are like gigantic aquariums. Bookstores in the main towns sell pamphlets containing photographs and descriptions of the creatures that will peer into your face mask. Humpback whales migrate to the islands from June to October, and sea turtles lay their eggs on some beaches from November through February.

Most South Pacific countries restrict the use of spear guns, so ask before you go in search of the catch of your life. Sea turtles and whales are on the list of endangered species, and many countries, including the United States, prohibit the importation of their shells, bones, and teeth.

SOME WARNINGS

Most of the South Pacific's marine creatures are harmless to humans, but there are some to avoid. Always **seek local advice** before snorkeling or swimming in a lagoon away from the hotel beaches. Many diving operators conduct snorkeling tours. If you don't know what you're doing, go with them.

Wash and apply a good antiseptic or antibacterial ointment to all **coral cuts and scrapes** as soon as possible.

Because coral cannot grow in fresh water, the flow of rivers and streams into the lagoon creates narrow channels known as **passes** through the reef. Currents can be very strong in the passes, so stay in the protected, shallow water of the inner lagoons.

Sharks are curious beasts that are attracted by bright objects such as watches and knives, so be careful what you wear in the water. Don't swim in areas where sewage or edible wastes are dumped, and never swim alone if you have any suspicion that sharks might be present. If you do see a shark, don't splash in the water or urinate. Calmly retreat and get out of the water as quickly as you can, without creating a disturbance.

Those round things on the rocks and reefs that look like pin cushions are **sea urchins,** and their calcium spikes can be more painful than needles. A sea-urchin puncture can result in burning, aching, swelling, and discoloration (black or purple) around the area where the spines entered your skin. The best thing to do is to pull any protruding spines out. The body will absorb the spines within 24 hours to 3 weeks, or the remainder of the spines will work themselves out. Contrary to popular advice, do not urinate or pour vinegar on the embedded spines—this will not help.

Jellyfish stings can hurt like the devil but are seldom life-threatening. You need to get any visible tentacles off your body right away, but not with your hands, unless you are wearing gloves. Use a stick or anything else that is handy. Then rinse the sting with salt- or freshwater, and apply ice to prevent swelling and to help control the pain. If you can find it at an island grocery store, Adolph's Meat Tenderizer is a great antidote.

The **stone fish** is so named because it looks like a piece of stone or coral as it lies buried in the sand on the lagoon bottom with only its back and 13 venomous spikes sticking out. Its venom can cause paralysis and even death. You'll know by the intense pain if you're stuck. Serum is available, so get to a hospital at once. **Sea snakes, cone shells, crown-of-thorns starfish, moray eels, lionfish,** and **demon stingers** also can be painful, if not deadly. The last thing any of these creatures wants to do is to tangle with a human, so keep your hands to yourself.

Index

AARP, 34
Accommodations
surfing for, 37–38
tips on, 51–53
Active vacations, 49–51
Adventure Eagle Tours (Tahiti), 228
Adventures Fiji, 50, 101
Adventures in Paradise Fiji (Coral Coast), 100, 130
Aehautai Marae (Bora Bora), 270
Afareaitu (Moorea), 251
Aggie's Gift Shop (Samoa), 378
Aggressor Fleet, 70, 200
Aiga, 355–356
Airfares, 36–37, 43
discounters and consolidators, 45
Air Fiji, 85
Air France, 41
Airlines, 1, 41–43
baggage allowances, 42–43
Air Moorea (French Polynesia), 195
Air New Zealand, 41
"Go As You Please" program, 52
Air Pacific, 41–42
Airports, 40–41
security procedures, 44
Air Tahiti, 195
Air Tahiti Nui, 1, 42, 46
Air Tahiti Pass, 196
Air Tickets Direct, 45
Aitutaki (Cook Islands), 5, 11, 21, 343–350
Akitua (Cook Islands), 346
Alao (American Samoa), 401
Albert Tours (Moorea), 247, 252
Aleipata (Samoa), 374, 383
Amazing Grace **(Fiji),** 89, 160, 170
American Express, Tahiti, 212

American Samoa, 391–405
accommodations, 403–404
brief description of, 22
climate, 394
clothing, 396
economy of, 392
emergencies, 396
entry requirements, 393
events and holidays, 394
exploring, 398–402
getting to and around, 394–395
government of, 392
healthcare, 396
history of, 392–393
Internet and e-mail access, 396
money matters, 393–394
National Park of American Samoa, 402–403
post office, 397
radio and TV, 397
restaurants, 405
safety, 397
suggested itinerary, 62–63
taxes, 397
telephone/fax, 397–398
time zone, 398
visitor information, 393
weights and measures, 398
what's new in, 3
American Samoa Archives Office (Pago Pago), 400
American Samoa Flag Day, 394
Anahulu Beach (Tonga), 426
Anau (Bora Bora), 270
Anini Marae (Huahine), 287
Aoa Bay (American Samoa), 401
Aora, Mount (Tahiti), 215
Apia (Samoa), 11, 366
accommodations, 378–382
day trip to American Samoa, 400
restaurants, 384–386
shopping, 378
sights and attractions, 369–377
Apia Weather Observatory (Samoa), 373

Apolima (Samoa), 388
Aqua Blue (Fiji), 102
Aquarium Adventures (Vava'u), 439, 440
Aqua Samoa Watersports, 377
Aquatica Dive Centre and Nautical Activities (Tahiti), 230
Aqua-Trek, 119, 138, 172, 173
Arahoho, 222
Arahurahu Marae (Tahiti), 215, 227
Arai-Te-Tonga (Rarotonga), 324–325
Aranui 3 **(French Polynesia),** 199
Archipel Croisiers, 201
Ariiura Camping (Huahine), 291
Arorangi (Rarotonga), 326
Art galleries, Moorea, 255
The Art of Tonga, 429
Arts Village (Pacific Harbour), 137
Arutanga (Aitutaki), 345
Atimaono (Tahiti), 226
Atimaono Golf Course (Tahiti), 229
Atiraa Waterfall (Moorea), 251
ATMs (automated teller machines), 26–27
Atwater, Dorence, grave of (Tahiti), 226
Aunu'u Island (American Samoa), 401
Austral Islands (French Polynesia), 180, 182
Avarua (Rarotonga), 21
restaurants, 340–342
sights and attractions, 323–324
Avea Bay (Huahine), 287
Avea Beach (Huahine), 6, 289
Awesome Adventures Fiji, 115

Ba **(Viti Levu),** 157
Baggage allowances, 42–43
Bain Loti (Loti's Pool; Tahiti), 221
Bali Hai Boys, 258

Baravi Handicrafts (Viti Levu), 131
The Barn (Suva), 156
Basilica of St. Anthony of Padua (Nuku'alofa), 425
Bathing Well at 'Ahau (Ha'apai), 445
Bathy's Club Moorea, 254
Ba Valley (Viti Levu), 157
Beach (Tahiti), 224
Beachcomber, Ltd., 323, 331
Beachcomber Day Cruises (Fiji), 116
Beaches. *See also specific beaches*
  best, 6–7
  Bora Bora, 270
  Fiji
    Malamala Island, 117
    Savusavu, 164
    Taveuni, 173
  Huahine, 289
  Moorea, 251, 254–255
  Samoa, 374, 376, 388
  Tonga, 426
Beach fales
  Manase Beach (Savai'i), 390
  Samoa, 16, 383
Beach on One Foot Island (Aitutaki), 7
Belvédère Lookout (Moorea), 250
Beqa Island (Fiji), 67, 68, 70, 137–140
Beqa Lagoon (Fiji), 137
Bergman & Sons (The Pearl Shop; Rarotonga), 331
Beverly Beach (Taveuni), 173
BiddingForTravel, 37
Biking, 49
  Moorea, 245
  Rarotonga, 319
  Savusavu (Vanua Levu), 162
  Tonga, 418
Birdland (Suva), 156
Bird Park, 425
Black pearls, 14, 232
  Bora Bora, 274
  Manihi, 305
  Moorea, 255–256
  Rangiroa, 302
  Rarotonga, 330
  Savusavu (Vanua Levu), 163
  Tahiti, 230
Black Rock (Rarotonga), 326
Blowholes (Tonga), 426–427
Blue Banana Studios (Tonga), 429

Blue Lagoon Cruises (Fiji), 118
The *Blue Lagoon* (films), 68, 124
Blue Lagoon (Rangiroa), 301
Blue Pacific Vacations, 46
Boat excursions and cruises. *See also* Ferries; Lagoon excursions; Sailing and yacht charters
  Fiji, 102
    Mamanuca and Yasawa Islands, 116, 118
  French Polynesia, 197–198
  Huahine, 289
  lagoon excursions
    Aitutaki, 346
    Bora Bora, 272–273
    Huahine, 288
    Moorea, 252–253
    Raiatea and Tahaa, 296–297
    Rangiroa, 301
    Rarotonga, 329
    Vava'u, 439
Boating (boat rentals). *See also* Kayaking; Sailing and yacht charters
  Rarotonga, 328
Books, recommended, 53–56
Bookstores
  Bora Bora, 268
  Moorea, 246
  Raiatea and Tahaa, 294
  Rarotonga (Cook Islands), 319
  Suva (Fiji), 142
  Tahiti, 212
  Tonga, 419
Bora Bora (French Polynesia), 5, 266–282
  accommodations, 274–280
  arriving in, 267
  drinking water, 268
  exploring, 270–272
  Internet and e-mail access, 268
  lagoon excursions, 272–273
  nightlife, 282
  restaurants, 280–282
  safari expeditions, 272
  shopping, 274
  transportation, 267–268
  visitor information, 268
Bora Bora Cruises, 200
Bora Bora Lagoonarium, 272
Bora Diving Center (Bora Bora), 273
Botanical Gardens (Tahiti), 217
Bougainville's Anchorage (Tahiti), 222–223
Bouma Falls (Taveuni), 171

Bouma National Heritage Park (Taveuni), 171–172
Bounty, HMS, 183–184, 448
Boutique Bora Bora, 274
Boutique Gauguin (Bora Bora), 274
Brendan Worldwide Vacations, 46
Bucket shops, 45

Camping
  Fiji, 167, 177
  Huahine, 291
  Moorea, 260–261
Captain Bligh Restaurant and Bar (Tahiti), 242
Captain Cook Cruises (Fiji), 116–118
Captain Cook's Landing Place (Tonga), 426
Captain Tama's AquaSports (Rarotonga), 328
Car-rental insurance, 31
Car rentals, surfing for, 38
Cascades de Tefaarumai (Faarumai Waterfalls; Tahiti), 222
Cathédrale de l'Immaculée Conception (Papeete), 220
Catholic Women's League Handicraft Centre (Tonga), 429
Cave de Rangiroa, 302
Caverne de Maui (Tahiti), 224
Cave swimming, 16
Cellphones, 39–40
Centenary Church (Nuku'alofa), 424
Centre Moana Nui (Tahiti), 230
Centre Vaima (Papeete), 217
Chan Mow & Co. (Apia), 372
Chapel Hill (Nuku'alofa), 423
Churchill Park (Lautoka), 98
Circle Island Tour (Tahiti), 220–229
Climate, 29. *See also under specific destinations*
Clothing, 15
  Fiji, 89
Club Bali Hai (Moorea), 264
The Cockscomb (American Samoa), 401
Colo—I-Suva Forest Park (Fiji), 149
Congregational Christian Church (Apia), 372
Connect Internet Services (Fiji), 90
Consolidators, 45

Cook, James, 10, 53, 54, 71, 180, 183, 184, 217, 222, 241, 309, 407, 409, 423, 444, 447–448, 450
  Captain Cook's Landing Place (Tonga), 426
The Cook Islands, 307–350. *See also* Rarotonga
  brief description of, 21
  calendar of events, 315–316
  climate, 314–315
  customs allowances, 313
  economy of, 308
  entry requirements, 313
  getting to Rarotonga and getting around, 316, 318–319
  government of, 308
  history of, 308–311
  holidays and seasons, 315
  languages of, 312
  money matters, 313–314
  natural environment, 307–308
  nightlife, 13–14
  people of, 311–312
  suggested itinerary, 61–62
  visitor information, 312–313
  what's new in, 2–3
Cook Islands Christian Church (Aitutaki), 345
Cook Islands Christian Church (Avarua), 323
Cook Islands Cultural Village (Rarotonga), 327
Cook Islands Game Fishing Club (Rarotonga), 329
Cook Islands Library and Museum (Avarua), 323–324
Cook's Bay (Moorea), 248
  accommodations, 256–259
  restaurants, 261–263
Copra Shed (Savusavu), 162–163
The Coral Coast (Viti Levu, Fiji), 67, 100, 126–137
  accommodations, 131–134
  emergencies, 127
  getting to and around, 127
  nightlife, 136–137
  restaurants, 135–136
  shopping, 131
  sights and activities, 127–131
Coral Coast Railway Co. (Viti Levu), 100, 128
Coral Sun Fiji (Nadi), 97
Courthouse (Apia), 372
Crafts, 14–15
  Fiji, 103–104, 131
    Suva, 149–150
  Rarotonga, 330, 331
  Tahiti, 231

Tonga, 429–430
Vava'u, 441
Credit cards, 28
  American Samoa, 394
  the Cook Islands, 314
  Fiji, 82
  French Polynesia, 192–193
  Samoa, 360–361
  Tonga, 415
Cross Island Road (Samoa), 375
Cross-Island Track (Rarotonga), 329
Cruise lines and ships, 45–46. *See also* Boat excursions and cruises; Lagoon excursions
  French Polynesia, 198–201
Cultural experiences, best, 10
Cumming Street (Suva), 146
Cunard Line, 45
Curly's Cruising/Bosun's Locker (Savusavu), 163
Currency and currency exchange, 26
  American Samoa, 394
  the Cook Islands, 313–314
  Fiji, 81–82
  French Polynesia, 192
  Samoa, 360
  Tonga, 414–415
Customs regulations, 24–26

Dance shows
  Aitutaki, 350
  Fiji, 100, 111, 114, 137
  Rarotonga, 343
  Tahiti, 241, 242
  Tonga, 436
Deep Blue Diving Centre (Tonga), 428
Deep-sea fishing, 49
  Bora Bora, 273
  Fiji
    Taveuni, 173
    Viti Levu, 101, 138
  French Polynesia, 200
  Huahine, 289
  Moorea, 254
  Rarotonga, 328–329
  Vava'u, 440–441
Denarau Golf & Racquet Club (Fiji), 101
Denarau Island (Fiji), 95
  accommodations, 104, 106–107
  restaurant, 111–112
Dengue fever, 31–32
The Diadème (Tahiti), 215, 221
Disabilities, travelers with, 33

Discover Fiji Tours, 138
Dive Savai'i (Samoa), 389
Diving, 49
  Aitutaki, 347
  best places for, 15
  Bora Bora, 273
  Fiji, 70
    Nadi, 102
    Savusavu, 163–164
    Taveuni, 172–173
    Viti Levu, 138
  Ha'apai, 445
  Huahine, 289
  Manihi, 305
  Moorea, 254–255
  Raiatea and Tahaa, 297
  Rangiroa, 302
  Rarotonga, 329–330
  Samoa, 377
  Savai'i, 389
  Tikehau, 304
  Tonga, 428
  Vava'u, 441
Dolphin-watching
  Moorea, 253
  Rangiroa, 302
Drug laws (Fiji), 90
Dry season, 29
Duty-free shopping, 24, 25
  Fiji, 83, 84, 103
Duty Free Tahiti, 230

Ecole de Surf Tura'i Mataare (Tahiti), 230
Ecotour Samoa, 50, 376–377, 388
Eglise Evangélique (Papeete), 218
Elderhostel, 34
E-mail, 38–39
  Aitutaki, 344
  Bora Bora, 268
  Fiji, 90
    the Coral Coast, 127
    Nadi, 96
    Savusavu, 162
    Suva, 142
  Huahine, 286
  Raiatea and Tahaa, 294
  Rarotonga (Cook Islands), 320
  Samoa, 367
  Tahiti, 213
  Tonga, 419–420
  Vava'u, 438
Entry requirements, 23–24
Environmental tours, Samoa, 376–377
Etiquette, Fiji, 77–78

'Eua (Tonga), 407
Eva Perles (Moorea), 256
Expedia, 36, 37

Faanui Bay (Bora Bora), 272
Faarumai Waterfalls (Cascades
    de Tefaarumai; Tahiti), 222
Faatautia Valley (Tahiti), 223
Fafa Island Resort (Tonga), 428
Faga (Savai'i), 388
Fagaloa Bay (Samoa), 374
Fagatogo Plaza (Pago Pago), 400
Fakarava (French Polynesia),
    15, 306
Faleata Golf Course (Samoa),
    377
Falefa Falls (Samoa), 374
Families with children, 34–35
    best islands for, 9–10
Fa'onelua Gardens (Nuku'alofa),
    423
Fare (Huahine), 284, 288
Fare Potee (Huahine), 286
Fare Ute (Papeete), 218
The Farm (Bora Bora), 274
Fautaua Valley (Tahiti), 221
Fautaua Waterfall (Tahiti), 221
Fehoko Art Creation (Tonga),
    429
Ferries
    American Samoa, 394
    Fiji, 88–89
    Moorea (French Polynesia),
        196–197
    Raiatea and Tahaa, 293
    Samoa, 364
    Tonga, 418–419
Fiafia, Samoa, 385
Fiji, 15, 66–178. *See also* Viti
    Levu; *And specific islands and
    groups of islands*
    accommodations and resorts,
        1–2, 122
    brief description of, 17, 20
    business hours, 89
    car rentals, 85–86
    climate, 82–83
    clothing, 89
    customs allowances, 81
    drinking water, 93
    driving rules, 86–87
    drugstores, 90
    economy, 71
    electricity, 90
    embassies and consulates, 90
    embassies or high commis-
        sions, in other countries, 81

emergencies, 90
entry requirements, 81
government, 71
healthcare, 90
history of, 71–74
holidays and special events, 83
honeymoon destinations in, 8
Internet and e-mail access, 90
    the Coral Coast, 127
    Nadi, 96
    Savusavu, 162
    Suva, 142
languages, 78–80
liquor laws, 91
money matters, 81–82
newspapers and magazines, 91
northern (Vanua Levu), 70–71,
    159–178. *See also* Savusavu;
    Taveuni
people of, 74–78
post office, 91
radio and TV, 91
regions of, 66–71
safety, 91–92
suggested itinerary, 57–59
taxes, 92
taxis, 87–88
telephone, 92
time zone, 93
tipping, 93
transportation, 84–89
traveling to, 83–84
visitor information, 80
what's new in, 1–2
Fiji Aggressor, 70
Fiji Airlines, 85
Fijian, 79
Fijian Village Visits, 10
Fiji Express, 87
Fiji Hindi, 79–80
Fiji Museum (Suva), 144, 148
Fiji Sugar Corporation
    (Lautoka), 98
Fiji Visitors Bureau (Nadi
    Airport), 80
Film, flying with, 48
Fire walking, 77
Fishing, 49
    Bora Bora, 273
    Fiji
        Taveuni, 173
        Viti Levu, 101, 138
    French Polynesia, 200
    Huahine, 289
    Moorea, 254
    Rarotonga, 328–329
    Vava'u, 440–441
Fish traps (Huahine), 287
Flights.com, 45

Flightseeing
    Fiji, 98
    Tahiti, 228
Flower Pot (American Samoa),
    401
Foa (Ha'apai), 444
Fono (American Samoa), 400
Fono (Samoa), 373
Forbidden Bay (American
    Samoa), 401
Freedom Air, 42
Free Wesleyan Church of Tonga
    (Nuku'alofa), 425
French Polynesia, 179–306. *See
    also specific islands*
    brief description of, 20–21
    calendar of events, 194–195
    climate, 193
    clothing, 203
    cruise ships and yachts,
        198–201
    drinking water, 206
    driving rules, 198
    economy of, 182–183
    electricity, 203
    embassies and consulates in,
        204
    entry requirements, 191
    etiquette, 204
    getting to and around, 195
    government of, 182
    healthcare, 204
    history of, 183–186
    holidays, 193–194
    honeymoon destinations in,
        8–9
    insects, 204
    Internet and e-mail access,
        203–204
    islands of, 180, 182
    languages of, 189–190
    liquor laws, 204
    mail, 204
    maps, 204–205
    money matters, 192–193
    newspapers and magazines,
        205
    nightlife, 13
    people of, 187
    radio and TV, 205
    restaurants, 201–202
    safety, 205
    suggested itinerary, 59–60
    taxes, 205
    telephone/fax, 205–206
    time zones, 206
    tipping, 206
    visitor information, 190–191
    what's new in, 2

Friendly Islands Kayak
  Company, 51
Frigate Passage (Fiji), 137
Frommers.com, 35
Fruits of Rarotonga, 325
Fugalei Street (Apia), 373

Galerie van der Heyde
  (Moorea), 255
Gambier Islands (French
  Polynesia), 182
Garden of the Sleeping Giant
  (Nadi), 97
Gare Maritime (Raiatea), 295
Gauguin, Paul, 54, 55, 185
Gauguin Museum (Tahiti),
  216, 225–226
Gauguin's Pearl Farm (Rangiroa),
  302
Gautavai Waterfall (Savai'i), 389
Gay and lesbian travelers, 34
  Nadi (Fiji), 114
Golf, 49–50
  Aitutaki, 347
  Fiji, 101, 102, 138, 157, 173
  Rarotonga, 329
  Samoa, 377
  Tahiti, 226, 229
  Tonga, 428
Good Samaritan Inn (Tonga),
  436
Go-Today, 46
Government Handicraft Centre
  (Suva), 149
Government House (Pago Pago),
  398
Government House (Suva), 148
Grande Danse de Tahiti, 242
Green Turtle Fiji (Nadi), 100–101
Green Turtle Tours, 376

Ha'amonga Trilithon (Tonga),
  426
Ha'apai (Tonga), 407, 444–446
Haapiti (Moorea), 250, 251
Ha'atafu (Tonga), 427
Handicrafts, 14–15
  Fiji, 103–104, 131
    Suva, 149–150
  Rarotonga, 330, 331
  Tahiti, 231
  Tonga, 429–430
  Vava'u, 441
Harrison W. Smith Botanical
  Gardens (Tahiti),
  217, 225–226

Haumana (French Polynesia),
  200
Hawaiian Airlines, 42
Health concerns, 31–32
Health insurance, 30–31
Herman Perles (Moorea), 255
Hibiscus Highway (Vanua Levu),
  159–160
High Court (Pago Pago), 400
Hiking, 50
  Aitutaki, 347
  Fiji
    Taveuni, 172
    Viti Levu, 101
  Moorea, 254
  Rarotonga, 329
  Samoa, 377
  Tahiti, 229–230
Hinakauea Beach Feast (Tonga),
  443
History, 447–451
Holidays and special events, 30
Holopeka Beach Quarry
  (Ha'apai), 445
Honeymoon destinations, best,
  7–9
Horseback riding, 50
  Fiji, 102
  Huahine, 289
  Moorea, 254
  Raiatea and Tahaa, 297
  Rarotonga, 329
Horseshoe Bay (Matagi
  Island), 6
Hostels
  Fiji, 104
  Moorea, 260
Hôtel de Ville (Papeete Town
  Hall), 220
Hotel Reservations Network, 52
Hotels and resorts
  surfing for, 37–38
  tips on, 51–53
Hotels.com, 38
Hot springs, Savusavu (Vanua
  Levu), 163
Hotwire, 37
House of Worship (Samoa), 375
Huahine (French Polynesia),
  11, 283–292
  accommodations, 290–291
  exploring, 286–288
  getting around, 284
  restaurants, 292
  shopping, 289
Huahine Nautique (Huahine),
  288
Huahine Nui Pearls & Pottery
  (Huahine), 287, 289

Hufangalupe Beach (Tonga), 426
Huluipaongo Tomb (Ha'apai),
  445

IFREMER: Le Centre
  Océanologique du Pacifique
  (Tahiti), 224
Impulse Fiji, 37
Impulse Trips Fiji (Nadi), 104
Indo-Fijians, 78
Inner Island Safari Tours
  (Moorea), 252
Insects, 33
  French Polynesia, 204
Insurance, 30–31
InterContinental Resort and Spa
  Moorea, sporting activities at,
  254
International date line, 411
International Gay & Lesbian
  Travel Association (IGLTA), 34
Internet and e-mail access,
  38–39
  Aitutaki, 344
  Bora Bora, 268
  Fiji, 90
    the Coral Coast, 127
    Nadi, 96
    Savusavu, 162
    Suva, 142
  Huahine, 286
  Raiatea and Tahaa, 294
  Rarotonga (Cook Islands), 320
  Samoa, 367
  Tahiti, 213
  Tonga, 419–420
  Vava'u, 438
InTouch USA, 40
Island Crafts (Rarotonga), 331
Island Eco Tours (Huahine), 287
Island Hoppers (Fiji), 85, 115
Island Hopper Vacations, 37
Islands in the Sun, 47
Itineraries, suggested, 57–65
  one-week
    Cook Islands, 61–62
    the Samoas, 62–63
    Tonga, 64–65
  two-week
    in Fiji, 57–59
    Tahiti and French Polyne-
      sia, 59–60

Jack's Handicrafts (Nadi), 104
James Norman Hall's Home
  (Tahiti), 215–216, 221
Japan Airlines, 42

Jardin Kellum (Moorea), 248, 250
Jardin Vaipehi (Tahiti), 226
Jean P. Haydon Museum (Pago Pago), 398, 400
Jetabout Island Vacations, 47
Jet boats, Fiji, 102
Jet lag, 44
Jet ski, Bora Bora, 274
John Williams Memorial (Apia), 372
Journey Pacific, 47
Judicial Building (Pago Pago), 400
Jus de Fruits de Moorea (Moorea Fruit Juices), 248

Kalevu South Pacific Cultural Centre (Viti Levu), 129
Kalia Handicrafts (FIMCO; Tonga), 429–430
Kao (Ha'apai), 444
Kava ceremony (Samoa), 356
Kayaking, 50–51
    Aitutaki, 346–347
    Bora Bora, 274
    Fiji, 138, 163–164
    Samoa, 377
    Vava'u, 441
King's Road (Viti Levu), 157
Korean Air, 42
Koro Sea, 67
Kula Eco Park (Viti Levu), 100, 130

Lagon Bleu (Rangiroa), 301
Lagoonarium de Moorea, 253
Lagoonarium de Tahiti (Punaauia), 215, 227
Lagoon excursions
    Aitutaki, 346
    Bora Bora, 272–273
    Huahine, 288
    Moorea, 252–253
    Raiatea and Tahaa, 296–297
    Rangiroa, 301
    Rarotonga, 329
Lake Lanoto'o National Park (Samoa), 375, 377
Lalomanu Beach (Samoa), 7, 374
La Maison James Norman Hall (Tahiti), 215–216, 221
LanChile Airlines, 42
Langafonua Handicrafts (Vava'u), 441
Langafonua Women's Association Handicraft Center (Nuku'alofa), 425, 430

Languages, 453
    Fiji, 78–80
Lapaha (Tonga), 426
La Plage de Maui (Tahiti), 224
Lautoka (Fiji), 98
Lautoka Market (Fiji), 98
Lavena (Taveuni), 171
Lavena Coastal Walk (Taveuni), 172
Lawai (Viti Levu), 129
Le Mafa Pass (Samoa), 374
Leone (American Samoa), 402
Leone Falls (American Samoa), 402
Le Petit Village (Moorea), 255
Le Pu'e, Mount (Samoa), 375
Le Royal Tahitien Hotel (Tahiti), 242
Lesiaceva Point (Vanua Levu), 159
Les Sables Rose (Rangiroa), 301
Le Tere Faati tour (Tahiti), 228
Levuka (Fiji), 11, 70, 152–153
Lifuka (Ha'apai), 444
Lindblad Expeditions, 46
Lion's Head (American Samoa), 401
Lost-luggage insurance, 31
Loti's Pool (Tahiti), 221
Lupepa'u International Airport (Vava'u), 437
Lycée Agricole d'Opunohu (Moorea), 250
Lyndon B. Johnson Tropical Medical Center (American Samoa), 401

Maeva (Huahine), 283, 286
Magasin Chin Lee (Bora Bora), 272
Magasin Vanira (Raiatea), 297
Mahaena Battlefield (Tahiti), 222
Mahana ATV Tours (Moorea), 252
Maharepa (Moorea), 248, 255
Maketi Talamahu (Nuku'alofa), 425
Maketi Talamahu (Tonga), 429
Malamala Island (Fiji), 117
Malololailai Island (Fiji), 117
Malololeilei Scenic View (Samoa), 375
Mamanuca Group (Fiji), 68, 114–126
    resorts in, 119–124
Manamo'ui Golf Course (Tonga), 428
Mana Rock Cafe (Tahiti), 242
Manase (Savai'i), 7, 388, 390

Manihi (French Polynesia), 15, 305
Manono (Samoa), 388
Manunu Marae (Huahine), 286
Maraa Grotto (Tahiti), 226
Mara'amu Sailing School (Huahine), 289
Marama Tours, 228
Marché Municipale (Moorea), 248
Marché Municipale (Municipal Market; Tahiti), 216
Mareto Plage Publique (Mareto Public Beach; Moorea), 255
Mariner's Cave (Vava'u), 439
Maroe Bay (Huahine), 287
Marotetini Marae (Bora Bora), 272
The Marquesas Islands (French Polynesia), 180
Martintar area (Nadi)
    accommodations, 107–109
    nightlife, 114
    restaurants, 113–114
Massacre Bay (American Samoa), 392, 402
Matafele Methodist Church (Apia), 372
Matagi Island (Fiji), 5, 177–178
Matairea Hill (Huahine), 286
Matavanu lava field (Savai'i), 388
Matavera (Rarotonga), 325
Matira Beach (Bora Bora), 6, 270
Matira Pearls (Bora Bora), 274
Mauaroa, Mount (Moorea), 248
Mauga (Savai'i), 388
Maui Pearls (Paka's Pearls; Rarotonga), 331
Maungapu, Mount (Aitutaki), 347
Maupiti (French Polynesia), 271
Mead, Margaret, 54, 357
MedicAlert Identification Tag, 32
Medical insurance, 30–31
Mekes, 111
Melanesians, 451–452
Melville, Herman, 54, 55, 182, 223, 247–248
Michener, James A., 5, 56, 68, 72, 73, 77, 78, 117, 141, 179, 215, 243, 244, 258, 266, 272, 308, 352, 379, 382
Mike's Divers (Viti Levu), 131
Momi Battery (Viti Levu), 128
Momi Bay (Viti Levu), 128
Moorea (French Polynesia), 5, 244–265
    accommodations, 256–261
    circle island tour, 247–251

Moorea *(cont.)*
  currency exchange, 246
  drinking water, 247
  drugstores, 246
  emergencies/police, 246
  exploring, 247–252
  Internet and e-mail access, 246
  nightlife, 264–265
  outdoor activities, 253–255
  post office, 246–247
  restaurants, 261–264
  safari tours, 252
  shopping, 255–256
  taxes, 247
  touring Tahiti from, 228
  transportation, 245
  visitor information, 246
Moorea Blue Nui Dive Center,
  254
Moorea Dolphin Center, 253
Moorea Explorer, 247, 252
Moorea Fruit Juices (Jus de
  Fruits de Moorea), 248
The Moorings, 51, 201, 440
Mosquitoes, 31–33
Motu Uta (Papeete), 218
Mo'unga Talau (Vava'u), 439
Mr. Lavalava (Samoa), 378
Mu'a (Tonga), 426
Mulinu'u Peninsula (Samoa), 373
Mulivai Catholic Cathedral
  (Apia), 372
Municipal Curio and Handicraft
  Centre (Suva), 146, 149
Municipal Market (Marché
  Municipale; Tahiti), 216
Municipal Market (Moorea), 248
Muri Beach (Rarotonga), 325
  accommodations, 332–334
  restaurants, 338–339
Musée de la Perle Robert Wan
  (Tahiti), 231
Musée de Tahiti et Ses Isles,
  216, 227
Musée Gauguin (Tahiti),
  216, 225–226
Museum of Samoa (Apia), 372
Mutiny on the Bounty (films),
  55, 186, 284
My Flower (Raiatea), 297

Nadi Airport Golf Club (Fiji),
  101
Nadi (Fiji), 67, 94–114
  accommodations, 104–110
  emergencies/police, 96
  exploring the Nadi area, 97–98
  exploring Viti Levu from Nadi,
    100–101
  healthcare, 96
  laundry and dry cleaning, 96
  nightlife, 114
  outdoor activities, 101–102
  post office, 96–97
  restaurants, 111–114
  shopping, 102–104
  transportation, 95
  visitor information, 96
Nadi International Airport (Fiji),
  arriving at, 83–84
Nagara (Taveuni), 171
Naiqaqi (Suva), 148
Nakabuta (Viti Levu), 129–130
Nakauvadra Range (Viti Levu),
  157
Namana Gallery (Viti Levu), 131
Namenalala Island (Fiji), 167–168
Nananu-I-Ra Island (Fiji),
  100, 158
Natadola Beach (Viti Levu),
  6, 100, 128
National Library (Avarua), 324
National Museum (Avarua), 324
National Park of American
  Samoa, 402–403
Nausori Airport (Suva), 84, 141
Nausori Highlands (Viti Levu),
  130
Navua River (Fiji), 100, 137
Neiafu (Vava'u), 11, 437
Nelson Memorial Public Library
  (Apia), 372
New Apia Market (Samoa), 373
Newmans South Pacific
  Vacations, 47
Ngatangiia (Rarotonga), 325
Nightlife, best, 13–14
Niuas Islands (Tonga), 407
Niukasa (Nuku'alofa), 424
Niutoua (Tonga), 426
Northern Fiji (Vanua Levu),
  70–71, 159–178. *See also*
  Savusavu; Taveuni
Nubukalou Creek (Suva), 141, 146
Nuku'alofa (Tonga),
  406, 422–425
  accommodations, 430–432
Nuku'alofa Club (Tonga), 423

Oceania Travel & Tours (Apia),
  400
Oholei Beach (Tonga), 426
Old Apia Market (Samoa),
  372–373, 378
O Le Pupu-Pue National Park
  (Samoa), 375, 377
Olovehi Tomb (Ha'apai), 445
Onenoa (American Samoa), 401
One Tree Hill (Tahiti), 222
Ootu Pass (Aitutaki), 346
Opunohu Agricultural School
  (Moorea), 250
Orbitz, 36
O'Reilly's (Suva), 156
Orient Lines, 46
Orohena, Mount (Tahiti), 214
Otemanu Tours (Bora Bora),
  267, 270
Ovalau (Fiji), 5, 70, 152
Ovalau (Nuku'alofa), 424

Pacific Blue, 1, 42
Pacific Blue Adventure
  (Huahine), 289
Pacific Destination Center, 47
Pacific Harbour (Viti Levu),
  67, 137–140
Pacific Islands Seaplanes,
  85, 115
Pacific Legends, 47
Pacific Transport Ltd., 87
Package deals, 46–48
PADI Travel Network, 49
Pago Pago (American Samoa),
  391, 398–400
  accommodations, 403–404
  restaurants, 405
Pai Moana Pearls (Moorea), 255
Palolo Deep Marine Reserve
  (Samoa), 377–378
Pangai (Ha'apai), 444
Pangai (Nuku'alofa), 423
Pangaimotu Island Resort
  (Tonga), 428
Pao Pao (Moorea), 248
Papaeari (Tahiti), 225
Papapai-tai Waterfalls (Samoa),
  375
Papase'a Sliding Rocks (Samoa),
  378
Papeete (Tahiti), 207
  walking tour, 217–220
Papeete Municipal Market
  (Tahiti), 231
Papenoo Valley (Tahiti), 222
Papetoai (Moorea), 250
Papetoai Temple Protestant
  (Moorea), 250
Papioi Hill (Raiatea), 296
Parc Bougainville (Papeete), 218
Parea (Huahine), 287

Parliament of Fiji (Suva), 144
Pa's nature walks (Rarotonga), 328
Patterson Shipping Services (Fiji), 89
Paul Gauguin (French Polynesia), 199
Peapea Cave (Samoa), 375
Pearls. *See* Black pearls
Pelorous Jack (Fiji), 117–118
Penang Golf Course (Vaileka), 157
Penang Mill (Viti Levu), 157
Peoples of the South Pacific, 451–454
Perfumes of Rarotonga, 331
Pets, traveling with, 36
Philatelic Bureau (Rarotonga), 330
Piano Bar (Tahiti), 242
Pink Sands (Rangiroa), 301
Piula Cave Pool (Samoa), 374, 378
Piula College (Samoa), 374
Place Jacques Chirac (Papeete), 218
Place Tarahoi (Papeete), 220
Place Toata (Papeete), 218
The Planter's Club (Savusavu), 169
Pleasant Holidays, 47
Pleasure Marine (Fiji), 101
Poetaina Cruises (Huahine), 288
Point Matira (Bora Bora), 266
Point Venus (Tahiti), 217, 222
Polynesia Hélicoptères, 228
Polynesian Airlines, 42
Polynesian Blue, 1, 42
Polynesians, 452–453
Pomare V, tomb of (Tahiti), 221
Poole, Dr. Michael, 253
Port of Refuge (Vava'u), 437
Povai Bay (Bora Bora), 270
Prescription medications, 32
Priceline, 37
Prime Minister's Office (Nuku'alofa), 423
Prince Charles Beach (Taveuni), 173
Princess Cruises, 46, 199–200
Pulemelei Mound (Savai'i), 388–389
Pulenu'u House (Apia), 372
Punanga Nui Market (Rarotonga), 324, 331
Punaruu Valley (Tahiti), 227
Pyramid Rock (American Samoa), 401

Qamea Island (Fiji), 5, 177–178
Qantas Airways, 42
The Quay (Papeete), 218
Queen Salote College (Nuku'alofa), 425
Queen Salote Memorial Hall (Nuku'alofa), 425
Quikbook.com, 38

Raemaru, Mount (Rarotonga), 326
Raiatea (French Polynesia), 15–16, 292–300
Raintree Square (Nuku'alofa), 423
Rakiraki (Viti Levu), 157–158
Ra Marama (Fiji), 116–117
Ranch Opunohu Valley (Moorea), 254
Rangiroa (French Polynesia), 15, 300–304
Raro Safari Tours, 327
Rarotonga (Cook Islands), 5, 10, 307. *See also* The Cook Islands
    accommodations, 332–338
    bookstores, 319
    clothing, 319
    cultural experiences, 327–328
    drinking water, 322–323
    drugstores, 320
    electricity, 320
    exploring, 323–328
    getting to and getting around, 316, 318–319
    Internet and e-mail access, 320
    newspapers and magazines, 321
    nightlife, 342–343
    outdoor activities, 328–330
    post office, 321
    restaurants, 338–342
    shopping, 330–332
    taxes, 322
    telephone/fax, 322
    time zone, 322
Rarotonga International Airport (Cook Islands), 316
Ravilevu Nature Preserve (Taveuni), 169
Restaurants, best, 11–13
Return to Paradise Beach (Samoa), 7, 376
Rev. Shirley Baker Monument (Ha'apai), 445
River rafting, 50
    Fiji, 100, 138
Rivers Fiji, 50, 138

RoadPost, 40
Robert Louis Stevenson Museum & Grave (near Apia), 369–370
Robinson Crusoe Island (Fiji), 128–129
Robinson's Cove (Moorea), 248
Ron Hall's Island Fashion Black Pearls (Moorea), 256
Rotoava (Fakarava), 306
Rotui, Mount (Moorea), 248
Roulottes
    Moorea, 263
    Tahiti, 237
Royal Palace (Ha'apai), 445
Royal Palace (Nuku'alofa), 423
Royal Samoan Golf Club (Samoa), 377
Royal Sunset Island Resort (Tonga), 428
Royal Tombs (Nuku'alofa), 425

Sadie Thompson Building (Pago Pago), 400
Safari expeditions
    Bora Bora, 272
    Huahine, 288
    Moorea, 252
    Raiatea and Tahaa, 296
    Rarotonga, 327
    Tahiti, 228–229
Safety, 32–33
Sailing and yacht charters, 50–51. *See also* Boat excursions and cruises
    best places for, 15–16
    Fiji, 117–118
    Raiatea and Tahaa, 297
    Tonga, 428
    Vava'u, 440
Sailing Safaris (Vava'u), 439
St. Joseph's Catholic Church (Moorea), 248
Salamumu (Samoa), 376
Samoa, 351–390. *See also* American Samoa
    accommodations, 378–384
    brief description of, 21–22
    car rentals, 364–365
    climate, 361
    clothing, 366
    as a cultural storehouse, 10
    drinking water, 369
    driving rules, 365
    economy of, 352
    electricity, 367
    entry requirements, 360
    exploring Apia and the rest of Upolu, 369–377

Samoa *(cont.)*
  geography of, 351–352
  getting to and around,
    362, 364–366
  government of, 352
  healthcare, 367
  history of, 353–355
  holidays, 362
  Internet and e-mail access, 367
  language, 358–359
  liquor laws, 367
  money matters, 360–361
  nightlife, 14, 386
  organized tours, 376–377
  people of, 355–358
  radio and TV, 367–368
  safety, 368
  special events, 361–362
  suggested itinerary, 62–63
  taxes, 368
  taxis, 366
  telephone/fax, 368
  time zone, 368
  tipping, 368
  visitor information, 359–360
  weights and measures, 369
  what's new in, 3
Samoa Scenic Tours, 376, 388
Savai'i (Samoa), 5, 11, 386–390
Savusavu (Vanua Levu), 159–169
  accommodations, 164–167
  exploring, 162–163
  getting around, 160, 162
  getting to, 160
  nightlife, 169
  restaurants, 168–169
Scuba diving, 49
  Aitutaki, 347
  best places for, 15
  Bora Bora, 273
  Fiji, 70
    Nadi, 102
    Savusavu, 163–164
    Taveuni, 172–173
    Viti Levu, 138
  Ha'apai, 445
  Huahine, 289
  Manihi, 305
  Moorea, 254–255
  Raiatea and Tahaa, 297
  Rangiroa, 302
  Rarotonga, 329–330
  Samoa, 377
  Savai'i, 389
  Tikehau, 304
  Tonga, 428
  Vava'u, 441
Scubapiti Moorea, 254
Sculpture Par Woody (Moorea),
  255

Seafari Cruise (Fiji), 117
SeaFiji, 116
Sea kayaking, 50–51
  Aitutaki, 346–347
  Bora Bora, 274
  Fiji, 138, 163–164
  Samoa, 377
  Vava'u, 441
Seasons, 29–30
Seaspray, MV (Fiji), 117
Senior travel, 34
Sharks, 16
  Bora Bora, 272
Shopping, best buys, 14–15
**Sia'atoutai Theological College
  (Nuku'alofa)**, 423
Sibani Perles Joallier (Tahiti),
  231
SideStep, 36
Sigatoka (Viti Levu), 129
**Sigatoka Agricultural Research
  Station (Viti Levu)**, 130
Sigatoka River (Viti Levu), 129
**Sigatoka Sand Dunes National
  Park (Viti Levu)**, 129
Sigatoka Valley (Viti Levu), 129
Single travelers, 36
**Sir Geoffrey Henry National Cul-
  tural Centre (Avarua)**, 324
Siufaga (Savai'i), 388
Skydiving, Fiji, 98
Smoking, 32
Snorkeling, 49
  Aitutaki, 347
  best places for, 15
  Fiji, 102, 138, 173, 174
  Huahine, 289
  Moorea, 254–255
  Rarotonga, 330
  Samoa, 377–378
  Savai'i, 389
  Tonga, 428
**The Society Islands (French
  Polynesia)**, 180
Solace, 47
Somosomo (Taveuni), 171
Sopo'aga Falls (Samoa), 375
South Pacific Airpass, 43
South Pacific Holidays, 47
**South Pacific World Music
  Festival (Fiji)**, 83
South Sea Cruises (Fiji),
  101, 115, 117
Star Cinema (Tonga), 436
STA Travel, 36, 45
Stevenson, Robert Louis,
  54, 188, 224, 354, 361,
  370, 372, 385, 450
    Museum & Grave (near Apia),
    369

Student travel, 35–36
**Subsurface Fiji Diving and
  Watersports**, 119
Suilven Shipping Ltd. (Fiji),
  88–89
Sukuna Park (Suva), 146
Sun Air (Fiji), 115
Sunbeam Transport Ltd., 87
Sunsail Yacht Charters, 51, 201
Sunspots International, 47
Sun Vacations, 37
Supersonics (Moorea), 255
Surfing, Tahiti, 230
Suva (Fiji), 68, 94, 140–156
  accommodations, 150–153
  arriving at, 84
  bookstores, 142
  currency exchange, 142
  day trips from Nadi to, 100
  emergencies/police, 143
  exploring, 144–149
  getting to and around,
    141–142
  healthcare, 143
  Internet and e-mail access, 142
  libraries, 143
  nightlife, 156
  post office, 143
  restaurants, 154–156
  restrooms, 143
  safety, 143
  shopping, 149–150
  telephone/fax, 143
  visitor information, 143
  walking tour, 144–148
Suva Municipal Market (Fiji),
  144, 146
Swallows Cave (Vava'u), 439
Swimming
  Huahine, 289
  Samoa, 377–378
Sword sellers, 103, 149

Tabua, 77
Taga Blowholes (Savai'i), 389
Tagimaucia, Lake (Taveuni),
  171, 172
Tahaa (French Polynesia),
  292–300
Taharuu Marae (Bora Bora), 270
Tahia Collins (Moorea), 255
Tahiti, 207–243. *See also* Tahiti
  Iti; Tahiti Nui
    accommodations, 2, 232–237
    American Express, 212
    arriving and getting around,
      208, 210–212
    bookstores, 212
    business hours, 212

car rentals, 211
circle island tour, 220–227
drinking water, 214
driving hints, 211–212
drugstores, 213
emergencies/police, 213
exploring, 214–229
golf, 229
healthcare, 213
hiking, 229–230
Internet and e-mail access, 213
nightlife, 242–243
parking, 212
post office, 214
restaurants, 237–242
safari expeditions, 228–229
safety, 214
shopping, 230–232
suggested itinerary, 59–60
taxis, 211
visitor information, 214
watersports, 230
what's new in, 2
Tahiti Aggressor, 200
Tahiti Discount Travel, 47
Tahiti Evasion (Moorea), 229, 254
Tahiti-Faaa International Airport, 208
Tahiti Iti, 214, 223
north coast of, 223–224
south coast of, 224
Tahiti Legends, 47
Tahiti Nui, 214
east coast of, 221–223
north coast of, 221–223
organized tours around the coastal road, 227–228
south coast of, 224
west coast of, 227
Tahiti Nui Travel, 37, 228
Tahiti Perles, 231
Tahiti Safari Expedition, 229
Tahiti Surf School, 230
Tahiti Tours, 212, 228
Tahiti Vacations, 47
Tahiti Yacht Charter, 201
Takamoa Theological College (Avarua), 324
Takitumu Conservation Area (Rarotonga), 326
Tamara Curios (Tahiti), 231
Taninuu Marae (Raiatea), 295
Tapuaetai (One Foot) Island (Cook Islands), 346
Taputapuatea Marae (Avarua), 323
Taputapuatea Marae (Raiatea), 293, 295
Taravao (Tahiti), 223

Taravao Plateau (Tahiti), 223
Taravao Plateau Overlook (Tahiti), 223
Taufa'ahau Road (Nuku'alofa), 425
Taufa'ahau Wharf (Ha'apai), 445
Tautira (Tahiti), 223–224
Taveuni (Fiji), 11, 159, 169–177
Taveuni Forest Preserve (Fiji), 169
TAV Ltd. (Rarotonga), 331–332
Tavua (Viti Levu), 157
Tavuni Hill Fortification (Viti Levu), 130
Taxes, 28
Teahupoo (Tahiti), 224
Tea Nui (Moorea), 254
Tefarerii (Huahine), 287
Temae (Moorea), 247–248
Temae Plage Publique (Moorea), 6, 251
Temae Plage Publique (Temae Public Beach; Moorea), 254
Temehani, Mount (Raiatea), 293
Tennis, 49–50
Fiji, 101, 173
Rarotonga, 330
Teremoana Tours (Bora Bora), 272
Tereora College (Rarotonga), 327
Te Rua Manga, Mount (Rarotonga), 326
Tetamanu (Fakarava), 306
Thurston Gardens (Suva), 148
Tiare apetahi, 294
Tikehau (French Polynesia), 304–305
Tiki Theatre Village (Moorea), 10, 251, 252, 264
Tipping, 28
Titikaveka (Rarotonga), 325
accommodations, 334–335
restaurants, 339
Titikaveka Beach (Rarotonga), 7
Titikaveka Lagoon (Rarotonga), 325
Titiroa Marae (Moorea), 250
Toatea Overlook (Moorea), 251
Tofua (Ha'apai), 444
Togitogiga Falls (Samoa), 375
Togitogiga National Forest (Samoa), 375
Togo Mangrove Estuary (Samoa), 376
Tohiea, Mount (Moorea), 248
Tonga, 15, 406–446. *See also* Vava'u
bookstores, 419
brief description of, 22

business hours, 419
car rentals, 416, 418
climate, 415
clothing, 419
customs regulations, 414
drinking water, 422
economy of, 407–408
electricity, 419
embassies and consulates, 420
entry requirements, 413–414
exploring Tongatapu, 422–427
festivals and events, 415
geography of, 407
getting to and around, 416, 418
government of, 407
healthcare, 420
history of, 408–410
holidays, 415
Internet and e-mail access, 419–420
island excursions, 427–428
language of, 412–413
liquor laws, 420
money matters, 414–415
newspapers and magazines, 420–421
nightlife, 14
organized tours, 427
people of, 410–412
post office, 421
radio and TV, 421
safety, 421
shopping, 429–430
suggested itinerary, 64–65
taxes, 421
taxis, 418
telephone/fax, 421
time zone, 421–422
tipping, 422
visitor information, 413
what's new in, 3
worshipping with the king, 16, 424
Tongan National Centre (Nuku'alofa), 10, 423, 434, 436
Tongan National Cultural Centre (Tonga), 422
Tongan Wildlife Centre, 425–426
Tongatapu (Tonga), 406
accommodations, 430–433
nightlife, 436
restaurants, 433–436
shopping, 429–430
touring, 425–427
Tonga Visitors Bureau (Nuku'alofa), 423
TOPdive (Moorea), 254
TOPdive Bora Bora, 273

Town Clock (Apia), 372
Trap's Bar (Suva), 156
TravelAxe, 38
Traveler's checks, 27–28
The Travel Insider, 40
Travel insurance, 30–31
Travelocity, 36, 38
Travelweb, 38
Treasury Building (Nuku'alofa), 423
The Triangle (Suva), 146
Trip-cancellation insurance, 30
Tuamotu Archipelago (French Polynesia), 180
Tuasivi (Savai'i), 388
Tuherahera (Tikehau), 304
Tui Tai Adventure Cruises (Fiji), 164
Tula (American Samoa), 401
Tupapa Sports Ground (Avarua), 324
Tupapa Stream (Rarotonga), 325
Turtle Airways (Fiji), 85, 98, 115
Turtle and Shark Point (American Samoa), 402
Turtle Conservatory (Savai'i), 388
Tutuila (American Samoa), 5, 22, 391
   sights and attractions, 400–402

Upolu (Samoa), 5
   exploring, 373–376
   nightlife, 386
Uturoa (Raiatea), 293, 295–297

Vaiare (Moorea), 251
Vaihiria, Lake (Tahiti), 226
Vaihiria River (Tahiti), 226
Vaileka (Viti Levu), 157
Vailima (near Apia), 369
Vaipehi Gardens (Tahiti), 226
Vaipito Valley (American Samoa), 400–401

Vaitape (Bora Bora), 267
Vaitogi (American Samoa), 402
Vanua Levu (Fiji), 70–71, 159–178. See also Savusavu; Taveuni
Vatia (American Samoa), 401
Vatulele Island (Fiji), 134–135
Vatulele Island Resort Beach (Fiji), 6
Vava'u (Tonga), 5, 16, 407, 436–444
   accommodations, 441–443
   exploring, 439–440
   getting to and around, 437–438
   healthcare, 438
   Internet and e-mail access, 438
   nightlife, 444
   outdoor activities, 440–441
   restaurants, 443–444
   shopping, 441
   visitor information, 438
Venu Shipping Ltd. (Fiji), 89
Victoria Parade (Suva), 141
Vidawa Rainforest Walk (Taveuni), 171
Video, flying with, 48
Village 6 Cinemas (Suva), 156
Virgin Falls (American Samoa), 401
Virgin's Grave (Savai'i), 388
Viseisei (Fiji), 97
Viseisei Village (Nadi), 97
Visitor information, 22–23. See also specific islands
Viti Levu (Fiji), 67, 94–158. See also specific towns, islands, and groups of islands
   the Coral Coast (Viti Levu, Fiji), 67, 100, 126–137
      accommodations, 131–134
      emergencies, 127
      getting to and around, 127
      nightlife, 136–137
      restaurants, 135–136

   shopping, 131
   sights and activities, 127–131
   northern, 68, 156–158
Vuna Road (Nuku'alofa), 424
Vuna Wharf (Nuku'alofa), 423

Waikiki (Taveuni), 171
Wailoaloa Beach (Fiji), accommodations, 107
Wainibau Falls (Taveuni), 172
Waitui Marina (Savusavu), 163
Waiyevo (Taveuni), 171
Wakaya Island (Fiji), 153–154
Water, drinking, 32
Watersports. See also specific sports
   Bora Bora, 273–274
   the Coral Coast (Viti Levu), 131
   Ha'apai, 445
   Samoa, 377–378
   Tahiti, 230
Waya Island (Fiji), 116
Weddings, 24
Wesley Arcade (Apia), 372
Wet season, 29
Whale's Tale (Fiji), 117
Whale-watching, Vava'u, 440
White Sunday (American Samoa), 394
Women travelers, 35

Yaqona (yong-gona or "grog"), 76
Yasawa Flyer (Fiji), 116
The Yasawa Islands (Fiji), 4–6, 68, 114–126
   cruising through, 118
   day trips from Nadi, 116–117
   getting to, 115–116
   resorts in, 124–126
   sailing through, 117–118